D1123525

STRAUSS
BRADLEY
SMITH

RUTGERS UNIVERSITY

Second Custom Edition for Math 135

VOLUME 1

CALCULUS

Taken from:

Calculus, Third Edition
by Monty J. Strauss, Gerald L. Bradley, and Karl J. Smith

Custom Publishing

New York   Boston   San Francisco
London   Toronto   Sydney   Tokyo   Singapore   Madrid
Mexico City   Munich   Paris   Cape Town   Hong Kong   Montreal

Cover Art: *Chadstone*, by Jessica Lamarre

Taken from:

Calculus, Third Edition
by Monty J. Strauss, Gerald L. Bradley, and Karl J. Smith
Copyright © 2002, 1999, 1995 by Pearson Education, Inc.
Published by Prentice Hall, Inc.
Upper Saddle River, New Jersey 07458

This special edition published in cooperation with Pearson Custom Publishing.

Printed in the United States of America
   8 9 10   VO88   10

2008360625

DE

Please visit our web site at www.pearsoncustom.com

**Pearson
Custom Publishing**
is a division of

www.pearsonhighered.com

ISBN 10: 0-536-80120-7
ISBN 13: 978-0-536-80120-3

Contents

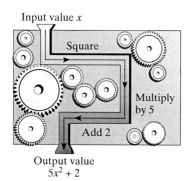
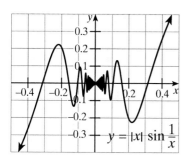

3 Differentiation   97

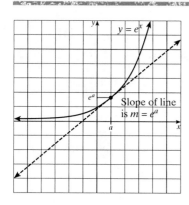

4 Additional Applications of the Derivative   183

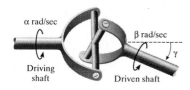

5 Integration   271

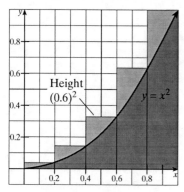

a. Partition into 5 subdivisions

Appendices

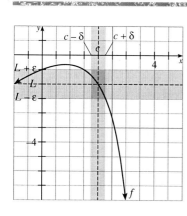

Preface

This text was developed to blend the best aspects of calculus reform with the reasonable goals and methodology of traditional calculus. It achieves this middle ground by providing sound development, stimulating problems, and well-developed pedagogy within a framework of a traditional structure. "Think, then do," is a fair summary of our approach.

New to this Edition

The acceptance and response from our first two editions has been most gratifying. For the third edition, we wanted to take a good book and make it even better. If you are familiar with the previous editions, the first thing you will notice is that we have added a new coauthor, Monty J. Strauss. His added expertise, and his attention to accuracy and detail, as well as his many years of experience teaching calculus, have added a new dimension to our exposition. Here is what is new in the third edition:

Organization

- In this edition we introduce e^x and $\ln x$ in Chapter 2 after we have defined the notion of a limit. This is beneficial because it allows the number e to be properly defined using limits. We also assume a knowledge of the conic sections and their graphs. A free *Student Mathematics Handbook* is available that provides review and reference material on these transcendental functions.
- l'Hôpital's Rule is now covered earlier in Chapter 4. This placement allows instructors to explore more interesting applications like curve sketching.
- A new section covering applications to business, economics, and the life sciences has been added to Chapter 6 on Applications of the Integral. This new material is designed to help students see how calculus relates to and is used in other disciplines.
- The chapter on polar coordinates and parametric forms has been distributed to other chapters in the book. The polar coordinate system and graphing in polar forms is in Chapter 6 in the context of the integration topic of finding areas. Parametric representation of curves now appears in the book where it is first needed, in Chapter 9.
- Modeling continues as a major theme in this edition. Modeling is now introduced in Section 3.4, and then appears in almost every section of the book. These applications are designated MODELING PROBLEMS. Some authors use the words "Modeling Problem" to refer to any applied problem. In the third edition of *Calculus*, we make a distinction between *modeling problems* and *application problems* by defining a modeling problem as follows. A **modeling problem** is a problem that requires that the reader make some assumptions about the real world in order to derive or come up

with the necessary mathematical formula or mathematical information to answer the question. These problems also include real-world examples of modeling by citing the source of the book or journal that shows the modeling process.

Problem Sets

- We have added a new major category of problems, called **counterexample problem**. A *counterexample* is an example that disproves a proposition or theorem, and in mathematics we are often faced with a proposition that is true or false, and our task is to prove the proposition true or to find a counterexample to disprove the proposition. In the third edition of *Calculus*, we attempt to build the student's ability with this type of situation to mean that the student must either find justification that the proposition is true or else find a counterexample. We believe this new form of problem to be important for preparing the student for future work in not only advanced mathematics courses, but also for analytically oriented courses.
- **Exploration Problems** explore concepts which may prove true or false and provide opportunities for innovative thinking.
- **Interpretation Problems** require exposition that requires a line of thinking that is not directly covered in the textbook.

Supplements

- **Interactive CD** (free with every new copy). The new CD-ROM is designed to enhance students' computational and conceptual understanding of calculus. This CD-ROM is not an add-on of extra material to the text but rather an incredibly useful expansion of the text. See the media supplement portion of the Walk-Through for a complete description of each CD.
- **TestGen-EQ.** This easy to use test generator contains all of the questions from the printed Test Item File.
- **Prentice Hall Online Homework Grader.** For more details, see the PH Homework Grader section in the Walk-Through.

Hallmark Features

Some of the distinguishing characteristics of the earlier editions are continued with this edition:

- It is possible to begin the course with either Chapter 1 or Chapter 2 (where the calculus topics begin).
- We believe that students *learn* mathematics by *doing* mathematics. Therefore, the **problems and applications** are perhaps the most important feature of any calculus book. You will find that the problems in this book extend from routine practice to challenging. The problem sets are divided into *A* Problems (routine), *B* Problems (requiring independent thought), and *C* Problems (theory problems). You will find the scope and depth of the problems in this book to be extraordinary while engineering and physics examples and problems play a prominent role, we include applications from a wide variety of fields, such as biology, economics, ecology, psychology, and sociology. In addition, the chapter summaries provide not only topical review, but also many miscellaneous exercises. Although the chapter reviews are typical of examinations, the miscellaneous problems are not presented as graded problems, but rather as a random list of problems loosely tied to the ideas of that chapter. In addition, there are cumulative reviews located at natural subdivision points in the text: Chapters 1–5, Chapters 6–8, Chapters 1–10, and Chapters 11–13. For a full description of each type of problem available, see pages xviii through xxi of Walk-Through.
- We understand that students often struggle with prerequisite material. Further, it is often frustrating for instructors to have to reteach material from previous courses. As

a result, we have created a unique **Student Mathematics Handbook**. This handbook functions as a **"Just-in-Time" Precalculus Review** that provides precalculus drill/review material, a catalog of curves, analytic geometry, and integral tables. Students are guided through the text to this handbook by a SMH symbol located in the text margin. This guide is entirely author-written and offered FREE with every new copy of the text.

- We have taken the introduction of **differential equations** seriously. Students in many allied disciplines need to use differential equations early in their studies and consequently cannot wait for a postcalculus course. We introduce differential equations in a natural and reasonable way. Slope fields are introduced as a geometric view of antidifferentiation in Section 5.1, and then are used to introduce a graphical solution to differential equations in Section 5.6. We consider separable differential equations in Chapter 5 and first-order linear equations in Chapter 7, and demonstrate the use of both modeling a variety of applied situations. Exact and homogeneous differential equations appear in Chapter 14, along with an introduction to second-order linear equations. The "early and often" approach to differential equations is intended to illustrate their value in continuous modeling and to provide a solid foundation for further study.

- **Visualization** is used to help students develop better intuition. Much of this visualization appears in the wide margins to accompany the text. Also, since tough calculus problems are often tough geometry (and algebra) problems, this emphasis on graphs will help students' problem-solving skills. Additional graphs are related to the student problems, including answer art.

- We have included dozens of "TECHNOLOGY NOTES" devoted to the use of technology. We strive to keep such references "platform neutral" because specific calculators and computer programs frequently change and are better considered in separate technology manuals. These references are designed to give insight into how technological advances can be used to help understand calculus. Problems requiring a graphing calculator or software and computer also appear in the exercises. On the other hand, problems that are not specially designated may still use technology (for example, to solve a higher-degree equation). Several technology manuals are also available at a discount price. See Instructor/Student Supplement section in the Walk-Through for details.

- **Guest essays** provide alternate viewpoints. The questions that follow are called MATHEMATICAL ESSAYS and are included to encourage individual writing assignments and mathematical exposition. We believe that students will benefit from individual writing and research in mathematics. Another pedagogical feature is the **"What this says:"** box in which we rephrase mathematical ideas in everyday language. In the problem sets we encourage students to summarize procedures and processes or to describe a mathematical result in everyday terms.

- **Group research projects**, each of which appears at the end of a chapter and involves intriguing questions whose mathematical content is tied loosely to the chapter just concluded. These projects have been developed and class-tested by their individual authors, to whom we are greatly indebted. Note that the complexity of these projects increases as we progress through the book and the mathematical maturity of the student is developed.

- We continue to utilize the **humanness** of mathematics. History is not presented as additional material to learn. Rather we have placed history into *problems* that lead the reader from the development of a concept to actually participating in the discovery process. The problems are designated as Historical Quest problems. The problems are not designed to be "add-on or challenge problems," but rather to become an integral part of the assignment. The level of difficulty of Quest problems ranges from easy to difficult. An extensive selection of biographies of noted mathematicians can be found on the internet site accompanying this text (www.prenhall.com/strauss)

Accuracy and Error Checking

Because of careful checking and proofing by several people besides each of the three authors, the authors and publisher believe this book to be substantially error free. For any errors remaining, the authors would be grateful if they were sent to Monty J. Strauss at **M.Strauss@ttu.edu** or Monty J. Strauss, Department of Mathematics and Statistics, Texas Tech University, Lubbock, TX 79409-1042.

Acknowledgments

The writing and publishing of a calculus book is a tremendous undertaking. We take this responsibility very seriously because a calculus book is instrumental in transmitting knowledge from one generation to the next. We would like to thank the many people who helped us in the preparation of this book. First, we thank our editor George Lobell, who led us masterfully through the development and publication of this book. We sincerely appreciate Henri Feiner, who not only worked all of the problems but also read and critiqued each word of the manuscript, and Carol Williams who transcribed our manuscript into TEX. We would like to thank Dennis Kletzing for his work in transforming the manuscript into finished pages. Finally, we would like to thank Lynn Savino Wendel, who led us through the production process.

Of primary concern is the accuracy of the book. We had the assistance of many: Henri Feiner, who read the entire manuscript and offered us many valuable suggestions; and Nancy and Mary Toscano, who were meticulous in their checking of our manuscript. Thanks also to the accuracy checkers of the previous editions, Jerry Alexanderson, Mike Ecker, Ken Sydel, Diana Gerardi, Kurt Norlin, Terri Bittner, Nancy Marsh, and Mary Toscano. We would also like to thank the following readers of the text for the many suggestions for improvement:

REVIEWERS OF THE THIRD EDITION:

Gregory Adams, Bucknell University

Robert Bakula, Ohio State University

J. Caggiano, Arkansas State Univery

James T. Campbell, University of Memphis

Lin Dearing, Clemson University

Stan Dick, George Mason University

Tevian Dray, Oregon State University

Michael W. Ecker, Pennsylvania State University, Wilkes-Barre Campus

Anda Gadidov, Gannon University

Ruth Gornet, Texas Tech University

Julia Hassett, Oakton Community College

Isom H. Herron, Rensselaer Polytechnic Institute

Michael G. Hilgers, University of Missouri–Rolla

Jason P. Huffman, Jacksonville State University

James E. Jamison, University of Memphis

Jeuel G. LaTorre, Clemson University

Ira Wayne Lewis, Texas Tech University

Maura B. Mast, University of Massachusetts–Boston

Mark Naber, Monroe County Community College

Chris Peterson, Colorado State University

Siew-Ching Pye, California State Polytechnic University–Pomona

Joe Rody, Arizona State University

Yongwu Rong, The George Washington University

Eric Rowley, Utah State University

John E. Santomas, Villanova University

Carl Seaquist, Texas Tech University

Dennis Wacker, Saint Louis University

W. Thurmon Whitley, University of New Haven

Teri Woodington, Colorado School of Mines

Cathleen M. Zucco-Teveloff, Trinity College

REVIEWERS OF THE FIRST TWO EDITIONS:

Gerald Alexanderson, Santa Clara University

David Arterburn, New Mexico Tech

Neil Berger, University of Illinois at Chicago

Michael L. Berry, West Virginia Wesleyan College

Linda A. Bolte, Eastern Washington University

Brian Borchers, New Mexico Tech

Barbara H. Briggs, Tennessee Technical University

Robert Broschat, South Dakota State University

Robert D. Brown, University of Kansas

Dan Chiddix, Ricks College

Philip Crooke, Vanderbilt University

Ken Dunn, Dalhousie University

Michael W. Ecker, Pennsylvania State University, Wilkes-Barre Campus

John H. Ellison, Grove City College

Mark Farris, Midwestern State University

Sally Fieschbeck, Rochester Institute of Technology

William P. Francis, Michigan Technological University

Stuart Goldenberg, California Polytechnic State University, San Luis Obispo Campus

Harvey Greenwald, California Polytechnic San Luis Obispo

Richard Hitt, University of South Alabama

Joel W. Irish, University of Southern Maine

Roger Jay, Tomball College

John H. Jenkins, Embry Riddle Aeronautical University

Clement T. Jeske, University of Wisconsin–Platteville

Kathy Kepner, Paducah Community College

Daniel King, Sarah Lawrence College

Lawrence Kratz, Idaho State University

Don Leftwich, Oklahoma Christian University

Sam Lessing, Northeast Missouri University

Estela S. Llinas, University of Pittsburgh at Greensburg

Pauline Lowman, Western Kentucky University

Ching Lu, Southern Illinois University at Edwardsville

William E. Mastrocola, Colgate University

Philip W. McCartney, Northern Kentucky University

E. D. McCune, Stephen F. Austin State University

John C. Michels, Chemeketa Community College

Judith Ann Miller, Delta College

Ann Morlet, Cleveland State University

Dena Jo Perkins, Oklahoma Christian University

Pamela B. Pierce, College of Wooster

Judith Reeves, California Polytechnic State Universty, Pomona Campus

Jim Roznowski, Delta College

Peter Salamon, San Diego State University

Connie Schrock, Emporia State University

Tatiana Shubin, San Jose State University

Jo Smith, Ketering University

Anita E. Solow, DePauw University

Lowell Stultz, Kalamazoo Valley Community College

Tingxiu Wang, Oakton Community College

Monty J. Strauss
Gerald L. Bradley
Karl J. Smith

1

Functions and Graphs

PREVIEW

This chapter uses several topics from algebra and trigonometry that are essential for the study of calculus. The necessary prerequisites for this course are reviewed in a companion book, *Student Mathematics Handbook*, and are briefly discussed in this chapter. This handbook is provided free with new copies of this textbook.

The concept of function is an especially important prerequisite for calculus. Even if you wish to skip most of this initial chapter, you should review the basic notions of functions and inverse functions in Sections 1.3 and 1.4.

PERSPECTIVE

Although modern science requires the use of many different skills and procedures, calculus is the primary mathematical tool for dealing with change. Sir Isaac Newton, one of the discoverers of calculus, once remarked that to accomplish his results, he "stood on the shoulders of giants." Indeed, calculus was not born in a moment of divine inspiration but developed gradually, as a variety of apparently different ideas and methods merged into a coherent pattern. The purpose of this initial chapter is to lay the foundation for the development of calculus.

1.1   Preliminaries

IN THIS SECTION   distance on a number line, absolute value, distance in the plane, trigonometry, solving trigonometric equations

Every mathematical book that is worth reading must be read "backwards and forwards," if I may use the expression. I would modify Lagrange's advice a little and say, "Go on, but often return to strengthen your faith." When you come on a hard and dreary passage, pass it over; come back to it after you have seen its importance or found its importance or found the need for it further on.

——George Chrystal,
Algebra, Part 2 (Edinburgh, 1889)

This section provides a quick review of some fundamental concepts and techniques from precalculus mathematics. If you have recently had a precalculus course, you may skip over this material.

Algebra, geometry, and trigonometry are important ingredients of calculus. Even though we will review many ideas from algebra, geometry, and trigonometry, we will not be able to develop every idea from these courses before we use it in calculus. For example, the law of cosines from trigonometry may be needed to solve a problem in a section that never mentions trigonometry in the exposition. For this reason, we have made available a separate reference manual, *Student Mathematics Handbook*, which includes the background material you will need for this course. We suggest that you keep it close at hand. References to this handbook are indicated by the logo **SMH**

DISTANCE ON A NUMBER LINE

SMH The real numbers, *along with these subsets, are found in Chapter 2 of the Student Mathematics Handbook.*

You are probably familiar with the set of **real numbers** and several of its subsets, including the counting or natural numbers, the integers, the rational numbers, and the irrational numbers.

The real numbers can be visualized most easily by using a **one-dimensional coordinate system** called a **real number line**, as shown in Figure 1.1.

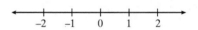

Figure 1.1   Real number line

Notice that a number a is less than a number b if it is to the left of b on a real number line, as shown in Figure 1.2. Similar definitions can be given for $a > b$, $a \leq b$, and $a \geq b$.

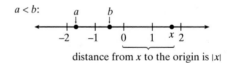

distance from x to the origin is $|x|$

Figure 1.2   Geometric definition of *less than*

The location of the number 0 is chosen arbitrarily, and a unit distance is picked (meters, feet, inches, ...). Numbers are ordered on the real number line according to the following order properties.

Order Properties

For all real numbers a, b, and c

Trichotomy law: Exactly one of the following is true:

$$a < b, \quad a > b, \quad \text{or} \quad a = b.$$

Transitive law of inequality: If $a < b$ and $b < c$, then $a < c$.

Additive law of inequality: If $a < c$ and $b < d$, then $a + b < c + d$.

Multiplicative law of inequality: If $a < b$, then

$$ac < bc \text{ if } c > 0 \quad \text{and} \quad ac > bc \text{ if } c < 0.$$

ABSOLUTE VALUE

Absolute Value

> The **absolute value** of a real number a, denoted by $|a|$, is
>
> $$|a| = \begin{cases} a & \text{if } a \geq 0 \\ -a & \text{if } a < 0 \end{cases}$$

The number x is located $|x|$ units away from 0 — to the right if $x > 0$ and to the left if $x < 0$.

Absolute value is used to describe the distance between points on a number line.

Distance Between Two Points on a Number Line

> The **distance** between the numbers x_1 and x_2 on a number line is
>
> $$|x_2 - x_1|$$

WARNING Note that $|x_2 - x_1| = |x_1 - x_2|$

For example, the distance between 2 and -3 is $|2 - (-3)| = 5$ units, and between -2 and -3 is $|-2 - (-3)| = 1$ unit.

Several properties of absolute value that you will need in this course are summarized in Table 1.1.

$x_2 - x_1: \quad |2 - (-3)| = |2 + 3| = 5$

$x_1 - x_2: \quad |-3 - 2| = 5$

TABLE 1.1 Properties of Absolute Value

Let a and b be any real numbers.	
Property	**Comment**
1. $|a| \geq 0$	1. Absolute value is nonnegative.
2. $|-a| = |a|$	2. The absolute value of a number and the absolute value of its opposite are equal.
3. $|a|^2 = a^2$	3. If an absolute value is squared, the absolute value signs can be dropped because both squares are nonnegative.
4. $|ab| = |a|\,|b|$	4. The absolute value of a product is the product of the absolute values.
5. $\left|\dfrac{a}{b}\right| = \dfrac{|a|}{|b|}, \quad b \neq 0$	5. The absolute value of a quotient is the quotient of the absolute values.
6. $-|a| \leq a \leq |a|$	6. This property is true because $|a|$ is either a or $-a$.
7. Let $b \geq 0$; $|a| = b$ if and only if $a = \pm b$	7. This property is useful in solving absolute value equations. See Example 1.
8. Let $b > 0$; $|a| < b$ if and only if $-b < a < b$	8. **and 9.** These are the main properties used in solving absolute value inequalities. See Example 2.
9. Let $b > 0$; $|a| > b$ if and only if $a > b$ or $a < -b$	
10. $|a + b| \leq |a| + |b|$	10. This property is called the **triangle inequality**. It is used in both theory and numerical computations involving inequalities.

WARNING *"p if and only if q"* is used to mean that both a statement and its converse are true. That is,

    if p, then q, and
    if q, then p.

For example, property 8 has two parts:

(i) If $|a| < b$, then $-b < a < b$;
(ii) If $-b < a < b$, then $|a| < b$.

Property 7 is sometimes stated for any a or b as $|a| = |b|$ if and only if $a = \pm b$. Since $|b| = \pm b$, it follows that this property is equivalent to property 7. Also, properties 8 and 9 are true for $\leq$ and $\geq$ inequalities. Specifically, if $b \geq 0$, then

$$|a| \leq b \quad \text{if and only if} \quad -b \leq a \leq b$$

and

$$|a| \geq b \quad \text{if and only if} \quad a \geq b \text{ or } a \leq -b$$

A convenient notation for representing intervals on a number line is called **interval notation** and is summarized in the accompanying table. Note that a solid dot (•) at an endpoint of an interval indicates that it is included in the interval, whereas an open dot (○) indicates that it is excluded. An interval is **bounded** if both of its endpoints are real numbers. A bounded interval is **open** if it includes neither of its endpoints, **half-open** if it includes only one endpoint, and **closed** if it includes both endpoints. The symbol "∞" (pronounced *infinity*) is used for intervals that are not limited in one direction or another. In particular, $(-\infty, \infty)$ denotes the entire real number line.

SMH   If this notation is new to you, please check the *Handbook* (Section 2.7) for further examples. We will use this interval notation to write the solutions of absolute value equations and absolute value inequality problems.

Name of Interval	Inequality Notation	Interval Notation	Graph
Closed interval	$a \leq x \leq b$	$[a, b]$	
	$a \leq x$ $x \geq a.$	$[a, \infty)$	
	$x \leq b$	$(-\infty, b]$	
Open interval	$a < x < b$	(a, b)	
	$a < x$	(a, ∞)	
	$x < b$	$(-\infty, b)$	
Half-open interval	$a < x \leq b$	$(a, b]$	
	$a \leq x < b$	$[a, b)$	
Real number line	All real numbers	$(-\infty, \infty)$	

Absolute Value Equations   Absolute value property 7 allows us to solve absolute value equations easily. For this reason property 7 is called the **absolute value equation property**.

EXAMPLE 1   Solving an equation with an absolute value on one side
Solve $|2x - 6| = x$.

Solution
If $2x - 6 \geq 0$, then $|2x - 6| = 2x - 6$ so that we solve

$$2x - 6 = x \quad \text{or} \quad x = 6 \qquad \text{Property 7}$$

If $2x - 6 < 0$, then $|2x - 6| = -(2x - 6)$ so that we solve

$$-(2x - 6) = x$$
$$-3x = -6$$
$$x = 2$$

The solutions are $x = 6$ and $x = 2$. ■

The absolute value expression $|x - a|$ can be interpreted as the distance between x and a on a number line. An equation of the form

$$|x - a| = b$$

is satisfied by two values of x that are a given distance b from a when represented on a number line. For example, $|x - 5| = 3$ states that x is 3 units from 5 on a number line. Thus, x is either 2 or 8.

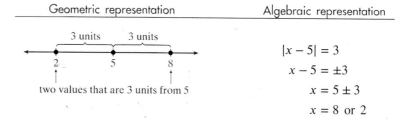

Absolute Value Inequalities Because $|x - 5| = 3$ states that the distance from x to 5 is 3 units, the inequality $|x - 5| < 3$ states that the distance from x to 5 is less than 3 units, whereas $|x - 5| > 3$ states that the distance from x to 5 is greater than 3 units.

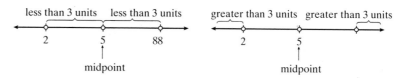

EXAMPLE 2 Solving an absolute value inequality

Solve $|2x - 3| \leq 4$.

Solution

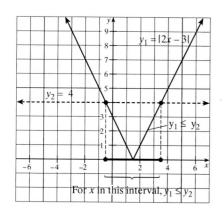

Figure 1.3 Solving an inequality by graphing

Algebraic solution:

$$-4 \leq 2x - 3 \leq 4 \qquad \text{Property 8}$$
$$-4 + 3 \leq 2x - 3 + 3 \leq 4 + 3$$
$$-1 \leq 2x \leq 7$$
$$-\frac{1}{2} \leq \frac{2x}{2} \leq \frac{7}{2}$$
$$-\frac{1}{2} \leq x \leq \frac{7}{2}$$

The solution is the interval $[-\frac{1}{2}, \frac{7}{2}]$.

Geometric solution: Graph $y_1 = |2x - 3|$ and $y_2 = 4$, as shown in Figure 1.3. Because we are looking for $|2x - 3| \leq 4$, we note those x-values on the real number line for which the graph of y_1 is below the graph of y_2. We see that the interval is $[-0.5, 3.5]$ or $[-\frac{1}{2}, \frac{7}{2}]$. ■

When absolute value is applied to measurement, it is called **tolerance.** Tolerance is an allowable deviation from a standard. For example, a cement bag whose weight w lb is "90 lb plus or minus 2 lb" might be described as having a weight given by $|w - 90| \leq 2$. When considered as a tolerance, the expression $|x - a| \leq b$ may be interpreted as x being compared to a with an **absolute error** of measurement of b units. Consider the following example.

EXAMPLE 3   Absolute value as a tolerance

Suppose you purchase a 90-lb bag of cement. It will not weigh exactly 90 lb. The material must be measured, and the measurement is approximate. Some bags will weigh as much as 2 lb over 90 lb, and some will weigh as much as 2 lb under 90 lb. If so, the bag could weigh as much as 92 lb or as little as 88 lb. State this as an absolute value inequality.

Solution

Let w = weight of the bag of cement in pounds. Then

$$90 - 2 \leq w \leq 90 + 2$$
$$-2 \leq w - 90 \leq 2$$

Equivalently, $|w - 90| \leq 2$. ∎

DISTANCE IN THE PLANE

Absolute value is used to find the distance between two points on a number line. To find the distance between two points in a coordinate plane, we use the *distance formula*, which is derived by using the Pythagorean theorem.

THEOREM 1.1   Distance between two points in the plane

The distance d between the points $P_1(x_1, y_1)$ and $P_2(x_2, y_2)$ in the plane is given by

$$d = \sqrt{(\Delta x)^2 + (\Delta y)^2} = \sqrt{(x_2 - x_1)^2 + (y_2 - y_1)^2}$$

where Δx (read "delta x") is the **horizontal change $x_2 - x_1$** (sometimes called *run*) and Δy (read "delta y") is the **vertical change $y_2 - y_1$** (sometimes called *rise*).

Proof   Using the two points, form a right triangle by drawing lines through the given points parallel to the coordinate axes, as shown in Figure 1.4.

The length of the horizontal side of the triangle is $|x_2 - x_1| = |\Delta x|$, and the length of the vertical side is $|y_2 - y_1| = |\Delta y|$. Then

$$d^2 = |\Delta x|^2 + |\Delta y|^2 \qquad \text{Pythagorean theorem}$$
$$d^2 = (\Delta x)^2 + (\Delta y)^2 \qquad \text{Absolute value property 3}$$
$$d = \sqrt{(\Delta x)^2 + (\Delta y)^2} \qquad \text{Solve for } d \qquad ❑$$

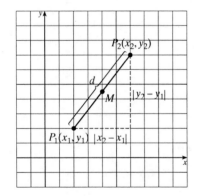

Figure 1.4 Distance formula

Midpoint formula   Related to the formula for the distance between two points is the formula for finding the midpoint of a line segment, as shown in Figure 1.4.

Midpoint Formula

> The **midpoint**, M, of the segment with endpoints $P_1(x_1, y_1)$ and $P_2(x_2, y_2)$ has coordinates
> $$M\left(\frac{x_1 + x_2}{2}, \frac{y_1 + y_2}{2}\right)$$

Notice that the coordinates of the midpoint of a segment are found by averaging the first and second components of the coordinates of the endpoints, respectively. You are asked to derive this formula in Problem 74.

Relationship between an equation and a graph **Analytic geometry** is that branch of geometry that ties together the geometric concept of position with an algebraic representation—namely, coordinates. For example, you remember from algebra that a line can be represented by an equation. Precisely what does this mean? Can we make such a statement that is true for any curve, not just for lines? We answer in the affirmative with the following definition.

Graph of an Equation

> The **graph of an equation** in two variables x and y is the collection of all points $P(x, y)$ whose coordinates (x, y) satisfy the equation.

There are two frequently asked questions in analytic geometry:

1. Given a graph (a geometrical representation), find the corresponding equation.
2. Given an equation (an algebraic representation), find the corresponding graph.

In Example 4, we use the distance formula to derive the equation of a circle. This means that if x and y are numbers that satisfy the equation, then the point (x, y) must lie on the circle. Conversely, the coordinates of any point on the circle will satisfy the equation.

EXAMPLE 4   Using the distance formula to derive an equation of a graph

Find the equation of a circle with center (h, k) and radius r.

Solution

Let (x, y) be any point on a circle. Recall that a circle is the set of all points in the plane a given distance from a given point. The given point (h, k) is the center and the given distance is the radius r.

$$r = \text{DISTANCE FROM } (h, k) \text{ TO } (x, y)$$
$$r = \sqrt{(x - h)^2 + (y - k)^2}$$
$$r^2 = (x - h)^2 + (y - k)^2, \quad \text{or} \quad (x - h)^2 + (y - k)^2 = r^2 \quad \blacksquare$$

A **unit circle** is a circle of radius 1 and center at the origin, so its equation is $x^2 + y^2 = 1$.

EXAMPLE 5   Finding the equation of a circle

Find the equation of the circle with center $(3, -5)$ that passes through the point $(1, 8)$.

Solution

See Figure 1.5. The radius is the distance from the center to the given point:

$$r = \sqrt{(1 - 3)^2 + [8 - (-5)]^2}$$
$$= \sqrt{4 + 169}$$
$$= \sqrt{173}$$

Thus, the equation of the circle is

$$(x - 3)^2 + [y - (-5)]^2 = (\sqrt{173})^2$$
$$(x - 3)^2 + (y + 5)^2 = 173 \quad \blacksquare$$

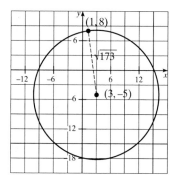

Figure 1.5 Circle with center $(3, -5)$ passing through $(1, 8)$

EXAMPLE 6   **Graphing a circle given its equation**

Sketch the graph of the circle whose equation is

$$4x^2 + 4y^2 - 4x + 8y - 5 = 0$$

Solution

We need to convert this equation into standard form. To do this we use a process called **completing the square** (see Section 2.6 of the *Student Mathematics Handbook*).

$$4x^2 + 4y^2 - 4x + 8y - 5 = 0$$

$$x^2 + y^2 - x + 2y = \tfrac{5}{4} \qquad \text{Coefficients of squared terms should be 1.}$$

$$(x^2 - x \quad) + (y^2 + 2y \quad) = \tfrac{5}{4} \qquad \text{Associate } x\text{-terms and } y\text{-terms.}$$

$$\left[x^2 - x + (-\tfrac{1}{2})^2\right] + (y^2 + 2y + 1^2) = \tfrac{5}{4} + \tfrac{1}{4} + 1 \qquad \text{Complete the squares by adding } \tfrac{1}{4} \text{ and 1 to both sides.}$$

$$(x - \tfrac{1}{2})^2 + (y + 1)^2 = \tfrac{10}{4} = \tfrac{5}{2}$$

This is a circle with center at $(\tfrac{1}{2}, -1)$ and radius $\sqrt{\tfrac{5}{2}}$. The graph is shown in Figure 1.6. ∎

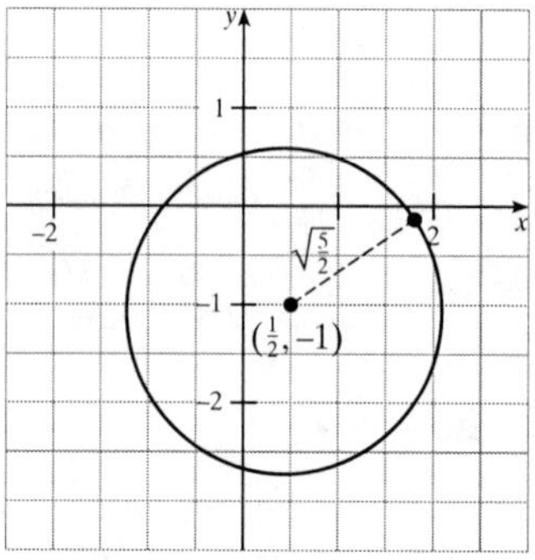

Figure 1.6 Sketch of
$4x^2 + 4y^2 - 4x + 8y - 5 = 0$

TRIGONOMETRY

One of the prerequisites for this book is trigonometry. If you need some review, consult a text on trigonometry or Chapter 4 of the *Student Mathematics Handbook* that accompanies this book. A summary of useful trigonometric formulas is found in Appendix E.

    Angles are commonly measured in degrees and radians. A **degree** is defined to be $\tfrac{1}{360}$ revolution and a **radian** $\tfrac{1}{2\pi}$ revolution. Thus, to convert between degree and radian measure use the following formula:

$$\frac{\theta \text{ measured in degrees}}{360} = \frac{\theta \text{ measured in radians}}{2\pi}$$

WARNING   In calculus, angles are usually measured in terms of radians rather than degrees since radian measure often leads to simpler formulas. You may assume that when we write expressions such as $\sin x$, $\cos x$, and $\tan x$, the angle x is in radians unless otherwise specified by a degree symbol.

EXAMPLE 7   **Converting degree measure to radian measure**

Convert $255°$ to radian measure.

Solution $\dfrac{255}{360} = \dfrac{\theta}{2\pi}$

$$\theta = \left(\frac{\pi}{180}\right)(255) \approx 4.450589593$$

EXAMPLE 8   **Converting radian measure to degree measure**

Express 1 radian in terms of degrees.

Solution $\dfrac{\theta}{360} = \dfrac{1}{2\pi}$

$$\theta = \left(\frac{180}{\pi}\right)(1)$$

$$\approx 57.29577951°$$

SOLVING TRIGONOMETRIC EQUATIONS

There will be many times in calculus when you will need to solve a trigonometric equation. As you may remember from trigonometry, solving a trigonometric equation is equivalent to evaluating an inverse trigonometric relation. Inverse functions will be introduced in Section 1.4; for now, we will solve trigonometric equations whose solutions involve the values in Table 1.2 (called a **table of exact values**). These exact values from trigonometry are reviewed in the *Student Mathematics Handbook*.

SMH

TABLE 1.2 Exact Trigonometric Values

Function \ Angle θ	0	$\frac{\pi}{6}$	$\frac{\pi}{4}$	$\frac{\pi}{3}$	$\frac{\pi}{2}$
$\cos\theta$	1	$\frac{\sqrt{3}}{2}$	$\frac{\sqrt{2}}{2}$	$\frac{1}{2}$	0
$\sin\theta$	0	$\frac{1}{2}$	$\frac{\sqrt{2}}{2}$	$\frac{\sqrt{3}}{2}$	1
$\tan\theta$	0	$\frac{\sqrt{3}}{3}$	1	$\sqrt{3}$	undefined

It is customary to use the values from Table 1.2 whenever possible. The approximate calculator values will be given only when necessary.

EXAMPLE 9 Evaluating trigonometric functions

Evaluate $\cos\frac{\pi}{3}$; $\sin\frac{5\pi}{6}$; $\tan(-\frac{5\pi}{4})$; $\sec 1.2$; $\csc(-4.5)$; and $\cot 180°$.

Solution

If you use a calculator, make certain it is in the proper mode (radian or degree).

$$\cos\frac{\pi}{3} = \frac{1}{2}$$ Exact value; Quadrant I

$$\sin\frac{5\pi}{6} = \frac{1}{2}$$ Exact value; Quadrant II

$$\tan\left(-\frac{5\pi}{4}\right) = -1$$ Exact value; Quadrant II

$$\sec 1.2 \approx 2.759703601$$ Approximate calculator value

$$\csc(-4.5) \approx 1.022986384$$ Approximate calculator value

$\cot 180°$ is not defined. ∎

EXAMPLE 10 Solving a trigonometric equation by factoring

Solve $2\cos\theta\sin\theta = \sin\theta$ on $[0, 2\pi)$.

Solution
$$2\cos\theta\sin\theta - \sin\theta = 0$$
$$\sin\theta(2\cos\theta - 1) = 0$$
$$\sin\theta = 0 \quad 2\cos\theta - 1 = 0$$
$$\theta = 0, \pi \quad \cos\theta = \frac{1}{2}$$
$$\theta = \frac{\pi}{3}, \frac{5\pi}{3}$$

WARNING Do not divide both sides by $\sin\theta$, because you might lose a solution. Notice that if $\theta = 0$ or π, then $\sin\theta = 0$. You cannot divide by 0. ∎

EXAMPLE 11 Solving a trigonometric equation using identities

Solve $\sin x + \sqrt{3}\cos x = 1$ on $[0, 2\pi)$.

Solution

For an algebraic solution,

$$\sqrt{3}\cos x = 1 - \sin x$$
$$3\cos^2 x = 1 - 2\sin x + \sin^2 x \qquad \text{Square both sides.}$$
$$3(1 - \sin^2 x) = 1 - 2\sin x + \sin^2 x$$
$$2 + 2\sin x - 4\sin^2 x = 0$$
$$2\sin^2 x - \sin x - 1 = 0$$
$$(2\sin x + 1)(\sin x - 1) = 0$$
$$\sin x = -\tfrac{1}{2} \qquad \sin x = 1$$
$$x = \tfrac{7\pi}{6}, \tfrac{11\pi}{6} \qquad x = \tfrac{\pi}{2}$$

However, since we squared both sides, we need to check for extraneous roots by substituting into the *original equation*, since squaring sometimes introduces extraneous solutions (that is, solutions that do not satisfy the given equation). Checking, we see that $x = \tfrac{7\pi}{6}$ is extraneous, and the solution is $x = \tfrac{\pi}{2}, \tfrac{11\pi}{6}$.

It is often worthwhile to check by finding a geometric solution. We graph the left and right sides of the equation on the same axes:

$$y_1 = \sin x + \sqrt{3}\cos x$$
$$y_2 = 1$$

The graphs are shown in Figure 1.7, and for a solution we look to the intersection points.

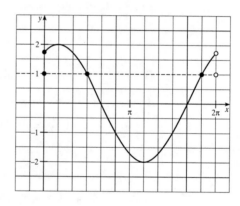

Figure 1.7 There are two intersection points, at $x = \tfrac{\pi}{2}$ and $x = \tfrac{11\pi}{6}$.

1.1   PROBLEM SET

A **1.** Fill in the missing parts in the table.

Inequality Notation	Interval Notation
$-3 < x < 4$	a.
b.	$[3, 5]$
c.	$[-2, 1)$
$2 < x \le 7$	d.

2. Fill in the missing parts in the table.

Inequality Notation	Interval Notation
a.	$(-\infty, -2)$
b.	$[\tfrac{\pi}{4}, \sqrt{2}]$
$x > -3$	c.
$-1 \le x \le 5$	d.

3. Represent each of the following on a number line.

   a. $-1 \le x < 4$ b. $-1 \le x \le 3$

   c. $(0, 2)$ d. $[-2, 1)$

4. Represent each of the following on a number line.

   a. $x > 2$ b. $x \le 4$

   c. $(-\infty, 2) \cup (2, \infty)$ d. $-2 < x \le 3$ or $x \ge 5$

In Problems 5–6, plot the given points P and Q on a Cartesian plane, find the distance between them, and find the coordinates of the midpoint of the line segment $\overline{PQ}$.

5. a. $P(2, 3)$, $Q(-2, 5)$ b. $P(-2, 3)$, $Q(4, 1)$

6. a. $P(-5, 3)$, $Q(-5, -7)$ b. $P(-4, 3)$, $Q(3, -4)$

SMH *Solve each equation in Problems 7–24. Assume that a, b, and c are known constants.*

7. $x^2 - x = 0$ 8. $2y^2 + y - 3 = 0$

9. $y^2 - 5y + 3 = 17$ 10. $x^2 + 5x + a = 0$

11. $3x^2 - bx = c$ 12. $4x^2 + 20x + 25 = 0$

13. $|2x + 4| = 16$ 14. $|5y + 2| = 12$

15. $|3 - 2w| = 7$ 16. $|5 - 3t| = 14$

17. $|3x + 1| = -4$ 18. $|1 - 5x| = -2$

19. $\sin x = -\frac{1}{2}$ on $[0, 2\pi)$

20. $(\sin x)(\cos x) = 0$ on $[0, 2\pi)$

21. $(2\cos x + \sqrt{2})(2\cos x - 1) = 0$ on $[0, 2\pi)$

22. $(3\tan x + \sqrt{3})(3\tan x - \sqrt{3}) = 0$ on $[0, 2\pi)$

23. $\cot x + \sqrt{3} = \csc x$ on $[0, 2\pi)$

24. $\sec^2 x - 1 = \sqrt{3}\tan x$ on $[0, 2\pi)$

Solve each inequality in Problems 25–34, and give your answer using interval notation.

25. $3x + 7 < 2$ 26. $5(3 - x) > 3x - 1$

27. $-5 < 3x < 0$ 28. $-3 < y - 5 \le 2$

29. $3 \le -y < 8$ 30. $-5 \le 3 - 2x < 18$

31. $t^2 - 2t \le 3$ 32. $s^2 + 3s - 4 > 0$

33. $|x - 8| \le 0.001$ 34. $|x - 5| < 0.01$

In Problems 35–38, find an equation of the circle with given center C and radius r.

35. $C(-1, 2)$; $r = 3$ 36. $C(3, 0)$; $r = 2$

37. $C(0, 1.5)$; $r = 0.25$ 38. $C(-1, -5)$; $r = 4.1$

In Problems 39–42, find the centers and radii of the circles and then graph.

39. $x^2 - 2x + y^2 + 2y + 1 = 0$

40. $4x^2 + 4y^2 + 4y - 15 = 0$

41. $x^2 + y^2 + 2x - 10y + 25 = 0$

42. $2x^2 + 2y^2 + 2x - 6y - 9 = 0$

SMH *Use the sum and difference formulas from trigonometry to find the exact values of the expressions in Problems 43–46. Check by finding a calculator approximation.*

43. $\sin\left(-\frac{\pi}{12}\right)$ 44. $\cos\frac{7\pi}{12}$

45. $\tan\frac{\pi}{12}$ 46. $\sin 165°$

B 47. **WHAT DOES THIS SAY?*** Describe a process for solving a quadratic equation.

---

*Many problems in this book are labeled **What Does This Say?** Following the question will be a question for you to answer in your own words, or a statement for you to rephrase in your own words. These problems are intended to be similar to the "What This Says" boxes.

48. **WHAT DOES THIS SAY?** Describe a process for solving absolute value equations.

49. **WHAT DOES THIS SAY?** Describe a process for solving absolute value inequalities.

50. **WHAT DOES THIS SAY?** Describe a process for solving trigonometric equations.

SMH *Specify the period for each graph in Problems 51–56. Also graph each curve.*

51. a. $y = \sin x$ b. $y = \cos x$ c. $y = \tan x$

52. a. $y = 2\sin 2\pi x$ b. $y = 3\cos 3\pi x$ c. $y = 4\tan\left(\frac{\pi x}{5}\right)$

53. $y = \tan(2x - \frac{\pi}{2})$ 54. $y = 2\cos(3x + 2\pi) - 2$

55. $y = 4\sin(\frac{1}{2}x + 2) - 1$ 56. $y = \tan(\frac{1}{2}x + \frac{\pi}{3})$

57. The current I (in amperes) in a certain circuit (for some convenient unit of time) generates the following set of data points:

Time	Current	Time	Current
0	-60.00000	10	30.00000
1	-58.68886	11	40.14784
2	-54.81273	12	48.54102
3	-48.54102	13	54.81273
4	-40.14784	14	58.68886
5	-30.00000	15	60.00000
6	-18.54102	16	58.68886
7	-6.27171	17	54.81273
8	6.27171	18	48.54102
9	18.54102	19	40.14784
		20	30.00000

Plot the data points and draw a smooth curve passing through these points. Determine possible values of A, B, C, and D so that the graph of these data is approximated by the equation $y - A = B\sin C(x - D)$.

58. Suppose that a point P on a water wheel with a 30-ft radius is d units from the waterline. If the water wheel turns at 6 revolutions per minute, the height of the point P above the waterline is given by the following set of data points:

Time	Height, d	Time	Height, d
0	-1.000	10	-1.000
1	4.729	11	4.729
2	19.729	12	19.729
3	38.271	13	38.270
4	53.271	14	53.270
5	59.000	15	59.000
6	53.271	16	53.271
7	38.271	17	38.271
8	19.729	18	19.730
9	4.729	19	4.730
		20	-1.000

Plot the data points and draw a smooth curve passing through these points. Determine possible values of A, B, C, and D so that the graph of these data is approximated by the equation

$$y - A = B\cos C(x - D)$$

Determine a possible equation of a curve that is generated by this water wheel.

59. The sun and moon tide curves are shown here.* During a new moon, the sun and moon tidal bulges are centered at the same longitude, so their effects are added to produce maximum high tides and minimum low tides. This produces maximum tidal range (the distance between the low and high tides).

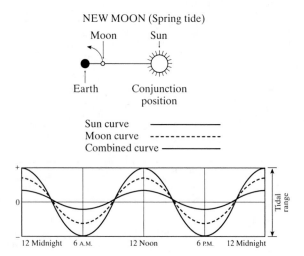

Write possible equations for the sun curve, the moon curve, and the combined curve. Assume the tidal range is 10 ft and the period is 12 hours.

60. The sun and moon tide curves are shown in the figure. During the third quarter (neap tide), the sun and moon tidal bulges are at right angles to each other. Thus, the sun tide reduces the effect of the moon tide.

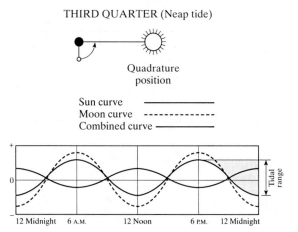

Write possible equations for the sun curve, the moon curve, and the combined curve. Assume the tidal range is 4 ft and the period is 12 hours.

61. A person is swimming at a depth of d units beneath the surface of the water. Because the light is refracted by the water, a viewer standing above the waterline sees the swimmer at an apparent depth of s units. (See Figure 1.8.)

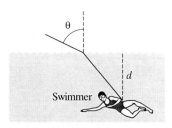

Figure 1.8 Refracted light when viewing an underwater swimmer

In physics,[†] it is shown that if the person is viewed from an angle of incidence θ, then

$$s = \frac{3d \cos \theta}{\sqrt{7 + 9 \cos^2 \theta}}$$

a. If $d = 5.0$ meters and $\theta = 37°$, what is the apparent depth of the swimmer?

b. If the actual depth is $d = 5.0$ meters, what angle of incidence yields an apparent depth of $s = 2.5$ meters?

62. Journal problem   *The Mathematics Student Journal* by Murray Klamkin[‡] ■ Determine all the roots of the quartic equation $x^4 - 4x = 1$.

63. HISTORICAL QUEST   The division of one revolution into 360 equal parts (called degrees) is no doubt due to the sexagesimal (base 60) numeration system used by the Babylonians. Several explanations have been put forward to account for the choice of this number. (For example, see Howard Eves's *In Mathematical Circles*, Boston: Prindle, Weber & Schmidt, 1969.) One possible explanation is put forth by Otto Neugebauer, scholar and authority on early Babylonian mathematics and astronomy. In early Sumerian times, there existed a Babylonian mile, equal to about seven of our miles. Sometime in the first millennium B.C., when Babylonian astronomy reached the stage in which systematic records of the stars were kept, the Babylonian mile was adapted for measuring spans of time. Since a complete day was found to be equal to 12 time-miles, and one complete day is equivalent to one revolution of the sky, a complete circuit was divided into 12 equal parts. Then, for convenience, the Babylonian mile was subdivided into 30 equal parts. One complete circuit therefore has (12)(30) = 360 equal parts. ■

Show that the radius of a circle can be applied exactly six times to its circumference as a chord.

---

*From *Introductory Oceanography*, 5th ed., by H. V. Thurman, p. 253. Reprinted with permission of Merrill, an imprint of Macmillan Publishing Company. Copyright ©1988 Merrill Publishing Company, Columbus, Ohio.

[†]R. A. Serway, *Physics*, 3rd ed., Philadelphia: Saunders, 1992, p. 1007.

[‡]Most mathematics journals have problem sections that solicit interesting problems and solutions for publication. From time to time, we will reprint a problem from a mathematics journal. If you have difficulty solving a journal problem, you may wish to use a library to find the problem and solution as printed in the journal. The title of the journal is included as part of the problem, and we will generally give you a reference as a footnote. This problem is found in the named journal in Volume 28 (1980), issue 3, p. 2.

64. HISTORICAL QUEST The numeration system we use (base 10) evolved over a long period of time. It is often called the *Hindu-Arabic* system because its origins can be traced back to the Hindus in Bactria (now Afghanistan). Later, in A.D. 700, India was invaded by the Arabs who used and modified the Hindu numeration system, and, in turn, introduced it to Western civilization. The Hindu Brahmagupta stated the rules for operations with positive and negative numbers in the seventh century A.D. There are some indications that the Chinese had some knowledge of negative numbers as early as 200 B.C. On the other hand, the Western mathematician Girolamo Cardan (1501–1576) was calling numbers such as (−1) absurd as late as 1545. ∎

Write a paper on the history of the real number system.

65. Exploration Problem If $ax + b = 0$, what effect does changing the sign of b have on the solution ($a \neq 0$; keep a fixed)?

66. Exploration Problem If $ax^2 + bx + c = 0$, what effect does changing c have on the solution ($a \neq 0$, keep a and b fixed)?

67. Exploration Problem If $\sin ax = b$, what effect does changing a have on the solution ($a \neq 0$; keep b fixed)?

68. If $c \geq 0$, show that $|x| \leq c$ if and only if $-c \leq x \leq c$.

69. Show that $-|x| \leq x \leq |x|$ for any number x.

70. Prove that $|a| = |b|$ if and only if $a = b$ or $a = -b$.

71. Prove that if $|a| < b$ and $b > 0$, then $-b < a < b$.

72. Prove the triangle inequality:

$$|x + y| \leq |x| + |y|$$

73. Show that $||x| - |y|| \leq |x - y|$ for all x and y.

74. Derive the **midpoint formula**

$$M\left(\frac{x_1 + x_2}{2}, \frac{y_1 + y_2}{2}\right)$$

for the midpoint of a segment with endpoints $P(x_1, y_1)$ and $Q(x_2, y_2)$.

1.2   Lines in the Plane

IN THIS SECTION   slope of a line, forms for the equation of a line, parallel and perpendicular lines

SLOPE OF A LINE

A distinguishing feature of a line is the fact that its *inclination* with respect to the horizontal is constant. It is common practice to specify inclination by means of a concept called *slope*. A carpenter might describe a roof line that rises 1 ft for every 3 ft of horizontal "run" as having a slope or pitch of 1 to 3.

Let Δx and Δy represent, as before, the amount of change in the variables x and y, respectively. Then a nonvertical line L that rises (or falls) Δy units (measured from bottom to top) for every Δx units of run (measured from left to right) is said to have a *slope* of $m = \Delta y / \Delta x$. (If Δy is negative, then the "rise" is actually a fall; and if Δx is negative, then the run is actually right to left.) In particular, if $P(x_1, y_1)$ and $Q(x_2, y_2)$ are two distinct points on L, then the changes in the variables x and y are given by $\Delta x = x_2 - x_1$ and $\Delta y = y_2 - y_1$, and the slope of L is

$$m = \frac{\Delta y}{\Delta x} = \frac{y_2 - y_1}{x_2 - x_1} \quad \text{for } \Delta x \neq 0 \qquad \text{See Figure 1.9.}$$

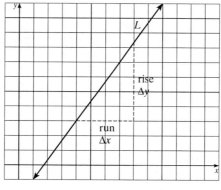

a. The slope of L is $m = \dfrac{\Delta y}{\Delta x}$.

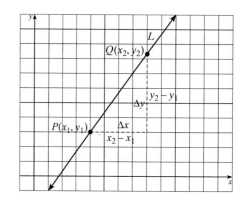

b. The slope is given by $m = \dfrac{y_2 - y_1}{x_2 - x_1}$.

Figure 1.9   The slope of a line

Slope of a Line

> A nonvertical line that contains the points $P(x_1, y_1)$ and $Q(x_2, y_2)$ has **slope**
>
> $$m = \frac{\Delta y}{\Delta x} = \frac{y_2 - y_1}{x_2 - x_1}$$

We say that a line with slope m is *rising* (when viewed from left to right) if $m > 0$, *falling* if $m < 0$, and *horizontal* if $m = 0$.

There is a useful trigonometric formulation of slope. The **angle of inclination** of a line L is defined to be the nonnegative angle ϕ ($0 \le \phi < \pi$) formed between L and the positive x-axis.

Angle of Inclination

WARNING Sometimes we say a vertical line has **infinite slope.**

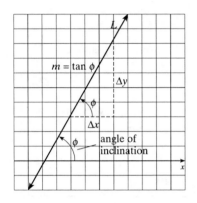

Figure 1.10 Trigonometric form for the slope of a line

> The **angle of inclination** of a line L is the angle ϕ ($0 \le \phi < \pi$) between L and the positive x-axis. Then the **slope** of L with inclination ϕ is
>
> $$m = \tan \phi$$

We see that the line L is *rising* if $0 < \phi < \frac{\pi}{2}$ and is *falling* if $\frac{\pi}{2} < \phi < \pi$. The line is *horizontal* if $\phi = 0$ and is *vertical* if $\phi = \frac{\pi}{2}$. Notice that if $\phi = \frac{\pi}{2}$, $\tan \phi$ is not defined; therefore the slope, m, is undefined for a vertical line.

To derive the trigonometric representation for slope we need to find the slope of the line through $P(x_1, y_1)$ and $Q(x_2, y_2)$, where ϕ is the angle of inclination. From the definition of the tangent, we have

$$\tan \phi = \frac{y_2 - y_1}{x_2 - x_1} = \frac{\Delta y}{\Delta x} = m \quad \text{See Figure 1.10.}$$

Lines with various slopes are shown in Figure 1.11.

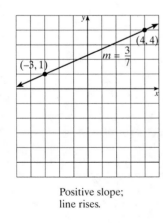

Positive slope; line rises.

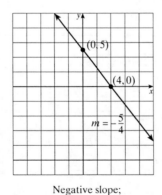

Negative slope; line falls.

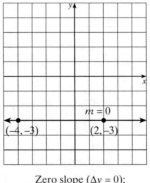

Zero slope ($\Delta y = 0$); line is horizontal.

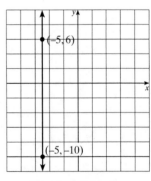

Slope is undefined; ($\Delta x = 0$) line is vertical.

Figure 1.11   Examples of slope

FORMS FOR THE EQUATION OF A LINE

In algebra you studied several forms of the equation of a line. The derivations of some of these are reviewed in the problems. Here is a summary of the forms most frequently used in calculus.

Forms of Linear Equations

Standard Form:	$Ax + By + C = 0$	A, B, C constants
		(A and B not both 0)
Slope-intercept Form:	$y = mx + b$	Slope m, y-intercept $(0, b)$
Point-slope Form:	$y - k = m(x - h)$	Slope m, through point (h, k)
Two-intercept Form:	$\dfrac{x}{a} + \dfrac{y}{b} = 1$	Intercepts $(a, 0)$ and $(0, b)$
Horizontal line:	$y = k$	Slope 0
Vertical line:	$x = h$	Slope undefined

EXAMPLE 1   Deriving the two-intercept form of the equation of a line

Derive the equation of the line with intercepts $(a, 0)$ and $(0, b)$, $a \neq 0$, $b \neq 0$.

Solution

The slope of the equation passing through the given points is

$$m = \frac{b - 0}{0 - a} = -\frac{b}{a}$$

Use the point-slope form with $h = 0$, $k = b$. (You can use either of the given points.)

$$y - b = -\frac{b}{a}(x - 0)$$
$$ay - ab = -bx$$
$$bx + ay = ab$$
$$\frac{x}{a} + \frac{y}{b} = 1 \qquad \text{Divide both sides by } ab. \quad \blacksquare$$

Two quantities x and y that satisfy a linear equation $Ax + By + C = 0$ (A and B not both 0) are said to be *linearly related*. This terminology is illustrated in Example 2.

EXAMPLE 2   Linearly related variables

When a weight is attached to a helical spring, it causes the spring to lengthen. According to Hooke's law, the length d of the spring is linearly related to the weight w.* If $d = 4$ cm when $w = 3$ g and $d = 6$ cm when $w = 6$ g, what is the original length of the spring, and what weight will cause the spring to lengthen to 5 cm?

Solution

Because d is linearly related to w, we know that points (w, d) lie on a line, and the given information tells us that two such points are $(3, 4)$ and $(6, 6)$ as shown in Figure 1.12. We first find the slope of the line and then use the point-slope form to derive its equation.

$$m = \frac{6 - 4}{6 - 3} = \frac{2}{3}$$

Next, substitute into the point-slope form with $h = 3$ and $k = 4$:

$$d - 4 = \tfrac{2}{3}(w - 3)$$
$$d = \tfrac{2}{3}w + 2$$

The original length of the spring is found for $w = 0$:

$$d = \tfrac{2}{3}(0) + 2 = 2$$

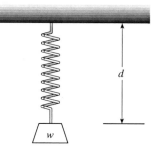

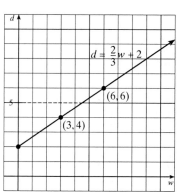

Figure 1.12 The length d of the spring is linearly related to the weight w of the attached object.

*Hooke's law is useful for small displacements, but for larger displacements, it may not be a good model.

The original length was 2 cm. To find the weight that corresponds to $d = 5$, we solve the equation

$$5 = \tfrac{2}{3}w + 2$$
$$\tfrac{9}{2} = w$$

Therefore, the weight that corresponds to a length of 5 cm is 4.5 g.   ■

PARALLEL AND PERPENDICULAR LINES

It is often useful to know whether two given lines are either parallel or perpendicular. A vertical line can be parallel only to other vertical lines and perpendicular only to horizontal lines. Cases involving nonvertical lines may be handled by the criteria given in the following box.

Slope Criteria for Parallel and Perpendicular Lines

If L_1 and L_2 are nonvertical lines with slopes m_1 and m_2, then

L_1 and L_2 are **parallel** if and only if $m_1 = m_2$;

L_1 and L_2 are **perpendicular** if and only if $m_1 m_2 = -1$, or $m_1 = -\dfrac{1}{m_2}$.

➤ **What This Says**   Nonvertical and nonhorizontal lines are parallel if and only if their slopes are equal. They are perpendicular if and only if their slopes are negative reciprocals of each other.

The key ideas behind these two slope criteria are displayed in Figure 1.13.

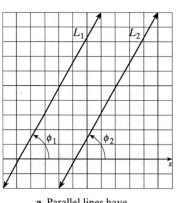

a. Parallel lines have equal slope: $m_1 = m_2$.

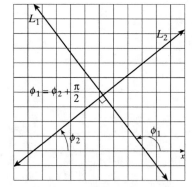

b. Perpendicular lines have negative reciprocal slopes: $m_1 m_2 = -1$.

Figure 1.13

EXAMPLE 3   Finding equations for parallel and perpendicular lines

Let L be the line $3x + 2y = 5$.

a. Find an equation of the line that is parallel to L and passes through $P(4, 7)$.
b. Find an equation of the line that is perpendicular to L and passes through $P(4, 7)$.

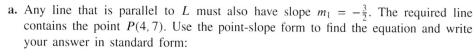

Solution

By rewriting the equation of L as $y = -\frac{3}{2}x + \frac{5}{2}$, we see that the slope of L is $m = -\frac{3}{2}$.

a. Any line that is parallel to L must also have slope $m_1 = -\frac{3}{2}$. The required line contains the point $P(4,7)$. Use the point-slope form to find the equation and write your answer in standard form:

$$y - 7 = -\tfrac{3}{2}(x - 4)$$
$$2y - 14 = -3x + 12$$
$$3x + 2y - 26 = 0$$

b. Any line perpendicular to L must have slope $m_2 = \frac{2}{3}$ (negative reciprocal of the slope of L). Once again, the required line contains the point $P(4,7)$, and we find

$$y - 7 = \tfrac{2}{3}(x - 4)$$
$$3y - 21 = 2x - 8$$
$$2x - 3y + 13 = 0$$

These lines are shown in Figure 1.14. ∎

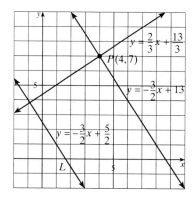

Figure 1.14 Graph of lines parallel and perpendicular to the given line $3x + 2y = 5$

1.2 PROBLEM SET

Ⓐ 1. WHAT DOES THIS SAY? Outline a procedure for graphing a linear equation.

In Problems 2–15, find the equation in standard form for the line that satisfies the given requirements.

2. passing through $(1,4)$ and $(3,6)$
3. passing through $(-1,7)$ and $(-2,9)$
4. horizontal line through $(-2,-5)$
5. passing through the point $(1,\frac{1}{2})$ with slope 0
6. slope 2 and y-intercept $(0,5)$
7. vertical line through $(-2,-5)$
8. slope -3, x-intercept $(5,0)$
9. x-intercept $(7,0)$ and y-intercept $(0,-8)$
10. x-intercept $(4.5,0)$ and y-intercept $(0,-5.4)$
11. passing through $(-1,8)$ parallel to $3x + y = 7$
12. passing through $(4,5)$ parallel to the line passing through $(2,1)$ and $(5,9)$
13. passing through $(3,-2)$ perpendicular to $4x - 3y + 2 = 0$
14. passing through $(-1,6)$ perpendicular to the line through the origin with slope 0.5
15. perpendicular to the line whose equation is $x - 4y + 5 = 0$ where it intersects the line whose equation is $2x + 3y - 1 = 0$

In Problems 16–29, find, if possible, the slope, the y-intercept, and the x-intercept of the line whose equation is given. Sketch the graph of each equation.

16. $y = \frac{2}{3}x - 8$
17. $y = -\frac{5}{7}x + 3$
18. $y - 4 = 4.001(x - 2)$
19. $y - 9 = 6.001(x - 3)$
20. $5x + 3y - 15 = 0$
21. $3x + 5y + 15 = 0$
22. $2x - 3y - 2{,}550 = 0$
23. $6x - 10y - 3 = 0$
24. $\frac{x}{4} + \frac{y}{6} = 1$
25. $\frac{x}{2} - \frac{y}{3} = 1$
26. $y = 2x$
27. $x = 5y$
28. $y - 5 = 0$
29. $x + 3 = 0$

Ⓑ 30. Find an equation for a vertical line(s) L such that a region bounded by L, the x-axis, and the line $2y - 3x = 6$ has area 3.

31. Find an equation for a horizontal line(s) M such that the region bounded by M, the y-axis, and the line $2y - 3x = 6$ has an area of 3.

32. Find the equation of the perpendicular line passing through the midpoint of the line segment connecting $(-3,7)$ and $(4,-1)$.

33. Three vertices of a parallelogram are $A(1,3)$, $C(4,11)$, and $B(3,-2)$. If A and B lie on the same side, what is the fourth vertex?

Use a graphing calculator in Problems 34–45 to solve the systems of equations graphically, and approximate the coordinates of the intersection point. Some calculators have an INTERSECT feature. Check your owner's manual. Then solve the system algebraically and compare the results.

34. $\begin{cases} 2x - 3y = -8 \\ x + y = 6 \end{cases}$
35. $\begin{cases} 2x - 3y = -8 \\ 4x - 6y = 0 \end{cases}$
36. $\begin{cases} 2x - 3y = -8 \\ y = \frac{2}{3}x + \frac{8}{3} \end{cases}$
37. $\begin{cases} 3x - 4y = 16 \\ -x + 2y = -6 \end{cases}$
38. $\begin{cases} y = 3x + 1 \\ x - 2y = 8 \end{cases}$
39. $\begin{cases} 2x + 3y = 12 \\ -4x + 6y = 18 \end{cases}$
40. $\begin{cases} 2x + 3y = 15 \\ y = \frac{2}{3}x - 20 \end{cases}$
41. $\begin{cases} x + y = 12 \\ 0.6y = 0.5(40) \end{cases}$
42. $\begin{cases} x + 3y = \cos^2 \frac{\pi}{3} \\ x + y = -\sin^2 \frac{\pi}{3} \end{cases}$
43. $\begin{cases} x^2 + y^2 = 4 \\ x - y = 0 \end{cases}$

44. $\begin{cases} x^2 + y^2 = 10 \\ (x-3)^2 + y^2 = 9 \end{cases}$ **45.** $\begin{cases} x^2 + y^2 = 15 \\ (x+4)^2 + y^2 = 16 \end{cases}$

46. A life insurance table indicates that a woman who is now A years old can expect to live E years longer. Suppose that A and E are linearly related and that $E = 50$ when $A = 24$ and $E = 20$ when $A = 60$.

   a. At what age may a woman expect to live 30 years longer?

   b. What is the life expectancy of a newborn female child?

   c. At what age is the life expectancy zero?

47. On the Fahrenheit temperature scale, water freezes at $32°$ and boils at $212°$; the corresponding temperatures on the Celsius scale are $0°$ and $100°$. Given that the Fahrenheit and Celsius temperatures are linearly related, first find numbers r and s so that $F = rC + s$, and then answer these questions.

   a. Mercury freezes at $-39°C$. What is the corresponding Fahrenheit temperature?

   b. For what value of C is $F = 0$?

   c. What temperature is the same in both scales?

48. The average SAT mathematics scores of incoming students at an eastern liberal arts college have been declining in recent years. In 1996, the average SAT score was 575; in 2001, it was 545. Assuming the average SAT score varies linearly with time, answer these questions.

   a. Express the average SAT score in terms of time measured from 1996.

   b. If the trend continues, what will the average SAT score of incoming students be in 2014?

   c. When will the average SAT score be 455?

*__49.__ **Spy Problem** An internationally famous spy has escaped from the headquarters of a diamond smuggling ring in the tiny Mediterranean country of Azusa. Our hero, driving a stolen milk truck at 72 km/hr, has a 40-minute head start on his pursuers, who are chasing him in a Ferrari going 168 km/hr. The distance from the smugglers' headquarters in Azusa to freedom in the neighboring country of Duarte is 83.8 km. Is this the end of the Spy, or does he live to return in Chapter 2?

50. A certain car rental agency charges $40 per day with 100 free miles plus 34¢ per mile after the first 100 miles. First express the cost of renting a car from this agency for one day in terms of the number of miles driven. Then draw the graph and use it to check your answers to these questions.

   a. How much does it cost to rent a car for a 1-day trip of 50 mi?

   b. How many miles were driven if the daily rental cost was $92.36?

51. A manufacturer buys $200,000 worth of machinery that depreciates linearly so that its trade-in value after 10 years will be $10,000. Express the value of the machinery as a function of its age and draw the graph. What is the value of the machinery after 4 years?

52. Show that if the point $P(x, y)$ is equidistant from $A(1, 3)$ and $B(-1, 2)$, its coordinates must satisfy the equation $4x + 2y - 5 = 0$. Sketch the graph of this equation.

53. Let $P_1(2, 6)$, $P_2(-1, 3)$, $P_3(0, -2)$, and $P_4(a, b)$ be points in the plane that are located so that $P_1 P_2 P_3 P_4$ is a parallelogram.

   a. There are three possible choices for P_4. One is $A(3, 1)$. What are the others, which we will call B and C?

   b. The centroid of a triangle is the point where its three medians intersect. Find the centroid of $\triangle ABC$ and of $\triangle P_1 P_2 P_3$. Do you notice anything interesting?

54. **Exploration Problem** Ethyl alcohol is metabolized by the human body at a constant rate (independent of concentration). Suppose the rate is 10 mL per hour.

   a. Express the time t (in hours) required to metabolize the effects of drinking ethyl alcohol in terms of the amount A of ethyl alcohol consumed.

   b. How much time is required to eliminate the effects of a liter of beer containing 3% ethyl alcohol?

   c. Discuss how the function in part **a** can be used to determine a reasonable "cutoff" value for the amount of ethyl alcohol A that each individual may be served at a party.

55. Since the beginning of the month, a local reservoir has been losing water at a constant rate (that is, the amount of water in the reservoir is a linear function of time). On the 12th of the month, the reservoir held 200 million gallons of water; on the 21st, it held only 164 million gallons. How much water was in the reservoir on the 8th of the month?

56. To encourage motorists to form car pools, the transit authority in a certain metropolitan area has been offering a special reduced rate at toll bridges for vehicles containing four or more persons. When the program began 30 days ago, 157 vehicles qualified for the reduced rate during the morning rush hour. Since then, the number of vehicles qualifying has increased at a constant rate (that is, the number is a linear function of time), and 247 vehicles qualified today. If the trend continues, how many vehicles will qualify during the morning rush hour 14 days from now?

57. **Exploration Problem** The value of a certain rare book doubles every 10 years. The book was originally worth $3.

   a. How much is the book worth when it is 30 years old? When it is 40 years old?

   b. Is the relationship between the value of the book and its age linear? Explain.

58. HISTORICAL QUEST The region between the Tigris and Euphrates Rivers (present day Iraq) is rightly known as the Cradle of Civilization. During the so-called Babylonian period (roughly 2000–600 B.C.),[†] important mathematical ideas began to germinate in the region, including positional notation for numeration. Unlike their Egyptian contemporaries who usually wrote on fragile papyrus, Babylonian mathematicians recorded their ideas on clay tablets. One of these tablets, in the Yale Collection, shows a system equivalent to

$$\begin{cases} xy = 600 \\ (x+y)^2 - 150(x-y)^2 = 100 \end{cases} \blacksquare$$

Find a positive solution ($x > 0$, $y > 0$) for this system correct to the nearest tenth.

---

*Take note: The Spy will accompany us on our journey through this book, if he can survive (which, of course, will require your help).

[†]For an interesting discussion of Mesopotamian mathematics, see *A History of Mathematics*, 2nd ed., by Carl B. Boyer, revised by Uta C. Merzbach, John Wiley and Sons, Inc., New York, 1968, pp. 26-47.

59. HISTORICAL QUEST   The Louvre Tablet from the Babylonian civilization is dated about 1500 B.C. It shows a system equivalent to

$$\begin{cases} xy = 1 \\ x + y = a \end{cases} \blacksquare$$

Solve this system for x and y in terms of a.

⊙ 60. Show that, in general, a line passing through $P(h, k)$ with slope m has the equation

$$y - k = m(x - h)$$

61. If $A(x_1, y_1)$ and $B(x_2, y_2)$ with $x_1 \neq x_2$ are two points on the graph of the line $y = mx + b$, show that

$$m = \frac{y_2 - y_1}{x_2 - x_1}$$

Use this fact to show that the graph of $y = mx + b$ is a line with slope m and then show that the line has y-intercept $(0, b)$.

62. Show that the distance s from the point (x_0, y_0) to the line $Ax + By + C = 0$ is given by the formula

$$s = \frac{|Ax_0 + By_0 + C|}{\sqrt{A^2 + B^2}}$$

63. Let L_1 and L_2 have slopes m_1 and m_2, respectively, and let ϕ be the angle between L_1 and L_2, as shown in Figure 1.15. Show that $\tan \phi = \dfrac{m_2 - m_1}{1 + m_1 m_2}$.

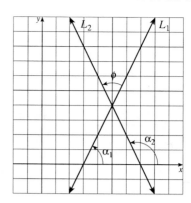

Figure 1.15   Angle ϕ between given lines

64. Journal Problem *Ontario Secondary School Mathematics Bulletin*[*] ■ Show that there is just one line in the family $y - 8 = m(x + 1)$ that is five units from the point $(2, 4)$.

65. The *centroid* of a triangle with vertices $A(x_1, y_1)$, $B(x_2, y_2)$, $C(x_3, y_3)$ is the point where its three medians intersect. It can be shown that the centroid $P(x_0, y_0)$ is located 2/3 the distance from each vertex to the midpoint of the opposite side. Use this fact to show that

$$x_0 = \frac{x_1 + x_2 + x_3}{3} \quad \text{and} \quad y_0 = \frac{y_1 + y_2 + y_3}{3}$$

1.3   Functions and Graphs

IN THIS SECTION   definition of a function, functional notation, domain of a function, composition of functions, graph of a function, classification of functions

Scientists, economists, and other researchers study relationships between quantities. For example, an engineer may need to know how the illumination from a light source on an object is related to the distance between the object and the source; a biologist may wish to investigate how the population of a bacterial colony varies with time in the presence of a toxin; an economist may wish to determine the relationship between consumer demand for a certain commodity and its market price. The mathematical study of such relationships involves the concept of a *function*.

DEFINITION OF A FUNCTION

Function

> A **function** f is a rule that assigns to each element x of a set X a unique element y of a set Y. The element y is called the **image** of x under f and is denoted by $f(x)$ (read as "f of x"). The set X is called the **domain** of f, and the set of all images of elements of X is called the **range** of the *function*.

A function whose *name* is f can be thought of as the set of ordered pairs (x, y) for which each member x of the domain is associated with exactly one member $y = f(x)$ of the range. The function can also be regarded as a rule that assigns a unique "output"

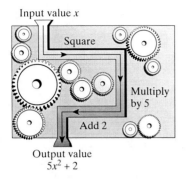

Figure 1.16 A function machine

in the set Y to each "input" from the set X, just as the function "machine" shown in Figure 1.16 generates an output of $5x^2 + 2$ for each input x.

→ **What This Says**   To be called a function, the rule must have the property that it assigns to each legitimate input one and only one output. For instance, -2 is not a legitimate input for the function that computes the square root because we are working in the set of real numbers.

A visual representation of a function is shown in Figure 1.17.

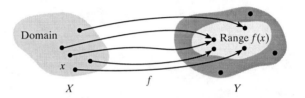

Figure 1.17   A function as a mapping

Note that it is quite possible for two different elements in the domain X to map into the same element in the range, and that it is possible for Y to include elements not in the range of f. If, however, the range of f does consist of all of Y, then f is said to map **X onto Y**. Furthermore, if each element in the range is the image of one and only one element in the domain, then f is said to be a **one-to-one function.** A function f is said to be **bounded** on $[a, b]$ if there exists a number B so that $|f(x)| \leq B$ for all x in $[a, b]$.

Most of our work will be with real-valued functions of a real variable; that is, functions whose domain and range are both sets of real numbers.*

FUNCTIONAL NOTATION

Functions can be represented in various ways, but usually they are specified by using a mathematical formula. It is traditional to let x denote the input and y the corresponding output, and to write an equation relating x and y. The letters x and y that appear in such an equation are called **variables.** Because the value of the variable y is determined by that of the variable x, we call y the **dependent variable** and x the **independent variable.**

In this book, when we define a function by an expression such as $f(x) = x^2 + 4x + 5$, we mean the function f is the set of all ordered pairs (x, y) satisfying the equation $y = x^2 + 4x + 5$. To **evaluate** a function f means to find the value of f for some particular value in the domain. For example, to evaluate f at $x = 2$ is to find $f(2)$.

EXAMPLE 1   Using functional notation

Suppose $f(x) = 2x^2 - x$. Find $f(-1)$, $f(0)$, $f(2)$, $f(\pi)$, $f(x + h)$, and

$$\frac{f(x + h) - f(x)}{h},$$

where x and h are real numbers and $h \neq 0$.

---

*Most functions that appear in this book belong to a very special class of **elementary functions**, defined by Joseph Liouville (1809–1882). Certain functions that appear in physics and higher mathematics are not elementary functions.

Solution

In this case, the defined function f tells us to subtract the independent variable x from twice its square. Thus, we have

$$f(-1) = 2(-1)^2 - (-1) = 3$$
$$f(0) = 2(0)^2 - (0) = 0$$
$$f(2) = 2(2)^2 - 2 = 6$$
$$f(\pi) = 2\pi^2 - \pi$$

To find $f(x + h)$ we begin by writing the formula for f in more neutral terms, say as

$$f(\square) = 2(\square)^2 - (\square)$$

Then we insert the expression $x + h$ inside each box, obtaining

$$f(\boxed{x + h}) = 2(\boxed{x + h})^2 - (\boxed{x + h})$$
$$= 2(x^2 + 2xh + h^2) - (x + h)$$
$$= 2x^2 + 4xh + 2h^2 - x - h$$

Finally, if $h \neq 0$,

$$\frac{f(x + h) - f(x)}{h} = \frac{[2x^2 + 4xh + 2h^2 - x - h] - [2x^2 - x]}{h}$$
$$= \frac{4xh + 2h^2 - h}{h}$$
$$= 4x + 2h - 1$$

Note: The expression $\dfrac{f(x + h) - f(x)}{h}$ is called a **difference quotient** and is used in Chapter 3 to compute the *derivative*.

Certain functions are defined differently on different parts of their domain and are thus more naturally expressed in terms of more than one formula. We refer to such functions as **piecewise-defined functions**.

EXAMPLE 2   Evaluating a piecewise-defined function

If

$$f(x) = \begin{cases} x \sin x & \text{if } x < 2 \\ 3x^2 + 1 & \text{if } x \geq 2 \end{cases}$$

find $f(-0.5)$, $f(\frac{\pi}{2})$, and $f(2)$.

Solution

To find $f(-0.5)$, we use the first line of the formula because $-0.5 < 2$:

$$f(-0.5) = -0.5 \sin(-0.5) = 0.5 \sin 0.5 \quad \text{This is the exact value.}$$
$$\approx 0.2397 \qquad\qquad\qquad \text{This is the approximate value.}$$

To find $f(\frac{\pi}{2})$, we use the first line of the formula because $\frac{\pi}{2} \approx 1.57 < 2$:

$$f(\frac{\pi}{2}) = \frac{\pi}{2} \sin \frac{\pi}{2} = \frac{\pi}{2} \quad \text{This is the exact value.}$$

Finally, because $2 \geq 2$, we use the second line of the formula to find $f(2)$.

$$f(2) = 3(2)^2 + 1 = 13$$

Functional notation can be used in a wide variety of applied problems, as shown by Example 3 and again in the problem set.

EXAMPLE 3   Applying functional notation

It is known that an object dropped from a height in a vacuum will fall a distance of s ft in t seconds according to the formula

$$s(t) = 16t^2, \qquad t \geq 0$$

a. How far will the object fall in the first second? In the *next* 2 seconds?
b. How far will it fall during the time interval $t = 1$ to $t = 1 + h$ seconds?
c. What is the average rate of change of distance (in feet per second) during the time $t = 1$ sec to $t = 3$ sec?
d. What is the average rate of change of distance during the time $t = x$ seconds to $t = x + h$ seconds?

Solution

a. $s(1) = 16(1)^2 = 16$. In the first second the object will fall 16 ft. In the next two seconds the object will fall

$$s(1 + 2) - s(1) = s(3) - s(1) = 16(3)^2 - 16(1)^2 = 128$$

The object will fall 128 ft in the next 2 sec.

b. $s(1 + h) - s(1) = 16(1 + h)^2 - 16(1)^2$
$\qquad\qquad\qquad\quad = 16 + 32h + 16h^2 - 16 = 32h + 16h^2$

c. AVERAGE RATE $= \dfrac{\text{CHANGE IN DISTANCE}}{\text{CHANGE IN TIME}} = \dfrac{s(3) - s(1)}{3 - 1} = \dfrac{128}{2} = 64.$

The average rate of change is 64 ft/sec.

d. $\dfrac{s(x + h) - s(x)}{(x + h) - x} = \dfrac{s(x + h) - s(x)}{h}$ Does this look familiar? See Example 1.

$= \dfrac{16(x + h)^2 - 16x^2}{h} = \dfrac{16x^2 + 32xh + 16h^2 - 16x^2}{h} = 32x + 16h$ ∎

DOMAIN OF A FUNCTION

In this book, unless otherwise specified, the domain of a function is the set of real numbers for which the function is defined. We call this the **domain convention** and it will be used throughout this text. If a function f is **undefined** at x, it means that x is not in the domain of f. The most frequent exclusions from the domain are those values that cause division by 0 or negative values under a square root. In applications, the domain is often specified by the context. For example, if x is the number of people on an elevator, the context requires that negative numbers and nonintegers be excluded from the domain; therefore, x must be an integer such that $0 \leq x \leq c$, where c is the maximum capacity of the elevator.

EXAMPLE 4   Domain of a function

Find the domain for the given functions.

a. $f(x) = 2x - 1$ **b.** $g(x) = 2x - 1, \; x \neq -3$

c. $h(x) = \dfrac{(2x - 1)(x + 3)}{x + 3}$ **d.** $F(x) = \sqrt{x + 2}$ **e.** $G(x) = \dfrac{4}{5 - \cos x}$

Solution

a. All real numbers; $(-\infty, \infty)$
b. All real numbers except -3. This can be written as $(-\infty, -3) \cup (-3, \infty)$.
c. Because the expression is meaningful for all $x \neq -3$, the domain is all real numbers except -3.

d. F has meaning if and only if $x + 2$ is nonnegative; therefore, the domain is $x \geq -2$, or $[-2, \infty)$.

e. G is defined whenever $5 - \cos x \neq 0$. This imposes no restriction on x since $|\cos x| \leq 1$. Thus, the domain of G is the set of all real numbers; this can be written $(-\infty, \infty)$.   ∎

Equality of Functions

> Two functions f and g are **equal** if and only if both
>
> **1.** f and g have the same domain.
> **2.** $f(x) = g(x)$ for all x in the domain.

EXAMPLE 5   Equality of functions

Consider again the functions from Example 4:

$$f(x) = 2x - 1 \qquad g(x) = 2x - 1 \text{ for } x \neq -3 \qquad h(x) = \frac{(2x - 1)(x + 3)}{x + 3}$$

Does $h(x)$ equal $f(x)$ or $g(x)$?

Solution

A common mistake is to "reduce" the function h to obtain the function f:

$$\text{WRONG:} \quad h(x) = \frac{(2x - 1)(x + 3)}{x + 3} = 2x - 1 = f(x)$$

This is wrong because the functions f and h have different domains. In particular, -3 is a valid input for f, but it is not a valid input for h. We say that the function h has a **hole** at $x = -3$. In other words, this WRONG calculation is valid only if $x \neq -3$, so the correct answer is

$$\text{RIGHT:} \quad h(x) = \frac{(2x - 1)(x + 3)}{x + 3} = 2x - 1, \; x \neq -3$$

Therefore, $h(x) = g(x)$.   ∎

COMPOSITION OF FUNCTIONS

There are many situations in which a quantity is given as a function of one variable that, in turn, can be written as a function of a second variable. Suppose, for example, that your job is to ship x packages of a product via Federal Express to a variety of addresses. Let x be the number of packages to ship, and let $f(x)$ be the weight of the x objects and $g(w)$ be the cost of shipping a package of weight w. Then

Weight is a function $f(x)$ of the number of objects x.

Cost is a function $g[f(x)]$ of the weight.

So we have expressed cost as a function of the number of packages. This process of evaluating a function of a function is known as *functional composition*.

Composition of Functions

The **composite function** $f \circ g$ is defined by

$$(f \circ g)(x) = f[g(x)]$$

for each x in the domain of g for which $g(x)$ is in the domain of f.

→ **What This Says**   To visualize how functional composition works, think of $f \circ g$ in terms of an "assembly line" in which g and f are arranged in series, with output $g(x)$ becoming the input of f, as illustrated in Figure 1.18.

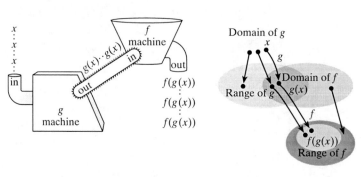

Figure 1.18   Composition of functions

EXAMPLE 6   Finding the composition of functions

If $f(x) = 3x + 5$ and $g(x) = \sqrt{x}$, find the composite functions $f \circ g$ and $g \circ f$.

Solution

The function $f \circ g$ is defined by $f[g(x)]$.

$$(f \circ g)(x) = f[g(x)] = f(\sqrt{x}) = 3\sqrt{x} + 5$$

The function $g \circ f$ is defined by $g[f(x)]$.

$$(g \circ f)(x) = g[f(x)] = g(3x + 5) = \sqrt{3x + 5}$$

WARNING   Example 6 illustrates that functional composition is not commutative.

That is, $f \circ g$ is not, in general, the same as $g \circ f$.

EXAMPLE 7   An application of composite functions

Air pollution is a problem for many metropolitan areas. Suppose a study conducted in a certain city indicates that when the population is p hundred thousand people, then the average daily level of carbon monoxide in the air is given by the formula

$$L(p) = 0.70\sqrt{p^2 + 3}$$

parts per million (ppm). A second study predicts that t years from now, the population will be $p(t) = 1 + 0.02t^3$ hundred thousand people. Assuming these formulas are correct, what level of air pollution should be expected in 4 years?

Solution

The level of pollution is $L(p) = 0.70\sqrt{p^2 + 3}$, where $p(t) = 1 + 0.02t^3$. Thus, the pollution level at time t is given by the composite function

$$(L \circ p)(t) = L[p(t)] = L(1 + 0.02t^3) = 0.70\sqrt{(1 + 0.02t^3)^2 + 3}$$

In particular, when $t = 4$, we have

$$(L \circ p)(4) = 0.70\sqrt{[1 + 0.02(4)^3]^2 + 3} \approx 2.00 \text{ ppm}$$

In calculus, it is frequently necessary to express a function as the composite of two simpler functions. Here is an example that illustrates how this can be done.

EXAMPLE 8   Expressing a given function as a composite of two functions

Express each of the following functions as the composite of two functions u and g so that $f(x) = g[u(x)]$.

a. $f(x) = (x^2 + 5x + 1)^5$ **b.** $f(x) = \cos^3 x$

c. $f(x) = \sin x^3$ **d.** $f(x) = \sqrt{5x^2 - x}$

Solution

There are often many ways to express $f(x)$ as a composite $g[u(x)]$. Perhaps the most natural is to choose u to represent the "inner" portion of f and g as the "outer" portion. Such choices are indicated in the following table.

Given Function $f(x) = g[u(x)]$	Inner Function $u(x)$	Outer Function $g(u)$
a. $f(x) = (x^2 + 5x + 1)^5$	$u(x) = x^2 + 5x + 1$	$g(u) = u^5$
b. $f(x) = \cos^3 x$	$u(x) = \cos x$	$g(u) = u^3$
c. $f(x) = \sin x^3$	$u(x) = x^3$	$g(u) = \sin u$
d. $f(x) = \sqrt{5x^2 - x}$	$u(x) = 5x^2 - x$	$g(u) = \sqrt{u}$

GRAPH OF A FUNCTION

Graphs have visual impact. They also reveal information that may not be evident from verbal or algebraic descriptions. Two graphs depicting practical relationships are shown in Figure 1.19.

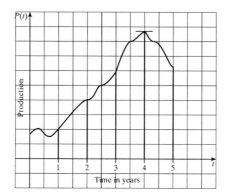

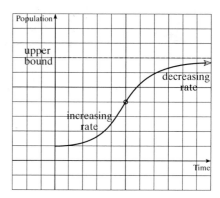

a. A production function
This graph describes the variation in total industrial production in a certain country over a five year time span. The fact that the graph has a peak suggests that production is greatest at the corresponding time.

b. Bounded population growth
This graph represents the growth of a population when environmental factors impose an upper bound on the possible size of the population. It indicates that the rate of population growth increases at first and then decreases as the size of the population gets closer and closer to the upper bound.

Figure 1.19   Two graphs with practical interpretations

To represent a function $y = f(x)$ geometrically as a graph, it is traditional to use a Cartesian coordinate system on which units for the independent variable x are marked on the horizontal axis and units for the dependent variable y on the vertical axis.

Graph of a Function

> The **graph** of a function f consists of points whose coordinates (x, y) satisfy $y = f(x)$, for all x in the domain of f.

In Chapter 4, we will discuss efficient techniques involving calculus that you can use to draw accurate graphs of functions. In algebra you began sketching lines by plotting points, but you quickly discovered that this is not a very efficient way to draw more complicated graphs, especially without the aid of a graphing calculator or computer. Table 1.3 includes a few common graphs you have probably encountered in previous courses. We will assume that you are familiar with their general shape and know how to sketch each of them either by hand or with the assistance of your graphing calculator. There are, however, certain functions, such as $f(x) = \sin \frac{1}{x}$, that are hard to graph even with a calculator or computer. That said, be assured that most functions that appear in this text or in practical applications can be graphed.

Vertical Line Test By definition of a function, for a given x in the domain there is only one number y in the range. Geometrically, this means that any vertical line $x = a$ crosses the graph of a function at most once. This observation leads to the following useful criterion.

> **The Vertical Line Test**
>
> A curve in the plane is the graph of a function if and only if it intersects no vertical line more than once.

Look at Figure 1.20 for examples of the vertical line test.

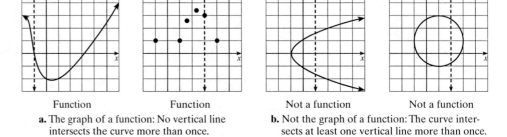

| Function | Function | Not a function | Not a function |

a. The graph of a function: No vertical line intersects the curve more than once.   **b.** Not the graph of a function: The curve intersects at least one vertical line more than once.

Figure 1.20   The vertical line test

Intercepts The points where a graph intersects the coordinate axes are called *intercepts*. Here is a definition.

Intercepts

> If the number zero is in the domain of f and $f(0) = b$, then the point $(0, b)$ is called the **y-intercept** of the graph of f. If a is a real number in the domain of f such that $f(a) = 0$, then $(a, 0)$ is an **x-intercept** of f.

> ➡ **What This Says** To find the x-intercepts, set y equal to 0 and solve for x. To find the y-intercept, set x equal to 0 and solve for y.

TABLE 1.3 Directory of Curves

Identity Function $y = x$	Standard Quadratic Function $y = x^2$	Standard Cubic Function $y = x^3$

Absolute Value Function $y = |x|$	Square Root Function $y = \sqrt{x}$	Cube Root Function $y = \sqrt[3]{x}$

Standard Reciprocal Function $y = \dfrac{1}{x}$	Standard Reciprocal Squared Function $y = \dfrac{1}{x^2}$	Standard Square Root Reciprocal Function $y = \dfrac{1}{\sqrt{x}}$

Cosine Function $y = \cos x$	Sine Function $y = \sin x$	Tangent Function $y = \tan x$

Secant Function $y = \sec x$	Cosecant Function $y = \csc x$	Cotangent Function $y = \cot x$
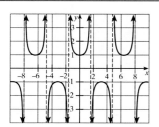	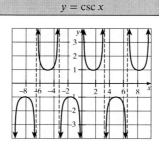	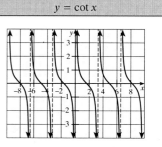

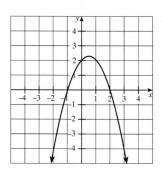

Figure 1.21 Graph of $f(x) = -x^2 + x + 2$ using the intercepts

EXAMPLE 9   Finding intercepts

Find all intercepts of the graph of the function $f(x) = -x^2 + x + 2$.

Solution

The y-intercept is $(0, f(0)) = (0, 2)$. To find the x-intercepts, solve the equation $f(x) = 0$. Factoring, we find that

$$-x^2 + x + 2 = 0$$
$$x^2 - x - 2 = 0$$
$$(x + 1)(x - 2) = 0$$
$$x = -1 \text{ or } x = 2$$

Thus, the x-intercepts are $(-1, 0)$ and $(2, 0)$, and the y-intercept is $(0, 2)$. The graph of f is shown in Figure 1.21.   ■

Symmetry   There are two kinds of symmetry that help in graphing a function, as shown in Figure 1.22 and defined in the following box.

Symmetry

> The graph of $y = f(x)$ is **symmetric with respect to the y-axis** if whenever $P(x, y)$ is a point on the graph, so is the point $(-x, y)$ that is the mirror image of P about the y-axis. Thus, y-axis symmetry occurs if and only if $f(-x) = f(x)$ for all x in the domain of f. A function with this property is called an **even function**.
>
> The graph of $y = f(x)$ is **symmetric with respect to the origin** if whenever $P(x, y)$ is on the graph, so is $(-x, -y)$, the mirror image of P about the origin. Symmetry with respect to the origin occurs when $f(-x) = -f(x)$ for all x. A function that satisfies this condition is called an **odd function**.

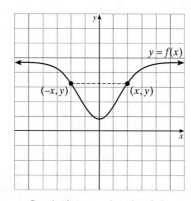

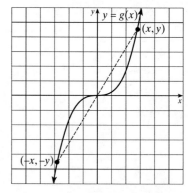

a. Graph of an even function f. Symmetry with respect to the y-axis: $f(-x) = f(x)$

b. Graph of an odd function g. Symmetry with respect to the origin: $g(-x) = -g(x)$

Figure 1.22   Graphs of even and odd functions

WARNING   The graph of a nonzero function cannot be symmetric with respect to the x-axis. In other words, if the curve is symmetric with respect to the x-axis, such as the circle, then it will not be a function.

There are many functions that are neither odd nor even. You may wonder why we have said nothing about symmetry with respect to the x-axis, but such symmetry would require $f(x) = -f(x)$, which is precluded by the vertical line test (do you see why?).

EXAMPLE 10   Even and odd functions

Classify the given functions as even, odd, or neither.

a. $f(x) = x^2$ **b.** $g(x) = x^3$ **c.** $h(x) = x^2 + 5x$

Solution

a. $f(x) = x^2$ is *even*, because

$$f(-x) = (-x)^2 = x^2 = f(x)$$

b. $g(x) = x^3$ is *odd*, because

$$g(-x) = (-x)^3 = -x^3 = -g(x)$$

c. $h(x) = x^2 + 5x$ is *neither* even nor odd because

$$h(-x) = (-x)^2 + 5(-x) = x^2 - 5x$$

Note that $h(-x) \neq h(x)$ and $h(-x) \neq -h(x)$.

The graphs of these three functions are shown in Figure 1.23. Note the symmetry in the first two graphs and the lack of symmetry with respect to the axis or the origin in the third.

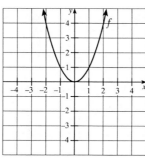
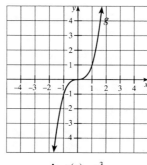
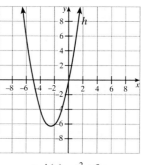

a. $f(x) = x^2$ **b.** $g(x) = x^3$ **c.** $h(x) = x^2 + 5x$

Figure 1.23   Three graphs illustrating the concept of symmetry   ■

CLASSIFICATION OF FUNCTIONS

We will now describe some of the common types of functions used in this text.

Polynomial Function

A **polynomial function** is a function of the form

$$f(x) = a_n x^n + a_{n-1} x^{n-1} + \cdots + a_2 x^2 + a_1 x + a_0$$

where n is a nonnegative integer and $a_n, \ldots, a_2, a_1, a_0$ are constants. If $a_n \neq 0$, the integer n is called the **degree** of the polynomial. The constant a_n is called the **leading coefficient** and the constant a_0 is called the **constant term** of the polynomial function. In particular,

A **constant function** is zero degree: $f(x) = a$
   Example: $f(x) = 5$

A **linear function** is first degree: $f(x) = ax + b$
   Example: $f(x) = 2x - \sqrt{2}$

A **quadratic function** is second degree: $f(x) = ax^2 + bx + c$
   Example: $f(x) = 3x^2 + 5x - \frac{1}{2}$

A **cubic function** is third degree: $f(x) = ax^3 + bx^2 + cx + d$
Example: $f(x) = \sqrt{2}x^3 - \pi x$

A **quartic function** is fourth degree: $f(x) = ax^4 + bx^3 + cx^2 + dx + e$
Example: $f(x) = 3x^4 - \frac{\sqrt{2}}{2}$

Rational Function

A **rational function** is the quotient of two polynomial functions, $p(x)$ and $d(x)$, which can be written in the form

$$f(x) = \frac{p(x)}{d(x)}, \qquad d(x) \neq 0$$

Examples: $f(x) = x^{-1}$; $\quad f(x) = \dfrac{x-5}{x^2 + 2x - 3}$; $\quad f(x) = x^{-3} + \sqrt{2}\,x$

When we write $d(x) \neq 0$, we mean that all values c for which $d(c) = 0$ are excluded from the domain of d.

If r is any nonzero real number, the function $f(x) = x^r$ is called a **power function** with exponent r. You should be familiar with the following cases:

Integer powers ($r = n$, a positive integer): $f(x) = x^n = \underbrace{x \cdot x \cdot \ldots \cdot x}_{n \text{ factors}}$

Example: $f(x) = x^6$

Reciprocal powers (r is a negative integer): $f(x) = x^{-n} = \dfrac{1}{x^n}$ for $x \neq 0$

Example: $f(x) = x^{-4}$

Roots ($r = \frac{m}{n}$ is a nonzero rational number): $f(x) = x^{m/n} = \sqrt[n]{x^m} = (\sqrt[n]{x})^m$ for all x if n odd, for $x \geq 0$ if n even, $n \neq 0$ ($\frac{m}{n}$ is reduced)

Examples: $f(x) = x^{3/4}$; $f(x) = \sqrt[5]{x^2}$

Power functions can also have irrational exponents (such as $\sqrt{2}$ or π), but such functions must be defined in a special way (see Section 2.4).

A function is called **algebraic** if it can be constructed using a finite number of algebraic operations (such as adding, subtracting, multiplying, dividing, or taking roots) starting with polynomials. Functions that are not algebraic are called **transcendental**. The following are transcendental functions:

Trigonometric functions are the functions sine, cosine, tangent, secant, cosecant, and cotangent. The basic forms of these functions are reviewed in Chapter 4 of the *Student Mathematics Handbook*. You can also review these functions by consulting a trigonometry or precalculus textbook.

SMH

Exponential functions are functions of the form $f(x) = b^x$, where b is a positive constant, $b \neq 1$. We will introduce these functions in Section 2.4.

Logarithmic functions are functions of the form $f(x) = \log_b x$, where b is a positive constant, $b \neq 1$. We will also study these functions in Section 2.4.

1.3 PROBLEM SET

In Problems 1–12, find the domain of f and compute the indicated values or state that the corresponding x-value is not in the domain. Tell whether any of the indicated values are zeros of the function, that is, values of x that cause the functional value to be 0.

Ⓐ 1. $f(x) = 2x + 3$; $f(-2)$, $f(1)$, $f(0)$

2. $f(x) = -x^2 + 2x + 3$; $f(0)$, $f(1)$, $f(-2)$

3. $f(x) = 3x^2 + 5x - 2$; $f(1)$, $f(0)$, $f(-2)$

4. $f(x) = x + \dfrac{1}{x}$; $f(-1)$, $f(1)$, $f(2)$

5. $f(x) = \dfrac{(x + 3)(x - 2)}{x + 3}$; $f(2)$, $f(0)$, $f(-3)$

6. $f(x) = (2x - 1)^{-3/2}$; $f(1)$, $f(\frac{1}{2})$, $f(13)$

7. $f(x) = \sqrt{x^2 + 2x}$; $f(-1)$, $f(\frac{1}{2})$, $f(1)$

8. $f(x) = \sqrt{x^2 + 5x + 6}$; $f(0)$, $f(1)$, $f(-2)$

9. $f(x) = \sin(1 - 2x)$; $f(-1)$, $f(\frac{1}{2})$, $f(1)$

10. $f(x) = \sin x - \cos x$; $f(0)$, $f(-\frac{\pi}{2})$, $f(\pi)$

11. $f(x) = \begin{cases} -2x + 4 & \text{if } x \le 1 \\ x + 1 & \text{if } x > 1 \end{cases}$; $f(3)$, $f(1)$, $f(0)$

12. $f(x) = \begin{cases} 3 & \text{if } x < -5 \\ x + 1 & \text{if } -5 \le x \le 5 \\ \sqrt{x} & \text{if } x > 5 \end{cases}$; $f(-6)$, $f(-5)$, $f(16)$

In Problems 13–20, evaluate the difference quotient $\dfrac{f(x + h) - f(x)}{h}$ for the given function.

13. $f(x) = 9x + 3$

14. $f(x) = 5 - 2x$

15. $f(x) = 5x^2$

16. $f(x) = 3x^2 + 2x$

17. $f(x) = |x|$ if $x < -1$ and $0 < h < 1$

18. $f(x) = |x|$ if $x > 1$ and $0 < h < 1$

19. $f(x) = \dfrac{1}{x}$

20. $f(x) = \dfrac{x + 1}{x - 1}$

State whether the functions f and g in Problems 21–26 are equal.

21. $f(x) = \dfrac{2x^2 + x}{x}$; $g(x) = 2x + 1$

22. $f(x) = \dfrac{2x^2 + x}{x}$; $g(x) = 2x + 1$, $x \ne 0$

23. $f(x) = \dfrac{2x^2 - x - 6}{x - 2}$; $g(x) = 2x + 3$, $x \ne 2$

24. $f(x) = \dfrac{3x^2 - 7x - 6}{x - 3}$; $g(x) = 3x + 2$, $x \ne 3$

25. $f(x) = \dfrac{3x^2 - 5x - 2}{x - 2}$; $g(x) = 3x + 1$

26. $f(x) = \dfrac{(3x + 1)(x - 2)}{x - 2}$, $x \ne 6$;

$g(x) = \dfrac{(3x + 1)(x - 6)}{x - 6}$, $x \ne 2$

Classify the functions defined in Problems 27–34 as even, odd, or neither.

27. $f_1(x) = x^2 + 1$

28. $f_2(x) = \sqrt{x^2}$

29. $f_3(x) = \dfrac{1}{3x^3 - 4}$

30. $f_4(x) = x^3 + x$

31. $f_5(x) = \dfrac{1}{(x^3 + 3)^2}$

32. $f_6(x) = \dfrac{1}{(x^3 + x)^2}$

33. $f_7(x) = |x|$

34. $f_8(x) = |x + x^3|$

In Problems 35–40, find the composite functions $f \circ g$ and $g \circ f$.

35. $f(x) = x^2 + 1$ and $g(x) = 2x$

36. $f(x) = \sin x$ and $g(x) = 1 - x^2$

37. $f(t) = \sqrt{t}$ and $g(t) = t^2$

38. $f(u) = \dfrac{u - 1}{u + 1}$ and $g(u) = \dfrac{u + 1}{1 - u}$

39. $f(x) = \sin x$ and $g(x) = 2x + 3$

40. $f(x) = \dfrac{1}{x}$ and $g(x) = \tan x$

In Problems 41–50, express f as the composition of two functions u and g such that $f(x) = g(u)$, where u is a function of x.

41. $f(x) = (2x^2 - 1)^4$

42. $f(x) = (x^2 + 1)^3$

43. $f(x) = |2x + 3|$

44. $f(x) = \sqrt{5x - 1}$

45. $f(x) = \tan^2 x$

46. $f(x) = \tan x^2$

47. $f(x) = \sin \sqrt{x}$

48. $f(x) = \sqrt{\sin x}$

49. $f(x) = \sin\left(\dfrac{x + 1}{2 - x}\right)$

50. $f(x) = \tan\left(\dfrac{2x}{1 - x}\right)$

51. If point A in Figure 1.24 has coordinates $(2, f(2))$, what are the coordinates of P and Q?

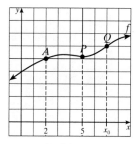
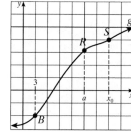

| Problem 51 | Problem 52 |

Figure 1.24

52. If point B in Figure 1.24 has coordinates $(3, g(3))$, what are the coordinates of R and S?

Find the x-intercepts, if any, for the functions given in Problems 53–60.

53. $f(x) = 3x^2 - 5x - 2$

54. $f(x) = 6x^2 + 5x - 6$

55. $f(x) = (x - 15)(2x + 25)(3x - 65)(4x + 1)$

56. $f(x) = (x^2 - 10)(x^2 - 12)(x^2 - 20)$

57. $f(x) = 5x^3 - 3x^2 + 2x$

58. $f(x) = x^4 - 41x^2 + 400$

59. $f(x) = \dfrac{x^2 - 1}{x^2 + 2}$

60. $f(x) = \dfrac{x(x^2 - 3)}{x^2 + 5}$

B **61.** Suppose the total cost (in dollars) of manufacturing q units of a certain commodity is given by

$$C(q) = q^3 - 30q^2 + 400q + 500$$

  a. Compute the cost of manufacturing 20 units.

  b. Compute the cost of manufacturing the 20th unit.

62. An efficiency study of the morning shift at a certain factory indicates that an average worker who arrives on the job at 8:00 A.M. will have assembled

$$f(x) = -x^3 + 6x + 15x^2$$

CD players x hours later ($0 \leq x \leq 8$).

  a. How many players will such a worker have assembled by 10:00 A.M.?

  b. How many players will such a worker assemble between 9:00 A.M. and 10:00 A.M.?

63. In physics, a light source of luminous intensity K candles is said to have *illuminance* $I = K/s^2$ on a flat surface s ft away. Suppose a small, unshaded lamp of luminous intensity 30 candles is connected to a rope that allows it to be raised and lowered between the floor and the top of a 10-ft-high ceiling. Assume that the lamp is being raised and lowered in such a way that at time t (in min) it is $s = 6t - t^2$ ft above the floor.

  a. Express the illuminance on the floor as a composite function of t for $0 < t < 6$.

  b. What is the illuminance when $t = 1$? When $t = 4$?

64. Biologists have found that the speed of blood in an artery is a function of the distance of the blood from the artery's central axis. According to *Poiseuille's law*, the speed (cm^3/sec) of blood that is r cm from the central axis of an artery is given by the function

$$S(r) = C \cdot (R^2 - r^2)$$

where C is a constant and R is the radius of the artery.[*] Suppose that for a certain artery, $C = 1.76 \times 10^5$ cm/sec and $R = 1.2 \times 10^{-2}$ cm. (See Figure 1.25.)

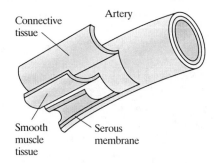

Figure 1.25 Artery

  a. Compute the speed of the blood at the central axis of this artery.

  b. Compute the speed of the blood midway between the artery's wall and central axis.

*[*] The law and the unit *poise*, a unit of viscosity, are both named for the French physician Jean Louis Poiseuille (1799–1869).

65. At a certain factory, the total cost of manufacturing q units during the daily production run is $C(q) = q^2 + q + 900$ dollars. On a typical workday, the number of units manufactured during the first t hours of a production run can be modeled by the function $q(t) = 25t$.

  a. Express the total manufacturing cost as a function of t.

  b. How much will have been spent on production by the end of the third hour?

  c. When will the total manufacturing cost reach \$11,000?

66. A ball is thrown directly upward from the edge of a cliff in such a way that t seconds later, it is

$$s = -16t^2 + 96t + 144$$

feet above the ground at the base of the cliff. Sketch the graph of this equation (making the t-axis the horizontal axis) and then answer these questions:

  a. How high is the cliff?

  b. When (to the nearest tenth of a second) does the ball hit the ground at the base of the cliff?

  c. Estimate the time it takes for the ball to reach its maximum height. What is the maximum height?

67. Charles's law for gases states that if the pressure remains constant, then

$$V(T) = V_0 \cdot \left(1 + \frac{T}{273}\right)$$

where V is the volume (in.^{3}), V_0 is the initial volume (in.^{3}), and T is the temperature (in degrees Celsius).

  a. Sketch the graph of $V(T)$ for $V_0 = 100$ and $T \geq -273$.

  b. What is the temperature needed for the volume to double?

68. To study the rate at which animals learn, a psychology student performed an experiment in which a rat was sent repeatedly through a laboratory maze. Suppose that the time (in minutes) required for the rat to traverse the maze on the nth trial was approximately

$$f(n) = 3 + \frac{12}{n}$$

  a. What is the domain of the function $f(x) = 3 + \dfrac{12}{x}$?

  b. For what values of n does $f(n)$ have meaning in the context of the psychology experiment?

  c. How long did it take the rat to traverse the maze on the third trial?

  d. On which trial did the rat first traverse the maze in 4 minutes or less?

  e. According to the function f, what will happen to the time required for the rat to traverse the maze as the number of trials increases? Will the rat ever be able to traverse the maze in less than 3 minutes?

69. The trajectory of a cannonball shot from the origin with initial velocity v and angle of inclination α (measured from level ground), is given by the equation

$$y = mx - 16v^{-2}(1 + m^2)x^2$$

where $m = \tan \alpha$. For this problem assume the initial velocity is $v = 200$ ft/s and that the angle of inclination is $42°$.

  a. Using a graphing utility of a calculator, determine the maximum height reached by the cannonball.

  b. Estimate the point where the cannonball will hit the ground.

c. Which curve in Table 1.3 shows the basic shape of this graph?

70. Draw the path of a cannonball (see Problem 69) for an angle of inclination of 47°. Determine the angle α that will maximize the distance the cannonball will travel.

71. It is estimated that t years from now, the population of a certain suburban community will be

$$P(t) = 20 - \frac{6}{t+1}$$

thousand people.

a. What will the population of the community be nine years from now?

b. By how much will the population increase during the ninth year?

c. What will happen to the size of the population in the "long run"?

72. Journal problem: *The Mathematics Student Journal.*[*] ■ Given that $f(11) = 11$ and

$$f(x+3) = \frac{f(x) - 1}{f(x) + 1}$$

for all x, find $f(2000)$.

*[*]Volume 28 (1980), issue 3, p. 2. Note that the journal problem requests $f(1979)$, which, no doubt, was related to the publication date. We have taken the liberty of updating the requested value.

73. HISTORICAL QUEST One of the best known mathematical theorems is the **Pythagorean theorem**, named after the Greek philosopher Pythagoras. Very little is known about the life of Pythagoras, but we do know he was born on the island of Samos. He founded a secret brotherhood called the Pythagoreans that continued for at least 100 years after Pythagoras was murdered for political reasons. Even though the cult was called a "brotherhood," it did admit women. According to Lynn Osen in *Women in Mathematics,*[†] the order was carried on by his wife and daughters after his death. In fact, women were probably more welcome in the centers of learning in ancient Greece than in any other age from that time until now. ■

State and prove the Pythagorean theorem.

PYTHAGORAS
ca. 500 B.C.

*[†]MIT Press, Cambridge MA, 1975.

1.4 Inverse Functions; Inverse Trigonometric Functions

IN THIS SECTION inverse functions, criteria for the existence of an inverse f^{-1}, graph of f^{-1}, inverse trigonometric functions, inverse trigonometric identities

INVERSE FUNCTIONS

WARNING The symbol f^{-1} means the inverse of f and does not mean reciprocal, $1/f$.

For a given function f, we write $y_0 = f(x_0)$ to indicate that f maps the number x_0 in its domain into the corresponding number y_0 in its range. If f has an inverse f^{-1}, it is the function that reverses the effect of f in the sense that

$$f^{-1}(y_0) = x_0$$

For example, if

$$f(x) = 2x - 3, \text{ then } f(0) = -3, \; f(1) = -1, \; f(2) = 1,$$

and the inverse f^{-1} reverses f so that

$$
\begin{array}{lll}
f(0) = -3 & \mathbf{f^{-1}(-3) = 0} & \text{that is, } f^{-1}[f(0)] = 0 \\
f(1) = -1 & \mathbf{f^{-1}(-1) = 1} & \text{that is, } f^{-1}[f(1)] = 1 \\
f(2) = 1 & \mathbf{f^{-1}(1) = 2} & \text{that is, } f^{-1}[f(2)] = 2
\end{array}
$$

In the case where the inverse of a function is itself a function, we have the following definition.

Inverse Function

Let f be a function with domain D and range R. Then the function f^{-1} with domain R and range D is the **inverse of f** if

$$f^{-1}[f(x)] = x \qquad \text{for all } x \text{ in } D$$

and

$$f[f^{-1}(y)] = y \qquad \text{for all } y \text{ in } R$$

→ **What This Says**   Suppose we consider a function defined by a set of ordered pairs (x, y) where $y = f(x)$. The image of x is y, as shown in Figure 1.26.

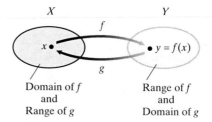

Figure 1.26   Inverse functions f and g

If y is a member of the domain of the function $g = f^{-1}$, then $g(y) = x$. This means that f matches each element of x to exactly one y, and g matches those same elements of y back to the original values of x. If you think of a function as a set of ordered pairs (x, y), the inverse of f is the set of ordered pairs with the components (y, x).

The inverse function f^{-1} reverses the effect of f. This relationship can be illustrated by function "machines," as shown in Figure 1.27. Note that the value input into the first "f machine" is x and the output $f(x)$ from this machine is the input into a second "f^{-1} machine" whose output is the original input value, x.

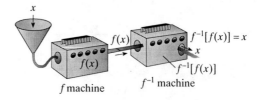

Figure 1.27   Inverse machines

The language of this definition suggests that there is only one inverse function of f. Indeed, it can be shown (see Problem 54) that if f has an inverse, then the inverse is unique.

EXAMPLE 1   Inverse of a given function defined as a set of ordered pairs

Let $f = \{(0, 3), (1, 5), (3, 9), (5, 13)\}$; find f^{-1}, if it exists.

Solution

The inverse simply reverses the ordered pairs:

$$f^{-1} = \{(3, 0), (5, 1), (9, 3), (13, 5)\}$$ ∎

EXAMPLE 2 Inverse of a given function defined by an equation

Let $f(x) = 2x - 3$; find f^{-1}, if it exists.

Solution

To find f^{-1}, let $y = f(x)$, then interchange the x and y variables, and finally solve for y.

Given function: $y = 2x - 3$ Then $x = 2y - 3$

$$2y = x + 3$$

Inverse: $y = \frac{1}{2}(x + 3)$

Thus, we represent the inverse function as $f^{-1}(x) = \frac{1}{2}(x + 3)$. To verify that these functions are inverses of each other, we note that

$$f[f^{-1}(x)] = f\left[\tfrac{1}{2}(x + 3)\right] = 2\left[\tfrac{1}{2}(x + 3)\right] - 3 = x + 3 - 3 = x$$

and

$$f^{-1}[f(x)] = f^{-1}(2x - 3) = \tfrac{1}{2}[(2x - 3) + 3] = \tfrac{1}{2}(2x) = x$$

for all x. ■

CRITERIA FOR EXISTENCE OF AN INVERSE f^{-1}

The inverse of a function may not exist. For example, both the functions

$$f = \{(0,0), (1,1), (-1,1), (2,4), (-2,4)\} \quad \text{and} \quad g(x) = x^2$$

do not have inverses because if we attempt to find the inverses, we obtain relations that are not functions. In the first case, we find

Possible inverse of f: $\{(0,0), (1,1), (1,-1), (4,2), (4,-2)\}$

This is not a function because not every member of the domain is associated with a single member in the range: $(1,1)$ and $(1,-1)$, for example.

In the second case, if we interchange the x and y in the equation for the function g where $y = x^2$ and then solve for y, we find

$$x = y^2 \quad \text{or} \quad y = \pm\sqrt{x} \quad \text{for } x \geq 0$$

But this is not a function of x, because for any positive value of x, there are two corresponding values of y, namely, $\sqrt{x}$ and $-\sqrt{x}$.

A function f will have an inverse f^{-1} on the interval I when there is exactly one number in the domain associated with each number in the range. That is, f^{-1} exists if $f(x_1)$ and $f(x_2)$ are equal only when $x_1 = x_2$. A function with this property is said to be **one-to-one**. This is equivalent to the graphical criterion, called the *horizontal line test*, shown in Figure 1.28.

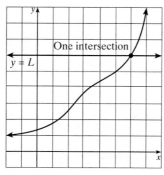

a. A function that has an inverse

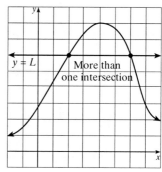

b. A function that does not have an inverse

Figure 1.28 Horizontal line test

> **Horizontal Line Test**
>
> A function f has an inverse if and only if no horizontal line intersects the graph of $y = f(x)$ at more than one point.

A function is said to be **strictly increasing** on an interval I if its graph is always rising on I, and **strictly decreasing** on I if the graph always falls on I. It is called **strictly monotonic** on I if it is either strictly increasing or strictly decreasing throughout that interval. A strictly monotonic function must be one-to-one and hence must have an inverse. For example, if f is strictly increasing on the interval I, we know that

$$x_1 > x_2 \quad \text{implies} \quad f(x_1) > f(x_2)$$

so there is no way to have $f(x_1) = f(x_2)$ unless $x_1 = x_2$. This observation is formalized in the following theorem.

THEOREM 1.2 A strictly monotonic function has an inverse

Let f be a function that is strictly monotonic on an interval I. Then f^{-1} exists and is monotonic on I (increasing if f is increasing and decreasing if f is decreasing).

Proof We have already commented on why f^{-1} exists. To show that f^{-1} is strictly increasing whenever f is increasing, let y_1 and y_2 be numbers in the range of f, with $y_2 > y_1$. We will show that $f^{-1}(y_2) > f^{-1}(y_1)$. Because y_1, y_2 are in the range of f, there exist numbers x_1, x_2 in the domain I such that $y_1 = f(x_1)$ and $y_2 = f(x_2)$. Because $y_2 > y_1$, it follows that $f(x_2) > f(x_1)$, and because f is strictly increasing, we must have $x_2 > x_1$. Thus, $f^{-1}(y_2) > f^{-1}(y_1)$, and f^{-1} is strictly increasing. Similarly, if f is strictly decreasing, then so is f^{-1}. (The details are left for the reader.) ❑

GRAPH OF f^{-1}

The graphs of f and its inverse f^{-1} are closely related. In particular, if (a, b) is a point on the graph of f, then $b = f(a)$ and $a = f^{-1}(b)$, so (b, a) is on the graph of f^{-1}. It can be shown that (a, b) and (b, a) are reflections of one another in the line $y = x$. (See Figure 1.29.) These observations yield the following procedure for sketching the graph of an inverse function.

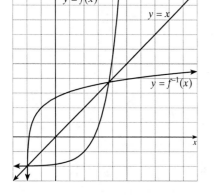

Figure 1.29 The graphs of f and f^{-1} are reflections in the line $y = x$

> **Procedure for Obtaining the Graph of f^{-1}**
>
> If f^{-1} exists, its graph may be obtained by reflecting the graph of f in the line $y = x$.

INVERSE TRIGONOMETRIC FUNCTIONS

The trigonometric functions are not one-to-one, so their inverses do not exist. However, if we restrict the domains of the trigonometric functions, then the inverses exist on those domains. In trigonometry you probably distinguished between the sine curve with unrestricted domain and the sine curve with restricted domain by writing $y = \sin x$ and $y = \operatorname{Sin} x$, respectively. In calculus, it is not customary to make such a distinction by using a capital letter.

Let us consider the sine function first. We know that the sine function is strictly increasing on the closed interval $[-\frac{\pi}{2}, \frac{\pi}{2}]$, and if we restrict $\sin x$ to this interval, it does have an inverse, as shown in Figure 1.30.

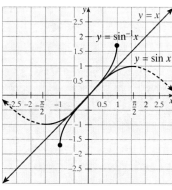

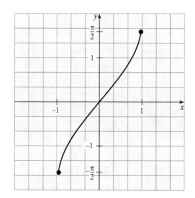

a. The graph of $y = \sin^{-1}x$ is obtained by reflecting the part of the sine on $\left[-\frac{\pi}{2}, \frac{\pi}{2}\right]$ about $y = x$.

b. The graph of the inverse sine function, $y = \sin^{-1}x$.

Figure 1.30   Inverse sine function

Inverse Sine Function

$$y = \sin^{-1} x \quad \text{if and only if} \quad x = \sin y \quad \text{and} -\frac{\pi}{2} \le y \le \frac{\pi}{2}$$

The function $\sin^{-1} x$ is sometimes written $\arcsin x$.

WARNING The function $\sin^{-1} x$ is NOT the reciprocal of $\sin x$. To denote the reciprocal, write $(\sin x)^{-1}$. In other words, $\sin^{-1} x \ne \dfrac{1}{\sin x}$, whereas $(\sin x)^{-1} = \dfrac{1}{\sin x}$.

Inverses of the other five trigonometric functions may be constructed in a similar manner. For example, by restricting $\tan x$ to the open interval $\left(-\frac{\pi}{2}, \frac{\pi}{2}\right)$ where it is one-to-one, we can define the inverse tangent function as follows.

Inverse Tangent Function

$$y = \tan^{-1} x \quad \text{if and only if} \quad x = \tan y \quad \text{and} \quad -\frac{\pi}{2} < y < \frac{\pi}{2}$$

The function $\tan^{-1} x$ is sometimes written $\arctan x$.

The graph of $y = \tan^{-1} x$ is shown in Figure 1.31.

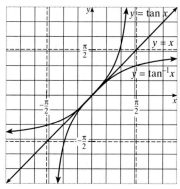

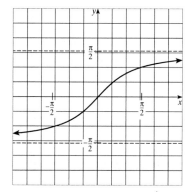

a. The graph of $y = \tan^{-1}x$ is obtained by reflecting the part of the tangent graph on $\left(-\frac{\pi}{2}, \frac{\pi}{2}\right)$ about the line $y = x$.

b. The graph of $y = \tan^{-1}x$

Figure 1.31   Graph of the inverse tangent function

Definitions and graphs of four other fundamental inverse trigonometric functions are given in Table 1.4 and Figure 1.32, respectively.

WARNING It is easier to remember the restrictions on the domain and range if you do so in terms of quadrants, as shown in Table 1.4.

TABLE 1.4 Definition of Inverse Trigonometric Functions

Inverse Function	Domain	Range
$y = \sin^{-1} x$	$-1 \leq x \leq 1$	$-\frac{\pi}{2} \leq y \leq \frac{\pi}{2}$ Quadrants I and IV
$y = \cos^{-1} x$	$-1 \leq x \leq 1$	$0 \leq y \leq \pi$ Quadrants I and II
$y = \tan^{-1} x$	$-\infty < x < +\infty$	$-\frac{\pi}{2} < y < \frac{\pi}{2}$ Quadrants I and IV
$y = \csc^{-1} x$	$x \geq 1$ or $x \leq -1$	$-\frac{\pi}{2} \leq y \leq \frac{\pi}{2}, y \neq 0$ Quadrants I and IV
$y = \sec^{-1} x$	$x \geq 1$ or $x \leq -1$	$0 \leq y \leq \pi, y \neq \frac{\pi}{2}$ Quadrants I and II
$y = \cot^{-1} x$	$-\infty < x < +\infty$	$0 < y < \pi$ Quadrants I and II

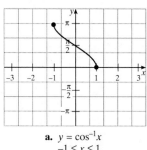

a. $y = \cos^{-1} x$
$-1 \leq x \leq 1$
$0 \leq y \leq \pi$

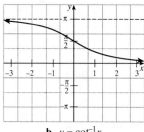

b. $y = \cot^{-1} x$
all x
$0 < y < \pi$

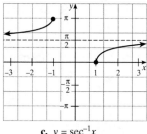

c. $y = \sec^{-1} x$
$|x| \geq 1$
$0 \leq y \leq \pi, y \neq \frac{\pi}{2}$

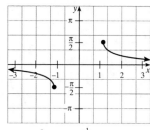

d. $y = \csc^{-1} x$
$|x| \geq 1$
$-\frac{\pi}{2} \leq y \leq \frac{\pi}{2}, y \neq 0$

Figure 1.32 Graphs of four inverse trigonometric functions

EXAMPLE 3 **Evaluating inverse trigonometric functions**

Evaluate the given functions.

a. $\sin^{-1}\left(\frac{-\sqrt{2}}{2}\right)$ **b.** $\sin^{-1} 0.21$ **c.** $\cos^{-1} 0$ **d.** $\tan^{-1}\left(\frac{1}{\sqrt{3}}\right)$

Solution

a. $\sin^{-1}\left(\frac{-\sqrt{2}}{2}\right) = -\frac{\pi}{4}$ Think: $x = \frac{-\sqrt{2}}{2}$ is negative, so y is in Quadrant IV; the reference angle is the angle whose sine is $\frac{\sqrt{2}}{2}$; it is $\frac{\pi}{4}$, so in Quadrant IV the angle is $-\frac{\pi}{4}$.

b. $\sin^{-1} 0.21 \approx 0.2115750$ By calculator; be sure to use radian mode and inverse sine (not reciprocal).

c. $\cos^{-1} 0 = \frac{\pi}{2}$ Memorized exact value.

d. $\tan^{-1}\left(\frac{1}{\sqrt{3}}\right) = \frac{\pi}{6}$ Think: $x = \frac{1}{\sqrt{3}}$ is positive, so y is in Quadrant I; the reference angle is the same as the value of the inverse tangent in Quadrant I. ∎

INVERSE TRIGONOMETRIC IDENTITIES

The definition of inverse functions yields four formulas, which we call the inversion formulas for sine and tangent.

WARNING The inversion formulas for $\sin^{-1}$ and $\tan^{-1}$ are valid only on the specified domains.

Inversion Formulas

$$\sin(\sin^{-1} x) = x \qquad \text{for } -1 \le x \le 1$$

$$\sin^{-1}(\sin y) = y \qquad \text{for } -\frac{\pi}{2} \le y \le \frac{\pi}{2}$$

$$\tan(\tan^{-1} x) = x \qquad \text{for all } x$$

$$\tan^{-1}(\tan y) = y \qquad \text{for } -\frac{\pi}{2} < y < \frac{\pi}{2}$$

EXAMPLE 4 Inversion formula for x inside and outside domain

Evaluate the given functions.

a. $\sin(\sin^{-1} 0.5)$ **b.** $\sin(\sin^{-1} 2)$ **c.** $\sin^{-1}(\sin 0.5)$ **d.** $\sin^{-1}(\sin 2)$

Solution

a. $\sin(\sin^{-1} 0.5) = 0.5$, because $-1 \le 0.5 \le 1$.
b. $\sin(\sin^{-1} 2)$ does not exist, because 2 is not between -1 and 1.
c. $\sin^{-1}(\sin 0.5) = 0.5$, because $-\frac{\pi}{2} \le 0.5 \le \frac{\pi}{2}$.
d. $\sin^{-1}(\sin 2) = 1.1415927$, by calculator.

For exact values, notice that

$$\sin 2 = \sin(\pi - 2) \quad (\text{and } -\tfrac{\pi}{2} \le \pi - 2 \le \tfrac{\pi}{2})$$

so that we have $\sin^{-1}(\sin 2) = \sin^{-1}[\sin(\pi - 2)] = \pi - 2$. ∎

Some trigonometric identities correspond to inverse trigonometric identities, but others do not. For example,

$$\sin(-x) = -\sin x \quad \text{and} \quad \cos(-x) = \cos x$$

It is true that

$$\sin^{-1}(-x) = -\sin^{-1}(x)$$

but in general,

$$\cos^{-1}(-x) \ne \cos^{-1} x$$

(For a counterexample, try $x = 1$: $\cos^{-1}(-1) = \pi$; and $\cos^{-1} 1 = 0$.)

EXAMPLE 5 Proving inverse trigonometric identities

For $-1 \le x \le 1$, show that

a. $\sin^{-1}(-x) = -\sin^{-1} x$ **b.** $\cos(\sin^{-1} x) = \sqrt{1 - x^2}$

Solution

a. Let

$$y = \sin^{-1}(-x)$$
$$\sin y = -x \qquad \qquad \text{Definition of inverse sine}$$
$$-\sin y = x$$
$$\sin(-y) = x \qquad \qquad \text{Opposite angle identity}$$
$$-y = \sin^{-1} x \qquad \qquad \text{Definition of inverse sine}$$
$$y = -\sin^{-1} x$$

Thus, $\sin^{-1}(-x) = -\sin^{-1} x$.

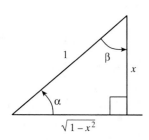

Figure 1.33 A reference triangle

b. Let $\alpha = \sin^{-1} x$, so $\sin \alpha = x$, where $-\dfrac{\pi}{2} \le \alpha \le \dfrac{\pi}{2}$. Here we consider the case where $0 \le \alpha \le \dfrac{\pi}{2}$, and the other case where $-\dfrac{\pi}{2} \le \alpha < 0$ is handled similarly. Construct a right triangle with an acute angle α and hypotenuse 1, as shown in Figure 1.33. We call this triangle a **reference triangle**.

The side opposite α is x (since $\sin \alpha = x$), and by the Pythagorean theorem, the adjacent side is $\sqrt{1 - x^2}$. Thus, we have

$$\cos(\sin^{-1} x) = \cos \alpha$$
$$= \frac{\pm\sqrt{1 - x^2}}{1}$$
$$= \sqrt{1 - x^2} \qquad \text{Substitute } \cos \alpha = x \text{ and choose the positive value for the radical because } \alpha \text{ is in Quadrant I.} \qquad \blacksquare$$

Reference triangles, such as the one shown in Figure 1.33, are extremely useful devices for obtaining inverse trigonometric identities. For instance, let α and β be angles of a right triangle with hypotenuse 1. If the side opposite α is x (so that $\sin \alpha = x$), then $\alpha = \sin^{-1} x$ and $\beta = \cos^{-1} x$ so that

$$\sin^{-1} x + \cos^{-1} x = \alpha + \beta = \frac{\pi}{2} \quad \text{for } 0 \le x \le 1$$

since the acute angles of a right triangle must sum to $\pi/2$. The same reasoning can also be used to show that

$$\tan^{-1} x + \cot^{-1} x = \frac{\pi}{2}$$

and

$$\sec^{-1} x + \csc^{-1} x = \frac{\pi}{2}$$

Identities involving inverse trigonometric functions have a variety of uses. For instance, most calculators have keys for evaluating $\sin^{-1} x$, $\cos^{-1} x$, and $\tan^{-1} x$, but what about the other three inverse trigonometric functions? The answer is given by the following theorem, which allows us to compute $\sec^{-1} x$, $\csc^{-1} x$, and $\cot^{-1} x$ using reciprocal identities involving the three inverse trigonometric functions the calculator does have.

THEOREM 1.3   Reciprocal identities for inverse trigonometric functions

$$\sec^{-1} x = \cos^{-1} \frac{1}{x} \quad \text{if } |x| \ge 1$$
$$\csc^{-1} x = \sin^{-1} \frac{1}{x} \quad \text{if } |x| \ge 1$$
$$\cot^{-1} x = \frac{\pi}{2} - \tan^{-1} x$$

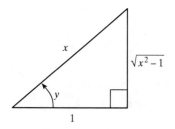

Figure 1.34 Reference triangle

Proof   We will prove that $\sec^{-1} x = \cos^{-1} \dfrac{1}{x}$ and leave the other two parts as an exercise. Let $y = \sec^{-1} x$. Then $\sec y = x$ and by using the reference triangle in Figure 1.34, we see that $\cos y = \dfrac{1}{x}$ so that

$$y = \sec^{-1} x = \cos^{-1} \frac{1}{x}$$

Note that the reference triangle is valid only if $|x| \ge 1$.   ❑

EXAMPLE 6 Evaluating inverse reciprocal functions

Evaluate the given inverse functions using the inverse identities and a calculator.

a. $\sec^{-1}(-3)$ **b.** $\csc^{-1} 7.5$ **c.** $\cot^{-1} 2.4747$

Solution

a. $\sec^{-1}(-3) = \cos^{-1}(-\frac{1}{3}) \approx 1.910633236$
b. $\csc^{-1} 7.5 = \sin^{-1}(\frac{1}{7.5}) \approx 0.1337315894$
c. $\cot^{-1} 2.4747 = \frac{\pi}{2} - \tan^{-1} 2.4747 \approx 0.3840267299$ ∎

1.4 PROBLEM SET

A 1. **Exploration Problem** Discuss the restrictions on the domain and range in the definition of the inverse trigonometric functions.

2. **Exploration Problem** Discuss the use of reference triangles with respect to the inverse trigonometric functions.

Determine which pairs of functions defined by the equations in Problems 3–8 are inverses of each other.

3. $f(x) = 5x + 3$; $g(x) = \dfrac{x-3}{5}$

4. $f(x) = \frac{2}{3}x + 2$; $g(x) = \frac{3}{2}x + 3$

5. $f(x) = \frac{4}{5}x + 4$; $g(x) = \frac{5}{4}x + 3$

6. $f(x) = \dfrac{1}{x}$, $x \neq 0$; $g(x) = \dfrac{1}{x}$, $x \neq 0$

7. $f(x) = x^2$, $x < 0$; $g(x) = \sqrt{x}$, $x > 0$

8. $f(x) = x^2$, $x \geq 0$; $g(x) = \sqrt{x}$, $x \geq 0$

Find the inverse (if it exists) of each function given in Problems 9–18.

9. $f = \{(4,5), (6,3), (7,1), (2,4)\}$

10. $g = \{(3,9), (-3,9), (4,16), (-4,16)\}$

11. $f(x) = 2x + 3$ 12. $g(x) = -3x + 2$

13. $f(x) = x^2 - 5$, $x \geq 0$ 14. $g(x) = x^2 - 5$, $x < 0$

15. $F(x) = \sqrt{x} + 5$ 16. $G(x) = 10 - \sqrt{x}$

17. $h(x) = \dfrac{2x-6}{3x+3}$ 18. $h(x) = \dfrac{2x+1}{x}$

Give the exact values for functions in Problems 19–30.

19. **a.** $\cos^{-1} \frac{1}{2}$ **b.** $\sin^{-1}(-\frac{\sqrt{3}}{2})$

20. **a.** $\sin^{-1}(-\frac{1}{2})$ **b.** $\cos^{-1}(-\frac{1}{2})$

21. **a.** $\tan^{-1}(-1)$ **b.** $\cot^{-1}(-\sqrt{3})$

22. **a.** $\sec^{-1}(-\sqrt{2})$ **b.** $\csc^{-1}(-\sqrt{2})$

23. **a.** $\sin^{-1}(-\frac{\sqrt{3}}{2})$ **b.** $\sec^{-1}(-1)$

24. **a.** $\sec^{-1}(\frac{2}{\sqrt{3}})$ **b.** $\cot^{-1}(-1)$

25. $\cos(\sin^{-1} \frac{1}{2})$ 26. $\sin(\cos^{-1} \frac{1}{\sqrt{2}})$

27. $\cot(\tan^{-1} \frac{1}{3})$ 28. $\tan(\sin^{-1} \frac{1}{3})$

29. $\cos(\sin^{-1} \frac{1}{5} + 2\cos^{-1} \frac{1}{5})$

SMH *Hint*: Use the addition law for $\cos(\alpha + \beta)$.

30. $\sin(\sin^{-1} \frac{1}{5} + \cos^{-1} \frac{1}{4})$

SMH *Hint*: Use the addition law for $\sin(\alpha + \beta)$.

31. Suppose that α is an acute angle of a right triangle where

$$\sin \alpha = \frac{s^2 - t^2}{s^2 + t^2} \quad (s > t > 0)$$

Show that $\alpha = \tan^{-1}\left(\dfrac{s^2 - t^2}{2st}\right)$.

32. If $\sin \alpha + \cos \alpha = s$ and $\sin \alpha - \cos \alpha = t$, where α is an acute angle, show that

$$\alpha = \tan^{-1}\left(\frac{s+t}{s-t}\right)$$

B *Sketch the graph of f in Problems 33–38 and then use the horizontal line test to determine whether f has an inverse. If f^{-1} exists, sketch its graph.*

33. $f(x) = x^2$, for all x 34. $f(x) = x^2$, $x \leq 0$

35. $f(x) = \sqrt{1 - x^2}$, on $(-1, 1)$

36. $f(x) = x(x-1)(x-2)$, on $[1, 2]$

37. $f(x) = \cos x$, on $[0, \pi]$

38. $f(x) = \tan x$, on $(-\frac{\pi}{2}, \frac{\pi}{2})$

Simplify each expression in Problems 39–44.

39. $\sin(2\tan^{-1} x)$ 40. $\tan(2\tan^{-1} x)$

41. $\tan(\cos^{-1} x)$ 42. $\cos(2\sin^{-1} x)$

43. $\sin(\sin^{-1} x + \cos^{-1} x)$ 44. $\cos 2(\sin^{-1} x + \cos^{-1} x)$

45. Use reference triangles, if necessary, to justify each of the following identities.

a. $\cot^{-1} x = \frac{\pi}{2} - \tan^{-1} x$ for all x

b. $\csc^{-1} x = \sin^{-1}\left(\dfrac{1}{x}\right)$ for all $|x| \geq 1$

46. Use the identities in Theorem 1.3 to evaluate each function rounded to four decimal places.

a. $\cot^{-1} 0.67$ **b.** $\sec^{-1} 1.34$

c. $\csc^{-1} 2.59$ **d.** $\cot^{-1}(-1.54)$

47. Use the identities in Theorem 1.3 to evaluate each function rounded to four decimal places.

a. $\cot^{-1} 1.5$ **b.** $\cot^{-1}(-1.5)$

c. $\sec^{-1}(-1.7)$ **d.** $\csc^{-1}(-1.84)$

48. A painting 3 ft high is hung on a wall in such a way that its lower edge is 7 ft above the floor. An observer whose eyes are 5 ft above the floor stands x ft away from the wall. Express the angle θ subtended by the painting as a function of x.

49. To determine the height of a building (see Figure 1.35), select a point P and find the angle of elevation to be α. Then move out a distance of x units (on a level plane) to point Q and find that the angle of elevation is now β. Find the height h of the building, as a function of x.

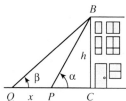

Figure 1.35   Determining height

50. a. Find $\tan^{-1} 1 + \tan^{-1} 2 + \tan^{-1} 3$ using a calculator. Make a conjecture about the exact value. Prove your conjecture using reference triangles.
  b. Prove the conjecture from part **a** using trigonometric identities. *Hint*: Find $\tan(\tan^{-1} 1 + \tan^{-1} 2 + \tan^{-1} 3)$.

51. Prove the conjecture from Problem 50a using right triangles as follows. You may use the figure shown in Figure 1.36; assume that $\triangle ABC$, $\triangle ABD$, and $\triangle DEF$ are all right triangles with lengths of sides as shown in the figure.

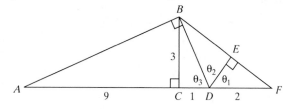

Figure 1.36 $\theta_1 + \theta_2 + \theta_3 = \pi$

52. We proved the identity

$$\csc^{-1} x = \sin^{-1}\left(\frac{1}{x}\right) \text{ for all } |x| \geq 1$$

By examining the graph of $y = \csc^{-1} x$, conjecture an identity of the form

$$\csc^{-1}(-x) = A + B \csc^{-1} x \text{ for } x > 1$$

Prove this identity, and then use it to evaluate $\csc^{-1}(-9.38)$.

53. Counterexample Problem   In Theorem 1.3 we proved the dentity

$$\sec^{-1} x = \cos^{-1}\left(\frac{1}{x}\right) \text{ for all } x \geq 1$$

The graph of $y = \sec^{-1} x$ suggests that

$$\sec^{-1}(-x) = \pi + \sec^{-1} x \text{ for } x > 1$$

Either prove this identity or find a counterexample.

54. Show that if f^{-1} exists, it is unique. *Hint*: If g_1 and g_2 both satisfy

$$g_1[f(x)] = x = f[g_1(x)]$$
$$g_2[f(x)] = x = f[g_2(x)]$$

then $g_1(x) = g_2(x)$.

55. Suppose that $\triangle ABC$ is *not* a right triangle but has an obtuse angle γ. Draw $\overline{BD}$ perpendicular to $\overline{AC}$, forming right triangles $\triangle ABD$ and $\triangle BDC$ (with right angles at D). Show that

$$\frac{\sin \alpha}{a} = \frac{\sin \gamma}{c}$$

CHAPTER 1 REVIEW

Proficiency Examination

CONCEPT PROBLEMS

1. Characterize the following sets of numbers: natural numbers ($\mathbb{N}$), whole numbers ($\mathbb{W}$), integers ($\mathbb{Z}$), rational numbers ($\mathbb{Q}$), irrational numbers ($\mathbb{Q}'$), and real numbers ($\mathbb{R}$).

2. Define absolute value.

3. State the triangle inequality.

4. State the distance formula for points $P(x_1, y_1)$ and $Q(x_2, y_2)$.

5. Define slope in terms of angle of inclination.

6. List the following forms of the equation of a line:
  a. standard form
  b. slope-intercept form
  c. point-slope form
  d. horizontal line
  e. vertical line

7. State the slope criteria for parallel and for perpendicular lines.

8. Define function.

9. Define the composition of functions.

10. What is meant by the graph of a function?

11. Draw a quick sketch of an example of each of the following functions.
  a. identity function
  b. standard quadratic function
  c. standard cubic function
  d. absolute value function
  e. cube root function
  f. standard reciprocal function
  g. standard reciprocal squared function
  h. cosine function
  i. sine function
  j. tangent function
  k. secant function
  l. cosecant function
  m. cotangent function
  n. inverse cosine function

o. inverse sine function

p. inverse tangent function

q. inverse secant function

r. inverse cosecant function

s. inverse cotangent function

12. What is a polynomial function?

13. What is a rational function?

14. a. Define an inverse function.

b. What is the procedure for graphing the inverse of a given function?

15. What is the horizontal line test?

16. State the inversion formulas for sine and tangent.

17. State the reciprocal inverse trigonometric identities.

PRACTICE PROBLEMS

18. Find an equation for the lines satisfying the given conditions:

a. through $(-\frac{1}{2}, 5)$ with slope $m = -\frac{3}{4}$

b. through $(-3, 5)$ and $(7, 2)$

c. with x-intercept $(4, 0)$ and y-intercept $(0, -\frac{3}{7})$

d. through $(-\frac{1}{2}, 5)$ and parallel to the line $2x + 5y - 11 = 0$

e. the perpendicular bisector of the line segment joining $P(-3, 7)$ and $Q(5, 1)$

Sketch the graph of each of the equations in Problems 19–26.

19. $3x + 2y - 12 = 0$

20. $y - 3 = |x + 1|$

21. $y - 3 = -2(x - 1)^2$

22. $y = x^2 - 4x - 10$

23. $y = 2\cos(x - 1)$

24. $y + 1 = \tan(2x + 3)$

25. $y = \sin^{-1}(2x)$

26. $y = \tan^{-1} x^2$

27. If $f(x) = \dfrac{1}{x + 1}$, what value(s) of x satisfy

$$f\left(\frac{1}{x+1}\right) = f\left(\frac{2x+1}{2x+4}\right)?$$

28. If $f(x) = \sqrt{\dfrac{x}{x-1}}$ and $g(x) = \dfrac{\sqrt{x}}{\sqrt{x-1}}$, does $f = g$? Why or why not?

29. If $f(x) = \sin x$ and $g(x) = \sqrt{1 - x^2}$, find the composite functions $f \circ g$ and $g \circ f$.

30. An open box with a square base is to be built for $96. The sides of the box will cost $3/ft^2 and the base will cost $8/ft^2. Express the volume of the box as a function of the length of its base.

Supplementary Problems*

In Problems 1–3, find the perimeter and area of the given figure.

1. the right triangle with vertices $(-1, 3)$, $(-1, 8)$, and $(11, 8)$

2. the triangle bounded by the lines $y = 5$, $3y - 4x = 11$, and $12x + 5y = 25$

3. the trapezoid with vertices $A(-3, 0)$, $B(5, 0)$, $C(2, 8)$, and $D(0, 8)$

In Problems 4–7, find an equation for the indicated line or circle.

4. the vertical line through the point where the line $y = 2x - 7$ intersects the parabola $y = x^2 + 6x - 3$

5. the circle that is tangent to the x-axis and is centered at $(5, 4)$

6. the circle with center on the y-axis that passes through the origin and is tangent to the line $3x + 4y - 40 = 0$

7. the line through the two points where the circles $x^2 + y^2 - 5x + 7y = 3$ and $x^2 + y^2 + 4y = 0$ intersect

8. Find constants A and B so that $\tan\left(x + \dfrac{\pi}{3}\right) = \dfrac{A + \tan x}{1 + B\tan x}$.

9. Find constants A and B so that $\sin^3 x = A\sin 3x + B\sin x$.

10. In a triangle, the perpendicular segment drawn from a given vertex to the opposite side is called the *altitude* on that side. Consider the triangle with vertices $(-2, 1)$, $(5, 6)$, and $(3, -2)$. Find an equation for each line containing an altitude of this triangle.

11. Show that the three lines found in Problem 10 intersect at the same point. Find the coordinates of this point. Is this the same point where the three medians meet?

12. Let $f(x) = x^2 + 5x - 9$. For what values of x is it true that $f(2x) = f(3x)$?

13. If an object is shot upward from the ground with an initial velocity of 256 ft/sec, its distance in feet above the ground at the end of t seconds is given by $s(t) = 256t - 16t^2$ (neglecting air resistance). What is the highest point for this projectile?

14. It is estimated that t years from now, the population of a certain suburban community will be

$$P(t) = \frac{11t + 12}{2t + 3}$$

thousand people. What is the current population of the community? What will the population be in 6 years? When will there be 5,000 people in the community?

15. Evaluate each of the given numbers (calculator approximations).

a. $\tan^{-1} 2$ b. $\cot^{-1} 2$ c. $\sec^{-1}(-3.1)$

16. Evaluate each of the given numbers (exact values).

a. $\sin(\cos^{-1} \frac{\sqrt{5}}{4})$ b. $\sin(2\tan^{-1} 3)$

c. $\sin\left(\cos^{-1} \frac{3}{5} + \sin^{-1} \frac{5}{13}\right)$

17. Solve $\sqrt{x} = \cos^{-1} 0.317 + \sin^{-1} 0.317$

In Problems 18–21, find f^{-1} if it exists.

18. $f(x) = 2x^3 - 7$

19. $f(x) = \sqrt[7]{2x + 1}$, $x \geq -\frac{1}{2}$

20. $f(x) = \sqrt{\sin x}$, $0 < x < \frac{\pi}{2}$

21. $f(x) = \dfrac{x + 5}{x - 7}$, $x \neq 7$

22. Show that for any constant $a \neq 1$, the function $f(x) = \dfrac{x + a}{x - 1}$ is its own inverse.

23. Let $f(x) = \dfrac{ax + b}{cx + d}$, for constants a, b, c, and d. Find $f^{-1}(x)$ in terms of a, b, c, and d.

24. Find $f^{-1}(x)$ if $f(x) = \dfrac{x + 1}{x - 1}$. What is the domain of f^{-1}?

25. First show that $\tan^{-1} x + \tan^{-1} y = \tan^{-1}\left(\dfrac{x + y}{1 - xy}\right)$ for $xy \neq 1$ whenever $-\dfrac{\pi}{2} < \tan^{-1}\left(\dfrac{x + y}{1 - xy}\right) < \dfrac{\pi}{2}$. Then establish the following equations.

a. $\tan^{-1} \frac{1}{2} + \tan^{-1} \frac{1}{3} = \frac{\pi}{4}$ b. $2\tan^{-1} \frac{1}{3} + \tan^{-1} \frac{1}{7} = \frac{\pi}{4}$

c. $4\tan^{-1} \frac{1}{5} - \tan^{-1} \frac{1}{239} = \frac{\pi}{4}$

Note: The identity in part **c** will be used in Chapter 8 to estimate the value of π.

---

*The supplementary problems are presented in a somewhat random order, not necessarily in order of difficulty.

26. **Counterexample Problem**   Each of the following equations may be either true or false. In each case, either show that the equation is generally true or find a counterexample.

   a. $\tan^{-1} x = \dfrac{\sin^{-1} x}{\cos^{-1} x}$ **b.** $\tan^{-1} x = \dfrac{1}{\tan x}$

   c. $\cot^{-1} x = \frac{\pi}{2} - \tan^{-1} x$ **d.** $\cos(\sin^{-1} x) = \sqrt{1 - x^2}$

   e. $\sec^{-1}\left(\frac{1}{x}\right) = \cos^{-1} x$

27. Many materials, such as brick, steel, aluminum, and concrete, expand with increases in temperature. This is why spaces are placed between the cement slabs in sidewalks. Suppose you have a 100-ft length of material securely fastened at both ends, and assume that the buckle is linear. (It is not, but this assumption will serve as a worthwhile approximation.) If the height of the buckle is x ft and the percentage of swelling is y, then x and y are related as shown in Figure 1.37. Find the amount of buckling (to the nearest inch) for the following materials:

   a. brick; $y = 0.03$ [This means $(0.03\%)(100 \text{ ft}) = 0.03$ ft, which is y in Figure 1.37.]

   b. steel; $y = 0.06$

   c. aluminum; $y = 0.12$ **d.** concrete; $y = 0.05$

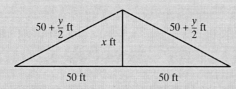

Figure 1.37   Buckling of a given material

28. A ball has been dropped from the top of a building. Its height (in feet) after t seconds is given by the function

$$h(t) = -16t^2 + 256$$

   a. How high will the ball be after 2 sec?
   b. How far will the ball travel during the third second?
   c. How tall is the building?
   d. When will the ball hit the ground?

29. Suppose the number of worker-hours required to distribute new telephone books to x percent of the households in a certain rural community is given by the function

$$f(x) = \frac{600x}{300 - x}$$

   a. What is the domain of the function f?
   b. For what values of x does $f(x)$ have a practical interpretation in this context?
   c. How many worker-hours were required to distribute new telephone books to the first 50% of the households?
   d. How many worker-hours were required to distribute new telephone books to the entire community?
   e. What percentage of the households in the community had received new telephone books by the time 150 worker-hours had been expended?

30. Find the area of each of the following plane figures:
   a. the circle with $P(0,0)$ and $Q(2,3)$ endpoints of a diameter
   b. the trapezoid with vertices $A(0,0)$, $B(4,0)$, $C(1,3)$, and $D(2,3)$

31. Find the volume and the surface area of each of the following solid figures:
   a. a sphere with radius 4
   b. a rectangular parallelepiped (box) with sides of length 2, 3, and 5
   c. a right circular cylinder (including top and bottom) with height 4 and radius 2
   d. an inverted cone with height 5 and top radius 3 (lateral surface only)

32. Consider the triangle with vertices $A(-1,4)$, $B(3,2)$, and $C(3,-6)$. Determine the midpoints M_1 and M_2 of sides $\overline{AB}$ and $\overline{AC}$, respectively, and show that the line segment $\overline{M_1 M_2}$ is parallel to side $\overline{BC}$ with half its length.

33. Generalize the procedure of Problem 32 to show that the line segment joining the midpoints of any two sides of a given triangle is parallel to the third side and has half its length.

34. Let $ABCD$ be a quadrilateral in the plane, and let P, Q, R, and S be the midpoints of sides $\overline{AB}$, $\overline{BC}$, $\overline{CD}$, and $\overline{DA}$, as shown in Figure 1.38. Show that $PQRS$ is a parallelogram.

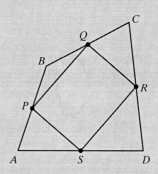

Figure 1.38   Problem 34

35. Find a constant c that guarantees that the graph of the equation

$$x^2 + xy + cy = 4$$

will have a y-intercept of $(0, -5)$. What are the x-intercepts of the graph?

36. A bus charter company offers a travel club the following arrangements: If no more than 100 people go on a certain tour, the cost will be $500 per person, but the cost per person will be reduced by $4 for each person in excess of 100 who takes the tour.
   a. Express the total revenue R obtained by the charter company as a function of the number of people who go on the tour.
   b. Sketch the graph of R. Estimate the number of people that results in the greatest total revenue for the charter company.

37. A mural 7 feet high is hung on a wall in such a way that its lower edge is 5 feet higher than the eye of an observer standing 12 feet from the wall. (See Figure 1.39.) Find the angle θ subtended by the mural at the observer's eye.

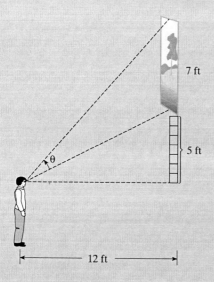

Figure 1.39 Problem 37

38. In Figure 1.40, ship *A* is at point *P* at noon and sails due east at 9 km/hr. Ship *B* arrives at point *P* at 1:00 P.M. and sails at 7 km/hr along a course that forms an angle of 60° with the course of ship *A*. Find a formula for the distance $s(t)$ separating the ships *t* hours after noon ($t \geq 1$). Approximately how far apart (to the nearest kilometer) are the ships at 4:00 P.M.?

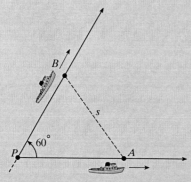

Figure 1.40 Problem 38

39. A manufacturer estimates that when the price for each unit is *p* dollars, the profit will be $N = -p^2 + 14p - 48$ thousand dollars. Sketch the graph of the profit function and answer these questions.

a. For what values of *p* is this a profitable operation? (That is, when is $N > 0$?)

b. What price results in maximum profit? What is the maximum profit?

40. Two jets bound for Los Angeles leave New York 30 minutes apart. The first travels 550 mph, and the second flies at 650 mph. How long will it take the second plane to pass the first?

41. To raise money, a service club has been collecting used bottles that it plans to deliver to a local glass company for recycling. Since the project began 8 days ago, the club has collected 2,400 pounds of glass, for which the glass company currently offers 15¢ per pound. However, since bottles are

accumulating faster than they can be recycled, the company plans to reduce the price it pays by 1¢ per pound each day until the price reaches 0¢ fifteen days from now. Assuming that the club can continue to collect bottles at the same rate and that transportation costs make more than one trip to the glass company unfeasible, express the club's revenue from its recycling project as a function of the number of additional days the project runs. Draw the graph and estimate when the club should conclude the project and deliver the bottles in order to maximize its revenue.

42. An open box with a square base is to be built for $48. The sides of the box will cost $3/ft² and the base will cost $4/ft². Express the volume of the box as a function of the length of its base.

43. A closed box with a square base is to have a volume of 250 cubic feet. The material for the top and bottom of the box costs $2/ft², and the material for the sides costs $1/ft². Express the construction cost of the box as a function of the length of its base.

44. The famous author John Uptight must decide between two publishers who are vying for the rights to his new book, *Zen and the Art of Taxidermy*. Publisher *A* offers royalties of 1% of net proceeds on the first 30,000 copies sold and 3.5% on all copies in excess of that figure, and expects to net $2 on each copy sold. Publisher *B* will pay no royalties on the first 4,000 copies sold but will pay 2% on the net proceeds of all copies sold in excess of 4,000 copies, and expects to net $3 on each copy sold.

a. Express the revenue John should expect if he signs with Publisher *A* (as a function P_A of the number of books sold, *x*). Likewise, find the revenue function P_B associated with Publisher *B*.

b. Sketch the graphs of $P_A(x)$ and $P_B(x)$ on the same coordinate axes.

c. For what value(s) of *x* are the two offers equivalent?

d. With whom should he sign if he expects to sell 5,000 copies? 100,000 copies? 200,000 copies?

e. State a simple criterion for determining which publisher he should choose if he expects to sell *N* copies.

*45. **Putnam Examination Problem** If *f* and *g* are real-valued functions of one real variable, show that there exist numbers *x*, *y* such that

$$0 \leq x \leq 1, \ 0 \leq y \leq 1, \ \text{and} \ |xy - f(x) - g(y)| \geq \tfrac{1}{4}$$

*46. **Putnam Examination Problem** Consider a polynomial $f(x)$ with real coefficients having the property $f(g(x)) = g(f(x))$ for every polynomial $g(x)$ with real coefficients. What is $f(x)$?

---

*The Putnam Examination is a national annual examination given under the auspices of the Mathematical Association of America and is designed to recognize mathematically talented college and university students. We include Putnam examination problems, which should be considered optional, to encourage students to consider taking the examination. Putnam problems used by permission of the Mathematical Association of America. Solutions to Putnam Examinations generally appear in *The American Mathematical Monthly*, approximately one year after the examination.

Calculus Was Inevitable

By John L. Troutman, Professor of Mathematics at Syracuse University

The invention of calculus is now credited jointly to Isaac Newton (1642–1727) and Gottfried W. Leibniz (1646–1716), when they produced their separate publications. However (around 1685) there was a bitter controversy throughout Europe as to whose work had been done first. Part of the explanation for this is the fact that each had done his actual work earlier (Newton in 1669; Leibniz, a little later); some can be attributed to the rivalry between scientists in England who championed Newton and those in Europe who supported Leibniz; but much simply reflects how ripe the intellectual climate was for the blooming of calculus. Indeed, even if neither of these great mathematicians had existed, it seems almost certain that the principles of calculus—including the fundamental theorem (introduced in Chapter 5)—would have been announced by the end of the seventeenth century.

Emergence of calculus was effectively demanded by the philosophical spirit of the times. Natural philosophers had long believed that the universe was constructed according to understandable mathematical principles, although they disagreed about just what these principles were and how they might be formulated. For example, the Pythagorean school (ca. 600 B.C.) maintained that everything consisted of (whole) numbers and their ratios; hence their consternation upon discovering that different entities such as $\sqrt{2}$ could be constructed. Next, the early astronomers announced that heavenly bodies move in circular orbits around the earth as center, and later that the earth itself must be a perfect sphere to reflect the divine hand of its Creator. Both of these assertions are now known to be false, and by 1612, Kepler had already explained why. Galileo (1564–1642) announced that the distance traveled by a heavy body falling from rest is proportional to the square of the elapsed time, and Fermat asserted (in 1657) that light moves along those paths that minimize the time of travel (we will discuss this principle in Chapter 4). The question was whether such laws could be formulated and justified mathematically, and what kind of mathematics would be appropriate to describe these phenomena.

For already from antiquity there was the warning of Zeno (ca. 450 B.C.), in the form of paradoxes, against unwise speculation about phenomena whose analysis involved infinite processes. In particular, he "proved" that motion was impossible if time consisted of individual "instants," and conversely, that covering a given distance was impossible if length was capable of infinite subdivision (see Chapter 8). Thus, although seventeenth-century scientists and philosophers might propose such principles, it was evident that there must be underlying subtleties in the mathematics required to support them (that, in fact, required another two centuries for satisfactory clarification).

To understand better how the mathematics developed, we must examine some of the previous attempts to solve the twin problems of classical origin that motivated the emergence of the calculus—those of finding the tangent line to a given planar geometrical curve and finding the area under the curve. Newton himself acknowledged that his greater vision resulted from his "standing on the shoulders of giants." Who were these giants, and what had they contributed? First, there were the efforts of the Greek mathematicians, principally Eudoxus, Euclid, and Archimedes, who had originated the geometric concepts of tangency and area between 400 B.C. and 200 B.C., together with examples of each, such as the construction of tangent lines to a circle and the area under a parabolic curve. The Hindu and Arabic mathematicians had extended the number system and the formal language of algebra with certain of its laws by 1300 A.D., but it was not until Newton's own era that the methods of algebra and geometry were combined satisfactorily in the analytic geometry of René Descartes (1596–1650) to produce the recognition that a geometrical curve could be regarded as the locus of points whose coordinates satisfied an algebraic equation. This provided potential numerical exactitude to geometric constructions as well as the possibility of giving geometric proofs for limiting algebraic arguments. Since Euclidian geometry was then generally regarded as the only reliable mathematics, it was the latter direction that was most frequently taken. And it was this direction that was taken in the seventeenth century by de Roberval, Fermat, Cavalieri, Huygens, Wallis, and others, not the least of whom was Newton's own teacher at Cambridge, Isaac Barrow (1630–1677). These giants, as Newton called them, obtained equations for tangent lines to, and the (correct) areas under, polynomial curves with equations $y = x^n$ for $n = 1, 2, 3, \ldots, 9$, and certain other geometrically defined curves such as the spiral and the cycloid.

In his analysis of tangency, Barrow incorporated the approximating infinitesimal triangle with sides Δx, Δy, Δs that is now standard in expositions of calculus, and Cavalieri attempted to "count" an indefinite number of parallel equidistant lines to obtain areas. It was known that in specific cases these problems were related, and that they were equivalent, respectively, to the kinematic problems of characterizing velocity and distance traveled during a motion, problems which directly confronted the paradoxes of Zeno.

All that remained was for some mathematicians to sense the generality underlying these specific constructions and to devise a usable notation for presenting the results. This was accomplished essentially independently by Newton (who, justly mistrusting the required limiting arguments, suppressed his own contributions until he could validate them geometrically) and by the only slightly less cautious Leibniz. However, as we have argued, by this time (about 1670), it was almost inevitable that someone should do so.

What calculus has provided is a mathematical language that, by means of the derivative, can describe the rates of change used to characterize various physical processes (such as velocity) and, by means of the integral, can show how macroscopic entities (such as area or distance) can emerge from properly assembled microscopic elements. Moreover, the fundamental theorem, which states that these are inverse operations, supplies an exact method for passing between these types of description. Finally, the ability to relate the results of limiting arguments by simple algebraic formulas permits the correct use of calculus while retaining skepticism regarding its foundations. This has enabled applications to go forward while mathematicians have sought an appropriate axiomatic basis.

Our present technological age attests to the success of this endeavor, and to the value of calculus.

Mathematical Essays

Use a library or references other than this textbook to research the information necessary to answer the questions in Problems 1–10.

1. HISTORICAL QUEST Sir Isaac Newton was one of the greatest mathematicians of all time. He was a genius of the highest order but was often absent-minded. One story about Newton is that, when he was a boy, he was sent to cut a hole in the bottom of the barn door for the cats to go in and out. He cut two holes, a large one for the cat and a small one for the kittens.

ISAAC NEWTON
1642–1727

   Newton considered himself a theologian rather than a mathematician or a physicist. He spent years searching for clues about the end of the world and the geography of hell. One of Newton's quotations about himself is, "I seem to have been only like a boy playing on the seashore and diverting myself in now and then finding a smoother pebble or prettier shell than ordinary, whilst the great ocean of truth lay all undiscovered before me." ■

   Write an essay about Isaac Newton and his discovery of calculus. This essay should be at least 500 words.

2. HISTORICAL QUEST At the age of 14, Gottfried Leibniz attempted to reform Aristotelian logic. He wanted to create a general method of reasoning by calculation. At the age of 20, he applied for his doctorate at the university in Leipzig and was refused (because, officials said, he was too young). He received his doctorate the next year at the University of Altdorf, where he made

GOTTFRIED LEIBNIZ
1646–1716

   such a favorable impression that he was offered a professorship, which he declined, saying he had very different things in view. Leibniz went on to invent calculus, but not without a bitter controversy developing between Leibniz and Newton. Most historians agree that the bitterness over who invented calculus materially affected the history of mathematics. J. S. Mill characterized Leibniz by saying, "It would be difficult to name a man more remarkable for the greatness and universality of his intellectual powers than Leibniz." ■

   Write a 500-word essay about Gottfried Leibniz and his discovery of calculus.

3. HISTORICAL QUEST Write a 500-word essay about the controversy surrounding the discovery of calculus by Newton and Leibniz.

4. The Greek mathematicians mentioned in this guest essay include Eudoxus, Euclid, and Archimedes. Write a short paper about contributions they made that might have been used by Newton.

5. What is the definition of elementary functions as given by Joseph Liouville?

6. The guest essay mentions the contributions of de Roberval, Fermat, Cavalieri, Huygens, Wallis, and Barrow toward the invention of calculus. Write a short paper about these contributions.

7. In this guest essay, Troutman argues that the invention of calculus was inevitable, and even if Newton and Leibniz had not invented it, someone else would have. Write a 500-word essay either defending or refuting this thesis.

8. HISTORICAL QUEST Sophie Germain was one of the first women to publish original mathematical research in number theory. In her time, women were not admitted to first-rate universities and were not, for the most part, taken seriously, so she wrote at first under the pseudonym LeBlanc. The situation is not too different from that portrayed by Barbra Streisand in the movie *Yentl*. Even

SOPHIE GERMAIN
1776–1831

though Germain's most important research was in number theory, she was awarded the prize of the French Academy for a paper entitled "Memoir on the Vibrations of Elastic Plates." ■

   As we progress through this book we will profile many mathematicians in the history of mathematics, and you will notice that most of them are white males. Why? Write a paper on the history of women mathematicians and their achievements. Your paper should include a list of many prominent women mathematicians and their primary contributions. It should also include a lengthy profile of at least one woman mathematician.

9. HISTORICAL QUEST The Navajo are a Native American people who, despite considerable interchange and assimilation with the surrounding dominant culture, maintain a world view that remains vital and distinctive. The Navajo believe in a dynamic universe. Rather than consisting of objects and situations, the universe is made up of processes. Central to our Western mode of thought is the idea that things are separable entities that can be subdivided into smaller discrete units. For us, things that change through time do so by going from one specific state to another specific state. While we believe time to be continuous, we often even break it into discrete units or freeze it and talk about an instant or point in time. Among the Navajo, where the focus is on process, change is ever present; interrelationship and motion are of primary significance. These incorporate and subsume space and time.

   There are, in every culture, groups or individuals who think more about some ideas than do others. For other cultures, we know about the ideas of some professional groups or some ideas of the culture at large. We know little, however, about the mathematical thoughts of individuals in those cultures who are specially inclined toward mathematical ideas. In Western culture, on the other hand, we focus on, and record much about, those special individuals while including little about everyone else. Realization of this difference should make us particularly wary of any comparisons across cultures. Even more important, it should encourage finding out more about the ideas of mathematically oriented innovators in other cultures and, simultaneously, encourage expanding the scope of Western history to recognize and include mathematical ideas held by different groups within our culture or by our culture as a whole.* ■

   Write a paper discussing this quotation.

10. **Book Report** "Ethnomathematics, as it is being addressed here, has the goal of broadening the history of mathematics to one that has a multicultural, global perspective." Read the book *Ethnomathematics* by Marcia Ascher (Pacific Grove: Brooks/Cole, 1991), and prepare a book report.

---

*From *Ethnomathematics* by Marcia Ascher, pp. 128–129 and 188–189.

Limits and Continuity

PREVIEW

Calculus is the mathematics of motion and change, while algebra, geometry, and trigonometry are more static in nature. The development of calculus in the seventeenth century by Newton, Leibniz, and others grew out of attempts by these and earlier mathematicians to answer certain fundamental questions about dynamic real-world situations. These investigations led to two fundamental procedures, *differentiation* and *integration*, which can be formulated in terms of a concept called the *limit*. We will introduce the limit in this chapter and study its basic properties. In addition, we will continue the investigation of functions begun in Chapter 1 by exploring the concept of functional continuity, and using limits to introduce exponential and logarithmic functions.

PERSPECTIVE

The limit is a mathematical tool for studying the tendency of a function as its independent variable approaches some value. For instance, in the guest essay at the end of Chapter 1, John Troutman mentions Zeno's paradoxes, which involve infinite processes. One such paradox can be stated as follows:

> Archilles fires an arrow, but it can never reach its target. Why? Because if the arrow takes T seconds to travel half the distance to the target, it will take $T/2$ seconds to finish half the rest, and so on for each half. No matter how close the arrow is to the target, it will take finite time to travel half the distance that remains, so the arrow will never reach its destination.

Common sense tells that the arrow will strike home in $2T$ seconds, so where is the error in reasoning? If we measure the total time of the arrow's flight by the "half, then half of that, and so on," approach of the paradox, it will take

$$T + \frac{T}{2} + \frac{T}{4} + \cdots$$

seconds for the arrow to strike the target; that is, an infinite sum of finite time intervals. The Greeks of Zeno's time assumed that such a sum would have to be infinite. However, the limit process can be used to show that this particular sum is not only finite, but equals $2T$, as common sense would suggest. We will study infinite sums in Chapter 8, but first it is necessary to introduce and explore a different kind of limit, the *limit of a function*, and that is the goal of this chapter.

In a very real sense, the concept of limit is the threshold to modern mathematics. You are about to cross that threshold, and beyond lies the fascinating world of calculus.

2.1   The Limit of a Function

IN THIS SECTION   informal computation of limits, one-sided limits, limits that do not exist, formal definition of a limit

The goal of this section is to define and explore what is meant by the *limit of a function*. We will begin with an informal discussion of the limit concept, emphasizing graphical and numerical computations. Then in Section 2.2, we will develop algebraic techniques for computing limits more systematically.

The development of the limit concept was a major breakthrough in the history of mathematics, and you should not be surprised or disappointed if certain aspects of this concept seem difficult to comprehend or apply. Be patient and this crucial concept will soon become part of your mathematical toolkit.

INFORMAL COMPUTATION OF LIMITS

The limit of a function f is a tool for investigating the behavior of $f(x)$ as x gets closer and closer to a particular number c. That is, the limit concerns the *tendency* of $f(x)$ for x near c rather than the *value* of f at $x = c$. The following example illustrates how such a tendency can be used to compute velocity.

EXAMPLE 1   Computing velocity as a limit

A freely falling body experiencing no air resistance falls $s(t) = 16t^2$ feet in t seconds. Express the body's velocity at time $t = 2$ as a limit.

Solution

What we want is the *instantaneous velocity* after 2 seconds, which can be thought of as the "speedometer reading" of the falling body at $t = 2$. To approximate the instantaneous velocity, we compute the average velocity of the body over smaller and smaller time intervals, either ending with or beginning with $t = 2$. For instance, over the time interval $1.9 \leq t \leq 2$, the average velocity, $\bar{v}(t)$, is

$$\bar{v}(t) = \frac{\text{DISTANCE TRAVELED}}{\text{ELAPSED TIME}} \qquad \text{\small Where distance is in ft}$$

$$\text{\small and time is in seconds}$$

$$= \frac{s(2) - s(1.9)}{2 - 1.9}$$

$$= \frac{16(2)^2 - 16(1.9)^2}{0.1}$$

$$= 62.4 \text{ ft/s}$$

Similar computations of average velocity over short time intervals ending or beginning with time $t = 2$ are contained in the following table:

Time interval	$1.8 \leq t \leq 2$	$1.9 \leq t \leq 2$	$1.99 \leq t \leq 2$	$1.999 \leq t \leq 2$	$2 \leq t \leq 2.0001$	$2 \leq t \leq 2.001$	$2 \leq t \leq 2.01$
Interval length (sec)	0.2	0.1	0.01	0.001	0.0001	0.001	0.01
Average velocity (ft/s)	60.8	62.4	63.84	63.98	64.0016	64.016	64.16

Examining the bottom row of this table, we see that the average velocity seems to be approaching the value 64 as the time intervals become smaller and smaller. Thus, it is reasonable to expect the velocity at the instant when $t = 2$ to be 64 ft/s.

In symbols, the average velocity of the falling body over the time interval $2 \leq t \leq 2 + h$ is given by

$$\frac{s(2 + h) - s(2)}{(2 + h) - 2} = \frac{16(2 + h)^2 - 16(2)^2}{h}$$

We say that the average velocity has a limiting value of 64 as the length h of the time interval tends to zero (gets smaller and smaller), and we denote this tendency by writing

$$\lim_{h \to 0} \frac{16(2 + h)^2 - 16(2)^2}{h} = 64 \qquad \blacksquare$$

Here is a general, though informal, definition of the limit of a function.

**Limit of a Function
(Informal Definition)**

The notation

$$\lim_{x \to c} f(x) = L$$

is read "the limit of $f(x)$ as x approaches c is L" and means that the functional values $f(x)$ can be made arbitrarily close to a unique number L by choosing x sufficiently close to c (but not equal to c).

➤ **What This Says** If $f(x)$ becomes arbitrarily close to a single number L as x approaches c from either side, then we say that L is the limit of $f(x)$ as x approaches c. It means that the functional values of f "home in" on the number L as x gets closer and closer to c. The values of x can approach c from either side, but $x = c$ itself is excluded.

Notation: Sometimes we will find it convenient to represent the limit statement

$$\lim_{x \to c} f(x) = L$$

by writing $f(x) \to L$ as $x \to c$.

This informal definition of limit cannot be used in proofs until we give precise meaning to terms such as "arbitrarily close to L" and "sufficiently close to c." This will be done at the end of this section. For now, we will use this informal definition to explore a few basic features of the limiting process.

EXAMPLE 2 Informal computation of a limit

Use a table to guess the value of

$$L = \lim_{x \to -2} \frac{x^2 + x - 2}{x + 2}$$

Solution

It would be nice if we could simply substitute $x = -2$ into the formula for

$$f(x) = \frac{x^2 + x - 2}{x + 2}$$

but note that $f(-2)$ is not defined. This is of no consequence since the limit process is concerned only when x *approaches* -2 and has nothing to do with the value of f at $x = -2$. We form a table of values of $f(x)$ for x near -2:

x	-2.3	-2.1	-2.05	-2.001	-2	-1.9997	-1.995
$f(x)$	-3.3	-3.1	-3.05	-3.001	undefined	-2.9997	-2.995

The numbers on the bottom row of this table suggest that $f(x) \to -3$ as $x \to -2$; that is,

$$L = \lim_{x \to -2} \frac{x^2 + x - 2}{x + 2} = -3$$

The graph of f is shown in Figure 2.1. Notice that the graph is a line with a "hole" at the point $(-2, -3)$. $\blacksquare$

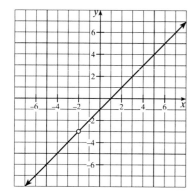

Figure 2.1 Graph of
$f(x) = \dfrac{x^2 + x - 2}{x + 2}$

EXAMPLE 3   Finding limits of trigonometric functions

Evaluate $\lim_{x \to 0} \sin x$ and $\lim_{x \to 0} \cos x$.

Solution

We can evaluate these limits by table.

x	1	0.5	0.1	0.01	−0.01	−0.1	−0.5
$\sin x$	0.84	0.48	0.0998	0.0099998	−0.0099998	−0.0998	−0.48
$\cos x$	0.54	0.88	0.9950	0.9999500	0.99995	0.9950	0.88

The pattern of numbers in the table suggests that

$$\lim_{x \to 0} \sin x = 0 = \sin 0 \qquad \text{and} \qquad \lim_{x \to 0} \cos x = 1 = \cos 0 \qquad ■$$

EXAMPLE 4   A computational dilemma

Use a table to guess the value of

$$L = \lim_{x \to 0} \frac{2\sqrt{x + 1} - x - 2}{x^2}$$

Solution

Form a table of values of

$$f(x) = \frac{2\sqrt{x + 1} - x - 2}{x^2}$$

for x near 0:

x	−0.5	−0.1	−0.01	−0.001	0	0.001	0.005
$f(x)$	−0.3431	−0.2633	−0.2513	−0.2501	undefined	−0.2499	−0.2494

The numbers on the bottom line suggest that the limit is $L = -0.25$. ■

In Example 4, note that if you decide to try $x = 0.0000001$ just to make sure you have taken numbers close enough to 0, you may find that the calculator gives the value 0. Does this mean the limit is actually 0 instead of −0.25? No, the problem is that the numerator $2\sqrt{x + 1} - x - 2$ is so close to 0 when $x = 0.0000001$ that the calculator gives a false value for f.

The point is this: When you use your calculator to estimate limits, always be aware that this method can introduce errors. In the next section, we will develop an algebraic approach for computing limits that is more reliable. The three basic approaches (examining appropriate data by using a calculator and/or a table, drawing a graph to find a limit, or using algebraic rules) each has its virtues and faults. As you study this section and the next, you need to learn all three approaches, along with their virtues and faults, and this knowledge will serve you well for the rest of your mathematical course work.

ONE-SIDED LIMITS

Sometimes we will be interested in the limiting behavior of a function from only one side; that is, the limit as x approaches a number c from the left or the analogous limit from the right.

One-Sided Limits

Right-hand limit We write $\lim\limits_{x \to c^+} f(x) = L$ if we can make the number $f(x)$ as close to L as we please by choosing x sufficiently close to c on a small interval (c, b) *immediately to the right of c.*

Left-hand limit We write $\lim\limits_{x \to c^-} f(x) = L$ if we can make the number $f(x)$ as close to L as we please by choosing x sufficiently close to c on a small interval (a, c) *immediately to the left of c.*

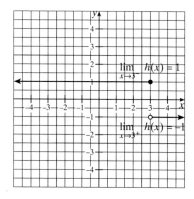

Figure 2.2 Graph of

$$h(x) = \begin{cases} 1 & \text{if } x \le 3 \\ -1 & \text{if } x > 3, \end{cases}$$

a graph illustrating one-sided limits

For instance, note that the graph in Figure 2.2 is "broken" at $x = 3$. The limit as x approaches 3 from the left is 1, while the limit from the right at the same point is -1.

Observe that the "two-sided" limit, $\lim\limits_{x \to 3} h(x)$, defined earlier in this section, does not exist since $h(x)$ does not tend toward a single limiting value L as x approaches $c = 3$ from either side. It should be clear that, in general, a two-sided limit cannot exist if the corresponding pair of one-sided limits are different. Conversely, it can be shown that if the two one-sided limits of a given function f as $x \to c^-$ and $x \to c^+$ both exist and are equal, then the two-sided limit $\lim\limits_{x \to c} f(x)$ must also exist. These observations are so important that we state them in the form of a theorem.

THEOREM 2.1 One-sided limit theorem

The two-sided limit $\lim\limits_{x \to c} f(x)$ exists if and only if the two one-sided limits $\lim\limits_{x \to c^-} f(x) = L$ and $\lim\limits_{x \to c^+} f(x)$ both exist and are equal. Furthermore, if $\lim\limits_{x \to c^-} f(x) = L = \lim\limits_{x \to c^+} f(x)$, then $\lim\limits_{x \to c} f(x) = L$. ❑

One-sided and two-sided limits are illustrated in Figure 2.3.

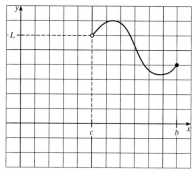

a. Left-hand limit
$\lim\limits_{x \to c^-} f(x) = L$

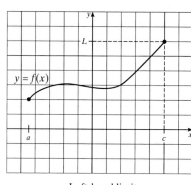

b. Right-hand limit
$\lim\limits_{x \to c^+} f(x) = L$

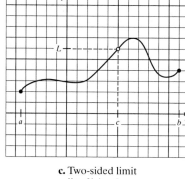

c. Two-sided limit
$\lim\limits_{x \to c} f(x) = L$

Figure 2.3 We say that $\lim\limits_{x \to c} f(x) = L$ if and only if $\lim\limits_{x \to c^-} f(x) = \lim\limits_{x \to c^+} f(x) = L$.

EXAMPLE 5 Estimating limits by graphing

Given the functions defined by the graphs in Figure 2.4, find the requested limits by inspection, if they exist.

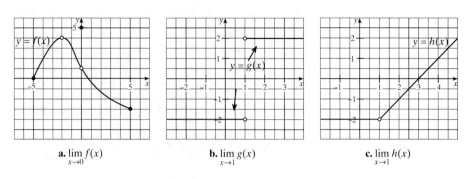

a. $\lim_{x \to 0} f(x)$ **b.** $\lim_{x \to 1} g(x)$ **c.** $\lim_{x \to 1} h(x)$

Figure 2.4 Limits from a graph

Solution

a. Take a good look at the given graph; notice the open circles on the graph at $x = 0$ and $x = -2$ and also notice that $f(0) = 5$. To find $\lim_{x \to 0} f(x)$ we need to look at both the left-hand and right-hand limits. Look at Figure 2.4a to find

$$\lim_{x \to 0^-} f(x) = 1 \quad \text{and} \quad \lim_{x \to 0^+} f(x) = 1$$

so $\lim_{x \to 0} f(x)$ exists and $\lim_{x \to 0} f(x) = 1$. Notice here that *the value of the limit as $x \to 0$ is not the same as the value of the function at $x = 0$.*

b. Look at Figure 2.4b to find

$$\lim_{x \to 1^-} g(x) = -2 \quad \text{and} \quad \lim_{x \to 1^+} g(x) = 2$$

so the *limit as $x \to 1$ does not exist.*

c. Look at Figure 2.4c to find

$$\lim_{x \to 1^-} h(x) = -2 \quad \text{and} \quad \lim_{x \to 1^+} h(x) = -2$$

so $\lim_{x \to 1} h(x) = -2$. ∎

EXAMPLE 6   Evaluating a trigonometric limit using a table

Evaluate $\lim_{x \to 0} \dfrac{\sin x}{x}$.

Solution

$f(x) = \dfrac{\sin x}{x}$ is an even function because

$$f(-x) = \frac{\sin(-x)}{-x} = \frac{-\sin x}{-x} = \frac{\sin x}{x} = f(x)$$

This means that we need to find only the right-hand limit at 0 because the limiting behavior from the left will be the same as that from the right. Consider the following table.

x	0.1 ‑ ‑ ‑ ‑▶	0.05 ‑ ‑ ‑ ‑ ‑▶	0.01 ‑ ‑ ‑ ‑ ‑▶	0.001 ‑ ‑ ‑ ‑ ‑▶	0
$f(x)$	0.998334	0.999583	0.9999833	0.999999833	Undefined

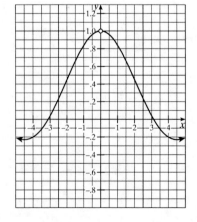

Figure 2.5 Graph of $f(x) = \dfrac{\sin x}{x}$

The table suggests that $\lim_{x \to 0^+} \dfrac{\sin x}{x} = 1$ and hence that $\lim_{x \to 0} \dfrac{\sin x}{x} = 1$. We will revisit this limit in Section 2.2. The graph of $f(x) = \dfrac{\sin x}{x}$ is shown in Figure 2.5. ∎

LIMITS THAT DO NOT EXIST

It may happen that a function f does not have a (finite) limit as $x \to c$. When $\lim_{x \to c} f(x)$ fails to exist, the functional values $f(x)$ are said to **diverge** as $x \to c$.

EXAMPLE 7   A function that diverges

Evaluate $\lim_{x \to 0} \dfrac{1}{x^2}$.

Solution

As $x \to 0$, the corresponding functional values of $f(x) = \dfrac{1}{x^2}$ grow arbitrarily large, as indicated in the following table.

	x approaches 0 from the left; $x \to 0^-$				*x* approaches 0 from the right; $x \to 0^+$		
x	$-0.1 \dashrightarrow$	$-0.05 \dashrightarrow$	$-0.001 \dashrightarrow$	0	$\dashleftarrow 0.001$	$\dashleftarrow 0.005$	$\dashleftarrow 0.01$
$f(x) = \dfrac{1}{x^2}$	100	400	1×10^6	undefined	1×10^6	4×10^4	1×10^4

The graph of f is shown in Figure 2.6.

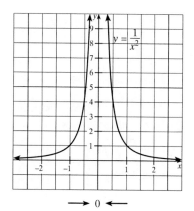

$$\longrightarrow \ 0 \ \longleftarrow$$

Figure 2.6 $\lim_{x \to 0} \dfrac{1}{x^2}$ does not exist, and the graph illustrates that f rises without bound.

Geometrically, the graph of $y = f(x)$ rises without bound as $x \to 0$. Thus, $\lim_{x \to 0} \dfrac{1}{x^2}$ does not exist. ∎

Infinite Limits

WARNING   It is important to remember that ∞ is *not* a number, but is merely a symbol denoting unrestricted growth in the magnitude of the function.

A function f that increases or decreases without bound as x approaches c is said to **tend to infinity** (∞) at c. We indicate this behavior by writing

$$\lim_{x \to c} f(x) = +\infty \qquad \text{if } f \text{ increases without bound}$$

and by

$$\lim_{x \to c} f(x) = -\infty \qquad \text{if } f \text{ decreases without bound}$$

Using this notation, we can rewrite the answer to Example 7 as

$$\lim_{x \to 0} \dfrac{1}{x^2} = +\infty$$

EXAMPLE 8   A function that diverges by oscillation

Evaluate $\lim\limits_{x \to 0} \sin \dfrac{1}{x}$.

Solution

Note this is not the same as $\lim\limits_{x \to 0} \dfrac{\sin x}{x}$. The values of $f(x) = \sin \dfrac{1}{x}$ oscillate infinitely often between 1 and -1 as x approaches 0. For example, $f(x) = 1$ for $x = \frac{2}{\pi}, \frac{2}{5\pi}, \frac{2}{9\pi}, \dots$, and $f(x) = -1$ for $x = \frac{2}{3\pi}, \frac{2}{7\pi}, \frac{2}{11\pi}, \dots$. The graph of $f(x)$ is shown in Figure 2.7.

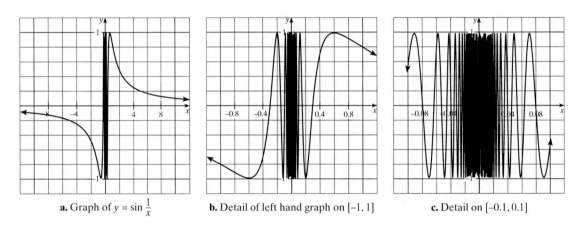

a. Graph of $y = \sin \frac{1}{x}$ **b.** Detail of left hand graph on $[-1, 1]$ **c.** Detail on $[-0.1, 0.1]$

Figure 2.7 $\sin \frac{1}{x}$ diverges by oscillation as $x \to 0$.

Because the values of $f(x)$ do not approach a unique number L as $x \to 0$, the limit does not exist. This kind of limiting behavior is called **divergence by oscillation**.   ■

In the next section, we will introduce some properties of limits that will help us evaluate limits efficiently. In the following problem set remember that the emphasis is on an intuitive understanding of limits, including their evaluation by graphing and by table.

FORMAL DEFINITION OF A LIMIT

Our informal definition of the limit provides valuable intuition and allows you to develop a working knowledge of this fundamental concept. For theoretical work, however, the intuitive definition will not suffice, because it gives no precise, quantifiable meaning to the terms "arbitrarily close to L" and "sufficiently close to c." In the nineteenth century, leading mathematicians, including Augustin-Louis Cauchy (1789–1857) and Karl Weierstrass (1815–1897), sought to put calculus on a sound logical foundation by giving precise definitions for the foundational ideas of calculus. The following definition, derived from the work of Cauchy and Weierstrass, gives precision to the limit notion.

**Limit of a Function
(Formal definition)**

The limit statement
$$\lim_{x \to c} f(x) = L$$
means that for each number $\epsilon > 0$, there corresponds a number $\delta > 0$ with the property that
$$|f(x) - L| < \epsilon \quad \text{whenever} \quad 0 < |x - c| < \delta$$

We show this definition graphically in Figure 2.8.

For each ε > 0	**there is a δ > 0**	**such that**	**if 0 < |x − c| < δ,**	**then |f(x) − L| < ε.**
This forms an interval around L on the y-axis.	This forms an interval around c on the x-axis.		This says that if x is in the δ-interval on the x-axis...	... then $f(x)$ is in the ε-interval on the y-axis.

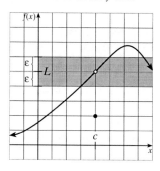 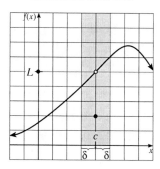 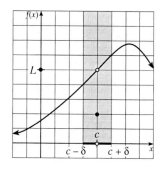 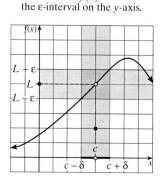

Figure 2.8 Formal definition of limit: $\lim_{x \to c} f(x) = L$

Because the Greek letters ϵ (epsilon) and δ (delta) are traditionally used in this context, the formal definition of limit is sometimes called the **epsilon-delta** definition of the limit. The goal of this section is to show how this formal definition embodies our intuitive understanding of the limit process and how it can be used rigorously to establish a variety of results.

Do not be discouraged if this material seems difficult—it is. Probably your best course of action is to read this section carefully and examine the details of a few examples closely. Then, using the examples as models, try some of the exercises. This material often takes several attempts, but if you persevere, you should come away with an appreciation of the epsilon-delta process—and with it, a better understanding of calculus.

Behind the formal language is a fairly straightforward idea. In particular, to establish a specific limit, say $\lim_{x \to c} f(x) = L$, a number $\epsilon > 0$ is chosen first to establish a desired degree of proximity to L, and then a number $\delta > 0$ is found that determines how close x must be to c to ensure that $f(x)$ is within ϵ units of L.

The situation is summarized in Figure 2.9, which shows a function that satisfies the conditions of the definition. Notice that whenever x is within δ units of c (but not equal to c), the point $(x, f(x))$ on the graph of f must lie in the rectangle (shaded region) formed by the intersection of the horizontal band of width 2ϵ centered at L and the vertical band of width 2δ centered at c. The smaller the ϵ-interval around the proposed limit L, generally the smaller the δ-interval will need to be for $f(x)$ to lie in the ϵ-interval. If such a δ can be found no matter how small ϵ is, then $f(x)$ and L are arbitrarily close, so L must be the limit. The following examples illustrate epsilon-delta proofs, one in which the limit exists and one in which it does not.

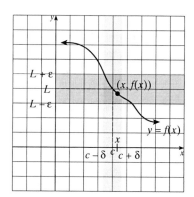

Figure 2.9 The epsilon-delta definition of limit

EXAMPLE 9 An epsilon-delta proof of a limit statement

Show that $\lim_{x \to 2}(4x - 3) = 5$.

Solution

From the graph of $f(x) = 4x - 3$ (see Figure 2.10), we guess that the limit as $x \to 2$ is 5. The object of this example is to *prove* that the limit is 5. We have

$$|f(x) - L| = |4x - 3 - 5|$$
$$= |4x - 8|$$
$$= \underbrace{4|x - 2|}$$

This must be less than ϵ whenever $|x - 2| < \delta$.

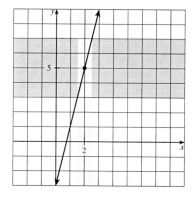

Figure 2.10 $\lim_{x \to 2}(4x - 3) = 5$

For a given $\epsilon > 0$, choose $\delta = \dfrac{\epsilon}{4}$; then

$$|f(x) - L| = 4\,|x - 2| < 4\delta = 4\left(\dfrac{\epsilon}{4}\right) = \epsilon \qquad\blacksquare$$

EXAMPLE 10   An epsilon-delta proof that a limit does not exist

Show that $\displaystyle\lim_{x \to 0} \dfrac{1}{x}$ does not exist.

Solution

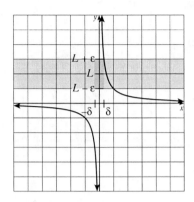

Figure 2.11 $\displaystyle\lim_{x \to 0} \dfrac{1}{x}$

Let $f(x) = \dfrac{1}{x}$ and L be any number. Suppose that $\displaystyle\lim_{x \to 0} f(x) = L$. Look at the graph of f, as shown in Figure 2.11. It would seem that no matter what value of ϵ is chosen, it would be impossible to find a corresponding δ. Consider the absolute value expression required by the definition of limit: If

$$|f(x) - L| < \epsilon, \quad \text{or, for this example,} \quad \left|\dfrac{1}{x} - L\right| < \epsilon$$

then

$$-\epsilon < \dfrac{1}{x} - L < \epsilon \qquad \text{Property of absolute value (Table 1.1, p. 3)}$$

and

$$L - \epsilon < \dfrac{1}{x} < L + \epsilon$$

If $\epsilon = 1$ (not a particularly small ϵ), then

$$\left|\dfrac{1}{x}\right| < |L| + 1$$

$$|x| > \dfrac{1}{|L| + 1}$$

In general, given any $\epsilon > 0$, then no matter how $\delta > 0$ is chosen, there will always be numbers x in the interval $0 < |x - 0| < \delta$ such that $\dfrac{1}{|x|} > L + \epsilon$. Since L was chosen arbitrarily, it follows that the limit does not exist. $\qquad\blacksquare$

Appendix B gives many of the important proofs in calculus, and if you look there, you will see many of them are given in ϵ-δ form. In the following problem set, remember that the emphasis is on an intuitive understanding of limits, including their evaluation by graphing and by table.

2.1 PROBLEM SET

A *Given the functions defined by the graphs in Figure 2.12, find the limits in Problems 1–6.*

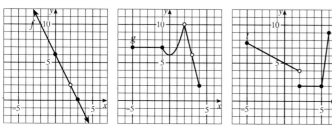

Graph of *f*   Graph of *g*   Graph of *t*

Figure 2.12 Graphs of the functions *f*, *g*, and *t*

1. **a.** $\lim_{x \to 3} f(x)$ **b.** $\lim_{x \to 2} f(x)$ **c.** $\lim_{x \to 0} f(x)$

2. **a.** $\lim_{x \to -3} g(x)$ **b.** $\lim_{x \to -1} g(x)$ **c.** $\lim_{x \to 4^-} g(x)$

3. **a.** $\lim_{x \to 4} t(x)$ **b.** $\lim_{x \to -4} t(x)$ **c.** $\lim_{x \to -5^+} t(x)$

4. **a.** $\lim_{x \to 2^-} f(x)$ **b.** $\lim_{x \to 2^+} f(x)$ **c.** $\lim_{x \to 2} f(x)$

5. **a.** $\lim_{x \to 3^-} g(x)$ **b.** $\lim_{x \to 3^+} g(x)$ **c.** $\lim_{x \to 3} g(x)$

6. **a.** $\lim_{x \to 2^-} t(x)$ **b.** $\lim_{x \to 2^+} t(x)$ **c.** $\lim_{x \to 2} t(x)$

Find the limits by filling in the appropriate values in the tables in Problems 7–9.

7. $\lim_{x \to 5^-} f(x)$, where $f(x) = 4x - 5$

$$x \to 5^-$$

x	2	3	4	4.5	4.9	4.99
$f(x)$	3					

$$f(x) \to ?$$

8. $\lim_{x \to 2^-} g(x)$, where $g(x) = \dfrac{x^3 - 8}{x^2 + 2x + 4}$

$$x \to 2^-$$

x	1	1.5	1.9	1.99	1.999	1.9999
$g(x)$	−1					

$$g(x) \to ?$$

9. $\lim_{x \to 2} h(x)$, where $h(x) = \dfrac{3x^2 - 2x - 8}{x - 2}$

	$x \to 2^-$				$2^+ \leftarrow x$			
x	1	1.9	1.99	1.999	2.001	2.1	2.5	3
$h(x)$	7							

$$h(x) \to ? \leftarrow h(x)$$

10. Find $\lim_{x \to 0} \dfrac{\tan 2x}{\tan 3x}$ using the following procedure based on the fact that $f(x) = \tan x$ is an odd function.

If $f(x) = \dfrac{\tan 2x}{\tan 3x}$, then

$$f(-x) = \frac{\tan(-2x)}{\tan(-3x)} = \frac{-\tan 2x}{-\tan 3x} = f(x).$$

Thus, we simply need to check for $x \to 0^+$. Find the limit by completing the following table.

	$x \to 0^+$				
x	1	0.5	0.1	0.01	0.001
$f(x)$	15.33				

$$f(x) \to ?$$

Describe each illustration in Problems 11–16 using a limit statement.

11.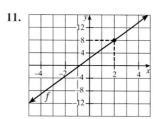

12.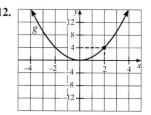

13.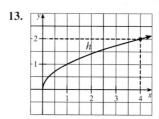

14.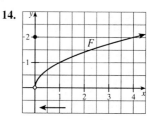

15.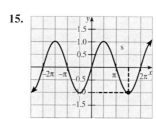

16.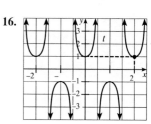

B **17. WHAT DOES THIS SAY?** *Explain a process for finding a limit.

Evaluate the limits in Problems 18–44 to two decimal places by graphing or by using a table of values, and check your answer using a calculator. If the limit does not exist, explain why.

18. $\lim_{x \to 0^+} x^4$

19. $\lim_{x \to 0^+} \cos x$

20. $\lim_{x \to 2^-} (x^2 - 4)$

21. $\lim_{x \to 3^-} (x^2 - 4)$

22. $\lim_{x \to 1^+} \dfrac{1}{x - 3}$

23. $\lim_{x \to -3^+} \dfrac{1}{x - 3}$

24. $\lim_{x \to 3} \dfrac{1}{x - 3}$

25. $\lim_{x \to \pi/2} \tan x$

---

*Many problems in this book are labeled What Does This Say? Following the question will be a question for you to answer in your own words, or a statement for you to rephrase in your own words. These problems are intended to be similar to the "What This Says" boxes.

26. a. $\displaystyle\lim_{x\to 0}\frac{\cos x}{x}$

    b. $\displaystyle\lim_{x\to \pi}\frac{\cos x}{x}$

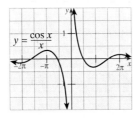

$y = \dfrac{\cos x}{x}$

27. a. $\displaystyle\lim_{x\to 0}\frac{1-\cos x}{x}$

    b. $\displaystyle\lim_{x\to \pi}\frac{1-\cos x}{x}$

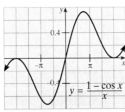

$y = \dfrac{1-\cos x}{x}$

28. a. $\displaystyle\lim_{x\to 0.4}|x|\sin\frac{1}{x}$

    b. $\displaystyle\lim_{x\to 0}|x|\sin\frac{1}{x}$

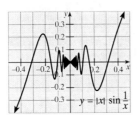

$y = |x|\sin\dfrac{1}{x}$

29. $\displaystyle\lim_{x\to 3}\frac{x^2+3x-10}{x-2}$

30. $\displaystyle\lim_{x\to 3}\frac{x^2+3x-10}{x-3}$

31. $\displaystyle\lim_{x\to \pi/2}\frac{2x-\pi}{\cos x}$

32. $\displaystyle\lim_{x\to 1}\frac{\sin\frac{\pi}{x}}{x-1}$

33. $\displaystyle\lim_{x\to 9}\frac{\sqrt{x}-3}{x-9}$

34. $\displaystyle\lim_{x\to 9}\frac{\sqrt{x}-3}{x-3}$

35. $\displaystyle\lim_{x\to 2}\frac{\sqrt{x+2}-2}{x-2}$

36. $\displaystyle\lim_{x\to 1}\frac{\sqrt[3]{x}-1}{\sqrt{x}-1}$

37. $\displaystyle\lim_{x\to 3^+}\frac{\sqrt{x-3}+x}{3-x}$

38. $\displaystyle\lim_{x\to 4^+}\frac{\frac{1}{\sqrt{x}}-\frac{1}{2}}{x-4}$

39. $\displaystyle\lim_{x\to 0}\frac{\sin 2x}{x}$

40. $\displaystyle\lim_{x\to 0}\frac{\sin 3x}{x}$

41. $\displaystyle\lim_{x\to 0}\frac{1-\frac{1}{x+1}}{x}$

42. $\displaystyle\lim_{x\to 1}\frac{1-\frac{1}{x}}{x-1}$

43. $\displaystyle\lim_{x\to 0}\cos\frac{1}{x}$

44. $\displaystyle\lim_{x\to 0}\tan\frac{1}{x}$

45. A ball is thrown directly upward from the edge of a cliff and travels in such a way that t seconds later, its height (in feet) above the ground at the base of the cliff is

$$s(t) = -16t^2 + 40t + 24$$

a. Compute the limit

$$v(t) = \lim_{x\to t}\frac{s(x)-s(t)}{x-t}$$

to find the instantaneous velocity of the ball at time t.

b. What is the ball's initial velocity?

c. When does the ball hit the ground, and what is its impact velocity at time $t = 0$?

d. When does the ball have velocity 0? What physical interpretation should be given to this time?

46. Tom and Sue are driving along a straight, level road in a car whose speedometer needle is broken but that has a trip odometer that can measure the distance traveled from an arbitrary starting point in tenths of a mile. At 2:50 P.M., Tom says he would like to know how fast they are traveling at 3:00 P.M., so Sue takes down the odometer readings listed in the table, makes a few calculations, and announces the desired velocity. What is her result?

time t	2:50	2:55	2:59	3:00	3:01	3:03	3:06
odometer reading	33.9	38.2	41.5	42.4	43.2	44.9	47.4

In Problems 47–48, estimate the limits by plotting points or by using tables.

47. $\displaystyle\lim_{x\to 13}\frac{x^3-9x^2-45x-91}{x-13}$

48. $\displaystyle\lim_{x\to 13}\frac{x^3-9x^2-39x-86}{x-13}$

49. HISTORICAL QUEST   By the second half of the 1700s, it was generally accepted that without logical underpinnings, calculus would be limited. Augustin-Louis Cauchy developed an acceptable theory of limits, and in doing so removed much doubt about the logical validity of calculus. Cauchy is described by the historian Howard Eves not only as a first-rate mathematician with tremendous mathematical productivity but also as a lawyer (he practiced law for 14 years), a mountain climber, and a painter (he worked in watercolors). Among other characteristics that distinguished him from his contemporaries, he advocated respect for the environment.

AUGUSTIN–LOUIS CAUCHY 1789–1857

Cauchy wrote a treatise on integrals in 1814 that is considered a classic, and in 1816 his paper on wave propagation in liquids won a prize from the French Academy. It has been said that with his work the modern era of analysis began. In all, he wrote over 700 papers, which are, today, considered no less than brilliant. ∎

Cauchy did not formulate the ϵ-δ definition of limit that we use today, but formulated instead a purely arithmetical definition. Consult some history of mathematics books to find a translation of Cauchy's definition, which appeared in his monumental treatise, *Cours d'Analyse de l'Ecole Royale Polytechnique* (1821). As part of your research, find when and where the ϵ-δ definition of limit was first used.

⊙ *In Problems 50–55, use the formal definition of the limit to prove or disprove the given limit statement.*

50. $\displaystyle\lim_{x\to 2}(x+3)=5$

51. $\displaystyle\lim_{t\to 0}(3t-1)=0$

52. $\displaystyle\lim_{x\to -2}(3x+7)=1$

53. $\displaystyle\lim_{x\to 1}(2x-5)=-3$

54. $\displaystyle\lim_{x\to 2}(x^2+2)=6$

55. $\displaystyle\lim_{x\to 2}\frac{1}{x}=\frac{1}{2}$

56. The tabular approach is a convenient device for discussing limits informally, but if it is not used very carefully, it can be misleading. For example, for $x \neq 0$, let

$$f(x) = \sin\frac{1}{x}$$

a. Construct a table showing the values of $f(x)$ for $x = \frac{-2}{\pi}, \frac{-2}{9\pi}, \frac{-2}{13\pi}, \frac{2}{19\pi}, \frac{2}{7\pi}, \frac{2}{3\pi}$. Based on this table, what would you say about $\lim\limits_{x \to 0} f(x)$?

b. Construct a second table, this time showing the values of $f(x)$ for $x = \frac{-1}{2\pi}, \frac{-1}{11\pi}, \frac{-1}{20\pi}, \frac{1}{50\pi}, \frac{1}{30\pi}, \frac{1}{5\pi}$. Now what would you say about $\lim\limits_{x \to 0} f(x)$?

c. Based on the results in parts **a** and **b**, what do you conclude about $\lim\limits_{x \to 0} \sin \frac{1}{x}$?

2.2 Algebraic Computation of Limits

IN THIS SECTION computations with limits, using algebra to find limits, two special trigonometric limits, limits of piecewise-defined functions

COMPUTATIONS WITH LIMITS

In Section 2.1, we observed that finding limits by tables or by graphing is risky. In this section, we will explore a more exact way of computing limits that is based on the following properties.

Basic Properties and Rules for Limits

For any real number c, suppose the functions f and g both have limits at $x = c$.

Constant rule $\quad \lim\limits_{x \to c} k = k$ for any constant k

Limit of x rule $\quad \lim\limits_{x \to c} x = c$

Multiple rule $\quad \lim\limits_{x \to c} [k f(x)] = k \lim\limits_{x \to c} f(x)$ for any constant k

The limit of a constant times a function is the constant times the limit of the function.

Sum rule $\quad \lim\limits_{x \to c} [f(x) + g(x)] = \lim\limits_{x \to c} f(x) + \lim\limits_{x \to c} g(x)$

The limit of a sum is the sum of the limits.

Difference rule $\quad \lim\limits_{x \to c} [f(x) - g(x)] = \lim\limits_{x \to c} f(x) - \lim\limits_{x \to c} g(x)$

The limit of a difference is the difference of the limits.

Product rule $\quad \lim\limits_{x \to c} [f(x)g(x)] = \left[\lim\limits_{x \to c} f(x)\right]\left[\lim\limits_{x \to c} g(x)\right]$

The limit of a product is the product of the limits.

Quotient rule $\quad \lim\limits_{x \to c} \dfrac{f(x)}{g(x)} = \dfrac{\lim\limits_{x \to c} f(x)}{\lim\limits_{x \to c} g(x)}$ if $\lim\limits_{x \to c} g(x) \neq 0$

The limit of a quotient is the quotient of the limits, as long as the limit of the denominator is not zero.

Power rule $\quad \lim\limits_{x \to c} [f(x)]^n = \left[\lim\limits_{x \to c} f(x)\right]^n$ $\quad n$ is a rational number and the limit on the right exists.

The limit of a power is the power of the limit.

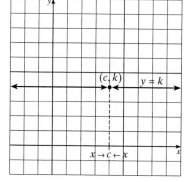

a. Limit of a constant: $\lim\limits_{x \to c} k = k$

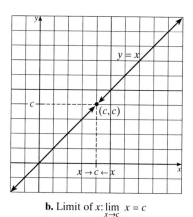

b. Limit of x: $\lim\limits_{x \to c} x = c$

Figure 2.13 Two basic limits

It is fairly easy to justify graphically the rules for the limit of a constant and the limit of x, as shown in Figure 2.13. All of these properties of limits (including the two basic limits shown in Figure 2.13) can be proved using the formal definition of limit.

EXAMPLE 1   **Finding the limit of a polynomial function**

Evaluate $\lim\limits_{x\to 2}(2x^5 - 9x^3 + 3x^2 - 11)$.

Solution

$$\lim_{x\to 2}(2x^5 - 9x^3 + 3x^2 - 11) = \lim_{x\to 2}(2x^5) - \lim_{x\to 2}(9x^3) + \lim_{x\to 2}(3x^2) - \lim_{x\to 2}(11)$$

Sum and difference rules

$$= 2\left[\lim_{x\to 2} x^5\right] - 9\left[\lim_{x\to 2} x^3\right] + 3\left[\lim_{x\to 2} x^2\right] - 11$$

Multiple and constant rules

$$= 2\left[\lim_{x\to 2} x\right]^5 - 9\left[\lim_{x\to 2} x\right]^3 + 3\left[\lim_{x\to 2} x\right]^2 - 11$$

Power rule

$$= 2(2)^5 - 9(2)^3 + 3(2)^2 - 11 = -7$$

Limit of x rule   ■

Comment: If you consider Example 1 carefully, it is easy to see that if P is any polynomial, then the limit at $x = c$ can be found by substituting $x = c$ into the formula for $P(x)$.

Limit of a Polynomial Function

If P is a polynomial function, then

$$\lim_{x\to c} P(x) = P(c)$$

EXAMPLE 2   **Finding the limit of a rational function**

Evaluate $\lim\limits_{z\to -1}\dfrac{z^3 - 3z + 7}{5z^2 + 9z + 6}$.

Solution

$$\lim_{z\to -1}\frac{z^3 - 3z + 7}{5z^2 + 9z + 6} = \frac{\lim\limits_{z\to -1}(z^3 - 3z + 7)}{\lim\limits_{z\to -1}(5z^2 + 9z + 6)} \qquad \text{Quotient rule}$$

$$= \frac{(-1)^3 - 3(-1) + 7}{5(-1)^2 + 9(-1) + 6}$$

$$= \frac{9}{2} \qquad \begin{array}{l}\text{Both numerator and denominator}\\\text{are polynomial functions.}\end{array} \qquad ■$$

WARNING You must be careful as to when you write the word "limit" and when you do not; pay particular attention to this when looking at the examples in this section.

Notice that if the denominator of the rational function is not zero, the limit can be found by substitution. If the limit of the denominator is zero, we find ourselves dividing by zero, an illegal operation.

Limit of a Rational Function

If Q is a rational function defined by $Q(x) = \dfrac{P(x)}{D(x)}$, then

$$\lim_{x\to c} Q(x) = \frac{P(c)}{D(c)}$$

provided $\lim\limits_{x\to c} D(x) \neq 0$.

EXAMPLE 3   Finding the limit of a power (or root) function

Evaluate $\lim\limits_{x \to -2} \sqrt[3]{x^2 - 3x - 2}$.

Solution
$$\lim_{x \to -2} \sqrt[3]{x^2 - 3x - 2} = \lim_{x \to -2} (x^2 - 3x - 2)^{1/3}$$

$$= \left[\lim_{x \to -2} (x^2 - 3x - 2) \right]^{1/3} \qquad \text{Power rule}$$

$$= [(-2)^2 - 3(-2) - 2]^{1/3} = 8^{1/3} = 2 \qquad \blacksquare$$

Once again, for values of the function for which $f(c)$ is defined, the limit can be found by substitution.

In the previous section we used a table to find that $\lim\limits_{x \to 0} \sin x = 0$ and $\lim\limits_{x \to 0} \cos x = 1$. In the following example we use this information, along with the properties of limits, to find other trigonometric limits.

EXAMPLE 4   Finding trigonometric limits algebraically

Given that $\lim\limits_{x \to 0} \sin x = 0$ and $\lim\limits_{x \to 0} \cos x = 1$, evaluate:

a. $\lim\limits_{x \to 0} \sin^2 x$ **b.** $\lim\limits_{x \to 0} (1 - \cos x)$

Solution

a. $\lim\limits_{x \to 0} \sin^2 x = \left[\lim\limits_{x \to 0} \sin x \right]^2$ Power rule

$$= 0^2 \qquad \lim_{x \to 0} \sin x = 0$$

$$= 0$$

b. $\lim\limits_{x \to 0} (1 - \cos x) = \lim\limits_{x \to 0} 1 - \lim\limits_{x \to 0} \cos x$ Difference rule

$$= 1 - 1 \qquad \text{Constant rule and} \lim_{x \to 0} \cos x = 1$$

$$= 0 \qquad \blacksquare$$

The following theorem states that we can find limits of trigonometric functions by direct substitution, as long as the number that x is approaching is in the domain of the given function. Proofs of several parts are outlined in the problem set, and in fact an examination of the graphs of the functions indicates why they are true.

THEOREM 2.2   Limits of trigonometric functions

If c is any number in the domain of the given function, then

$$\lim_{x \to c} \cos x = \cos c \qquad \lim_{x \to c} \sin x = \sin c \qquad \lim_{x \to c} \tan x = \tan c$$

$$\lim_{x \to c} \sec x = \sec c \qquad \lim_{x \to c} \csc x = \csc c \qquad \lim_{x \to c} \cot x = \cot c$$

Proof   We will show that $\lim\limits_{x \to c} \sin x = \sin c$. The other limit formulas may be proved in a similar fashion (see Problems 63–64). Let $h = x - c$. Then $x = h + c$, so $x \to c$ as $h \to 0$. Thus,

$$\lim_{x \to c} \sin x = \lim_{h \to 0} \sin(h + c)$$

Using the trigonometric identity

$$\sin(A + B) = \sin A \cos B + \cos A \sin B$$

and the limit formulas for sums and products, we find that

$$\lim_{x \to c} \sin x = \lim_{h \to 0} \sin(h + c)$$

$$= \lim_{h \to 0} [\sin h \cos c + \cos h \sin c]$$

$$= \lim_{h \to 0} \sin h \cdot \lim_{h \to 0} \cos c + \lim_{h \to 0} \cos h \cdot \lim_{h \to 0} \sin c$$

$$= 0 \cdot \cos c + 1 \cdot \sin c \qquad \lim_{h \to 0} \sin h = 0 \text{ and } \lim_{h \to 0} \cos h = 1$$

$$= \sin c$$

Note that $\sin c$ and $\cos c$ do not change as $h \to 0$ because these are constants with respect to h. ❏

EXAMPLE 5   Finding limits of trigonometric functions

Evaluate the following limits:

a. $\lim_{x \to 1}(x^2 \cos \pi x)$ **b.** $\lim_{x \to 0} \dfrac{x}{\cos x}$

Solution

a. $\lim_{x \to 1}(x^2 \cos \pi x) = \left[\lim_{x \to 1} x\right]^2 \cdot \left[\lim_{x \to 1} \cos \pi x\right] = 1^2 \cos \pi = -1$

b. $\lim_{x \to 0} \dfrac{x}{\cos x} = \dfrac{\lim\limits_{x \to 0} x}{\lim\limits_{x \to 0} \cos x} = \dfrac{0}{1} = 0$ ■

USING ALGEBRA TO FIND LIMITS

Sometimes the limit of $f(x)$ as $x \to c$ *cannot* be evaluated by direct substitution. In such a case, we look for another function that agrees with f for all values of x *except at the troublesome value $x = c$.* We illustrate this procedure with some examples.

EXAMPLE 6   Evaluating a limit using fractional reduction

Evaluate $\lim\limits_{x \to 2} \dfrac{x^2 + x - 6}{x - 2}$.

Solution

If you try substitution on this limit, you will obtain

If $x = 2$, then $x^2 + x - 6 = 0$.

$$\downarrow$$

$$\lim_{x \to 2} \dfrac{x^2 + x - 6}{x - 2} = \dfrac{0}{0}$$

$$\uparrow$$

If $x = 2$, then $x - 2 = 0$.

The form $\frac{0}{0}$ is called an **indeterminate form** because the value of the limit cannot be determined without further analysis.

If the expression is a rational expression, the next step is to try to simplify the function by factoring and checking to see if the reduced form is a polynomial.

$$\lim_{x \to 2} \dfrac{x^2 + x - 6}{x - 2} = \lim_{x \to 2} \dfrac{(x + 3)(x - 2)}{x - 2} = \lim_{x \to 2}(x + 3)$$

This simplification is valid only if $x \neq 2$. Now complete the evaluation of the reduced function by direct substitution. This is not a problem, because the limit is concerned with values *as x approaches* 2, not the value where $x = 2$. In the preceding expression

$$\lim_{x \to 2} \dfrac{x^2 + x - 6}{x - 2} = \lim_{x \to 2}(x + 3) = 5$$ ■

Another algebraic technique for finding limits is to rationalize either the numerator or the denominator to obtain an algebraic form that is not indeterminate.

EXAMPLE 7 Evaluating a limit by rationalizing

Evaluate $\lim\limits_{x \to 4} \dfrac{\sqrt{x} - 2}{x - 4}$.

Solution

Once again, notice that both the numerator and denominator of this rational expression are 0 when $x = 4$, so we cannot evaluate the limit by direct substitution. Instead, rationalize the numerator:

$$\lim_{x \to 4} \frac{\sqrt{x} - 2}{x - 4} = \lim_{x \to 4} \frac{\sqrt{x} - 2}{x - 4} \cdot \frac{\sqrt{x} + 2}{\sqrt{x} + 2} \qquad \text{Multiply by 1.}$$

$$= \lim_{x \to 4} \frac{x - 4}{(x - 4)(\sqrt{x} + 2)}$$

$$= \lim_{x \to 4} \frac{1}{\sqrt{x} + 2}$$

$$= \frac{1}{\sqrt{4} + 2} = \frac{1}{4} \qquad \blacksquare$$

WARNING This method will work only if the resulting numerator allows the fraction to be simplified. Pay close attention to this example because it illustrates a procedure we will use over and over.

LIMITS OF PIECEWISE-DEFINED FUNCTIONS

In Section 1.3 we discussed *piecewise-defined functions*. To evaluate $\lim\limits_{x \to c} f(x)$ where the domain of f is divided into pieces, we first look to see whether c is a value separating two of the pieces. If so, we need to consider one-sided limits, as illustrated by the following examples.

EXAMPLE 8 Limit of a piecewise-defined function

Find $\lim\limits_{x \to 0} f(x)$, where $f(x) = \begin{cases} x + 5 & \text{if } x > 0 \\ x & \text{if } x < 0 \end{cases}$.

Solution

Notice that $f(0)$ is not defined, and that it is necessary to consider left- and right-hand limits because $f(x)$ is defined differently on each side of $x = 0$. We have

$$\lim_{x \to 0^-} f(x) = \lim_{x \to 0^-} x \qquad f(x) = x \text{ to the left of } 0.$$
$$= 0$$
$$\lim_{x \to 0^+} f(x) = \lim_{x \to 0^+} (x + 5) \qquad f(x) = x + 5 \text{ to the right of } 0.$$
$$= 5$$

Because the left- and right-hand limits are not the same, we conclude that $\lim\limits_{x \to 0} f(x)$ does not exist. If we look at the graph, as shown in Figure 2.14, it is easy to see that the left- and right-hand limits are not the same. $\blacksquare$

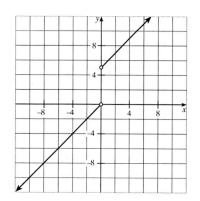

Figure 2.14 Graph of f

EXAMPLE 9 Limit of a piecewise-defined function

Find $\lim\limits_{x \to 0} g(x)$, where $g(x) = \begin{cases} x + 1 & \text{if } x > 0 \\ x^2 + 1 & \text{if } x < 0 \end{cases}$.

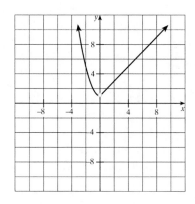

Figure 2.15 Graph of g

Solution

$$\lim_{x \to 0^-} g(x) = \lim_{x \to 0^-} (x^2 + 1) = 1$$

$$\lim_{x \to 0^+} g(x) = \lim_{x \to 0^+} (x + 1) = 1$$

Because the left- and right-hand limits are equal, we conclude that $\lim_{x \to 0} g(x) = 1$. This time, by looking at the graph in Figure 2.15, we see that the left- and right-hand limits are the same (even though the function is not defined at $x = 0$). Compare this graph with the graph in Example 8. ∎

TWO SPECIAL TRIGONOMETRIC LIMITS

The following theorem contains two additional limits that play an important role in calculus. We evaluated the first of these limits by table and graphically in Example 6 of Section 2.1.

THEOREM 2.3 Special limits involving sine and cosine

$$\lim_{h \to 0} \frac{\sin h}{h} = 1 \qquad \lim_{h \to 0} \frac{\cos h - 1}{h} = 0$$

Proof A geometric argument justifying these rules is given at the end of this section. ❑

For now, let us concentrate on illustrating how these rules can be used.

EXAMPLE 10 Evaluation of trigonometric and inverse trigonometric limits

Find each of the following limits.

a. $\lim\limits_{x \to 0} \dfrac{\sin 3x}{5x}$ **b.** $\lim\limits_{x \to 0} \dfrac{\sin^{-1} x}{x}$ **c.** $\lim\limits_{h \to 0} \dfrac{\cos h - 1}{h^2}$

Solution

a. We prepare the limit for evaluation by Theorem 2.3 by writing

$$\frac{\sin 3x}{5x} = \frac{3}{5} \left(\frac{\sin 3x}{3x} \right) \qquad \textbf{WARNING} \longrightarrow \quad \sin 3x \neq 3 \sin x$$

Since $3x \to 0$ as $x \to 0$, we can set $h = 3x$ in Theorem 2.3 to obtain

$$\lim_{x \to 0} \frac{\sin 3x}{5x} = \lim_{x \to 0} \frac{3}{5} \left(\frac{\sin 3x}{3x} \right) = \frac{3}{5} \lim_{h \to 0} \frac{\sin h}{h} = \frac{3}{5}(1) = \frac{3}{5}$$

b. Let $u = \sin^{-1} x$, so $\sin u = x$. Thus $u \to 0$ as $x \to 0$, and

$$\lim_{x \to 0} \frac{\sin^{-1} x}{x} = \lim_{u \to 0} \frac{u}{\sin u} = 1$$

c. We begin by writing

$$\frac{\cos h - 1}{h^2} = \frac{(\cos h - 1)(\cos h + 1)}{h^2(\cos h + 1)}$$

$$= \frac{\cos^2 h - 1}{h^2(\cos h + 1)}$$

$$= \frac{-\sin^2 h}{h^2(\cos h + 1)} \qquad \text{Since } \sin^2 h + \cos^2 h = 1$$

Thus, we have

$$\lim_{h \to 0} \frac{\cos h - 1}{h^2} = \lim_{h \to 0} \frac{-\sin^2 h}{h^2(\cos h + 1)}$$

$$= -\left[\lim_{h \to 0} \frac{\sin^2 h}{h^2}\right]\left[\lim_{h \to 0} \frac{1}{\cos h + 1}\right]$$

$$= -\left[\lim_{h \to 0} \frac{\sin h}{h}\right]^2\left[\lim_{h \to 0} \frac{1}{\cos h + 1}\right]$$

$$= -(1)^2\left(\frac{1}{1 + 1}\right)$$

$$= -\frac{1}{2}$$

We conclude this section with a justification of Theorem 2.3. Our argument is based on the following useful property that is proved in Appendix A.

Squeeze Rule*

If $g(x) \le f(x) \le h(x)$ on an open interval containing c, and if

$$\lim_{x \to c} g(x) = \lim_{x \to c} h(x) = L, \text{ then } \lim_{x \to c} f(x) = L$$

➡ **What This Says** If a function can be squeezed between two functions whose limits at a particular point c have the same value L, then that function must also have limit L at $x = c$.

With this squeeze rule in our toolkit, we are now ready to justify Theorem 2.3.

Proof Proof that $\lim_{h \to 0} \dfrac{\sin h}{h} = 1$.

To prove the sine limit theorem requires some principles that are not entirely obvious. However, we can demonstrate its plausibility by considering Figure 2.16, in which AOC is a sector of a circle of radius 1 with angle h measured in radians. The line segments $\overline{AD}$ and $\overline{BC}$ are drawn perpendicular to segment $\overline{OC}$.

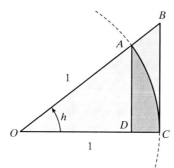

Assume $0 < h < \frac{\pi}{2}$; that is, h is in Quadrant I.

$$\left|\widehat{AC}\right| = h$$

$$\left|\overline{AD}\right| = \sin h$$

$$\left|\overline{BC}\right| = \tan h = \frac{\sin h}{\cos h}$$

$$\left|\overline{OD}\right| = \cos h$$

Figure 2.16 Trigonometric relationships in the proof that $\lim_{h \to 0} \dfrac{\sin h}{h} = 1$

---

*This rule is sometimes known as the **sandwich rule**.

Now, compare the area of the sector AOC with those of $\triangle AOD$ and $\triangle BOC$. In particular, since the area of the circular sector of radius r and central angle θ is $\frac{1}{2}r^2\theta$ (see the *Student Mathematics Handbook*), sector AOC must have area

$$\tfrac{1}{2}(1)^2 h = \tfrac{1}{2}h$$

We also find that $\triangle AOD$ has area

$$\tfrac{1}{2}\left|\overline{OD}\right|\left|\overline{AD}\right| = \tfrac{1}{2}\cos h \sin h,$$

and $\triangle BOC$ has area

$$\tfrac{1}{2}\left|\overline{BC}\right|\left|\overline{OC}\right| = \tfrac{1}{2}\left|\overline{BC}\right|(1) = \frac{1}{2}\frac{\sin h}{\cos h}$$

By comparing areas (see Figure 2.16), we have

AREA OF $\triangle AOD$		AREA OF SECTOR AOC		AREA OF $\triangle BOC$	
$\frac{1}{2}\cos h \sin h$	$\leq$	$\frac{1}{2}h$	$\leq$	$\dfrac{\sin h}{2\cos h}$	
$\cos h$	$\leq$	$\dfrac{h}{\sin h}$	$\leq$	$\dfrac{1}{\cos h}$	Divide by $\frac{1}{2}\sin h$.
$\dfrac{1}{\cos h}$	$\geq$	$\dfrac{\sin h}{h}$	$\geq$	$\cos h$	Take reciprocals (reverse order).
$\cos h$	$\leq$	$\dfrac{\sin h}{h}$	$\leq$	$\dfrac{1}{\cos h}$	Interchange left and right sides (reverse order again).

This same inequality holds in the interval $(-\frac{\pi}{2}, 0)$, which is Quadrant IV for the angle h. This can be shown by using the trigonometric identities $\cos(-h) = \cos h$ and $\sin(-h) = -\sin h$. Finally, we take the limit of all parts as $h \to 0$ to find

$$\lim_{h\to 0}\cos h \leq \lim_{h\to 0}\frac{\sin h}{h} \leq \lim_{h\to 0}\frac{1}{\cos h}$$

By Theorem 2.2, $\lim\limits_{h\to 0}\cos h = \cos 0 = 1$. Thus,

$$1 \leq \lim_{h\to 0}\frac{\sin h}{h} \leq \frac{1}{1}$$

From the squeeze rule, we conclude that $\lim\limits_{h\to 0}\dfrac{\sin h}{h} = 1$.

You are asked to prove the second part of this theorem in Problem 59.   ❑

2.2   PROBLEM SET

Ⓐ *In Problems 1–32, evaluate each limit.*

1. $\lim\limits_{x\to -2}(x^2 + 3x - 7)$

2. $\lim\limits_{t\to 0}(t^3 - 5t^2 + 4)$

3. $\lim\limits_{x\to 3}(x + 5)(2x - 7)$

4. $\lim\limits_{x\to 0}\dfrac{\sin^{-1}x}{x - 1}$

5. $\lim\limits_{z\to 1}\dfrac{z^2 + z - 3}{z + 1}$

6. $\lim\limits_{x\to 3}\dfrac{x^2 + 3x - 10}{3x^2 + 5x - 7}$

7. $\lim\limits_{x\to \pi/3}\sec x$

8. $\lim\limits_{x\to \pi/4}\dfrac{1 + \tan x}{\csc x + 2}$

9. $\lim\limits_{x\to 1/3}\dfrac{x \sin \pi x}{1 + \cos \pi x}$

10. $\lim\limits_{x\to 6}\dfrac{\tan(\pi/x)}{x - 1}$

11. $\lim\limits_{u\to -2}\dfrac{4 - u^2}{2 + u}$

12. $\lim\limits_{x\to 2}\dfrac{x^2 - 4x + 4}{x^2 - x - 2}$

13. $\lim\limits_{x\to 1} \dfrac{\frac{1}{x} - 1}{x - 1}$

14. $\lim\limits_{x\to 0} \dfrac{(x+1)^2 - 1}{x}$

15. $\lim\limits_{x\to 1} \left(\dfrac{x^2 - 3x + 2}{x^2 + x - 2} \right)^2$

16. $\lim\limits_{x\to 3} \sqrt{\dfrac{x^2 - 2x - 3}{x - 3}}$

17. $\lim\limits_{x\to 1} \dfrac{\sqrt{x} - 1}{x - 1}$

18. $\lim\limits_{y\to 2} \dfrac{\sqrt{y+2} - 2}{y - 2}$

19. $\lim\limits_{x\to 0} \dfrac{\sqrt{x+1} - 1}{x}$

20. $\lim\limits_{x\to 0} \dfrac{\sqrt{x^2+4} - 2}{x}$

21. $\lim\limits_{x\to 0^+} \dfrac{\sin x}{\sqrt{x}}$

22. $\lim\limits_{x\to 0^+} \dfrac{1 - \cos\sqrt{x}}{x}$

23. $\lim\limits_{x\to 0} \dfrac{\sin 2x}{x}$

24. $\lim\limits_{x\to 0} \dfrac{\sin 4x}{9x}$

25. $\lim\limits_{t\to 0} \dfrac{\tan 5t}{\tan 2t}$

26. $\lim\limits_{x\to 0} \dfrac{\cot 3x}{\cot x}$

27. $\lim\limits_{x\to 0} \dfrac{1 - \cos x}{\sin x}$

28. $\lim\limits_{x\to 0} \dfrac{\sin^2 x}{2x}$

29. $\lim\limits_{x\to 0} \dfrac{\sin^2 x}{x^2}$

30. $\lim\limits_{x\to 0} \dfrac{x^2 \cos 2x}{1 - \cos x}$

31. $\lim\limits_{x\to 0} \dfrac{\sec x - 1}{x \sec x}$

32. $\lim\limits_{x\to \pi/4} \dfrac{1 - \tan x}{\sin x - \cos x}$

33. **WHAT DOES THIS SAY?** How do you find the limit of a polynomial function?

34. **WHAT DOES THIS SAY?** How do you find the limit of a rational function?

35. **WHAT DOES THIS SAY?** How do you find

$$\lim\limits_{x\to 0} \dfrac{\sin ax}{x}$$

for $a \neq 0$?

B *In Problems 36–43, compute the one-sided limit or use one-sided limits to find the given limit, if it exists.*

36. $\lim\limits_{x\to 2^-} (x^2 - 2x)$

37. $\lim\limits_{x\to 1^+} \dfrac{\sqrt{x-1} + x}{1 - 2x}$

38. $\lim\limits_{x\to 2} |x - 2|$

39. $\lim\limits_{x\to 3} |3 - x|$

40. $\lim\limits_{x\to 0} \dfrac{|x|}{x}$

41. $\lim\limits_{x\to -2} \dfrac{|x + 2|}{x + 2}$

42. $\lim\limits_{x\to 2} f(x)$, where $f(x) = \begin{cases} 3 - 2x & \text{if } x \leq 2 \\ x^2 - 5 & \text{if } x > 2 \end{cases}$

43. $\lim\limits_{s\to 1} g(s)$, where $g(s) = \begin{cases} \dfrac{s^2 - s}{s - 1} & \text{if } s > 1 \\ \sqrt{1 - s} & \text{if } s \leq 1 \end{cases}$

WHAT DOES THIS SAY? *In Problems 44–51, explain why the given limit does not exist.*

44. $\lim\limits_{x\to 1} \dfrac{1}{x - 1}$

45. $\lim\limits_{x\to 2^+} \dfrac{1}{\sqrt{x - 2}}$

46. $\lim\limits_{t\to 2} \dfrac{t^2 - 4}{t^2 - 4t + 4}$

47. $\lim\limits_{x\to 3} \dfrac{x^2 + 4x + 3}{x - 3}$

48. $\lim\limits_{x\to 1} f(x)$, where $f(x) = \begin{cases} 2 & \text{if } x \geq 1 \\ -5 & \text{if } x < 1 \end{cases}$

49. $\lim\limits_{t\to -1} g(t)$, where $g(t) = \begin{cases} 2t + 1 & \text{if } t \geq -1 \\ 5t^2 & \text{if } t < -1 \end{cases}$

50. $\lim\limits_{x\to \pi/2} \tan x$

51. $\lim\limits_{x\to 1} \csc \pi x$

In Problems 52–57, either evaluate the limit or explain why it does not exist.

52. $\lim\limits_{x\to 1} \dfrac{\frac{1}{x} - 1}{\sqrt{x} - 1}$

53. $\lim\limits_{x\to 0} \left(\dfrac{1}{x} - \dfrac{1}{x^2} \right)$

54. $\lim\limits_{x\to 5} f(x)$, where $f(x) = \begin{cases} x + 3 & \text{if } x \neq 5 \\ 4 & \text{if } x = 5 \end{cases}$

55. $\lim\limits_{x\to 2} g(t)$, where $g(t) = \begin{cases} t^2 & \text{if } -1 \leq t < 2 \\ 3t - 2 & \text{if } t \geq 2 \end{cases}$

56. $\lim\limits_{x\to 2} f(x)$, where $f(x) = \begin{cases} 2(x + 1) & \text{if } x < 3 \\ 4 & \text{if } x = 3 \\ x^2 - 1 & \text{if } x > 3 \end{cases}$

57. $\lim\limits_{x\to 3} f(x)$, where $f(x) = \begin{cases} 2(x + 1) & \text{if } x < 3 \\ 4 & \text{if } x = 3 \\ x^2 - 1 & \text{if } x > 3 \end{cases}$

58. **Interpretation Problem** Evaluate $\lim\limits_{x\to 0} \left[x^2 - \dfrac{\cos x}{1{,}000{,}000{,}000} \right]$. Explain why a calculator solution may lead to an incorrect conclusion about the limit.

C 59. Prove the second part of Theorem 2.3: $\lim\limits_{h\to 0} \dfrac{\cos h - 1}{h} = 0$.

60. **Counterexample Problem** Give an example for which neither $\lim\limits_{x\to c} f(x)$ nor $\lim\limits_{x\to c} g(x)$ exists, but $\lim\limits_{x\to c} [f(x) + g(x)]$ does exist.

61. Let $f(x) = \dfrac{1}{x^2}$ with $x \neq 0$, and let L be any fixed positive integer. Show that

$$f(x) > 100L \text{ if } |x| < \dfrac{1}{10\sqrt{L}}$$

What does this imply about $\lim\limits_{x\to 0} f(x)$?

62. Use the sum rule to show that if $\lim\limits_{x\to c} [f(x) + g(x)]$ and $\lim\limits_{x\to c} f(x)$ both exist, then so does $\lim\limits_{x\to c} g(x)$.

63. Show that $\lim\limits_{x\to x_0} \cos x = \cos x_0$. *Hint*: You will need to use the trigonometric identity $\cos(A + B) = \cos A \cos B - \sin A \sin B$.

64. Show that $\lim\limits_{x\to x_0} \tan x = \tan x_0$ whenever $\cos x_0 \neq 0$.

2.3   Continuity

IN THIS SECTION   intuitive notion of continuity, definition of continuity, continuity theorems, continuity on an interval, the intermediate value theorem

INTUITIVE NOTION OF CONTINUITY

$\lim\limits_{x \to c} f(x)$ exists and is equal to $f(c)$.

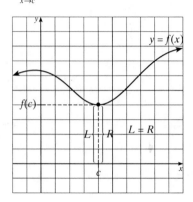

Figure 2.17 A function continuous at a point $x = c$

The idea of *continuity* may be thought of informally as the quality of having parts that are in immediate connection with one another, as shown in Figure 2.17. The idea evolved from the vague or intuitive notion of a curve "without breaks or jumps" to a rigorous definition first given toward the end of the nineteenth century (see Historical Quest Problem 45).

We begin with a discussion of *continuity at a point*. It may seem strange to talk about continuity *at a point*, but it should seem natural to talk about a curve being "discontinuous at a point." A few such discontinuities are illustrated by Figure 2.18.

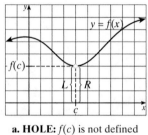

a. HOLE: $f(c)$ is not defined $\lim\limits_{x \to c} f(x)$ exists

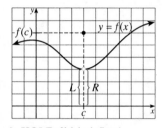

b. HOLE: $f(c)$ is defined $\lim\limits_{x \to c} f(x)$ exists and is not equal to $f(c)$

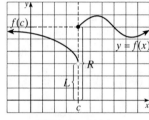

c. JUMP: $\lim\limits_{x \to c^-} f(c)$ is not the same as $\lim\limits_{x \to c^+} f(x)$

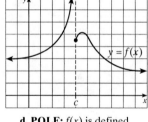

d. POLE: $f(x)$ is defined at $x = c$; $\lim\limits_{x \to c^-} f(x) = +\infty$

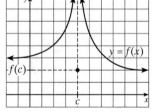

e. POLE: $f(x)$ is defined at $x = c$; $\lim\limits_{x \to c^-} f(x) = +\infty$ and $\lim\limits_{x \to c^+} f(x) = +\infty$

Figure 2.18   Types of discontinuity: holes, poles, and jumps

DEFINITION OF CONTINUITY

Let us consider the conditions that must be satisfied for a function f to be continuous at a point c. First, $f(c)$ must be defined or we have a "hole" in the graph, as shown in Figure 2.18a. (An open dot indicates an excluded point.) In Figure 2.18b, there is a "hole" even though $f(c)$ is defined. If $\lim\limits_{x \to c} f(x)$ has one value as $x \to c^-$ and another as $x \to c^+$, then $\lim\limits_{x \to c} f(x)$ does not exist and there will be a "jump" in the graph of f, as shown in Figure 2.18c. Finally, if one or both of the one-sided limits at c are infinite ($+\infty$ or $-\infty$), there will be a "pole" at $x = c$, as shown in Figures 2.18d and e.

**Continuity of a Function
at a Point**

A function f is **continuous at a point** $x = c$ if the following three conditions are satisfied:

1. $f(c)$ is defined;

2. $\lim\limits_{x \to c} f(x)$ exists;

3. $\lim\limits_{x \to c} f(x) = f(c)$.

A function that is not continuous at c is said to have a **discontinuity** at that point.

➡ **What This Says**   The third condition $\lim\limits_{x \to c} f(x) = f(c)$ summarizes the idea behind continuity. It says that if x is close to c, then $f(x)$ must be close to $f(c)$.

If f is continuous at c, the points $(x, f(x))$ converge to $(c, f(c))$ as $x \to c$.

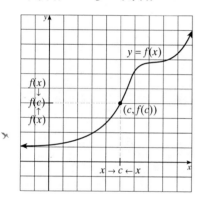

Figure 2.19 The geometric interpretation of continuity

WARNING   Do not rely on graphing calculators to test for continuity. For example, the graph of $y = \dfrac{x-2}{x-2}$ looks like a constant function when done with a calculator; it does not show the discontinuity at $x = 2$.

If f is continuous at $x = c$, the difference between $f(x)$ and $f(c)$ is small whenever x is close to c because $\lim\limits_{x \to c} f(x) = f(c)$. Geometrically, this means that the points $(x, f(x))$ on the graph of f converge to the point $(c, f(c))$ as $x \to c$, and this is what guarantees that the graph is unbroken at $(c, f(c))$ with no "gap" or "hole," as shown in Figure 2.19.

We should note that not every continuous function can be graphed (for example, see Example 2e later in this section), so you cannot test continuity by graphing, even though graphing can help for many functions.

EXAMPLE 1   Testing continuity

Test the continuity of each of the following functions at $x = 1$. If the given function is not continuous at $x = 1$, explain.

a. $f(x) = \dfrac{x^2 + 2x - 3}{x - 1}$

b. $g(x) = \dfrac{x^2 + 2x - 3}{x - 1}$ if $x \neq 1$ and $g(x) = 6$ if $x = 1$

c. $h(x) = \dfrac{x^2 + 2x - 3}{x - 1}$ if $x \neq 1$ and $h(x) = 4$ if $x = 1$

d. $F(x) = \dfrac{x + 3}{x - 1}$ if $x \neq 1$ and $F(x) = 4$ if $x = 1$

e. $G(x) = 7x^3 + 3x^2 - 2$

f. $H(x) = 2\sin x - \tan x$

Solution

a. The function f is not continuous at $x = 1$ [hole; $f(1)$ not defined] because it is not defined at this point.

b. 1. $g(1)$ is defined; $g(1) = 6$.

   2. $\lim\limits_{x \to 1} g(x) = \lim\limits_{x \to 1} \dfrac{x^2 + 2x - 3}{x - 1}$

   $= \lim\limits_{x \to 1} \dfrac{(x - 1)(x + 3)}{x - 1}$

   $= \lim\limits_{x \to 1} (x + 3) = 4$

   3. $\lim\limits_{x \to 1} g(x) \neq g(1)$, so g is not continuous at $x = 1$ [hole; $g(1)$ defined].

c. Compare h with g of part **b.** We see that all three conditions of continuity are satisfied, so h is continuous at $x = 1$.

d. 1. $F(1)$ is defined; $F(1) = 4$.

2. $\lim_{x \to 1} F(x) = \lim_{x \to 1} \dfrac{x + 3}{x - 1}$; the limit does not exist.

The function F is not continuous at $x = 1$ (pole).

e. 1. $G(1)$ is defined; $G(1) = 8$.

2. $\lim_{x \to 1} G(x) = 7 \left(\lim_{x \to 1} x \right)^3 + 3 \left(\lim_{x \to 1} x \right)^2 - \lim_{x \to 1} 2 = 8$.

3. $\lim_{x \to 1} G(x) = G(1)$.

Because the three conditions of continuity are satisfied, G is continuous at $x = 1$.

f. 1. $H(1)$ is defined; $H(1) = 2 \sin 1 - \tan 1$.

2. $\lim_{x \to 1} H(x) = 2 \lim_{x \to 1} \sin x - \lim_{x \to 1} \tan x = 2 \sin 1 - \tan 1$.

3. $\lim_{x \to 1} H(x) = H(1)$.

Because the three conditions of continuity are satisfied, H is continuous at $x = 1$.
∎

CONTINUITY THEOREMS

It is often difficult to determine whether a given function is continuous at a specified number. However, many common functions are continuous wherever they are defined.

THEOREM 2.4 Continuity theorem

If f is a polynomial or a rational function, a power function, a trigonometric function, or an inverse trigonometric function, then f is continuous at any number $x = c$ for which $f(c)$ is defined.

Proof The proof of the continuity theorem is based on the limit properties stated in the previous section. For instance, a polynomial is a function of the form

$$P(x) = a_n x^n + a_{n-1} x^{n-1} + \cdots + a_1 x + a_0$$

where $a_0, a_1, \ldots, a_n$ are constants. We know that $\lim_{x \to c} a_0 = a_0$ and that $\lim_{x \to c} x^m = c^m$ for $m = 1, 2, \ldots, n$. This is precisely the statement that the function $g(x) = ax^m$ is continuous at any number $x = c$, or simply continuous. Because P is a sum of functions of this form and a constant function, it follows from the limit properties that P is continuous.

The proofs of the other parts follow similarly. ❑

The limit properties of the previous section can also be used to prove a second continuity theorem. This theorem tells us that continuous functions may be combined in various ways *without creating a discontinuity*.

THEOREM 2.5 Properties of continuous functions

If f and g are functions that are continuous at $x = c$, then the following functions are also continuous at $x = c$.

Scalar multiple	sf	for any constant s (called a *scalar*)
Sum and difference	$f + g$ and $f - g$	
Product	fg	
Quotient	$\dfrac{f}{g}$	provided $g(c) \neq 0$
Composition	$f \circ g$	provided g is continuous at c and f is continuous at $g(c)$

Proof The first four properties in this theorem follow directly from the basic limit rules given in Section 2.2. For instance, to prove the product property, note that since f and g are given to be continuous at $x = c$, we have

$$\lim_{x \to c} f(x) = f(c) \quad \text{and} \quad \lim_{x \to c} g(x) = g(c)$$

If $P(x) = (fg)(x) = f(x)g(x)$, then

$$\lim_{x \to c} P(x) = \lim_{x \to c} f(x)g(x)$$
$$= \left[\lim_{x \to c} f(x)\right]\left[\lim_{x \to c} g(x)\right]$$
$$= f(c)g(c) = P(c)$$

so $P(x)$ is continuous at $x = c$, as required. ❑

The continuous composition property is proved in a similar fashion, but requires the following limit rule, which we state without proof.

Composition Limit Rule

If $\lim_{x \to c} g(x) = L$ and f is a function continuous at L, then $\lim_{x \to c} f[g(x)] = f(L)$. That is,

$$\lim_{x \to c} f[g(x)] = f(L) = f\left(\lim_{x \to c} g(x)\right)$$

This property applies in the same way to other kinds of limits, in particular to one-sided limits.

Now we can prove the continuous composition property of Theorem 2.5. Let $h(x) = (f \circ g)(x)$. Then we have

$$\lim_{x \to c}(f \circ g)(x) = \lim_{x \to c} f[g(x)] \qquad \text{Definition of composition}$$
$$= f\left[\lim_{x \to c} g(x)\right] \qquad \text{Composition limit rule}$$
$$= f[g(c)] \qquad g \text{ is continuous at } x = c.$$
$$= (f \circ g)(c) \qquad \text{Definition of composition} \quad ❑$$

➡ **What This Says** The limit of a continuous function is the function of the limiting value. The continuous composition property says that a continuous function of a continuous function is continuous.

We need to talk about a function being continuous on an interval. To do so, we must first know how to handle continuity at the endpoints of the interval, which leads to the following definition.

One-Sided Continuity

> The function f is **continuous from the right at** a if and only if
>
> $$\lim_{x \to a^+} f(x) = f(a)$$
>
> and it is **continuous from the left at** b if and only if
>
> $$\lim_{x \to b^-} f(x) = f(b)$$

CONTINUITY ON AN INTERVAL

The function f is said to be **continuous on the open interval** (a, b) if it is continuous at each number in this interval. Also note that the endpoints are not part of open intervals. If f is also continuous from the right at a, we say it is **continuous on the half-open interval** $[a, b)$. Similarly, f is **continuous on the half-open interval** $(a, b]$ if it is continuous at each number between a and b and is continuous from the left at the endpoint b. Finally, f is **continuous on the closed interval** $[a, b]$ if it is continuous at each number between a and b and is both continuous from the right at a and continuous from the left at b.

EXAMPLE 2   Testing for continuity on an interval

Find the intervals on which each of the given functions is continuous.

a. $f_1(x) = \dfrac{x^2 - 1}{x^2 - 4}$ **b.** $f_2(x) = \left| x^2 - 4 \right|$ **c.** $f_3(x) = \csc x$

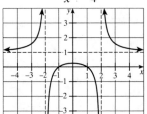   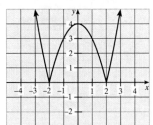   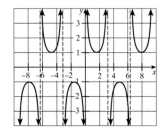

d. $f_4(x) = \sin \dfrac{1}{x}$ **e.** $f_5(x) = \begin{cases} x \sin \frac{1}{x} & \text{if } x \neq 0 \\ 0 & \text{if } x = 0 \end{cases}$

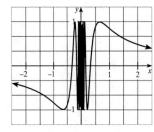   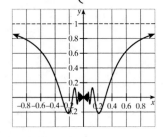

Solution

a. Function f_1 is not defined when $x^2 - 4 = 0$; that is, when $x = 2$ or $x = -2$. The function is continuous on $(-\infty, -2) \cup (-2, 2) \cup (2, \infty)$.

b. Function f_2 is continuous on $(-\infty, \infty)$.

c. The cosecant function is not defined at $x = n\pi$, n an integer. At all other points it is continuous.

d. Because $1/x$ is continuous except at $x = 0$ and the sine function is continuous everywhere, we need only check continuity at $x = 0$

$$\lim_{x \to 0} \sin \frac{1}{x} \quad \text{does not exist}$$

Therefore, $f(x) = \sin \frac{1}{x}$ is continuous on $(-\infty, 0) \cup (0, \infty)$.

e. It can be shown that since

$$-1 \le \sin \frac{1}{x} \le 1$$

then

$$-|x| \le x \sin \frac{1}{x} \le |x|, \quad x \ne 0$$

We can now use the squeeze rule. Because $\lim_{x \to 0} |x| = 0$ and $\lim_{x \to 0} (-|x|) = 0$, it follows that $\lim_{x \to 0} x \sin \frac{1}{x} = 0$. Because $f_5(0) = 0$ we see that f is continuous at $x = 0$ and therefore is continuous on $(-\infty, \infty)$. ∎

Usually there are only a few points in the domain of a given function f where a discontinuity can occur. We use the term **suspicious point** for a number c where either

1. The defining rule for f changes.
2. Substitution of $x = c$ causes division by 0 in the function.

For Example 2, the suspicious points can be listed:

a. $\dfrac{x^2 - 1}{x^2 - 4}$ has suspicious points for division by zero when $x = 2$ and $x = -2$.

b. $\left| x^2 - 4 \right| = x^2 - 4$ when $x^2 - 4 \ge 0$ and $\left| x^2 - 4 \right| = 4 - x^2$ when $x^2 - 4 < 0$. This means the definition of the function changes when $x^2 - 4 = 0$, namely, when $x = 2$ and $x = -2$.

c. There are no suspicious points; we know the function cannot be continuous at places where the function is not defined.

d. $\sin \frac{1}{x}$ has a suspicious point when $x = 0$ (division by 0).

e. $x \sin \frac{1}{x}$ has a suspicious point when $x = 0$ (division by 0).

EXAMPLE 3 Checking continuity at suspicious points

Let $f(x) = \begin{cases} 3 - x & \text{if } -5 \le x < 2 \\ x - 2 & \text{if } 2 \le x < 5 \end{cases}$ and $g(x) = \begin{cases} 2 - x & \text{if } -5 \le x < 2 \\ x - 2 & \text{if } 2 \le x < 5 \end{cases}$.

Find the intervals on which f and g are continuous.

Solution

We find that the domain for both functions is $[-5, 5)$; the continuity theorem tells us both functions are continuous everywhere on that interval except possibly at the suspicious points. Consider the graphs of f and g as shown in Figure 2.20. Examining f, we see

$$\lim_{x \to 2^-} f(x) = \lim_{x \to 2^-} (3 - x) = 1 \quad \text{and} \quad \lim_{x \to 2^+} f(x) = \lim_{x \to 2^+} (x - 2) = 0$$

so $\lim_{x \to 2} f(x)$ does not exist and f is discontinuous at $x = 2$. Thus, f is continuous for $-5 \le x < 2$ and for $2 < x < 5$.

For g, the domain is also $-5 \le x < 5$, and again, the only suspicious point is $x = 2$. We have $g(2) = 0$ and

$$\lim_{x \to 2^-} g(x) = \lim_{x \to 2^-} (2 - x) = 0 \quad \text{and} \quad \lim_{x \to 2^+} g(x) = \lim_{x \to 2^+} (x - 2) = 0$$

Therefore, $\lim_{x \to 2} g(x) = 0 = g(2)$, and g is continuous at $x = 2$. Hence, g is continuous throughout the interval $[-5, 5)$. ∎

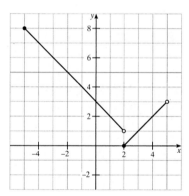

Although a graph is not part of the derivation, it can often be helpful in finding suspicious points. This is the graph of the function f.

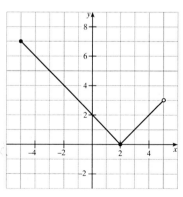

This is the graph of g. Does the graph reinforce our conclusions?

Figure 2.20 Graphs of f and g

THE INTERMEDIATE VALUE THEOREM

Intuitively, if f is continuous throughout an entire interval, its graph on that interval may be drawn "without the pencil leaving the paper." That is, if $f(x)$ varies continuously from $f(a)$ to $f(b)$ as x increases from a to b, then it must hit every number L between $f(a)$ and $f(b)$, as shown in Figure 2.21.

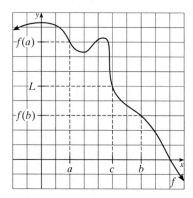

Figure 2.21 If L lies between $f(a)$ and $f(b)$, then $f(c) = L$ for some c between a and b.

To illustrate the property shown in Figure 2.21, suppose f is a function defined as the weight of a person at age x. If we assume that weight varies continuously with time, a person who weighs 50 pounds at age 6 and 120 pounds at age 15 must weigh 100 pounds at some time between ages 6 and 15.

This feature of continuous functions is known as the *intermediate value property*. A formal statement of this property is contained in the following theorem.

THEOREM 2.6   The intermediate value theorem

If f is a continuous function on the closed interval $[a, b]$ and L is some number strictly between $f(a)$ and $f(b)$, then there exists at least one number c on the open interval (a, b) such that $f(c) = L$.

Proof   This theorem is intuitively obvious, but it is not at all easy to prove. A proof may be found in most advanced calculus textbooks.   ❑

> ➜ **What This Says**   If f is a continuous function (with emphasis on the word *continuous*) on some *closed* interval $[a, b]$, then $f(x)$ must take on all values between $f(a)$ and $f(b)$.

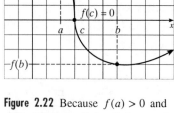

Figure 2.22 Because $f(a) > 0$ and $f(b) < 0$, then $f(c) = 0$ for some c between a and b.

The intermediate value theorem can be used to estimate roots of the equation $f(x) = 0$. Suppose $f(a) > 0$ and $f(b) < 0$, so the graph of f is above the x-axis at $x = a$ and below for $x = b$. Then, if f is continuous on the closed interval $[a, b]$, there must be a point $x = c$ between a and b where the graph crosses the x-axis, that is, where $f(c) = 0$. The same conclusion would be drawn if $f(a) < 0$ and $f(b) > 0$. The key is that $f(x)$ changes sign between $x = a$ and $x = b$. This is shown in Figure 2.22 and is summarized in the following theorem.

THEOREM 2.7   Root location theorem

If f is continuous on the closed interval $[a, b]$ and if $f(a)$ and $f(b)$ have opposite algebraic signs (one positive and the other negative), then $f(c) = 0$ for at least one number c on the open interval (a, b).

Proof   This follows directly from the intermediate value theorem (see Figure 2.22). The details of this proof are left as a problem. ❑

EXAMPLE 4   Using the root location theorem

Show that $\cos x = x^3 - x$ has at least one solution on the interval $[\frac{\pi}{4}, \frac{\pi}{2}]$.

Solution

We can use a graphing utility to estimate the point of intersection, as shown in Figure 2.23.

We will now use the root location theorem to confirm the intersection point shown in Figure 2.23. By calculator, we estimate $c \approx 1.16$.

Notice that the function $f(x) = \cos x - x^3 + x$ is continuous on $[\frac{\pi}{4}, \frac{\pi}{2}]$. We find that

$$f(\tfrac{\pi}{4}) = \cos \tfrac{\pi}{4} - \left(\tfrac{\pi}{4}\right)^3 + \tfrac{\pi}{4} \approx 1.008$$

$$f(\tfrac{\pi}{2}) = \cos \tfrac{\pi}{2} - \left(\tfrac{\pi}{2}\right)^3 + \tfrac{\pi}{2} \approx -2.305$$

Therefore, by the root location theorem there is at least one number c on $(\frac{\pi}{4}, \frac{\pi}{2})$ for which $f(c) = 0$, and it follows that $\cos c = c^3 - c$. ∎

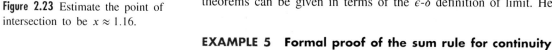

Figure 2.23 Estimate the point of intersection to be $x \approx 1.16$.

Since the definition of continuity involves the limit, formal proofs of continuity theorems can be given in terms of the $\epsilon\text{-}\delta$ definition of limit. Here is an example.

EXAMPLE 5   Formal proof of the sum rule for continuity

Show that if f and g are continuous at $x = x_0$, then $f + g$ is also continuous at $x = x_0$.

Solution

The continuity of f and g at $x = x_0$ says that

$$\lim_{x \to x_0} f(x) = f(x_0) \quad \text{and} \quad \lim_{x \to x_0} g(x) = g(x_0)$$

This means that if $\epsilon > 0$ is given, there exist numbers δ_1 and δ_2 such that

$$|f(x) - f(x_0)| < \frac{\epsilon}{2} \quad \text{whenever} \quad 0 < |x - x_0| < \delta_1$$

and

$$|g(x) - g(x_0)| < \frac{\epsilon}{2} \quad \text{whenever} \quad 0 < |x - x_0| < \delta_2$$

Let δ be the smaller of δ_1 and δ_2; that is, $\delta = \min(\delta_1, \delta_2)$. Then

$$0 < |x - x_0| < \delta_1 \quad \text{and} \quad 0 < |x - x_0| < \delta_2$$

must both be true whenever $0 < |x - x_0| < \delta$ so that (by the triangle inequality)

$$
\begin{aligned}
|[f(x) + g(x)] - [f(x_0) + g(x_0)]| &= |[f(x) - f(x_0)] + [g(x) - g(x_0)]| \\
&\le |f(x) - f(x_0)| + |g(x) - g(x_0)| \\
&< \frac{\epsilon}{2} + \frac{\epsilon}{2} = \epsilon
\end{aligned}
$$

Thus, $|(f + g)(x) - (f + g)(x_0)| < \epsilon$ whenever $0 < |x - x_0| < \delta$, and it follows from the definition of limit that

$$\lim_{x \to x_0} [f(x) + g(x)] = f(x_0) + g(x_0)$$

In other words, $f + g$ is continuous at $x = x_0$, as claimed. ∎

2.3 PROBLEM SET

Ⓐ *Which of the functions described in Problems 1–4 represent continuous functions? State the domain, if possible, for each example.*

1. the temperature on a specific day at a given location considered as a function of time

2. the humidity on a specific day at a given location considered as a function of time

3. the charges for a taxi ride across town considered as a function of mileage

4. the charges to mail a package as a function of its weight

Identify all suspicious points and determine all points of discontinuity in Problems 5–14.

5. $f(x) = x^3 - 7x + 3$

6. $f(x) = \dfrac{3x + 5}{2x - 1}$

7. $f(x) = \dfrac{3x}{x^2 - x}$

8. $f(t) = 3 - (5 + 2t)^3$

9. $h(x) = \sqrt{x} + \dfrac{3}{x}$

10. $f(u) = \sqrt[3]{u^2 - 1}$

11. $f(x) = \begin{cases} x^2 - 2 & \text{if } x > 1 \\ 2x - 3 & \text{if } x \le 1 \end{cases}$

12. $g(t) = \begin{cases} 3t + 2 & \text{if } t \le 1 \\ 5 & \text{if } 1 < t \le 3 \\ 3t^2 - 1 & \text{if } t > 3 \end{cases}$

13. $f(x) = 3 \tan x - 5 \sin x \cos x$

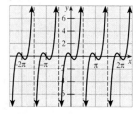

14. $g(x) = \dfrac{\cot x}{\sin x - \cos x}$

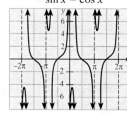

In Problems 15–20, the given function is defined for all x > 0, except at x = 2. In each case, find the value that should be assigned to f(2), if any, to guarantee that f will be continuous at 2.

15. $f(x) = \dfrac{x^2 - x - 2}{x - 2}$

16. $f(x) = \sqrt{\dfrac{x^2 - 4}{x - 2}}$

17. $f(x) = \dfrac{\sin(\pi x)}{x - 2}$

18. $f(x) = \dfrac{\cos \frac{\pi}{x}}{x - 2}$

19. $f(x) = \begin{cases} 2x + 5 & \text{if } x > 2 \\ 15 - x^2 & \text{if } x < 2 \end{cases}$

20. $f(x) = \dfrac{\frac{1}{x} - 1}{x - 2}$

In Problems 21–25, determine whether or not the given function is continuous on the prescribed interval.

21. **a.** $f(x) = \dfrac{1}{x}$ on $[1, 2]$ **b.** $f(x) = \dfrac{1}{x}$ on $[0, 1]$

22. $f(x) = \begin{cases} x^2 & \text{if } 0 \le x < 2 \\ 3x + 1 & \text{if } 2 \le x < 5 \end{cases}$

23. $g(t) = \begin{cases} 15 - t^2 & \text{if } -3 < t \le 0 \\ 2t & \text{if } 0 < t \le 1 \end{cases}$

24. $f(x) = x \sin x$ on $(0, \pi)$

25. $f(x) = \dfrac{\cos x - 1}{x}$ on $[-\pi, \pi]$

Ⓑ 26. Let $f(x) = \begin{cases} x & \text{if } x \ne 0 \\ 2 & \text{if } x = 0 \end{cases}$ and $g(x) = \begin{cases} 3x & \text{if } x \ne 0 \\ -2 & \text{if } x = 0 \end{cases}$
   Show that $f + g$ is continuous at $x = 0$ even though f and g are both discontinuous there.

In Problems 27–32, show that the given equation has at least one solution on the indicated interval.

27. $\sqrt[3]{x} = x^2 + 2x - 1$ on $(0, 1)$

28. $\dfrac{1}{x + 1} = x^2 - x - 1$ on $(1, 2)$

29. $\sqrt[3]{x - 8} + 9x^{2/3} = 29$ on $(0, 8)$

30. $\tan x = 2x^2 - 1$ on $(-\frac{\pi}{4}, 0)$

31. $\cos x - \sin x = x$ on $(0, \frac{\pi}{2})$

32. $\cos x = x^2 - 1$ on $(0, \pi)$

33. Let $f(x) = \begin{cases} x^2 & \text{if } x > 2 \\ x + 1 & \text{if } x \le 2 \end{cases}$
   Show that f is continuous from the left at 2, but not from the right.

34. Find constants a and b such that $f(2) + 3 = f(0)$ and f is continuous at $x = 1$.
$$f(x) = \begin{cases} ax + b & \text{if } x > 1 \\ 3 & \text{if } x = 1 \\ x^2 - 4x + b + 3 & \text{if } x < 1 \end{cases}$$

35. **Interpretation Problem**   Use the intermediate value theorem to explain why the hands of a clock coincide at least once every hour.

36. **Interpretation Problem**   The graph shown in Figure 2.24 models how the growth rate of a bacterial colony changes with temperature.*

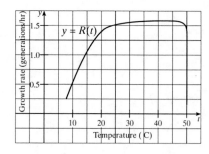

Figure 2.24   Growth rate of a bacterial colony

*Michael D. La Grega, Philip L. Buckingham, and Jeffery C. Evans, *Hazardous Waste Management*, New York: McGraw-Hill, 1994, pp. 565–566.

What happens when the temperature reaches 45°C? Does it make sense to compute $\lim_{t \to 50} R(t)$? Write a paragraph describing how temperature affects the growth rate of a species.

37. A fish swims upstream at a constant speed v relative to the water, which in turn flows at a constant speed v_w ($v_w < v$) relative to the ground. The energy expended by the fish in traveling to a point upstream is given by

$$E(v) = \frac{Cv^k}{v - v_w}$$

where $C > 0$ is a physical constant and $k > 0$ is a number that depends on the type of fish.*

a. Compute $\lim_{v \to v_w} E(v)$. Interpret your result in words.

b. What happens to $E(v)$ as $v \to +\infty$? Interpret your result in words.

38. The population (in thousands) of a colony of bacteria t minutes after the introduction of a toxin is given by the function

$$P(t) = \begin{cases} t^2 + 1 & \text{if } 0 \le t < 5 \\ -8t + 66 & \text{if } t \ge 5 \end{cases}$$

a. When does the colony die out?

b. Show that at some time between $t = 2$ and $t = 7$, the population is 9,000.

In Problems 39–44, find constants a and b so that the given function will be continuous for all x.

39. $f(x) = \begin{cases} ax + 3 & \text{if } x > 5 \\ 8 & \text{if } x = 5 \\ x^2 + bx + 1 & \text{if } x < 5 \end{cases}$

40. $f(x) = \begin{cases} \dfrac{ax - 4}{x - 2} & \text{if } x \ne 2 \\ b & \text{if } x = 2 \end{cases}$

41. $f(x) = \begin{cases} \dfrac{\sqrt{x} - a}{x - 1} & \text{if } x > 1 \\ b & \text{if } x \le 1 \end{cases}$

42. $f(x) = \begin{cases} 2\sin(a\cos^{-1} x) & \text{if } x > 0 \\ \sqrt{3} & \text{if } x = 0 \\ ax + b & \text{if } x < 0 \end{cases}$

43. $g(x) = \begin{cases} \dfrac{\sin ax}{x} & \text{if } x < 0 \\ 5 & \text{if } x = 0 \\ x + b & \text{if } x > 0 \end{cases}$

44. $f(x) = \begin{cases} \dfrac{\tan ax}{\tan bx} & \text{if } x < 0 \\ 4 & \text{if } x = 0 \\ ax + b & \text{if } x > 0 \end{cases}$

45. HISTORICAL QUEST   The first modern formulation of the notion of continuity appeared in a pamphlet published by Bernard Bolzano, a Czechoslovakian priest whose mathematical work was, for the most part, overlooked by his contemporaries. In explaining the concept of continuity, Bolzano said that one must understand the phrase, "A function $f(x)$ (that) varies according to the law of continuity for all values of x which lie inside or outside certain limits, is nothing other than this: If x is any such value, the difference

BERNARD BOLZANO
1781–1848

$$f(x + \omega) - f(x)$$

can be made smaller than any given quantity, if one makes ω as small as one wishes."

In his book, *Cours d'Analyse*, Cauchy (see Historical Quest Problem 49, Section 2.1) introduces the concept of continuity for a function defined on an interval in essentially the same way as Bolzano. In this book Cauchy points out that the continuity of many functions is easily verified. As an example, he argues that $\sin x$ is continuous on every interval because "the numerical value of $\sin \frac{1}{2}\alpha$, and consequently that of the difference

$$\sin(x + \alpha) - \sin x = 2\sin \tfrac{1}{2}\alpha \cos(x + \tfrac{1}{2}\alpha)$$

decreases indefinitely with that of α."[†]

Show that $\sin x$ is continuous, and also show that the given expression decreases as claimed by Cauchy.

We conclude this Historical Quest by noting that the formal ϵ-δ definition of limits and continuity that we use today was first done by Karl Weierstrass (1815–1897), a German secondary school teacher who did his research at night. The historian David Burton describes Weierstrass as "the world's greatest analyst during the last third of the nineteenth century—the father of modern analysis."

46. Let f be a continuous function and suppose that $f(a)$ and $f(b)$ have opposite signs. The root location theorem tells us that at least one root of $f(x) = 0$ lies between $x = a$ and $x = b$.

a. Let $c = (a + b)/2$ be the midpoint of the interval $[a, b]$. Explain how the root location theorem can be used to determine whether the root lies in $[a, c]$ or in $[c, b]$. Does anything special have to be said about the case where the interval $[a, b]$ contains more than one root?

b. Based on your observation in part **a**, describe a procedure for approximating a root of $f(x) = 0$ more and more accurately. This is called the *bisection method* for root location.

c. Apply the bisection method to locate at least one root of $x^3 + x - 1 = 0$ on $[0, 1]$. Check your answer using your calculator.

47. Apply the bisection method (see Problem 46) to locate at least one root of each of the given equations, and then check your answer using your calculator.

a. $\sin x + \cos x = x$ on $[0, \frac{\pi}{2}]$

b. $\cos(x + 1) = \sin(x - 1)$ on $[0, 1]$

---

*E. Batschelet, *Introduction to Mathematics for Life Scientists*, 2nd ed., New York: Springer-Verlag, 1976, p. 280.

[†]A. L. Cauchy, *Cours d'Analyse de l'Ecole Royale Polytechnique, Oeuvres*, Ser. 2, Vol. 3. Paris: Gauthier-Villars, 1897, p. 44.

48. Counterexample Problem   Find functions f and g such that f is discontinuous at $x = 1$ but fg is continuous there.

49. Counterexample Problem   Give an example of a function defined for all real numbers that is continuous at only one point.

50. Prove the root location theorem, assuming the intermediate value theorem.

51. Show that f is continuous at c if and only if it is both continuous from the right and continuous from the left at c.

52. Show that if f and g are both continuous at $x = c$ and $g(c) \neq 0$, then f/g must also be continuous there.

53. Let $u(x) = x$ and $f(x) = \begin{cases} 0 & \text{if } x \neq 0 \\ 1 & \text{if } x = 0 \end{cases}$.

Show that $\lim\limits_{x \to 0} f[u(x)] \neq f\left[\lim\limits_{x \to 0} u(x)\right]$.

2.4   Exponential and Logarithmic Functions

IN THIS SECTION   exponential functions, logarithmic functions, natural exponential and logarithmic functions, continuous compounding of interest

In Chapter 1, we introduced polynomial and rational functions, power functions, trigonometric functions, and inverse trigonometric functions. In this section, we will complete our list of the elementary functions typically used in calculus by using limits to introduce exponential functions and their inverses, the logarithmic functions.

EXPONENTIAL FUNCTIONS

Recall that if n is a natural number, then

$$b^n = \underbrace{b \cdot b \cdot b \cdot \cdots \cdot b}_{n \text{ factors}}$$

If $b \neq 0$, then $b^0 = 1$, $b^{-n} = \dfrac{1}{b^n}$, and furthermore, if $b > 0$, then $b^{1/n} = \sqrt[n]{b}$. Also, if m and n are any integers, and m/n is a reduced fraction, then

$$b^{m/n} = (b^{1/n})^m$$

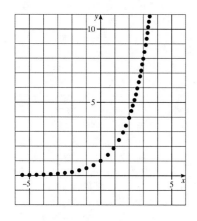

Figure 2.25 Graph of $y = 2^x$ for rational exponents

This definition tells us what b^x means for rational values of x. However, we now wish to enlarge the domain of x to include all real numbers. To get a feeling for what is involved in this problem, let us examine the special case where $b = 2$. In Figure 2.25, we have plotted several points with coordinates $(r, 2^r)$, where r is a rational number. We must now attach meaning to b^x if x is not a rational number by filling those holes or spaces to make the graph continuous for all x. We use the following fundamental fact about the real number system, called the **completeness property**.

For any real number x, there exist rational numbers r_n such that

$$x = \lim_{n \to \infty} r_n$$

which means that for any number $\epsilon > 0$, there exists a number N such that $|x - r_n| < \epsilon$ whenever $n > N$.

Another way of expressing the completeness property is to say that *each real number x can be approximated to any degree of accuracy by a rational number.* Using the completeness property, we can now define an exponential function.

Exponential Function

Let x be a real number, and let r_n be a sequence of rational numbers such that $x = \lim_{n \to \infty} r_n$. Then the **exponential function** with base $b > 0$ $(b \neq 1)$ is given by

$$b^x = \lim_{n \to \infty} b^{r_n}$$

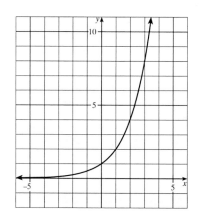

Figure 2.26 Graph of $y = 2^x$

For example, the number $\sqrt{3}$ has an infinite decimal representation

$$\sqrt{3} \approx 1.732050808\cdots$$

which means that $\sqrt{3}$ can be approximated to any desired degree of accuracy by members of the sequence of rational numbers

$$r_1 = 1, \; r_2 = 1.7, \; r_3 = 1.73, \; r_4 = 1.732, \; r_5 = 1.7320, \; r_6 = 1.73205, \ldots$$

Therefore, the exponential number $2^{\sqrt{3}}$ is given by the limit of the sequence of numbers

$$2^1, \; 2^{1.7}, \; 2^{1.73}, \; 2^{1.732}, \; 2^{1.7320}, \; 2^{1.73205}, \ldots$$

In this fashion, we can fill the holes and gaps shown in Figure 2.25 to obtain the continuous graph of $y = 2^x$, as shown in Figure 2.26.

The shape of the graph of $y = b^x$ for any $b > 1$ is essentially the same as that of $y = 2^x$. The graph of $y = b^x$ for a typical base $b > 1$ is shown in Figure 2.27a and is rising (when viewed from left to right). For a base b where $0 < b < 1$ the graph is falling, as shown in Figure 2.27b.

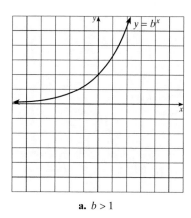 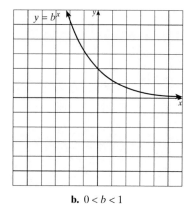

a. $b > 1$ **b.** $0 < b < 1$

Figure 2.27 Graph of $y = b^x$

We summarize the basic properties of exponential functions with the following theorem. Many of these properties for bases with rational exponents should be familiar from previous courses.

THEOREM 2.8 Properties of exponential functions

Let x, y be real numbers, a and b positive real numbers.

Equality rule	If $b \neq 1$, then $b^x = b^y$ if and only if $x = y$.
Inequality rules	If $x > y$ and $b > 1$, then $b^x > b^y$.
	If $x > y$ and $0 < b < 1$, then $b^x < b^y$.
Product rule	$b^x b^y = b^{x+y}$
Quotient rule	$\dfrac{b^x}{b^y} = b^{x-y}$
Power rules	$(b^x)^y = b^{xy}$; $(ab)^x = a^x b^x$; $\left(\dfrac{a}{b}\right)^x = \dfrac{a^x}{b^x}$

> **Graphical Properties**
>
> The function $y = b^x$ is continuous for all x. Furthermore, its graph is always above the x-axis ($b^x > 0$), and is always rising for $b > 1$ and always falling for $0 < b < 1$.

Several parts of this theorem are used in the following example.

EXAMPLE 1   Exponential equations

Solve each of the following exponential equations.

a. $2^{x^2+3} = 16$ **b.** $2^x 3^{x+1} = 108$ **c.** $(\sqrt{2})^{x^2} = \dfrac{8^x}{4}$

Solution

a. $2^{x^2+3} = 16$

$\quad\quad 2^{x^2+3} = 2^4$ *Write 16 as 2^4 so that the equality rule can be used.*

$\quad x^2 + 3 = 4,$ or $x = \pm 1$

b. $2^x 3^{x+1} = 108$

$\quad\quad 2^x 3^x 3 = 3 \cdot 36$ *Product rule*

$\quad\quad (2 \cdot 3)^x = 36$ *Divide both sides by 3 and then use the power rule.*

$\quad\quad\quad 6^x = 6^2$

$\quad\quad\quad\quad x = 2$ *Equality rule*

c. $(\sqrt{2})^{x^2} = \dfrac{8^x}{4}$

$\quad\quad (2^{1/2})^{x^2} = \dfrac{(2^3)^x}{2^2}$

$\quad\quad\quad 2^{x^2/2} = 2^{3x-2}$

$\quad\quad\quad\quad \dfrac{x^2}{2} = 3x - 2$ *Equality rule*

$\quad x^2 - 6x + 4 = 0$

$$x = \frac{6 \pm \sqrt{36 - 4(1)(4)}}{2} = 3 \pm \sqrt{5} \qquad \blacksquare$$

LOGARITHMIC FUNCTIONS

Since the exponential function $y = b^x$ for $b > 0$, $b \neq 1$ is monotonic (its graph is either always rising for all x or always falling), it must have an inverse that is itself monotonic. This inverse function is called the **logarithm of x to the base b**. Here is a definition, with some notation.

Logarithmic Function

> If $b > 0$ and $b \neq 1$, the **logarithm of x to the base b** is the function $y = \log_b x$ that satisfies $b^y = x$; that is,
>
> $$y = \log_b x \quad \text{means} \quad b^y = x$$

> ➡ **What This Says**   It is useful to think of a logarithm as an exponent. That is, consider the following sequence of interpretations:
>
> $\quad\quad y = \log_b x$
>
> $\quad\quad y$ is the logarithm to the base b of x.
>
> $\quad\quad y$ is the **exponent to the base b** that gives x.
>
> $\quad\quad b^y = x$

Notice that $y = \log_b x$ is defined only for $x > 0$ because $b^y > 0$ for all y. We have sketched the graph of $y = \log_b x$ for $b > 1$ in Figure 2.28 by reflecting the graph of $y = b^x$ in the line $y = x$.

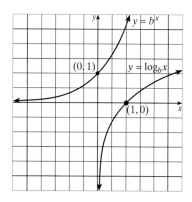

Figure 2.28 The graph of $y = \log_b x$ for $b > 1$

Because $y = b^x$ is a continuous, increasing function that satisfies $b^x > 0$ for all x, $\log_b x$ must also be continuous and increasing, and its graph must lie entirely to the right of the y-axis.

Also, because $b^0 = 1$ and $b^1 = b$, we have

$$\log_b 1 = 0 \quad \text{and} \quad \log_b b = 1$$

so $(1, 0)$ and $(b, 1)$ lie on the logarithmic curve.

Theorem 2.9 lists several general properties of logarithms.

WARNING Remember that $\log_b x$ is defined only for $x > 0$. Any undefined values for $\log_b x$ are excluded.

THEOREM 2.9 Basic properties of logarithmic functions

Assume $b > 0$ and $b \neq 1$.

Equality rule	$\log_b x = \log_b y$ if and only if $x = y$.
Inequality rules	If $x > y$ and $b > 1$, then $\log_b x > \log_b y$.
	If $x > y$ and $0 < b < 1$, then $\log_b x < \log_b y$.
Product rule	$\log_b(xy) = \log_b x + \log_b y$
Quotient rule	$\log_b \left(\dfrac{x}{y} \right) = \log_b x - \log_b y$
Power rule	$\log_b x^p = p \log_b x$ for any real number p
Inversion rules	$b^{\log_b x} = x$ and $\log_b b^x = x$
Special values	$\log_b b = 1$ and $\log_b 1 = 0$

Proof Each part of this theorem can be derived by using the definition of the logarithm in conjunction with a suitable property of exponentials. (See Problems 73–75.) ❑

EXAMPLE 2 Evaluating a logarithmic expression

Evaluate $\log_2(\frac{1}{8}) + \log_2 128$.

Solution

Using Theorem 2.9, we find that

$$\log_2 \left(\tfrac{1}{8} \right) + \log_2 128 = \log_2 (2)^{-3} + \log_2 2^7$$
$$= \log_2 [2^{-3}(2^7)] = \log_2 2^4 = 4 \log_2 2 = 4(1) = 4$$

What we have shown here is longer than what you would do in your work, which would probably be shortened as follows:

$$\log_2\left(\tfrac{1}{8}\right) + \log_2 128 = \log_2 16 \qquad \text{Because } \left(\tfrac{1}{8}\right)(128) = 16$$
$$= 4 \qquad \text{Because 4 is the exponent on 2 that yields 16} \qquad \blacksquare$$

EXAMPLE 3 Logarithmic equation

Solve the equation $\log_3(2x + 1) - 2\log_3(x - 3) = 2$.

Solution

Use Theorem 2.9, and remember that both $2x + 1 > 0$ and $x - 3 > 0$.

$$\log_3(2x + 1) - 2\log_3(x - 3) = 2$$
$$\log_3(2x + 1) - \log_3(x - 3)^2 = 2$$
$$\log_3 \frac{2x + 1}{(x - 3)^2} = 2$$
$$3^2 = \frac{2x + 1}{(x - 3)^2}$$
$$9(x - 3)^2 = 2x + 1$$
$$9x^2 - 56x + 80 = 0$$
$$(x - 4)(9x - 20) = 0$$
$$x = 4, \tfrac{20}{9}$$

Notice that $x - 3 < 0$ if $x = \tfrac{20}{9}$. The given logarithmic equation has only $x = 4$ as a solution because we cannot take the logarithm of a negative number. $\blacksquare$

NATURAL EXPONENTIAL AND LOGARITHMIC FUNCTIONS

In elementary algebra you probably studied logarithms to base 10 or possibly to base 2, but in calculus, it turns out to be convenient to use the number e defined by the limit*

$$e = \lim_{n \to \infty} \left(1 + \frac{1}{n}\right)^n$$

which can be thought of as the number approached by expressions of the form $(1 + \frac{1}{n})^n$ as n grows large without bound.

"But wait," you may be thinking, "as n grows large without bound, the expression $1 + 1/n$ tends toward 1 and since $1^n = 1$ for all n, no matter how large the number n, e must equal 1." However, the limit process does not work that way, and as you can see from Table 2.1, e is a number slightly less than 3. In fact, to twelve decimal places,

$$e \approx 2.71828182845\cdots$$

The letter e was chosen to represent this number in honor of the great Swiss mathematician Leonhard Euler (1707–1783), who discovered many of its special properties and investigated applications in which e plays a vital role.

The number e is called the **natural exponential base** because many formulas in calculus assume an especially simple or "natural" form when expressed in terms of exponentials or logarithms to the base e. For this reason, e^x is called the **natural exponential function,** and $\log_e x$ is the **natural logarithm.** We will have more to say about what makes these functions "natural" in Chapter 3. Here is some special notation and terminology associated with these functions.

WARNING You must be careful when using software to reach conclusions in calculus. For example, on most software or calculators, if you input

$$\left(1 + \frac{1}{10^{20}}\right)^{10^{20}}$$

the output is 1 (which, of course, is incorrect). We know (from the definition of e) that $\lim_{n \to \infty}(1 + \frac{1}{n})^n = e > 1$.

```
Y1目(1+1/X)^X
   X      Y1
  1       2
  2       2.25
  3       2.3704
  4       2.4414
  5       2.4883
  10      2.5937
  50      2.6916
  100     2.7048
  1000    2.7169
  5000    2.718
  10000   2.7181
  1E6     2.7183
  X=12    2.7183
```

TABLE 2.1 Calculator approximations of e

*Limits such as $n \to \infty$ are called "limits at infinity" and will be discussed in detail in Chapter 4.

EXP NOTATION

The natural exponential function e^x is sometimes denoted by $\exp(x)$.

COMMON LOGARITHM

The **common logarithm**, $\log_{10} x$, is denoted by **log** x.

NATURAL LOGARITHM

The **natural logarithm**, $\log_e x$, is denoted by **ln** x.
($\ln x$ is pronounced "ell n x" or "lawn x.")

The "exp" notation for the natural exponential function is especially useful for representing composite functions. For instance, the awkward expression

$$e^{3x^2 - 2\sin x + 8}$$

can be expressed more compactly as

$$\exp(3x^2 - 2\sin x + 8)$$

The following theorem summarizes the key properties of natural exponential and logarithmic functions.

THEOREM 2.10   Basic properties of the natural logarithm

a. $\ln 1 = 0$ **b.** $\ln e = 1$

c. $e^{\ln x} = x$ for all $x > 0$ **d.** $\ln e^y = y$ for all y

e. $b^x = e^{x \ln b}$ for any $b > 0$ ($b \neq 1$)

Proof   Parts **a** and **b** follow immediately from the definitions of $\ln x$ and e^x. Parts **c** and **d** are just the inversion rules for base e.

We show the proof of part **e**.

$$e^{x \ln b} = e^{\ln b^x} \qquad \text{Power rule (Theorem 2.9)}$$
$$= b^x \qquad \text{Property of natural log (Theorem 2.10c)} \qquad \square$$

On calculators, there are usually two logarithm keys, $\boxed{\text{LOG}}$ and $\boxed{\text{LN}}$. For other logarithms, you will need the useful conversion formula contained in the following theorem.

THEOREM 2.11   Change-of-base theorem

$$\log_b x = \frac{\ln x}{\ln b} \quad \text{for any } b > 0 \ (b \neq 1)$$

Proof   Let $y = \log_b x$. Then

$$b^y = x \qquad \text{Definition of logarithm}$$
$$\ln b^y = \ln x \qquad \text{Equality rule of logarithms}$$
$$y \ln b = \ln x \qquad \text{Power rule of logarithms}$$
$$y = \frac{\ln x}{\ln b} \qquad \text{Divide both sides by } \ln b. \qquad \square$$

WARNING If you are using a software package such as *Mathematica, Derive,* or *Maple,* sometimes referred to as CAS (Computer Algebra System), be careful about the notation. Some versions do not distinguish between $\log x$ (common logarithm) and $\ln x$ (natural logarithm). All logarithms on these versions are assumed to be natural logarithms, so to evaluate a common logarithm requires using the change-of-base theorem.

EXAMPLE 4   Solving an exponential equation using the change-of-base theorem

Solve $6^x = 200$.

Solution

$$6^x = 200$$

$$x = \log_6 200 \qquad \text{Definition of exponent}$$

$$= \frac{\ln 200}{\ln 6} \qquad \text{Change-of-base theorem}$$

$$\approx 2.957047225 \qquad \text{Approximate with a calculator.} \qquad \blacksquare$$

EXAMPLE 5   Finding a velocity

An object moves along a straight line in such a way that after t seconds, its velocity is given by

$$v(t) = 10 \log_5 t + 3 \log_2 t$$

ft/s. How long will it take for the velocity to reach 20 ft/s?

Solution

We want to solve the equation

$$10 \log_5 t + 3 \log_2 t = 20$$

$$10 \frac{\ln t}{\ln 5} + 3 \frac{\ln t}{\ln 2} = 20 \qquad \text{Change-of-base formula}$$

$$\left(\frac{10}{\ln 5} + \frac{3}{\ln 2} \right) \ln t = 20 \qquad \text{Factor.}$$

$$\ln t = 20 \left(\frac{10}{\ln 5} + \frac{3}{\ln 2} \right)^{-1} \approx 1.89727$$

$$t \approx e^{1.89727} \approx 6.6677$$

Thus, it takes about 6.67 seconds for the velocity to reach 20 ft/s. $\qquad \blacksquare$

EXAMPLE 6   Changing an exponential from base b to base e

Change 10^{2x} to an exponential to the natural base.

Solution

We wish to find N for

$$10^{2x} = e^N$$

$$\ln 10^{2x} = \ln e^N \qquad \text{Log of both sides}$$

$$2x \ln 10 = N \ln e \qquad \text{Power rule of logarithms}$$

$$2x \ln 10 = N \qquad \ln e = 1$$

Thus, $10^{2x} = e^{2x \ln 10}$. $\qquad \blacksquare$

EXAMPLE 7   Solving an exponential equation with base e

Solve $\frac{1}{2} = e^{-0.000425t}$.

Solution

We have

$$\frac{1}{2} = e^{-0.000425t}$$

$$-0.000425t = \ln 0.5 \qquad \text{Remember that } -0.000425t \text{ is the exponent on base } e \text{ that equals } \frac{1}{2} = 0.5$$

$$t = \frac{\ln 0.5}{-0.000425} \approx 1630.934542 \qquad \blacksquare$$

EXAMPLE 8 Exponential growth

A biological colony grows in such a way that at time t (in minutes), the population is

$$P(t) = P_0 e^{kt}$$

where P_0 is the initial population and k is a positive constant. Suppose the colony begins with 5,000 individuals and contains a population of 7,000 after 20 min. Find k and determine the population (rounded to the nearest hundred individuals) after 30 min.

Solution

Because $P_0 = 5,000$, the population after t minutes will be

$$P(t) = 5,000 e^{kt}$$

In particular, because the population is 7,000 after 20 min,

$$P(20) = 5,000 e^{k(20)}$$
$$7,000 = 5,000 e^{20k}$$
$$\tfrac{7}{5} = e^{20k}$$
$$20k = \ln(\tfrac{7}{5})$$
$$k = \tfrac{1}{20} \ln(\tfrac{7}{5})$$
$$\approx 0.0168236$$

Finally, to determine the population after 30 min, substitute this value for k to find

$$P(30) = 5,000 e^{30k}$$
$$\approx 8,282.5117$$

The expected population is approximately 8,300. ■

CONTINUOUS COMPOUNDING OF INTEREST

One reason e is called the "natural" exponential base is that many natural growth phenomena can be described in terms of e^x. As an illustration of this fact, we close this section by showing how e^x can be used to describe the accounting procedure called *continuous compounding of interest*.

Suppose a sum of money is invested and the interest is compounded once during a particular period. If P is the initial investment (the **present value** or **principal**) and i is the **interest rate** during the period, then the **future value** (in dollars), A, after the interest is added will be

$$A = \underset{\uparrow}{P} + \underset{\uparrow}{Pi} = P(1 + i)$$
$$\text{principal} \quad \text{interest}$$

Thus, to compute the balance at the end of an interest period, we multiply the balance at the beginning of the period by the expression $1 + i$.

Interest is usually compounded more than once a year. The interest added to the account during one period will itself earn interest during subsequent periods. If the annual interest rate is r and the interest is compounded n times per year, then the year is divided into n equal interest periods and the interest rate during each such period is $i = \frac{r}{n}$. To compute the balance at the end of any period, you multiply the balance at the beginning of that period by the expression $1 + \frac{r}{n}$, so the balance at the end of the first period is

$$A_1 = P\left(1 + \frac{r}{n}\right)$$

At the end of the second period, the balance is

$$A_2 = A_1\left(1 + \frac{r}{n}\right) = \left[P\left(1 + \frac{r}{n}\right)\right]\left(1 + \frac{r}{n}\right) = P\left(1 + \frac{r}{n}\right)^2$$

At the end of the third period, the balance is

$$A_3 = A_2\left(1 + \frac{r}{n}\right) = \left[P\left(1 + \frac{r}{n}\right)^2\right]\left(1 + \frac{r}{n}\right) = P\left(1 + \frac{r}{n}\right)^3$$

and so on. At the end of t years, the interest has been compounded nt times, and the future value is

$$A(t) = P\left(1 + \frac{r}{n}\right)^{nt}$$

The first two graphs in Figure 2.29 show how an amount of money in an account over a one-year period of time grows, first with quarterly compounding and then with monthly compounding. Notice that these are "step" graphs, with jumps occurring at the end of each compounding period.

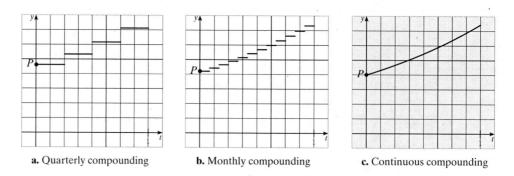

a. Quarterly compounding   **b.** Monthly compounding   **c.** Continuous compounding

Figure 2.29   The growth of an account over a one-year period with different compounding frequencies

With continuous compounding, we compound interest not quarterly, or monthly, or daily, or even every second, but *instantaneously*, so that the future amount of money A in the account grows continuously, as shown in Figure 2.29c. In other words, for a one-year period we compute A as the limiting value of

$$P\left(1 + \frac{r}{n}\right)^n$$

as the number of compounding periods n grows without bound. We denote by $A(t)$, the future value after t years, as with the definition of e, by the limit notation $n \to \infty$:

$$A(t) = \lim_{n \to \infty} P\left(1 + \frac{r}{n}\right)^{nt}$$ Let $k = \frac{n}{r}$, so that $krt = nt$ and $\frac{r}{n} = \frac{1}{k}$; also $k \to \infty$ as $n \to \infty$.

$$= \lim_{k \to \infty} P\left(1 + \frac{1}{k}\right)^{krt}$$

$$= \lim_{k \to \infty} P\left[\left(1 + \frac{1}{k}\right)^k\right]^{rt}$$

$$= P\left[\lim_{k \to \infty} \left(1 + \frac{1}{k}\right)^k\right]^{rt}$$ Scalar rule for limits

$$= Pe^{rt}$$ Definition of e

These observations are now summarized.

Future Value

If P dollars are compounded n times per year at an annual rate r, then the future value after t years is given by

$$A(t) = P\left(1 + \frac{r}{n}\right)^{nt}$$

and if the compounding is continuous, the future value is

$$A(t) = Pe^{rt}$$

EXAMPLE 9   Continuous compounding of interest

If \$12,000 is invested for 5 years at 18%, find the future value at the end of 5 years if interest is compounded

a. monthly.   **b.** continuously.

c. If the interest is compounded continuously, how long will it take for the money to double?

Solution

$P = \$12,000$; $t = 5$; and $r = 18\% = 0.18$ are given.

a. $n = 12$; $A = P\left(1 + \frac{r}{n}\right)^{nt} = \$12,000\left(1 + \frac{0.18}{12}\right)^{12 \cdot 5} \approx \$29,318.64$

b. $A = \$12,000e^{0.18(5)} \approx \$29,515.24$

c. The account doubles when $A(t) = 2P = \$24,000$; that is, when

$$12,000e^{0.18t} = 24,000$$

$$e^{0.18t} = 2$$

$$0.18t = \ln 2 \quad \text{Definition of logarithm}$$

$$t = \frac{\ln 2}{0.18} \approx 3.851$$

This is about 3 years and 10 months.   ∎

2.4 PROBLEM SET

A *Sketch the graph of the functions in Problems 1–4.*

1. $y = 3^x$

2. $y = 4^{-x}$

3. $y = -e^{-x}$

4. $y = -e^x$

Evaluate the expressions (with calculator accuracy) in Problems 5–12.

5. $32^{2/5} + 9^{3/2}$

6. $(1 + 4^{3/2})^{-1/2}$

7. $e^3e^{2.3}$

8. $\dfrac{(e^{1.3})^2}{e^{1.3} + \sqrt{e^{-1.4}}}$

9. $5,000\left(1 + \frac{0.135}{12}\right)^{12(5)}$

10. $145,000\left(1 + \frac{0.073}{365}\right)^{-365(5)}$

11. $2,589e^{0.45(6)}$

12. $850,000e^{-0.04(10)}$

Evaluate the expressions given in Problems 13–22.

13. $\log_2 4 + \log_3 \frac{1}{9}$

14. $2^{\log_2 3 - \log_2 5}$

15. $5\log_3 9 - 2\log_2 16$

16. $\left(\log_2 \frac{1}{8}\right)(\log_3 27)$

17. $(3^{\log_7 1})(\log_5 0.04)$

18. $e^{5\ln 2}$

19. $\log_3 3^4 - \ln e^{0.5}$

20. $\ln(\log 10^e)$

21. $\exp(\ln 3 - \ln 10)$

22. $\exp(\log_{e^2} 25)$

Solve the logarithmic and exponential equations to calculator accuracy in Problems 23–40.

23. $\log_x 16 = 2$

24. $\log x = 5.1$

25. $e^{-3x} = 0.5$

26. $\ln x^2 = 9$

27. $7^{-x} = 15$

28. $e^{2x} = \ln(4 + e)$

29. $\frac{1}{2}\log_3 x = \log_2 8$

30. $\log_2(x^{\log_2 x}) = 4$

31. $3^{x^2-x} = 9$

32. $4^{x^2+x} = 16$

33. $2^x 5^{x+2} = 25,000$

34. $3^x 4^{x+(1/2)} = 3,456$

35. $(\sqrt[3]{2})^{x+10} = 2^{x^2}$

36. $(\sqrt[3]{5})^{x+2} = 5^{x^2}$

37. $e^{2x+3} = 1$

38. $\dfrac{e^{x^2}}{e^{x+6}} = 1$

39. $\log_3 x + \log_3(2x + 1) = 1$

40. $\ln\left(\dfrac{x^2}{1-x}\right) = \ln x + \ln\left(\dfrac{2x}{1+x}\right)$

In Problems 41–46, evaluate the given limits.

41. a. $\displaystyle\lim_{x \to 0^+} x^2 e^{-x}$ **b.** $\displaystyle\lim_{x \to 1} x^2 e^{-x}$

42. a. $\displaystyle\lim_{x \to 0} e^{-x^3}$ **b.** $\displaystyle\lim_{x \to 1} e^{-x^3}$

43. a. $\displaystyle\lim_{x \to 0^+} (1 + x)^{1/x}$ **b.** $\displaystyle\lim_{x \to 1} (1 + x)^{1/x}$

44. a. $\displaystyle\lim_{x \to 0^-} e^{1/x}$ **b.** $\displaystyle\lim_{x \to 0^+} \ln x$

45. $\displaystyle\lim_{x \to e} x \ln x^2$ **46.** $\displaystyle\lim_{x \to e} \frac{\ln \sqrt{x}}{x}$

Ⓑ 47. If $\log_b 1{,}296 = 4$, what is $\left(\frac{3}{2}b\right)^{3/2}$?

48. If $\log_{\sqrt{b}} 106 = 2$, what is $\sqrt{b - 25}$?

49. Solve $\log_2 x + \log_5(2x + 1) = \ln x$ correct to the nearest tenth.

50. Solve $\log_x 2 = \log_3 x$ correct to the nearest tenth.

Data points with a curve fit to those points are shown in Problems 51–54. Decide whether the data are better modeled by an exponential or a logarithmic function.

51.

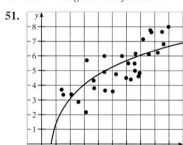

52.

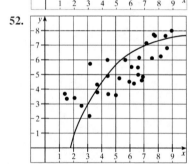

53.

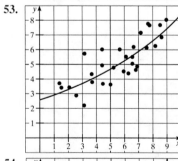

54.

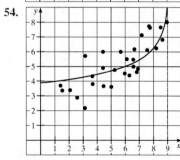

55. According to the *Bouguer–Lambert law*, a beam of light that strikes the surface of a body of water with intensity I_0 will have intensity I at a depth of x meters, where

$$I = I_0 e^{kx}, \qquad k > 0$$

The constant k, called the *absorption coefficient*, depends on such things as the wavelength of the beam of light and the purity of the water. Suppose a given beam of light is only 5% as intense at a depth of 2 meters as it is at the surface. Find k and determine at what depth (to the nearest meter) the intensity is 1% of the intensity at the surface. (This explains why plant life exists only in the top 10 m of a lake or sea.)

56. A certain bank pays 6% interest compounded continuously. How long will it take for $835 to double?

57. If an amount of money is compounded continuously at an annual rate r, how long will it take for that amount of money to double?

58. First National Bank pays 7% interest compounded monthly, and World Savings pays 6.95% interest compounded continuously. Which bank offers a better deal?

59. A person invests $8,500 in a bank that compounds interest continuously. If the investment doubles in 10 years, what is the (annual) rate of interest (correct to the nearest hundredth percent)?

60. In 1626, Peter Minuit traded trinkets worth $24 for land on Manhattan Island. Assume that in 2000 the same land was worth $43.9 billion. Find the annual rate of interest compounded continuously at which the $24 would have had to be invested during this time to yield the same amount.

61. Biologists estimate that the population of a bacterial colony is

$$P(t) = P_0 2^{kt}$$

at time t (in minutes). Suppose the population is found to be 1,000 after 20 minutes and that it doubles every hour.

a. Find P_0 and k.

b. When (to the nearest minute) will the population be 5,000?

62. Spy Problem   Having escaped from the smugglers (Problem 49, Section 1.2), the Spy receives an e-mail message that his best friend, Sigmund ("Siggy") Leiter, has been found murdered, the body stuffed unceremoniously in a freezer. Fighting back tears of grief, he remembers that t hours after death, a body has temperature

$$T = A + (B - A)e^{-0.03t}$$

where A is the air temperature and B is the temperature of the body at the time of death. The police inform the Spy that at the time of discovery, 1:00 P.M. on Thursday, the corpse had temperature 40°F, and the freezer 10°F . The Spy knows the deed was done by either Coldfinger or André Scélérat. If Coldfinger was in jail from Monday until Wednesday noon and Scélérat was at a villains' convention in Las Vegas from noon on Wednesday until Friday, who "iced" Siggy and when? (By the way, one of the few normal things about Siggy was his body temperature, 98.6°F.)

63. The *Richter scale* measures the intensity of earthquakes. Specifically, if E is the energy (watt/cm³) released by a quake, then it is said to have *magnitude* M, where

$$M = \frac{\log E - 11.4}{1.5}$$

a. Express E in terms of M.

b. How much more energy is released in an $M = 8.5$ earthquake (such as the devastating Alaska quake of 1964) than in an average quake of magnitude $M = 6.5$ (the Los Angeles quake of 1994)?

64. Exploration Problem In the definition of the exponential function $f(x) = b^x$, we require that b be a positive constant. What happens if $b < 0$, for example, if $b = -2$? For what values of x is f defined? Describe the graph of f in this case.

65. Let $E(x) = 2^{x^2 - 2x}$.

a. Use a calculator to sketch $E(x)$.

b. Where does the graph cross the y-axis? What happens to the graph as $x \to +\infty$ and as $x \to -\infty$?

c. Use a calculator utility to find the value of x that minimizes $E(x)$. What is the minimum value?

66. A manufacturer of car batteries estimates that p percent of the batteries will work for at least t months, where

$$p(t) = 100e^{-0.03t}$$

a. What percent of the batteries can be expected to last at least 40 months?

b. What percent can be expected to *fail* before 50 months?

c. What percent can be expected to *fail* between the 40th and 50th months?

67. If \$3,600 is invested at 15% compounded daily, how much money will there be in 7 years?

a. Use a 365-day year; this is known as *exact interest*.

b. Use a 360-day year; this is known as *ordinary interest*.

68. If P dollars are borrowed for a total of N months compounded monthly at an annual interest rate of r, then the monthly payment is found by the formula

$$m = \frac{P\left(\frac{r}{12}\right)}{1 - \left(1 + \frac{r}{12}\right)^{-N}}$$

a. Use this formula to determine the monthly car payment for a new car costing \$17,487 with a down payment of \$7,487. The car is financed for 4 years at 12%.

b. A home loan is made for \$210,000 at 8% interest for 30 years. What is the monthly payment with a 20% down payment?

69. A cool drink is removed from a refrigerator and is placed in a room where the temperature is 70°F. According to a result in physics known as *Newton's law of cooling*, the temperature of the drink in t minutes will be

$$F(t) = 70 - Ae^{-kt}$$

where A and k are positive constants. Suppose the temperature of the drink was 35°F when it left the refrigerator, and 30 minutes later, it was 50°F [that is, $F(0) = 35$ and $F(30) = 50$].

a. Find A and e^{-30k}.

b. What will the temperature of the drink be after one hour (to the nearest degree)?

c. What would you expect to happen to the temperature as $t \to +\infty$?

70. HISTORICAL QUEST John Napier was a Scottish landowner who was the Isaac Asimov of his day, having envisioned the tank, the machine gun, and the submarine. He also predicted that the end of the world would occur between 1688 and 1700. He is best known today as the inventor of logarithms, which until the advent of the calculator were used extensively with complicated calculations. Napier's logarithms are not identical to the logarithms we use today. Napier chose to use $1 - 10^{-7}$ as his given number, and then he multiplied by 10^7. That is, if

JOHN NAPIER
1550–1617

$$N = 10^7 \left(1 - \frac{1}{10^7}\right)^L$$

then L is Napier's logarithm of the number N; that is, $L = \text{nog } N$ means $N = 10^7(1 - 10^{-7})^L$. ∎

One difference between Napier's logarithms (which for clarity we will call a nog) and modern logarithms is apparent when stating the product, quotient, and power rules for logarithms.

a. Show that if $L_1 = \text{nog } N_1$ and $L_2 = \text{nog } N_2$, then

$$\text{nog } N_1 + \text{nog } N_2 = \text{nog}\left(\frac{N_1 N_2}{10^7}\right).$$

b. State and prove similar results for a quotient rule and a power rule for Napier logarithms.

c. What is nog 10^7?

d. If nog $N = 10^7$, then $N \approx e^r$ for some rational number r. What is r?

e. Fortunately, Napier's 1614 paper on logarithms was read by a true mathematician, Henry Briggs (1561–1630), and together they decided that base 10 made a lot more sense. In the year Napier died, Briggs published a table of common logarithms (base 10) that at the time was a major accomplishment. In this paper he used the words "mantissa" and "characteristic." What is the meaning that Briggs gave to these words?

f. Who was the first person to publish a table of natural logarithms (base e)?

71. For $b > 0$ and all positive integers m and n, show that

a. $b^m b^n = b^{m+n}$ **b.** $\dfrac{b^m}{b^n} = b^{m-n}$

72. For $b > 0$ and all positive integers m and n, show that

a. $(b^m)^n = b^{mn}$ **b.** $(\sqrt[n]{b})^m = \sqrt[n]{b^m}$

73. Prove:

a. $\log_b x + \log_b y = \log_b(xy)$

b. $\log_b x - \log_b y = \log_b \dfrac{x}{y}$

74. Let b be any positive number other than 1. Show that

$$x^x = b^{x \log_b x}$$

75. Let a and b be any positive numbers other than 1. Show that

a. $\log_a x = \dfrac{\log_b x}{\log_b a}$ **b.** $(\log_a b)(\log_b a) = 1$

CHAPTER 2 REVIEW

Proficiency Examination

CONCEPT PROBLEMS

1. State the informal definition of a limit of a function. Discuss this informal definition.

2. State the formal definition of a limit.

3. State the following basic rules for limits:
   - **a.** limit of a constant
   - **b.** multiple rule
   - **c.** sum rule
   - **d.** difference rule
   - **e.** product rule
   - **f.** quotient rule
   - **g.** power rule
   - **h.** limit of a polynomial function
   - **i.** limit of a rational function
   - **j.** limit of a transcendental function

4. State the squeeze rule.

5. What are the values of the given limits?
   - **a.** $\lim\limits_{x\to 0} \dfrac{\sin x}{x}$
   - **b.** $\lim\limits_{x\to 0} \dfrac{\cos x - 1}{x}$

6. Define the continuity of a function at a point and discuss.

7. State the continuity theorem.

8. State the composition limit rule.

9. State the intermediate value theorem.

10. State the root location theorem.

11. State the completeness property.

12. **a.** What is an exponential function?
    b. How is such a function related to a logarithmic function?

13. Define e.

14. **a.** What is a logarithmic function?
    b. What is a common logarithm?
    c. What is a natural logarithm?

15. Draw a quick sketch of:
    a. An exponential function b^x for $b > 1$.
    b. An exponential function b^x for $0 < b < 1$.

16. Draw a quick sketch of:
    a. A logarithmic function $\log_b x$ for $b > 1$.
    b. A logarithmic function $\log_b x$ for $0 < b < 1$.

17. State each of the following exponential properties:
    - **a.** Equality rule
    - **b.** Inequality rules
    - **c.** Product rule
    - **d.** Quotient rule
    - **e.** Power rules

18. Complete the statement of each of the following natural logarithm properties:
    - **a.** $\ln 1 = $ _____
    - **b.** $\ln e = $ _____
    - **c.** $e^{\ln x} = $ _____
    - **d.** $\ln e^y = $ _____
    - **e.** $b^x = $ _____ (write as a power of e)

PRACTICE PROBLEMS

Evaluate the limits in Problems 19–24.

19. $\lim\limits_{x\to 3} \dfrac{x^2 - 4x + 9}{x^2 + x - 8}$

20. $\lim\limits_{x\to 4} \dfrac{\sqrt{x} - 2}{x - 4}$

21. $\lim\limits_{x\to 2} \dfrac{x^2 - 5x + 6}{x^2 - 4}$

22. $\lim\limits_{x\to 0} \dfrac{1 - \cos x}{2\tan x}$

23. $\lim\limits_{x\to 0} \dfrac{\sin 9x}{\sin 5x}$

24. $\lim\limits_{x\to \frac{1}{2}^-} \dfrac{|2x - 1|}{2x - 1}$

25. Decide whether each of the curves is exponential or logarithmic.

a. 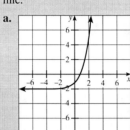 **b.**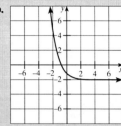

c. 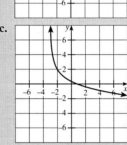 **d.**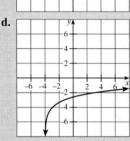

Determine whether the functions given in Problems 26–27 are continuous on the interval $[-5, 5]$.

26. $f(t) = \dfrac{1}{t} - \dfrac{3}{t + 1}$

27. $g(x) = \dfrac{x^2 - 1}{x^2 + x - 2}$

28. How quickly will \$2,000 grow to \$5,000 when invested at an annual rate of 8% if interest is compounded:
    - **a.** quarterly?
    - **b.** monthly?
    - **c.** continuously?

29. Find constants A and B such that f is continuous for all x:
$$f(x) = \begin{cases} Ax + 3 & \text{if } x < 1 \\ 2 & \text{if } x = 1 \\ x^2 + B & \text{if } x > 1 \end{cases}$$

30. Show that the equation
$$x + \sin x = \frac{1}{\sqrt{x} + 3}$$
has at least one solution on the interval $(0, \pi)$.

Supplementary Problems*

1. Evaluate each of the given numbers (calculator approximations for parts **a** and **b**).
   - **a.** $\ln 4.5$
   - **b.** $e^{2.8}$
   - **c.** $e^{\ln \pi}$
   - **d.** $\ln e^{\sqrt{2}}$

Solve each equation in Problems 2–8 for x.

2. $4^{x-1} = 8$

3. $2^{x^2 + 4x} = \frac{1}{16}$

4. $\log_2 2^{x^2} = 4$

5. $\log_4 \sqrt{x(x - 15)} = 1$

6. $\log_2 x + \log_2 (x - 15) = 4$

7. $3^{2x-1} = 6^x 3^{1-x}$

8. $\ln(x - 1) + \ln(x + 1) = 2 \ln \sqrt{12}$

In Problems 9–28, evaluate the given limit.

9. $\lim\limits_{x \to 2} \dfrac{3x^2 - 7x + 2}{x - 2}$

10. $\lim\limits_{x \to -3} \dfrac{4x^2 + 11x - 3}{x^2 - x - 12}$

11. $\lim\limits_{x \to 1^+} \sqrt{\dfrac{x^2 - x}{x - 1}}$

12. $\lim\limits_{x \to 1} \dfrac{x^3 - 1}{x^2 - 1}$

13. $\lim\limits_{x \to 4} |4 - x|$

14. $\lim\limits_{x \to 0^-} \dfrac{|x|}{x}$

15. $\lim\limits_{x \to 1} \dfrac{x^2 - 3x + 2}{x^2 - 1}$

16. $\lim\limits_{x \to 1/\pi} \dfrac{1 + \cos \frac{1}{x}}{\pi x - 1}$

17. $\lim\limits_{x \to 0^+} (1 + x)^{4/x}$

18. $\lim\limits_{x \to 0^+} (1 + 2x)^{1/x}$

19. $\lim\limits_{x \to 1} \dfrac{x^5 - 1}{x - 1}$

20. $\lim\limits_{x \to e^2} \dfrac{(\ln x)^3 - 8}{\ln x - 2}$

21. $\lim\limits_{x \to 0} \dfrac{\sin 3x}{\sin 2x}$

22. $\lim\limits_{t \to 0} \dfrac{\tan^{-1} t}{\sin^{-1} t}$

23. $\lim\limits_{x \to 0} \dfrac{\sin(\cos x)}{\sec x}$

24. $\lim\limits_{x \to 0} \tan 2x \cot x$

25. $\lim\limits_{x \to 0} \dfrac{1 - \sin x}{\cos^2 x}$

26. $\lim\limits_{x \to 0} \dfrac{1 - 2\cos x}{\sqrt{3} - 2\sin x}$

27. $\lim\limits_{x \to 0} \dfrac{e^{3x} - 1}{e^x - 1}$

28. $\lim\limits_{x \to 3} \dfrac{\frac{1}{x} - \frac{1}{3}}{x - 3}$

Evaluate $\lim\limits_{\Delta x \to 0} \dfrac{f(x + \Delta x) - f(x)}{\Delta x}$ *for the function f in Problems 29–36.*

29. $f(x) = 7$

30. $f(x) = 3x + 5$

31. $f(x) = \sqrt{2x}$

32. $f(x) = x(x + 1)$

33. $f(x) = \dfrac{4}{x}$

34. $f(x) = \sin x$

35. $f(x) = e^x$

36. $f(x) = \ln x$

Decide whether the functions in Problems 37–40 are continuous on the given intervals. If not, define or redefine the function at one point to make it continuous everywhere on the given interval, or else explain why that cannot be done.

37. $f(x) = \dfrac{x + 4}{x - 8}$ on $[-5, 5]$

38. $f(x) = \dfrac{x + 4}{x - 8}$ on $[0, 10]$

39. $f(x) = \dfrac{\sqrt{x} - 8}{x - 64}$ on $\mathbb{R}$

40. $f(x) = \dfrac{\sqrt{x} - 6}{x - 36}$ on $[-5, 5]$

Decide whether the functions in Problems 41–44 are continuous on the given intervals. Check all of the suspicious points.

41. $r(x) = \begin{cases} 1 & \text{if } x \text{ is rational} \\ -1 & \text{if } x \text{ is irrational} \end{cases}$

42. $f(x) = |x - 2|$ on $[-5, 5]$

43. a. $f(x) = \dfrac{x^2 - x - 6}{x + 2}$ on $[0, 5]$

b. $f(x) = \dfrac{x^2 - x - 6}{x + 2}$ on $[-5, 5]$

c. $f(x) = \begin{cases} \dfrac{x^2 - x - 6}{x + 2} & \text{on } [-5,5],\ x \neq -2 \\ -4 & \text{for } x = -2 \end{cases}$

d. $f(x) = \begin{cases} \dfrac{x^2 - x - 6}{x + 2} & \text{on } [-5,5],\ x \neq -2 \\ -5 & \text{for } x = -2 \end{cases}$

44. a. $g(x) = \dfrac{x^2 - 3x - 10}{x + 2}$ on $[0, 5]$

b. $g(x) = \dfrac{x^2 - 3x - 10}{x + 2}$ on $[-5, 5]$

c. $g(x) = \begin{cases} \dfrac{x^2 - 3x - 10}{x + 2} & \text{for } -5 \leq x < -2 \\ -7 & \text{for } x = -2 \\ x - 5 & \text{for } -2 < x \leq 5 \end{cases}$

*The **greatest integer function** $f(x) = [\![\, x \,]\!]$ is the largest integer that is less than or equal to x. This definition is used in Problems 45–47.*

45. a. Graph $f(x) = [\![\, x \,]\!]$ on $[-3, 6]$.

b. Find $\lim\limits_{x \to 3} f(x)$.

c. For what values of a does $\lim\limits_{x \to a} f(x)$ exist?

46. Repeat Problem 45 for $f(x) = [\![\, \frac{x}{2} \,]\!]$.

47. Let $f(x) = [\![\, x^2 + 1 \,]\!]^{[\![\, x + 1 \,]\!]}$; find $\lim\limits_{x \to 1} f(x)$.

48. Find constants A and B such that f is continuous for all x:

$$f(x) = \begin{cases} Ax + 3 & \text{if } x < 1 \\ 5 & \text{if } x = 1 \\ x^2 + B & \text{if } x > 1 \end{cases}$$

49. Find numbers a and b so that

$$\lim\limits_{x \to 0} \frac{\sqrt{ax + b} - 1}{x} = 1$$

50. Find a number c so that

$$\lim\limits_{x \to 3} \frac{x^3 + cx^2 + 5x + 12}{x^2 - 7x + 12}$$

exists. Then find the corresponding limit.

51. A manufacturer of lightbulbs estimates that the fraction $F(t)$ of bulbs that remain burning after t weeks is given by

$$F(t) = e^{-kt}$$

where k is a positive constant. Suppose twice as many bulbs are burning after 5 weeks as after 9 weeks.

a. Find k and determine the fraction of bulbs still burning after 7 weeks.

b. What fraction of the bulbs burn out before 10 weeks?

c. What fraction of the bulbs can be expected to burn out between the 4th and 5th weeks?

52. How much should you invest now at an annual interest rate of 6.25% so that your balance 10 years from now will be $2,000 if interest is compounded

a. quarterly?   **b.** continuously?

53. A *decibel* (named for Alexander Graham Bell) is the smallest increase of the loudness of a sound that is detectable by the human ear. In physics, it is shown that when two sounds of intensity I_1 and I_2 (watts/cm^3) occur, the difference in loudness is D decibels, where

$$D = 10 \log \left(\frac{I_1}{I_2} \right)$$

When sound is rated in relation to the threshold of human hearing ($I_0 = 10^{-16}$), the level of normal conversation is 50 decibels, whereas that of a rock concert is 110 decibels. Show that a rock concert is 60 times as loud as normal conversation but a million times as intense.

54. If a function f is not continuous at $x = c$, but can be made continuous at c by being given a new value at the point, it is said to have a *removable discontinuity* at $x = c$. Which of the following functions has a removable discontinuity at $x = c$?

    a. $f(x) = \dfrac{2x^2 + x - 15}{x + 3}$ at $c = -3$

    b. $f(x) = \dfrac{x - 2}{|x - 2|}$ at $c = 2$

    c. $f(x) = \dfrac{2 - \sqrt{x}}{4 - x}$ at $c = 4$

55. If $f(x) = x^3 - x^2 + x + 1$, show that there is a number c such that $f(c) = 0$.

56. Prove that $\sqrt{x + 3} = e^x$ has at least one real root, and then use a graphing utility to find the root correct to the nearest tenth.

57. Show that the tangent line to the circle $x^2 + y^2 = r^2$ at the point (x_0, y_0) has the equation $y_0 y + x_0 x = r^2$. *Hint*: Recall that the tangent line at a point P on a circle with center C is the line that passes through P and is perpendicular to the line segment $\overline{CP}$.

58. **Counterexample Problem**   It is not necessarily true that $\lim\limits_{x \to c} f(x)$ and $\lim\limits_{x \to c} g(x)$ exist whenever $\lim\limits_{x \to c}[f(x) \cdot g(x)]$ exists. Find functions f and g such that $\lim\limits_{x \to c}[f(x) \cdot g(x)]$ exists and $\lim\limits_{x \to c} g(x) = 0$, but $\lim\limits_{x \to c} f(x)$ does not exist.

59. **Counterexample Problem**   It is not necessarily true that $\lim\limits_{x \to c} f(x)$ and $\lim\limits_{x \to c} g(x)$ exist whenever $\lim\limits_{x \to c} \dfrac{f(x)}{g(x)}$ exists. Find functions f and g such that $\lim\limits_{x \to 0} \dfrac{f(x)}{g(x)}$ exists, but neither $\lim\limits_{x \to 0} f(x)$ nor $\lim\limits_{x \to 0} g(x)$ exists.

60. When analyzing experimental data involving two variables, a useful procedure is to pass a smooth curve through a number of plotted data points and then perform computations as if the curve were the graph of an equation relating the variables. Suppose the following data are gathered as a result of a physiological experiment in which skin tissue is subjected to external heat for t seconds, and a measurement is made of the change in temperature ΔT required to cause a change of $2.5°C$ at a depth of 0.5 mm in the skin:

t (sec)	1	2	3	4	10	20	25	30
ΔT (°C)	12.5	7.5	5.8	5.0	4.5	3.5	2.9	2.8

Plot the data points in a coordinate plane and then answer these questions.

    a. What temperature difference ΔT would be expected if the exposure time is 2.2 sec?

    b. Approximately what exposure time t corresponds to a temperature difference $\Delta T = 8.0°C$?

61. **Journal Problem**   The theorem

$$\lim_{h \to 0} \frac{\sin h}{h} = 1$$

stated in this chapter has been the subject of much discussion in mathematical journals:

W. B. Gearhart and H. S. Schultz, "The Function $\sin x/x$," *College Mathematics Journal* (1990): 90–99.

L. Gillman, "π and the Limit of $(\sin \alpha)/\alpha$," *American Mathematical Monthly* (1991): 345–348.

F. Richman, "A Circular Argument," *College Mathematics Journal* (1993): 160–162.

D. A. Rose, "The Differentiability of $\sin x$," *College Mathematics Journal* (1991): 139–142.

P. Ungar, "Reviews," *American Mathematical Monthly* (1986): 221–230.

Some of these articles argue that the demonstration shown in the text is circular, since we use the fact that the area of a circle is πr^2. How do we know the area of a circle? The answer, of course, is that we learned it in elementary school, but that does not constitute a proof. On the other hand, some of these articles argue that the reasoning is not necessarily circular. Read one or more of these journal articles and write a report.

62. a. Show that $\sin x < x$ if $0 < x < \frac{\pi}{2}$. Refer to Figure 2.30. *Hint*: Compare the area of an appropriate triangle and sector.

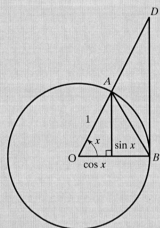

Figure 2.30   Figure for Problems 62 and 63

    b. Show that $|\sin x| < |x|$ if $0 < |x| < \frac{\pi}{2}$.

    c. Use the definition of continuity to show that $\sin x$ is continuous at $x = 0$.

    d. Use the formula

$$\sin(\alpha + \beta) = \sin \alpha \cos \beta + \cos \alpha \sin \beta$$

to show that $\sin x$ is continuous for all real x.

63. Follow the procedure outlined in Problem 62 to show that $\cos x$ is continuous for all x. *Hint*: After showing that

$$\lim_{x \to 0} \cos x = 1$$

you may need the identity

$$\cos(\alpha + \beta) = \cos \alpha \cos \beta - \sin \alpha \sin \beta$$

to show that $\cos x$ is continuous for $x \neq 0$.

64. A regular polygon of n sides is inscribed in a circle of radius R, as shown in Figure 2.31.

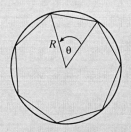

Figure 2.31 A regular polygon of seven sides with central angle θ (Problem 64)

a. Show that the perimeter of the polygon is given by $P(\theta) = \dfrac{4\pi R}{\theta} \sin \dfrac{\theta}{2}$, where $\theta = \dfrac{2\pi}{n}$ is the central angle subtended by one side of the polygon.

b. Use the formula in part **a** together with the fact that $\lim\limits_{x \to 0} \dfrac{\sin x}{x} = 1$ to show that a circle of radius R has circumference $2\pi R$.

c. Modify the approach suggested in parts **a** and **b** to show that a circle of radius R has area πR^2. *Hint*: First express the area of the shaded polygon in Figure 2.31 as a function of θ.

65. **Exploration Problem** A cylindrical tank containing 50 L of water is drained into an empty rectangular trough that can hold 75 L. Explain why there must be a time when the height of water in the tank is the same as that in the trough.

66. The radius of the earth is roughly 4,000 mi, and an object located x miles from the center of the earth weighs w lb, where

$$w(x) = \begin{cases} Ax & \text{if } x \le 4{,}000 \\[2mm] \dfrac{B}{x^2} & \text{if } x > 4{,}000 \end{cases}$$

where A and B are positive constants. Assuming that w is continuous for all x, what must be true about A and B?

67. The windchill temperature in degrees is a function of the air temperature T (in degrees Fahrenheit) and the wind speed v (in mi/h).* If we hold T constant and consider the windchill as a function of v, we have

$$W(v) = \begin{cases} T & \text{if } 0 \le v \le 4 \\[2mm] 91.4 + (91.4 - T)(0.0203v - 0.304\sqrt{v} - 0.474) \\[1mm] \qquad\qquad \text{if } 4 < v < 45 \\[2mm] 1.6T - 55 & \text{if } v \ge 45 \end{cases}$$

a. If $T = 30$, what is the windchill for $v = 20$? What is it for $v = 50$?

b. For $T = 30$, what wind speed corresponds to a windchill temperature of $0°$ Fahrenheit?

c. For what value of T is the windchill function continuous at $v = 4$? At $v = 45$?

68. Based on the estimate that there are 10 billion acres of arable land on the earth and that each acre can produce enough food to feed 4 people, some demographers believe that the earth can support a population of no more than 40 billion people.

The population of the earth reached approximately 5 billion in 1986 and 6 billion in 1999. If the population of the earth were growing according to the formula

$$P(t) = P_0 e^{rt}$$

where t is the time after the population is P_0 and r is the growth rate, when would the population reach the theoretical limit of 40 billion?

69. A function f is said to satisfy a *Lipschitz condition* (named for the nineteenth century mathematician Rudolf Lipschitz, 1832–1903) on a given interval if there is a positive constant M such that

$$|f(x) - f(y)| < M\,|x - y|$$

for all x and y in the interval (with $x \ne y$). Suppose f satisfies a Lipschitz condition on an interval and let c be a fixed number chosen arbitrarily from the interval. Use the formal definition of limit to prove that f is continuous at c.

70. A population model employed at one time by the U.S. Census Bureau uses the formula

$$P(t) = \frac{202.31}{1 + e^{3.98 - 0.314t}}$$

to estimate the population of the United States (in millions) for every tenth year from the base year of 1790. For example, if $t = 0$, then the year is 1790, and if $t = 20$, the year is 1990.

a. Draw the graph using this population model and predict the population in the year 2000.

b. Consult an almanac or some other source to find the actual population figures for the years from 1790 to present.

c. What happens to the population P "in the long run," that is, as t increases without bound?

*71. **Putnam Examination Problem** Evaluate

$$\lim_{x \to +\infty} \left[\frac{1}{x} \cdot \frac{a^x - 1}{a - 1} \right]^{1/x} \qquad \text{where } a > 0, a \ne 1$$

*72. **Putnam Examination Problem** Figure 2.32 shows a rectangle of base b and height h inscribed in a circle of radius 1, surmounted by an isosceles triangle. Find $\lim\limits_{h \to 2/5} \dfrac{A(h)}{bh}$.

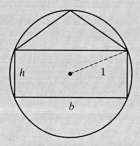

Figure 2.32 Putnam problem

---

*From William Bosch and L. G. Cobb, "Windchill," *UMAP Module No. 658*, (1984), pp. 244–247.

*The Putnam Examination is a national annual examination given under the auspices of the Mathematical Association of America and is designed to recognize mathematically talented college and university students. We include Putnam examination problems, which should be considered optional, to encourage students to consider taking the examination. Putnam problems used by permission of the American Mathematical Association. Solutions to Putnam Examinations generally appear in *The American Mathematical Monthly*, approximately one year after the examination.

3
Differentiation

PREVIEW

In this chapter, we develop the main ideas of differential calculus. We begin by defining the *derivative*, which is the central concept of differential calculus. Then we develop a list of rules and formulas for finding the derivative of a variety of expressions involving polynomials, rational and root functions, and trigonometric, logarithmic, and inverse trigonometric functions. Along the way, we will see how the derivative can be used to find slopes of tangent lines and rates of change.

PERSPECTIVE

A *calculus* is a body of calculation or reasoning associated with a certain concept. For *differential calculus*, that concept is the *derivative*, one of the fundamental ideas in all mathematics and, arguably, a cornerstone of modern scientific thought. The basic ideas of what we now call calculus had been fermenting in intellectual circles throughout much of the seventeenth century. The genius of Newton and Leibniz (see the guest essay at the end of Chapter 1) centered not so much on the discovery of those ideas as on their systematization.

In this chapter, we will consider various ways of efficiently computing derivatives. We will also see how the derivative can be used to find rates of change and to measure the direction (slope) at each point on a graph. Falling body problems in physics and marginal analysis from economics are examples of applied topics to be discussed, and we will also explore several topics involving basic concepts. It is fair to say that your success with differential calculus hinges on understanding this material.

3.1   An Introduction to the Derivative: Tangents

IN THIS SECTION   tangent lines, the derivative, relationship between the graphs of f and f', existence of derivatives, continuity and differentiability, derivative notation

TANGENT LINES

Since classical times, mathematicians have known that the tangent line at a given point on a circle has the property that it is the only line that intersects the circle exactly once, but the same principle cannot be applied to finding tangent lines to more general curves. Indeed, as shown in Figure 3.1, the line we may intuitively think of as being tangent to the graph of $y = f(x)$ at point P can intersect the curve at other points, and for that matter, there may be many lines that intersect the curve only at P, but are clearly not tangent lines.

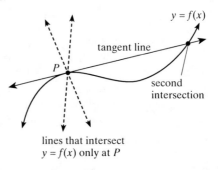

Figure 3.1   Tangent line at P

We begin this section by computing the slope of a tangent line as a limit, using a procedure originally developed by the French mathematician Pierre de Fermat (1601–1665). Fermat's use of the "dynamic" limit process rather than the "static" procedures of classical geometry and algebra was a breakthrough in thinking that eventually led to the development of differential calculus by Isaac Newton (1642–1727) and Gottfried Leibniz (1646–1716) in the latter half of the seventeenth century. Following in the footsteps of these giants, we, too, will use what we discover about tangent lines as a springboard for introducing the derivative and studying its basic properties.

Suppose we wish to find the slope of the tangent line to $y = f(x)$ at the point $P(x_0, f(x_0))$. The strategy is to approximate the tangent line by other lines whose slopes can be computed directly. In particular, consider the line joining the given point P to the neighboring point Q on the graph of f, as shown in Figure 3.2. This line is called a **secant line.** Compare the secant lines shown in Figure 3.2.

WARNING   Do not confuse *secant line* (a line that intersects a curve in two or more points) with the *secant function* of trigonometry.

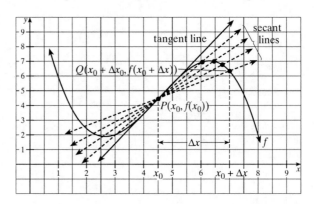

Figure 3.2   The secant line $\overline{PQ}$

Notice that a secant line is a good approximation to the tangent line at point P as long as Q is close to P.

Δx is a single symbol and does not mean delta times x. Do not forget that as $\Delta x \to 0$, Δx is getting close to 0, but is not equal to 0.

To compute the slope of a secant line, first label the coordinates of the neighboring point Q, as indicated in Figure 3.2. In particular, let Δx denote the change in the x-coordinate between the given point $P(x_0, f(x_0))$ and the neighboring point $Q(x_0 + \Delta x, f(x_0 + \Delta x))$.

The slope of this secant line, m_{sec}, is easy to calculate:

$$m_{\text{sec}} = \frac{\Delta y}{\Delta x} = \frac{f(x_0 + \Delta x) - f(x_0)}{\Delta x}$$

To bring the secant line closer to the tangent line, let Q approach P *on the graph of f* by letting Δx approach 0. As this happens, the slope of the secant line should approach the slope of the tangent line at P. We denote the slope of the tangent line by m_{tan} to distinguish it from the slope of a secant line. These observations suggest the following definition.

Slope of a Line Tangent to a Graph at a Point

At the point $P(x_0, f(x_0))$, the tangent line to the graph of f has **slope** given by the formula

$$m_{\text{tan}} = \lim_{\Delta x \to 0} \frac{f(x_0 + \Delta x) - f(x_0)}{\Delta x}$$

provided this limit exists.

EXAMPLE 1   Slope of a tangent line at a particular point

Find the slope of the tangent line to the graph of $f(x) = x^2$ at the point $P(-1, 1)$.

Solution

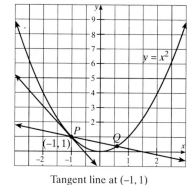

Tangent line at $(-1, 1)$

Figure 3.3 Tangent line to the graph of $y = x^2$ at $(-1, 1)$

Figure 3.3 shows the tangent line to f at $x = -1$. The slope of the tangent line is given by

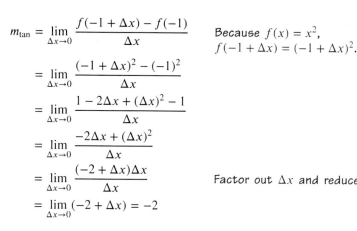

$$m_{\text{tan}} = \lim_{\Delta x \to 0} \frac{f(-1 + \Delta x) - f(-1)}{\Delta x}$$ Because $f(x) = x^2$, $f(-1 + \Delta x) = (-1 + \Delta x)^2$.

$$= \lim_{\Delta x \to 0} \frac{(-1 + \Delta x)^2 - (-1)^2}{\Delta x}$$

$$= \lim_{\Delta x \to 0} \frac{1 - 2\Delta x + (\Delta x)^2 - 1}{\Delta x}$$

$$= \lim_{\Delta x \to 0} \frac{-2\Delta x + (\Delta x)^2}{\Delta x}$$

$$= \lim_{\Delta x \to 0} \frac{(-2 + \Delta x)\Delta x}{\Delta x}$$ Factor out Δx and reduce.

$$= \lim_{\Delta x \to 0} (-2 + \Delta x) = -2$$ ∎

In Example 1, we found the slope of the tangent line to the graph of $y = x^2$ at the point $(-1, 1)$. In Example 2, we perform the same calculation again, this time representing the given point algebraically as (x, x^2). This is the situation shown in Figure 3.4 for the slope of the tangent line to $y = x^2$ at *any* point (x, x^2).

EXAMPLE 2   Slope of a tangent line at an arbitrary point

Derive a formula for the slope of the tangent line to the graph of $f(x) = x^2$, and then use the formula to compute the slope at $(4, 16)$.

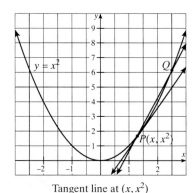

Tangent line at (x, x^2)

Figure 3.4 Tangent line to the graph of $y = x^2$ at (x, x^2)

Solution

Figure 3.4 shows a tangent line at an arbitrary point $P(x, x^2)$ on the curve. From the definition of slope of the tangent line,

$$
\begin{aligned}
m_{\tan} &= \lim_{\Delta x \to 0} \frac{f(x + \Delta x) - f(x)}{\Delta x} && \text{Because } f(x) = x^2, \\
&&& f(x + \Delta x) = (x + \Delta x)^2. \\
&= \lim_{\Delta x \to 0} \frac{(x + \Delta x)^2 - x^2}{\Delta x} \\
&= \lim_{\Delta x \to 0} \frac{x^2 + 2x\Delta x + (\Delta x)^2 - x^2}{\Delta x} \\
&= \lim_{\Delta x \to 0} \frac{2x\Delta x + (\Delta x)^2}{\Delta x} \\
&= \lim_{\Delta x \to 0} \frac{(2x + \Delta x)\Delta x}{\Delta x} && \text{Factor and reduce.} \\
&= \lim_{\Delta x \to 0} (2x + \Delta x) = 2x
\end{aligned}
$$

At the point $(4, 16)$, $x = 4$, so $m_{\tan} = 2(4) = 8$.   ∎

The result of Example 2 gives a general formula for the slope of a line tangent to the graph of $f(x) = x^2$, namely, $m_{\tan} = 2x$. The answer from Example 1 can now be verified using this formula; if $x = -1$, then $m_{\tan} = 2(-1) = -2$.

THE DERIVATIVE

The expression

$$
\frac{f(x + \Delta x) - f(x)}{\Delta x}
$$

which gives a formula for the slope of a secant line to the graph of a function f, is called the **difference quotient** of f. The limit of the difference quotient

$$
\lim_{\Delta x \to 0} \frac{f(x + \Delta x) - f(x)}{\Delta x}
$$

which gives a formula for the slope of the tangent line to the graph of f at the point $(x, f(x))$, is called the **derivative** of f and is frequently denoted by the symbol $f'(x)$ (read "eff prime of x"). To **differentiate** a function f at x means to find its derivative at the point $(x, f(x))$.

Derivative

> The **derivative** of f at x is given by
>
> $$
> f'(x) = \lim_{\Delta x \to 0} \frac{f(x + \Delta x) - f(x)}{\Delta x}
> $$
>
> provided this limit exists.

Alternatively, we can write

$$
f'(x) = \lim_{t \to x} \frac{f(t) - f(x)}{t - x}
$$

where $t = x + \Delta x$. Occasionally, this form is easier to use in computations.

The derivative is one of the fundamental concepts in calculus, and it is important to make some observations regarding this definition.

1. If the limit for the difference quotient exists, then we say that the function f is **differentiable at** x.

2. The value of a derivative depends only on the limit process and not on the symbols used in that process. In Example 2, we found that if $f(x) = x^2$, then $f'(x) = 2x$. This means that we also know

$$\text{If } g(t) = t^2, \text{ then } g'(t) = 2t.$$
$$\text{If } h(u) = u^2, \text{ then } h'(u) = 2u.$$
$$\vdots$$

3. Notice that the derivative of a function is itself a function.

Finding the slope of a tangent line is just one of several applications of the derivative that we will discuss in this chapter. In Section 3.4, we will examine rectilinear motion and other rates of change, and in Section 3.8, marginal analysis from economics. In Chapter 4 we will examine more complex applications such as curve sketching and optimization.

EXAMPLE 3 Derivative using the definition

Differentiate $f(t) = \sqrt{t}$.

WARNING Notice that $f(t) = \sqrt{t}$ is defined for all $t \geq 0$, whereas its derivative $f'(t) = 1/(2\sqrt{t})$ is defined for all $t > 0$. This shows that a function need not be differentiable throughout its entire domain.

Solution

$$\begin{aligned}
f'(t) &= \lim_{\Delta t \to 0} \frac{f(t + \Delta t) - f(t)}{\Delta t} \\
&= \lim_{\Delta t \to 0} \frac{\sqrt{t + \Delta t} - \sqrt{t}}{\Delta t} \\
&= \lim_{\Delta t \to 0} \frac{\sqrt{t + \Delta t} - \sqrt{t}}{\Delta t} \left(\frac{\sqrt{t + \Delta t} + \sqrt{t}}{\sqrt{t + \Delta t} + \sqrt{t}} \right) \quad \text{Rationalize numerator.} \\
&= \lim_{\Delta t \to 0} \frac{(t + \Delta t) - t}{\Delta t(\sqrt{t + \Delta t} + \sqrt{t})} \\
&= \lim_{\Delta t \to 0} \frac{\Delta t}{\Delta t(\sqrt{t + \Delta t} + \sqrt{t})} \\
&= \lim_{\Delta t \to 0} \frac{1}{\sqrt{t + \Delta t} + \sqrt{t}} \quad \text{Reduce fraction.} \\
&= \frac{1}{2\sqrt{t}} \quad \text{For } t > 0 \quad \blacksquare
\end{aligned}$$

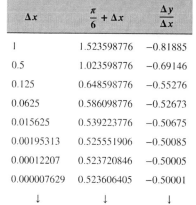

Δx	$\frac{\pi}{6} + \Delta x$	Difference quotient $\frac{\Delta y}{\Delta x}$
1	1.523598776	−0.81885
0.5	1.023598776	−0.69146
0.125	0.648598776	−0.55276
0.0625	0.586098776	−0.52673
0.015625	0.539223776	−0.50675
0.00195313	0.525551906	−0.50085
0.00012207	0.523720846	−0.50005
0.000007629	0.523606405	−0.50001
↓	↓	↓
0	$\frac{\pi}{6} \approx$	$-\frac{1}{2}$
0	0.5235987756	$-\frac{1}{2}$

EXAMPLE 4 Estimating a derivative using a table

Estimate the derivative of $f(x) = \cos x$ at $x = \frac{\pi}{6}$ by evaluating the difference quotient

$$\frac{\Delta y}{\Delta x} = \frac{f(x + \Delta x) - f(x)}{\Delta x}$$

near the point $x = \frac{\pi}{6}$.

Solution $\quad \dfrac{\Delta y}{\Delta x} = \dfrac{\cos(\frac{\pi}{6} + \Delta x) - \cos \frac{\pi}{6}}{\Delta x}$

Choose a sequence of values for $\Delta x \to 0$: say $1, \frac{1}{2}, \frac{1}{4}, \frac{1}{8}, \ldots$ and use a calculator (or a computer) to estimate the difference quotient by table. We show selected elements from this sequence of calculations in the margin.

A similar table for negative values of Δx should also be considered. From the table, we would guess that $f'(\frac{\pi}{6}) = -0.5$. $\quad \blacksquare$

An encouraging word is necessary after reading this first example of finding a derivative. By now you are aware of the fact that the derivative concept is one of the main ideas of calculus, and the previous example indicates that finding a derivative can be long and tedious. In the next section, we will begin to simplify the *process* of finding derivatives, so that you can quickly and efficiently find the derivatives of many functions (without using this definition directly). For now, however, we focus on the derivative *concept* and *definition*.

THEOREM 3.1   Equation of a line tangent to a curve at a point

If f is a differentiable function at x_0, the graph of $y = f(x)$ has a tangent line at the point $P(x_0, f(x_0))$ with slope $f'(x_0)$ and equation

$$y = f'(x_0)(x - x_0) + f(x_0)$$

Proof   To find the equation of the tangent line to the curve $y = f(x)$ at the point $P(x_0, y_0)$, we use the fact that the slope of the tangent line is the derivative $f'(x_0)$ and apply the point-slope formula for the equation of a line:

$$y - k = m(x - h) \qquad \text{Point-slope formula}$$
$$y - y_0 = m(x - x_0) \qquad \text{Given point } (x_0, y_0)$$
$$y - f(x_0) = f'(x_0)(x - x_0) \qquad y_0 = f(x_0) \text{ and } m_{\tan} = f'(x_0)$$
$$y = f'(x_0)(x - x_0) + f(x_0) \qquad \text{Add } f(x_0) \text{ to both sides.} \qquad \square$$

EXAMPLE 5   Finding the equation of a tangent line

Find an equation for the tangent line to the graph of $f(x) = \frac{1}{x}$ at the point where $x = 2$.

Solution

The graph of the function $y = \frac{1}{x}$, the point where $x = 2$, and the tangent line at the point are shown in Figure 3.5. First, find $f'(x)$:

$$f'(x) = \lim_{\Delta x \to 0} \frac{f(x + \Delta x) - f(x)}{\Delta x} \qquad \text{Definition of derivative}$$

$$= \lim_{\Delta x \to 0} \frac{\dfrac{1}{x + \Delta x} - \dfrac{1}{x}}{\Delta x} \qquad f(x) = \frac{1}{x}; \; f(x + \Delta x) = \frac{1}{x + \Delta x}$$

$$= \lim_{\Delta x \to 0} \frac{x - (x + \Delta x)}{x \Delta x (x + \Delta x)} \qquad \text{Simplify the fraction.}$$

$$= \lim_{\Delta x \to 0} \frac{-1}{x(x + \Delta x)}$$

$$= \frac{-1}{x^2}$$

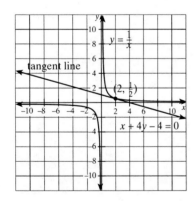

Figure 3.5 Tangent line to $y = \frac{1}{x}$ at $(2, \frac{1}{2})$

WARNING   The slope of f at x_0 is not the derivative f' but the value of the derivative at x_0. In Example 5 the function is defined by $f(x) = 1/x$, the derivative is $f'(x) = -1/x^2$, and the slope at $x = 2$ is the number $f'(2) = -\frac{1}{4}$.

Next, find the slope of the tangent line at $x = 2$: $m_{\tan} = f'(2) = -\frac{1}{4}$. Since $f(2) = \frac{1}{2}$, the equation of the tangent line can now be found by using Theorem 3.1:

$$y = -\frac{1}{4}(x - 2) + \frac{1}{2}, \quad \text{or in standard form,} \quad x + 4y - 4 = 0 \qquad \blacksquare$$

EXAMPLE 6   Finding a line that is perpendicular to a tangent line

Find the equation of the line that is perpendicular to the tangent line to $f(x) = \frac{1}{x}$ at $x = 2$ and intersects it at the point of tangency.

Solution

In Example 5, we found that the slope of the tangent line is $f'(2) = -\frac{1}{4}$ and that the point of tangency is $(2, \frac{1}{2})$. In Section 1.2, we saw that two lines are perpendicular if and only if their slopes are negative reciprocals of each other. Thus, the perpendicular line we seek has slope 4 (the negative reciprocal of $m = -\frac{1}{4}$). The desired equation is

$$y - \frac{1}{2} = 4(x - 2) \qquad \textit{Point-slope formula}$$

In standard form, $4x - y - \frac{15}{2} = 0$; compare the coefficients of the variables in the tangent and perpendicular lines. ∎

The perpendicular line we found in Example 6 has a name.

Normal Line to a Graph

> The **normal line** to the graph of f at the point P is the line that is perpendicular to the tangent line to the graph at P.

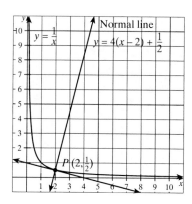

Figure 3.6 Graph of $y = \frac{1}{x}$ along with its normal $y = 4(x - 2) + \frac{1}{2}$

Figure 3.6 shows the graph of the function from Example 6, along with the graph of its normal line.

RELATIONSHIP BETWEEN THE GRAPHS OF f AND f'

It is important to take some time to study the relationship between the graph of a function and its derivative. Since slope is measured by f', it follows that at points x where $f'(x) > 0$, the tangent line must be tilted upward, and the graph is rising. Similarly, where $f'(x) < 0$, the tangent line is tilted downward, and the graph is falling. If $f'(x) = 0$, the tangent line is horizontal at x, so the graph "flattens." These observations are illustrated in Figure 3.7.

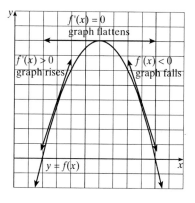

Figure 3.7 How the sign of f' determines whether the tangent line slants up, down, or is horizontal

EXAMPLE 7   **Sketching the graph of f', given the graph of f**

The graph of a function f is shown in Figure 3.8. Sketch a possible graph for the derivative f'.

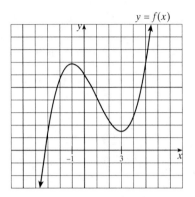

Figure 3.8   Graph of a function f

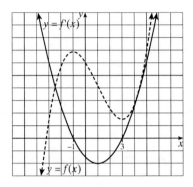

Figure 3.9 A possible graph for the derivative of the function whose graph is given in Figure 3.8

Solution

Notice that the graph of f is rising for $x < -1$ and for $x > 3$; it is falling for $-1 < x < 3$; and it has horizontal tangent lines at $x = -1$ and $x = 3$. Thus, the graph of f' is above the x-axis ($f'(x) > 0$) for $x < -1$ and $x > 3$, below the axis for $-1 < x < 3$ ($f'(x) < 0$), and crosses the axis at $x = -1$ and at $x = 3$. One possible graph with these features is shown in Figure 3.9.   ∎

EXISTENCE OF DERIVATIVES

We observed that a function is differentiable only if *the limit* in the definition of derivative exists. At points where a function f is not differentiable, we say that *the derivative of f does not exist*. Three common ways for a derivative to fail to exist at a point $(c, f(c))$ in the domain of f are shown in Figure 3.10.

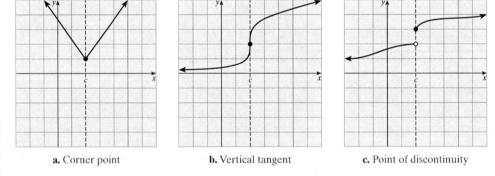

a. Corner point   **b.** Vertical tangent   **c.** Point of discontinuity

Figure 3.10   Common examples where a derivative does not exist

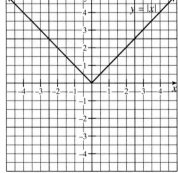

Figure 3.11 $f(x) = |x|$ is not differentiable at $x = 0$ because the slope from the left does not equal the slope from the right

EXAMPLE 8   **A function that does not have a derivative because of a corner**

Show that the absolute value function $f(x) = |x|$ is not differentiable at $x = 0$.

Solution

The graph of $f(x) = |x|$ is shown in Figure 3.11. Note that because the slope "from the left" at $x = 0$ is -1 while the slope "from the right" is $+1$, the graph has a corner at the origin, which prevents a unique tangent line from being drawn there.

We can show this algebraically by using the definition of derivative:

$$f'(0) = \lim_{\Delta x \to 0} \frac{f(0 + \Delta x) - f(0)}{\Delta x}$$

$$= \lim_{\Delta x \to 0} \frac{f(\Delta x) - f(0)}{\Delta x}$$

$$= \lim_{\Delta x \to 0} \frac{|\Delta x|}{\Delta x}$$

We must now consider one-sided limits, because

$$|\Delta x| = \Delta x \text{ when } \Delta x > 0, \text{ and } |\Delta x| = -\Delta x \text{ when } \Delta x < 0$$

$$\lim_{\Delta x \to 0^-} \frac{|\Delta x|}{\Delta x} = \lim_{\Delta x \to 0^-} \frac{-\Delta x}{\Delta x} = -1 \qquad \text{Derivative from the left}$$

$$\lim_{\Delta x \to 0^+} \frac{|\Delta x|}{\Delta x} = \lim_{\Delta x \to 0^+} \frac{\Delta x}{\Delta x} = 1 \qquad \text{Derivative from the right}$$

The left- and right-hand limits are not the same; therefore, the limit does not exist. This means that the derivative does not exist at $x = 0$. ∎

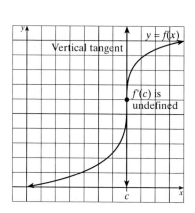

Figure 3.12 Vertical tangent line at $x = c$

The continuous function $f(x) = |x|$ in Example 8 failed to be differentiable at $x = 0$ because the one-sided limits of its difference quotient were unequal. A continuous function may also fail to be differentiable at $x = c$ if its difference quotient diverges to infinity. In this case, the function is said to have a *vertical tangent line* at $x = c$, as illustrated in Figure 3.12. We will have more to say about such functions when we discuss curve sketching with derivatives in Chapter 4.

CONTINUITY AND DIFFERENTIABILITY

If the graph of a function has a tangent line at a point, we would expect to be able to draw the graph continuously (without the pencil leaving the paper). In other words, we expect the following theorem to be true.

THEOREM 3.2   Differentiability implies continuity

If a function f is differentiable at c, then it is also continuous at c.

Proof   Recall that for f to be continuous at $x = c$: (1) $f(c)$ must be defined; (2) $\lim_{x \to c} f(x)$ exists; and (3) $\lim_{x \to c} f(x) = f(c)$. Thus, continuity can be established by showing that $\lim_{\Delta x \to 0} f(c + \Delta x) = f(c)$ or, equivalently,

$$\lim_{\Delta x \to 0} [f(c + \Delta x) - f(c)] = 0$$

Because f is a differentiable function at $x = c$, $f'(c)$ exists and

$$\lim_{\Delta x \to 0} \frac{f(c + \Delta x) - f(c)}{\Delta x} = f'(c)$$

Therefore, by applying the product rule for limits, we find that

$$\lim_{\Delta x \to 0} [f(c + \Delta x) - f(c)] = \lim_{\Delta x \to 0} \left[\frac{f(c + \Delta x) - f(c)}{\Delta x} \cdot \Delta x \right]$$

$$= \left[\lim_{\Delta x \to 0} \frac{f(c + \Delta x) - f(c)}{\Delta x} \right] \left[\lim_{\Delta x \to 0} \Delta x \right]$$

$$= f'(c) \cdot 0 = 0$$

Thus, $\lim_{x \to c} f(x) = f(c)$, and we see that the conditions for continuity are satisfied. ❑

WARNING Be sure you understand what we have just shown with Example 8 and Theorem 3.2: If a function is differentiable at $x = c$, then it must be continuous at that point. The converse is not true: If a function is continuous at $x = c$, then it may or may not be differentiable at that point. Finally, if a function is discontinuous at $x = c$, then it cannot possibly have a derivative at that point. (See Figure 3.13c.)

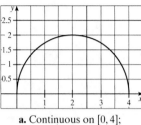

a. Continuous on $[0, 4]$; differentiable on $(0, 4)$

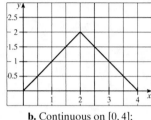

b. Continuous on $[0, 4]$; not differentiable at $x = 2$

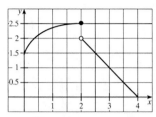

c. Discontinuous at $x = 2$; cannot be differentiable at $x = 2$

Figure 3.13 A function continuous at $x = 2$ may or may not be differentiable at $x = 2$. A function discontinuous at $x = 2$ cannot be differentiable at $x = 2$.

DERIVATIVE NOTATION

In certain situations, it is convenient or suggestive to denote the derivative of $y = f(x)$ by $\dfrac{dy}{dx}$ instead of $f'(x)$. This notation is called the *Leibniz notation* because Leibniz was the first to use it.

For example, if $y = x^2$, the derivative is $y' = 2x$ or, using Leibniz notation, $\dfrac{dy}{dx} = 2x$. The symbol $\dfrac{dy}{dx}$ is read "the derivative of y with respect to x." When we wish to denote the value of the derivative at c in the Leibniz notation, we will write

$$\frac{dy}{dx}\bigg|_{x=c}$$

For instance, we would evaluate $\dfrac{dy}{dx} = 4x^2$ at $x = 3$ by writing

$$\frac{dy}{dx}\bigg|_{x=3} = 4x^2\big|_{x=3} = 4(3)^2 = 36$$

Another notation omits reference to y and f altogether, and we can write

$$\frac{d}{dx}(x^2) = 2x$$

which is read "the derivative of x^2 with respect to x is $2x$."

WARNING Despite its appearance, $\frac{dy}{dx}$ is a single symbol and is *not a fraction*. In Section 3.8, we introduce a concept called a *differential* that will provide independent meaning to symbols like dy and dx, but for now, these symbols have meaning only in connection with the Leibniz derivative symbol $\frac{dy}{dx}$.

EXAMPLE 9   Derivative at a point with Leibniz notation

Find $\dfrac{dy}{dx}\bigg|_{x=-1}$ if $y = x^3$.

Solution

$$\frac{dy}{dx} = \frac{d}{dx}(x^3)$$

$$= \lim_{\Delta x \to 0} \frac{(x + \Delta x)^3 - x^3}{\Delta x}$$

$$= \lim_{\Delta x \to 0} \frac{[x^3 + 3x^2\Delta x + 3x(\Delta x)^2 + (\Delta x)^3] - x^3}{\Delta x}$$

$$= \lim_{\Delta x \to 0} [3x^2 + 3x(\Delta x) + (\Delta x)^2]$$

$$= 3x^2$$

At $x = -1$, $\left.\dfrac{dy}{dx}\right|_{x=-1} = 3x^2\Big|_{x=-1} = 3$. ■

```
nDeriv(X^3,X,-1)
        3.000001
```

Figure 3.14 Typical calculator output for $\dfrac{dy}{dx}\Big|_{x=-1}$, where $y = x^3$

If you are using technology to find derivatives, most formats require that you input not only the function, but the variable in the expression and the value at which you wish to find the derivative. The usual format is nDeriv(*expression, variable, value*). The symbol "nDeriv" depends on the calculator or software, and sometimes is "nDer" (TI-85/86), "d" (TI-92), "diff" (Maple V), or "Dif" (Derive). This notation is used in Figure 3.14. Some software and calculators will find the exact value of a derivative, whereas some will do a numerical evaluation (as shown in Figure 3.14).

3.1 PROBLEM SET

Ⓐ **1. WHAT DOES THIS SAY?** Describe the process of finding a derivative using the definition.

2. WHAT DOES THIS SAY? What is the definition of a derivative?

3. WHAT DOES THIS SAY? Discuss the truth or falsity of the following statements:

If a function f is continuous on (a, b), then it is differentiable on (a, b).

If a function f is differentiable on (a, b), then it is continuous on (a, b).

4. WHAT DOES THIS SAY? Discuss the relationship between the derivative of a function f at a point $x = x_0$ and the tangent line at that same point.

In each of Problems 5–10, the graph of a function f is given. Sketch a graph of f'.

5.

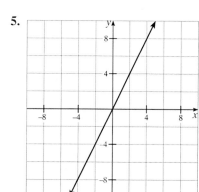

6.

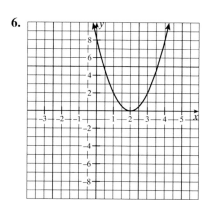

7.

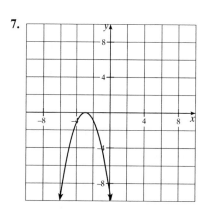

8. 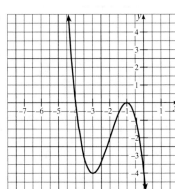   **9.** 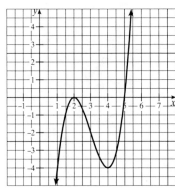   **10.**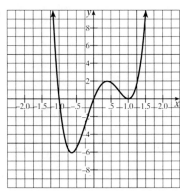

In each of Problems 11–16, a function f is given along with a number c in its domain.

a. *Find the difference quotient of f.*

b. *Find f'(c) by computing the limit of the difference quotient.*

11. $f(x) = 3$ at $c = -5$ **12.** $f(x) = x$ at $c = 2$

13. $f(x) = 2x$ at $c = 1$ **14.** $f(x) = 2x^2$ at $c = 1$

15. $f(x) = 2 - x^2$ at $c = 0$ **16.** $f(x) = -x^2$ at $c = 2$

Use the definition to differentiate the functions given in Problems 17–28, and then describe the set of all numbers for which the function is differentiable.

17. $f(x) = 5$ **18.** $g(x) = 3x$

19. $f(x) = 3x - 7$ **20.** $g(x) = 4 - 5x$

21. $g(x) = 3x^2$ **22.** $h(x) = 2x^2 + 3$

23. $f(x) = x^2 - x$ **24.** $g(t) = 4 - t^2$

25. $f(s) = (s - 1)^2$ **26.** $f(x) = \dfrac{1}{2x}$

27. $f(x) = \sqrt{5x}$ **28.** $f(x) = \sqrt{x + 1}$

Find an equation for the tangent line to the graph of the function at the specified point in Problems 29–34.

29. $f(x) = 3x - 7$ at $(3, 2)$ **30.** $g(x) = 3x^2$ at $(-2, 12)$

31. $f(s) = s^3$ at $s = -\frac{1}{2}$ **32.** $g(t) = 4 - t^2$ at $t = 0$

33. $f(x) = \dfrac{1}{x + 3}$ at $x = 2$ **34.** $g(x) = \sqrt{x - 5}$ at $x = 9$

Find an equation of the normal line to the graph of the function at the specified point in Problems 35–38.

35. $f(x) = 3x - 7$ at $(3, 2)$ **36.** $g(x) = 4 - 5x$ at $(0, 4)$

37. $f(x) = \dfrac{1}{x + 3}$ at $x = 3$ **38.** $f(x) = \sqrt{5x}$ at $x = 5$

Find $\left.\dfrac{dy}{dx}\right|_{x=c}$ for the functions and values of c given in Problems 39–42.

39. $y = 2x$, $c = -1$ **40.** $y = 4 - x$, $c = 2$

41. $y = 1 - x^2$, $c = 0$ **42.** $y = \dfrac{4}{x}$, $c = 1$

Ⓑ 43. Suppose $f(x) = x^2$.

a. Compute the slope of the secant line joining the points on the graph of f whose x-coordinates are -2 and -1.9.

b. Use calculus to compute the slope of the line that is tangent to the graph when $x = -2$ and compare this slope with your answer in part **a**.

44. Suppose $f(x) = x^3$.

a. Compute the slope of the secant line joining the points on the graph of f whose x-coordinates are 1 and 1.1.

b. Use calculus to compute the slope of the line that is tangent to the graph when $x = 1$ and compare this slope to your answer from part **a**.

45. Sketch the graph of the function $y = x^2 - x$. Determine the value(s) of x for which the derivative is 0. What happens to the graph at the corresponding point(s)?

46. a. Find the derivative of $f(x) = x^2 - 3x$.

b. Show that the parabola whose equation is $y = x^2 - 3x$ has one horizontal tangent line. Find the equation of this line.

c. Find a point on the graph of f where the tangent line is parallel to the line $3x + y = 11$.

d. Sketch the graph of the parabola whose equation is $y = x^2 - 3x$. Display the horizontal tangent line and the tangent line found in part **c**.

47. a. Find the derivative of $f(x) = 4 - 2x^2$.

b. The graph of f has one horizontal tangent line. What is its equation?

c. At what point on the graph of f is the tangent line parallel to the line $8x + 3y = 4$?

48. Show that the function $f(x) = |x - 2|$ is not differentiable at $x = 2$.

49. Is the function $f(x) = 2|x + 1|$ differentiable at $x = 1$?

50. Let $f(x) = \begin{cases} -x^2 & \text{if } x < 0 \\ x^2 & \text{if } x \geq 0 \end{cases}$.

Does $f'(0)$ exist? *Hint:* Find the difference quotient and take the limit as $\Delta x \to 0$ from the left and from the right.

51. Let $f(x) = \begin{cases} -2x & \text{if } x < 1 \\ \sqrt{x} - 3 & \text{if } x \geq 1 \end{cases}$.

a. Sketch the graph of f.

b. Show that f is continuous but not differentiable at $x = 1$.

52. Counterexample Problem Give an example of a function that is continuous on $(-\infty, \infty)$ but is not differentiable at $x = 5$.

Estimate the derivative $f'(c)$ in Problems 53–58 by evaluating the difference quotient

$$\frac{\Delta y}{\Delta x} = \frac{f(c + \Delta x) - f(c)}{\Delta x}$$

at a succession of numbers near c.

53. $f(x) = (2x - 1)^2$ for $c = 1$ **54.** $f(x) = \dfrac{1}{x+1}$ for $c = 2$

55. $f(x) = \sin x$ for $c = \frac{\pi}{3}$ **56.** $f(x) = \cos x$ for $c = \frac{\pi}{3}$

57. $f(x) = \sqrt{x}$ for $c = 4$ **58.** $f(x) = \sqrt[3]{x}$ for $c = 8$

59. Show that the tangent line to the parabola $y = Ax^2$ (for $A \neq 0$) at the point where $x = c$ will intersect the x-axis at the point $(\frac{c}{2}, 0)$. Where does it intersect the y-axis?

60. Find the point(s) on the graph of $f(x) = -x^2$ such that the tangent line at that point passes through the point $(0, -9)$.

61. Interpretation Problem

  a. Find the derivatives of the functions $y = x^2$ and $y = x^2 - 3$ and account geometrically for their similarity.

  b. Without further computation, find the derivative of $y = x^2 + 5$.

62. Interpretation Problem

  a. Find the derivative of $f(x) = x^2 + 3x$.

  b. Find the derivatives of the functions $g(x) = x^2$ and $h(x) = 3x$ separately. How are these derivatives related to the derivative in part **a**?

  c. In general, if $f(x) = g(x) + h(x)$, what would you guess is the relationship between the derivative of f and the derivatives of g and h?

63. Consider a graph of the function defined by $f(x) = x^{2/3}$.

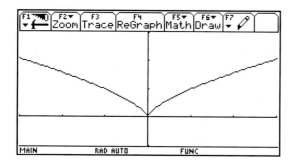

There is a tangent utility on many calculators that will draw tangent lines at a given point. Use this utility or use the preceding simulated graph to draw tangent lines as $x \to 0^-$. Next, draw tangent lines as $x \to 0^+$. Describe what happens, and use this description to support the conclusion that there is no tangent line at $x = 0$.

64. Consider the function

$$f(x) = (x - 2)^{2/3} + 2x^3$$

which gives trouble in seeking the tangent line at $(2, f(2))$. Attempt to compute $f'(2)$, either "by hand" or using a calculator. Describe what happens; in particular, do you see why the tangent line there is meaningless?

65. Compute the difference quotient for the function defined by

$$f(x) = \begin{cases} \dfrac{\sin x}{x} & \text{if } x \neq 0 \\ 1 & \text{if } x = 0 \end{cases}$$

Do you think $f(x)$ is differentiable at $x = 0$? If so, what is the equation of the tangent line at $x = 0$?

66. HISTORICAL QUEST In the quest essay at the end of Chapter 1, it was noted that Isaac Newton, who invented calculus at the same time as Leibniz, considered Fermat as "one of the giants" on whose shoulders he stood. Fermat was a lawyer by profession, but he liked to do mathematics in his spare time. He wrote well over 3,000 mathematical papers and notes. Fermat developed a general procedure for finding tangent lines that is a precursor to the methods of Newton and Leibniz. ∎

PIERRE DE FERMAT
1601–1665

We will explore this procedure by finding a tangent line to the curve

$$x^3 + y^3 - 2xy = 0$$

A graph is shown in Figure 3.15.

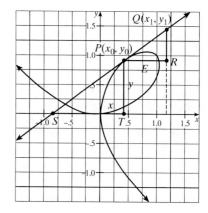

Figure 3.15 Fermat's method of subtangents

  a. Let $P(x_0, y_0)$ be a given point on the curve, and let S be the x-axis intercept of the tangent line at P. Let $Q(x_1, y_1)$ be another point on the tangent line and let T and R be located so $\triangle STP$ and $\triangle PRQ$ are right triangles. Finally, let $A = \left| \overline{ST} \right|$ and $E = \left| \overline{PR} \right|$. Express x_1 and y_1 in terms of x_0, y_0, A, and E.

  b. Fermat reasoned that if E were very small, then Q would "almost" be on the curve. Substitute the values for x_1 and y_1 you found in part **a** into the equation

$$x^3 + y^3 - 2xy = 0$$

That is, substitute the (x, y) values you found in part **a** into this equation.

  c. With the answer from part **b**, you can follow the steps of Fermat by dividing both sides of the equation by E. Fermat reasoned that since E was close to 0, this step should be permitted. Now, after doing this, Fermat further reasoned that since E was close to 0, he could now set $E = 0$ and solve for A. Carry out these steps to write A in terms of x_0 and y_0.

  d. Fermat then constructed the tangent line at P by joining P to S. Draw the tangent line for the given curve at the point $(0.5, 0.93)$ by plotting the point corresponding to the calculated value of A. Find an equation for the tangent line to the curve

$$x^3 + y^3 - 2xy = 0$$

at the point $P(0.5, 0.93)$.

67. HISTORICAL QUEST   The groundwork for much of the mathematics we do today, and certainly a necessity for calculus, is the development of analytic geometry by Descartes and Pierre de Fermat (see Problem 66). Descartes ideas for analytic geometry were published in 1637 as one of three appendices to his *Discourse on the Method* (of Reasoning Well and Seeking Truth in the Sciences). In that same

RENÉ DESCARTES
1596–1650

year, Fermat sent an essay entitled *Introduction to Plane and Solid Loci* to Paris, and in this essay he laid the foundation for analytic geometry. Fermats paper was more complete and systematic, but Descartes was published first. Descartes is generally credited with the discovery of analytic geometry, and we speak today of the Cartesian coordinate system and Cartesian geometry to honor Descartes discovery. Today we describe analytic geometry from two viewpoints: (1) Given a curve, describe it by an equation (Descartes viewpoint); and (2) given an equation, describe it by a curve (Fermats viewpoint).

In this Historical Quest we will describe Descartes circle method for finding a tangent line to a given curve. This method uses algebra and geometry rather than limits. Descartes method for finding the tangent line to the curve $y = f(x)$ at the point $P(x_0, f(x_0))$ involved first finding the point $Q(x_1, 0)$, which is the point of intersection of the normal line to the curve at P with the x-axis, as shown in Figure 3.16.

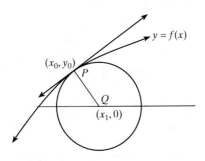

Figure 3.16   Descartes' circle method for finding tangent lines

Descartes then wrote the equation of the circle with center Q passing through P:

$$(x - x_1)^2 + y^2 = (x_0 - x_1)^2 + y_0^2$$

Descartes next step was to use the equation of the given curve $y = f(x)$ (actually any equation involving two variables) to eliminate one of the variables (usually y) from the equation of the circle. Descartes reasoned that the circle will cut the given curve in two places except when $\overline{PQ}$ is normal, in which case the two intersection points will coincide and the circle will be tangent line to the curve at P. That is, Descartes imposed the condition that the resulting equation (after substitution) has only one root to solve for x_1. The point Q is thus found and the normal line was then known to Descartes. The tangent line can be taken as the perpendicular through P to the normal line. ▪

Carry out Descartes circle method for the parabola $y^2 = 4x$ at the point $(4, 4)$.

68. HISTORICAL QUEST   Pierre de Fermat (see Problem 66) also obtained the first method for differentiating polynomials, but his real love was number theory. His most famous problem has come to be known as Fermats last theorem. He wrote in the margin of a text: *"To divide a cube into two cubes, a fourth power, or in general, any power whatever above the second, into powers of the same denominations, is impossible, and I have assuredly found an admirable proof of this, but the margin is too narrow to contain it."* ▪

In 1993 an imaginative, but lengthy, proof was constructed by Andrew Wiles, and in 1997 Wiles was awarded the Wolfskehl Prize for proving this theorem. An engaging book, *Fermat's Enigma*, shows how a great mathematical puzzle of our age was solved: Lock yourself in a room and emerge seven years later. Write a paper on the history of Fermat's last theorem, including some discussion of the current status of its proof. [You might begin with "Fermat's Last Theorem, The Four Color Conjecture, and Bill Clinton for April Fools' Day," by Edward B. Burger and Frank Morgan, *American Mathematical Monthly*, March 1997, pp. 246–250. Next, see the NOVA film, *The Proof*, which was shown in 1997 on many PBS stations (check with your library or PBS Online). Finally, see "Fermat's Last Stand" by Simon Singh and Kenneth A. Ribet, *Scientific American*, November 1997, pp. 68–73.]

Ⓒ 69. If $f'(c) \neq 0$, what is the equation of the normal line to $y = f(x)$ at the point $P(c, f(c))$? What is the equation if $f'(c) = 0$?

70. Suppose a parabola is given in the plane along with its axis of symmetry. Explain how you could construct the tangent line at a given point P on the parabola using only compass and straightedge methods. *Hint*: You may assume that the parabola has an equation of the form $y = Ax^2$ in which the y-axis is the axis of symmetry and the vertex of the parabola is at the origin. Then use the result of Problem 59.

3.2   Techniques of Differentiation

IN THIS SECTION   derivative of a constant function, derivative of a power function, procedural rules for finding derivatives, higher-order derivatives

If we had to compute the limit of a difference quotient every time we wished to find a derivative, differentiation would not be the valuable tool that it is. Fortunately, there is a better way, and in this section, we will derive several formulas that will enable us to compute derivatives indirectly, without evaluating any limits.

DERIVATIVE OF A CONSTANT FUNCTION

We begin by proving that the derivative of any constant function is zero. Notice that this is plausible because the graph of the constant function $f(x) = k$ is a horizontal line, and its slope is zero. Thus, for example, if $f(x) = 5$, then $f'(x) = 0$.

THEOREM 3.3 Constant rule

A constant function $f(x) = k$ has derivative $f'(x) = 0$; in Leibniz notation,

$$\frac{d}{dx}(k) = 0$$

Proof   Note that if $f(x) = k$, then $f(x + \Delta x) = k$ for all Δx. Therefore, the difference quotient is

$$\frac{f(x + \Delta x) - f(x)}{\Delta x} = \frac{k - k}{\Delta x} = 0$$

and

$$f'(x) = \lim_{\Delta x \to 0} \frac{f(x + \Delta x) - f(x)}{\Delta x} = \lim_{\Delta x \to 0} 0 = 0$$

as claimed.   ❑

WARNING   Remember $\Delta x \neq 0$ even though $\Delta x \to 0$.

DERIVATIVE OF A POWER FUNCTION

Recall that a **power function** is a function of the form $f(x) = x^n$, where n is a real number. For example, $f(x) = x^2$, $g(x) = x^{-3}$, $h(x) = x^{1/2}$ are all power functions. So are

$$F(x) = \frac{1}{x^2} = x^{-2} \quad \text{and} \quad G(x) = \sqrt[3]{x^2} = x^{2/3}$$

Here is a simple rule for finding the derivative of any power function.

THEOREM 3.4 Power rule

For any real number n, the power function $f(x) = x^n$ has the derivative $f'(x) = nx^{n-1}$; in Leibniz notation,

$$\frac{d}{dx}(x^n) = nx^{n-1}$$

Proof   If the exponent n is a positive integer, we can prove the power rule by using the binomial theorem with the definition of derivative. Begin with the difference quotient:

$$\frac{f(x + \Delta x) - f(x)}{\Delta x} = \frac{(x + \Delta x)^n - x^n}{\Delta x}$$

$$= \frac{\left[x^n + nx^{n-1}\Delta x + \frac{n(n-1)}{2}x^{n-2}(\Delta x)^2 + \cdots + (\Delta x)^n \right] - x^n}{\Delta x}$$

$$= \frac{nx^{n-1}\Delta x + \frac{n(n-1)}{2}x^{n-2}(\Delta x)^2 + \cdots + (\Delta x)^n}{\Delta x}$$

$$= nx^{n-1} + \frac{n(n-1)}{2}x^{n-2}\Delta x + \cdots + (\Delta x)^{n-1}$$

Note that Δx is a factor of every term in this expression except the first. Hence, as $\Delta x \to 0$, we have

$$f'(x) = \lim_{\Delta x \to 0} \frac{f(x + \Delta x) - f(x)}{\Delta x}$$

$$= \lim_{\Delta x \to 0} \left[nx^{n-1} + \frac{n(n-1)}{2}x^{n-2}\Delta x + \cdots + (\Delta x)^{n-1} \right]$$

$$= nx^{n-1}$$

If $n = 0$, then $f(x) = x^0 = 1$, so $f'(x) = 0$. We will prove the power rule for negative integer exponents later in this section, and we will deal with the case in which the exponent is any real number in Section 3.6. Note, however, that we have already verified the power rule for $n = 3$ in Example 9 of Section 3.1 and for the rational exponent $\frac{1}{2}$ in Example 3 of Section 3.1, when we showed that the derivative of $f(t) = \sqrt{t} = t^{1/2}$ is

$$f'(t) = \frac{1}{2}t^{-1/2} = \frac{1}{2\sqrt{t}} \quad \text{for } t > 0$$

For the following examples, and the problems at the end of this section, you may assume that the power rule is valid when the exponent n is any real number.   ❏

EXAMPLE 1   Using the power rule to find a derivative

Differentiate each of the following functions.

a. $f(x) = x^8$ **b.** $g(x) = x^{3/2}$ **c.** $h(x) = \dfrac{\sqrt[3]{x}}{x^2}$

Solution

a. Applying the power rule with $n = 8$, we find that

$$\frac{d}{dx}(x^8) = 8x^{8-1} = 8x^7$$

b. Applying the power rule with $n = \frac{3}{2}$, we get

$$\frac{d}{dx}(x^{3/2}) = \frac{3}{2}x^{3/2-1} = \frac{3}{2}x^{1/2} = \frac{3}{2}\sqrt{x}$$

c. For this part you need to recognize that $h(x) = \dfrac{x^{1/3}}{x^2} = x^{-5/3}$. Applying the power rule with $n = -\frac{5}{3}$, we find that

$$\frac{d}{dx}(x^{-5/3}) = -\frac{5}{3}x^{-5/3-1} = -\frac{5}{3}x^{-8/3}$$ ∎

PROCEDURAL RULES FOR FINDING DERIVATIVES

The next theorem expands the class of functions that we can differentiate easily by giving rules for differentiating certain combinations of functions, such as sums, differences, products, and quotients. We will see that the derivative of a sum (difference) is the sum (difference) of derivatives, but the derivative of a product (or quotient) does not have such a simple form. For example, to convince yourself that the derivative of a product is not the product of the separate derivatives, consider the power functions

$$f(x) = x \quad \text{and} \quad g(x) = x^2$$

and their product

$$p(x) = f(x)g(x) = x^3$$

WARNING   Note the derivative of a product is not the product of derivatives. A similar warning applies to the derivative of a quotient. (See Theorem 3.5.)

Because $f'(x) = 1$ and $g'(x) = 2x$, the product of the derivatives is

$$f'(x)g'(x) = (1)(2x) = 2x$$

whereas the actual derivative of $p(x) = x^3$ is $p'(x) = 3x^2$. The product rule tells us how to find the derivative of a product.

THEOREM 3.5 Basic rules for combining derivatives—Procedural forms

If f and g are differentiable functions at all x, and a, b, and c are any real numbers, then the functions cf, $f + g$, fg, and f/g (for $g(x) \neq 0$) are also differentiable, and their derivatives satisfy the following formulas:

Name of Rule	Function Notation	Leibniz Notation
Constant multiple	$[cf(x)]' = cf'(x)$	$\dfrac{d}{dx}(cf) = c\dfrac{df}{dx}$
Sum rule	$[f(x) + g(x)]' = f'(x) + g'(x)$	$\dfrac{d}{dy}(f + g) = \dfrac{df}{dx} + \dfrac{dg}{dx}$
Difference rule	$[f(x) - g(x)]' = f'(x) - g'(x)$	$\dfrac{d}{dx}(f - g) = \dfrac{df}{dx} - \dfrac{dg}{dx}$

The constant multiple, sum, and difference rules can be combined into a single rule, which is called the *linearity rule*.

Linearity rule	$[af(x) + bg(x)]' = af'(x) + bg'(x)$	$\dfrac{d}{dx}(af + bg) = a\dfrac{df}{dx} + b\dfrac{dg}{dx}$
Product rule	$[f(x)g(x)]' = f(x)g'(x) + f'(x)g(x)$	$\dfrac{d}{dx}(fg) = f\dfrac{dg}{dx} + g\dfrac{df}{dx}$
Quotient rule	$\left[\dfrac{f(x)}{g(x)}\right]' = \dfrac{g(x)f'(x) - f(x)g'(x)}{[g(x)]^2}$	$\dfrac{d}{dx}\left(\dfrac{f}{g}\right) = \dfrac{g\dfrac{df}{dx} - f\dfrac{dg}{dx}}{g^2}$

WARNING Note that the order of terms in the quotient rule matters because

$$gf' - fg' \neq fg' - gf'$$

Proof We will prove the product rule in detail, leaving the other rules as problems.

Let $f(x)$ and $g(x)$ be differentiable functions of x and let $p(x) = f(x)g(x)$. We will add and subtract the term $f(x + \Delta x)g(x)$ to the numerator of the difference quotient for $p(x)$ to create difference quotients for $f(x)$ and $g(x)$. Thus,

$$p'(x) = \frac{dp}{dx} = \lim_{\Delta x \to 0} \frac{p(x + \Delta x) - p(x)}{\Delta x}$$

$$= \lim_{\Delta x \to 0} \frac{f(x + \Delta x)g(x + \Delta x) - f(x)g(x)}{\Delta x}$$

$$= \lim_{\Delta x \to 0} \frac{f(x + \Delta x)g(x + \Delta x) - f(x + \Delta x)g(x) + f(x + \Delta x)g(x) - f(x)g(x)}{\Delta x}$$

$$= \lim_{\Delta x \to 0} \left[f(x + \Delta x)\left[\frac{g(x + \Delta x) - g(x)}{\Delta x}\right] + g(x)\left[\frac{f(x + \Delta x) - f(x)}{\Delta x}\right] \right]$$

$$= \lim_{\Delta x \to 0} f(x + \Delta x) \underbrace{\lim_{\Delta x \to 0}\left[\frac{g(x + \Delta x) - g(x)}{\Delta x}\right]}_{\text{This is the derivative of } g.} + \lim_{\Delta x \to 0} g(x) \underbrace{\lim_{\Delta x \to 0}\left[\frac{f(x + \Delta x) - f(x)}{\Delta x}\right]}_{\text{This is the derivative of } f.}$$

$$= f(x)g'(x) + g(x)f'(x) \qquad \lim_{\Delta x \to 0} f(x + \Delta x) = f(x) \text{ because } f \text{ is continuous.} \qquad \square$$

Note that in each part of Theorem 3.5, we prove the differentiability of the appropriate functional combination at the same time we are establishing the differentiation formula.

EXAMPLE 2   Using the basic rules to find derivatives

Differentiate each of the following functions.

a. $f(x) = 2x^2 - 5\sqrt{x}$

b. $p(x) = (3x^2 - 1)(7 + 2x^3)$

c. $q(x) = \dfrac{4x - 7}{3 - x^2}$

d. $g(x) = (4x + 3)^2$

e. $F(x) = \dfrac{2}{3x^2} - \dfrac{x}{3} + \dfrac{4}{5} + \dfrac{x + 1}{x}$

Solution

a. Apply the linearity rule (constant multiple, sum, and difference) and power rules:

$$f'(x) = 2(x^2)' - 5(x^{1/2})' = 2(2x) - 5\left(\tfrac{1}{2}\right)(x^{-1/2}) = 4x - \tfrac{5}{2}x^{-1/2}$$

b. Apply the product rule; then apply the linearity and power rules:

$$\begin{aligned}
p'(x) &= (3x^2 - 1)(7 + 2x^3)' + (3x^2 - 1)'(7 + 2x^3) \\
&= (3x^2 - 1)[0 + 2(3x^2)] + [3(2x) - 0](7 + 2x^3) \\
&= (3x^2 - 1)(6x^2) + (6x)(7 + 2x^3) \\
&= 6x(5x^3 - x + 7)
\end{aligned}$$

c. Apply the quotient rule, then the linearity and power rules:

$$\begin{aligned}
q'(x) &= \frac{(3 - x^2)(4x - 7)' - (4x - 7)(3 - x^2)'}{(3 - x^2)^2} \\
&= \frac{(3 - x^2)(4 - 0) - (4x - 7)(0 - 2x)}{(3 - x^2)^2} \\
&= \frac{12 - 4x^2 + 8x^2 - 14x}{(3 - x^2)^2} = \frac{4x^2 - 14x + 12}{(3 - x^2)^2}
\end{aligned}$$

d. Apply the product rule:

$$\begin{aligned}
g'(x) &= (4x + 3)(4x + 3)' + (4x + 3)'(4x + 3) \\
&= (4x + 3)(4) + (4)(4x + 3) = 8(4x + 3)
\end{aligned}$$

Sometimes when the exponent is 2, it is easier to expand before differentiating:

$$g(x) = (4x + 3)^2 = 16x^2 + 24x + 9$$
$$g'(x) = 32x + 24$$

e. Write the function using negative exponents for reciprocal powers:

$$F(x) = \tfrac{2}{3}x^{-2} - \tfrac{1}{3}x + \tfrac{4}{5} + 1 + x^{-1}$$

Then apply the power rule term by term to obtain

$$\begin{aligned}
F'(x) &= \tfrac{2}{3}(-2x^{-3}) - \tfrac{1}{3} + 0 + 0 + (-1)x^{-2} \\
&= -\tfrac{4}{3}x^{-3} - \tfrac{1}{3} - x^{-2}
\end{aligned}$$

∎

In applying the power rule term by term in Example 2e, we really used the following generalization of the linearity rule.

COROLLARY TO THEOREM 3.5   The extended linearity rule

If $f_1, f_2, \ldots, f_n$ are differentiable functions and $a_1, a_2, \ldots, a_n$ are constants, then

$$\frac{d}{dx}[a_1 f_1 + a_2 f_2 + \cdots + a_n f_n] = a_1 \frac{df_1}{dx} + a_2 \frac{df_2}{dx} + \cdots + a_n \frac{df_n}{dx}$$

Proof   The proof is a straightforward extension (using mathematical induction) of the proof of the linearity rule of Theorem 3.5.   ❑

Example 3 illustrates how the extended linearity rule can be used to differentiate a polynomial.

EXAMPLE 3   Derivative of a polynomial function

Differentiate the polynomial function $p(x) = 2x^5 - 3x^2 + 8x - 5$.

Solution

$$
\begin{aligned}
p'(x) &= \frac{d}{dx}[2x^5 - 3x^2 + 8x - 5] \\
&= 2\frac{d}{dx}(x^5) - 3\frac{d}{dx}(x^2) + 8\frac{d}{dx}(x) - \frac{d}{dx}(5) \qquad \text{Extended linearity rule} \\
&= 2(5x^4) - 3(2x) + 8(1) - 0 \qquad\qquad\qquad \text{Power rule; constant rule} \\
&= 10x^4 - 6x + 8
\end{aligned}
$$

EXAMPLE 4   Derivative of a product of polynomials

Differentiate $p(x) = (x^3 - 4x + 7)(3x^5 - x^2 + 6x)$.

Solution

We could expand the product function $p(x)$ as a polynomial and proceed as in Example 3, but it is easier to use the product rule.

$$
\begin{aligned}
p'(x) &= (x^3 - 4x + 7)(3x^5 - x^2 + 6x)' + (x^3 - 4x + 7)'(3x^5 - x^2 + 6x) \\
&= (x^3 - 4x + 7)(15x^4 - 2x + 6) + (3x^2 - 4)(3x^5 - x^2 + 6x)
\end{aligned}
$$

This form is an acceptable answer, but if you are using software or an algebraic calculator, more than likely you will obtain the expanded formula

$$
p'(x) = 24x^7 - 72x^5 + 100x^4 + 24x^3 + 12x^2 - 62x + 42
$$

EXAMPLE 5   Equation of a tangent line

Find the standard form equation for the line tangent to the graph of

$$
f(x) = \frac{3x^2 + 5}{2x^2 + x - 3}
$$

at the point where $x = -1$.

Solution

Evaluating $f(x)$ at $x = -1$, we find that $f(-1) = -4$ (verify); therefore, the point of tangency is $(-1, -4)$. The slope of the tangent line at $(-1, -4)$ is $f'(-1)$. Find $f'(x)$ by applying the quotient rule:

$$
\begin{aligned}
f'(x) &= \frac{(2x^2 + x - 3)(3x^2 + 5)' - (3x^2 + 5)(2x^2 + x - 3)'}{(2x^2 + x - 3)^2} \\
&= \frac{(2x^2 + x - 3)(\mathbf{6x}) - (3x^2 + 5)(\mathbf{4x + 1})}{(2x^2 + x - 3)^2}
\end{aligned}
$$

The slope of the tangent line is

$$
f'(-1) = \frac{(2 - 1 - 3)(-6) - (3 + 5)(-4 + 1)}{(2 - 1 - 3)^2} = \frac{(-2)(-6) - (8)(-3)}{(-2)^2} = 9
$$

From the formula (Theorem 3.1) $y = f'(x_0)(x - x_0) + f(x_0)$, we find that an equation for the tangent line at $(-1, -4)$ is

$$
y = 9(x + 1) + (-4)
$$

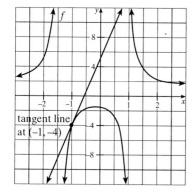

Figure 3.17 Graph of f and the tangent line at the point $(-1, -4)$

or in standard form $9x - y + 5 = 0$. The graphs of both f and its tangent line at $(-1, -4)$ are shown in Figure 3.17.

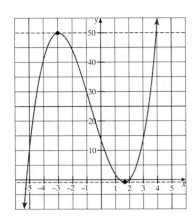

Figure 3.18 Graph of curve and the horizontal tangent lines

EXAMPLE 6   Finding horizontal tangent lines

Let $y = (x - 2)(x^2 + 4x - 7)$. Find all points on this curve where the tangent line is horizontal.

Solution

The tangent line will be horizontal when $dy/dx = 0$, because the derivative dy/dx measures the slope and a horizontal line has slope 0 (see Figure 3.18). Applying the product rule, we find

$$\frac{dy}{dx} = (x - 2)(x^2 + 4x - 7)' + (x - 2)'(x^2 + 4x - 7)$$
$$= (x - 2)(2x + 4) + (1)(x^2 + 4x - 7)$$
$$= 2x^2 - 8 + x^2 + 4x - 7$$
$$= 3x^2 + 4x - 15 = (3x - 5)(x + 3)$$

Thus, $\dfrac{dy}{dx} = 0$ when $x = \frac{5}{3}$ or $x = -3$. The corresponding points $(\frac{5}{3}, -\frac{22}{27})$ and $(-3, 50)$ are the points on the curve at which the tangent line is horizontal.   ■

In the following example, we use the quotient rule to extend the proof of the power rule to the case in which the exponent n is a negative integer.

EXAMPLE 7   Proof of the power rule for negative exponents

Show that $\dfrac{d}{dx}(x^n) = nx^{n-1}$ if $n = -m$, where m is a positive integer.

Solution

We have $f(x) = x^n = x^{-m} = 1/x^m$, so apply the quotient rule:

$$\frac{d}{dx}(x^n) = \frac{d}{dx}\left(\frac{1}{x^m}\right) = \frac{x^m(1)' - (1)(x^m)'}{(x^m)^2} = \frac{x^m(0) - mx^{m-1}}{x^{2m}}$$
$$= -mx^{(m-1)-2m} = -mx^{-m-1} = nx^{n-1} \qquad \text{Substitute } -m = n. \qquad ■$$

HIGHER-ORDER DERIVATIVES

Occasionally, it is useful to differentiate the derivative of a function. In this context, we will refer to f' as the **first derivative** of f and to the derivative of f' as the **second derivative** of f. We could denote the second derivative by $(f')'$, but for simplicity we write f''. Other higher-order derivatives are defined and denoted similarly. Thus, the **third derivative** of f is the derivative of f'' and is denoted by f'''. In general, for $n > 3$, the **nth derivative** of f is denoted by $f^{(n)}$; $f^{(4)}$ or $f^{(5)}$, for example. In Leibniz notation, higher-order derivatives for $y = f(x)$ are denoted as follows:

			Leibniz notation		
First derivative:	y'	$f'(x)$	$\dfrac{dy}{dx}$	or	$\dfrac{d}{dx}f(x)$
Second derivative:	y''	$f''(x)$	$\dfrac{d}{dx}\left(\dfrac{dy}{dx}\right) = \dfrac{d^2y}{dx^2}$	or	$\dfrac{d^2}{dx^2}f(x)$
Third derivative:	y'''	$f'''(x)$	$\dfrac{d}{dx}\left(\dfrac{d^2y}{dx^2}\right) = \dfrac{d^3y}{dx^3}$	or	$\dfrac{d^3}{dx^3}f(x)$

Leibniz notation

Fourth derivative: $y^{(4)}$ $f^{(4)}(x)$ $\dfrac{d^4y}{dx^4}$ or $\dfrac{d^4}{dx^4}f(x)$

$\vdots$ $\vdots$ $\vdots$ $\vdots$ $\vdots$

nth derivative $y^{(n)}$ $f^{(n)}(x)$ $\dfrac{d^ny}{dx^n}$ or $\dfrac{d^n}{dx^n}f(x)$

→ What This Says Because the derivative of a function is a function, differentiation can be applied over and over, as long as the derivative itself is a differentiable function. That is, we can take derivatives of derivatives.

Notice also that for derivatives of higher order than the third, the parentheses distinguish a derivative from a power. For example, $f^4 \neq f^{(4)}$.

You should note that all higher-order derivatives of a polynomial $p(x)$ will also be polynomials, and if p has degree n, then $p^{(k)}(x) = 0$ for $k \geq n+1$, as illustrated in the following example.

EXAMPLE 8 Higher-order derivatives for a polynomial function

Find the derivatives of all orders of

$$p(x) = -2x^4 + 9x^3 - 5x^2 + 7$$

Solution

$$p'(x) = -8x^3 + 27x^2 - 10x; \quad p''(x) = -24x^2 + 54x - 10;$$
$$p'''(x) = -48x + 54; \quad p^{(4)}(x) = -48; \quad p^{(5)}(x) = 0; \dots \quad p^{(k)}(x) = 0 \ (k \geq 5)$$

■

3.2 PROBLEM SET

A *To demonstrate the power of the theorems of this section, Problems 1–4 ask you to go back and rework some problems in Section 3.1, using the material of this section instead of the definition of derivative.*

1. Find the derivatives of the functions given in Problems 11–16 of Problem Set 3.1.

2. Find the derivatives of the functions given in Problems 17–22 of Problem Set 3.1.

3. Find the derivatives of the functions given in Problems 23–27 of Problem Set 3.1.

4. Find the derivatives of the functions given in Problems 39–42 of Problem Set 3.1.

Differentiate the functions given in Problems 5–20. Assume that C is a constant.

5. **a.** $f(x) = 3x^4 - 9$ **b.** $g(x) = 3(9)^4 - x$

6. **a.** $f(x) = 5x^2 + x$ **b.** $g(x) = \pi^3$

7. **a.** $f(x) = x^3 + C$ **b.** $g(x) = C^2 + x$

8. **a.** $f(t) = 10t^{-1}$ **b.** $g(t) = \dfrac{7}{t}$

9. $r(t) = t^2 - \dfrac{1}{t^2} + \dfrac{5}{t^4}$ 10. $f(x) = \pi^3 - 3\pi^2$

11. $f(x) = \dfrac{7}{x^2} + x^{2/3} + C$ 12. $g(x) = \dfrac{1}{2\sqrt{x}} + \dfrac{x^2}{4} + C$

13. $f(x) = \dfrac{x^3 + x^2 + x - 7}{x^2}$ 14. $g(x) = \dfrac{2x^5 - 3x^2 + 11}{x^3}$

15. $f(x) = (2x+1)(1-4x^3)$ 16. $g(x) = (x+2)(2\sqrt{x} + x^2)$

17. $f(x) = \dfrac{3x+5}{x+9}$ 18. $f(x) = \dfrac{x^2+3}{x^2+5}$

19. $g(x) = x^2(x+2)^2$ 20. $f(x) = x^2(2x+1)^2$

In Problems 21–24, find f', f'', f''', and $f^{(4)}$.

21. $f(x) = x^5 - 5x^3 + x + 12$

22. $f(x) = \frac{1}{4}x^8 - \frac{1}{2}x^6 - x^2 + 2$

23. $f(x) = \dfrac{-2}{x^2}$ 24. $f(x) = \dfrac{4}{\sqrt{x}}$

25. Find $\dfrac{d^2y}{dx^2}$, where $y = 3x^3 - 7x^2 + 2x - 3$.

26. Find $\dfrac{d^2y}{dx^2}$, where $y = (x^2+4)(1-3x^3)$.

In Problems 27–32, find the standard form equation for the tangent line to $y = f(x)$ at the specified point.

27. $f(x) = x^2 - 3x - 5$, where $x = -2$

28. $f(x) = x^5 - 3x^3 - 5x + 2$, where $x = 1$

29. $f(x) = (x^2 + 1)(1 - x^3)$, where $x = 1$

30. $f(x) = \dfrac{x+1}{x-1}$, where $x = 0$

31. $f(x) = \dfrac{x^2 + 5}{x + 5}$, where $x = 1$

32. $f(x) = 1 - \dfrac{1}{x} + \dfrac{2}{\sqrt{x}}$, where $x = 4$

Find the coordinates of each point on the graph of the given function where the tangent line is horizontal in Problems 33–39.

33. $f(x) = 2x^3 - 7x^2 + 8x - 3$

34. $f(t) = t^4 + 4t^3 - 8t^2 + 3$ 35. $g(x) = (3x - 5)(x - 8)$

36. $f(t) = \dfrac{1}{t^2} - \dfrac{1}{t^3}$ 37. $f(x) = \sqrt{x}(x - 3)$

38. $h(u) = \dfrac{1}{\sqrt{u}}(u + 9)$ 39. $h(x) = \dfrac{4x^2 + 12x + 9}{2x + 3}$

B 40. **a.** Differentiate the function $f(x) = 2x^2 - 5x - 3$.

  b. Factor the function in part **a** and differentiate by using the product rule. Show that the two answers are the same.

41. **a.** Use the quotient rule to differentiate $f(x) = \dfrac{2x - 3}{x^3}$.

  b. Rewrite the function in part **a** as $f(x) = x^{-3}(2x - 3)$ and differentiate by using the product rule.

  c. Rewrite the function in part **a** as $f(x) = 2x^{-2} - 3x^{-3}$ and differentiate.

  d. Show that the answers to parts **a**, **b**, and **c** are all the same.

42. Find numbers a, b, and c that guarantee that the graph of the function $f(x) = ax^2 + bx + c$ will have x-intercepts at $(0, 0)$ and $(5, 0)$ and a tangent line with slope 1 where $x = 2$.

43. Find the equation for the tangent line to the curve with equation $y = x^4 - 2x + 1$ that is parallel to the line $2x - y - 3 = 0$.

44. Find equations for two tangent lines to the graph of $f(x) = \dfrac{3x + 5}{1 + x}$ that are perpendicular to the line $2x - y = 1$.

45. Let $f(x) = (x^3 - 2x^2)(x + 2)$.

  a. Find an equation for the tangent line to the graph of f at the point where $x = 1$.

  b. Find an equation for the normal line to the graph of f at the point where $x = 0$.

46. Find an equation for a normal line to the graph of $f(x) = (x^3 - 2x^2)(x + 2)$ that is parallel to the line $x - 16y + 17 = 0$.

47. Find all points (x, y) on the graph of $y = 4x^2$ with the property that the tangent line at (x, y) passes through the point $(2, 0)$.

48. Find the equations of all the tangent lines to the graph of the function $f(x) = x^2 - 4x + 25$ that pass through the origin.

Determine which (if any) of the functions $y = f(x)$ given in Problems 49–52 satisfy the equation

$$y''' + y'' + y' = x + 1$$

49. $f(x) = x^2 + 2x - 3$ 50. $f(x) = x^3 + x^2 + x$

51. $f(x) = \frac{1}{2}x^2 + 3$ 52. $f(x) = 2x^2 + x$

53. HISTORICAL QUEST When working with rational expressions, we need to be careful about division by zero. One of the earliest recorded treatments of division by zero is attributed to the Hindu mathematician Āryabhata (476–550), in whose honor the first Indian satellite was named. He also gave rules for approximations of square roots and sums of arithmetic progressions as well as rules for basic algebraic manipulations. One example of his work is the following calculation for π: "Add four to one hundred, multiply by eight and add again sixty-two thousand; the result is the approximate value of the circumference of a circle whose diameter is twenty-thousand."

  Follow the steps of Āryabhata's approximation for π. After you have completed this demonstration, discuss the procedure and technology you used and contrast it with the tools that Āryabhata must have had available.

C 54. What is the relationship between the degree of a polynomial function P and the value of k for which $P^{(k)}(x)$ is first equal to 0?

55. Prove the constant multiple rule $(cf)' = cf'$.

56. Prove the sum rule $(f + g)' = f' + g'$.

57. Use the definition of the derivative to find the derivative of f^2, given that f is a differentiable function.

58. Prove the product rule by using the result of Problem 57 and the identity

$$fg = \tfrac{1}{2}\left[(f + g)^2 - f^2 - g^2\right]$$

59. Prove the quotient rule

$$\left(\frac{f}{g}\right)' = \frac{gf' - fg'}{g^2}$$

where $g(x) \neq 0$. *Hint:* First show that the difference quotient for f/g can be expressed as

$$\frac{\frac{f}{g}(x + \Delta x) - \frac{f}{g}(x)}{\Delta x} = \frac{f(x + \Delta x)g(x) - f(x)g(x + \Delta x)}{(\Delta x)g(x + \Delta x)g(x)}$$

and then subtract and add the term $g(x)f(x)$ in the numerator.

60. Show that the reciprocal function $r(x) = 1/f(x)$ has the derivative $r'(x) = -f'(x)/[f(x)]^2$ at each point x where f is differentiable and $f(x) \neq 0$.

61. If f, g, and h are differentiable functions, show that the product fgh is also differentiable and

$$(fgh)' = fgh' + fg'h + f'gh$$

62. Let f be a function that is differentiable at x.

  a. If $g(x) = [f(x)]^3$, show that $g'(x) = 3[f(x)]^2 f'(x)$.
    Hint: Write $g(x) = [f(x)]^2 f(x)$ and use the product rule.

  b. Show that $p(x) = [f(x)]^4$ has the derivative

$$p'(x) = 4[f(x)]^3 f'(x).$$

63. Find constants A, B, and C so that $y = Ax^3 + Bx + C$ satisfies the equation

$$y''' + 2y'' - 3y' + y = x$$

3.3 Derivatives of Trigonometric, Exponential, and Logarithmic Functions

IN THIS SECTION derivatives of the sine and cosine functions, differentiation of the other trigonometric functions, derivatives of exponential and logarithmic functions

DERIVATIVES OF THE SINE AND COSINE FUNCTIONS

In calculus we assume that the trigonometric functions are functions of real numbers or of angles measured in radians.

We make this assumption because the trigonometric differentiation formulas rely on limit formulas that become complicated if degree measurement is used instead of radian measure.

Before stating the theorem for the derivatives of the sine and cosine functions, suppose we look at the graph of the difference quotient. Consider $f(x) = \sin x$. Then

$$\frac{\sin(x + \Delta x) - \sin x}{\Delta x} = \frac{\sin(x + 0.01) - \sin x}{0.01}$$

is the difference quotient for $\Delta x = 0.01$. To graph this difference quotient, shown in Figure 3.19, we input to a calculator as

$$Y1 = (\text{SIN}(X+.01) - \text{SIN } X)/.01$$

From the graph of this difference quotient, it appears that the derivative of $f(x) = \sin x$ is $f'(x) = \cos x$. We now verify this with the following theorem, which uses the following limits established earlier in Theorem 2.3:

$$\lim_{h \to 0} \frac{\sin h}{h} = 1 \qquad \lim_{h \to 0} \frac{\cos h - 1}{h} = 0$$

Y1⊟(sin (X+.01)-
sin X)/.01

Xmin=-9.424777...
Xmax=9.4247779...
Xscl=1.5707963...
Ymin=-1
Ymax=1
Yscl=.1

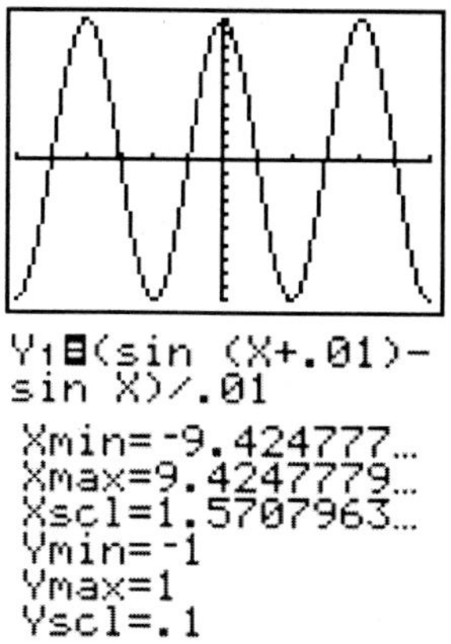

Figure 3.19 Calculator graph of the difference quotient for $y = \sin x$

THEOREM 3.6 Derivatives of the sine and cosine functions

The functions $\sin x$ and $\cos x$ are differentiable for all x and

$$\frac{d}{dx} \sin x = \cos x \qquad \frac{d}{dx} \cos x = -\sin x$$

Proof The proofs of these two formulas are similar. We will prove the first using the trigonometric identity

$$\sin(\alpha + \beta) = \sin \alpha \cos \beta + \cos \alpha \sin \beta$$

and leave the proof of the second formula as a problem. From the definition of the derivative

$$\frac{d}{dx} \sin x = \lim_{\Delta x \to 0} \frac{\sin(x + \Delta x) - \sin x}{\Delta x}$$

$$= \lim_{\Delta x \to 0} \frac{\sin x \cos \Delta x + \cos x \sin \Delta x - \sin x}{\Delta x}$$

$$= \lim_{\Delta x \to 0} \left[\sin x \left(\frac{\cos \Delta x}{\Delta x} \right) + \cos x \left(\frac{\sin \Delta x}{\Delta x} \right) - \frac{\sin x}{\Delta x} \right]$$

$$= (\sin x) \lim_{\Delta x \to 0} \left(\frac{\cos \Delta x - 1}{\Delta x} \right) + (\cos x) \lim_{\Delta x \to 0} \frac{\sin \Delta x}{\Delta x}$$

$$= (\sin x)(0) + (\cos x)(1)$$

$$= \cos x \qquad\qquad ❑$$

EXAMPLE 1 Derivative involving a trigonometric function

Differentiate $f(x) = 2x^4 + 3\cos x + \sin a$, for constant a.

Solution

$$f'(x) = \frac{d}{dx}(2x^4 + 3\cos x + \sin a)$$

$$= 2\frac{d}{dx}(x^4) + 3\frac{d}{dx}(\cos x) + \frac{d}{dx}(\sin a) \quad \text{Extended linearity rule}$$

$$= 2(4x^3) + 3(-\sin x) + 0 \quad \begin{array}{l}\text{Power rule, derivative of cosine,} \\ \text{and derivative of a constant}\end{array}$$

$$= 8x^3 - 3\sin x \qquad\qquad\qquad\qquad\qquad\qquad \blacksquare$$

EXAMPLE 2   Derivative of a trigonometric function with product rule

Differentiate $f(x) = x^2 \sin x$.

Solution

$$f'(x) = \frac{d}{dx}(x^2 \sin x)$$

$$= x^2\frac{d}{dx}(\sin x) + \sin x\frac{d}{dx}(x^2) \quad \text{Product rule}$$

$$= x^2\cos x + 2x\sin x \qquad\qquad \text{Power rule and derivative of sine} \qquad \blacksquare$$

EXAMPLE 3   Derivative of a trigonometric function with quotient rule

Differentiate $h(t) = \dfrac{\sqrt{t}}{\cos t}$.

Solution

Write $\sqrt{t}$ as $t^{1/2}$. Then

$$h'(t) = \frac{d}{dt}\left[\frac{t^{1/2}}{\cos t}\right]$$

$$= \frac{\cos t\dfrac{d}{dt}(t^{1/2}) - t^{1/2}\dfrac{d}{dt}\cos t}{\cos^2 t} \quad \text{Quotient rule}$$

$$= \frac{\frac{1}{2}t^{-1/2}\cos t - t^{1/2}(-\sin t)}{\cos^2 t} \quad \text{Power rule and derivative of sine}$$

$$= \frac{\frac{1}{2}t^{-1/2}(\cos t + 2t\sin t)}{\cos^2 t} \quad \text{Common factor } \frac{1}{2}t^{-1/2}$$

$$= \frac{\cos t + 2t\sin t}{2\sqrt{t}\cos^2 t} \qquad\qquad\qquad\qquad\qquad \blacksquare$$

DIFFERENTIATION OF THE OTHER TRIGONOMETRIC FUNCTIONS

You will need to be able to differentiate not only the sine and cosine functions, but also the other trigonometric functions. To find the derivatives of these functions you will need the following identities, which are given in the *Student Mathematics Handbook* and Appendix E.

$$\tan x = \frac{\sin x}{\cos x} \qquad\qquad \cot x = \frac{\cos x}{\sin x}$$

$$\sec x = \frac{1}{\cos x} \qquad\qquad \csc x = \frac{1}{\sin x}$$

You will also need the following identities:

$$\cos^2 x + \sin^2 x = 1, \quad 1 + \tan^2 x = \sec^2 x, \quad \cot^2 x + 1 = \csc^2 x$$

THEOREM 3.7   Derivatives of the trigonometric functions

The six basic trigonometric functions $\sin x$, $\cos x$, $\tan x$, $\csc x$, $\sec x$, and $\cot x$ are all differentiable wherever they are defined, and

$$\frac{d}{dx}\sin x = \cos x \qquad\qquad \frac{d}{dx}\cos x = -\sin x$$

$$\frac{d}{dx}\tan x = \sec^2 x \qquad\qquad \frac{d}{dx}\cot x = -\csc^2 x$$

$$\frac{d}{dx}\sec x = \sec x \tan x \qquad\qquad \frac{d}{dx}\csc x = -\csc x \cot x$$

Proof   The derivatives for the sine and cosine functions were given in Theorem 3.6. All the other derivatives in this theorem are proved by using the quotient rule along with formulas for the derivatives of the sine and cosine functions. We will obtain the derivative of the tangent function and leave the rest as problems (see Problems 56–59).

$$\frac{d}{dx}\tan x = \frac{d}{dx}\frac{\sin x}{\cos x} \qquad\qquad \text{Trigonometric identity}$$

$$= \frac{\cos x \dfrac{d}{dx}\sin x - \sin x \dfrac{d}{dx}\cos x}{\cos^2 x} \qquad\qquad \text{Quotient rule}$$

$$= \frac{\cos x(\cos x) - \sin x(-\sin x)}{\cos^2 x} \qquad\qquad \text{Derivative of }\sin x\text{ and }\cos x$$

$$= \frac{\cos^2 x + \sin^2 x}{\cos^2 x}$$

$$= \frac{1}{\cos^2 x} \qquad\qquad \cos^2 x + \sin^2 x = 1$$

$$= \sec^2 x \qquad\qquad 1/\cos^2 x = \sec^2 x \qquad ❑$$

EXAMPLE 4   Derivative of a trigonometric function with the product rule

Differentiate $f(\theta) = 3\theta \sec \theta$.

Solution
$$f'(\theta) = \frac{d}{d\theta}(3\theta \sec \theta)$$
$$= 3\theta\frac{d}{d\theta}\sec \theta + \sec \theta\frac{d}{d\theta}(3\theta) \qquad \text{Product rule}$$
$$= 3\theta \sec \theta \tan \theta + 3\sec \theta \qquad\qquad ■$$

EXAMPLE 5   Derivative of a product of trigonometric functions

Differentiate $f(x) = \sec x \tan x$.

Solution
$$f'(x) = \frac{d}{dx}(\sec x \tan x)$$
$$= \sec x\frac{d}{dx}\tan x + \tan x\frac{d}{dx}\sec x \qquad \text{Product rule}$$
$$= \sec x(\sec^2 x) + \tan x(\sec x \tan x)$$
$$= \sec^3 x + \sec x \tan^2 x \qquad\qquad ■$$

EXAMPLE 6   Equation of a tangent line involving a trigonometric function

Find the equation of the tangent line to the curve $y = \cot x - 2\csc x$ at the point where $x = \frac{2\pi}{3}$.

Solution

When $x = \frac{2\pi}{3}$, we have

$$\cot \frac{2\pi}{3} - 2 \csc \frac{2\pi}{3} = \frac{-\sqrt{3}}{3} - 2\left(\frac{2\sqrt{3}}{3}\right) = \frac{-5\sqrt{3}}{3}$$

so the point of tangency is $P\left(\frac{2\pi}{3}, \frac{-5\sqrt{3}}{3}\right)$. To find the slope of the tangent line at P, we first compute the derivative $\frac{dy}{dx}$:

$$\begin{aligned}
\frac{dy}{dx} &= \frac{d}{dx}(\cot x - 2\csc x) \\
&= \frac{d}{dx}\cot x - 2\frac{d}{dx}\csc x \qquad \text{Linearity rule} \\
&= -\csc^2 x - 2(-\csc x \cot x) \\
&= 2\csc x \cot x - \csc^2 x
\end{aligned}$$

Then the slope of the tangent line is given by

$$\begin{aligned}
\frac{dy}{dx}\bigg|_{x=2\pi/3} &= 2\csc \frac{2\pi}{3} \cot \frac{2\pi}{3} - \csc^2 \frac{2\pi}{3} \\
&= 2\left(\frac{2}{\sqrt{3}}\right)\left(\frac{-1}{\sqrt{3}}\right) - \left(\frac{2}{\sqrt{3}}\right)^2 \\
&= \frac{-8}{3}
\end{aligned}$$

so the tangent line at $\left(\frac{2\pi}{3}, \frac{-5\sqrt{3}}{3}\right)$ with slope $-\frac{8}{3}$ is

$$y + \frac{5\sqrt{3}}{3} = -\frac{8}{3}\left(x - \frac{2\pi}{3}\right)$$

$$24x + 9y + 15\sqrt{3} - 16\pi = 0 \qquad\blacksquare$$

DERIVATIVES OF EXPONENTIAL AND LOGARITHMIC FUNCTIONS

The next theorem, which is easy to prove and remember, is one of the most important results in all of differential calculus.

THEOREM 3.8 Derivative rule for the natural exponential

The natural exponential function e^x is differentiable for all x, with derivative

$$\frac{d}{dx}(e^x) = e^x$$

Proof   We will proceed informally. Recall the definition of e:

$$\lim_{n\to\infty}\left(1 + \frac{1}{n}\right)^n = e$$

Let $n = \frac{1}{\Delta x}$, so that $\lim_{\Delta x\to 0}(1 + \Delta x)^{1/\Delta x} = e$. This means that for Δx very small, $e \approx (1 + \Delta x)^{1/\Delta x}$ or $e^{\Delta x} \approx 1 + \Delta x$, so that $e^{\Delta x} - 1 \approx \Delta x$. Thus, $\lim_{\Delta x\to 0}\dfrac{e^{\Delta x} - 1}{\Delta x} = 1$. Finally, using the limit in the definition of derivative for e^x, we obtain

$$\begin{aligned}
\frac{d}{dx}(e^x) &= \lim_{\Delta x\to 0}\frac{e^{(x+\Delta x)} - e^x}{\Delta x} \\
&= \lim_{\Delta x\to 0}\frac{e^x(e^{\Delta x} - 1)}{\Delta x} \\
&= e^x \lim_{\Delta x\to 0}\frac{e^{\Delta x} - 1}{\Delta x} \\
&= e^x(1) = e^x \qquad\qquad\square
\end{aligned}$$

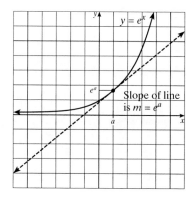

Figure 3.20 The slope of $y = e^x$ at each point (a, e^a) is $m = e^a$.

Note: An easier proof of the derivative formula in Theorem 3.8 is given in Example 6 of Section 3.6 using methods developed in that section.

The fact that $\dfrac{d}{dx}(e^x) = e^x$ means that the slope of the graph of $y = e^x$ at any point (a, e^a) is $m = e^a$, the y-coordinate of the point, as shown in Figure 3.20. This is one of the features of the exponential function $y = e^x$ that makes it "natural."

EXAMPLE 7 A derivative involving e^x

Differentiate $f(x) = x^2 e^x$. For what values of x does $f'(x) = 0$?

Solution

Using the product rule, we find

$$f'(x) = \frac{d}{dx}(x^2 e^x)$$

$$= x^2 \left[\frac{d}{dx} e^x\right] + \left[\frac{d}{dx} x^2\right] e^x$$

$$= x^2 e^x + 2x e^x \qquad \text{Exponential and power rules}$$

To find where $f'(x) = 0$, we solve

$$x^2 e^x + 2x e^x = 0$$

$$x(x + 2)e^x = 0$$

$$x(x + 2) = 0 \qquad \text{Since } e^x \neq 0 \text{ for all } x$$

$$x = 0, -2 \qquad\qquad\qquad\qquad \blacksquare$$

EXAMPLE 8 A second derivative involving e^x

For $f(x) = e^x \sin x$, find $f'(x)$ and $f''(x)$.

Solution

Apply the product rule twice:

$$f'(x) = e^x(\sin x)' + (e^x)' \sin x$$

$$= e^x(\cos x) + e^x(\sin x)$$

$$= e^x(\cos x + \sin x)$$

$$f''(x) = e^x(\cos x + \sin x)' + (e^x)'(\cos x + \sin x)$$

$$= e^x(-\sin x + \cos x) + e^x(\cos x + \sin x)$$

$$= 2e^x \cos x \qquad\qquad\qquad\qquad \blacksquare$$

THEOREM 3.9 Derivative rule for the natural logarithmic function

The natural logarithmic function $\ln x$ is differentiable for all $x > 0$, with derivative

$$\frac{d}{dx}(\ln x) = \frac{1}{x}$$

Proof According to the definition of the derivative, we have

$$\frac{d}{dx}(\ln x) = \lim_{\Delta x \to 0} \frac{\ln(x + \Delta x) - \ln x}{\Delta x}$$

$$= \lim_{\Delta x \to 0} \frac{1}{\Delta x} \ln\left(\frac{x + \Delta x}{x}\right)$$

$$= \lim_{\Delta x \to 0} \frac{1}{\Delta x} \ln\left(1 + \frac{\Delta x}{x}\right) \qquad \text{Let } h = \frac{x}{\Delta x}, \text{ so } \Delta x = \frac{x}{h}.$$

$$= \lim_{h \to +\infty} \frac{h}{x} \ln \left(1 + \frac{1}{h} \right) \qquad h \to +\infty \text{ as } \Delta x \to 0$$

$$= \frac{1}{x} \left[\lim_{h \to +\infty} h \ln \left(1 + \frac{1}{h} \right) \right]$$

$$= \frac{1}{x} \left[\lim_{h \to +\infty} \ln \left(1 + \frac{1}{h} \right)^h \right] \qquad \text{Power rule for logarithms}$$

$$= \frac{1}{x} \ln \left[\lim_{h \to +\infty} \left(1 + \frac{1}{h} \right)^h \right] \qquad \begin{array}{l} \text{Since } \ln x \text{ is continuous,} \\ \text{use the composition limit rule.} \end{array}$$

$$= \frac{1}{x} \ln e \qquad \text{Definition of } e$$

$$= \frac{1}{x} \qquad \ln e = 1 \qquad \Box$$

EXAMPLE 9   Derivative of a quotient involving a natural logarithm

Differentiate $f(x) = \dfrac{\ln x}{\sin x}$.

Solution   We use the quotient rule.

$$f'(x) = \frac{(\sin x)\frac{d}{dx}(\ln x) - (\ln x)\frac{d}{dx}(\sin x)}{\sin^2 x}$$

$$= \frac{(\sin x)\left(\frac{1}{x}\right) - (\ln x)(\cos x)}{\sin^2 x}$$

$$= \frac{\sin x - x \ln x \cos x}{x \sin^2 x} \qquad \blacksquare$$

TECHNOLOGY NOTE

When you are using calculators or computer programs such as *Mathematica*, *Derive*, or *Maple*, the form of the derivative may vary. For example, you might obtain

$$\frac{d}{dx}(\tan x) = \tan^2 x + 1$$

instead of $\sec^2 x$ as found in this section;

$$\frac{d}{dx}(\cot x) = -\cot^2 x - 1$$

instead of $-\csc^2 x$;

$$\frac{d}{dx}(\sec x) = \frac{\sin x}{\cos^2 x}$$

instead of $\sec x \tan x$; and

$$\frac{d}{dx}(\csc x) = -\frac{\cos x}{\sin^2 x}$$

instead of $-\csc x \cot x$. A solution to Example 9, using a TI-92, is shown in Figure 3.21.

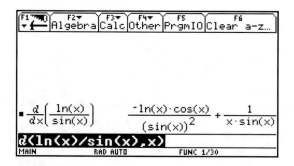

Figure 3.21   Sample output for Example 9. Notice that the form of the answer differs from that shown in the text.

Although the form of this calculator solution is different from the form shown in the example, you should notice that they are equivalent by using algebra (and recalling some of the fundamental identities from trigonometry).

A good test for your calculator is to try to find the derivative of $|x|$ at $x = 0$, which we know does not exist. Many calculators will give the incorrect answer of 0.

3.3 PROBLEM SET

A *Differentiate the functions given in Problems 1–32.*

1. $f(x) = \sin x + \cos x$
2. $f(x) = 2 \sin x + \tan x$
3. $g(t) = t^2 + \cos t + \cos \frac{\pi}{4}$
4. $g(t) = 2 \sec t + 3 \tan t - \tan \frac{\pi}{3}$
5. $f(t) = \sin^2 t$ *Hint*: Use the product rule.
6. $g(x) = \cos^2 x$ *Hint*: Use the product rule.
7. $f(x) = \sqrt{x} \cos x + x \cot x$
8. $f(x) = 2x^3 \sin x - 3x \cos x$
9. $p(x) = x^2 \cos x$
10. $p(t) = (t^2 + 2) \sin t$
11. $q(x) = \dfrac{\sin x}{x}$
12. $r(x) = \dfrac{e^x}{\sin x}$
13. $h(t) = e^t \csc t$
14. $f(\theta) = \dfrac{\sec \theta}{2 - \cos \theta}$
15. $f(x) = x^2 \ln x$
16. $g(x) = \dfrac{\ln x}{x^2}$
17. $h(x) = e^{2x}(\sin x - \cos x)$
18. $f(x) = \dfrac{\ln x}{x}$
19. $f(x) = \dfrac{\sin x}{e^x}$
20. $g(x) = \dfrac{x \cos x}{e^x}$
21. $f(x) = \dfrac{\tan x}{1 - 2x}$
22. $g(t) = \dfrac{1 + \sin t}{\sqrt{t}}$
23. $f(t) = \dfrac{2 + \sin t}{t + 2}$
24. $f(\theta) = \dfrac{\theta - 1}{2 + \cos \theta}$
25. $f(x) = \dfrac{\sin x}{1 - \cos x}$
26. $f(x) = \dfrac{x}{1 - \sin x}$
27. $f(x) = \dfrac{1 + \sin x}{2 - \cos x}$
28. $g(x) = \dfrac{\cos x}{1 + \cos x}$
29. $f(x) = \dfrac{\sin x + \cos x}{\sin x - \cos x}$
30. $f(x) = \dfrac{x^2 + \tan x}{3x + 2 \tan x}$
31. $g(x) = \sec^2 x - \tan^2 x + \cos x$
32. $g(x) = \cos^2 x + \sin^2 x + \sin x$

Find the second derivative of each function given in Problems 33–44.

33. $f(\theta) = \sin \theta$
34. $f(\theta) = \cos \theta$
35. $f(\theta) = \tan \theta$
36. $f(\theta) = \cot \theta$
37. $f(\theta) = \sec \theta$
38. $f(\theta) = \csc \theta$
39. $f(x) = \sin x + \cos x$
40. $f(x) = x \sin x$
41. $f(x) = e^x \cos x$
42. $g(t) = t^3 e^t$
43. $h(t) = \sqrt{t} \ln t$
44. $f(t) = \dfrac{\ln t}{t}$

B *Find an equation for the tangent line at the prescribed point for each function in Problems 45–52.*

45. $f(\theta) = \tan \theta$ at $(\frac{\pi}{4}, 1)$
46. $f(\theta) = \sec \theta$ at $(\frac{\pi}{3}, 2)$
47. $f(x) = \sin x$, where $x = \frac{\pi}{6}$
48. $f(x) = \cos x$, where $x = \frac{\pi}{3}$
49. $y = x + \sin x$, where $x = 0$
50. $y = x \sec x$, where $x = 0$
51. $y = e^x \cos x$, where $x = 0$
52. $y = x \ln x$, where $x = 1$
53. Which of the following functions satisfy $y'' + y = 0$?
    a. $y_1 = 2 \sin x + 3 \cos x$
    b. $y_2 = 4 \sin x - \pi \cos x$
    c. $y_3 = x \sin x$
    d. $y_4 = e^x \cos x$
54. For what values of A and B does $y = A \cos x + B \sin x$ satisfy $y'' + 2y' + 3y = 2 \sin x$?
55. For what values of A and B does $y = Ax \cos x + Bx \sin x$ satisfy $y'' + y = -3 \cos x$?

C 56. Complete the proof of Theorem 3.6 by showing that $\dfrac{d}{dx} \cos x = -\sin x$. *Hint*: You will need to use the identity $\cos(\alpha + \beta) = \cos \alpha \cos \beta - \sin \alpha \sin \beta$.

Prove the requested parts of Theorem 3.7 in Problems 57–59.

57. $\dfrac{d}{dx} \cot x = -\csc^2 x$
58. $\dfrac{d}{dx} \sec x = \sec x \tan x$
59. $\dfrac{d}{dx} \csc x = -\csc x \cot x$
60. Use the limit of a difference quotient to prove that

$$\frac{d}{dx} \tan x = \sec^2 x$$

61. **Exploration Problem** Write a short paper on the difficulties of differentiating trigonometric functions measured in degrees.*

---

*See, for example, "Fallacies, Flaws, and Flimflam," *The College Mathematics Journal*, Vol. 23, No. 3, May 1992, and Vol. 24, No. 4, September 1993. Another very understandable article, "Why Use Radians in Calculus?", by Carl E. Crockett, can be found in *The AMATYC Review*, Vol.19, No. 2, Spring 1998, pp. 44–47.

3.4 Rates of Change: Modeling Rectilinear Motion

IN THIS SECTION average and instantaneous rate of change, introduction to mathematical modeling, rectilinear motion (modeling in physics), falling body problems

The speed of a car or airplane; interest rates; the growth rate of a population; the drip rate of an intravenous injection—these are examples of the many situations in which rates of change are an important consideration in practical problems. In this section, we begin by showing how rates of change can be computed using differentiation. Then we discuss the general notion of mathematical modeling and conclude by demonstrating modeling principles in a variety of practical problems involving motion along a line.

AVERAGE AND INSTANTANEOUS RATE OF CHANGE

The graph of a linear function $f(x) = ax + b$ is the line $y = ax + b$, whose slope $m = a$ can be thought of as the rate at which y is changing with respect to x (see Figure 3.22a). However, for another function g that is *not* linear, the average (and instantaneous) rate of change of $y = g(x)$ with respect to x varies from point to point, as shown in Figure 3.22b.

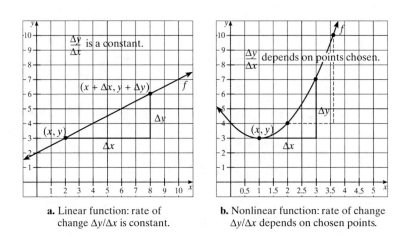

a. Linear function: rate of change $\Delta y/\Delta x$ is constant.

b. Nonlinear function: rate of change $\Delta y/\Delta x$ depends on chosen points.

Figure 3.22 Rate of change is measured by the slope of a tangent line

Because the slope of the tangent line is given by the derivative of the function, the preceding geometric observations suggest that the rate of change of a function is measured by its derivative. This connection will be made more precise in the following discussion.

Suppose y is a function of x, say $y = f(x)$. Corresponding to a change from x to $x + \Delta x$ the variable y changes from $f(x)$ to $f(x + \Delta x)$. The change in y is $\Delta y = f(x + \Delta x) - f(x)$, and the **average rate of change of y with respect to x** is

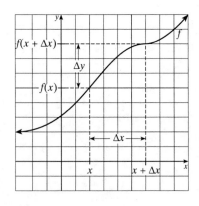

Figure 3.23 A change in Δy corresponding to a change Δx

$$\text{AVERAGE RATE OF CHANGE} = \frac{\text{CHANGE IN } y}{\text{CHANGE IN } x} = \frac{\Delta y}{\Delta x} = \frac{f(x + \Delta x) - f(x)}{\Delta x}$$

WARNING   This formula for the change in y is important. Find Δy in Figure 3.23.

As the interval over which we are averaging becomes shorter (that is, as $\Delta x \to 0$), the average rate of change approaches what we would intuitively call the **instantaneous rate of change of y with respect to x**, and the difference quotient approaches the derivative $\dfrac{dy}{dx}$. Thus, we have

$$\begin{array}{c}\text{INSTANTANEOUS} \\ \text{RATE OF CHANGE}\end{array} = \lim_{\Delta x \to 0} \frac{\Delta y}{\Delta x} = \lim_{\Delta x \to 0} \frac{f(x + \Delta x) - f(x)}{\Delta x} = f'(x)$$

To summarize,

Instantaneous Rate of Change

Suppose $f(x)$ is differentiable at $x = x_0$. Then the **instantaneous rate of change** of $y = f(x)$ with respect to x at x_0 is the value of the derivative of f at x_0. That is,

$$\text{INSTANTANEOUS RATE OF CHANGE} = f'(x_0) = \frac{dy}{dx}\bigg|_{x=x_0}$$

EXAMPLE 1 Instantaneous rate of change

Find the rate at which the function $y = x^2 \sin x$ is changing with respect to x when $x = \pi$.

Solution

For any x, the instantaneous rate of change is the derivative,

$$\frac{dy}{dx} = 2x \sin x + x^2 \cos x$$

Thus, the rate when $x = \pi$ is

$$\frac{dy}{dx}\bigg|_{x=\pi} = 2\pi \sin \pi + \pi^2 \cos \pi = 2\pi(0) + \pi^2(-1) = -\pi^2$$

The negative sign indicates that when $x = \pi$, the function is *decreasing* at the rate of $\pi^2 \approx 9.9$ units of y for each one-unit increase in x. ■

Let us consider an example comparing the average rate of change with the instantaneous rate of change.

EXAMPLE 2 Comparison between average rate and instantaneous rate of change

Let $f(x) = x^2 - 4x + 7$.

a. Find the average rate of change of f with respect to x between $x = 3$ and 5.
b. Find the instantaneous rate of change of f at $x = 3$.

Solution

a. The (average) rate of change from $x = 3$ to $x = 5$ is found by dividing the change in f by the change in x. The change in f from $x = 3$ to $x = 5$ is

$$f(5) - f(3) = [5^2 - 4(5) + 7] - [3^2 - 4(3) + 7] = 8$$

Thus, the average rate of change is

$$\frac{f(5) - f(3)}{5 - 3} = \frac{8}{2} = 4$$

The slope of the secant line is 4, as shown in Figure 3.24.

b. The derivative of the function is

$$f'(x) = 2x - 4$$

Thus, the instantaneous rate of change of f at $x = 3$ is

$$f'(3) = 2(3) - 4 = 2$$

The tangent line at $x = 3$ has slope 2, as shown in Figure 3.24. ■

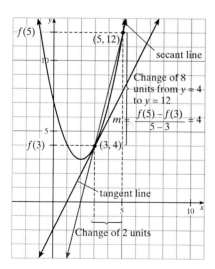

Figure 3.24 Comparison of the instantaneous rate of change and the average rate of change from 3 to 5

Often we are not as interested in the instantaneous rate of change of a quantity as its relative rate of change, defined as follows:

$$\text{RELATIVE RATE} = \frac{\text{INSTANTANEOUS RATE OF CHANGE}}{\text{SIZE OF QUANTITY}}$$

For instance, if you are earning \$15,000/yr and receive a \$3,000 raise, you would probably be very pleased. However, that \$3,000 raise might be much less meaningful if you were earning \$100,000/yr. In both cases, the change is the quantity \$3,000, but in the first case the relative rate of change is $3,000/15,000 = 20\%$, whereas in the second, it is a much smaller $3,000/100,000 = 3\%$.

In terms of the derivative, the relative rate of change may be defined as follows:

Relative Rate of Change

> The **relative rate of change** of $y = f(x)$ at $x = x_0$ is given by the ratio
>
> $$\text{RELATIVE RATE OF CHANGE} = \frac{f'(x_0)}{f(x_0)}$$

EXAMPLE 3   Relative rate of change

The aerobic rate is the rate of a person's oxygen consumption and is sometimes modeled by the function A defined by

$$A(x) = 110\left[\frac{\ln x - 2}{x}\right]$$

where x is the person's age. What is the relative rate of change of the aerobic rating of a 20-year-old person? A 50-year-old person?

Solution

Applying the quotient rule, we obtain the derivative of $A(x)$:

$$A'(x) = 110\left[\frac{x(1/x) - (\ln x - 2)(1)}{x^2}\right] = 110\left[\frac{3 - \ln x}{x^2}\right]$$

Thus, the relative rate of change of A at age x is

$$\text{RELATIVE RATE} = \frac{A'(x)}{A(x)} = \frac{110\left[\dfrac{3 - \ln x}{x^2}\right]}{110\left[\dfrac{\ln x - 2}{x}\right]} = \frac{3 - \ln x}{(\ln x - 2)x}$$

In particular, when $x = 20$, the relative rate is

$$\frac{A'(20)}{A(20)} = \frac{3 - \ln 20}{(\ln 20 - 2)20} \approx 0.0002143$$

In other words, at age 20, the person's aerobic rating is increasing at the rate of 0.02%/yr. However, at age 50, the relative rate is

$$\frac{A'(50)}{A(50)} = \frac{3 - \ln 50}{(\ln 50 - 2)50} \approx -0.0095399$$

and the person's aerobic rating is *decreasing* (because of the negative sign) at the relative rate of 0.95%/yr. ∎

INTRODUCTION TO MATHEMATICAL MODELING

A real-life situation is usually far too complicated to be precisely and mathematically defined. When confronted with a problem in the real world, therefore, it is usually necessary to develop a mathematical framework based on certain assumptions about the real world. This framework can then be used to find a solution to the real-world problem. The process of developing this body of mathematics is referred to as **mathematical modeling**.

Some mathematical models are quite accurate, particularly many used in the physical sciences. For example, one of the models we will consider in calculus is a model for the path of a projectile. Other rather precise models predict such things as the time of sunrise and sunset, or the distance which an object falls in a vacuum. Some mathematical models, however, are less accurate, especially those that involve examples from the life sciences and social sciences. Only recently has modeling in these disciplines become precise enough to be expressed in terms of calculus.

What, exactly, is a mathematical model? Sometimes, mathematical modeling can mean nothing more than a textbook word problem. But mathematical modeling can also mean choosing appropriate mathematics to solve a problem that has previously been unsolved. In this book, we use the term "mathematical modeling" to mean something between these two extremes. That is, it is a process we will apply to some real-life problem that does not have an obvious solution. It usually cannot be solved by applying a single formula.

Learning to use modeling techniques is an important part of your mathematical education. The first step in the modeling process involves *abstraction*, in which certain assumptions about a given practical problem are made in order to formulate a version of the problem in abstract terms. Next, the abstract version of the problem is *analyzed* using appropriate mathematical methods such as calculus, and finally, results derived from the abstract analysis are *interpreted* in terms of the original problem. The results obtained from the model often lead to predictions about the "real-world" situations related to the given problem. Data can be gathered to check the accuracy of these predictions and to modify the initial assumptions of the model to make it more precise. The process continues until a model is obtained that fits "reality" with acceptable accuracy. The steps in the modeling process are demonstrated in Figure 3.25. You may also find it interesting to read the article on modeling weather from *Scientific American* quoted in the margin.

HOW GLOBAL CLIMATE IS MODELED

We find a good example of mathematical modeling by looking at the work being done with weather prediction. In theory, if the correct assumptions could be programmed into a computer, along with appropriate mathematical statements of the ways global climate conditions operate, we would have a model to predict the weather throughout the world. In the global climate model, a system of equations calculates time-dependent changes in wind as well as temperature and moisture changes in the atmosphere and on the land. The model may also predict alterations in the temperature of the ocean's surface. At the National Center for Atmospheric Research, a CRAY supercomputer is used to do this modeling.

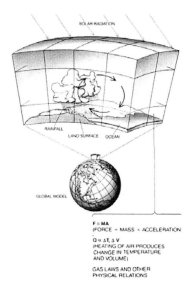

From *Scientific American*, March 1991

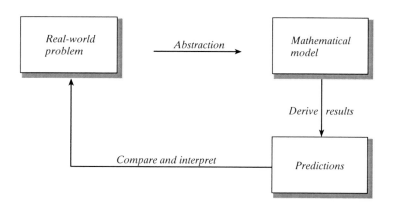

Figure 3.25 Mathematical modeling

EXAMPLE 4 Identifying models

It is common to gather data when studying most phenomena. Classifying the data by comparing with known models is an important mathematical skill. Identify each of the data sets as an example of a linear model, a quadratic model, a cubic model, a logarithmic model, an exponential model, or a sinusoidal model.

a.

x	y
−4	2.00
−3	1.28
−2	0.72
−1	0.32
0	0.08
1	0.00
2	0.08
3	0.32
4	0.72

b.

x	y
−4	−20.7
−3	−16.5
−2	−12.3
−1	−8.2
0	−3.8
1	0.4
2	4.7
3	8.9
4	13.12

c.

x	y
0.0	0.0
1.0	1.7
1.5	2.0
2.5	1.2
3.5	−0.7
4.5	−1.9
5.5	−1.4
6.0	−0.6
6.5	0.4

d.

x	y
−4	0.27
−3	0.30
−2	0.33
−1	0.36
0	0.40
1	0.44
2	0.49
3	0.52
4	0.60

e.

x	y
3	0.00
4	0.69
5	1.10
6	1.39
7	1.61
8	1.79
9	1.95
10	2.08
11	2.20
12	2.30

Solution

Sketch each graph and observe the pattern (if any) of the graphs.

a. Quadratic model

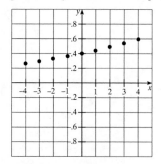

b. Linear model

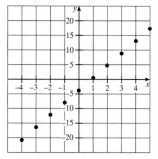

c. The data points seem to form a pattern, and we hypothesize that the data points are periodic, namely a sinusoidal model.

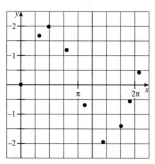

d. The data points look almost linear (but not quite), so we hypothesize that the data points may indicate an exponential model.

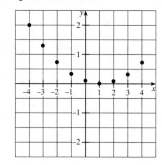

e. The data points seem to indicate a logarithmic model.

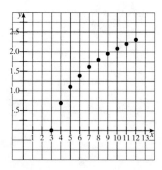

Mathematical models will appear in both examples and exercises throughout this text. In the next subsection, we begin our work with modeling by studying rectilinear motion, an important topic from physics.

RECTILINEAR MOTION (MODELING IN PHYSICS)

Rectilinear motion is motion along a straight line. For example, the up and down motion of a yo-yo may be regarded as rectilinear, as may the motion of a rocket early in its flight.

When studying rectilinear motion, we may assume that the object is moving along a coordinate line. The *position* of the object on the line is a function of time t and is often expressed as $s(t)$. The rate of change of $s(t)$ with respect to time is the object's **velocity** $v(t)$, and the rate of change of the velocity with respect to t is its **acceleration** $a(t)$. The absolute value of the velocity is called **speed**. Thus,

$$\text{Velocity is } v(t) = \frac{ds}{dt}$$

$$\text{Speed is } |v(t)| = \left| \frac{ds}{dt} \right|$$

$$\text{Acceleration is } a(t) = \frac{dv}{dt} = \frac{d^2 s}{dt^2}$$

If $v(t) > 0$, we say that the object is *advancing*, and if $v(t) < 0$, it is *retreating*. If $v(t) = 0$, the object is neither advancing nor retreating, and we say it is *stationary*. The object is *accelerating* when $a(t) > 0$ and is *decelerating* when $a(t) < 0$. The significance of the acceleration is that it gives the rate at which the velocity is changing. When you are riding in a car, you do not feel the velocity, but you do feel the acceleration. That is, you feel *changes* in the velocity.

These ideas are summarized in the following box.

Rectilinear Motion

An object that moves along a straight line with *position* $s(t)$ has *velocity* $v(t) = \dfrac{ds}{dt}$ and *acceleration* $a(t) = \dfrac{dv}{dt} = \dfrac{d^2 s}{dt^2}$ when these derivatives exist. The *speed* of the object is $|v(t)|$.

WARNING   Rectilinear motion involves *position, velocity,* and *acceleration.* Sometimes there is confusion between the words "speed" and "velocity." Because speed is the absolute value of the velocity, it indicates how fast an object is moving, whereas velocity indicates both speed and direction (relative to a given coordinate system).

Notational comment: If distance is measured in meters and time in seconds, then velocity is measured in meters per second (m/s). Acceleration is recorded in meters per second per second (m/s/s). The notation m/s/s is awkward, so m/s^2 is more commonly used. Similarly, if distance is measured in feet, then velocity is measured in feet per second (ft/s) and acceleration in feet per second per second (ft/s^2).

EXAMPLE 5 The position, velocity, and acceleration of a moving object

Assume that the position at time t of an object moving along a line is given by

$$s(t) = 3t^3 - 40.5t^2 + 162t$$

for t on $[0, 8]$. Find the initial position, velocity, and acceleration for the object and discuss the motion. Compute the total distance traveled.

Solution

The position at time t is given by the function s. The initial position occurs at time $t = 0$, so

$$s(0) = 0 \qquad \textit{The object starts at the origin.}$$

The velocity is determined by finding the derivative of the position function.

$$v(t) = s'(t) = 9t^2 - 81t + 162$$
$$= 9(t^2 - 9t + 18)$$
$$= 9(t-3)(t-6) \qquad \textit{The initial velocity is } v(0) = 162.$$

When $t = 3$ and when $t = 6$, the velocity v is 0, which means the *object is stationary* at those times. Furthermore,

$$v(t) > 0 \quad \text{on} \quad [0, 3) \qquad \textit{Object is advancing.}$$
$$v(t) < 0 \quad \text{on} \quad (3, 6) \qquad \textit{Object is retreating.}$$
$$v(t) > 0 \quad \text{on} \quad (6, 8] \qquad \textit{Object is advancing.}$$

For the acceleration,

$$a(t) = s''(t) = v'(t) = 18t - 81$$
$$= 18(t - 4.5) \qquad \textit{The initial acceleration is } a(0) = -81.$$

We see that

$$a(t) < 0 \quad \text{on} \quad [0, 4.5) \qquad \textit{Velocity is decreasing;}$$
$$\textit{that is, the object is decelerating.}$$
$$a(t) = 0 \quad \text{at} \quad t = 4.5 \qquad \textit{Velocity is not changing.}$$
$$a(t) > 0 \quad \text{on} \quad (4.5, 8] \qquad \textit{Velocity is increasing;}$$
$$\textit{so the object is accelerating.}$$

The table in the margin gives certain values for s, v, and a. We use these values to plot a few points, as shown in Figure 3.26. The actual path of the object is back and forth on the axis and the figure is for clarification only.

t	s	v	a
0	0	162	−81
1	124.5	90	−63
2	186	36	−45
3	202.5	0	−27
4	192	−18	−9
4.5	182.25	−20.25	0
5	172.5	−18	9
6	162	0	27
7	178.5	36	45
8	240	90	63

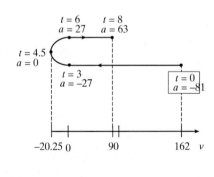

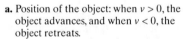

a. Position of the object: when $v > 0$, the object advances, and when $v < 0$, the object retreats.

b. Velocity of the object: when $a > 0$, the velocity increases, and when $a < 0$, the velocity decreases.

Figure 3.26 Analysis of rectilinear motion

Recall that the *speed* of the object is the absolute value of its velocity. The speed decreases from 162 to 0 between $t = 0$ and $t = 3$ and increases from 0 to 20.25 as the velocity becomes negative between $t = 3$ and $t = 4.5$. Then for $4.5 < t < 6$, the object slows down again, from 20.25 to 0, after which it speeds up.

The total distance traveled is

$$|s(3) - s(0)| + |s(6) - s(3)| + |s(8) - s(6)| = 202.5 + 40.5 + 78 = 321 \qquad \blacksquare$$

A common mistake is to think that a particle moving on a straight line speeds up when its acceleration is positive and slows down when the acceleration is negative, but this is not quite correct. Instead, the following is generally true:

The speed *increases* (particle speeds up) when the velocity and acceleration have the same signs.

The speed *decreases* (particle slows down) when the velocity and acceleration have opposite signs.

FALLING BODY PROBLEMS

As a second example of rectilinear motion, we will consider a *falling body problem*. In such a problem, it is assumed that an object is projected (that is, thrown, fired, dropped, etc.) vertically in such a way that the only acceleration acting on the object is the constant downward acceleration g due to gravity, which on the earth near sea level is approximately 32 ft/s^2 or 9.8 m/s^2.* Thus, we disregard air resistance. At time t, the height of the projectile is given by the following formula:

Formula for the height of a projectile

v_0 is the initial velocity.
$\downarrow$
$$h(t) = -\tfrac{1}{2}gt^2 + v_0 t + s_0 \leftarrow s_0 \text{ is the initial height.}$$
$\uparrow$
g is the acceleration due to gravity.

---

where s_0 and v_0 are the projectile's initial height and velocity, respectively. You are asked to derive this formula for earth's gravity and a particular initial velocity and a particular initial position in a problem in Section 5.1.

EXAMPLE 6   Position, velocity, and acceleration of a falling object

Suppose a person standing at the top of the Tower of Pisa (176 ft high) throws a ball directly upward with an initial speed of 96 ft/s.

a. Find the ball's height, its velocity, and acceleration at time t.
b. When does the ball hit the ground, and what is its impact velocity?
c. How far does the ball travel during its flight?

Solution

First, draw a picture such as the one shown in Figure 3.27 to help you understand the problem.

a. Substitute the known values into the formula for the height of an object:

$$v_0 = 96 \text{ ft/s: Initial velocity}$$
$$\downarrow$$
$$h(t) = -\tfrac{1}{2}(32)t^2 + 96t + 176 \leftarrow h_0 = 176 \text{ ft is the height of tower}$$
$$\uparrow$$
$$g = 32 \text{ ft/s}^2\text{: Constant downward gravitational acceleration}$$

$$h(t) = -16t^2 + 96t + 176 \qquad \textsf{This is the position function.}$$
$$\textsf{It gives the height of the ball.}$$

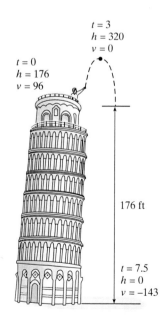

$t = 3$
$h = 320$
$v = 0$

$t = 0$
$h = 176$
$v = 96$

176 ft

$t = 7.5$
$h = 0$
$v = -143$

Figure 3.27 The motion of a ball thrown upward from the Tower of Pisa

---

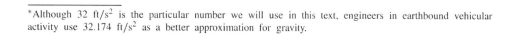

*Although 32 ft/s^2 is the particular number we will use in this text, engineers in earthbound vehicular activity use 32.174 ft/s^2 as a better approximation for gravity.

The velocity at time t is the derivative:

$$v(t) = \frac{dh}{dt} = -32t + 96$$

The acceleration is the derivative of the velocity function:

$$a(t) = \frac{dv}{dt} = \frac{d^2h}{dt^2} = -32$$

This means that the acceleration of the ball is always decreasing at the rate of 32 ft/s^2.

b. The ball hits the ground when $h(t) = 0$. Solve the equation

$$-16t^2 + 96t + 176 = 0$$

to find that this occurs when $t \approx -1.47$ and $t \approx 7.47$. Disregarding the negative value, we see that impact occurs at $t \approx 7.47$ sec. The impact velocity is

$$v(7.47) \approx -143 \text{ ft/s}$$

The negative sign here means the ball is coming down at the moment of impact.

c. The ball travels upward for some time and then falls downward to the ground, as shown in Figure 3.27. We need to find the distance it travels upward plus the distance it falls to the ground. The turning point at the top (the highest point) occurs when the velocity is zero. Solve the equation

$$-32t + 96 = 0$$

to find that this occurs when $t = 3$. The ball starts at $h(0) = 176$ ft and rises to a maximum height when $t = 3$. Thus, the maximum height is

$$h(3) = -16(3)^2 + 96(3) + 176 = 320$$

and the total distance traveled is

$$\underbrace{(320 - 176)}_{\text{Upward distance}} + \underbrace{320}_{\text{Downward distance}} = 464$$
$$\uparrow$$
$$\text{Initial height}$$

The total distance traveled is 464 ft. ∎

3.4 PROBLEM SET

Ⓐ 1. WHAT DOES THIS SAY? What is a mathematical model?

2. Interpretation Problem Why are mathematical models necessary or useful?

For each function f given in Problems 3–16, find the rate of change with respect to x at $x = x_0$.

3. $f(x) = x^2 - 3x + 5$ when $x_0 = 2$

4. $f(x) = 14 + x - x^2$ when $x_0 = 1$

5. $f(x) = -2x^2 + x + 4$ for $x_0 = 1$

6. $f(x) = \dfrac{-2}{x+1}$ for $x_0 = 1$

7. $f(x) = \dfrac{2x-1}{3x+5}$ when $x_0 = -1$

8. $f(x) = (x^2 + 2)(x + \sqrt{x})$ when $x_0 = 4$

9. $f(x) = x \cos x$ when $x_0 = \pi$

10. $f(x) = (x+1)\sin x$ when $x_0 = \frac{\pi}{2}$

11. $f(x) = x \ln \sqrt{x}$ when $x_0 = 1$

12. $f(x) = \dfrac{x^2}{e^x}$ when $x_0 = 0$

13. $f(x) = \sin x \cos x$ when $x_0 = \frac{\pi}{2}$

14. $f(x) = \dfrac{x^2}{x^2 + 1}$ when $x_0 = 1$

15. $f(x) = \left(x - \dfrac{2}{x}\right)^2$ when $x_0 = 1$

16. $f(x) = \sin^2 x$ when $x_0 = \frac{\pi}{4}$

The function $s(t)$ in Problems 17–24 gives the position of an object moving along a line. In each case,

a. *Find the velocity at time t.*

b. *Find the acceleration at time t.*

c. Describe the motion of the object; that is, tell when it is advancing and when it is retreating. Compute the total distance traveled by the object during the indicated time interval.

d. Tell when the object is accelerating and when it is decelerating.

SMH For a review of solving equations, see Sections 2.5 and 4.7 of the Student Mathematics Handbook.

17. $s(t) = t^2 - 2t + 6$ on $[0, 2]$

18. $s(t) = 3t^2 + 2t - 5$ on $[0, 1]$

19. $s(t) = t^3 - 9t^2 + 15t + 25$ on $[0, 6]$

20. $s(t) = t^4 - 4t^3 + 8t$ on $[0, 4]$

21. $s(t) = \dfrac{2t + 1}{t^2}$ for $1 \le t \le 3$

22. $s(t) = t^2 + t \ln t$ for $1 \le t \le e$

23. $s(t) = 3 \cos t$ for $0 \le t \le 2\pi$

24. $s(t) = 1 + \sec t$ for $0 \le t \le \frac{\pi}{4}$

Modeling Problems *Identify each of the data sets in Problems 25–34 as an example of a linear model, a quadratic model, a cubic model, a logarithmic model, an exponential model, or a sinusoidal model.*

25.

x	y
−4	−140
−3	−96
−2	−60
−1	−32
0	−12
1	0
2	4
3	0
4	−12

26.

x	y
−4	−10.2
−3	−8.0
−2	−5.8
−1	−3.6
0	−1.4
1	0.8
2	3.0
3	5.2
4	7.4

27.

x	y
−4	−0.019531
−3	−0.078125
−2	−0.3125
−1	−1.25
0	−5
1	−20
2	−80
3	−320
4	−1280

28.

x	y
−4	−0.0003
−3	−0.0009
−2	−0.0027
−1	−0.0082
0	−0.0247
1	−0.0741
2	−0.2222
3	−0.6667
4	−2.0000

29.

x	y
−4	238
−3	173
−2	118
−1	73
0	38
1	13
2	−2
3	−7
4	−2

30.

x	y
−4	4.84
−3	2.46
−2	−1.41
−1	−4.42
0	−4.76
1	−2.20
2	1.68
3	4.55
4	4.66

31.

x	y
−2.0	−28.0
−1.5	−8.5
−1.0	1.0
−0.5	3.5
0.0	2.0
0.5	−0.5
1.0	−1.0
1.5	3.5
2.0	16.0

32.

x	y
−4	−3.5
−3	−2.4
−2	−1.3
−1	−0.2
0	0.9
1	2.0
2	3.1
3	4.2
4	5.3

33.

x	y
2	0.0
3	−1.2
4	−1.9
5	−2.4
6	−2.8
7	−3.1
8	−3.4
9	−3.6
10	−3.8

34.

x	y
1	4.2
2	5.6
3	6.4
4	7.0
5	7.4
6	7.8
7	8.1
8	8.4
9	8.6

Ⓑ 35. It is estimated that x years from now, $0 \le x \le 10$, the average SAT score of the incoming students at a certain eastern liberal arts college will be

$$f(x) = -6x + 1,082$$

a. Derive an expression for the rate at which the average SAT score will be changing with respect to time x years from now.

b. What is the significance of the fact that the expression in part **a** is a negative constant?

36. A particle moving on the x-axis has position

$$x(t) = 2t^3 + 3t^2 - 36t + 40$$

after an elapsed time of t seconds.

a. Find the velocity of the particle at time t.

b. Find the acceleration at time t.

c. What is the total distance traveled by the particle during the first 3 seconds?

37. An object moving on the x-axis has position

$$x(t) = t^3 - 9t^2 + 24t + 20$$

after t seconds. What is the total distance traveled by the object during the first 8 seconds?

38. A car has position

$$s(t) = 50t \ln t + 80$$

ft after t seconds of motion. What is its acceleration (to the nearest hundredth ft/s^2) after 10 seconds?

39. An object moves along a straight line so that after t minutes, its position relative to its starting point (in meters) is

$$s(t) = 10t + \frac{t}{e^t}$$

a. At what speed (to the nearest thousandth m/min) is the object moving at the end of 4 min?

b. How far (to the nearest thousandth m) does the object actually travel during the fifth minute?

40. A bucket containing 5 gal of water has a leak. After t seconds, there are

$$Q(t) = 5\left(1 - \frac{t}{25}\right)^2$$

gallons of water in the bucket.

a. At what rate (to the nearest hundredth gal) is water leaking from the bucket after 2 seconds?

b. How long does it take for all the water to leak out of the bucket?

c. At what rate is the water leaking when the last drop leaks out?

Modeling Problems   *In Problems 41–48, set up and solve an appropriate model to answer the given question. Be sure to state your assumptions.*

41. A person standing at the edge of a cliff throws a rock directly upward. It is observed that 2 seconds later the rock is at its maximum height (in ft) and that 5 seconds after that, it hits the ground at the base of the cliff.

a. What is the initial velocity of the rock?

b. How high is the cliff?

c. What is the velocity of the rock at time t?

d. With what velocity does the rock hit the ground?

42. A projectile is shot upward from the earth with an initial velocity of 320 ft/s.

a. What is its velocity after 5 seconds?

b. What is its acceleration after 3 seconds?

43. A rock is dropped from a height of 90 ft. One second later another rock is dropped from height H. What is H (to the nearest foot) if the two rocks hit the ground at the same time?

44. A ball is thrown vertically upward from the ground with an initial velocity of 160 ft/s.

a. When will the ball hit the ground?

b. With what velocity will the ball hit the ground?

c. When will the ball reach its maximum height?

45. An object is dropped (initial velocity $v_0 = 0$) from the top of a building and falls 3 seconds before hitting the pavement below. Determine the height of the building in ft.

46. An astronaut standing at the edge of a cliff on the moon throws a rock directly upward and observes that it passes her on the way down exactly 4 seconds later. Three seconds after that, the rock hits the ground at the base of the cliff. Use this information to determine the initial velocity v_0 and the height of the cliff. *Note*: $g = 5.5$ ft/s^2 on the moon.

47. Answer the question in Problem 46 assuming the astronaut is on Mars, where $g = 12$ ft/s^2.

48. A car is traveling at 88 ft/s (60 mi/h) when the driver applies the brakes to avoid hitting a child. After t seconds, the car is $s(t) = 88t - 8t^2$ feet from the point where the brakes were first applied. How long does it take for the car to come to a stop, and how far does it travel before stopping?

49. It is estimated that t years from now, the circulation of a local newspaper can be modeled by the formula

$$C(t) = 100t^2 + 400t + 50t \ln t$$

a. Find an expression for the rate at which the circulation will be changing with respect to time t years from now.

b. At what rate will the circulation be changing with respect to time 5 years from now?

c. By how much will the circulation actually change during the sixth year?

50. An efficiency study of the morning shift at a certain factory indicates that an average worker who arrives on the job at 8:00 A.M. will have assembled

$$f(x) = -\tfrac{1}{3}x^3 + \tfrac{1}{2}x^2 + 50x$$

units x hours later.

a. Find a formula for the rate at which the worker will be assembling the units after x hours.

b. At what rate will the worker be assembling units at 9:00 A.M.?

c. How many units will the worker actually assemble between 9:00 A.M. and 10:00 A.M.?

51. An environmental study of a certain suburban community suggests that t years from now, the average level of carbon monoxide in the air can be modeled by the formula

$$q(t) = 0.05t^2 + 0.1t + 3.4$$

parts per million.

a. At what rate will the carbon monoxide level be changing with respect to time one year from now?

b. By how much will the carbon monoxide level change in the first year?

c. By how much will the carbon monoxide level change over the next (second) year?

52. According to *Newton's law of universal gravitation*, if an object of mass M is separated by a distance r from a second object of mass m, then the two objects are attracted to one another by a force that acts along the line joining them and has magnitude

$$F = \frac{GmM}{r^2}$$

where G is a positive constant. Show that the rate of change of F with respect to r is inversely proportional to r^3.

53. The population of a bacterial colony is approximately

$$P(t) = P_0 + 61t + 3t^2$$

thousand t hours after observation begins, where P_0 is the initial population. Find the rate at which the colony is growing after 5 hours.

54. The gross domestic product (GDP) of a certain country is

$$g(t) = t^2 + 5t + 106$$

billion dollars t years after 2001.

a. At what rate does the GDP change in 2003?

b. At what percentage rate does the GDP change in 2003?

55. It is projected that x months from now, the population of a certain town will be

$$P(x) = 2x + 4x^{3/2} + 5,000$$

a. At what rate will the population be changing with respect to time 9 months from now?

b. At what percentage rate will the population be changing with respect to time 9 months from now?

56. Assume that your starting salary is \$30,000 and you get a raise of \$3,000 each year.

a. Express the percentage rate of change of your salary as a function of time.

b. At what percentage rate will your salary be increasing after one year?

c. What will happen to the percentage rate of change of your salary in the long run?

57. The GDP of a certain country is growing at a constant rate. In 1999 the GDP was 125 billion dollars, and in 2001 it was 155 billion dollars. At what percentage rate did the GDP grow in 2000?

58. If y is a linear function of x, what will happen to the percentage rate of change of y with respect to x as x increases without bound?

59. According to Debye's formula in physical chemistry, the orientation polarization P of a gas satisfies

$$P = \frac{4}{3}\pi N \left(\frac{\mu^2}{3kT} \right)$$

where μ, k, and N are constants and T is the temperature of the gas. Find the rate of change of P with respect to T.

60. A disease is spreading in such a way that after t weeks, for $0 \le t \le 6$, it has affected

$$N(t) = 5 - t^2(t - 6)$$

hundred people. Health officials declare that this disease will reach epidemic proportions when the percentage rate of increase of $N(t)$ at the start of a particular week is at least 30% per week. The epidemic designation level is dropped when the percentage rate falls below this level.

a. Find the percentage rate of change of $N(t)$ at time t.

b. Between what weeks is the disease at the epidemic level?

61. An object attached to a helical spring is pulled down from its equilibrium position and then released, as shown in Figure 3.28.

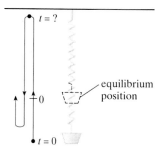

Figure 3.28 Helical spring

Suppose that t seconds later, its position (in centimeters, measured relative to the equilibrium position) is modeled by

$$s(t) = 7 \cos t$$

a. Find the velocity and acceleration of the object at time t.

b. Find the length of time required for one complete oscillation. This is called the *period* of the motion.

c. What is the distance between the highest point reached by the object and the lowest point? Half of this distance is called the *amplitude* of the motion.

62. Two cars leave a town at the same time and travel at constant speeds along straight roads that meet at an angle of 60° in the town. If one car travels twice as fast as the other and the distance between them increases at the rate of 45 mi/h, how fast is the slower car traveling?

63. Spy Problem In an attempt to divert the Spy from seeking revenge for the death of his friend Siggy (Problem 62, Section 2.4), his superior, Lord Newton Fleming (affectionately known as the "Flamer"), assigns him to a mission in space. However, an encounter with an enemy agent leaves him with a mild concussion that causes him to forget where he is. Fortunately, he remembers the values of g for various heavenly bodies (32 ft/s^2 on earth, 5.5 ft/s^2 on the moon, 12 ft/s^2 on Mars, and 28 ft/s^2 on Venus). To deduce his whereabouts, he throws a rock directly upward (from ground level) and notes that it reaches a maximum height of 37.5 ft and hits the ground 5 s after leaving his hand. Where is he?

64. Find the rate of change of the volume of a cube with respect to the length of one of its edges. How is this rate related to the surface area of the cube?

65. Show that the rate of change of the volume of a sphere with respect to its radius is equal to its surface area.

66. Van der Waal's equation states that a gas that occupies a volume V at temperature T (Kelvin) exerts pressure P, where

$$\left(P + \frac{A}{V^2} \right)(V - B) = kT$$

and A, B, and k are physical constants. Find the rate of change of pressure with respect to volume, assuming fixed temperature.

3.5   The Chain Rule

IN THIS SECTION   introduction to the chain rule, extended derivative formulas, justification of the chain rule

INTRODUCTION TO THE CHAIN RULE

Suppose it is known that the carbon monoxide pollution in the air is changing at the rate of 0.02 ppm (parts per million) for each person in a town whose population is growing at the rate of 1,000 people per year. To find the rate at which the level of pollution is increasing with respect to time, we form the product

$$(0.02 \text{ ppm/person}) \ (1,000 \text{ people/year}) = 20 \text{ ppm/year}$$

In this example, the level of pollution L is a function of the population P, which is itself a function of time t. Thus, L is a composite function of t, and

$$\begin{bmatrix} \text{RATE OF CHANGE OF } L \\ \text{WITH RESPECT TO } t \end{bmatrix} = \begin{bmatrix} \text{RATE OF CHANGE OF } L \\ \text{WITH RESPECT TO } P \end{bmatrix} \begin{bmatrix} \text{RATE OF CHANGE OF } P \\ \text{WITH RESPECT TO } t \end{bmatrix}$$

Expressing each of these rates in terms of an appropriate derivative in Leibniz form, we obtain the following equation:

$$\frac{dL}{dt} = \frac{dL}{dP}\frac{dP}{dt}$$

These observations anticipate the following important theorem.

THEOREM 3.10   Chain rule

If $y = f(u)$ is a differentiable function of u and u in turn is a differentiable function of x, then $y = f(u(x))$ is a differentiable function of x and its derivative is given by the product

$$\frac{dy}{dx} = \frac{dy}{du}\frac{du}{dx}$$

Proof   A rigorous proof involves a few details that make it inappropriate to include at this point in the text. A justification (partial proof) is given at the end of this section, and a full proof of the chain rule is included in Appendix B.

WARNING   Recall our earlier warning in Section 3.1 against thinking of $\frac{dy}{dx}$ as a fraction. That said, there are certain times when this incorrect reasoning can be used as a mnemonic device. For instance, "canceling du," as indicated below, makes it easy to remember the chain rule:

$$\frac{dy}{dx} = \frac{dy}{du}\frac{du}{dx}$$ ❑

EXAMPLE 1   The chain rule

Find $\frac{dy}{dx}$ if $y = u^3 - 3u^2 + 1$ and $u = x^2 + 2$.

Solution

Because $\frac{dy}{du} = 3u^2 - 6u$ and $\frac{du}{dx} = 2x$, it follows from the chain rule that

$$\frac{dy}{dx} = \frac{dy}{du}\frac{du}{dx} = (3u^2 - 6u)(2x)$$

Notice that this derivative is expressed in terms of the variables x and u. To express dy/dx in terms of x alone, we substitute $u = x^2 + 2$ as follows:

$$\frac{dy}{dx} = [3(x^2 + 2)^2 - 6(x^2 + 2)](2x) = 6x^3(x^2 + 2)$$ ■

The chain rule is actually a rule for differentiating composite functions. In particular, if $y = f(u)$ and $u = u(x)$, then y is the composite function $y = (f \circ u)(x) = f[u(x)]$, and the chain rule can be rewritten as follows:

THEOREM 3.10a   The chain rule (alternate form)

If u is differentiable at x and f is differentiable at $u(x)$, then the composite function $f \circ u$ is differentiable at x and

$$\frac{d}{dx} f[u(x)] = \frac{d}{du} f(u) \frac{du}{dx}$$

or

$$(f \circ u)'(x) = f'[u(x)]u'(x)$$

> ➡ **What This Says**   In Section 1.3 when we introduced composite functions, we talked about the "inner" and "outer" functions. With this terminology, the chain rule says that the derivative of the composite function $f[u(x)]$ is equal to the derivative of the inner function u times the derivative of the outer function f evaluated at the inner function.

❑

EXAMPLE 2   The chain rule applied to a power

Differentiate $y = (3x^4 - 7x + 5)^3$.

Solution

Here, the "inner" function is $u(x) = 3x^4 - 7x + 5$ and the "outer" function is u^3, so we have

$$
\begin{aligned}
y' &= (u^3)'[u(x)]' \\
&= (3u^2)(12x^3 - 7) \\
&= 3(3x^4 - 7x + 5)^2(12x^3 - 7)
\end{aligned}
$$

■

With a lot of work, you could have found the derivative in Example 2 without using the chain rule either by expanding the polynomial or by using the product rule. The answer would be the same but would involve much more algebra. The chain rule allows us to find derivatives that would otherwise be very difficult to handle.

EXAMPLE 3   Differentiation with quotient rule inside the chain rule

Differentiate $g(x) = \sqrt[4]{\dfrac{x}{1 - 3x}}$.

Solution

Write $g(x) = \left(\dfrac{x}{1 - 3x}\right)^{1/4} = u^{1/4}$, where $u = \dfrac{x}{1 - 3x}$ is the inner function and $u^{1/4}$ is the outer function. Then

$$g'(x) = (u^{1/4})'u'(x) = \tfrac{1}{4} u^{-3/4} u'(x)$$

and we have

$$
\begin{aligned}
g'(x) &= \frac{1}{4}\left(\frac{x}{1 - 3x}\right)^{-3/4}\left(\frac{x}{1 - 3x}\right)' \\
&= \frac{1}{4}\left(\frac{x}{1 - 3x}\right)^{-3/4}\left[\frac{(1 - 3x)(1) - x(-3)}{(1 - 3x)^2}\right] \qquad \text{Quotient rule}
\end{aligned}
$$

$$= \frac{1}{4}\left(\frac{x}{1-3x}\right)^{-3/4}\left[\frac{1}{(1-3x)^2}\right]$$

$$= \frac{1}{4x^{3/4}(1-3x)^{5/4}}$$ ∎

EXTENDED DERIVATIVE FORMULAS

The chain rule can be used to obtain generalized differentiation formulas for the standard functions, as displayed in the following box.

If u is a differentiable function of x, then

Extended Power Rule

$$\frac{d}{dx}u^n = nu^{n-1}\frac{du}{dx}$$

Extended Trigonometric Rules

$$\frac{d}{dx}\sin u = \cos u\frac{du}{dx} \qquad\qquad \frac{d}{dx}\cos u = -\sin u\frac{du}{dx}$$

$$\frac{d}{dx}\tan u = \sec^2 u\frac{du}{dx} \qquad\qquad \frac{d}{dx}\cot u = -\csc^2 u\frac{du}{dx}$$

$$\frac{d}{dx}\sec u = \sec u\tan u\frac{du}{dx} \qquad\qquad \frac{d}{dx}\csc u = -\csc u\cot u\frac{du}{dx}$$

Extended Exponential and Logarithmic Rules

$$\frac{d}{dx}e^u = e^u\frac{du}{dx} \qquad\qquad \frac{d}{dx}\ln u = \frac{1}{u}\frac{du}{dx}$$

EXAMPLE 4   Chain rule with a trigonometric function

Differentiate $f(x) = \sin(3x^2 + 5x - 7)$.

Solution

Think of this as $f(u) = \sin u$, where $u = 3x^2 + 5x - 7$, and apply the chain rule:

$$f'(x) = \cos(3x^2 + 5x - 7) \cdot (3x^2 + 5x - 7)'$$
$$= (6x + 5)\cos(3x^2 + 5x - 7)$$ ∎

EXAMPLE 5   Chain rule with other rules

Differentiate $g(x) = \cos x^2 + 5\left(\frac{3}{x} + 4\right)^6$.

Solution
$$\frac{dg}{dx} = \frac{d}{dx}\cos x^2 + 5\frac{d}{dx}(3x^{-1} + 4)^6$$
$$= -\sin x^2\frac{d}{dx}(x^2) + 5\left[6(3x^{-1} + 4)^5\frac{d}{dx}(3x^{-1} + 4)\right]$$
$$= (-\sin x^2)(2x) + 30(3x^{-1} + 4)^5(-3x^{-2})$$
$$= -2x\sin x^2 - 90x^{-2}(3x^{-1} + 4)^5$$ ∎

EXAMPLE 6   Extended power and cosine rules

Differentiate $y = \cos^4(3x + 1)^2$.

Solution

$$\frac{dy}{dx} = 4\cos^3(3x+1)^2 \frac{d}{dx}\cos(3x+1)^2 \qquad \text{Extended power rule}$$

$$= 4\cos^3(3x+1)^2 \cdot [-\sin(3x+1)^2] \cdot \frac{d}{dx}(3x+1)^2 \qquad \text{Extended cosine rule}$$

$$= -4\cos^3(3x+1)^2 \sin(3x+1)^2 \cdot 2(3x+1)(3) \qquad \text{Extended power rule}$$

$$= -24(3x+1)\cos^3(3x+1)^2 \sin(3x+1)^2 \qquad \blacksquare$$

EXAMPLE 7   Extended power rule inside quotient rule

Differentiate $p(x) = \dfrac{\tan 7x}{(1-4x)^5}$.

Solution

$$\frac{dp}{dx} = \frac{(1-4x)^5 \left[\dfrac{d}{dx}\tan 7x\right] - \tan 7x \left[\dfrac{d}{dx}(1-4x)^5\right]}{[(1-4x)^5]^2}$$

$$= \frac{(1-4x)^5(\sec^2 7x)\dfrac{d}{dx}(7x) - (\tan 7x)[5(1-4x)^4 \dfrac{d}{dx}(1-4x)]}{(1-4x)^{10}}$$

$$= \frac{(1-4x)^5(\sec^2 7x)(7) - (\tan 7x)(5)(1-4x)^4(-4)}{(1-4x)^{10}}$$

$$= \frac{(1-4x)^4[7(1-4x)\sec^2 7x + 20\tan 7x]}{(1-4x)^{10}}$$

$$= \frac{7(1-4x)\sec^2 7x + 20\tan 7x}{(1-4x)^6} \qquad \blacksquare$$

EXAMPLE 8   Extended exponential rule within product rule

Differentiate $e^{-3x}\sin x$.

Solution

Use the product rule:

$$\frac{d}{dx}[e^{-3x}\sin x] = e^{-3x}\left[\frac{d}{dx}(\sin x)\right] + \left[\frac{d}{dx}(e^{-3x})\right]\sin x \qquad \text{Product rule}$$

$$= e^{-3x}(\cos x) + [e^{-3x}(-3)]\sin x$$

$$= e^{-3x}(\cos x - 3\sin x) \qquad \blacksquare$$

EXAMPLE 9   Finding a horizontal tangent line

Find the x-coordinate of each point on the graph of

$$f(x) = x^2(4x+5)^3$$

where the tangent line is horizontal.

Solution

Because horizontal tangent lines have zero slope, we need to solve the equation $f'(x) = 0$. We find that

$$f'(x) = [x^2(4x+5)^3]'$$

$$= [x^2]'(4x+5)^3 + x^2[(4x+5)^3]' \qquad \text{Product rule}$$

$$= [2x](4x + 5)^3 + x^2[3(4x + 5)^2(4)] \qquad \textit{Extended power rule}$$

$$= 2x(4x + 5)^2[4x + 5 + 6x] \qquad \textit{Common factor}$$

$$= 2x(4x + 5)^2(10x + 5)$$

$$= 10x(4x + 5)^2(2x + 1)$$

From the factored form of the derivative, we see that $f'(x) = 0$ when $x = 0$, $x = -\frac{5}{4}$, and $x = -\frac{1}{2}$, so these are the x-coordinates of the points on the graph of f where horizontal tangent lines occur. ■

EXAMPLE 10   A modeling problem using the chain rule

An environmental study of a certain suburban community suggests that the average daily level of carbon monoxide in the air may be modeled by the formula

$$C(p) = \sqrt{0.5p^2 + 17}$$

parts per million when the population is p thousand. It is estimated that t years from now, the population of the community will be

$$p(t) = 3.1 + 0.1t^2$$

thousand. At what rate will the carbon monoxide level be changing with respect to time 3 years from now?

Solution

$$\frac{dC}{dt} = \frac{dC}{dp}\frac{dp}{dt} = \left[\frac{1}{2}(0.5p^2 + 17)^{-1/2}(0.5)(2p)\right][0.2t]$$

When $t = 3$, $p(3) = 3.1 + 0.1(3)^2 = 4$, so

$$\left.\frac{dC}{dt}\right|_{t=3} = \left[\frac{1}{2}(0.5 \cdot 4^2 + 17)^{-1/2}(4)\right][0.2(3)] = 0.24$$

The carbon monoxide level will be changing at the rate of 0.24 parts per million. It will be increasing because the sign of dC/dt is positive. ■

JUSTIFICATION OF THE CHAIN RULE

To get a better feel for why the chain rule is true, suppose x is changed by a small amount Δx. This will cause u to change by an amount Δu, which, in turn, will cause y to change by an amount Δy. *If Δu is not zero*, we can write

$$\frac{\Delta y}{\Delta x} = \frac{\Delta y}{\Delta u}\frac{\Delta u}{\Delta x}$$

By letting $\Delta x \to 0$, we force Δu to approach zero as well, since

$$\Delta u = \left(\frac{\Delta u}{\Delta x}\right)\Delta x \quad \text{so} \quad \lim_{\Delta x \to 0}\Delta u = \left(\frac{du}{dx}\right)(0) = 0$$

It follows that

$$\lim_{\Delta x \to 0}\frac{\Delta y}{\Delta x} = \left(\lim_{\Delta u \to 0}\frac{\Delta y}{\Delta u}\right)\left(\lim_{\Delta x \to 0}\frac{\Delta u}{\Delta x}\right)$$

or, equivalently,

$$\frac{dy}{dx} = \frac{dy}{du}\frac{du}{dx}$$

Unfortunately, there is a flaw in this "proof" of the chain rule. At the beginning we assumed that $\Delta u \neq 0$. However, it is theoretically possible for a small change in x to produce no change in u so that $\Delta u = 0$. This is the case that we consider in the proof in Appendix B.

Historical Note

A calculus book written by the famous mathematician G. H. Hardy (1877–1947) contained essentially this "incorrect" proof rather than the one given in Appendix B. It is even more remarkable that the error was not noticed until the fourth edition.

3.5 PROBLEM SET

A **1. WHAT DOES THIS SAY?** What is the chain rule?

2. WHAT DOES THIS SAY? When do you need to use the chain rule?

In Problems 3–8, use the chain rule to compute the derivative dy/dx and write your answer in terms of x only.

3. $y = u^2 + 1$; $u = 3x - 2$

4. $y = 2u^2 - u + 5$; $u = 1 - x^2$

5. $y = \dfrac{2}{u^2}$; $u = x^2 - 9$

6. $y = \cos u$; $u = x^2 + 7$

7. $y = u \tan u$; $u = 3x + \dfrac{6}{x}$

8. $y = u^2$; $u = \ln x$

Differentiate each function in Problems 9–12 with respect to the given variable of the function.

9. a. $g(u) = u^3$ **b.** $u(x) = x^2 + 1$
   c. $f(x) = (x^2 + 1)^3$

10. a. $g(u) = u^5$ **b.** $u(x) = 3x - 1$
   c. $f(x) = (3x - 1)^5$

11. a. $g(u) = u^7$ **b.** $u(x) = 5 - 8x - 12x^2$
   c. $f(x) = (5 - 8x - 12x^2)^7$

12. a. $g(u) = u^{15}$ **b.** $u(x) = 3x^2 + 5x - 7$
   c. $f(x) = (3x^2 + 5x - 7)^{15}$

In Problems 13–40, find the derivative of the given function.

13. $f(x) = (5x - 2)^5$
14. $f(x) = (x^4 - 7x)^{15}$
15. $f(x) = (3x^2 - 2x + 1)^4$
16. $f(x) = (3 - x^2 - x^4)^{11}$
17. $s(\theta) = \sin(4\theta + 2)$
18. $c(\theta) = \cos(5 - 3\theta)$
19. $f(x) = e^{-x^2 + 3x}$
20. $y = e^{x^3 - \pi}$
21. $y = e^{\sec x}$
22. $g(x) = e^{\sin x}$
23. $f(t) = \exp(t^2 + t + 5)$
24. $g(t) = t^2 e^{-t} + (\ln t)^2$
25. $g(x) = x \sin 5x$
26. $h(x) = \dfrac{\tan 3x}{x^2}$
27. $f(x) = \left(\dfrac{1}{1 - 2x}\right)^3$
28. $f(x) = \sqrt[3]{\dfrac{1}{2 - 3x}}$
29. $f(x) = xe^{1 - 2x}$
30. $g(x) = \ln(3x^4 + 5x)$
31. $p(x) = \sin x^2 \cos x^2$
32. $f(x) = \csc^2(\sqrt{x})$
33. $f(x) = x^3(2 - 3x)^2$
34. $f(x) = x^4(2 - x - x^2)^3$
35. $f(x) = \sqrt{\dfrac{x^2 + 3}{x^2 - 5}}$
36. $f(x) = \sqrt{\dfrac{2x^2 - 1}{3x^2 + 2}}$
37. $f(x) = \sqrt[3]{x + \sqrt{2x}}$
38. $g(x) = \ln(\ln x)$
39. $f(x) = \ln(\sin x + \cos x)$
40. $T(x) = \ln(\sec x + \tan x)$

Find the x-coordinate of each point in Problems 41–46 where the graph of the given function has a horizontal tangent line.

41. $f(x) = x\sqrt{1 - 3x}$
42. $g(x) = x^2(2x + 3)^2$
43. $q(x) = \dfrac{(x - 1)^2}{(x + 2)^3}$
44. $f(x) = (2x^2 - 7)^3$
45. $T(x) = x^2 e^{1 - 3x}$
46. $V(x) = \dfrac{\ln \sqrt{x}}{x^2}$

B **47.** The graphs of $u = g(x)$ and $y = f(u)$ are shown in Figure 3.29.

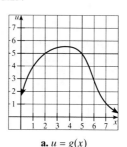 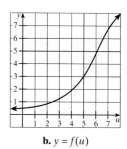

a. $u = g(x)$ **b.** $y = f(u)$

Figure 3.29 Find the slope of $y = f[g(x)]$.

a. Find the approximate value of u at $x = 2$. What is the slope of the tangent line at that point?

b. Find the approximate value of y at $x = 5$. What is the slope of the tangent line at that point?

c. Find the slope of $y = f[g(x)]$ at $x = 2$.

48. The graphs of $y = f(x)$ and $y = g(x)$ are shown in Figure 3.30.

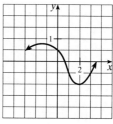 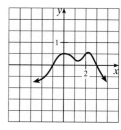

a. $y = f(x)$ **b.** $y = g(x)$

Figure 3.30 Problem 48

Let $h(x) = f[g(x)]$.
a. Estimate $h'(-1)$ **b.** $h'(1)$ **c.** $h'(3)$

49. Repeat Problem 48 for $h(x) = g[f(x)]$.

50. If $g(x) = f[f(x)]$, use the table to find the value of $g'(2)$.

x	0.0	1.0	2.0	3.0	4.0	5.0
$f(x)$	18.5	9.4	4.0	2.6	8.3	14.0

51. If $h(x) = f[g(x)]$, use the table to find the value of $h'(1)$.

x	0.0	1.0	2.0	3.0	4.0	5.0
$f(x)$	6.9	4.3	3.1	2.8	2.2	2.0
$g(x)$	0.8	2.0	2.5	1.8	0.9	0.4

52. Assume that a spherical snowball melts in such a way that its radius decreases at a constant rate (that is, the radius is a linear function of time). Suppose it begins as a sphere with radius 10 cm and takes 2 hours to disappear.

a. What is the rate of change of its volume after 1 hour? (Recall $V = \frac{4}{3}\pi r^3$.)

b. At what rate is its surface area changing after 1 hour? (Recall $S = 4\pi r^2$.)

53. It is estimated that t years from now, the population of a certain suburban community is modeled by the formula

$$p(t) = 20 - \frac{6}{t+1}$$

where $p(t)$ is in thousands of people. A separate environmental study indicates that the average daily level of carbon monoxide in the air will be

$$L(p) = 0.5\sqrt{p^2 + p + 58}$$

ppm when the population is p thousand. Find the rate at which the level of carbon monoxide will be changing with respect to time two years from now.

54. At a certain factory, the total cost of manufacturing q units during the daily production run is

$$C(q) = 0.2q^2 + q + 900$$

dollars. From experience, it has been determined that approximately

$$q(t) = t^2 + 100t$$

units are manufactured during the first t hours of a production run. Compute the rate at which the total manufacturing cost is changing with respect to time one hour after production begins.

55. An importer of Brazilian coffee estimates that local consumers will buy approximately

$$D(p) = \frac{4,374}{p^2}$$

pounds of the coffee per week when the price is p dollars per pound. It is estimated that t weeks from now, the price of Brazilian coffee will be

$$p(t) = 0.02t^2 + 0.1t + 6$$

dollars per pound. At what rate will the weekly demand for the coffee be changing with respect to time 10 weeks from now? Will the demand be increasing or decreasing?

56. When electric blenders are sold for p dollars apiece, local consumers will buy

$$D(p) = \frac{8,000}{p}$$

blenders per month. It is estimated that t months from now, the price of the blenders will be

$$p(t) = 0.04t^{3/2} + 15$$

dollars. Compute the rate at which the monthly demand for the blenders will be changing with respect to time 25 months from now. Will the demand be increasing or decreasing?

When a point source of light of luminous intensity K (candles) shines directly on a point on a surface s meters away, the illuminance on the surface is given by the formula $I = Ks^{-2}$. Use this formula to answer the questions in Problems 57–58. (Note that 1 lux = 1 candle/m².)

57. Suppose a person carrying a 20-candlepower light walks toward a wall in such a way that at time t (seconds) the distance to the wall is $s(t) = 28 - t^2$ meters.

a. How fast is the illuminance on the wall increasing when the person is 19 m from the wall?

b. How far is the person from the wall when the illuminance is changing at the rate of 1 lux/s?

58. A lamp of luminous intensity 40 candles is 20 m above the floor of a room and is being lowered at the constant rate of 2 m/s. At what rate will the illuminance at the point on the floor directly under the lamp be increasing when the lamp is 15 m above the floor? Your answer should be in lux/s rounded to the nearest hundredth.

59. To form a *simple pendulum*, a weight is attached to a rod that is then suspended by one end in such a way that it can swing freely in a vertical plane. Let θ be the angular displacement of the rod from the vertical, as shown in Figure 3.31.

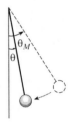

Figure 3.31 Problem 59

It can be shown that as long as the maximum displacement θ_M is small, it is reasonable to assume that $\theta = \theta_M \sin kt$ at time t, where k is a constant that depends on the length of the rod and θ_M is a constant. Show that

$$\frac{d^2\theta}{dt^2} + k^2\theta = 0$$

60. A lighthouse is located 2 km directly across the sea from a point O on the shoreline, as shown in Figure 3.32.

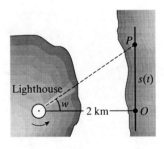

Figure 3.32 Problem 60

A beacon in the lighthouse makes 3 complete revolutions (that is, 6π radians) each minute, and during part of each revolution, the light sweeps across the face of a row of cliffs lining the shore.

a. Show that t minutes after it passes point O, the beam of light is at a point P located $s(t) = 2\tan(6\pi t)$ km from O.

b. How fast is the beam of light moving at the time it passes a point on the cliff that is 4 km from the lighthouse?

61. The average Fahrenheit temperature t hours after midnight in a certain city is modeled by the formula

$$T(t) = 58 + 17\sin\left(\frac{\pi t}{10} - \frac{5}{6}\right)$$

At what rate is the temperature changing with respect to time at 2 A.M.? Is it getting hotter or colder at that time?

62. In physics, it is shown that when an object is viewed at depth d under water from an angle of incidence θ, then refraction causes the apparent depth of the object to be

$$s(\theta) = \frac{3d\cos\theta}{\sqrt{7 + 9\cos^2\theta}}$$

(see Figure 3.33). At what rate is the apparent depth changing with respect to θ when $d = 2$ m and $\theta = \frac{\pi}{6}$?

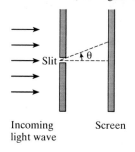

Figure 3.33 Light refraction

63. In the study of Frauenhofer diffraction in optics, a light beam of intensity I_0 from a source L passes through a narrow slit and is diffracted onto a screen (see Figure 3.34.)

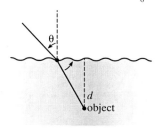

Figure 3.34 Optical diffraction

Experiments indicate that the intensity $I(\theta)$ of light on the screen depends on the diffraction angle θ shown in Figure 3.34 in such a way that

$$I(\beta) = I_0\left(\frac{\sin\beta}{\beta}\right)^2$$

where $\beta = \pi a\sin(\theta/\lambda)$, λ is the wavelength of the light, and a is a constant related to the width of the screen. Use the chain rule to find $dI/d\theta$, the rate of change of intensity with respect to θ.

64. A worker pushes a heavy crate across a warehouse floor at a constant velocity. If the crate weighs W pounds and the worker applies a force F at an angle θ, as shown in Figure 3.35, then

$$F(\theta) = \frac{\mu W\sec\theta}{1 + \mu\tan\theta}$$

where μ is a constant (the coefficient of friction). For the case where $W = 100$ lb and $\mu = 0.25$, find $\frac{dF}{d\theta}$ when $\theta = 27°$.

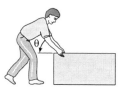

Figure 3.35 Pushing a crate with variable force

C 65. Using only the formula

$$\frac{d}{dx}\sin u = \cos u\frac{du}{dx}$$

and the identities $\cos x = \sin(\frac{\pi}{2} - x)$ and $\sin x = \cos(\frac{\pi}{2} - x)$, show that

$$\frac{d}{dx}\cos u = -\sin u\frac{du}{dx}$$

66. Let $g(x) = f[u(x)]$, where $u(-3) = 5$, $u'(-3) = 2$, $f(5) = 3$, and $f'(5) = -3$. Find an equation for the tangent line to the graph of g at the point where $x = -3$.

67. Let f be a function for which

$$f'(x) = \frac{1}{x^2 + 1}$$

a. If $g(x) = f(3x - 1)$, what is $g'(x)$?

b. If $h(x) = f\left(\frac{1}{x}\right)$, what is $h'(x)$?

68. Let f be a function for which $f(2) = -3$ and $f'(x) = \sqrt{x^2 + 5}$. If $g(x) = x^2 f\left(\frac{x}{x-1}\right)$, what is $g'(2)$?

69. a. If $F(x) = \ln|\cos x|$, show that $F'(x) = -\tan x$.

b. If $F(x) = \ln|\sec x + \tan x|$, show that $F'(x) = \sec x$.

70. If $\frac{df}{dx} = \frac{\sin x}{x}$ and $u(x) = \cot x$, what is $\frac{df}{du}$?

71. Use the chain rule to find

$$\frac{d}{dx}f'[f(x)] \quad \text{and} \quad \frac{d}{dx}f[f'(x)]$$

assuming these derivatives exist.

72. Show that if a particle moves along a straight line with position $s(t)$ and velocity $v(t)$, then its acceleration satisfies

$$a(t) = v(t)\frac{dv}{ds}$$

Use this formula to find $\frac{dv}{ds}$ in the case where

$$s(t) = -2t^3 + 4t^2 + t - 3$$

3.6   Implicit Differentiation

IN THIS SECTION   general procedure for implicit differentiation, derivative formulas for the inverse trigonometric functions, logarithmic differentiation

GENERAL PROCEDURE FOR IMPLICIT DIFFERENTIATION

The equation $y = \sqrt{1 - x^2}$ **explicitly** defines $y = f(x) = \sqrt{1 - x^2}$ as a function of x for $-1 \leq x \leq 1$, but the same function can also be defined **implicitly** by the equation $x^2 + y^2 = 1$, as long as we restrict y by $0 \leq y \leq 1$ so that the vertical line test is satisfied. To find the derivative of the explicit form, we use the chain rule:

$$\frac{d}{dx}\sqrt{1 - x^2} = \frac{d}{dx}(1 - x^2)^{1/2} = \frac{1}{2}(1 - x^2)^{-1/2}(-2x) = \frac{-x}{\sqrt{1 - x^2}}$$

To obtain the derivative of the same function in its implicit form, we simply differentiate across the equation $x^2 + y^2 = 1$, remembering that y is a function of x:

$$\frac{d}{dx}(x^2 + y^2) = \frac{d}{dx}(1) \qquad \text{Derivative of both sides}$$

$$2x + 2y\frac{dy}{dx} = 0 \qquad \text{Chain rule for the derivative of } y$$

$$\frac{dy}{dx} = -\frac{x}{y} \qquad \text{Solve for } \frac{dy}{dx}.$$

$$= -\frac{x}{\sqrt{1 - x^2}} \qquad \text{Write as a function of } x, \text{ if desired.}$$

The procedure we have just illustrated is called **implicit differentiation**. Our illustrative example was simple, but consider a differentiable function $y = f(x)$ defined by the equation

$$x^2y^3 - 6 = 5y^3 + x$$

Implicit differentiation tells us that

$$x^2\frac{d}{dx}(y^3) + y^3\frac{d}{dx}(x^2) - \frac{d}{dx}(6) = 5\frac{d}{dx}(y^3) + \frac{d}{dx}(x)$$

$$x^2\left(3y^2\frac{dy}{dx}\right) + y^3(2x) - 0 = 5\left(3y^2\frac{dy}{dx}\right) + 1$$

$$(3x^2y^3 - 15y^2)\frac{dy}{dx} = 1 - 2xy^3$$

$$\frac{dy}{dx} = \frac{1 - 2xy^3}{3x^2y^2 - 15y^2}$$

You may think that we are not finished since the derivative involves both x and y, but for many applications, that is enough as we may know both x and y simultaneously at a point. In this example, we could have found y as an explicit function of x, namely

$$y = \left(\frac{x + 6}{x^2 - 5}\right)^{1/3}$$

and then found dy/dx by the chain rule.

Now consider a differentiable function $y = f(x)$ defined by the equation

$$x^2y + 2y^3 = 3x + 2y$$

Finding y as an explicit function of x is very difficult in this case, and it is not at all hard to imagine similar situations where solving for y in terms of x would be impossible or at least not worth the effort. We begin our work with implicit differentiation by using it to find the slope of a tangent line at a point on a circle.

EXAMPLE 1   Slope of a tangent line using implicit differentiation

Find the slope of the tangent line to the circle $x^2 + y^2 = 10$ at the point $P(-1, 3)$.

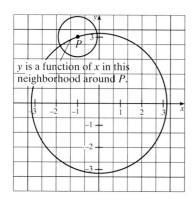

Figure 3.36 Graph of $x^2 + y^2 = 10$ showing a neighborhood about $P(-1, 3)$

Solution

We recognize the graph of $x^2 + y^2 = 10$ as not being the graph of a function. However, if we look at a small neighborhood around the point $(-1, 3)$, as shown in Figure 3.36, we see that this part of the graph *does pass the vertical line test* for functions. Thus, the required slope can be found by evaluating the derivative dy/dx at $(-1, 3)$. Instead of solving for y and finding the derivative, we *take the derivative of both sides of the equation*:

$$x^2 + y^2 = 10 \qquad \text{Given equation}$$

$$\frac{d}{dx}(x^2 + y^2) = \frac{d}{dx}(10) \qquad \text{Derivative of both sides}$$

$$2x + 2y\frac{dy}{dx} = 0 \qquad \text{Do not forget that } y \text{ is a function of } x.$$

$$\frac{dy}{dx} = -\frac{x}{y} \qquad \text{Solve the equation for } \frac{dy}{dx}.$$

The slope of the tangent line at $P(-1, 3)$ is

$$\left.\frac{dy}{dx}\right|_P = \left.-\frac{x}{y}\right|_{(-1,3)} = -\frac{-1}{3} = \frac{1}{3} \qquad \blacksquare$$

Here is a general description of the procedure for implicit differentiation.

Procedure for Implicit Differentiation

Suppose an equation defines y implicitly as a differentiable function of x. To find $\frac{dy}{dx}$:

Step 1. Differentiate both sides of the equation with respect to x. Remember that y is really a function of x for part of the curve and use the chain rule when differentiating terms containing y.

Step 2. Solve the differentiated equation algebraically for $\frac{dy}{dx}$.   ■

EXAMPLE 2   Implicit differentiation

If $y = f(x)$ is a differentiable function of x such that

$$x^2 y + 2y^3 = 3x + 2y$$

find $\frac{dy}{dx}$.

Solution

The process is to differentiate both sides of the given equation with respect to x. To help remember that y is a function of x, replace y by the symbol $y(x)$:

$$x^2 y(x) + 2[y(x)]^3 = 3x + 2y(x)$$

Differentiate both sides of this equation term by term with respect to x:

$$\frac{d}{dx}\left\{x^2 y(x) + 2[y(x)]^3\right\} = \frac{d}{dx}\{3x + 2y(x)\}$$

$$\frac{d}{dx}[x^2 y(x)] + 2\frac{d}{dx}[y(x)]^3 = 3\frac{d}{dx}x + 2\frac{d}{dx}y(x)$$

$$\underbrace{x^2\frac{d}{dx}y(x) + y(x)\frac{d}{dx}x^2}_{\text{Product rule}} + 2\underbrace{\left\{3[y(x)]^2\frac{d}{dx}y(x)\right\}}_{\text{Extended power rule}} = 3 + 2\frac{d}{dx}y(x)$$

$$x^2\frac{d}{dx}y(x) + 2xy(x) + 6[y(x)]^2\frac{d}{dx}y(x) = 3 + 2\frac{d}{dx}y(x)$$

Now replace $y(x)$ by y and $\frac{d}{dx}y(x)$ by $\frac{dy}{dx}$ and rewrite the equation:

$$x^2\frac{dy}{dx} + 2xy + 6y^2\frac{dy}{dx} = 3 + 2\frac{dy}{dx}$$

Finally, solve this equation for $\frac{dy}{dx}$:

$$x^2\frac{dy}{dx} + 6y^2\frac{dy}{dx} - 2\frac{dy}{dx} = 3 - 2xy$$

$$(x^2 + 6y^2 - 2)\frac{dy}{dx} = 3 - 2xy$$

$$\frac{dy}{dx} = \frac{3 - 2xy}{x^2 + 6y^2 - 2}$$

Notice that the formula for dy/dx contains both the independent variable x and the dependent variable y. This is usual when derivatives are computed implicitly.   ■

WARNING   It is important to realize that implicit differentiation is a technique for finding dy/dx that is valid only if y is a differentiable function of x, and careless application of the technique can lead to errors. For example, there is clearly no real-valued function $y = f(x)$ that satisfies the equation $x^2 + y^2 = -1$, yet formal application of implicit differentiation yields the "derivative" $dy/dx = -x/y$. To be able to evaluate this "derivative," we must find some values of x and y for which $x^2 + y^2 = -1$. Because no such values exist, the derivative does not exist.

In Example 2 it was suggested that you temporarily replace y by $y(x)$, so you would not forget to use the chain rule when first learning implicit differentiation. In the following example, we eliminate this unnecessary step and differentiate the given equation directly. Just keep in mind that y is really a function of x and remember to use the chain rule (or extended power rule) when it is appropriate.

EXAMPLE 3   Implicit differentiation; simplified notation

Find $\dfrac{dy}{dx}$ if y is a differentiable function of x that satisfies

$$\sin(x^2 + y) = y^2(3x + 1)$$

Solution

There is no obvious way to solve the given equation explicitly for y. Differentiate implicitly to obtain

$$\frac{d}{dx}[\sin(x^2 + y)] = \frac{d}{dx}[y^2(3x + 1)]$$

$$\underbrace{\cos(x^2 + y)\frac{d}{dx}(x^2 + y)}_{\text{Chain rule}} = \underbrace{y^2 \frac{d}{dx}(3x + 1) + (3x + 1)\frac{d}{dx}y^2}_{\text{Product rule}}$$

$$\cos(x^2 + y)\left(2x + \frac{dy}{dx}\right) = y^2(3) + (3x + 1)\left(2y\frac{dy}{dx}\right)$$

Finally, solve for $\dfrac{dy}{dx}$:

$$2x\cos(x^2 + y) + \cos(x^2 + y)\frac{dy}{dx} = 3y^2 + 2y(3x + 1)\frac{dy}{dx}$$

$$[\cos(x^2 + y) - 2y(3x + 1)]\frac{dy}{dx} = 3y^2 - 2x\cos(x^2 + y)$$

$$\frac{dy}{dx} = \frac{3y^2 - 2x\cos(x^2 + y)}{\cos(x^2 + y) - 2y(3x + 1)}$$ ∎

EXAMPLE 4 Slope of a tangent line using implicit differentiation

Find the slope of a line tangent to the circle $x^2 + y^2 = 5x + 4y$ at the point $P(5, 4)$.

Solution

The slope of a curve $y = f(x)$ is $\dfrac{dy}{dx}$, which we find implicitly.

$$x^2 + y^2 = 5x + 4y$$

$$\frac{d}{dx}(x^2 + y^2) = \frac{d}{dx}(5x + 4y)$$

$$2x + 2y\frac{dy}{dx} = 5 + 4\frac{dy}{dx}$$

$$2y\frac{dy}{dx} - 4\frac{dy}{dx} = 5 - 2x$$

$$(2y - 4)\frac{dy}{dx} = 5 - 2x$$

$$\frac{dy}{dx} = \frac{5 - 2x}{2y - 4}$$

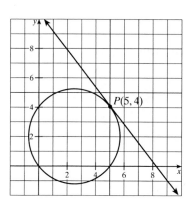

Figure 3.37 Graph of circle and tangent line

At $(5, 4)$, the slope of the tangent line is

$$\frac{dy}{dx}\bigg|_{(5,4)} = \frac{5 - 2x}{2y - 4}\bigg|_{(5,4)} = \frac{5 - 2(5)}{2(4) - 4} = -\frac{5}{4}$$

Note that the expression is undefined at $y = 2$; this makes sense when you see that the tangent line is vertical there. Look at the graph in Figure 3.37 and see whether you should exclude any other values. ∎

EXAMPLE 5 Second derivative by implicit differentiation

Find $\dfrac{d^2y}{dx^2}$ if $x^2 + y^2 = 10$.

Solution

In Example 1 we found (implicitly) that $\dfrac{dy}{dx} = -\dfrac{x}{y}$. Thus,

$$\frac{d^2y}{dx^2} = \frac{d}{dx}\left(\frac{-x}{y}\right) = \underbrace{\frac{y\frac{d}{dx}(-x) - (-x)\frac{d}{dx}y}{y^2}}_{\text{Quotient rule}} = \frac{-y + x\frac{dy}{dx}}{y^2}$$

Note that the expression for the second derivative contains the first derivative dy/dx. To simplify the answer, substitute the algebraic expression previously found for dy/dx:

$$\frac{-y + x\dfrac{dy}{dx}}{y^2} = \frac{-y + x\left(\dfrac{-x}{y}\right)}{y^2} \qquad \text{Substitute } \frac{dy}{dx} = -\frac{x}{y}.$$

$$= \frac{-y^2 - x^2}{y^3}$$

$$= \frac{-(x^2 + y^2)}{y^3}$$

$$= \frac{-10}{y^3} \qquad \text{Substitute } x^2 + y^2 = 10.$$

Thus, $\dfrac{d^2y}{dx^2} = \dfrac{-10}{y^3}$. ∎

In Section 3.3, we found the derivative of $f(x) = e^x$ (Theorem 3.8). This derivative is more easily found using implicit differentiation, as shown in the following example.

EXAMPLE 6   Derivative rule for the natural exponential

Show that

$$\frac{d}{dx}(e^x) = e^x$$

Solution

Let $v = e^x$, so that $x = \ln v$. Then

$$\frac{d}{dx}(x) = \frac{d}{dx}(\ln v) \qquad \text{Derivative of both sides of } x = \ln v$$

$$1 = \frac{1}{v}\frac{dv}{dx} \qquad \text{Implicit differentiation}$$

$$v = \frac{dv}{dx}$$

$$e^x = \frac{dv}{dx} = \frac{d}{dx}(e^x) \qquad \text{Because } v = e^x$$ ∎

Implicit differentiation is a valuable theoretical tool. For example, in Section 3.2 we proved the power rule for the case where the exponent is an integer. Implicit differentiation now allows us to extend the proof for all real exponents.

EXAMPLE 7   Proof of power rule for real (rational and irrational) exponents

Prove that $\dfrac{d}{dx}(x^r) = rx^{r-1}$ holds for all real numbers r if $x > 0$.

Solution

If $y = x^r$, then $y = e^{r \ln x}$, so that

$$\ln y = r \ln x \qquad \text{Definition of exponent}$$

$$\frac{1}{y}\frac{dy}{dx} = r\left(\frac{1}{x}\right) \qquad \text{Implicit differentiation}$$

$$\frac{dy}{dx} = y\left(\frac{r}{x}\right) \qquad \text{Solve for } \frac{dy}{dx}.$$

$$= x^r\left(\frac{r}{x}\right) \qquad \text{Substitute } y = x^r.$$

$$= rx^{r-1} \qquad \text{Property of exponents} \qquad \blacksquare$$

Notice in Example 7 that $y = x^r = e^{r \ln x}$ is differentiable because it is defined as the composition of the differentiable functions $y = e^u$ and $u = r \ln x$.

DERIVATIVE FORMULAS FOR THE INVERSE TRIGONOMETRIC FUNCTIONS

Next, we will use implicit differentiation to obtain differentiation formulas for the six inverse trigonometric functions. Note that these derivatives are not inverse trigonometric functions or even trigonometric functions, but are instead rational functions or roots of rational functions. In fact, the usefulness of inverse trigonometric functions in many areas is related to the simplicity of their derivatives.

THEOREM 3.11   Differentiation formulas for six inverse trigonometric functions

If u is a differentiable function of x, then

$$\frac{d}{dx}(\sin^{-1} u) = \frac{1}{\sqrt{1 - u^2}}\frac{du}{dx} \qquad\qquad \frac{d}{dx}(\cos^{-1} u) = \frac{-1}{\sqrt{1 - u^2}}\frac{du}{dx}$$

$$\frac{d}{dx}(\tan^{-1} u) = \frac{1}{1 + u^2}\frac{du}{dx} \qquad\qquad \frac{d}{dx}(\cot^{-1} u) = \frac{-1}{1 + u^2}\frac{du}{dx}$$

$$\frac{d}{dx}(\sec^{-1} u) = \frac{1}{|u|\sqrt{u^2 - 1}}\frac{du}{dx} \qquad\qquad \frac{d}{dx}(\csc^{-1} u) = \frac{-1}{|u|\sqrt{u^2 - 1}}\frac{du}{dx}$$

WARNING Note that the derivative of each inverse trigonometric function $y = \cos^{-1} x$, $y = \cot^{-1} x$, and $y = \csc^{-1} x$ is the opposite of the derivative of the corresponding inverse cofunction $y = \sin^{-1} x$, $y = \tan^{-1} x$, and $y = \sec^{-1} x$.

Proof   We will prove the first formula and leave the others as problems. Let $\alpha = \sin^{-1} x$, so $x = \sin \alpha$. Because the sine function is one-to-one and differentiable on $[-\pi/2, \pi/2]$, the inverse sine function is also differentiable. To find its derivative, we proceed implicitly:

$$\sin \alpha = x$$

$$\frac{d}{dx}(\sin \alpha) = \frac{d}{dx}(x)$$

$$\cos \alpha \frac{d\alpha}{dx} = 1$$

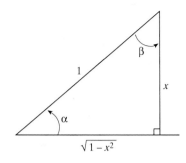

Figure 3.38 $\sin\alpha = x$ and $\cos\alpha = \sqrt{1-x^2}$

Since $-\frac{\pi}{2} \le \alpha \le \frac{\pi}{2}$, $\cos\alpha \ge 0$, so

$$\frac{d\alpha}{dx} = \frac{1}{\cos\alpha} = \frac{1}{\sqrt{1-\sin^2\alpha}} = \frac{1}{\sqrt{1-x^2}}$$

Note the reference triangle in Figure 3.38.

If u is a differentiable function of x, then the chain rule gives

$$\frac{d}{dx}(\sin^{-1}u) = \frac{d}{dx}(\sin^{-1}u)\frac{du}{dx} = \frac{1}{\sqrt{1-u^2}}\frac{du}{dx}$$

EXAMPLE 8   **Derivatives involving inverse trigonometric functions**

Differentiate each of the following functions.

a. $f(x) = \tan^{-1}\sqrt{x}$ **b.** $g(t) = \sin^{-1}(1-t)$ **c.** $h(x) = \sec^{-1}e^{2x}$

Solution

a. Let $u = \sqrt{x}$ in the formula for $\dfrac{d}{dx}(\tan^{-1}u)$:

$$f'(x) = \frac{d}{dx}(\tan^{-1}\sqrt{x})$$

$$= \frac{1}{1+(\sqrt{x})^2}\frac{d}{dx}(\sqrt{x}) = \frac{1}{1+x}\left(\frac{1}{2}\frac{1}{\sqrt{x}}\right) = \frac{1}{2\sqrt{x}(1+x)}$$

b. Let $u = (1-t)$:

$$g'(t) = \frac{d}{dt}\left[\sin^{-1}(1-t)\right]$$

$$= \frac{1}{\sqrt{1-(1-t)^2}}\frac{d}{dt}(1-t) = \frac{-1}{\sqrt{1-(1-t)^2}} = \frac{-1}{\sqrt{2t-t^2}}$$

c. Let $u = e^{2x}$:

$$h'(x) = \frac{d}{dx}\left[\sec^{-1}e^{2x}\right] = \frac{1}{\left|e^{2x}\right|\sqrt{(e^{2x})^2-1}}\frac{d}{dx}(e^{2x})$$

$$= \frac{1}{e^{2x}\sqrt{e^{4x}-1}}(2e^{2x}) = \frac{2}{\sqrt{e^{4x}-1}}$$

The derivatives of b^u and $\log_b u$ for a differentiable function $u = u(x)$ and a base b other than e can be obtained using the chain rule and the change-of-base formulas from Chapter 2. We summarize the results in the following theorem.

THEOREM 3.12   **Derivatives of exponential and logarithmic functions with base b**

Let u be a differentiable function of x and b be a positive number (other than 1). Then

$$\frac{d}{dx}b^u = (\ln b)b^u\frac{du}{dx}$$

$$\frac{d}{dx}(\log_b u) = \frac{1}{\ln b}\cdot\frac{1}{u}\frac{du}{dx}$$

WARNING $\dfrac{d}{dx}b^u \ne ub^{u-1}\dfrac{du}{dx}$ since b^u is a constant to a variable power, not a variable to a constant power.

Proof   Because $b^u = e^{u\ln b}$, we can apply the chain rule as follows:

$$\frac{d}{dx}b^u = \frac{d}{dx}(e^{u\ln b}) = e^{u\ln b}\frac{d}{dx}(u\ln b) = e^{u\ln b}\left(\ln b\frac{du}{dx}\right) = (\ln b)b^u\frac{du}{dx}$$

To differentiate the logarithm, recall the change-of-base formula $\log_b u = \dfrac{\ln u}{\ln b}$ so that

$$\frac{d}{dx}\log_b u = \frac{d}{dx}\left(\frac{\ln u}{\ln b}\right) = \frac{1}{\ln b}\cdot\frac{1}{u}\frac{du}{dx}$$

➡ **What This Says** The derivatives of b^x and $\log_b x$ are the same as the derivatives of e^x and $\ln x$, respectively, except for a factor of $\ln b$ that appears as a multiplier in the formula

$$\frac{d}{dx}(b^x) = (\ln b)b^x$$

and as a divisor in the formula

$$\frac{d}{dx}(\log_b x) = \frac{1}{(\ln b)x}$$

EXAMPLE 9 **Derivative of an exponential function with base $b \neq e$**

Differentiate $f(x) = x(2^{1-x})$.

Solution

Apply the product rule:

$$f'(x) = \frac{d}{dx}(x2^{1-x}) = x\frac{d}{dx}(2^{1-x}) + 2^{1-x}\frac{d}{dx}(x)$$
$$= x(\ln 2)(2^{1-x})(-1) + 2^{1-x}(1) = 2^{1-x}(1 - x\ln 2)$$ ■

The following theorem will prove useful in Chapter 5.

THEOREM 3.13 **Derivative of $\ln|u|$**

If $f(x) = \ln|x|$, $x \neq 0$, then $f'(x) = \frac{1}{x}$. Also, if u is a differentiable function of x, then

$$\frac{d}{dx}\ln|u| = \frac{1}{u}\frac{du}{dx}$$

Proof Using the definition of absolute value,

$$f(x) = \begin{cases} \ln x & \text{if } x > 0 \\ \ln(-x) & \text{if } x < 0 \end{cases}$$

so

$$f'(x) = \begin{cases} \dfrac{1}{x} & \text{if } x > 0 \\ \dfrac{1}{-x}(-1) = \dfrac{1}{x} & \text{if } x < 0 \end{cases}$$

Thus, $f'(x) = \frac{1}{x}$ for all $x \neq 0$.

The second part of the theorem (for u, a differentiable function of x) follows from the chain rule. ❑

LOGARITHMIC DIFFERENTIATION

Logarithmic differentiation is a procedure in which logarithms are used to trade the task of differentiating products and quotients for that of differentiating sums and differences. It is especially valuable as a means for handling complicated product or quotient functions and exponential functions where variables appear in both the base and the exponent.

EXAMPLE 10   **Logarithmic differentiation**

Find the derivative of $y = \dfrac{e^{2x}(2x - 1)^6}{(x^3 + 5)^2(4 - 7x)}$ if $y > 0$.

Solution

The procedure called logarithmic differentiation requires that we first take the logarithm of both sides and then apply properties of logarithms before attempting to take the derivative.

$$y = \frac{e^{2x}(2x - 1)^6}{(x^3 + 5)^2(4 - 7x)}$$

$$\ln y = \ln\left[\frac{e^{2x}(2x - 1)^6}{(x^3 + 5)^2(4 - 7x)}\right]$$

$$= \ln e^{2x} + \ln(2x - 1)^6 - \ln(x^3 + 5)^2 - \ln(4 - 7x)$$

$$= 2x + 6\ln(2x - 1) - 2\ln(x^3 + 5) - \ln(4 - 7x)$$

Next, differentiate both sides with respect to x and then solve for $\dfrac{dy}{dx}$:

$$\frac{1}{y}\frac{dy}{dx} = 2 + 6\left[\frac{1}{2x - 1}(2)\right] - 2\left[\frac{1}{x^3 + 5}(3x^2)\right] - \left[\frac{1}{4 - 7x}(-7)\right]$$

$$\frac{dy}{dx} = y\left[2 + \frac{12}{2x - 1} - \frac{6x^2}{x^3 + 5} + \frac{7}{4 - 7x}\right]$$

This is the derivative in terms of x and y. If we want the derivative in terms of x alone, we can substitute the expression for y:

$$\frac{dy}{dx} = \frac{e^{2x}(2x - 1)^6}{(x^3 + 5)^2(4 - 7x)}\left[2 + \frac{12}{2x - 1} - \frac{6x^2}{x^3 + 5} + \frac{7}{4 - 7x}\right] \qquad \blacksquare$$

EXAMPLE 11   **Derivative with variables in both the base and the exponent**

Find $\dfrac{dy}{dx}$, where $y = (x + 1)^{2x}$.

Solution $y = (x + 1)^{2x}$

$$\ln y = \ln\left[(x + 1)^{2x}\right] = 2x\ln(x + 1)$$

Differentiate both sides of this equation:

$$\frac{1}{y}\frac{dy}{dx} = 2x\left\{\frac{d}{dx}[\ln(x + 1)]\right\} + \left[\frac{d}{dx}(2x)\right]\ln(x + 1) \qquad \text{Product rule}$$

$$= 2x\left[\frac{1}{x + 1}(1)\right] + 2\ln(x + 1)$$

$$= \frac{2x}{x + 1} + 2\ln(x + 1)$$

Finally, multiply both sides by $y = (x + 1)^{2x}$:

$$\frac{dy}{dx} = \left[\frac{2x}{x + 1} + 2\ln(x + 1)\right](x + 1)^{2x} \qquad \blacksquare$$

3.6 PROBLEM SET

A *Find $\dfrac{dy}{dx}$ by implicit differentiation in Problems 1–14.*

1. $x^2 + y^2 = 25$

2. $x^2 + y = x^3 + y^3$

3. $xy = 25$

4. $xy(2x + 3y) = 2$

5. $x^2 + 3xy + y^2 = 15$

6. $x^3 + y^3 = x + y$

7. $\dfrac{1}{y} + \dfrac{1}{x} = 1$

8. $(2x + 3y)^2 = 10$

9. $\sin(x + y) = x - y$

10. $\tan \dfrac{x}{y} = y$

11. $\cos xy = 1 - x^2$

12. $e^{xy} + 1 = x^2$

13. $\ln(xy) = e^{2x}$

14. $e^{xy} + \ln y^2 = x$

In Problems 15–18, find $\dfrac{dy}{dx}$ in two ways:

a. By implicit differentiation of the equation

b. By differentiating an explicit formula for y

15. $x^2 + y^3 = 12$

16. $xy + 2y = x^2$

17. $x + \dfrac{1}{y} = 5$

18. $xy - x = y + 2$

Find the derivative $\dfrac{dy}{dx}$ in Problems 19–32.

19. $y = \sin^{-1}(2x + 1)$

20. $y = \cos^{-1}(4x + 3)$

21. $y = \tan^{-1}\sqrt{x^2 + 1}$

22. $y = \cot^{-1} x^2$

23. $y = (\sin^{-1} 2x)^3$

24. $y = (\tan^{-1} x^2)^4$

25. $y = \sec^{-1}(e^{-x})$

26. $y = \ln \left| \sin^{-1} x \right|$

27. $y = \tan^{-1}\left(\dfrac{1}{x}\right)$

28. $y = \cos^{-1}(\sin x)$, $\sin x \geq 0$

29. $y = \sin^{-1}(\cos x)$, $\cos x \geq 0$

30. $y = \ln[\sin^{-1}(e^x)]$

31. $x \sin^{-1} y + y \tan^{-1} x = x$

32. $\sin^{-1} y + y = 2xy$

In Problems 33–38, find an equation of the tangent line to the graph of each equation at the prescribed point.

33. $x^2 + y^2 = 13$ at $(-2, 3)$

34. $x^3 + y^3 = y + 21$ at $(3, -2)$

35. $\sin(x - y) = xy$ at $(0, \pi)$

36. $3^x + \log_2(xy) = 10$ at $(2, 1)$

37. $x \tan^{-1} y = x^2 + y$ at $(0, 0)$

38. $\sin^{-1}(xy) + \dfrac{\pi}{2} = \cos^{-1} y$ at $(1, 0)$

Find the slope of the tangent line to the graph at the points indicated in Problems 39–42.

39. bifolium:
$(x^2 + y^2)^2 = 4x^2 y$
at $(1, 1)$

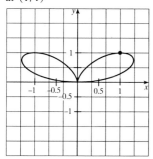

40. lemniscate of Bernoulli:
$(x^2 + y^2)^2 = \dfrac{25}{3}(x^2 - y^2)$
at $(2, 1)$

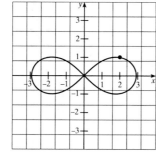

41. folium of Descartes:
$x^3 + y^3 - \dfrac{9}{2}xy = 0$
at $(2, 1)$

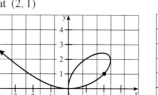

42. cissoid of Diocles:
$y^2(6 - x) = x^3$ at $(3, 3)$

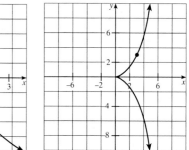

43. Find an equation of the normal line to the curve $x^2 + 2xy = y^3$ at $(1, -1)$.

44. Find an equation of the normal line to the curve $x^2\sqrt{y - 2} = y^2 - 3x - 5$ at $(1, 3)$.

Use implicit differentiation to find the second derivative y'' of the functions given in Problems 45–46.

45. $7x + 5y^2 = 1$

46. $x^2 + 2y^3 = 4$

B 47. **Interpretation Problem** Compare and contrast the derivatives of the following functions:

  a. $y = x^2$ b. $y = 2^x$ c. $y = e^x$ d. $y = x^e$

48. **Interpretation Problem** Compare and contrast the derivatives of the following functions:

  a. $y = \log x$ b. $y = \ln x$

49. **Interpretation Problem** Discuss logarithmic differentiation.

Use logarithmic differentiation in Problems 50–55 to find dy/dx. You may express your answer in terms of both x and y, and you do not need to simplify the resulting rational expressions.

50. $y = \sqrt[18]{(x^{10} + 1)^3 (x^7 - 3)^8}$

51. $y = \dfrac{(2x - 1)^5}{\sqrt{x - 9}(x + 3)^2}$

52. $y = \dfrac{e^{2x}}{(x^2 - 3)^2 \ln \sqrt{x}}$

53. $y = \dfrac{e^{3x^2}}{(x^3 + 1)^2 (4x - 7)^{-2}}$

54. $y = x^x$

55. $y = x^{\ln \sqrt{x}}$

56. Let $\dfrac{u^2}{a^2} + \dfrac{v^2}{b^2} = 1$, where a and b are nonzero constants. Find

  a. $\dfrac{du}{dv}$ b. $\dfrac{dv}{du}$

57. Show that the tangent line at the point (a, b) on the curve whose equation is $2x^2 + 3xy + y^2 = -2$ is horizontal if $4a + 3b = 0$. Find two such points on the curve.

58. Find two points on the curve whose equation is $x^2 - 3xy + 2y^2 = -2$, where the tangent line is vertical.

59. Let g be a differentiable function of x that satisfies $g(x) < 0$ and $x^2 + g^2(x) = 10$ for all x.

  a. Use implicit differentiation to show that $\dfrac{dg}{dx} = \dfrac{-x}{g(x)}$.

b. Show that $g(x) = -\sqrt{10 - x^2}$ satisfies the given requirements. Then use the chain rule to verify that

$$\frac{dg}{dx} = \frac{-x}{g(x)}$$

60. Find the equation of the tangent line and the normal line to the curve

$$x^3 + y^3 = 2Axy$$

at the point (A, A), where A is a nonzero constant.

61. Counterexample Problem

a. If $x^2 + y^2 = 6y - 10$ and $\dfrac{dy}{dx}$ exists, show that $\dfrac{dy}{dx} = \dfrac{x}{3 - y}$.

b. Show that there are no real numbers x, y that satisfy the equation $x^2 + y^2 = 6y - 10$.

c. What can you conclude from the result found in part **a** in light of the observation in part **b**?

62. Find all points on the lemniscate

$$(x^2 + y^2)^2 = 4(x^2 - y^2)$$

where the tangent line is horizontal. (See Figure 3.39.)

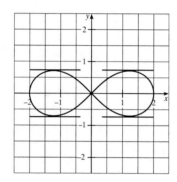

Figure 3.39   Lemniscate $(x^2 + y^2)^2 = 4(x^2 - y^2)$

63. Find all points on the cardioid

$$x^2 + y^2 = \sqrt{x^2 + y^2} + x$$

where the tangent line is vertical. (See Figure 3.40)

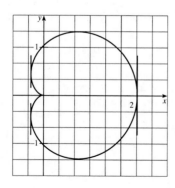

Figure 3.40   Cardioid $x^2 + y^2 = \sqrt{x^2 + y^2} + x$

64. The tangent line to the curve $x^{2/3} + y^{2/3} = 8$ at the point $(8, 8)$ and the coordinate axes form a triangle, as shown in Figure 3.41. What is the area of this triangle?

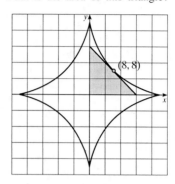

Figure 3.41   Graph of $x^{2/3} + y^{2/3} = 8$

65. Modeling Problem   A worker stands 4 m from a hoist being raised at the rate of 2 m/s, as shown in Figure 3.42. Model the worker's angle of sight θ using an inverse trigonometric function, and then determine how fast θ is changing at the instant when the hoist is 1.5 m above eye level.

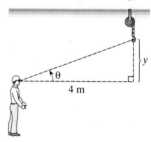

Figure 3.42   Modeling an angle of elevation

66. Find two differentiable functions f that satisfy the equation

$$x - [f(x)]^2 = 9$$

Give the explicit form of each function, and sketch its graph.

67. Show that the tangent line to the ellipse

$$\frac{x^2}{a^2} + \frac{y^2}{b^2} = 1$$

at the point (x_0, y_0) is

$$\frac{x_0 x}{a^2} + \frac{y_0 y}{b^2} = 1$$

(See Figure 3.43.)

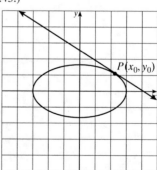

Figure 3.43   Ellipse $\dfrac{x^2}{a^2} + \dfrac{y^2}{b^2} = 1$

68. Find an equation of the tangent line to the hyperbola $\dfrac{x^2}{a^2} - \dfrac{y^2}{b^2} = 1$ at the point (x_0, y_0). (See Figure 3.44.)

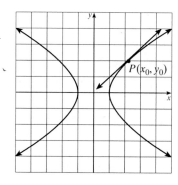

Figure 3.44   Hyperbola $\dfrac{x^2}{a^2} - \dfrac{y^2}{b^2} = 1$

69. Use implicit differentiation to find the second derivative y'', where y is a differentiable function of x that satisfies $ax^2 + by^2 = c$ (a, b, and c are constants).

70. Show that the sum of the x-intercept and the y-intercept of any tangent line to the curve $\sqrt{x} + \sqrt{y} = C$ is equal to C^2.

*The **angle between curves C_1 and C_2** at the point of intersection P is defined as the angle $0 \leq \theta \leq \frac{\pi}{2}$ between the tangent lines at P. Specifically, the angle between C_1 and C_2 is the angle between the tangent line to C_1 at P and the tangent line to C_2 at P as shown in Figure 3.45.*

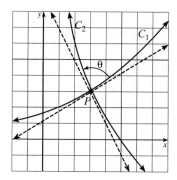

Figure 3.45   The angle θ between C_1 and C_2 at P

Use this information for Problems 71–72.

71. If θ is the angle between curve C_1 and curve C_2 at P and the tangent lines to C_1 and C_2 at P have slopes m_1 and m_2, respectively, show that

$$\tan \theta = \frac{|m_2 - m_1|}{1 + m_1 m_2}$$

72. Find the angle between the circle $x^2 + y^2 = 1$ and the circle $x^2 + (y - 1)^2 = 1$ at each of the two points of intersection.

73. Journal Problem *The Pi Mu Epsilon Journal* by Bruce W. King* : ■ When a professor asked the calculus class to find the derivative of y^2 with respect to x^2 for the function $y = x^2 - x$, one student found

$$\frac{dy}{dx} \cdot \frac{y}{x}$$

Was this answer correct? Suppose

$$y = x^3 - 3x^2 + \frac{7}{x}$$

What is the derivative of y^2 with respect to x^2 for this function?

74. Use implicit differentiation to obtain the differentiation formulas for $y = \tan^{-1} u$ and $y = \sec^{-1} u$.

75. Use the identity $\sin^{-1} u + \cos^{-1} u = \frac{\pi}{2}$ to obtain the differentiation formula for $y = \cos^{-1} u$. Similar identities can be used to obtain differentiation formulas for $y = \cot^{-1} u$ and $y = \csc^{-1} u$.

3.7   Related Rates and Applications

Certain practical problems involve a functional relationship $y = f(x)$ in which both x and y are themselves functions of another variable, such as time t. Implicit differentiation is then used to relate the rate of change dy/dt to the rate dx/dt. In this section, we will examine a variety of such **related rate problems**.

When working a related rate problem, you must distinguish between the general situation and the specific situation. The *general situation* comprises properties that are true at *every* instant of time, whereas the *specific situation* refers to those properties that are guaranteed to be true only at the *particular* instant of time that the problem investigates. Here is an example.

EXAMPLE 1   An application involving related rates

A spherical balloon is being filled with a gas in such a way that when the radius is 2 ft, the radius is increasing at the rate of 1/6 ft/min. How fast is the volume changing at this time?

Solution

The general situation: Let V denote the volume and r the radius, both of which are functions of time t (minutes). Since the container is a sphere, its volume is given by

$$V = \tfrac{4}{3}\pi r^3$$

Differentiating both sides implicitly with respect to time t yields

$$\frac{dV}{dt} = \frac{d}{dt}\left(\frac{4}{3}\pi r^3\right)$$

$$= 4\pi r^2 \frac{dr}{dt} \qquad \text{Do not forget to use the chain rule because } r \text{ is also a function of time.}$$

The specific situation: Our goal is to find $\dfrac{dV}{dt}$ at the time when $r = 2$ ft and $\dfrac{dr}{dt} = \dfrac{1}{6}$.

$$\frac{dV}{dt}\bigg|_{r=2} = 4\pi(2)^2\left(\frac{1}{6}\right) = \frac{8\pi}{3}$$

This means that the volume of the container is increasing at about 8.38 ft³/min when the radius is 2 ft. ∎

Although each related rate problem has its own "personality," many can be handled by the following summary:

Procedure for Solving Related Rate Problems

The General Situation

Step 1.   *Draw a figure, if appropriate, and assign variables to the quantities that vary.* Be careful not to label a quantity with a number unless it *never* changes in the problem.

Step 2.   *Find a formula or equation that relates the variables.* Eliminate unnecessary variables; some of these "extra" variables may be constants, but others may be eliminated because of given relationships among the variables.

Step 3.   *Differentiate the equations.* You will usually differentiate implicitly with respect to time.

The Specific Situation

Step 4.   *Substitute specific numerical values and solve algebraically for any required rate.* List the known quantities; list as unknown the quantity you wish to find. Substitute all values into the formula. The only remaining variable should be the unknown, which may be a variable or a rate. Solve for the unknown.

EXAMPLE 2   Moving shadow problem

A person 6 ft tall is walking away from a streetlight 20 ft high at the rate of 7 ft/s. At what rate is the length of the person's shadow increasing?

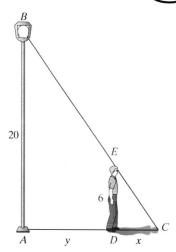

Figure 3.46 A person walking away from a streetlamp

(SMH) *Solution*

The general situation: (See *Student Mathematics Handbook*, Problem 37, Problem Set 1.)

Step 1. Let x denote the length (in feet) of the person's shadow, and y, the distance between the person and the street light, as shown in Figure 3.46. Let t denote the time (in seconds).

Step 2. Since $\triangle ABC$ and $\triangle DEC$ are similar, we have

$$\frac{x + y}{20} = \frac{x}{6}$$

Step 3. Write this equation as $x + y = \frac{20}{6}x$, or $y = \frac{7}{3}x$, and differentiate both sides with respect to t.

$$\frac{dy}{dt} = \frac{7}{3}\frac{dx}{dt}$$

The specific situation:

Step 4. List the known quantities. We know that $dy/dt = 7$. Our goal is to find dx/dt. Substitute and then solve for the unknown value:

$$\frac{dy}{dt} = \frac{7}{3}\frac{dx}{dt}$$

$$7 = \frac{7}{3}\frac{dx}{dt} \qquad \text{Substitute.}$$

$$3 = \frac{dx}{dt} \qquad \text{Multiply both sides by } \tfrac{3}{7}.$$

The length of the person's shadow is increasing at the rate of 3 ft/s. ∎

EXAMPLE 3   Leaning ladder problem

A bag is tied to the top of a 5-m ladder resting against a vertical wall. Suppose the ladder begins sliding down the wall in such a way that the foot of the ladder is moving away from the wall. How fast is the bag descending at the instant the foot of the ladder is 4 m from the wall and the foot is moving away at the rate of 2 m/s?

(SMH) *Solution*

The general situation: Let x and y be the distances from the base of the wall to the foot and top of the ladder, respectively, as shown in Figure 3.47. (See *Student Mathematics Handbook*, Problem 38, Problem Set 1.)

Notice that $\triangle TOB$ is a right triangle, so a relevant formula is the Pythagorean theorem:

$$x^2 + y^2 = 25$$

Differentiate both sides of this equation with respect to t:

$$2x\frac{dx}{dt} + 2y\frac{dy}{dt} = 0$$

The specific situation: At the particular instant in question, $x = 4$ and $y = \sqrt{25 - 4^2} = 3$. We also know that $\dfrac{dx}{dt} = 2$, and the goal is to find $\dfrac{dy}{dt}$ at this instant. We have

$$2(4)(2) + 2(3)\frac{dy}{dt} = 0$$

$$\frac{dy}{dt} = -\frac{8}{3}$$

This tells us that, at the instant in question, the bag is descending (since dy/dt is negative) at the rate of $8/3 \approx 2.7$ m/sec. ∎

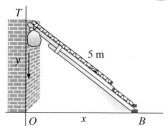

Figure 3.47 A ladder sliding down a wall

EXAMPLE 4   Modeling a physical application involving related rates

When air expands *adiabatically* (that is, with no change in heat), the pressure P and the volume V satisfy the relationship

$$PV^{1.4} = C$$

where C is a constant. At a certain instant, the pressure is 20 lb/in.^{2} and the volume is 280 in.^{3}. If the volume is decreasing at the rate of 5 in.^{3}/s at this instant, what is the rate of change of the pressure?

Solution

The general situation: The required equation was given, so we begin by differentiating both sides with respect to t. Remember, because C is a constant, its derivative with respect to t is zero.

$$1.4PV^{0.4}\frac{dV}{dt} + V^{1.4}\frac{dP}{dt} = 0 \qquad \text{Product rule}$$

The specific situation: At the instant in question, $P = 20$, $V = 280$, and $dV/dt = -5$ (negative because the volume is decreasing). The goal is to find dP/dt. First substitute to obtain

$$(20)(1.4)(280)^{0.4}(-5) + (280)^{1.4}\frac{dP}{dt} = 0$$

Now, solve for $\dfrac{dP}{dt}$:

$$\frac{dP}{dt} = \frac{5(20)(1.4)(280)^{0.4}}{(280)^{1.4}} = 0.5$$

Thus, at the instant in question, the pressure is increasing (because its derivative is positive) at the rate of 0.5 lb/in.^{2} per second. ∎

EXAMPLE 5   The water level in a cone-shaped tank

A tank filled with water is in the shape of an inverted cone 20 ft high with a circular base (on top) whose radius is 5 ft. Water is running out of the bottom of the tank at the constant rate of 2 ft^3/min. How fast is the water level falling when the water is 8 ft deep?

Solution

The general situation: Consider a conical tank with height 20 ft and circular base of radius 5 ft, as shown in Figure 3.48. Suppose that the water level is h ft and that the radius of the surface of the water is r.

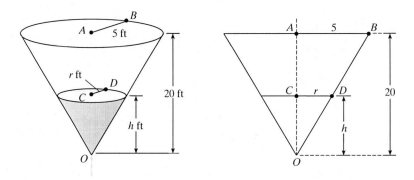

Figure 3.48   A conical water tank

Let V denote the volume of water in the tank after t minutes. We know that

$$V = \tfrac{1}{3}\pi r^2 h$$

(See *Student Mathematics Handbook*, Problem 39, Problem Set 1.) Once again, we use similar triangles (see Figure 3.48) to write $\frac{5}{20} = \frac{r}{h}$, or $r = \frac{h}{4}$. We substitute this into the formula to obtain

$$V = \frac{1}{3}\pi\left(\frac{h}{4}\right)^2 h = \frac{1}{48}\pi h^3$$

and then differentiate both sides of this equation with respect to t.

$$\frac{dV}{dt} = \frac{\pi}{16}h^2\frac{dh}{dt}$$

WARNING A common error in solving related rate problems is to substitute numerical values too soon or, equivalently, to use relationships that apply only at a particular moment in time. This is the reason we have separated related rate problems into two distinct parts. Be careful to work with general relationships among the variables and substitute specific numerical values only after you have found general rate relationships by differentiation.

The specific situation: Begin with the known quantities: We know that $dV/dt = -2$ (negative, because the volume is decreasing). The goal is to find dh/dt. At the particular instant in question, $h = 8$; we substitute to find

$$-2 = \frac{\pi}{16}(8)^2\frac{dh}{dt}$$

$$\frac{-1}{2\pi} = \frac{dh}{dt}$$

At the instant when the water is 8 ft deep, the water level is falling (since dh/dt is negative) at a rate of $\frac{1}{2\pi} \approx 0.16$ ft/min ≈ 2 in./min. ■

EXAMPLE 6 Modeling with an angle of elevation

Every day, a flight to Los Angeles flies directly over my home at a constant altitude of 4 mi. If I assume that the plane is flying at a constant speed of 400 mi/h, at what rate is the angle of elevation of my line of sight changing with respect to time when the horizontal distance between the approaching plane and my location is exactly 3 mi?

Solution

The general situation: Let x denote the horizontal distance between the plane and the observer, as shown in Figure 3.49. The height of the observer is insignificant when compared to the height of the plane.

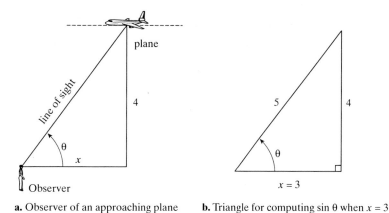

a. Observer of an approaching plane   **b.** Triangle for computing $\sin\theta$ when $x = 3$

Figure 3.49 Angle of elevation problem

Then the angle of observation θ can be modeled by

$$\cot\theta = \frac{x}{4} \qquad \text{or} \qquad \theta = \cot^{-1}\left(\frac{x}{4}\right)$$

Differentiate both sides of this last equation with respect to t to obtain

$$\frac{d\theta}{dt} = \frac{-1}{1 + (\frac{x}{4})^2}\left(\frac{1}{4}\right)\frac{dx}{dt} = \frac{-4}{16 + x^2}\frac{dx}{dt}$$

The specific situation: At the instant when $x = 3$, we are given that $\dfrac{dx}{dt} = -400$ (negative because the distance is decreasing). Thus, the angle of elevation is changing at the rate of

$$\frac{d\theta}{dt} = \frac{-4}{16 + 3^2}(-400) = 64 \text{ rad/hr}$$

The angle of elevation is changing at the rate of 64 radians per hour or, equivalently,

$$(64 \text{ rad/hr}) \left(\frac{360 \text{ deg}}{2\pi \text{ rad}} \right) \left(\frac{1 \text{ hr}}{3,600 \text{ s}} \right) \approx 1.02 \text{ deg/sec} \qquad \blacksquare$$

3.7   PROBLEM SET

Ⓐ *Find the indicated rate in Problems 1–9, given the other information. Assume $x > 0$ and $y > 0$.*

1. If $x^2 + y^2 = 25$ and $\dfrac{dx}{dt} = 4$, find $\dfrac{dy}{dt}$ when $x = 3$.

2. If $x^2 + y^2 = 25$ and $\dfrac{dy}{dt} = 2$, find $\dfrac{dx}{dt}$ when $x = 4$.

3. If $5x^2 - y = 100$ and $\dfrac{dx}{dt} = 10$, find $\dfrac{dy}{dt}$ when $x = 10$.

4. If $4x^2 - y = 100$ and $\dfrac{dy}{dt} = -6$, find $\dfrac{dx}{dt}$ when $x = 1$.

5. If $y = 2\sqrt{x} - 9$ and $\dfrac{dy}{dt} = 5$, find $\dfrac{dx}{dt}$ when $x = 9$.

6. If $y = 5\sqrt{x + 9}$ and $\dfrac{dx}{dt} = 2$, find $\dfrac{dy}{dt}$ when $x = 7$.

7. If $xy = 10$, and $\dfrac{dx}{dt} = -2$, find $\dfrac{dy}{dt}$ when $x = 5$.

8. If $5xy = 10$, and $\dfrac{dx}{dt} = -2$, find $\dfrac{dy}{dt}$ when $x = 1$.

9. If $x^2 + xy - y^2 = 11$ and $\dfrac{dy}{dt} = 5$, find $\dfrac{dx}{dt}$ when $x = 4$ and $y > 0$.

In physics, Hooke's law says that when a spring is stretched x units beyond its natural length, the elastic force $F(x)$ exerted by the spring is $F(x) = -kx$, where k is a constant that depends on the spring. Assume $k = 12$ in Problems 10 and 11.

10. If a spring is stretched at the constant rate of $\frac{1}{4}$ in./s, how fast is the force $F(x)$ changing when $x = 2$ in.?

11. If a spring is stretched at the constant rate of $\frac{1}{4}$ in./s, how fast is the force $F(x)$ changing when $x = 3$ in.?

12. A particle moves along the parabolic path given by $y^2 = 4x$ in such a way that when it is at the point $(1, -2)$, its horizontal velocity (in the direction of the x-axis) is 3 ft/s. What is its vertical velocity (in the direction of the y-axis) at this instant?

13. A particle moves along the elliptical path given by $4x^2 + y^2 = 4$ in such a way that when it is at the point $(\sqrt{3}/2, 1)$, its x-coordinate is increasing at the rate of 5 units per second. How fast is the y-coordinate changing at that instant?

14. A rock is dropped into a lake and an expanding circular ripple results. When the radius of the ripple is 8 in., the radius is increasing at a rate of 3 in./s. At what rate is the area enclosed by the ripple changing at this time?

15. A pebble dropped into a pond causes a circular ripple. Find the rate at which the radius of the ripple is changing at a time when the radius is one foot and the area enclosed by the ripple is increasing at the rate of 4 ft^2/s.

16. An environmental study of a certain community indicates that there will be $Q(p) = p^2 + 3p + 1,200$ units of a harmful pollutant in the air when the population is p thousand. The population is currently 30,000 and is increasing at a rate of 2,000 per year. At what rate is the level of air pollution increasing currently?

17. It is estimated that the annual advertising revenue received by a certain newspaper will be $R(x) = 0.5x^2 + 3x + 160$ thousand dollars when its circulation is x thousand. The circulation of the paper is currently 10,000 and is increasing at a rate of 2,000 per year. At what rate will the annual advertising revenue be increasing with respect to time 2 years from now?

18. Hospital officials estimate that approximately $N(p) = p^2 + 5p + 900$ people will seek treatment in the emergency room each year if the population of the community is p thousand. The population is currently 20,000 and is growing at the rate of 1,200 per year. At what rate is the number of people seeking emergency room treatment increasing?

19. Boyle's law states that when gas is compressed at constant temperature, the pressure P of a given sample satisfies the equation $PV = C$, where V is the volume of the sample and C is a constant. Suppose that at a certain time the volume is 30 in.^{3}, the pressure is 90 lb/in.^{2}, and the volume is increasing at the rate of 10 in.^{3}/s. How fast is the pressure changing at this instant? Is it increasing or decreasing?

Ⓑ **20. Interpretation Problem** What do we mean by a related rate problem?

21. Interpretation Problem Outline a procedure for solving related-rate problems.

22. The volume of a spherical balloon is increasing at a constant rate of 3 in.^{3}/s. At what rate is the radius of the balloon increasing when the radius is 2 in.?

23. The surface area of a sphere is decreasing at the constant rate of 3π cm^2/s. At what rate is the volume of the sphere decreasing at the instant its radius is 2 cm?

24. A person 6 ft tall walks away from a streetlight at the rate of 5 ft/s. If the light is 18 ft above ground level, how fast is the person's shadow lengthening?

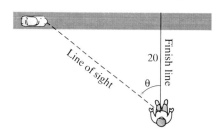

Figure 3.52 Problem 31

25. A ladder 13 ft long rests against a vertical wall and is sliding down the wall at the rate of 3 ft/s at the instant the foot of the ladder is 5 ft from the base of the wall. At this instant, how fast is the foot of the ladder moving away from the wall?

26. A car traveling north at 40 mi/h and a truck traveling east at 30 mi/h leave an intersection at the same time. At what rate will the distance between them be changing 3 hours later?

27. A person is standing at the end of a pier 12 ft above the water and is pulling in a rope attached to a rowboat at the waterline at the rate of 6 ft of rope per minute, as shown in Figure 3.50. How fast is the boat moving in the water when it is 16 ft from the pier?

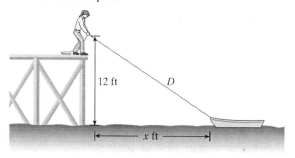

Figure 3.50 Problem 27

28. One end of a rope is fastened to a boat and the other end is wound around a windlass located on a dock at a point 4 m above the level of the boat. If the boat is drifting away from the dock at the rate of 2 m/min, how fast is the rope unwinding at the instant when the length of the rope is 5 m?

29. A ball is dropped from a height of 160 ft. A light is located at the same level, 10 ft away from the initial position of the ball. How fast is the ball's shadow moving along the ground one second after the ball is dropped?

30. A person 6 ft tall stands 10 ft from point P directly beneath a lantern hanging 30 ft above the ground, as shown in Figure 3.51.

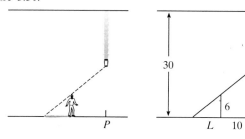

Figure 3.51 Problem 30

The lantern starts to fall, thus causing the person's shadow to lengthen. Given that the lantern falls $16t^2$ ft in t seconds, how fast will the shadow be lengthening when $t = 1$?

31. A race official is watching a race car approach the finish line at the rate of 200 km/h. Suppose the official is sitting at the finish line, 20 m from the point where the car will cross, and let θ be the angle between the finish line and the official's line of sight to the car, as shown as Figure 3.52. At what rate is θ changing when the car crosses the finish line? Give your answer in terms of rad/s.

Modeling Problems: *In Problems 32–35, set up and solve an appropriate model to answer the given question. Be sure to state your assumptions.*

32. Consider a piece of ice in the shape of a sphere that is melting at the rate of 5 in.^{3}/min. Model the volume of ice by a function of the radius r. How fast is the radius changing at the instant when the radius is 4 in.? How fast is the surface area of the sphere changing at the same instant?

33. A certain medical procedure requires that a balloon be inserted into the stomach and then inflated. Model the shape of the balloon by a sphere of radius r. If r is increasing at the rate of 0.3 cm/min, how fast is the volume changing when the radius is 4 cm?

34. Model a water tank by a cone 40 ft high with a circular base of radius 20 ft at the top. Water is flowing into the tank at a constant rate of 80 ft^3/min. How fast is the water level rising when the water is 12 ft deep? Give your answer to the nearest hundredth of a foot per minute.

35. In Problem 34, suppose that water is also flowing out the bottom of the tank. At what rate should the water be allowed to flow out so that the water level will be rising at a rate of only 0.05 ft/min when the water is 12 ft deep? Give your answer to the nearest tenth of a cubic foot per minute.

36. The air pressure $p(s)$ at a height of s meters above sea level is modeled by the formula $p(s) = e^{-0.000125s}$ atmospheres. An instrument box carrying a device for measuring pressure is dropped into the ocean from a plane and falls in such a way that after t seconds it is

$$s(t) = 3,000 - 49t - 245(e^{-t/5} - 1)$$

meters above the ocean's surface.

a. Find ds/dt and then use the chain rule to find dp/dt. How fast is the air pressure changing 2 seconds after the box begins to fall?

b. When (to the nearest second) does the box hit the water? How fast is the air pressure changing at the time of impact?

What assumptions are you making in this model?

37. At noon on a certain day, a truck is 250 mi due east of a car. The truck is traveling west at a constant speed of 25 mi/h, while the car is traveling north at 50 mi/h.

a. At what rate is the distance between them changing at time t?

b. At what time is the distance between the car and the truck neither increasing nor decreasing?

c. What is the minimal distance between the car and the truck? *Hint*: This distance must occur at the time found in part **b**. Do you see why?

38. A weather balloon is rising vertically at the rate of 10 ft/s. An observer is standing on the ground 500 ft horizontally from the point where the balloon was released. At what rate is the distance between the observer and the balloon changing when the balloon is 400 ft high?

39. An observer watches a plane approach at a speed of 500 mi/h and an altitude of 3 mi. At what rate is the angle of elevation of the observer's line of sight changing with respect to time when the horizontal distance between the plane and the observer is 4 mi? Give your answer in radians per minute.

40. A person 6 ft tall is watching a streetlight 18 ft high while walking toward it at a speed of 5 ft/s, as shown in Figure 3.53. At what rate is the angle of elevation of the person's line of sight changing with respect to time when the person is 9 ft from the base of the light?

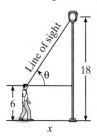

Figure 3.53 Streetlight problem

41. A revolving searchlight in a lighthouse 2 mi offshore is following a beachcomber along the shore, as shown in Figure 3.54.

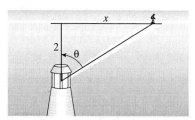

Figure 3.54 Problem 41

When the beachcomber is 1 mi from the point on the shore that is closest to the lighthouse, the searchlight is turning at the rate of 0.25 rev/h. How fast is the beachcomber walking at that moment? *Hint:* Note that 0.25 rev/h is the same as $\frac{\pi}{2}$ rad/h.

42. A water trough is 2 ft deep and 10 ft long. It has a trapezoidal cross section with base lengths 2 ft and 5 ft, as shown in Figure 3.55.

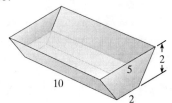

Figure 3.55 Water trough

a. Find a relationship between the volume of water in the trough at any given time and the depth of the water at that time.

b. If water enters the trough at the rate of 10 ft^3/min, how fast is the water level rising (to the nearest $\frac{1}{2}$ in./min) when the water is 1 ft deep?

43. At noon, a ship sails due north from a point P at 8 knots (nautical miles per hour). Another ship, sailing at 12 knots, leaves the same point 1 h later on a course 60° east of north. How fast is the distance between the ships increasing at 2 P.M.? At 5 P.M.? *Hint:* Use the law of cosines.

44. A swimming pool is 60 ft long and 25 ft wide. Its depth varies uniformly from 3 ft at the shallow end to 15 ft at the deep end, as shown in Figure 3.56.

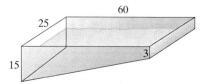

Figure 3.56 Swimming pool

Suppose the pool is being filled with water at the rate of 800 ft^3/min. At what rate is the depth of water increasing at the deep end when it is 5 ft deep at that end?

45. Suppose a water bucket is modeled by the frustum of a cone with height 1 ft and upper and lower radii of 1 ft and 9 in., respectively, as shown in Figure 3.57.

Figure 3.57 Water bucket

If water is leaking from the bottom of the bucket at the rate of 8 in.^{3}/min, at what rate is the water level falling when the depth of water in the bucket is 6 in.? *Hint:* The volume of the frustum of a cone with height h and base radii r and R is
$$V = \frac{\pi h}{3}(R^2 + rR + r^2).$$

46. A lighthouse is located 2 km directly across the sea from a point S on the shoreline. A beacon in the lighthouse makes 3 complete revolutions (6π radians) each minute, and during part of each revolution, the light sweeps across the face of a row of cliffs lining the shore.

a. Show that t minutes after it passes point S, the beam of light is at a point P located $s(t) = 2 \tan 6\pi t$ km from S.

b. How fast is the beam of light moving at the time it passes a point on the cliff located 4 km from the lighthouse?

47. Modeling Problem A car is traveling at the rate of 40 ft/s along a straight, level road that parallels the seashore. A rock with a family of seals is located 50 yd offshore.

a. Model the angle θ between the road and the driver's line of sight as a function of the distance x to the point P directly opposite the rock.

b. As the distance x in Figure 3.58 approaches 0, what happens to $d\theta/dt$?

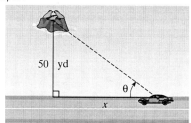

Figure 3.58 Problem 47

c. Suppose the car is traveling at v ft/s. Now what happens to $d\theta/dt$ as $x \to 0$? What effect does this have on a passenger looking at the seals if the car is traveling at a high rate of speed?

3.8 Linear Approximation and Differentials

IN THIS SECTION tangent line approximation, the differential, error propagation, marginal analysis in economics, the Newton–Raphson method for approximating roots

TANGENT LINE APPROXIMATION

If $f(x)$ is differentiable at $x = a$, the tangent line at a point $P(a, f(a))$ on the graph of $y = f(x)$ has slope $m = f'(a)$ and equation

$$\frac{y - f(a)}{x - a} = f'(a) \quad \text{or} \quad y = f(a) + f'(a)(x - a)$$

In the immediate vicinity of P, the tangent line closely approximates the shape of the curve $y = f(x)$. For instance, if $f(x) = x^3 - 2x + 5$, the tangent line at $P(1, 4)$ has slope $f'(1) = 3(1)^2 - 2 = 1$ and equation

$$y = 4 + (1)(x - 1) = x + 3$$

The graph of $y = f(x)$, the tangent line at $P(1, 4)$, and two enlargements showing how the tangent line approximates the graph of f near P are shown in Figure 3.59.

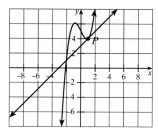 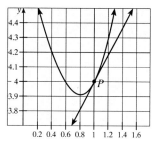 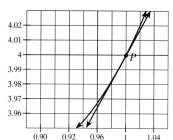

Figure 3.59 Tangent line approximation of $f(x) = x^3 - 2x + 5$ at $P(1, 4)$

Our observation about tangent lines suggests that if x_1 is near a, then $f(x_1)$ must be close to the point on the tangent line to $y = f(x)$ at $x = x_1$. That is,

$$f(x_1) \approx f(a) + f'(a)(x_1 - a)$$

We refer to this as a *linear approximation* of $f(x)$ at $x = a$, and the function
$$L(x) = f(a) + f'(a)(x - a)$$

is called a **linearization** of the function at a point $x = a$. We can use this line as an approximation of f as long as the line remains close to the graph of f, as shown in Figure 3.60.

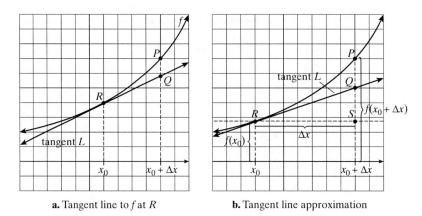

a. Tangent line to f at R **b.** Tangent line approximation

Figure 3.60 Tangent line approximation

Recall from Section 1.1, that for a line, we used the notation Δx for the horizontal change and Δy for the vertical change. Then, the linear approximation formula measures the vertical change from point R to point Q even though we really want the vertical change from the point R to the point P. If the distance Δx is small, then these two vertical distances should be approximately equal. This version of linear approximation is sometimes called the *incremental approximation formula*.

$$f(x_1) - f(a) \approx f'(a)(x_1 - a)$$
$$\Delta y \approx f'(a)\Delta x$$

EXAMPLE 1 Incremental approximation

Show that if $f(x) = \sin x$, the function $\dfrac{\Delta f}{\Delta x}$ approximates the function $f'(x) = \cos x$ for small values of Δx.

Solution

The approximation formula $\Delta f = f(x_0 + \Delta x) - f(x_0) \approx f'(x_0)\Delta x$ implies that

$$\frac{\Delta f}{\Delta x} = \frac{f(x_0 + \Delta x) - f(x_0)}{\Delta x} \approx f'(x_0)$$

Because $f(x) = \sin x$, $f'(x) = \cos x$, and

$$\frac{\sin(x + \Delta x) - \sin x}{\Delta x} \approx \cos x$$

Figure 3.61 shows the graphs for three different choices of Δx. Notice as Δx becomes smaller, it is more difficult to see the difference between f and g; in fact, for very small Δx, the graphs are virtually indistinguishable.

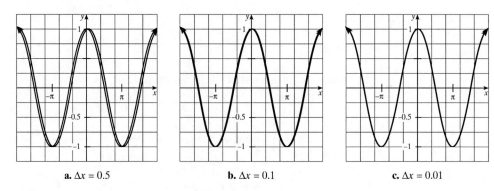

a. $\Delta x = 0.5$ **b.** $\Delta x = 0.1$ **c.** $\Delta x = 0.01$

Figure 3.61 Graphs of $f'(x) = \cos x$ and $g(x) = \dfrac{f(x + \Delta x) - f(x)}{\Delta x}$

THE DIFFERENTIAL

We have already observed that writing the derivative of $f(x)$ in the Leibniz notation df/dx suggests that the derivative may be incorrectly regarded as a quotient of "df" by "dx." It is a tribute to the genius of Leibniz that this erroneous interpretation of his notation often turns out to make good sense.

To give dx and dy meaning as separate quantities, let x be fixed and define dx to be an independent variable equal to Δx, the change in x. That is, define dx, called the **differential of x**, to be an independent variable equal to Δx, the change in x. Then, if f is differentiable at x, we define dy, called the **differential of y**, by the formula

$$dy = f'(x)\,dx \quad \text{or, equivalently,} \quad df = f'(x)\,dx$$

If we relate differentials to Figure 3.62, we see that $dx = \Delta x$ and that Δy is the rise of f that occurs for a change of Δx, whereas dy is the rise of a tangent line relative to the same change in x (Δy and dy are not the same thing). This is shown in Figure 3.62.

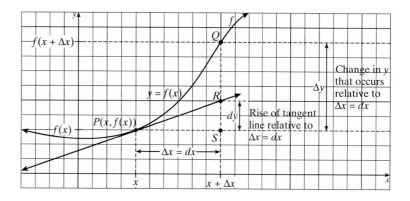

Figure 3.62 Geometrical definition of dx and dy

We now restate the standard rules and formulas for differentiation in terms of differentials. Remember that a and b are constants, while f and g are functions.

Differential rules

Linearity rule $d(af + bg) = a\,df + b\,dg$

Product rule $d(fg) = f\,dg + g\,df$

Quotient rule $d\left(\dfrac{f}{g}\right) = \dfrac{g\,df - f\,dg}{g^2} \qquad (g \neq 0)$

Power rule $d(x^n) = nx^{n-1}\,dx$

Trigonometric rules

$$d(\sin x) = \cos x\,dx \qquad\qquad d(\cos x) = -\sin x\,dx$$
$$d(\tan x) = \sec^2 x\,dx \qquad\qquad d(\cot x) = -\csc^2 x\,dx$$
$$d(\sec x) = \sec x \tan x\,dx \qquad d(\csc x) = -\csc x \cot x\,dx$$

Exponential and logarithmic rules

$$d(e^x) = e^x\,dx \qquad\qquad d(\ln x) = \frac{1}{x}\,dx$$

Differential rules (Continued)

Inverse trigonometric rules

$$d(\sin^{-1} x) = \frac{dx}{\sqrt{1 - x^2}} \qquad\qquad d(\cos^{-1} x) = \frac{-dx}{\sqrt{1 - x^2}}$$

$$d(\tan^{-1} x) = \frac{dx}{1 + x^2} \qquad\qquad d(\cot^{-1} x) = \frac{-dx}{1 + x^2}$$

$$d(\sec^{-1} x) = \frac{dx}{|x|\sqrt{x^2 - 1}} \qquad\qquad d(\csc^{-1} x) = \frac{-dx}{|x|\sqrt{x^2 - 1}}$$

Note that each of the above differential formulas resembles the earlier derivative formula, and they can be remembered by "multiplying through" the corresponding derivative formula by "dx."

EXAMPLE 2   Differential involving a product and a trigonometric function

Find $d(x^2 \sin x)$.

Solution

You can work with the differential, as follows:

$$d(x^2 \sin x) = x^2\, d(\sin x) + \sin x\, d(x^2)$$
$$= x^2 (\cos x\, dx) + \sin x (2x\, dx)$$
$$= (x^2 \cos x + 2x \sin x)\, dx$$

Or, you can work with the derivative, as shown:

$$\frac{d}{dx}(x^2 \sin x) = x^2 \cos x + 2x \sin x$$

so

$$d(x^2 \sin x) = (x^2 \cos x + 2x \sin x)\, dx \qquad\blacksquare$$

We can use differentials to approximate functional values, as shown in the following example.

EXAMPLE 3   Comparing differential and calculator approximations

Approximate $\frac{1}{3.98}$ using differentials, and compare with a calculator approximation.

Solution

Let $f(x) = \frac{1}{x} = x^{-1}$, so $f'(x) = -x^{-2}$. We know

$$f(x_0 + \Delta x) \approx f(x_0) + f'(x_0)\, dx$$

so we let $x_0 = 4$ and $\Delta x = dx = -0.02$ to find

$$\frac{1}{3.98} = \frac{1}{4 + (-0.02)}$$
$$\approx f(4) + f'(4)(-0.02)$$
$$= \frac{1}{4} + \frac{-1}{16}(-0.02)$$
$$= 0.25 + 0.00125$$
$$= 0.25125$$

By calculator, we find $\frac{1}{3.98} \approx 0.2512562814$. $\blacksquare$

ERROR PROPAGATION

In the next example, the approximation formula is used to study **propagation of error**, which is the term used to describe error that accumulates from other errors in an approximation. In particular, in the next example, the derivative is used to estimate the maximum error in a calculation that is based on figures obtained by imperfect measurement.

EXAMPLE 4   Propagation of error in a volume measurement

You measure the side of a cube and find it to be 10 cm long. From this you conclude that the volume of the cube is $10^3 = 1,000$ cm^3. If your original measurement of the side is accurate to within 2%, approximately how accurate is your calculation of the volume?

Solution

The volume of the cube is $V(x) = x^3$, where x is the length of a side. If you take the length of a side to be 10 when it is really $10 + \Delta x$, your error is Δx; and your corresponding error when computing the volume will be ΔV, given by

$$\Delta V = V(10 + \Delta x) - V(10) \approx V'(10)\Delta x$$

Now, $V'(x) = 3x^2$, so $V'(10) = 300$. Also, your measurement of the side can be off by as much as 2%—that is, by as much as $0.02(10) = 0.2$ cm in either direction. Substituting $\Delta x = \pm 0.2$ in the incremental approximation formula for ΔV, we get

$$\Delta V = 3(10)^2(\pm 0.2) \approx \pm 60$$

Thus, the propagated error in computing the volume is approximately ± 60 cm^3. Hence the maximum error in your measurement of the side is $|\Delta x| = 0.2$ and the corresponding maximum error in your calculation for the volume is

$$|\Delta V| \approx V'(10)\,|\Delta x| = 300(0.2) = 60$$

This says that, at worst, your calculation of the volume as $1,000$ cm^3 is off by 60 cm^3, or 6% of the calculated volume, when your maximum error in measuring the side is 2%. ∎

Error Propagation

If x_0 represents the measured value of a variable and $x_0 + \Delta x$ represents the exact value, then Δx is the **error in measurement**. The difference between $f(x + \Delta x)$ and $f(x)$ is called the **propagated error** at x and is defined by

$$\Delta f = f(x + \Delta x) - f(x)$$

Relative Error
The **relative error** is $\dfrac{\Delta f}{f} \approx \dfrac{df}{f}$.

Percentage Error
The **percentage error** is $100\left(\dfrac{\Delta f}{f}\right)$%.

In Example 4, the approximate propagated error in measuring volume is ± 60, and the approximate relative error is $\Delta V/V = \pm 60/10^3 = \pm 0.06$.

EXAMPLE 5   Estimating relative error and percentage error

A certain container is modeled by a right circular cylinder whose height is twice the radius of the base. The radius is measured to be 17.3 cm, with a maximum measurement error of 0.02 cm. Estimate the corresponding propagated error, the relative error, and the percentage error when calculating the surface area S.

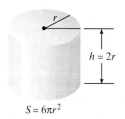

$$S = 6\pi r^2$$

Figure 3.63 Surface area of a right circular cylinder

Solution

Figure 3.63 shows the container. We have

$$S = \underbrace{2\pi r}_{\substack{\text{Circumference}}} \overbrace{2r}^{\text{Height}} + \underbrace{\pi r^2}_{\text{Top}} + \underbrace{\pi r^2}_{\text{Bottom}} = 6\pi r^2$$

$$\underbrace{\hphantom{2\pi r \; 2r}}_{\text{Lateral side}}$$

where r is the radius of the cylinder's base. Then the approximate *propagated error* is

$$\Delta S \approx S'(r)\Delta r = 12\pi r\Delta r = 12\pi(17.3)(\pm 0.02) \approx \pm 13.0438927$$

Thus, the maximum error in the measurement of the surface area is about 13.04 cm². Is this a large or a small error? The *relative error* is found by computing the ratio

$$\frac{\Delta S}{S} = \frac{12\pi r\Delta r}{6\pi r^2} = 2r^{-1}\Delta r = 2(17.3)^{-1}(\pm 0.02) \approx \pm 0.0023121$$

This tells us that the maximum error of approximately 13.04 is fairly small relative to the surface area S. The corresponding *percentage error* is found by

$$100\left(\frac{\Delta S}{S}\right)\% = 100(\pm 0.0023121387)\% = \pm 0.23121387\%$$

This means that the percentage error is about ±0.23%. ∎

MARGINAL ANALYSIS IN ECONOMICS

Marginal analysis is an area of economics concerned with estimating the effect on quantities such as cost, revenue, and profit when the level of production is changed by a unit amount. For example, if $C(x)$ is the cost of producing x units of a certain commodity, then the **marginal cost**, $MC(x)$, is the additional cost of producing one more unit and is given by the difference $MC(x) = C(x+1) - C(x)$. Using the linear approximation formula with $\Delta x = 1$, we see that

$$MC(x) = C(x+1) - C(x) \approx C'(x)(1)$$

and for this reason, we will compute marginal cost by the derivative $C'(x)$.

Similarly, if $R(x)$ is the revenue obtained from producing x units of a commodity, then the **marginal revenue**, $MR(x)$, is the additional revenue obtained from producing one more unit, and we compute MR by the derivative $R'(x)$. To summarize:

Marginal Cost And Marginal Revenue

The marginal cost of producing x units of a commodity is computed by the derivative $MC(x) = C'(x)$ and the marginal revenue of producing x units is computed by $MR(x) = R'(x)$.

EXAMPLE 6   Modeling change in cost and revenue

A manufacturer models the total cost (in dollars) of a particular commodity by the function

$$C(x) = \tfrac{1}{8}x^2 + 3x + 98$$

and the price per item (in dollars) by

$$p(x) = \tfrac{1}{3}(75 - x)$$

where x is the number of items produced ($0 \le x \le 50$). The function p is called the **demand function** which is the market price per unit when x units are produced.
a. Find the marginal cost and the marginal revenue.

b. Use marginal cost to estimate the cost of producing the 9th unit. What is the actual cost of producing the 9th unit?

c. Use marginal revenue to estimate the revenue derived from producing the 9th unit. What is the actual revenue derived from producing the 9th unit?

Solution

You can compare the values on $[0, 50]$ using a calculator in order to get a sense of the meaning of the problem.

No.	Total cost; Avg. cost	Price per item
0	$98.00	$25.00
5	$116.13; $23.23	$23.33
10	$140.50; $14.05	$21.67
15	$171.13; $11.41	$20.00
20	$208.00; $10.40	$18.33
25	$251.13; $10.05	$16.67
30	$300.50; $10.02	$15.00
35	$356.13; $10.18	$13.33
40	$418.00; $10.45	$11.67
45	$486.13; $10.80	$10.00
50	$560.50; $11.21	$8.33

a. The marginal cost is

$$C'(x) = \tfrac{1}{4}x + 3$$

To find the marginal revenue, we must first find the revenue function:

$$R(x) = xp(x) = x\left(\tfrac{1}{3}\right)(75 - x) = -\tfrac{1}{3}x^2 + 25x$$

Thus, the marginal revenue is

$$R'(x) = -\tfrac{2}{3}x + 25$$

b. The cost of producing the 9th unit is the change in cost as x increases from 8 to 9 and is estimated by

$$C'(8) = \tfrac{1}{4}(8) + 3 = 5$$

We estimate the cost of producing the 9th unit to be $5. The actual cost is

$$\Delta C = C(9) - C(8) = \left[\tfrac{1}{8}(9)^2 + 3(9) + 98\right] - \left[\tfrac{1}{8}(8)^2 + 3(8) + 98\right]$$
$$= 5\tfrac{1}{8} = 5.125 \quad \text{(that is, \$5.13)}$$

c. The revenue (to the nearest cent) obtained from the sale of the 9th unit is approximated by the marginal revenue:

$$R'(8) = -\tfrac{2}{3}(8) + 25 = \tfrac{59}{3} \approx 19.67 \quad \text{(that is, \$19.67)}$$

The actual revenue (to the nearest cent) obtained from the sale of the 9th unit is

$$\Delta R = R(9) - R(8) = \tfrac{58}{3} \approx 19.33 \quad \text{(that is, \$19.33)}$$ ∎

WARNING Remember that the marginal revenue from the sale of the 9th item is not the revenue derived from selling 9 items. Rather, it is the additional revenue the company has earned by selling the 9th item—that is, the total revenue of 9 items minus the total revenue of 8 items.

THE NEWTON-RAPHSON METHOD FOR APPROXIMATING ROOTS

The Newton–Raphson method is a different kind of tangent line approximation, one that uses tangent lines as a means for estimating roots of equations. The basic idea behind the procedure is illustrated in Figure 3.64. In this figure, r is a root of the equation $f(x) = 0$, x_0 is an approximation to r, and x_1 is a better approximation obtained by taking the x-intercept of the line that is tangent to the graph of f at $(x_0, f(x_0))$.

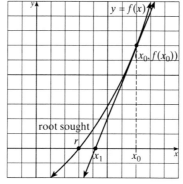
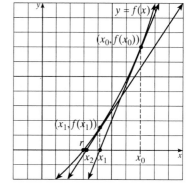

a. Estimating a root, r, of $y = f(x)$

b. First, second, and third estimates ($x_0, x_1,$ and x_2, respectively)

Figure 3.64 The Newton–Raphson method

THEOREM 3.14   The Newton–Raphson method

To approximate a root of the equation $f(x) = 0$, start with a preliminary estimate x_0 and generate a sequence $x_1, x_2, x_3, \ldots$ using the formula

$$x_{n+1} = x_n - \frac{f(x_n)}{f'(x_n)} \qquad f'(x_n) \neq 0$$

Either this sequence of approximations will approach a limit that is a root of the equation or else the sequence does not have a limit.

Proof   Rather than present a formal proof, we will present a geometric description of the procedure to help you understand what is happening. Let x_0 be an initial approximation such that $f'(x_0) \neq 0$. To find a formula for the improved approximation x_1, recall that the slope of the tangent line through $(x_0, f(x_0))$ is the derivative $f'(x_0)$. Therefore (see Figure 3.64b),

$$\underbrace{f'(x_0)}_{\text{Slope of the tangent line through } (x_0, f(x_0))} = \frac{\Delta y}{\Delta x} = \frac{f(x_0) - 0}{x_0 - x_1}$$

or, equivalently (by solving the equation for x_1),

$$x_1 = x_0 - \frac{f(x_0)}{f'(x_0)} \qquad f'(x_0) \neq 0$$

If this procedure is repeated using x_1 as the initial approximation, an even better approximation may often be obtained (see Figure 3.64b). This approximation, x_2, is related to x_1 as x_1 was related to x_0. That is,

$$x_2 = x_1 - \frac{f(x_1)}{f'(x_1)} \qquad f'(x_1) \neq 0$$

If this process produces a limit, it can be continued until the desired degree of accuracy is obtained. In general, the nth approximation x_n is related to the $(n-1)$st by the formula

$$x_n = x_{n-1} - \frac{f(x_{n-1})}{f'(x_{n-1})} \qquad f'(x_{n-1}) \neq 0 \qquad \square$$

Here is a step-by-step procedure for applying the Newton–Raphson method. A flowchart for the method appears in Figure 3.65.

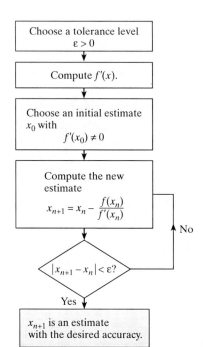

Figure 3.65 Flowchart for the Newton–Raphson method

Procedure for Applying the Newton–Raphson Method to Solve the Equation $f(x) = 0$

1. Choose a number $\epsilon > 0$ that determines the allowable tolerance for estimated solutions.
2. Compute $f'(x)$ and choose a number x_0 (with $f'(x_0) \neq 0$) "close" to a solution of $f(x) = 0$ as an initial estimate.
3. Compute a new approximation with the formula

$$x_{n+1} = x_n - \frac{f(x_n)}{f'(x_n)} \qquad f'(x_n) \neq 0$$

4. Repeat step 3 until $|x_{n+1} - x_n| < \epsilon$. The estimate $\overline{x} = x_{n+1}$ then has the required accuracy.

EXAMPLE 7   Estimating a root with the Newton–Raphson method

Approximate a real root of the equation $x^3 + x + 1 = 0$ on $[-2, 2]$.

Solution

Let $f(x) = x^3 + x + 1$. Our goal is to find a root of the equation $f(x) = 0$. The derivative of f is $f'(x) = 3x^2 + 1$, and so

$$x - \frac{f(x)}{f'(x)} = x - \frac{x^3 + x + 1}{3x^2 + 1} = \frac{2x^3 - 1}{3x^2 + 1}$$

Thus, for $n = 0, 1, 2, 3, \ldots,$

$$x_{n+1} = x_n - \frac{f(x_n)}{f'(x_n)} = \frac{2x_n^3 - 1}{3x_n^2 + 1}$$

A convenient choice for the preliminary estimate is $x_0 = -1$. Then

$$x_1 = \frac{2x_0^3 - 1}{3x_0^2 + 1} = -0.75$$ You will need a calculator or a spreadsheet to help you with these calculations.

$$x_2 = \frac{2x_1^3 - 1}{3x_1^2 + 1} \approx -0.6860465$$

$$x_3 = \frac{2x_2^3 - 1}{3x_2^2 + 1} \approx -0.6823396$$

So, to two decimal places, the root seems to be approximately $x_n \approx -0.68$. ■

In general, we will stop finding new estimates when successive approximations x_n and x_{n+1} are within a desired tolerance of each other. Specifically, if we wish to have the solutions to be within ϵ ($\epsilon > 0$) of each other, we compute approximations until $|x_{n+1} - x_n| < \epsilon$ is satisfied. Using the Newton–Raphson method (Theorem 3.14), we see that this condition is equivalent to

$$|x_{n+1} - x_n| = \left| \frac{-f(x_n)}{f'(x_n)} \right| < \epsilon$$

3.8 PROBLEM SET

A *Find the differentials indicated in Problems 1–16.*

1. $d(2x^3)$

2. $d(3 - 5x^2)$

3. $d(2\sqrt{x})$

4. $d(x^5 + \sqrt{x^2 + 5})$

5. $d(x \cos x)$

6. $d(x \sin 2x)$

7. $d\left(\frac{\tan 3x}{2x}\right)$

8. $d(xe^{-2x})$

9. $d(\ln|\sin x|)$

10. $d(x \tan^{-1} x)$

11. $d(e^x \ln x)$

12. $d\left(\frac{\sin^{-1} x}{e}\right)$

13. $d\left(\frac{x^2 \sec x}{x - 3}\right)$

14. $d(x\sqrt{x^2 - 1})$

15. $d\left(\frac{x - 5}{\sqrt{x + 4}}\right)$

16. $d\left(\frac{\ln \sqrt{x}}{x}\right)$

17. WHAT DOES THIS SAY? What is a differential?

18. Interpretation Problem Discuss error propagation, including relative error, and percentage error.

B *Use differentials to approximate the requested values in Problems 19–22 and then determine the error as compared to the calculator value.*

19. $\sqrt{0.99}$

20. $\cos(\frac{\pi}{2} + 0.01)$

21. $(3.01)^5 - 2(3.01)^3 + 3(3.01)^2 - 2$

22. $\sqrt[4]{4,100} + \sqrt[3]{4,100} + 3\sqrt{4,100}$

23. You measure the radius of a circle to be 12 cm and use the formula $A = \pi r^2$ to calculate the area. If your measurement of the radius is accurate to within 3%, approximately how accurate (to the nearest percent) is your calculation of the area?

24. Exploration Problem Suppose a 12-oz can of Coke® has a height of 4.5 in. If your measurement of the radius has an accuracy to within 1%, how accurate is your measurement for volume? Check your answer by examining a Coke can.

25. You measure the radius of a sphere to be 6 in. Use the formula $V = \frac{4}{3}\pi r^3$ to calculate the volume. If your measurement of the radius is accurate to within 1%, approximately how accurate (to the nearest percent) is your calculation of the volume?

26. It is projected that t years from now the circulation of a local newspaper will be

$$C(t) = 100t^2 + 400t + 5,000$$

Estimate the amount by which the circulation will increase during the next 6 months.

27. An environmental study suggests that t years from now, the average level of carbon monoxide in the air will be

$$Q(t) = 0.05t^2 + 0.1t + 3.4$$

parts per million (ppm). By approximately how much will the carbon monoxide level change during the next 6 months?

28. A manufacturer's total cost (in dollars) is

$$C(q) = 0.1q^3 - 0.5q^2 + 500q + 200$$

when the level of production is q units. The current level of production is 4 units, and the manufacturer is planning to decrease this to 3.9 units. Estimate how the total cost will change as a result.

29. At a certain factory, the daily output is

$$Q(L) = 60,000L^{1/3}$$

units, where L denotes the size of the labor force measured in worker-hours. Currently 1,000 worker-hours of labor are used each day. Estimate the effect on output that will be produced if the labor force is cut to 940 worker-hours.

30. Modeling Problem In a model developed by John Helms, the water evaporation $E(T)$ for a ponderosa pine is modeled by

$$E(T) = 4.6e^{17.3T/(T+237)}$$

where T (degrees Celsius) is the surrounding air temperature.* If the temperature is increased by 5% from 30°C, use differentials to estimate the corresponding percentage change in $E(T)$.

31. A soccer ball made of leather $\frac{1}{8}$ in. thick has an inner diameter of $8\frac{1}{2}$ in. Model the ball as a hollow sphere and estimate the volume of its leather shell.

32. A cubical box is to be constructed from three kinds of building materials. The material used in the four sides of the box costs 2¢ /in.^{2}, the material in the bottom costs 3¢ /in.^{2}, and the material used for the lid costs 4¢ /in.^{2}. Estimate the additional total cost of all the building materials if the length of a side is increased from 20 in. to 21 in.

33. In a healthy person of height x in., the average pulse rate in beats per minute is modeled by the formula

$$P(x) = \frac{596}{\sqrt{x}} \qquad 30 \le x \le 100$$

Estimate the change in pulse rate that corresponds to a height change from 59 to 60 in.

34. A drug is injected into a patient's bloodstream. The concentration of the drug in the bloodstream t hours after the drug is injected is modeled by the formula

$$C(t) = \frac{0.12t}{t^2 + t + 1}$$

milligrams per cubic centimeter. Estimate the change in concentration over the time period from 30 to 35 minutes after injection.

35. Modeling Problem According to Poiseuille's law, the speed of blood flowing along the central axis of an artery of radius R is modeled by the formula $S(R) = cR^2$, where c is a constant.[†] What percentage error (rounded to the nearest percent) will you make in the calculation of $S(R)$ from this formula if you make a 1% error in the measurement of R?

36. Modeling Problem One of the laws attributed to Poiseuille models the volume of a fluid flowing through a small tube in unit time under fixed pressure by the formula $V = kR^4$, where k is a positive constant and R is the radius of the tube. This formula is used in medicine to determine how wide a clogged artery must be opened to restore a healthy flow of blood. Suppose the radius of a certain artery is increased by 5%. Approximately what effect does this have on the volume of the blood flowing through the artery?[‡]

37. Modeling Problem A certain cell is modeled as a sphere. If the formulas $S = 4\pi r^2$ and $V = \frac{4}{3}\pi r^3$ are used to compute the surface area and volume of the sphere, respectively, estimate the effect on S and V produced by a 1% increase in the radius r.

38. The period of a pendulum is given by the formula

$$T = 2\pi\sqrt{\frac{L}{g}}$$

where L is the length of the pendulum in feet, $g = 32$ ft/s^2 is the acceleration due to gravity, and T is time in seconds. If the pendulum has been heated enough to increase its length by 0.4%, what is the approximate percentage change in its period?

39. The *thermal expansion coefficient* of an object is defined to be

$$\sigma = \frac{L'(T)}{L(T)}$$

where $L(T)$ is the length of the object when the temperature is T. Suppose a 75-ft span of a bridge is built with steel with $\sigma = 1.4 \times 10^{-5}$ per degree Celsius. Approximately how much will the length change during a year when the temperature varies from $-10°C$ in winter to $40°C$ in summer?

40. The radius R of a spherical ball is measured as 14 in.

  a. Use differentials to estimate the maximum propagated error in computing volume V if R is measured with a maximum error of $\frac{1}{8}$ inch.

  b. With what accuracy must the radius R be measured to guarantee an error of at most 2 in.^{3} in the calculated volume?

41. A thin horizontal beam of alpha particles strikes a thin vertical foil, and the scattered alpha particles will travel along a cone of vertex angle θ, as shown in Figure 3.66.

---

*John A. Helms, "Environmental Control of Net Photosynthesis in Naturally Grown Pinus Ponderosa Nets," *Ecology* (Winter 1972), p. 92.

[†] See *Introduction to Mathematics for Life Scientists*, 2nd edition. New York: Springer-Verlag (1976), pp. 102–103.

[‡] Ibid.

Time 1: Stream is focused.

Time 2: Stream hits foil.

Time 3: Stream is scattered after colliding with foil and disperses in the shape of a cone.

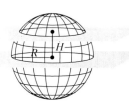

Figure 3.66   Paths of alpha particles

A vertical screen is placed at a fixed distance from the point of scattering. Physical theory predicts that the number N of alpha particles falling on a unit area of the screen is inversely proportional to $\sin^4\left(\frac{\theta}{2}\right)$. Suppose N is modeled by the formula

$$N = \frac{1}{\sin^4\left(\frac{\theta}{2}\right)}$$

Estimate the change in the number of alpha particles per unit area of the screen if θ changes from 1 to 1.1.

42. Suppose the total cost of manufacturing q units is

$$C(q) = 3q^2 + q + 500$$

dollars.

a. Use marginal analysis to estimate the cost of manufacturing the 41st unit.

b. Compute the actual cost of manufacturing the 41st unit.

43. A manufacturer's total cost is

$$C(q) = 0.1q^3 - 5q^2 + 500q + 200$$

dollars, where q is the number of units produced.

a. Use marginal analysis to estimate the cost of manufacturing the 4th unit.

b. Compute the actual cost of manufacturing the 4th unit.

44. Suppose the total cost of producing x units of a particular commodity is modeled by

$$C(x) = \frac{1}{7}x^2 + 4x + 100$$

and that each unit of the commodity can be sold for

$$p(x) = \frac{1}{4}(80 - x)$$

dollars.

a. What is the marginal cost?

b. What is the price when the marginal cost is 10?

c. Estimate the cost of producing the 11th unit.

d. Find the actual cost of producing the 11th unit.

45. At a certain factory, the daily output is modeled by the formula

$$Q(L) = 360L^{1/3}$$

units, where L is the size of the labor force measured in worker-hours. Currently, 1,000 worker-hours of labor are used each day. Use differentials to estimate the effect that one additional worker-hour will have on the daily output.

46. Approximate $\sqrt{2}$ to four decimal places by using the Newton–Raphson method.

47. Approximate $-\sqrt{2}$ to four decimal places by using the Newton–Raphson method.

48. Use the Newton–Raphson method to estimate a root of the equation $\cos x = x$. You may start with $x_0 = 1$.

49. Use the Newton–Raphson method to estimate a root of the equation $e^{-x} = x$. You may start with $x_0 = 1$.

50. Use the Newton–Raphson method to estimate a root of the equation

$$x^6 - x^5 + x^3 = 3$$

51. Let $f(x) = -2x^4 + 3x^2 + \frac{11}{8}$.

a. Show that the equation $f(x) = 0$ has at least two solutions. *Hint*: Use the intermediate value theorem.

b. Use $x_0 = 2$ in the Newton–Raphson method to find a root of the equation $f(x) = 0$.

c. Show that the Newton–Raphson method fails if you choose $x_0 = \frac{1}{2}$ as the initial estimate. *Hint*: You should obtain $x_1 = -x_0$, $x_2 = x_0$, ...

52. It can be shown that the volume of a spherical segment is given by

$$V = \frac{\pi}{3}H^2(3R - H)$$

where R is the radius of the sphere and H is the height of the segment, as shown in Figure 3.67.

Figure 3.67   Problem 52

If $V = 8$ and $R = 2$, use the Newton–Raphson method to estimate the corresponding H.

53. HISTORICAL QUEST   The Greek geometer Archimedes (see Essay Question 4 in Chapter 1) is acknowledged to be one of the greatest mathematicians of all time. Ten treatises of Archimedes have survived the rigors of time (as well as traces of some lost works) and are masterpieces of mathematical exposition. In one of these works, *On the Sphere and Cylinder*, Archimedes asks where a sphere should be cut in order to divide it into two pieces whose volumes have a given ratio. ∎

ARCHIMEDES
287–212 B.C.

Show that if a plane at distance x_c from the center of a sphere with $R = 1$ divides the sphere into two parts, one with volume twice that of the other, then

$$3x_c^3 - 9x_c^2 + 2 = 0$$

Use the Newton–Raphson method to estimate x_c.

54. Suppose the plane described in Problem 53 is located so that it divides the sphere in the ratio 1:3. Find an equation for x_c, and estimate the value of x_c by the Newton–Raphson method. *Hint*: You may need the result of Problem 52.

55. Show that if h is sufficiently small, then

a. $\sqrt{1+h}$ is approximately equal to $1 + \frac{h}{2}$.

b. $\dfrac{1}{1+h}$ is approximately equal to $1 - h$.

56. If h is sufficiently small, find an approximate value for $\sqrt[n]{A^n + h}$ for constant A.

57. Tangent line approximations are useful only if Δx is small. Illustrate this fact by trying to approximate $\sqrt{97}$ by regarding 97 as being near 81 (instead of 100).

58. Let $f(x) = -x^4 + x^2 + A$ for constant A. What value of A should be chosen that guarantees that if $x_0 = \frac{1}{3}$ is chosen as the initial estimate, the Newton–Raphson method produces $x_1 = -x_0$, $x_2 = x_0$, $x_3 = -x_0$, ...?

59. Suppose that when x units of a certain commodity are produced, the total cost is $C(x)$ and the total revenue is $R(x)$. Let $P(x) = R(x) - C(x)$ denote the total profit, and let

$$A(x) = \frac{C(x)}{x}$$

be the average cost.

a. Show that $P'(x) = 0$ when marginal revenue equals marginal cost.

b. Show that $A'(x) = 0$ when average cost equals marginal cost.

60. Can you solve the equation $\sqrt{x} = 0$ using the Newton–Raphson method with the initial estimate $x_0 = 0.05$? Does it make any difference if we choose another initial estimate (other than $x_0 = 0$)?

61. Interpretation Problem Suppose that when we try to use the Newton–Raphson method to approximate a solution of $f(x) = 0$, we find that $f(x_n) = 0$ but $f'(x_n) \neq 0$ for some x_n. What does this imply about $x_{n+1}, x_{n+2}, \ldots$? Explain.

62. HISTORICAL QUEST Among the peoples of the region between the Tigris and Euphrates rivers (at different times) during the period 2000–600 B.C. were Sumerians, Akkadians, Chaldeans, and Assyrians. Since the middle half of the nineteenth century, archeologists have found well over 50,000 clay tablets describing these great civilizations. Records show that they had highly developed religion, history, science (including alchemy, astronomy, botany, chemistry, mathematics, and zoology). ■

Mesopotamian culture had iterative formulas for computing algebraic quantities such as roots. In particular, they approximated $\sqrt{N}$ by repeatedly applying the formula

$$x_{n+1} = \frac{1}{2}\left(x_n + \frac{N}{x_n}\right) \quad \text{for } n = 0, 1, 2, 3, \ldots$$

a. Apply the Newton–Raphson method to $f(x) = x^2 - N$ to justify this formula.

b. Apply the formula to estimate $\sqrt{1,265}$ correct to five decimal places.

CHAPTER 3 REVIEW

Proficiency Examination

CONCEPT PROBLEMS

1. What is the slope of a tangent line? How does this compare to the slope of a secant line?
2. Define the derivative of a function.
3. What is a normal line to a graph?
4. What is the relationship between continuity and differentiability?
5. List and explain some of the notations for derivative.
6. State the following procedural rules for finding derivatives:
   a. constant multiple   b. sum rule
   c. difference rule   d. linearity rule
   e. product rule   f. quotient rule
   g. State each of these rules again, this time in differential form.
7. State the following derivative rules:
   a. constant rule   b. power rule
   c. trigonometric rules   d. exponential rule
   e. logarithmic rule   f. inverse trigonometric rules
8. What is a higher-order derivative? List some of the different notations for higher-order derivatives.
9. What is meant by rate of change? Distinguish between average and instantaneous rate of change.
10. What is relative rate of change?
11. How do you find the velocity and the acceleration for an object with position $s(t)$? What is speed?
12. State the chain rule.
13. Outline a procedure for logarithmic differentiation.
14. Outline a procedure for implicit differentiation.
15. Outline a procedure for solving related rate problems.
16. What is meant by tangent line approximation?
17. Define the differential of x and the differential of y for a function $y = f(x)$. Draw a sketch showing Δx, Δy, dx, and dy.
18. Define the terms propagated error, relative error, and percentage error.
19. What is meant by marginal analysis?
20. What is the Newton–Raphson method?

PRACTICE PROBLEMS

Find $\dfrac{dy}{dx}$ in Problems 21–30.

21. $x^3 + x\sqrt{x} + \cos 2x$
22. $y = \sqrt{3x} + \dfrac{3}{x^2}$
23. $y = \sqrt{\sin(3 - x^2)}$
24. $xy + y^3 = 10$
25. $y = x^2 e^{-\sqrt{x}}$
26. $y = \dfrac{\ln 2x}{\ln 3x}$
27. $y = \sin^{-1}(3x + 2)$
28. $y = \tan^{-1} 2x$
29. $y = \sin^2(x^{10} + \sqrt{x}) + \cos^2(x^{10} + \sqrt{x})$
30. $y = \dfrac{\ln(x^2 - 1)}{\sqrt[3]{x}(1 - 3x)^3}$
31. Find $\dfrac{d^2 y}{dx^2}$, the second derivative of $y = x^2(2x - 3)^3$.

32. Use the definition of the derivative to find $\dfrac{d}{dx}(x - 3x^2)$.
33. Find the equation of the tangent line to the graph of

$$y = (x^2 + 3x - 2)(7 - 3x)$$

at the point where $x = 1$.
34. Let $f(x) = \sin^2\left(\dfrac{\pi x}{4}\right)$. Find equations of the tangent line and the normal line to the graph of f at $x = 1$.
35. A rock tossed into a stream causes a circular ripple of water whose radius increases at a constant rate of 0.5 ft/s. How fast is the area contained inside of the ripple changing when the radius is 2 ft?

Supplementary Problems

Find dy/dx in Problems 1–36.

1. $y = x^4 + 3x^2 - 7x + 5$
2. $y = x^5 + 3x^3 - 11$
3. $y = \sqrt{\dfrac{x^2 - 1}{x^2 - 5}}$
4. $y = \dfrac{\cos x}{x + \sin x}$
5. $2x^2 - xy + 2y = 5$
6. $y = (x^2 + 3x - 5)^7$
7. $y = (x^3 + x)^{10}$
8. $y = \sqrt{x}(x^2 + 5)^{10}$
9. $y = \sqrt[3]{x}(x^3 + 1)^5$
10. $y = (x^2 + 3)^5 (x^3 - 5)^8$
11. $y = (x^4 - 1)^{10}(2x^4 + 3)^7$
12. $y = \sqrt{\sin 5x}$
13. $y = \sqrt{\cos \sqrt{x}}$
14. $y = (\sin x + \cos x)^3$
15. $y = (\sqrt{x} + \sqrt[3]{x})^5$
16. $y = \sqrt{\dfrac{x^3 - x}{4 - x^2}}$
17. $y = \exp(2x^2 + 5x - 3)$
18. $y = \ln(x^2 - 1)$
19. $y = x3^{2-x}$
20. $y = \log_3(x^2 - 1)$
21. $e^{xy} + 2 = \ln \dfrac{y}{x}$
22. $y = \sqrt{x} \sin^{-1}(3x + 2)$
23. $y = e^{\sin x}$
24. $y = 2^x \log_2 x$
25. $y = e^{-x} \log_5 3x$
26. $x2^y + y2^x = 3$
27. $\ln(x + y^2) = x^2 + 2y$
28. $y = e^{-x}\sqrt{\ln 2x}$
29. $y = \sin(\sin x)$
30. $y = \cos(\sin x)$
31. $x^{1/2} + y^{1/2} = x$
32. $4x^2 - 16y^2 = 64$
33. $\sin xy = y + x$
34. $\sin(x + y) + \cos(x - y) = xy$
35. $y = \dfrac{x}{\sin^{-1} x} + \dfrac{\tan^{-1} x}{x}$
36. $y = (\sin x)(\sin^{-1} x) + x \cot^{-1} x$

Find $d^2 y/dx^2$ in Problems 37–41.

37. $y = x^5 - 5x^4 + 7x^3 - 3x^2 + 17$
38. $y = \dfrac{x - 5}{2x + 3} + (3x - 1)^2$
39. $x^2 + y^3 = 10$
40. $x^2 + \sin y = 2$
41. $x^2 + \tan^{-1} y = 2$

In Problems 42–54, find an equation of the tangent line to the curve at the indicated point.

42. $y = x^4 - 7x^3 + x^2 - 3$ at $(0, -3)$
43. $y = (3x^2 + 5x - 7)^3$, where $x = 1$
44. $y = (x^3 - 3x^2 + 3)^3$, where $x = -1$
45. $y = x \cos x$, where $x = \dfrac{\pi}{2}$

46. $y = (\cos x)^2$, where $x = \pi$

47. $xy^2 + x^2 y = 2$ at $(1,1)$

48. $y = x \ln(ex)$, where $x = 1$

49. $y = xe^{2x-1}$, where $x = \frac{1}{2}$

50. $e^{xy} = x - y$ at $(1,0)$

51. $y = (1-x)^x$, where $x = 0$

52. $y = 2^x - \log_2 x$, where $x = 1$

53. $y = \dfrac{3x - 4}{3x^2 + x - 5}$, where $x = 1$

54. $x^{2/3} + y^{2/3} = 2$ at $(1,1)$

55. Let $f(x) = (x^3 - x^2 + 2x - 1)^4$. Find equations of the tangent and normal lines to the graph of f at $x = 1$.

56. Find equations for the tangent and normal lines to the graph of $y = \left(2x + \dfrac{1}{x}\right)^3$ at the point $(1, 27)$.

57. Use the chain rule to find $\dfrac{dy}{dt}$ when $y = x^3 - 7x$ and $x = t \sin t$.

58. Find $f''(x)$ if $f(x) = x^2 \sin x^2$.

59. Find $f^{(4)}(x)$ if $f(x) = x^4 - \dfrac{1}{x^4}$.

60. Find $f'''(x)$ if $f(x) = x(x^2 + 1)^{7/2}$.

61. Let $f(x) = \sqrt[3]{\dfrac{x^4 + 1}{x^4 - 2}}$. Find $f'(x)$ by implicitly differentiating $[f(x)]^3$.

62. Find y' if $x^3 y^3 + x - y = 1$. Leave your answer in terms of x and y.

63. Find y' and y'' if $x^2 + 4xy - y^2 = 8$. Your answer may involve x and y, but not y'.

64. Find the derivative of $f(x) = \begin{cases} x^2 + 5x + 4 & \text{for } x \le 0 \\ 5x + 4 & \text{for } 0 < x < 6 \\ x^2 - 2 & \text{for } x \ge 6 \end{cases}$

65. Advanced Placement Question *The following problem is found on the 1982 BC AP Exam.* Let f be the function defined by

$$f(x) = \begin{cases} x^2 \sin \dfrac{1}{x} & \text{for } x \ne 0 \\ 0 & \text{for } x = 0 \end{cases}$$

   a. Using the definition of the derivative, prove that f is differentiable at $x = 0$.

   b. Find $f'(x)$ for $x \ne 0$.

   c. Show that f' is not continuous at $x = 0$.

66. Use differentials to approximate $(16.01)^{3/2} + 2\sqrt{16.01}$.

67. Use differentials to approximate $\cos \frac{101\pi}{600}$.

68. Use differentials to estimate the change in the volume of a cone if the height of the cone is increased from 10 cm to 10.01 cm while the radius of the base stays fixed at 2 cm.

69. On New Year's Eve, a network TV camera is focusing on the descent of a lighted ball from the top of a building that is 600 ft away. The ball is falling at the rate of 20 ft/min. At what rate is the angle of elevation of the camera's line of sight changing with respect to time when the ball is 800 ft from the ground?

70. Suppose f is a differentiable function whose derivative satisfies $f'(x) = 2x^2 + 3$. Find $\dfrac{d}{dx} f(x^3 - 1)$.

71. Suppose f is a differentiable function such that $f'(x) = x^2 + x$. Find $\dfrac{d}{dx} f(x^2 + x)$.

72. Let $f(x) = 3x^2 + 1$ for all x. Use the chain rule to find $\dfrac{d}{dx}(f \circ f)(x)$.

73. Let $f(x) = \sin 2x + \cos 3x$ and $g(x) = x^2$. Use the chain rule to find $\dfrac{d}{dx}(f \circ g)(x)$.

74. Let $f(x) = \begin{cases} x \sin \dfrac{1}{x} & \text{if } x \ne 0 \\ 0 & \text{if } x = 0 \end{cases}$. Use the definition of the derivative to find $f'(0)$, if it exists.

75. A car and a truck leave an intersection at the same time. The car travels north at 60 mi/h and the truck travels east at 45 mi/h. How fast is the distance between them changing after 45 minutes?

76. A spherical balloon is being filled with air in such a way that its radius is increasing at a constant rate of 2 cm/s. At what rate is the volume of the balloon increasing at the instant when its surface has area 4π cm^2?

77. Suppose the total cost of producing x units of a particular commodity is

$$C(x) = \tfrac{2}{5}x^2 + 3x + 10$$

and that each unit of the commodity can be sold for

$$p(x) = \tfrac{1}{5}(45 - x)$$

dollars.

   a. What is the marginal cost?

   b. What is the price when the marginal cost is 23?

   c. Estimate the cost of producing the 11th unit.

   d. Find the actual cost of producing the 11th unit.

78. A block of ice in the shape of a cube originally having volume 1,000 cm^3 is melting in such a way that the length of each of its edges is decreasing at the rate of 1 cm/hr. At what rate is its surface area decreasing at the time its volume is 27 cm^3? Assume that the block of ice maintains its cubical shape.

79. Show that the rate of change of the area of a circle with respect to its radius is equal to the circumference.

80. A charged particle is projected into a linear accelerator. The particle undergoes a constant acceleration that changes its velocity from 1,200 m/s to 6,000 m/s in 2×10^{-3} seconds. Find the acceleration of the particle.

81. A rocket is launched vertically from a point on level ground that is 3,000 feet from an observer with binoculars. If the rocket is rising vertically at the rate of 750 ft/s at the instant it is 4,000 ft above the ground, how fast must the observer change the angle of elevation of her line of sight in order to keep the rocket in sight at that instant?

82. Modeling Problem Assume that a certain artery in the body is modeled by a circular tube whose cross section has radius 1.2 mm. Fat deposits are observed to build up uniformly on the inside wall of the artery. Find the rate at which the cross-sectional area of the artery is decreasing relative to the thickness of the fat deposit at the instant when the deposit is 0.3 mm thick.

83. A processor who sells a certain raw material has analyzed the market and determined that the unit price should be modeled by the formula

$$p(x) = 60 - x^2$$

(thousand dollars) for x tons ($0 \le x \le 7$) produced. Estimate the change in the unit price that accompanies each change in sales:

a. from 2 tons to 2.05 tons

b. from 1 ton to 1.1 tons

c. from 3 tons to 2.95 tons

84. A company sends out a truck to deliver its products. To estimate costs, the manager models gas consumption by the formula

$$G(x) = \frac{1}{300}\left(\frac{1,500}{x} + x\right)$$

gal/mi, under the assumption that the truck travels at a constant rate of x mi/h ($x \ge 5$). The driver is paid \$16 per hour to drive the truck 300 mi. Gasoline costs \$2 per gallon.

a. Find an expression for the total cost $C(x)$ of the trip.

b. Use differentials to estimate the additional cost if the truck is driven at 57 mi/h instead of 55 mi/h.

85. A viewer standing at ground level and 30 ft from a platform watches a balloon rise from that platform (at the same height as the viewer's eyes) at the constant rate of 3 ft/s. (See Figure 3.68) How fast is the angle of sight between the viewer and the object changing at the instant when $\theta = \frac{\pi}{4}$?

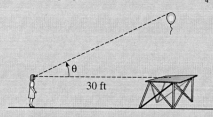

Figure 3.68 Problem 85

86. A lighthouse is 4,000 ft from a straight shore. Watching the beam on the shore from the point P on the shore that is closest to the lighthouse, an observer notes that the light is moving at the rate of 3 ft/s when it is 1,000 ft from P. How fast is the light revolving at this instant (in radians per second)?

87. A light is 4 miles from a straight shoreline. The light revolves at the rate of 2 rev/min. Find the speed of the spot of light along the shore when the light spot is 2 miles past the point on the shore closest to the source of light.

88. A particle of mass m moves along the x-axis. The velocity $v = \dfrac{dx}{dt}$ and position $x = x(t)$ satisfy the equation

$$m(v^2 - v_0^2) = k(x_0^2 - x^2)$$

where k, x_0, and v_0 are positive constants. The force F acting on the object is defined by $F = ma$, where a is the object's acceleration. Show that $F = -kx$.

89. The equation $\dfrac{d^2s}{dt^2} + ks = 0$ is called a **differential equation of simple harmonic motion.** Let A be any number. Show that the function $s(t) = A\sin 2t$ satisfies the equation

$$\frac{d^2s}{dt^2} + 4s = 0$$

90. Suppose $L(x)$ is a function with the property that $L'(x) = x^{-1}$. Use the chain rule to find the derivatives of the following functions.

a. $f(x) = L(x^2)$ **b.** $f(x) = L\left(\dfrac{1}{x}\right)$

c. $f(x) = L\left(\dfrac{2}{3\sqrt{x}}\right)$ **d.** $f(x) = L\left(\dfrac{2x+1}{1-x}\right)$

91. Let f and g be differentiable functions such that $f[g(x)] = x$ and $g[f(x)] = x$ for all x (that is, f and g are inverses). Show that

$$\frac{dg}{dx} = \frac{1}{\dfrac{df}{dx}}$$

92. A baseball player is stealing second base, as shown in Figure 3.69.

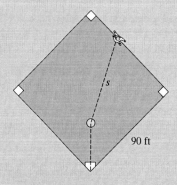

Figure 3.69 Baseball diamond

He runs at 30 ft/s and when he is 25 ft from second base, the catcher, while standing at home plate, throws the ball toward the base at a speed of 120 ft/s. At what rate is the distance between the ball and the player changing at the time the ball is thrown?

93. A connection rod $\overline{OA}$ 2 m long is rotating counterclockwise in a plane about O at the rate of 3 rev/s, as shown in Figure 3.70.

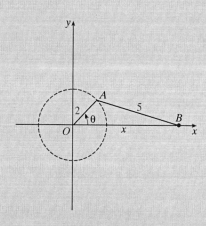

Figure 3.70 Connection rod

The rod $\overline{AB}$ is attached to $\overline{OA}$ at A, and the end B slides along the x-axis. Suppose $\overline{AB}$ is 5 meters long. What are the velocity and the acceleration of the motion of the point B along the x-axis?

94. The ideal gas law states that for an ideal gas, pressure P is given by the formula $P = kT/V$, where V is the volume, T is the temperature, and k is a constant. Suppose the temperature is kept fixed at $100°C$, and the pressure decreases at the rate of 7 lb/in.^{2} per min. At what rate is the volume changing at the instant the pressure is 25 lb/in.^{2} and the volume is 30 in.^{3}?

95. **Putnam Examination Problem**   Suppose $f(x) = ax^2 + bx + c$, where a, b, and c are real numbers and $|f(x)| \le 1$ for $x \le 1$. Show that $|f'(x)| \le 4$ for $|x| \le 1$.

96. **Putnam Examination Problem**   A point P is taken on the curve $y = x^3$. The tangent line at P meets the curve again at Q. Prove that the slope of the curve at Q is four times the slope at P.

97. **Putnam Examination Problem**   A particle of unit mass moves on a straight line under the action of a force that is a function $f(v)$ of the velocity v of the particle, but the form of this function is not known. A motion is observed, and the distance x covered in time t is found to be related to t by the formula $x = at + bt^2 + ct^3$, where a, b, and c have numerical values determined by observation of the motion. Find the function $f(v)$ for the range of v covered by this experiment.

Group Research Project

Chaos

This fractal image is an example of what is called mathematical chaos.

An exciting new topic in mathematics attempts to bring order to the universe by considering disorder. This topic is called **chaos theory**, and it shows how structures of incredible complexity and disorder really exhibit beauty and order.

Water flowing through a pipe offers one of the simplest physical models of chaos. Pressure is applied to the end of the pipe and the water flows in straight lines. More pressure increases the speed of the laminar flow until the pressure reaches a critical value, and a radically new situation evolves—turbulence. A simple laminar flow suddenly changes to a flow of beautiful complexity consisting of swirls within swirls. Before turbulence, the path of any particle was quite predictable. After a minute change in the pressure, turbulence occurs and predictability is lost. **Chaos** is concerned with systems in which minute changes suddenly transform predictability into unpredictability.*

For this research project begin with

$$f(x) = x^3 - x = x(x-1)(x+1)$$

Use the Newton–Raphson method to investigate what happens as you change the starting value, x_0, to solve $f(x) = 0$. What would you select as a starting value? Two important x-values in our study are

$$s_3 = \frac{1}{\sqrt{3}} \qquad \text{and} \qquad s_5 = \frac{1}{\sqrt{5}}$$

One would not want to pick x_0 as either $\pm s_3$. Why not? Also, what happens if one picks $x_0 = s_5$? That is, what are $x_1, x_2, \dots$?

Generate a good plot of $f(x)$ on $[-2, 2]$. Explain from the plots why you would *expect* that an initial value $x_0 > s_3$ would lead to $\lim_{n \to +\infty} x_n = 1$. (Also, by symmetry, $x_0 < -s_3$ leads to $\lim_{n \to +\infty} x_n = -1$.)

Explain why if $|x_0| < s_5$, you would expect $x_n \to 0$. Numerically verify your assertions. Now to see the "chaos," use the following x_0 values and take 6 to 10 iterations, until convergence occurs, and report what happens: 0.448955; 0.447503; 0.447262; 0.447222; 0.4472215; 0.4472213. Write a paper telling what you see and why.

Extended paper for further study   Attempt to define chaos. Your paper should include, but not be limited to, answers to the questions on this page. Some references (to get you started) are listed:

Chaos: Making a New Science, James Gleick, Penguin Books, 1988.

Chaos and Fractals: New Frontiers of Science, H. O. Peitgen, H. Jürgens, and D. Saupe, Springer-Verlag, 1992.

Newton's Method and Fractal Patterns, Phillip D. Straffin, Jr., UMAP Module 716, COMAP, 1991.

---

*Thanks to Jack Wadhams of Golden West College for this paragraph.

4

Additional Applications of the Derivative

PREVIEW

In Chapter 3, we used the derivative to find tangent lines and to compute rates of change. The primary goal of this chapter is to examine the use of calculus in curve sketching, optimization, and other applications.

PERSPECTIVE

Homing pigeons and certain other birds are known to avoid flying over large bodies of water whenever possible. The reason for this behavior is not entirely known. However, it is reasonable to speculate that it may have something to do with minimizing the energy expended in flight, because the air over a lake is often "heavier" than that over land. Suppose a pigeon is released from a boat at point B on the lake shown in the accompanying figure.* It will fly to its loft at point L on the lakeshore by heading across water to a point P on the shore and then flying directly from P to L along the shore. If the pigeon expends e_ω units of energy per mile over water and e_L units over land, where should P be located to minimize the total energy expended in flight?†

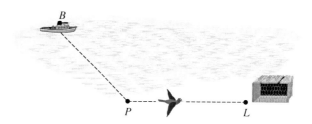

Optimization (finding the maximum or minimum values) is one of the most important applications we will study in calculus, from maximizing profit and minimizing cost to maximizing the strength of a structure and minimizing the distance traveled. Optimization problems are considered in depth in Sections 4.6 and 4.7.

*Edward Batschelet, *Introduction to Mathematics for Life Scientists,* 2nd ed. (New York: Springer-Verlag, 1979), pp. 276–277.
†See Problem 32, Section 4.7.

4.1   Extreme Values of a Continuous Function

IN THIS SECTION   extreme value theorem, relative extrema, absolute extrema, optimization

EXTREME VALUE THEOREM

One of the principal goals of calculus is to investigate the behavior of various functions. As part of this investigation, we will be laying the groundwork for solving a large class of problems that involve finding the maximum or minimum value of a function, if one exists. Such problems are called **optimization problems**. We begin by introducing some useful terminology.

Absolute Maximum and Minimum

> Let f be a function defined on an interval I that contains the number c. Then
>
> $f(c)$ is an **absolute maximum** of f on I if $f(c) \geq f(x)$ for all x in I
>
> $f(c)$ is an **absolute minimum** of f on I if $f(c) \leq f(x)$ for all x in I

Sometimes we just use the terms *maximum* and/or *minimum* if the context is clear. Together, the absolute maximum and minimum of f on the interval I are called the **extreme values**, or the **absolute extrema,** of f on I. A function does not necessarily have extreme values on a given interval. For instance, the continuous function $g(x) = x$ has neither a maximum nor a minimum on the open interval $(0, 1)$, as shown in Figure 4.1a.

The discontinuous function defined by

$$h(x) = \begin{cases} x^2 & \text{for } x \neq 0 \\ 1 & \text{for } x = 0 \end{cases}$$

has a maximum which is on the closed interval $[-1, 1]$, but no minimum, as shown in Figure 4.1b. Incidentally, this graph also illustrates the fact that a function may assume an absolute extremum at more than one point. In this case, the maximum occurs at the points $(-1, 1)$, $(0, 1)$, and $(1, 1)$. If a function f is continuous and the interval I is closed and bounded, it can be shown that both an absolute maximum and an absolute minimum *must* occur. This result, called the **extreme value theorem**, plays an important role in our work.

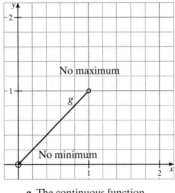

a. The continuous function $g(x) = x$ has no extrema on the open interval $(0, 1)$.

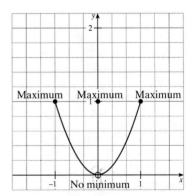

b. The discontinuous function h has a maximum, but not a minimum on the closed interval $[-1, 1]$.

Figure 4.1   Functions that lack one or both extreme values

THEOREM 4.1 The extreme value theorem

A function f has both an absolute maximum and an absolute minimum on any closed, bounded interval $[a, b]$ where it is continuous.

Proof Even though this result may seem quite reasonable (see Figure 4.2), its proof requires concepts beyond the scope of this text and will be omitted.

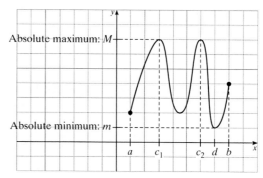

Absolute maximum at $x = c_1$ and $x = c_2$
Absolute minimum at $x = d$

Figure 4.2 Extreme value theorem ❑

If f is discontinuous or the interval is not both closed and bounded, you cannot conclude that f has both a largest and smallest value. You will be asked for appropriate counterexamples in the problem set. Sometimes there are extreme values even when the conditions of the theorem are not satisfied, but if the conditions hold, the extreme values are guaranteed.

Note that the maximum of a function occurs at the highest point on its graph and the minimum occurs at the lowest point. These properties are illustrated in Example 1.

EXAMPLE 1 Extreme values of a continuous function

The graph of a function f is shown in Figure 4.3. Locate the extreme values of f defined on the closed interval $[a, b]$.

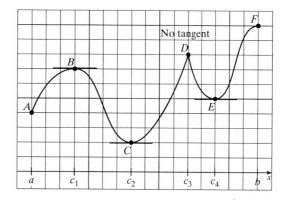

Figure 4.3 A continuous function on a closed interval $[a, b]$

Solution

The highest point on the graph occurs at the right endpoint F, and the lowest point occurs at C. Thus, the absolute maximum is $f(b)$, and the absolute minimum is $f(c_2)$.

■

In Example 1, the existence of maxima and minima as required by the extreme value theorem may seem obvious, but there are times when it seems that the extreme value theorem fails. If this occurs, you need to see which of the conditions of the extreme value theorem are not satisfied. Consider Example 2.

EXAMPLE 2 Conditions of the extreme value theorem

In each case, explain why the given function does not contradict the extreme value theorem:

a. $f(x) = \begin{cases} 2x & \text{if } 0 \leq x < 1 \\ 1 & \text{if } 1 \leq x \leq 2 \end{cases}$

b. $g(x) = x^2$ on $0 < x \leq 2$

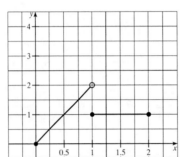

Does not have a maximum value.

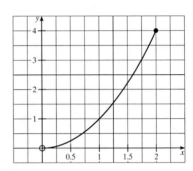

g does not have a minimum value
(but it does have a maximum value).

Solution

a. The function f has no maximum. It takes on all values less than, but arbitrarily close to, 2. However, it never reaches the value 2. This function does not contradict the extreme value theorem because f is not continuous on $[0, 2]$.

b. Although the functional values of $g(x)$ become arbitrarily small as x approaches 0, $g(x)$ never reaches the value 0 so g has no minimum. The function g is continuous on the interval $(0, 2]$, but the extreme value theorem is not contradicted because the interval is not closed. ∎

RELATIVE EXTREMA

Typically, the extrema of a continuous function occur either at endpoints of the interval or at points where the graph has a "peak" or a "valley" (points where the graph is higher or lower than all nearby points). For example, the function f in Figure 4.3 has "peaks" at B, D, and "valleys" at C, E. Peaks and valleys are what we call *relative extrema*.

Relative Maximum and Relative Minimum

> The function f is said to have a **relative maximum** at the point c if $f(c) \geq f(x)$ for all x in an open interval containing c. Likewise, f is said to have a **relative minimum** at d if $f(d) \leq f(x)$ for all x in an open interval containing d. Collectively, relative maxima and relative minima are called **relative extrema**.

WARNING Note that an extremum at an endpoint is, by definition, not a relative extremum, since there is not an open interval around the endpoint entirely contained in the domain of the function.

Next we will formulate a procedure for finding relative extrema. By looking at Figure 4.3, we see that there are horizontal tangents at B, C, and E, while no tangent can be defined at the point D. This suggests that the relative extrema of f occur either where the derivative is zero (horizontal tangent) or where the derivative does not exist (no tangent). This notion leads us to the following definition.

Critical Numbers and Critical Points

Suppose f is defined at c and either $f'(c) = 0$ or $f'(c)$ does not exist. Then the number c is called a **critical number** of f, and the point $P(c, f(c))$ on the graph of f is called a **critical point**.

WARNING Note that if $f(c)$ is not defined, then c **cannot** be a critical number.

EXAMPLE 3 Finding critical numbers

Find the critical numbers for the given functions.

a. $f(x) = 4x^3 - 5x^2 - 8x + 20$

b. $f(x) = \dfrac{e^x}{x - 2}$ Note that $x \neq 2$.

c. $f(x) = 2\sqrt{x}(6 - x)$ Note that $x \geq 0$.

Solution

a. $f'(x) = 12x^2 - 10x - 8$ is defined for all values of x. Solve

$$12x^2 - 10x - 8 = 0$$
$$2(3x - 4)(2x + 1) = 0$$
$$x = \tfrac{4}{3}, -\tfrac{1}{2} \quad \text{These are the critical numbers.}$$

b. $f'(x) = \dfrac{(x - 2)e^x - e^x(1)}{(x - 2)^2} = \dfrac{e^x(x - 3)}{(x - 2)^2}$ Note that $x \neq 2$.

The derivative is not defined at $x = 2$, but f is not defined at 2 either, so $x = 2$ is not a critical number. The actual critical numbers are found by solving $f'(x) = 0$:

$$\frac{e^x(x - 3)}{(x - 2)^2} = 0$$
$$x = 3 \quad \text{This is the only critical number since } e^x > 0.$$

c. Write $f(x) = 12x^{1/2} - 2x^{3/2}$ so $f'(x) = 6x^{-1/2} - 3x^{1/2}$. The derivative is not defined at $x = 0$. We have $f(0) = 12(0)^{1/2} - 2(0)^{3/2} = 0$, so we see that f is defined at $x = 0$, which means that $x = 0$ is a critical number. For other critical numbers, solve $f'(x) = 0$:

$$6x^{-1/2} - 3x^{1/2} = 0$$
$$3x^{-1/2}(2 - x) = 0$$
$$x = 2$$

The critical numbers are $x = 0, 2$. ∎

EXAMPLE 4 Critical numbers and critical points

Find the critical numbers and the critical points for the function

$$f(x) = (x - 1)^2(x + 2)$$

Solution

Because the function f is a polynomial, we know that it is continuous and that its derivative exists for all x. Thus, we find the critical numbers by using the product rule and extended power rule to solve the equation $f'(x) = 0$:

$$f'(x) = (x - 1)^2(1) + 2(x - 1)(1)(x + 2)$$
$$= (x - 1)[(x - 1) + 2(x + 2)]$$
$$= 3(x - 1)(x + 1)$$

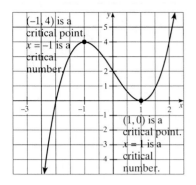

Figure 4.4 The graph of $f(x) = (x-1)^2(x+2)$

The critical numbers are $x = \pm 1$. To find the critical points, we need to find the y-coordinate for each critical number.

$$f(1) = (1-1)^2(1+2) = 0$$
$$f(-1) = (-1-1)^2(-1+2) = 4$$

Thus, the critical points are $(1,0)$ and $(-1,4)$. The graph of $f(x) = (x-1)^2(x+2)$ is shown in Figure 4.4. ∎

Note how the relative extrema occur at the critical points. Our observation that the relative extrema occur only at points on a graph where there is either a horizontal tangent line or no tangent at all is equivalent to the following result.

THEOREM 4.2   Critical number theorem

If a continuous function f has a relative extremum at c, then c must be a critical number of f.

> **➡ What This Says**   If a point is a relative maximum or a relative minimum value for a function, then either the derivative is 0 or the derivative does not exist at that point. We do not claim the converse.

Proof   Since f has a relative extremum at c, $f(c)$ is defined. If $f'(c)$ does not exist, then c is a critical number by definition. We will show that if $f'(c)$ exists and a relative maximum occurs at c, then $f'(c) = 0$. Our approach will be to examine the difference quotient. (The case where $f'(c)$ exists and a relative minimum occurs at c is handled similarly in Problem 61.)

Because a relative maximum occurs at c, we have $f(c) \geq f(x)$ for every number x in an open interval (a, b) containing c. Therefore, if Δx not equal to zero is small enough so $c + \Delta x$ is in (a, b), then

$$f(c) \geq f(c + \Delta x) \qquad \text{Because a relative maximum occurs at } c$$

$$f(c) - f(c + \Delta x) \geq 0$$
$$f(c + \Delta x) - f(c) \leq 0 \qquad \text{Multiply both sides by } -1, \text{ reversing the inequality.}$$

For the next step we want to divide both sides by Δx (to write the left side as a difference quotient). However, as this is an inequality, we need to consider two possibilities:

1. Suppose $\Delta x > 0$ (the inequality does not reverse):

$$\frac{f(c + \Delta x) - f(c)}{\Delta x} \leq 0 \qquad \text{Divide both sides by } \Delta x.$$

Now we take the limit of both sides as Δx approaches 0 from the right (because Δx is positive).

$$\underbrace{\lim_{\Delta x \to 0^+} \frac{f(c + \Delta x) - f(c)}{\Delta x}}_{f'(c)} \leq \underbrace{\lim_{\Delta x \to 0^+} 0}_{0}$$

$$f'(c) \leq 0$$

2. Next, suppose $\Delta x < 0$ (the inequality reverses). Then

$$\frac{f(c + \Delta x) - f(c)}{\Delta x} \geq 0$$

This time we take the limit of both sides as Δx approaches 0 from the left (because Δx is negative).

$$\lim_{\Delta x \to 0^-} \frac{f(c + \Delta x) - f(c)}{\Delta x} \geq \lim_{\Delta x \to 0^-} 0$$

$$f'(c) \geq 0$$

Because we have shown that $f'(c) \leq 0$ and $f'(c) \geq 0$, it follows that $f'(c) = 0$. □

WARNING Theorem 4.2 tells us that a relative extremum of a continuous function f can occur *only* at a critical number, but it does not say that a relative extremum must occur at each critical number.

For example, if $f(x) = x^3$, then $f'(x) = 3x^2$ and $f'(0) = 0$, so 0 is a critical number. But there is no relative extremum at $c = 0$ on the graph of f because the graph is rising for $x < 0$ and also for $x > 0$, as shown in Figure 4.5a. It is also quite possible for a continuous function g to have no relative extremum at a point c where $g'(x)$ does not exist (see Figure 4.5b).

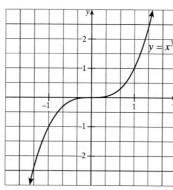

a. The graph of $f(x) = x^3$
No relative extremum occurs
at $c = 0$ even though $f'(0) = 0$.

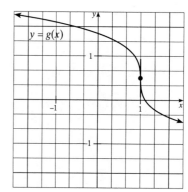

b. Although $g'(1)$ does not exist,
no relative extremum occurs
at $c = 1$.

Figure 4.5 A relative extremum may not occur at each critical number.

EXAMPLE 5 Critical numbers where the derivative does not exist

Find the critical numbers for $f(x) = |x + 1|$ on $[-5, 5]$. The graph is shown in Figure 4.6.

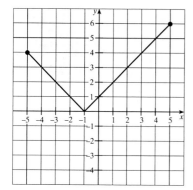

Figure 4.6 Graph of
$f(x) = |x + 1|$ on $[-5, 5]$

Solution

If $x > -1$, then $f(x) = x + 1$ and $f'(x) = 1$. However, if $x < -1$, then $f(x) = -x - 1$ and $f'(x) = -1$. We need to check what happens at $x = -1$.

$$f'(-1) = \lim_{\Delta x \to 0} \frac{f(-1 + \Delta x + 1) - f(-1 + 1)}{\Delta x}$$

$$= \lim_{\Delta x \to 0} \frac{|\Delta x| - |0|}{\Delta x}$$

$$= \lim_{\Delta x \to 0} \frac{|\Delta x|}{\Delta x}$$

We consider the left and right limits:

$$\lim_{\Delta x \to 0^+} \frac{|\Delta x|}{\Delta x} = \lim_{\Delta x \to 0^+} \frac{\Delta x}{\Delta x} = 1$$

and

$$\lim_{\Delta x \to 0^-} \frac{|\Delta x|}{\Delta x} = \lim_{\Delta x \to 0^-} \frac{-\Delta x}{\Delta x} = -1$$

Because these are not the same, this limit does not exist and thus the function $f(x) = |x + 1|$ is not differentiable at $x = -1$. Because $f(-1)$ is defined, it follows that -1 is the only critical number. ∎

ABSOLUTE EXTREMA

Suppose we are looking for the absolute extrema of a continuous function f on the closed, bounded interval $[a, b]$. Theorem 4.1 tells us that these extrema exist and Theorem 4.2 enables us to narrow the list of "candidates" for points where extrema can occur from the entire interval $[a, b]$ to just the endpoints $x = a$, $x = b$, and the critical numbers between a and b. This suggests the following procedure.

Procedure for Finding Absolute Extrema

To find the absolute extrema of a continuous function f on $[a, b]$:

Step 1.   Compute $f'(x)$ and find all critical numbers of f on $[a, b]$.
Step 2.   Evaluate f at the endpoints a and b and at each critical number c.
Step 3.   Compare the values in step 2.
            The largest value of f is the absolute maximum of f on $[a, b]$.
            The smallest value of f is the absolute minimum of f on $[a, b]$.

Figure 4.7 shows some of the possibilities in the application of this procedure.

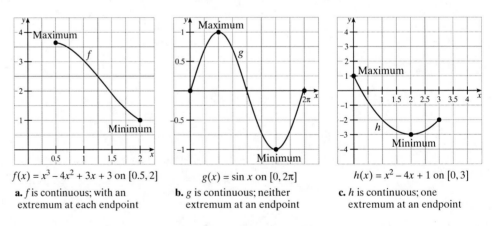

$f(x) = x^3 - 4x^2 + 3x + 3$ on $[0.5, 2]$

a. f is continuous; with an extremum at each endpoint

$g(x) = \sin x$ on $[0, 2\pi]$

b. g is continuous; neither extremum at an endpoint

$h(x) = x^2 - 4x + 1$ on $[0, 3]$

c. h is continuous; one extremum at an endpoint

Figure 4.7   Absolute extrema

EXAMPLE 6   Absolute extrema of a polynomial function

Find the absolute extrema of the function defined by the equation $f(x) = x^4 - 2x^2 + 3$ on the closed interval $[-1, 2]$.

Solution

Because f is a polynomial function, it is continuous on the closed interval $[-1, 2]$. Theorem 4.1 tells us that there must be an absolute maximum and an absolute minimum on the interval.

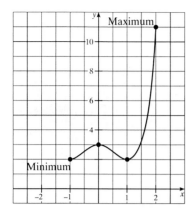

Figure 4.8 The graph of $f(x) = x^4 - 2x^2 + 3$ on $[-1, 2]$

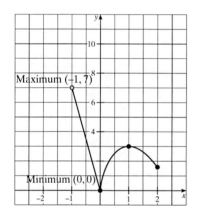

Figure 4.9 Graph of $f(x) = 5x^{2/3} - 2x^{5/3}$ on $[-1, 2]$

Step 1.
$$f'(x) = 4x^3 - 2(2x)$$
$$= 4x(x^2 - 1)$$
$$= 4x(x - 1)(x + 1)$$
The critical numbers are $x = 0$, 1, and -1.

Step 2. Values at endpoints: $f(-1) = 2$
$$f(2) = 11$$
Critical numbers: $f(0) = 3$
$$f(1) = 2$$

Step 3. The absolute maximum of f occurs at $x = 2$ and is $f(2) = 11$; the absolute minimum of f occurs at $x = 1$ and $x = -1$ and are $f(1) = f(-1) = 2$. The graph of f is shown in Figure 4.8. ■

EXAMPLE 7 Absolute extrema when the derivative does not exist

Find the absolute extrema of $f(x) = x^{2/3}(5 - 2x)$ on the interval $[-1, 2]$.

Solution

Step 1. To find the derivative, rewrite the given function as $f(x) = 5x^{2/3} - 2x^{5/3}$. Then
$$f'(x) = \tfrac{10}{3}x^{-1/3} - \tfrac{10}{3}x^{2/3} = \tfrac{10}{3}x^{-1/3}(1 - x)$$
Critical numbers are found by solving $f'(x) = 0$ and by locating the places where the derivative does not exist. First,
$$f'(x) = 0 \quad \text{when} \quad x = 1$$
Even though $f(0)$ exists, we note that $f'(x)$ does not exist at $x = 0$ (notice the division by zero when $x = 0$). Thus, the critical numbers are $x = 0$ and $x = 1$.

Step 2. Values at endpoints: $f(-1) = 7$
$$f(2) = 2^{2/3} \approx 1.587401052$$
Critical numbers: $f(0) = 0$
$$f(1) = 3$$

Step 3. The absolute maximum of f occurs at $x = -1$ and is $f(-1) = 7$; the absolute minimum of f occurs at $x = 0$ and is $f(0) = 0$. The graph of f is shown in Figure 4.9. ■

EXAMPLE 8 Absolute extrema for a trigonometric function

Find the absolute extrema of the continuous function
$$T(x) = \tfrac{1}{2}(\sin^2 x + \cos x) + 2\sin x - x$$
on the interval $[0, \tfrac{\pi}{2}]$.

Solution

Step 1. To find where $T'(x) = 0$, we begin by finding $T'(x)$:
$$T'(x) = \tfrac{1}{2}(2\sin x \cos x - \sin x) + 2\cos x - 1$$
$$= \tfrac{1}{2}(2\sin x \cos x - \sin x + 4\cos x - 2)$$
$$= \tfrac{1}{2}[2(\cos x)(\sin x + 2) - (\sin x + 2)]$$
$$= \tfrac{1}{2}[(\sin x + 2)(2\cos x - 1)]$$

Since the factor $(\sin x + 2)$ is never zero, it follows that $T'(x) = 0$ only when $2\cos x - 1 = 0$; that is, when $x = \tfrac{\pi}{3}$. This is the only critical number in $[0, \tfrac{\pi}{2}]$.

Step 2.   Evaluate the function at the endpoints:

$$T(0) = \tfrac{1}{2}(\sin^2 0 + \cos 0) + 2\sin 0 - 0 = \tfrac{1}{2}(0 + 1) + 2(0) - 0 = 0.5$$

$$T\left(\tfrac{\pi}{2}\right) = \tfrac{1}{2}\left(\sin^2\tfrac{\pi}{2} + \cos\tfrac{\pi}{2}\right) + 2\sin\tfrac{\pi}{2} - \tfrac{\pi}{2}$$

$$= \tfrac{1}{2}(1 + 0) + 2(1) - \tfrac{\pi}{2} = \tfrac{5}{2} - \tfrac{\pi}{2} \approx 0.9292036732$$

Evaluate the function at the critical number:

$$T\left(\tfrac{\pi}{3}\right) = \tfrac{1}{2}\left(\sin^2\tfrac{\pi}{3} + \cos\tfrac{\pi}{3}\right) + 2\sin\tfrac{\pi}{3} - \tfrac{\pi}{3}$$

$$= \tfrac{1}{2}\left(\tfrac{3}{4} + \tfrac{1}{2}\right) + 2\left(\tfrac{\sqrt{3}}{2}\right) - \tfrac{\pi}{3} = \tfrac{5}{8} + \sqrt{3} - \tfrac{\pi}{3} \approx 1.309853256$$

Step 3.   The absolute maximum of T is approximately 1.31 at $x = \tfrac{\pi}{3}$ and the absolute minimum of T is 0.5 at $x = 0$.   ■

OPTIMIZATION

In our next two examples, we examine applications involving optimization. Such problems are investigated in more depth in Sections 4.6 and 4.7.

EXAMPLE 9   An applied maximum value problem

A box with a square base is constructed so that the length of one side of the base plus the height is 10 in. What is the largest possible volume of such a box?

Solution

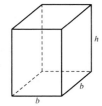

We let b be the length of one side of the base and h be the height of the box, as shown in Figure 4.10. The volume, V, is

$$V = b^2 h$$

Because our methods apply only to functions of one variable, it may seem that we cannot deal with V as a function of two variables. However, we know that $b + h = 10$; therefore, $h = 10 - b$, and we can now write V as a function of b alone:

$$V(b) = b^2(10 - b)$$

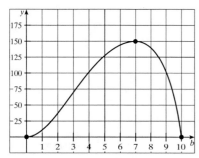

Figure 4.10 Volume of a box

The domain is not stated, but for physical reasons we must have $b \geq 0$ and $10 - b = h \geq 0$, so that $0 \leq b \leq 10$. Figure 4.10 shows the volume for various choices of b.

Now, find the value of b that produces the maximum volume. First, we find the critical numbers. Note that V is a polynomial function, so the derivative exists everywhere in the domain. Write $V(b) = 10b^2 - b^3$ and find $V'(b) = 20b - 3b^2$. Then

$$V'(b) = 0$$
$$20b - 3b^2 = 0$$
$$b(20 - 3b) = 0$$
$$b = 0, \tfrac{20}{3}$$

Checking the endpoints and the critical numbers, we have

$$V(0) = 0$$
$$V(10) = 10^2(10 - 10) = 0$$
$$V\left(\tfrac{20}{3}\right) = \left(\tfrac{20}{3}\right)^2\left(10 - \tfrac{20}{3}\right) = \tfrac{4,000}{27}$$

Alternatively, we could have solved the problem with V as a function of h: $V(h) = (10 - h)^2 h$, $0 \leq h \leq 10$, with the same result. We must write V as a function of one variable so that we can find its derivative.

Thus, the largest value for the volume V is $\tfrac{4,000}{27} \approx 148.1$ in.^{3}. It occurs when the square base has a side of length $\tfrac{20}{3}$ in. and the height is $h = 10 - \tfrac{20}{3} = \tfrac{10}{3}$ in.   ■

EXAMPLE 10 Maximum and minimum velocity of a moving particle

A particle moves along the s-axis with position

$$s(t) = t^4 - 8t^3 + 18t^2 + 60t - 8$$

Find the largest and smallest values of its velocity for $1 \le t \le 5$.

Solution

The velocity is

$$v(t) = s'(t) = 4t^3 - 24t^2 + 36t + 60$$

(**Note**: v is a polynomial function, so it has a derivative for all t.) To find the largest value of $v(t)$, we compute the derivative of v:

$$v'(t) = 12t^2 - 48t + 36$$
$$= 12(t-1)(t-3)$$

Setting $v'(t) = 0$, we find that the critical numbers of $v(t)$ are $t = 1, 3$. Now we evaluate v at the critical numbers and endpoints.

$t = 1$ is both a critical number and an endpoint:

$$v(1) = 4(1)^3 - 24(1)^2 + 36(1) + 60 = 76$$

$t = 5$ is an endpoint:

$$v(5) = 4(5)^3 - 24(5)^2 + 36(5) + 60 = 140$$

$t = 3$ is a critical number:

$$v(3) = 4(3)^3 - 24(3)^2 + 36(3) + 60 = 60$$

The largest value of the velocity is 140 at the endpoint where $t = 5$, and the smallest value is 60 when $t = 3$. ■

4.1 PROBLEM SET

Ⓐ *In Problems 1–14, find the critical numbers for each continuous function on the given closed, bounded interval, and then tell whether each yields a minimum, maximum, or neither.*

1. $f(x) = 5 + 10x - x^2$ on $[-3, 3]$
2. $f(x) = 10 + 6x - x^2$ on $[-4, 4]$
3. $f(x) = x^3 - 3x^2$ on $[-1, 3]$
4. $f(t) = t^4 - 8t^2$ on $[-3, 3]$
5. $f(x) = x^3$ on $\left[-\frac{1}{2}, 1\right]$
6. $g(x) = x^3 - 3x$ on $[-2, 2]$
7. $f(x) = x^5 - x^4$ on $[-1, 1]$
8. $g(t) = 3t^5 - 20t^3$ on $[-1, 2]$
9. $h(t) = te^{-t}$ on $[0, 2]$
10. $s(x) = \dfrac{\ln \sqrt{x}}{x}$ on $[1, 3]$
11. $f(x) = |x|$ on $[-1, 1]$
12. $f(x) = |x - 3|$ on $[-4, 4]$
13. $f(u) = \sin^2 u + \cos u$ on $[0, 2]$
14. $g(u) = \sin u - \cos u$ on $[0, \pi]$
15. **WHAT DOES THIS SAY?** Outline a procedure for finding the absolute extrema of a continuous function on a closed, bounded interval. Include in your outline a discussion of what is meant by critical numbers.

16. **Exploration Problem** Why is it important to check endpoints when finding an optimum value?

17. In Example 7, we found that the maximum value of $f(x) = x^{2/3}(5 - 2x)$ on $[-1, 2]$ is 7 and occurs at $x = -1$. The graph of this function on a leading brand of graphing calculator is shown:

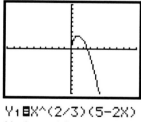

```
Y₁◘X^(2/3)(5-2X)
Xmin=-10 Ymin=-10
Xmax=10  Ymax=10
Xscl=1   Yscl=1
```

This graph is not correct. Can you explain the discrepancy? It is not our intent to "make up" problems to use with a calculator, but *whenever* you use a calculator or computer to assist you with calculus, you must understand the nature of the functions with which you are working, and not rely only on the calculator or computer output.

In Problems 18–29, find the absolute maximum and absolute minimum (largest and smallest values, respectively) of each continuous function on the closed, bounded interval. If the function is not continuous on the interval, then the extreme value theorem does not apply; if this is the case, so state.

18. $f(u) = 1 - u^{2/3}$ on $[-1, 1]$

19. $g(t) = (50 + t)^{2/3}$ on $[-50, 14]$

20. $g(x) = 2x^3 - 3x^2 - 36x + 4$ on $[-4, 4]$

21. $g(x) = x^3 + 3x^2 - 24x - 4$ on $[-4, 4]$

22. $f(x) = \frac{8}{3}x^3 - 5x^2 + 8x - 5$ on $[-4, 4]$

23. $f(x) = \frac{1}{6}(x^3 - 6x^2 + 9x + 1)$ on $[0, 2]$

24. $h(x) = \tan x + \sec x$ on $[0, 2\pi]$

25. $s(t) = t \cos t - \sin t$ on $[0, 2\pi]$

26. $f(x) = e^{-x} \sin x$ on $[0, 2\pi]$

27. $g(x) = \cot^{-1}\left(\frac{x}{9}\right) - \cot^{-1}\left(\frac{x}{5}\right)$ on $[0, 10]$

28. $f(x) = \begin{cases} 9 - 4x & \text{if } x < 1 \\ -x^2 + 6x & \text{if } x \geq 1 \end{cases}$ on $[0, 4]$

29. $f(x) = \begin{cases} 8 - 3x & \text{if } x < 2 \\ -x^2 + 3x & \text{if } x \geq 2 \end{cases}$ on $[-1, 4]$

Find the required extremum in Problems 30–35, or explain why it does not exist.

30. the smallest value of $f(x) = \dfrac{1}{x(x + 1)}$ on $[-0.5, 0)$

31. the smallest value of $g(x) = \dfrac{9}{x} + x - 3$ on $[1, 9]$

32. the smallest value of $g(x) = \dfrac{x^2 - 1}{x^2 + 1}$ on $[-1, 1]$

33. the largest value of $f(t) = \begin{cases} -t^2 - t + 2 & \text{if } t < 1 \\ 3 - t & \text{if } t \geq 1 \end{cases}$ on $[-2, 3]$

34. the smallest value of $f(x) = e^x + e^{-x} - x$ on $[0, 2]$

35. the largest value of $g(x) = \dfrac{\ln x}{\cos x}$ on $[2, 3]$ correct to the nearest tenth.

B In Problems 36–43, find the extrema (that is, the absolute maxima and minima).

36. $f(\theta) = \cos^3 \theta - 4\cos^2 \theta$ on $[-0.1, \pi + 0.1]$

37. $g(\theta) = \theta \sin \theta$ on $[-2, 2]$

38. $f(x) = 20 \sin(378\pi x)$ on $[-1, 1]$

39. $g(u) = 98u^3 - 4u^2 + 72u$ on $[0, 4]$

40. $f(w) = \sqrt{w}(w - 5)^{1/3}$ on $[0, 4]$

41. $h(x) = \sqrt[3]{x}\sqrt[3]{(x - 3)^2}$ on $[-1, 4]$

42. $h(x) = \cos^{-1} x \tan^{-1} x$ on $[0, 1]$

43. $f(x) = e^{-x}(\cos x + \sin x)$ on $[0, 2\pi]$

In Problems 44–47, find functions that satisfy the stated conditions and each of the following side conditions, if possible:

a. a minimum but no maximum

b. a maximum but no minimum

c. both a maximum and a minimum

d. neither a maximum nor a minimum

Note that in each problem, there may be a different solution function for each side condition.

44. Counterexample Problem For each of the four given conditions, find a function that is discontinuous and defined on an open interval.

45. Counterexample Problem For each of the four given conditions, find a function that is discontinuous and defined on a closed interval.

46. Counterexample Problem For each of the four given conditions, find a function that is continuous and defined on an open interval.

47. Counterexample Problem For each of the four given conditions, find a function that is continuous and defined on a closed interval.

48. Counterexample Problem Give a counterexample to show that the extreme value theorem does not necessarily apply if one disregards the condition that f be continuous.

49. Counterexample Problem Give a counterexample to show that the extreme value theorem does not necessarily apply if one disregards the condition that f be defined on a closed interval.

50. An object moves along the s-axis with position

$$s(t) = t^3 - 6t^2 - 15t + 11$$

Find the largest value of its velocity on $[0, 4]$.

51. An object moves along the s-axis with position

$$s(t) = t^4 - 2t^3 - 12t^2 + 60t - 10$$

Find the largest value of its velocity on $[0, 3]$.

52. Find two nonnegative numbers whose sum is 8 and the product of whose squares is as large as possible.

53. Find two nonnegative numbers such that the sum of one and twice the other is 12 if it is required that their product be as large as possible.

54. Under the condition that $3x + y = 80$, maximize xy^3 when $x \geq 0$, $y \geq 0$.

55. Under the condition that $3x + y = 126$, maximize xy when $x \geq 0$ and $y \geq 0$.

56. Under the condition that $2x - 5y = 18$, minimize $x^2 y$ when $x \geq 0$ and $y \leq 0$.

57. Show that if a rectangle with fixed perimeter P is to enclose the greatest area, it must be a square.

58. Find all points on the circle $x^2 + y^2 = a^2$ ($a \geq 0$) such that the product of the x-coordinate and the y-coordinate is as large as possible.

C **59. a.** Show that $\frac{1}{2}$ is the number that is greater than or equal to its own square by the greatest amount.

  b. Which nonnegative number is greater than or equal to its own cube by the greatest amount?

  c. Which nonnegative number is greater than or equal to its nth power ($n > 0$) by the greatest amount?

60. Given the constants $a_1, a_2, \ldots, a_n$, find the value of x that guarantees that the sum

$$S(x) = (a_1 - x)^2 + (a_2 - x)^2 + \cdots + (a_n - x)^2$$

will be as small as possible.

61. Without using Theorem 4.2, show that if $f'(c)$ exists and a

relative minimum occurs at c, then $f'(x) = 0$.

62. Explain why the function

$$f(\theta) = \frac{8}{\sin \theta} + \frac{27}{\cos \theta}$$

must attain a minimum in the open interval $(0, \frac{\pi}{2})$.

4.2   The Mean Value Theorem

IN THIS SECTION   Rolle's theorem, statement and proof of the mean value theorem, the zero-derivative theorem

If a car travels smoothly down a straight, level road with average velocity 60 mi/h, we would expect the speedometer reading to be exactly 60 mi/h at least once during the trip. After all, if the car's velocity were always above 60 mi/h, the average velocity would also be above that level, and the same reasoning applies if the velocity were always below 60 mi/h. More generally, if $s(t)$ is the car's position at time t during a trip over the time interval $a \leq t \leq b$, then there should be a time $t = c$ when the velocity $s'(c)$ equals the average velocity between times $t = a$ and $t = b$. That is, for some c with $a < c < b$,

$$\underbrace{\frac{s(b) - s(a)}{b - a}}_{\text{Average velocity}} = \underbrace{s'(c)}_{\text{Instantaneous velocity}}$$

This example illustrates a result called the mean value theorem for derivatives (abbreviated MVT) that is fundamental in the study of calculus. Our proof of the MVT is based on the following special case, which is named for the French mathematician, Michel Rolle (1652–1719), who gave a version of the result in an algebra text published in 1690.*

ROLLE'S THEOREM

The key to the proof of the mean value theorem is the following result, which is really just the MVT in the special case where $f(a) = f(b)$. In terms of our car example, Rolle's theorem says that if a moving car begins and ends at the same place, then somewhere during its journey, it must reverse direction, since $\dfrac{f(b) - f(a)}{b - a} = 0$ for $f(a) = f(b)$.

THEOREM 4.3   Rolle's theorem

Suppose f is continuous on the closed interval $[a, b]$ and differentiable on the open interval (a, b). If $f(a) = f(b)$, then there exists at least one number c between a and b such that $f'(c) = 0$.

Proof   To construct a formal proof, note that since f is continuous on the closed interval $[a, b]$, it follows from the extreme value theorem (Theorem 4.1) that f must have both a largest value and a smallest value on $[a, b]$. The case where f is constant on $[a, b]$ is easy since then $f'(x) = 0$ for all x in the interval (see Figure 4.11a).

---

*Incidentally, Rolle was a number theorist at heart and thoroughly distrusted the methods of calculus, which he regarded as a "collection of ingenious fallacies."

In the case where f is not constant throughout $[a, b]$, the largest and smallest values cannot be the same, and since $f(a) = f(b)$, we can conclude that at least one extreme value occurs at a number c that is not an endpoint; that is, $a < c < b$. Finally, since c is in the open interval (a, b) throughout which $f'(x)$ exists, it follows from the critical number theorem (Theorem 4.2) that $f'(c) = 0$. A graph illustrating this case is shown in Figure 4.11b.

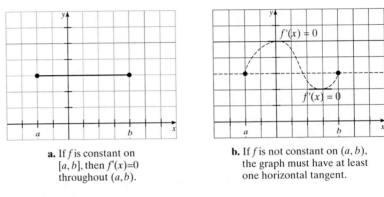

a. If f is constant on $[a, b]$, then $f'(x)=0$ throughout (a, b).

b. If f is not constant on (a, b), the graph must have at least one horizontal tangent.

Figure 4.11 A geometrical interpretation of Rolle's theorem

Note: Rolle's theorem asserts only that at least one number c exists between a and b such that $f'(c) = 0$. As illustrated in Figure 4.11b, there may be more than one such number.

STATEMENT AND PROOF OF THE MEAN VALUE THEOREM

Rolle's theorem can be interpreted as saying that there is at least one number c between a and b such that the tangent line to the graph of f at the point $(c, f(c))$ is parallel to the horizontal line through the points $(a, f(a))$ and $(b, f(b))$. It is reasonable to expect a similar result to hold if the endpoints of the graph are not necessarily at the same level of the graph; that is, if the graph in Figure 4.12a is tilted as shown in Figure 4.12b. This "tilted" version can be interpreted as showing that the line segment joining points $(a, f(a))$ and $(b, f(b))$ on the graph of a differentiable function $y = f(x)$ has the same slope as the tangent line to the graph at some point c between a and b. This observation leads to the following statement of the mean value theorem.

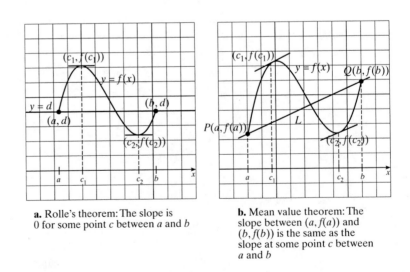

a. Rolle's theorem: The slope is 0 for some point c between a and b

b. Mean value theorem: The slope between $(a, f(a))$ and $(b, f(b))$ is the same as the slope at some point c between a and b

Figure 4.12 A geometrical comparison of Rolle's theorem with the mean value theorem

THEOREM 4.4   The mean value theorem for derivatives (MVT)

If f is continuous on the closed interval $[a, b]$ and differentiable on the open interval (a, b), then there exists in (a, b) at least one number c such that

$$\frac{f(b) - f(a)}{b - a} = f'(c)$$

Proof   Our strategy will be to apply Rolle's theorem to a function g related to f; namely the function

$$g(x) = \frac{f(b) - f(a)}{b - a}(x - a) + f(a) - f(x)$$

for $a \leq x \leq b$. Because f satisfies the hypotheses of the MVT, the function g is also continuous on the closed interval $[a, b]$ and differentiable on the open interval (a, b). In addition, we find that

$$g(a) = \left[\frac{f(b) - f(a)}{b - a}\right](a - a) + f(a) - f(a) = 0$$

$$g(b) = \left[\frac{f(b) - f(a)}{b - a}\right](b - a) + f(a) - f(b)$$

$$= [f(b) - f(a)] + f(a) - f(b) = 0$$

Thus, g satisfies the hypotheses of Rolle's theorem, so there exists at least one number c between a and b for which $g'(c) = 0$. Differentiating the function g, we find that

$$g'(x) = \frac{f(b) - f(a)}{b - a} - f'(x)$$

Because $g'(c) = 0$, we have

$$0 = g'(c) = \frac{f(b) - f(a)}{b - a} - f'(c)$$

This means that

$$f'(c) = \frac{f(b) - f(a)}{b - a}$$

as required.   ❏

The MVT asserts the existence of a number, c, but does not tell us how to find it. The following example illustrates one method for finding such a number c.

EXAMPLE 1   Finding the number c specified by the MVT

Show that the function $f(x) = x^3 + x^2$ satisfies the hypotheses of the MVT on the closed interval $[1, 2]$, and find a number c between 1 and 2 so that

$$f'(c) = \frac{f(2) - f(1)}{2 - 1}$$

Solution

Because f is a polynomial function, it is differentiable and also continuous on the entire interval $[1, 2]$. Thus, the hypotheses of the MVT are satisfied.

By differentiating f, we find that

$$f'(x) = 3x^2 + 2x$$

for all x. Therefore, we have $f'(c) = 3c^2 + 2c$, and the MVT equation

$$f'(c) = \frac{f(2) - f(1)}{2 - 1}$$

is satisfied when

$$3c^2 + 2c = \frac{f(2) - f(1)}{2 - 1} = \frac{12 - 2}{1} = 10$$

Solving the resulting equation $3c^2 + 2c - 10 = 0$ by the quadratic formula, we obtain

$$c = \frac{-1 \pm \sqrt{31}}{3}$$

The negative value is not in the open interval $(1, 2)$, but the positive value

$$c = \frac{-1 + \sqrt{31}}{3} \approx 1.522588121$$

satisfies the requirements of the MVT.   ∎

EXAMPLE 2   Using the MVT to prove a trigonometric inequality

Show that $|\sin x - \sin y| \leq |x - y|$ for all numbers x and y by applying the mean value theorem.

Solution

The inequality is true if $x = y$. Suppose $x \neq y$; then $f(\theta) = \sin\theta$ is differentiable and hence continuous for all θ, with $f'(\theta) = \cos\theta$. By applying the MVT to f on the closed interval with endpoints x and y, we see that

$$\frac{f(x) - f(y)}{x - y} = f'(c)$$

for some c between x and y. Because $f'(c) = \cos c$ and

$$f(x) - f(y) = \sin x - \sin y$$

it follows that

$$\frac{\sin x - \sin y}{x - y} = \cos c$$

Finally, we take the absolute value of the expression on each side, remembering that $|\cos c| \leq 1$ for any number c:

$$\left| \frac{\sin x - \sin y}{x - y} \right| = |\cos c| \leq 1$$

Thus, $|\sin x - \sin y| \leq |x - y|$, as claimed.   ∎

THE ZERO-DERIVATIVE THEOREM

The primary use of the MVT is as a tool for proving certain key theoretical results of calculus. For example, we know that the derivative of a constant is 0, and in Theorem 4.5, we prove a partial converse of this result by showing that a function whose derivative is 0 throughout the interval must be constant on that interval. This apparently simple result and its corollary (Theorem 4.6) turn out to be crucial to our development of integration in Chapter 5.

THEOREM 4.5   Zero-derivative theorem

Suppose f is a continuous function on the closed interval $[a, b]$ and is differentiable on the open interval (a, b), with $f'(x) = 0$ for all x on (a, b). Then the function f is constant on $[a, b]$.

Proof Let x_1 and x_2 be two distinct numbers ($x_1 \neq x_2$) chosen arbitrarily from the closed interval $[a, b]$. The function f satisfies the requirements of the MVT on the interval with endpoints x_1 and x_2, which means that there exists a number c between x_1 and x_2 such that

$$\frac{f(x_2) - f(x_1)}{x_2 - x_1} = f'(c)$$

By hypothesis, $f'(x) = 0$ throughout the open interval (a, b), and because c lies within this interval, we have $f'(c) = 0$. Thus, by substitution, we have

$$\frac{f(x_2) - f(x_1)}{x_2 - x_1} = 0$$

$$f(x_2) = f(x_1)$$

Because x_1 and x_2 were chosen arbitrarily from $[a, b]$, we conclude that $f(x) = k$, a constant, for all x, as required. ❑

THEOREM 4.6 Constant difference theorem

Suppose the functions f and g are continuous on the closed interval $[a, b]$ and differentiable on the open interval (a, b). Then if $f'(x) = g'(x)$ for all x in (a, b), there exists a constant C such that

$$f(x) = g(x) + C$$

for all x on $[a, b]$.

Proof Let $h(x) = f(x) - g(x)$; then

$$h'(x) = f'(x) - g'(x)$$
$$= 0 \qquad \text{Because } f'(x) = g'(x)$$

Thus, by Theorem 4.5, $h(x) = C$ for some constant C and all x on $[a, b]$, and because $h(x) = f(x) - g(x)$, it follows that

$$f(x) - g(x) = C$$
$$f(x) = g(x) + C \qquad \text{Add } g(x) \text{ to both sides.} \qquad ❑$$

> **➡ What This Says** Two functions with equal derivatives on an open interval differ by a constant on that interval.

4.2 PROBLEM SET

Ⓐ **1. Exploration Problem** What does Rolle's theorem say, and why is it important?

2. Exploration Problem State the hypotheses used in the proof of the MVT. How are the hypotheses used in the proof? Can the conclusion of the MVT be true if any or all of the hypotheses are not satisfied?

In Problems 3–20, verify that the given function f satisfies the hypotheses of the MVT on the given interval $[a, b]$. Then find all

numbers c between a and b for which

$$\frac{f(b) - f(a)}{b - a} = f'(c)$$

3. $f(x) = 2x^2 + 1$ on $[0, 2]$

4. $f(x) = -x^2 + 4$ on $[-1, 0]$

5. $f(x) = x^3 + x$ on $[1, 2]$

6. $f(x) = 2x^3 - x^2$ on $[0, 2]$

7. $f(x) = x^4 + 2$ on $[-1, 2]$

8. $f(x) = x^5 + 3$ on $[2, 4]$

9. $f(x) = \sqrt{x}$ on $[1, 4]$

10. $f(x) = \dfrac{1}{\sqrt{x}}$ on $[1, 4]$

11. $f(x) = \dfrac{1}{x + 1}$ on $[0, 2]$

12. $f(x) = 1 + \dfrac{1}{x}$ on $[1, 4]$

13. $f(x) = \cos x$ on $[0, \frac{\pi}{2}]$

14. $f(x) = \sin x + \cos x$ on $[0, 2\pi]$

15. $f(x) = e^x$ on $[0, 1]$

16. $f(x) = \frac{1}{2}(e^x + e^{-x})$ on $[0, 1]$

17. $f(x) = \ln x$ on $[\frac{1}{2}, 2]$ 18. $f(x) = \dfrac{\ln \sqrt{x}}{x}$ on $[1, 3]$

19. $f(x) = \tan^{-1} x$ on $[0, 1]$ 20. $f(x) = x \sin^{-1} x$ on $[0, 1]$

Decide whether Rolle's theorem can be applied to f on the interval indicated in Problems 21–30.

21. $f(x) = |x - 2|$ on $[0, 4]$ 22. $f(x) = \tan x$ on $[0, 2\pi]$

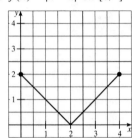
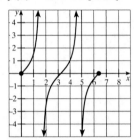

23. $f(x) = \sin x$ on $[0, 2\pi]$ 24. $f(x) = |x| - 2$ on $[0, 4]$

25. $f(x) = \sqrt[3]{x} - 1$ on $[-8, 8]$ 26. $f(x) = \dfrac{1}{x - 2}$ on $[-1, 1]$

27. $f(x) = \dfrac{1}{x - 2}$ on $[1, 2]$

28. $f(x) = 3x + \sec x$ on $[-\pi, \pi]$

29. $f(x) = \sin^2 x$ on $[-\frac{\pi}{2}, \frac{\pi}{2}]$

30. $f(x) = \sqrt{\ln x}$ on $[1, 2]$

31. Let $g(x) = 8x^3 - 6x + 8$. Find a function f with $f'(x) = g'(x)$ and $f(1) = 12$.

32. Let $g(x) = \sqrt{x^2 + 5}$. Find a function f with $f'(x) = g'(x)$ and $f(2) = 1$.

33. Show that $f(x) = \dfrac{x + 4}{5 - x}$ and $g(x) = \dfrac{-9}{x - 5}$ differ by a constant. Are the conditions of the constant difference theorem satisfied? Does $f'(x) = g'(x)$?

34. Let $f(x) = (x - 2)^3$ and $g(x) = (x^2 + 12)(x - 6)$. Use f and g to demonstrate the constant difference theorem.

35. Let $f(x) = (x - 1)^3$ and $g(x) = (x^2 + 3)(x - 3)$. Use f and g to demonstrate the constant difference theorem.

36. Let f be defined as shown in Figure 4.13.

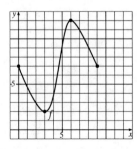

Figure 4.13   Function f on $[0, 9]$

Use the graph of f to estimate the values of c that satisfy the conclusion of Rolle's theorem on $[0, 9]$. What theorem would apply for the interval $[0, 5]$?

37. Let g be defined as shown in Figure 4.14.

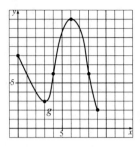

Figure 4.14   Function g on $[0, 9]$

Use the graph of g to estimate the values of c that satisfy the conclusion of the mean value theorem on $[0, 9]$. What theorem would apply for the interval $[4, 8]$?

38. **Alternative form of the mean value theorem:** If f is continuous on $[a, b]$ and differentiable on (a, b), then there exists a number c in (a, b) such that

$$f(b) = f(a) + (b - a)f'(c)$$

Prove this alternative form of the MVT.

39. Let u and v be any two numbers between $-\frac{\pi}{2}$ and $\frac{\pi}{2}$. Use the MVT to show that

$$|\tan u - \tan v| \geq |u - v|$$

40. If $f(x) = \dfrac{1}{x}$ on $[-1, 1]$, does the mean value theorem apply? Why or why not?

41. If $g(x) = |x|$ on $[-2, 2]$, does the mean value theorem apply? Why or why not?

42. **Counterexample Problem**   Is it true that

$$|\cos x - \cos y| \leq |x - y|$$

for all x and y? Either prove that the inequality is always valid or find a counterexample.

43. **Counterexample Problem**   Consider

$$f(x) = \begin{cases} 1 & \text{if } x \geq 0 \\ -1 & \text{if } x < 0 \end{cases}$$

$f'(x) = 0$ for all x in the domain, but f is not a constant. Does this example contradict the zero-derivative theorem? Why or why not?

44. **a.** Let n be a positive integer. Show that there is a number c between 0 and x for which

$$\frac{(1 + x)^n - 1}{x} = n(1 + c)^{n-1}$$

b. Use part **a** to evaluate

$$\lim_{x \to 0} \frac{(1 + x)^n - 1}{x}$$

45. **a.** Show that there is a number w between 0 and x for which

$$\frac{\cos x - 1}{x} = -\sin w$$

b. Use part **a** to evaluate

$$\lim_{x \to 0} \frac{\cos x - 1}{x}$$

46. Use the MVT to evaluate

$$\lim_{x \to \pi^+} \frac{\cos x + 1}{x - \pi}$$

47. Let $f(x) = 1 + \frac{1}{x}$. If a and b are constants such that $a < 0$ and $b > 0$, show that there is no number w between a and b for which

$$f(b) - f(a) = f'(w)(b - a)$$

48. Show that for any $x > 4$, there is a number w between 4 and x such that

$$\frac{\sqrt{x} - 2}{x - 4} = \frac{1}{2\sqrt{w}}$$

Use this fact to show that if $x > 4$, then

$$\sqrt{x} < 1 + \frac{x}{4}$$

49. Show that if an object moves along a straight line in such a way that its velocity is the same at two different times (that is, for a differentiable function v, we are given $v(t_1) = v(t_2)$ for $t_1 \neq t_2$), then there is some intermediate time when the acceleration is zero.

50. **Modeling Problem** Two radar patrol cars are located at fixed positions 6 mi apart on a long, straight road where the speed limit is 55 mi/h. A sports car passes the first patrol car traveling at 53 mi/h, and then 5 min later, it passes the second patrol car going 48 mi/h. Analyze a model of this situation to show that at some time between the two clockings, the sports car exceeded the speed limit. *Hint*: Use the MVT.

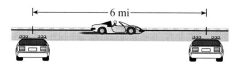

51. **Modeling Problem** Suppose two race cars begin at the same time and finish at the same time. Analyze a model to show that at some point in the race they had the same speed.

52. Use Rolle's theorem with

$$f(x) = (x - 1) \sin x$$

to show that the equation $\tan x = 1 - x$ has at least one solution for $0 < x < 1$.

53. Use the MVT to show that

$$\sqrt{1 + x} - 4 < \tfrac{1}{8}(x - 15)$$

if $x > 15$. *Hint*: Let $f(x) = \sqrt{1 + x}$.

54. Use the MVT to show that

$$\frac{1}{2x + 1} > \frac{1}{5} + \frac{2}{25}(2 - x)$$

if $0 \leq x \leq 2$.

55. Let $f(x) = \tan x$. Note that

$$f(\pi) = f(0) = 0$$

Show that there is no number w between 0 and π for which $f'(w) = 0$. Why does this fact not contradict the MVT?

56. Use Rolle's theorem or the MVT to show that there is no number a for which the equation

$$x^3 - 3x + a = 0$$

has *two* distinct solutions in the interval $[-1, 1]$.

57. If $a > 0$ is a constant, show that the equation

$$x^3 + ax - 1 = 0$$

has exactly one real solution. *Hint*: Let $f(x) = x^3 + ax - 1$ and use the intermediate value theorem to show that there is at least one root. Then assume there are two roots, and use Rolle's theorem to obtain a contradiction.

58. For constants a and b, $a > 0$, and n a positive integer, use Rolle's theorem or the MVT to show that the polynomial

$$p(x) = x^{2n+1} + ax + b$$

can have at most one real root.

59. Show that if $f''(x) = 0$ for all x, then f is a linear function. (That is, $f(x) = Ax + B$ for constants $A \neq 0$ and B.)

60. Show that if $f'(x) = Ax + B$ for constants $A \neq 0$ and B, then $f(x)$ is a quadratic function. (That is, $f(x) = ax^2 + bx + c$ for constants a, b, and c, where $a \neq 0$.)

4.3 Using Derivatives to Sketch the Graph of a Function

IN THIS SECTION increasing and decreasing functions, the first-derivative test, concavity and inflection points, the second-derivative test, curve sketching using the first and second derivatives

Our next goal is to see how information about the derivative f' and the second derivative f'' can be used to determine the shape of the graph of f. We begin by showing how the sign of f' is related to whether the graph of f is rising or falling.

INCREASING AND DECREASING FUNCTIONS

Suppose an ecologist has modeled the size of a population of a certain species as a function f of time t (months). If it turns out that the population is increasing until the end of the first year and is decreasing thereafter, it is reasonable to expect the population to be maximized at time $t = 12$ months and for the population curve to have a high point at $t = 12$, as shown in Figure 4.15. If the graph of a function f, such as this population curve, is rising throughout the interval $0 < x < 12$, we say that f is *strictly increasing* on that interval. Similarly, the graph of the function in Figure 4.15 is *strictly decreasing* on the interval $12 < t < 20$. These terms may be defined more formally as follows:

Strictly Increasing and Strictly Decreasing Functions

The function f is **strictly increasing** on an interval I if

$$f(x_1) < f(x_2) \quad \text{whenever} \quad x_1 < x_2$$

for x_1 and x_2 on I. Likewise, f is **strictly decreasing** on I if

$$f(x_1) > f(x_2) \quad \text{whenever} \quad x_1 < x_2$$

for x_1 and x_2 on I. (See Figure 4.16.)

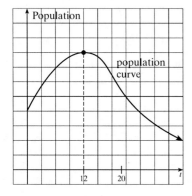

Figure 4.15 A population curve

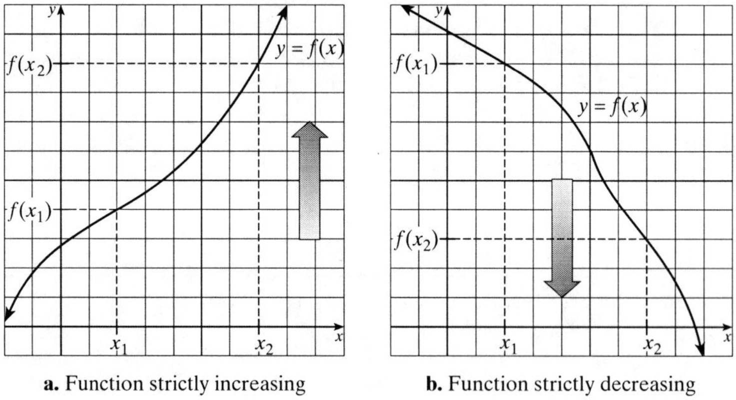

a. Function strictly increasing   **b.** Function strictly decreasing

Figure 4.16   Increasing and decreasing functions

Note that we do not use the word "strictly" every time we talk about a strictly monotonic function, or a strictly increasing function, or a strictly decreasing function.

A function f is said to be (strictly) **monotonic** on an interval I if it is either strictly increasing on all of I or strictly decreasing on all of I. The monotonic behavior is closely related to the sign of the derivative $f'(x)$. In particular, if the graph of a function has tangent lines with positive slope on I, the graph will be inclined upward and f will be increasing on I (see Figure 4.17). Since the slope of the tangent at each

WARNING A note on usage: We say that functions are **increasing** and that graphs are **rising**. For example, if $f(x) = x^2$, we say that the function f is increasing for $x > 0$ and that the graph is rising for $x > 0$.

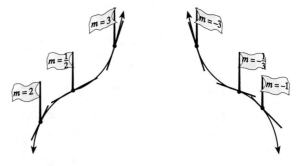

Figure 4.17   The graph is rising where $f' > 0$ and falling where $f' < 0$.
Notice that the small flags indicate the slope at various points on the graph.

point on the graph is measured by the derivative f', it is reasonable to expect f to be increasing on intervals where $f' > 0$. Similarly, it is reasonable to expect f to be decreasing on an interval when $f' < 0$. These observations are established formally in Theorem 4.7.

THEOREM 4.7   Monotone function theorem

Let f be differentiable on the open interval (a, b).

If $f'(x) > 0$ on (a, b), then f is strictly increasing on (a, b).

If $f'(x) < 0$ on (a, b), then f is strictly decreasing on (a, b).

Proof   We will prove that f is strictly increasing on (a, b) if $f'(x) > 0$ throughout the interval. The strictly decreasing case is similar and is left as an exercise for the reader.

Suppose $f'(x) > 0$ throughout the interval (a, b), and let x_1 and x_2 be two numbers chosen arbitrarily from this interval, with $x_1 < x_2$. The MVT tells us that

$$\frac{f(x_2) - f(x_1)}{x_2 - x_1} = f'(c) \quad \text{or} \quad f(x_2) - f(x_1) = f'(c)(x_2 - x_1)$$

for some number c between x_1 and x_2. Because both $f'(c) > 0$ and $x_2 - x_1 > 0$, it follows that $f'(c)(x_2 - x_1) > 0$, and therefore

$$f(x_2) - f(x_1) > 0 \quad \text{or} \quad f(x_2) > f(x_1)$$

That is, if x_1 and x_2 are any two numbers in (a, b) such that $x_1 < x_2$, then $f(x_1) < f(x_2)$, which means that f is strictly increasing on (a, b).   ❏

To determine where a function f is increasing or decreasing, we begin by finding the critical numbers (where the derivative is zero or does not exist). These numbers divide the x-axis into intervals, and we test the sign of $f'(x)$ in each of these intervals. If $f'(x) > 0$ in an interval, then f is increasing in that same interval, and if $f'(x) < 0$ in an interval, then f is decreasing in that same interval.

To indicate where a given function f is increasing and where it is decreasing, we will mark the critical values on a number line and use an up arrow (↑) to indicate an interval where f is increasing and a down arrow (↓) to indicate an interval where f is decreasing. Sometimes, when the full graph of f is displayed, we indicate the sign of f' on an interval bounded by critical numbers with a string of + signs if f is increasing on the interval or a string of − signs if f is decreasing there. This notation is illustrated in the following example.

EXAMPLE 1   Finding intervals of increase and decrease

Determine where the function defined by $f(x) = x^3 - 3x^2 - 9x + 1$ is strictly increasing and where it is strictly decreasing.

Solution

First, we find the derivative:

$$f'(x) = 3x^2 - 6x - 9 = 3(x + 1)(x - 3)$$

Next, we determine the critical numbers: $f'(x)$ exists for all x and $f'(x) = 0$ at $x = -1$ and $x = 3$. These critical numbers divide the x-axis into three parts, as shown in Figure 4.18a, and we select any arbitrary number from each of these intervals. For example, we select -2, 0, and 4, evaluate the derivative at these numbers, and mark each interval as increasing (↑) or decreasing (↓), according to whether the derivative is positive or negative, respectively. This is shown in Figure 4.18b. The function f is increasing for $x < -1$ and for $x > 3$; f is decreasing for $-1 < x < 3$.   ■

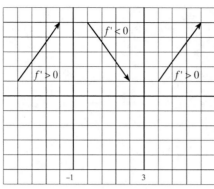

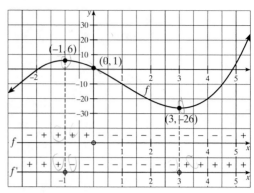

a. Intervals where f is increasing and where it is decreasing

b. The graph of f along with the sign graphs for f and f'

Figure 4.18 $f(x) = x^3 - 3x^2 - 9x + 1$

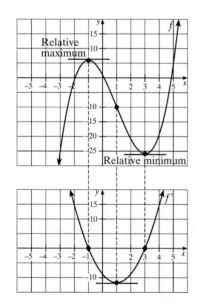

Figure 4.19 Graphs of f and f'

EXAMPLE 2 Comparing the graphs of a function and its derivative

Graph $f(x) = x^3 - 3x^2 - 9x + 1$ and $f'(x) = 3x^2 - 6x - 9$ and compare.

a. When $f' > 0$, what can be said about the graph of f?
b. When the graph of f is falling, what can be said about the graph of f'?
c. Where do the critical numbers of f appear on the graph of f?

Solution

The graphs of f and f' are shown in Figure 4.19.

a. When $f'(x) > 0$, the graph of f is rising. This occurs when $x < -1$ and when $x > 3$.
b. When the graph of f is falling (for $-1 < x < 3$), we have $f'(x) < 0$, so the graph of f' is below the x-axis.
c. The critical numbers of f are where $f'(x) = 0$; that is, at $x = -1$ and $x = 3$, so they are the x-intercepts of the graph of f'. ∎

THE FIRST-DERIVATIVE TEST

Every relative extremum is a critical point. However, as we saw in Section 4.1, not every critical point of a continuous function is necessarily a relative extremum. If the derivative is positive to the immediate left of a critical number and negative to its immediate right, the graph changes from increasing to decreasing and the critical point must be a relative maximum, as shown in Figure 4.20a. If the derivative is negative to the immediate left of a critical number and positive to its immediate right, the graph changes from decreasing to increasing and the critical point is a relative minimum (Figure 4.20b). However, if the sign of the derivative is the same on both immediate sides of the critical number, then it is neither a relative maximum nor a relative minimum (Figure 4.20c). These observations are summarized in a procedure called the *first-derivative test for relative extrema*.

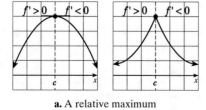

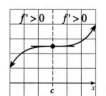
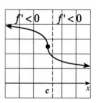

a. A relative maximum   **b.** A relative minimum   **c.** No extremum

Figure 4.20 Three patterns of behavior near a critical number

The First-Derivative Test for Relative Extrema

Step 1. Find all critical numbers of a continuous function f. That is, find all numbers c such that $f(c)$ is defined and either $f'(c) = 0$ or $f'(c)$ does not exist.

Step 2. Classify each critical point $(c, f(c))$ as follows:

a. The point $(c, f(c))$ is a **relative maximum** if

$f'(x) > 0$ (graph rising) for all x in an open interval (a, c) to the left of c, and

$f'(x) < 0$ (graph falling) for all x in an open interval (c, b) to the right of c.

b. The point $(c, f(c))$ is a **relative minimum** if

$f'(x) < 0$ (graph falling) for all x in an open interval (a, c) to the left of c, and

$f'(x) > 0$ (graph rising) for all x in an open interval (c, b) to the right of c.

or

c. The point $(c, f(c))$ is **not an extremum** if the derivative $f'(x)$ has the same sign for all x in open intervals (a, c) and (c, b) on each side of c.

Suppose we apply this first-derivative test to the polynomial $f(x) = x^3 - 3x^2 - 9x + 1$ In Example 2 we found that this function has the critical numbers -1 and 3 and that f is increasing when $x < -1$ and $x > 3$ and decreasing when $-1 < x < 3$ (see the arrow pattern above). The first-derivative test tells us there is a relative maximum at -1 ($\uparrow \downarrow$ pattern) and a relative minimum at 3 ($\downarrow \uparrow$ pattern).

EXAMPLE 3 Relative extrema using the first-derivative test

Find all critical numbers of $g(t) = t - 2\sin t$ for $0 \le t \le 2\pi$, and determine whether each corresponds to a relative maximum, a relative minimum, or neither. Sketch the graph of g.

Solution Because $g'(t) = 1 - 2\cos t$ exists for all t, the only critical numbers occur when $g'(t) = 0$; that is, when $\cos t = \frac{1}{2}$. Solving, we find that the critical numbers for $g(t)$ on the interval $[0, 2\pi]$ are $\frac{\pi}{3}$ and $\frac{5\pi}{3}$.

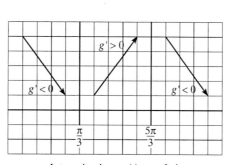

a. Intervals where $g(t) = t - 2\sin t$ is increasing or decreasing

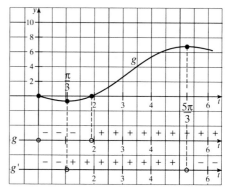

b. The graph of $g(t) = t - 2\sin t$ for $0 \le t \le 2\pi$

Figure 4.21 The first-derivative test for $g(t) = t - 2\sin t$

Next, we examine the sign of $g'(t)$. Thanks to the intermediate value theorem, because $g'(t)$ is continuous, it is enough to check the sign of $g'(t)$ at convenient numbers on each side of the critical numbers, as shown in Figure 4.21a. Notice that the arrows show the increasing and decreasing pattern for g. According to the first-derivative test, there is a relative minimum at $\frac{\pi}{3}$ and a relative maximum at $\frac{5\pi}{3}$. The graph of g is shown in Figure 4.21b. ■

CONCAVITY AND INFLECTION POINTS

Knowing where a given graph is rising and falling gives only a partial picture of the graph. For example, suppose we wish to sketch the graph of $f(x) = x^3 + 3x + 1$. The derivative $f'(x) = 3x^2 + 3$ is positive for all x so the graph is always rising. But in what *way* is it rising? Each of the graphs in Figure 4.22 is a possible graph of f, but they are quite different from one another.

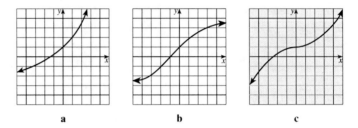

a   **b**   **c**

Figure 4.22   Which curve is the graph of $f(x) = x^3 + 3x + 1$?

Figure 4.22 shows three possibilities for the graph of f. All three are always rising, but they differ in the way they "bend" as they rise. The "bending" of a curve is measured by its *concavity*. If a curve lies above its tangent lines on some interval (a, b), then we say the curve is *concave up*, and if the curve lies below its tangent lines, we say it is *concave down* on (a, b). We will examine concavity, and then return in Example 4 to determine which of the three candidates in Figure 4.22 is indeed the graph of $f(x) = x^3 + 3x + 1$.

Concavity

> If the graph of a function f lies above all of its tangents on an interval I, then it is said to be **concave up** on I. If the graph of f lies below all of its tangents on I, it is said to be **concave down**.

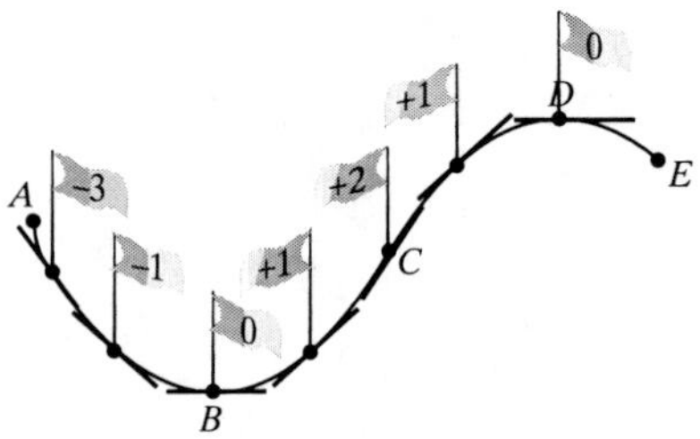

To be specific, a portion of a graph that is cupped upward is called *concave up*, and a portion that is cupped downward is *concave down*. Figure 4.23 shows a graph that is concave up between A and C and concave down between C and E. At various points on the graph, the slope is indicated by "flags," and we observe that the slope increases from A to C and decreases from C to E. This is no accident! *The slope of a graph increases on an interval where the graph is concave up and decreases where the graph is concave down.*

Conversely, a graph will be concave up on any interval where the slope is increasing and concave down where the slope is decreasing. Because the slope is found by computing the derivative, it is reasonable to expect the graph of a given function f to be concave up where the derivative f' is strictly increasing. According to the monotone function theorem (Theorem 4.7), this occurs when $(f')' > 0$, which means that the graph of f is concave up where the *second derivative* f'' satisfies $f'' > 0$. Similarly, the graph is concave down where $f'' < 0$. We use this observation to characterize concavity.

Figure 4.23 The slope of a graph increases or decreases, depending on its concavity.

> **Derivative Characterization of Concavity**
>
> The graph of a function f is **concave up** on any open interval I where $f''(x) > 0$, and it is **concave down** where $f''(x) < 0$.

When discussing the concavity of a function f, we will display a diagram in which a "cup" symbol ($\cup$) above an interval indicates that f is concave up on the interval and a "cap" symbol ($\cap$) indicates that f is concave down there. This convention is illustrated in the following example.

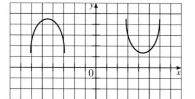

Figure 4.24 Intervals of concavity

EXAMPLE 4   Concavity for a polynomial function

Find where the graph of $f(x) = x^3 + 3x + 1$ is concave up and where it is concave down.

Solution

We find that $f'(x) = 3x^2 + 3$ and $f''(x) = 6x$. Therefore, $f''(x) < 0$ if $x < 0$ and $f''(x) > 0$ if $x > 0$, so the graph of f is concave down for $x < 0$ and concave up for $x > 0$, as indicated in Figure 4.24. Returning to Figure 4.22c, the graph is concave down to the left of $x = 0$ and concave up to the right. Hence, this is the graph of $f(x)$. ∎

In Figure 4.23, notice that the graph changes from concave up to concave down at the point C. It will be convenient to have a special name for such transition points.

Inflection Point

> A point $P(c, f(c))$ on a curve is called an **inflection point** if the graph is concave up on one side of P and concave down on the other side.

WARNING An inflection point must be on the graph, meaning $f(c)$ must be defined if there is an inflection point at $x = c$.

Returning to Example 4, notice that the graph of $f(x) = x^3 + 3x + 1$ has exactly one inflection point, at $(0, 1)$, where the concavity changes from down to up.

Various kinds of graphical behavior are illustrated in Figure 4.25. Note that the graph is rising on the interval $[a, c_1]$, falling on $[c_1, c_2]$, rising on $[c_2, c_3]$, falling on $[c_3, c_4]$, rising on $[c_4, c_5]$, and falling on $[c_5, b]$. The concavity is up on $[p_1, p_2]$, and down otherwise. In this figure, and elsewhere, when the graph of f is displayed, we will indicate the sign of f'' on an interval by a string of $+$ signs if $f'' > 0$ on the interval, and a string of $-$ signs if $f'' < 0$ there.

The graph has relative maxima at c_1, c_3, and c_5, and relative minima at c_2 and c_4. There are horizontal tangents ($f'(x) = 0$) at all of these points except at c_1 and c_3, where there are sharp points, called *corners* ($f'(c_1)$ and $f'(c_3)$ do not exist). There is a horizontal tangent at p_1; that is, $f'(p_1) = 0$, but no relative extremum appears there. Instead, we have points of inflection at p_1 and p_2, because the concavity changes direction at each of these points.

In general, the concavity of the graph of f will change only at points where $f''(x) = 0$ or $f''(x)$ does not exist—that is, at critical numbers of the derivative $f'(x)$. We will call the number c a **second-order critical number** if $f''(c) = 0$ or $f''(c)$ does not exist, and in this context an "ordinary" critical number (where $f'(c) = 0$ or $f'(c)$ does not exist) will be referred to as a **first-order critical number.** If we do not specify otherwise, a critical number is always a first-order critical number. Inflection points correspond to second-order critical numbers and must actually be on the graph

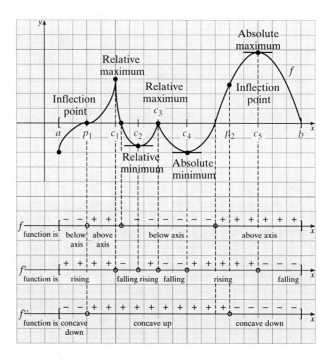

Figure 4.25 A graph of a function showing critical points and inflection points

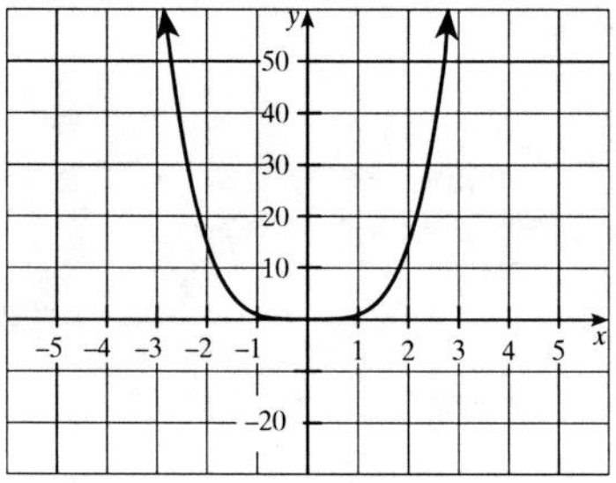

of f. Specifically, a number c such that $f''(c)$ is not defined and the concavity of f changes at c will correspond to an inflection point if and only if $f(c)$ is defined.

Here is an example of one way inflection points may appear in applications.

Figure 4.26 The graph of $f(x) = x^4$ has no inflection point at $(0, 0)$ even though $f''(0) = 0$.

WARNING A continuous function f need not have an inflection point at every number c where $f''(c) = 0$. For instance, if $f(x) = x^4$, we have $f''(0) = 0$, but the graph of f is always concave up (see Figure 4.26).

EXAMPLE 5 Peak worker efficiency

An efficiency study of the morning shift at a factory indicates that the number of units produced by an average worker t hours after 8:00 A.M. may be modeled by the formula $Q(t) = -t^3 + 9t^2 + 12t$. At what time in the morning is the worker performing most efficiently?

Solution

We assume that the morning shift runs from 8:00 A.M. until noon and that worker efficiency is maximized when the rate of production

$$R(t) = Q'(t) = -3t^2 + 18t + 12$$

is as large as possible for $0 \leq t \leq 4$. The derivative of R is

$$R'(t) = Q''(t) = -6t + 18$$

which is zero when $t = 3$; this is the critical number. Using the optimization criterion of Section 4.1, we know that the extrema of $R(t)$ on the closed interval $[0, 4]$ must occur at either the interior critical number 3 or at one (or both) of the endpoints (which are 0 and 4). We find that

$$R(0) = 12 \quad R(3) = 39 \quad R(4) = 36$$

so the rate of production $R(t)$ is greatest and the worker is performing most efficiently when $t = 3$; that is, at 11:00 A.M. The graphs of the production function Q and its derivative, the rate-of-production function R, are shown in Figure 4.27. Notice that the production curve is steepest and the rate of production is greatest when $t = 3$.

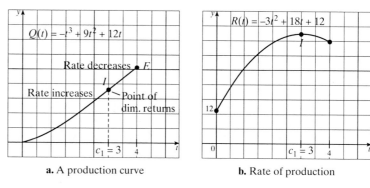

a. A production curve   **b.** Rate of production

Figure 4.27 Graph of a production curve showing the point of diminishing returns ■

In Example 5, note how the rate of production, as measured by the slope of the graph of the average worker's output, increases from 0 to the inflection point I and then decreases from I to E, as shown in Figure 4.27a. Because the point I marks the point where the rate of production "peaks out," it is natural to refer to I as a point of **diminishing returns.** It is also an inflection point on the graph of Q. Knowing that this point occurs at 11:00 A.M., the manager of the factory might be able to increase the overall output of the labor force by scheduling a break near this time, since the production rate changes from increasing to decreasing at this time.

THE SECOND-DERIVATIVE TEST

It is often possible to classify a critical point $P(c, f(c))$ on the graph of f by examining the sign of $f''(c)$. Specifically, suppose $f'(c) = 0$ and $f''(c) > 0$. Then there is a horizontal tangent line at P and the graph of f is concave up in the neighborhood of P. This means that the graph of f is cupped upward from the horizontal tangent at P, and it is reasonable to expect P to be a relative minimum, as shown in Figure 4.28a. Similarly, we expect P to be a relative maximum if $f'(c) = 0$ and $f''(c) < 0$, because the graph is cupped down beneath the critical point P, as shown in Figure 4.28b.

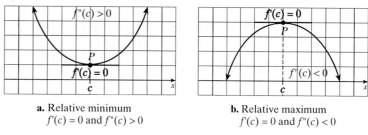

a. Relative minimum   **b.** Relative maximum
$f'(c) = 0$ and $f''(c) > 0$ $f'(c) = 0$ and $f''(c) < 0$

Figure 4.28 Second-derivative test for relative extrema

These observations lead to the *second-derivative test* for relative extrema.

The Second-Derivative Test for Relative Extrema

Let f be a function such that $f'(c) = 0$ and the second derivative exists on an open interval containing c.

If $f''(c) > 0$, there is a **relative minimum** at $x = c$.

If $f''(c) < 0$, there is a **relative maximum** at $x = c$.

If $f''(c) = 0$, then the second-derivative test **fails** (either a maximum, or a minimum, or neither may occur).

EXAMPLE 6   Using the second-derivative test

Use the second-derivative test to determine whether each critical number of the function $f(x) = 3x^5 - 5x^3 + 2$ corresponds to a relative maximum, a relative minimum, or neither.

Solution

Once again, we begin by finding the first and second derivatives:

$$f'(x) = 15x^4 - 15x^2 = 15x^2(x - 1)(x + 1)$$
$$f''(x) = 60x^3 - 30x = 30x(2x^2 - 1)$$

Solving $f'(x) = 0$, we find that the critical numbers are $x = 0$, $x = 1$, and $x = -1$. We plot these points on a number line, as shown in Figure 4.29. To apply the second-derivative test, we evaluate $f''(x)$ at each critical number.

$f''(0) = 0$; test fails at $x = 0$.

$f''(1) = 30 > 0$; positive, so the test tells us that there is a relative minimum at $x = 1$.

$f''(-1) = -30 < 0$; negative, so the test tells us that there is a relative maximum at $x = -1$.   ∎

When the second-derivative test fails, as at $x = 0$ in Example 6, the critical point can often be classified using the first-derivative test. For instance, the first derivative in Example 6 is

$$f'(x) = 15x^2(x - 1)(x + 1)$$

We see $f'(x) = 0$ at $x = -1$, 0, and 1. We can plot these points on a number line, shown in Figure 4.29, and then evaluate $f'(x)$ at test numbers just to the left and just to the right of each critical number.

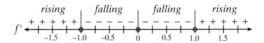

rising   falling   falling   rising

Figure 4.29   Sign graph for the derivative of $f(x) = 3x^5 - 5x^3 + 2$

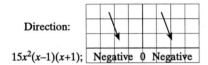

Direction:

$15x^2(x-1)(x+1)$; | Negative   0   Negative

Figure 4.30 The graph of $f(x) = 3x^5 - 5x^3 + 2$ is falling on both sides of $x = 0$.

We show a number line like this as part of the graph of many of our examples (as we did in Figure 4.25), but most often we show the derivative to the right and left of a critical number. For Example 6, the derivative is negative both to the immediate left and right of 0, which we illustrate as shown in Figure 4.30. Neither kind of extremum occurs at $x = 0$ (↓ ↓ pattern).

EXAMPLE 7   Finding inflection points

Find the inflection points for the function $f(x) = 3x^5 - 5x^3 + 2$, given in Example 6.

Solution

We begin with the second derivative (from Example 6):

$$f''(x) = 30x(2x^2 - 1)$$

To find the inflection points, we look at the second-order critical numbers, namely, where $f''(x) = 0$; that is, at $x = 0$ and $x = \pm\sqrt{\frac{1}{2}} = \pm\frac{\sqrt{2}}{2}$. We can show these on a sign graph of the second derivative, as in Figure 4.31. Notice that the inflection points occur where the sign of the second derivative changes.

The graph of f is shown in Figure 4.32, along with the sign graphs for both the first and second derivatives. Spend some time studying this figure to see how the signs of the first derivative indicate where the graph is rising and where it is falling, as well

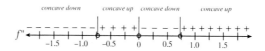

Figure 4.31 Sign graph for the second derivative of $f(x) = 3x^5 - 5x^3 + 2$

as how the signs of the second derivative show the concavity. For completeness, the figure also shows the sign graph for the function itself: The graph is above the x-axis where f is positive, below the x-axis where f is negative, and crosses the x-axis where $f(x) = 0$.

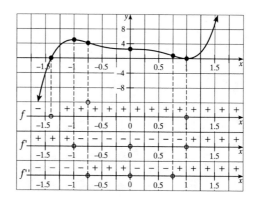

Figure 4.32 Graph of $f(x) = 3x^5 - 5x^3 + 2$ ■

Example 7 demonstrates both the strength and the weakness of the second-derivative test. In particular, when it is relatively easy to find the second derivative (as with a polynomial) and if the zeros of this function are easy to find, then the second-derivative test provides a quick means for classifying the critical points. However, if it is difficult to compute $f''(c)$ or if $f''(c) = 0$, it may be easier, or even necessary, to apply the first-derivative test.

CURVE SKETCHING USING THE FIRST AND SECOND DERIVATIVES

Now, we are ready to develop a procedure for curve sketching. The key ideas appear in Example 8.

EXAMPLE 8   Sketching the graph of a polynomial function

Determine where the function $f(x) = x^4 - 4x^3 + 10$ is increasing, where it is decreasing, where its graph is concave up, and where its graph is concave down. Find the relative extrema and inflection points, and sketch the graph of f.

Solution

The first derivative,

$$f'(x) = 4x^3 - 12x^2 = 4x^2(x - 3)$$

is zero when $x = 0$ and when $x = 3$. Because $4x^2 > 0$ for $x \neq 0$, we have $f'(x) < 0$ for $x < 3$ (except for $x = 0$) and $f'(x) > 0$ for $x > 3$. The pattern showing where f is increasing and where it is decreasing is displayed in Figure 4.33a.

Next, to determine the concavity of the graph we compute

$$f''(x) = 12x^2 - 24x = 12x(x - 2)$$

If $x < 0$ or $x > 2$, then $f''(x) > 0$ and the graph is concave up. It is concave down when $0 < x < 2$, because $f''(x) < 0$ on this interval. The concavity of the graph of f is shown in Figure 4.33b.

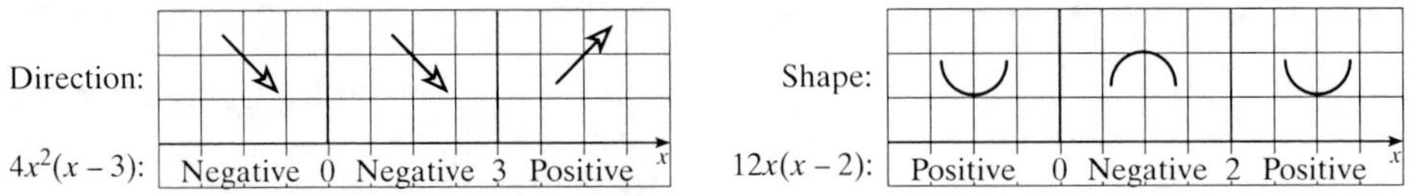

Direction:

Shape:

$4x^2(x - 3)$:   Negative 0 Negative 3 Positive

$12x(x - 2)$:   Positive 0 Negative 2 Positive

a. First derivative signs.   **b.** Second derivative signs.

Figure 4.33   Intervals of increase and decrease and concavity for $f(x) = x^4 - 4x^3 + 10$

The two diagrams in Figure 4.33 tell us that there is a relative minimum at $x = 3$ and inflection points at $x = 0$ and $x = 2$ (because the second derivative changes sign at these points).

To find the y-values of the critical points and the inflection points, evaluate f at $x = 0, 2,$ and 3:

$$f(0) = (0)^4 - 4(0)^3 + 10 = 10$$

$$f(2) = (2)^4 - 4(2)^3 + 10 = -6$$

$$f(3) = (3)^4 - 4(3)^3 + 10 = -17$$

Finally, to sketch the graph of f, we first place a "cup" ($\cup$) at the minimum point $(3, -17)$ and note that $(0, 10)$ and $(2, -6)$ are inflection points. Remember there is also a horizontal tangent at $(0, 10)$. The preliminary graph is shown in Figure 4.34a. Complete the sketch by passing a smooth curve through these points, using the two diagrams in Figure 4.33 as a guide for determining where the graph is rising and falling and where it is concave up and down. The completed graph is shown in Figure 4.34b.

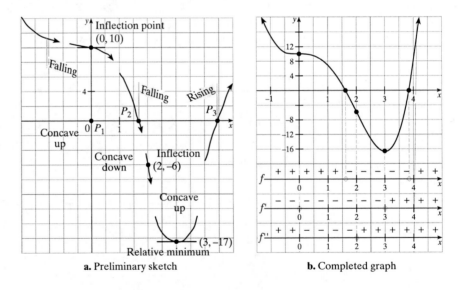

a. Preliminary sketch   **b.** Completed graph

Figure 4.34   Graphing $f(x) = x^4 - 4x^3 + 10$ ∎

EXAMPLE 9   Sketching the graph of an exponential function

Determine where the function

$$f(x) = \frac{1}{\sqrt{2\pi}} e^{-x^2/2}$$

is increasing, decreasing, concave up, and concave down. Find the relative extrema and inflection points and sketch the graph. This function plays an important role in statistics, where it is called the *standard normal density function*.

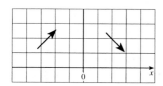

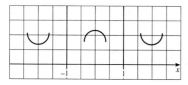

a. Intervals of increase and decrease for $f(x)$

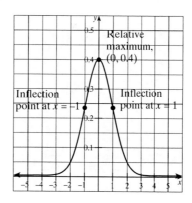

b. Concavity for $f(x)$

Figure 4.35 Intervals of increase, decrease, and concavity for
$$f(x) = \frac{1}{\sqrt{2\pi}}e^{-x^2/2}$$

Solution

The first derivative is

$$f'(x) = \frac{-x}{\sqrt{2\pi}}e^{-x^2/2}$$

Because $e^{-x^2/2}$ is always positive, $f'(x) = 0$ if and only if $x = 0$. Hence, the corresponding point

$$\left(0, \frac{1}{\sqrt{2\pi}}\right) \approx (0, 0.4)$$

is the only critical point. Checking the sign of f' on each side of 0, we find that f is increasing for $x < 0$ and decreasing for $x > 0$, so there is a relative maximum at $x = 0$, as indicated in Figure 4.35a.

We find that the second derivative of f is

$$f''(x) = \frac{x^2}{\sqrt{2\pi}}e^{-x^2/2} - \frac{1}{\sqrt{2\pi}}e^{-x^2/2} = \frac{1}{\sqrt{2\pi}}(x^2-1)e^{-x^2/2}$$

which is zero when $x = \pm1$. We find that $f(1) = f(-1) \approx 0.24$, and that the concavity of the graph of f is as indicated in Figure 4.35b.

Finally, we draw a smooth curve through the known points, as shown in Figure 4.36. The graph of f rises to the high point at approximately $(0, 0.4)$ and then falls indefinitely, approaching the x-axis arbitrarily closely because $e^{-x^2/2}$ approaches 0 as $|x|$ increases without bound. Note that the graph has no x-intercepts, because $e^{-x^2/2}$ is always positive.

Figure 4.36 Graph of $f(x) = \frac{1}{\sqrt{2\pi}}e^{-x^2/2}$

■

EXAMPLE 10   Sketching the graph of a trigonometric function

Sketch the graph of $T(x) = \sin x + \cos x$ on $[0, 2\pi]$.

Solution

You probably graphed this function in trigonometry by adding ordinates. However, with this example we wish to illustrate the power of calculus to draw the graph. Thus, we begin by finding the first and second derivatives.

$$T'(x) = \cos x - \sin x \qquad\qquad T''(x) = -\sin x - \cos x$$

We find the critical numbers (both T' and T'' are defined for all values of x):

$T'(x) = 0$ when $\cos x = \sin x$; thus, $x = \frac{\pi}{4}$ and $x = \frac{5\pi}{4}$.

$T''(x) = 0$ when $\cos x = -\sin x$; thus, $x = \frac{3\pi}{4}$ and $x = \frac{7\pi}{4}$.

The intervals of increase and decrease as well as the concavity pattern are shown in Figure 4.37.

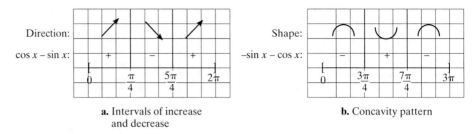

Direction:		Shape:	
$\cos x - \sin x$:	+ − +	$-\sin x - \cos x$:	− + −

a. Intervals of increase and decrease   **b.** Concavity pattern

Figure 4.37   Preliminary work for sketching $T(x) = \sin x + \cos x$

Find the critical points, the points of inflection, and the endpoints:

Relative maximum: $T\left(\frac{\pi}{4}\right) = \sqrt{2}$; the critical point is $(\frac{\pi}{4}, \sqrt{2})$.

Relative minimum: $T(\frac{5\pi}{4}) = -\sqrt{2}$; the critical point is $(\frac{5\pi}{4}, -\sqrt{2})$.

Inflection: $T(\frac{3\pi}{4}) = 0$; the inflection point is $(\frac{3\pi}{4}, 0)$.
$\quad\quad\quad\quad T(\frac{7\pi}{4}) = 0$; the inflection point is $(\frac{7\pi}{4}, 0)$.

Endpoints: $T(0) = 1$ and $T(2\pi) = 1$.

Finally, pass a smooth curve through these key points as indicated in the preliminary sketch in Figure 4.38a to obtain the completed graph shown in Figure 4.38b.

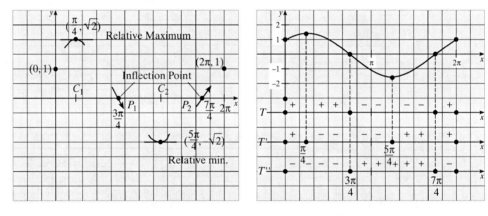

a. Preliminary sketch   **b.** Completed sketch

Figure 4.38   Graph of $T(x) = \sin x + \cos x$ on $[0, 2\pi]$ ■

4.3   PROBLEM SET

Ⓐ 1. **WHAT DOES THIS SAY?**   What is the first-derivative test?

2. **Exploration Problem**   What is the relationship between the graph of a function and the graph of its derivative?

3. **WHAT DOES THIS SAY?**   What is the second-derivative test?

4. **WHAT DOES THIS SAY?**   What is the relationship between concavity, points of inflection, and the second derivative?

5. **Exploration Problem**   The cartoon on page 209 exclaims, "Our prices are rising slower than any place in town." Restate using calculus.

In Problems 6–7, identify which curve represents a function f and which curve represents its derivative f'.

6.

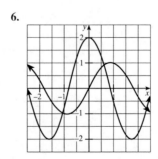

7.

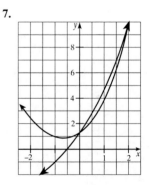

Draw a curve that represents the derivative of the function defined by the curves shown in Problems 8–11.

8.

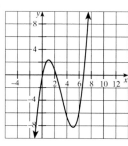

9.

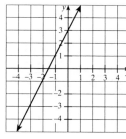

10.

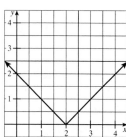

11.

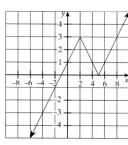

For the functions in Problems 12–19,

  a. *Find all critical numbers.*

  b. *Find where the function is increasing and decreasing.*

  c. *Find the critical points and identify each as a relative maximum, relative minimum, or neither.*

  d. *Find the second-order critical numbers and tell where the graph is concave up and where it is concave down.*

  e. *Sketch the graph.*

12. $f(x) = \frac{1}{3}x^3 - 9x + 2$ **13.** $f(x) = x^3 + 3x^2 + 1$

14. $f(x) = x^5 + 5x^4 - 550x^3 - 2{,}000x^2 + 60{,}000x$

15. $f(x) = x^3 + 35x^2 - 125x - 9{,}375$

16. $f(x) = x + \frac{1}{x}$ **17.** $f(x) = \frac{x-1}{x^2+3}$

18. $f(x) = x \ln x$ **19.** $f(t) = (t+1)^2(t-5)$

In Problems 20–35, determine the intervals of increase and decrease and concavity for the given function, and then use those intervals to help you sketch its graph.

20. $f(x) = (x-12)^4 - 2(x-12)^3$

21. $f(x) = 1 + 2x + 18/x$

22. $f(u) = 3u^4 - 2u^3 - 12u^2 + 18u - 5$

23. $g(u) = u^4 + 6u^3 - 24u^2 + 26$

24. $f(x) = \sqrt{x^2 + 1}$ **25.** $g(t) = (t^3 + t)^2$

26. $f(t) = (t^3 + 3t^2)^3$ **27.** $f(x) = \frac{x}{x^2+1}$

28. $f(t) = t - \ln t$ **29.** $f(t) = t^2 e^{-3t}$

30. $f(x) = e^x + e^{-x}$ **31.** $f(x) = (\ln x)^2$

32. $t(\theta) = \sin\theta - 2\cos\theta$ for $0 \le \theta \le 2\pi$

33. $t(\theta) = \theta + \cos 2\theta$ for $0 \le \theta \le \pi$

34. $f(x) = 2x - \sin^{-1} x$ for $-1 \le x \le 1$

35. $f(x) = x^3 + \sin x$ on $\left[-\frac{\pi}{2}, \frac{\pi}{2}\right]$

In Problems 36–39, use the first-derivative test to classify each of the given critical numbers as a relative minimum, a relative maximum, or neither.

36. $f(x) = (x^3 - 3x + 1)^7$ at $x = 1$, $x = -1$

37. $f(x) = \dfrac{e^{-x^2}}{3 - 2x}$ at $x = 1$, $x = \frac{1}{2}$

38. $f(x) = (x^2 - 4)^4(x^2 - 1)^3$ at $x = 1$, $x = 2$

39. $f(x) = \sqrt[3]{x^3 - 48x}$ at $x = 4$

In Problems 40–43, use the second-derivative test to classify each of the given critical numbers as a relative minimum, a relative maximum, or neither.

40. $f(x) = 2x^3 + 3x^2 - 12x + 11$ at $x = 1$, $x = -2$

41. $f(x) = \dfrac{x^2 - x + 5}{x + 4}$ at $x = -9$, $x = 1$

42. $f(x) = (x^2 - 3x + 1)e^{-x}$ at $x = 1$, $x = 4$

43. $f(x) = \sin x + \frac{1}{2}\cos 2x$ at $x = \frac{\pi}{6}$, $x = \frac{\pi}{2}$

B **44. Exploration Problem** Sketch the graph of a function with the following properties:

$$f'(x) > 0 \quad \text{when} \quad x < -1$$
$$f'(x) > 0 \quad \text{when} \quad x > 3$$
$$f'(x) < 0 \quad \text{when} \quad -1 < x < 3$$
$$f''(x) < 0 \quad \text{when} \quad x < 2$$
$$f''(x) > 0 \quad \text{when} \quad x > 2$$

45. Exploration Problem Sketch the graph of a function with the following properties:

$$f'(x) > 0 \quad \text{when} \quad x < 2 \quad \text{and when} \quad 2 < x < 5$$
$$f'(x) < 0 \quad \text{when} \quad x > 5$$
$$f'(2) = 0$$
$$f''(x) < 0 \quad \text{when} \quad x < 2 \quad \text{and when} \quad 4 < x < 7$$
$$f''(x) > 0 \quad \text{when} \quad 2 < x < 4 \quad \text{and when} \quad x > 7$$

46. Exploration Problem Sketch the graph of a function with the following properties:

$$f'(x) > 0 \quad \text{when} \quad x < 1$$
$$f'(x) < 0 \quad \text{when} \quad x > 1$$
$$f''(x) > 0 \quad \text{when} \quad x < 1$$
$$f''(x) > 0 \quad \text{when} \quad x > 1$$

What can you say about the derivative of f when $x = 1$?

47. Sketch the graph of a function with the following properties: There are relative extrema at $(-1, 7)$ and $(3, 2)$. There is an inflection point at $(1, 4)$. The graph is concave down only when $x < 1$. The x-intercept is $(-4, 0)$ and the y-intercept is $(0, 5)$.

48. Sketch a graph of a function f that satisfies the following conditions:

  (i) $f'(x) > 0$ when $x < -5$ and when $x > 1$.

  (ii) $f'(x) < 0$ when $-5 < x < 1$.

  (iii) $f(-5) = 4$ and $f(1) = -1$.

49. Sketch a graph of a function f that satisfies the following conditions:

  (i) $f'(x) < 0$ when $x < -1$.

  (ii) $f'(x) > 0$ when $-1 < x < 3$ and when $x > 3$.

  (iii) $f'(-1) = 0$ and $f'(3) = 0$.

50. In physics, the formula

$$I(\theta) = I_0 \left(\frac{\sin \theta}{\theta} \right)^2 \quad \text{where} \quad I(0) = \lim_{\theta \to 0} I(\theta)$$

and I_0 is a constant, is used to model light intensity in the study of Fraunhofer diffraction.

a. Show that $I(0) = I_0$.

b. Sketch the graph for $[-3\pi, 3\pi]$. What are the critical points on this interval?

51. At a temperature of T (in degrees Celsius), the speed of sound in air is modeled by the formula

$$v = v_0 \sqrt{1 + \frac{1}{273} T}$$

where v_0 is the speed at $0°C$. Sketch the graph of v for $T > 0$, and use calculus to check for critical points.

Modeling Problems: In Problems 52–53, set up an appropriate model to answer the given question. Be sure to state your assumptions.

52. At noon on a certain day, Frank sets out to assemble five stereo sets. His rate of assembly increases steadily throughout the afternoon until 4:00 P.M., at which time he has completed three sets. After that, he assembles sets at a slower and slower rate until he finally completes the fifth set at 8:00 P.M. Sketch a rough graph of a function that represents the number of sets Frank has completed after t hours of work.

53. An industrial psychologist conducts two efficiency studies at the Chilco appliance factory. The first study indicates that the average worker who arrives on the job at 8:00 A.M. will have assembled

$$-t^3 + 6t^2 + 13t$$

blenders in t hours (without a break), for $0 \le t \le 4$. The second study suggests that after a 15-minute coffee break, the average worker can assemble

$$-\tfrac{1}{3}t^3 + \tfrac{1}{2}t^2 + 25t$$

blenders in t hours after the break for $0 < t \le 4$. *Note:* The 15-minute break is not part of the work time.

a. Verify that if the coffee break occurs at 10:00 A.M., the average worker will assemble 42 blenders before the break and $49\frac{1}{3}$ blenders for the two hours after the break.

b. Suppose the coffee break is scheduled to begin x hours after 8:00 A.M. Find an expression for the total number of blenders $N(x)$ assembled by the average worker during the morning shift (8 A.M. to 12:15 P.M.).

c. At what time should the coffee break be scheduled so that the average worker will produce the maximum number of blenders during the morning shift? How is this optimum time related to the point of diminishing returns?

54. Research indicates that the power P required by a bird to maintain flight is given by the formula

$$P = \frac{w^2}{2\rho S v} + \frac{1}{2}\rho A v^3$$

where v is the relative speed of the bird, w is its weight, ρ is the density of air, and S and A are constants associated with the bird's size and shape.[*] What speed will minimize the power? You may assume that v, w, ρ, S, and A are all positive.

55. The deflection of a hardwood beam of length is given by

$$D(x) = \tfrac{9}{4}x^4 - 7\ell x^3 + 5\ell^2 x^2$$

where x is the distance from one end of the beam. What value of x yields the maximum deflection?

56. HISTORICAL QUEST   One of the most famous women in the history of mathematics is Maria Gatana Agnesi (pronounced n yā«zē). She was born in Milan, the first of 21 children. Her first publication was at age 9, when she wrote a Latin discourse defending higher education for women. Her most important work was a now-classic calculus textbook published in 1748. Maria Agnesi is primarily remembered for a curve defined by the equation

MARIA AGNESI
1718–1799

$$y = \frac{a^3}{x^2 + a^2}, \quad a \text{ a positive constant}$$

The curve was named *versiera* (from the Italian verb *to turn*) by Agnesi, but John Colson, an Englishman who translated her work, confused the word *versiera* with the word *avversiera*, which means "wife of the devil" in Italian; the curve has ever since been called the "witch of Agnesi." This was particularly unfortunate because Colson wanted Agnesi's work to serve as a model for budding young mathematicians, especially young women. ∎

Graph this curve and find the critical numbers, extrema, and points of inflection.

57. Journal Problem: *Mathematics Magazine*[†] ∎ Give an elementary proof that

$$f(x) = \frac{1}{\sin x} - \frac{1}{x}, \quad 0 < x \le \frac{\pi}{2}$$

is positive and increasing.

58. An important formula in physical chemistry is *van der Waals' equation*, which says that

$$\left(P + \frac{a}{V^2} \right)(V - b) = nRT$$

where P, V, and T are the pressure, volume, and temperature, respectively, of a gas, and a, b, n, and R are positive constants. The *critical temperature* T_C of the gas is the highest temperature at which the gaseous and liquid phases can exist as separate states.

a. When $T = T_C$, the pressure P can be expressed as a function $P(V)$ of V alone. Show how this can be done, and then find $P'(V)$ and $P''(V)$.

---

[*]C. J. Pennycuick, "The Mechanics of Bird Migration," *Ibis* III (1969), pp. 525–556.

[†]Volume 55 (1982), p. 300. "Elementary proof" in the question means that you should use only techniques from beginning calculus. For our purposes, you simply need to give a reasonable argument to justify the conclusion.

b. The *critical volume* V_C is the volume that satisfies $P'(V_C) = 0$ and $P''(V_C) = 0$. Find V_C.

c. Find T_C, the point where $P''(V) = 0$, using the V_C from part **b** to write it in terms of a, b, n, and R. Finally, find the *critical pressure* $P_C = P(V_C)$ in terms of a, b, n, and R.

d. Sketch P as a function of V.

59. Prove or disprove that if the graphs of the functions f and g are both concave up on an interval, then the graph of their sum $f + g$ is also concave up on that interval.

60. Use calculus to prove that for constants a, b, and c, the vertex (relative extremum) of the quadratic function

$$y = ax^2 + bx + c \qquad (a \neq 0)$$

occurs at $x = -b/(2a)$.

61. Find constants A, B, and C that guarantee that the function

$$f(x) = Ax^3 + Bx^2 + C$$

will have a relative extremum at $(2, 11)$ and an inflection point at $(1, 5)$. Sketch the graph of f.

62. Find constants a, b, and c that guarantee that the graph of

$$f(x) = x^3 + ax^2 + bx + c$$

will have a relative maximum at $(-3, 18)$ and a relative minimum at $(1, -14)$.

63. **Exploration Problem** Consider the graph of $y = x^3 + bx^2 + cx + d$ for constants b, c, and d. What happens to the graph as b changes?

64. Find constants A, B, C, and D that guarantee that the graph of

$$f(x) = 3x^4 + Ax^3 + Bx^2 + Cx + D$$

will have horizontal tangents at $(2, -3)$ and $(0, 7)$. There is a third point that has a horizontal tangent. Find this point. Then, for all three points, determine whether each corresponds to a relative maximum, a relative minimum, or neither.

4.4 Curve Sketching with Asymptotes: Limits Involving Infinity

IN THIS SECTION limits to infinity, infinite limits, graphs with asymptotes, vertical tangents and cusps, a general graphing strategy

LIMITS TO INFINITY

In applications, we are often concerned with "long run" behavior of a function. To indicate such behavior, we write

$$\lim_{x \to +\infty} f(x) = L$$

to indicate that $f(x)$ approaches the number L as x increases without bound. Similarly, we write

$$\lim_{x \to -\infty} f(x) = M$$

to indicate that $f(x)$ approaches the number M as x decreases without bound. Here are the formal definitions of these *limits to infinity*.

Limits to Infinity

WARNING Even though the symbols ∞ and $+\infty$ mean the same thing, for the time being we use $+\infty$ to help distinguish between $+\infty$ and $-\infty$.

> The limit statement $\lim_{x \to +\infty} f(x) = L$ means that for any number $\epsilon > 0$, there exists a number N_1 such that
>
> $$|f(x) - L| < \epsilon \quad \text{whenever} \quad x > N_1$$
>
> for x in the domain of f. Similarly, $\lim_{x \to -\infty} f(x) = M$ means that for any $\epsilon > 0$, there exists a number N_2 such that
>
> $$|f(x) - M| < \epsilon \quad \text{whenever} \quad x < N_2$$

This definition can be illustrated graphically, as shown in Figure 4.39.

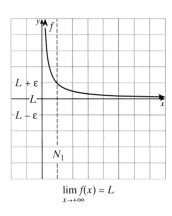
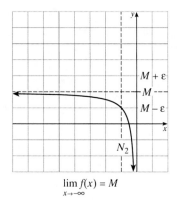

$$\lim_{x \to +\infty} f(x) = L \qquad\qquad \lim_{x \to -\infty} f(x) = M$$

Figure 4.39   Graphical representation of limits to infinity

With this formal definition, we can show that all the rules for limits established in Chapter 2 also apply to $\lim\limits_{x \to +\infty} f(x)$ and $\lim\limits_{x \to -\infty} f(x)$.

Limit Rules

If $\lim\limits_{x \to +\infty} f(x)$ and $\lim\limits_{x \to +\infty} g(x)$ exist, then for constants a and b:

Power rule: $\lim\limits_{x \to +\infty} [f(x)]^n = \left[\lim\limits_{x \to +\infty} f(x) \right]^n$

Linearity rule: $\lim\limits_{x \to +\infty} [af(x) + bg(x)] = a \lim\limits_{x \to +\infty} f(x) + b \lim\limits_{x \to +\infty} g(x)$

Product rule: $\lim\limits_{x \to +\infty} [f(x)g(x)] = \left[\lim\limits_{x \to +\infty} f(x) \right]\left[\lim\limits_{x \to +\infty} g(x) \right]$

Quotient rule: $\lim\limits_{x \to +\infty} \dfrac{f(x)}{g(x)} = \dfrac{\lim\limits_{x \to +\infty} f(x)}{\lim\limits_{x \to +\infty} g(x)}$ if $\lim\limits_{x \to +\infty} g(x) \ne 0$

Analogous results hold for $\lim\limits_{x \to -\infty} f(x)$, if it exists.

The following theorem will allow us to evaluate certain limits to infinity with ease.

THEOREM 4.8   Special limits to infinity

If A is any real number and r is a positive rational number, then

$$\lim_{x \to +\infty} \frac{A}{x^r} = 0$$

Furthermore, if r is such that x^r is defined for $x < 0$, then

$$\lim_{x \to -\infty} \frac{A}{x^r} = 0$$

Proof   We begin by proving that $\lim\limits_{x \to +\infty} \dfrac{1}{x} = 0$. For $\epsilon > 0$, let $N = \dfrac{1}{\epsilon}$. Then for $x > N$ we have

$$x > N = \frac{1}{\epsilon} \qquad \text{so that} \qquad \frac{1}{x} < \epsilon$$

This means that $\left| \dfrac{1}{x} - 0 \right| < \epsilon$, so that, from the definition of limit we have $\displaystyle\lim_{x \to +\infty} \dfrac{1}{x} = 0$. Now let r be a rational number, say $r = p/q$. Then

$$\lim_{x \to +\infty} \frac{A}{x^r} = \lim_{x \to +\infty} \frac{A}{x^{p/q}} = A \lim_{x \to +\infty} \left[\frac{1}{\sqrt[q]{x}} \right]^p$$

$$= A \left[\sqrt[q]{\lim_{x \to +\infty} \frac{1}{x}} \right]^p = A \left[\sqrt[q]{0} \right]^p = A \cdot 0 = 0$$

The proof for the analogous limit as $x \to -\infty$ follows similarly. ☐

When evaluating a limit of the form

$$\lim_{x \to +\infty} \frac{p(x)}{d(x)} \qquad \text{or} \qquad \lim_{x \to -\infty} \frac{p(x)}{d(x)}$$

where $p(x)$ and $d(x)$ are polynomials, it is often useful to divide both $p(x)$ and $d(x)$ by the highest power of x that occurs in either. The limit can then be found by applying Theorem 4.8. This process is illustrated by the following examples.

EXAMPLE 1 Evaluating a limit to infinity

Evaluate $\displaystyle\lim_{x \to +\infty} \dfrac{3x^3 - 5x + 9}{5x^3 + 2x^2 - 7}$.

Solution

We may assume that $x \neq 0$, because we are interested only in very large values of x. Dividing both the numerator and denominator of the given expressions by x^3, the highest power of x appearing in the fraction, we find

$$\frac{3x^3 - 5x + 9}{5x^3 + 2x^2 - 7} = \frac{3x^3 - 5x + 9}{5x^3 + 2x^2 - 7} \cdot \frac{\dfrac{1}{x^3}}{\dfrac{1}{x^3}} = \frac{3 - \dfrac{5}{x^2} + \dfrac{9}{x^3}}{5 + \dfrac{2}{x} - \dfrac{7}{x^3}}$$

Thus,

$$\lim_{x \to +\infty} \frac{3x^3 - 5x + 9}{5x^3 + 2x^2 - 7} = \lim_{x \to +\infty} \frac{3 - \dfrac{5}{x^2} + \dfrac{9}{x^3}}{5 + \dfrac{2}{x} - \dfrac{7}{x^3}}$$

$$= \frac{\displaystyle\lim_{x \to +\infty} \left(3 - \frac{5}{x^2} + \frac{9}{x^3} \right)}{\displaystyle\lim_{x \to +\infty} \left(5 + \frac{2}{x} - \frac{7}{x^3} \right)}$$

$$= \frac{3 - 0 + 0}{5 + 0 - 0} = \frac{3}{5}$$

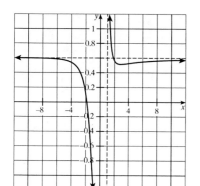

Figure 4.40 Graph of $y = \dfrac{3x^3 - 5x + 9}{5x^3 + 2x^2 - 7}$

The graph of the given rational function is shown in Figure 4.40. Notice how the curve seems to approach $y = \frac{3}{5}$ as $x \to +\infty$ and as $x \to -\infty$. ∎

Example 2 illustrates how Theorem 4.8 can be used along with the other limit properties to evaluate limits to infinity.

EXAMPLE 2 Evaluating limits to infinity

Evaluate

$$\lim_{x \to +\infty} \sqrt{\frac{3x - 5}{x - 2}} \qquad \text{and} \qquad \lim_{x \to -\infty} \left(\frac{3x - 5}{x - 2} \right)^3$$

Solution

Notice that for $x \neq 0$,

$$\frac{3x - 5}{x - 2} = \frac{x\left(3 - \dfrac{5}{x}\right)}{x\left(1 - \dfrac{2}{x}\right)} = \frac{3 - \dfrac{5}{x}}{1 - \dfrac{2}{x}}$$

Also, according to Theorem 4.8, we know that

$$\lim_{x \to +\infty} \frac{5}{x} = 0 \qquad \text{and} \qquad \lim_{x \to +\infty} \frac{2}{x} = 0$$

We now find the limits using the quotient rule, the power rule, and Theorem 4.8:

$$\lim_{x \to +\infty} \sqrt{\frac{3x - 5}{x - 2}} = \lim_{x \to +\infty} \left(\frac{3x - 5}{x - 2}\right)^{1/2} = \left(\lim_{x \to +\infty} \frac{3x - 5}{x - 2}\right)^{1/2}$$

$$= \left(\frac{\lim\limits_{x \to +\infty} \left(3 - \frac{5}{x}\right)}{\lim\limits_{x \to +\infty} \left(1 - \frac{2}{x}\right)}\right)^{1/2} = \left(\frac{3 - 0}{1 - 0}\right)^{1/2} = \sqrt{3}$$

Similarly,

$$\lim_{x \to -\infty} \left(\frac{3x - 5}{x - 2}\right)^3 = 3^3 = 27$$

■

EXAMPLE 3   Evaluating a limit to negative infinity

Evaluate $\displaystyle\lim_{x \to -\infty} \frac{95x^3 + 57x + 30}{x^5 - 1{,}000}$.

Solution

Dividing the numerator and the denominator by the highest power, x^5, we find that

$$\lim_{x \to -\infty} \frac{95x^3 + 57x + 30}{x^5 - 1{,}000} = \lim_{x \to -\infty} \frac{95x^3 + 57x + 30}{x^5 - 1{,}000} \cdot \frac{\dfrac{1}{x^5}}{\dfrac{1}{x^5}}$$

$$= \lim_{x \to -\infty} \frac{\dfrac{95}{x^2} + \dfrac{57}{x^4} + \dfrac{30}{x^5}}{1 - \dfrac{1{,}000}{x^5}}$$

$$= \frac{0 + 0 + 0}{1 - 0}$$

$$= 0$$

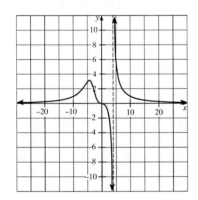

Figure 4.41 Graph of
$y = \dfrac{95x^3 + 57x + 30}{x^5 - 1{,}000}$

The graph of the rational function is shown in Figure 4.41.   ■

EXAMPLE 4   Evaluating a limit to infinity involving e^x

Find $\displaystyle\lim_{x \to +\infty} e^{-x} \cos x$.

Solution

We cannot use the product rule for limits since $\displaystyle\lim_{x \to +\infty} \cos x$ does not exist (it diverges by oscillation—do you see why?). Note, however, that the magnitude of

$$e^{-x} \cos x = \frac{\cos x}{e^x}$$

must become smaller and smaller as $x \to +\infty$ since the numerator $\cos x$ is bounded between -1 and 1, while the denominator e^x grows relentlessly larger with x. Thus by the squeeze rule,

$$\lim_{x \to +\infty} e^{-x} \cos x = 0$$

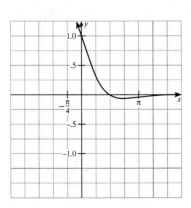

Figure 4.42 Graph of $y = e^{-x} \cos x$

The graph of $y = e^{-x} \cos x$ is shown in Figure 4.42.   ■

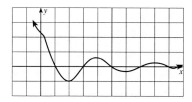

Try drawing the graph of $y = e^{-x} \cos x$ on your calculator, or other graphing software, and you will see that what you get does not properly illustrate the oscillatory behavior of this graph. This demonstrates the importance of *not* relying on technology for graphing. In fact, the accompanying graph (without scale) shows more clearly the behavior of the graph of the function $y = e^{-x} \cos x$ for large, positive values of x.

INFINITE LIMITS

In mathematics, the symbol ∞ is not a number, but is used to describe either the process of unrestricted growth or the result of such growth. Thus, a limit statement such as

$$\lim_{x \to c} f(x) = +\infty$$

means that the function f increases without bound as x approaches c from either side, while

$$\lim_{x \to c} g(x) = -\infty$$

means that g decreases without bound as x approaches c. Such limits may be defined formally as follows.

Infinite Limits

We write $\lim\limits_{x \to c} f(x) = +\infty$ if for any number $N > 0$ (no matter how large), it is possible to find a number $\delta > 0$ such that $f(x) > N$ whenever $0 < |x - c| < \delta$. Similarly, $\lim\limits_{x \to c} f(x) = -\infty$ if for any $N > 0$, it is possible to find a number $\delta > 0$ so that $f(x) < -N$ when $0 < |x - c| < \delta$.

➡ **What This Says** Remember, ∞ *is **not** a number*, so an infinite limit does not exist in the sense that limits were defined in Chapter 2. However, there are several ways for a limit not to exist (for example, $\lim\limits_{x \to \infty} \cos x$ fails to exist by oscillation), so saying that $\lim\limits_{x \to c} f(x) = +\infty$ or $\lim\limits_{x \to c} f(x) = -\infty$ conveys more information than simply observing that the limit does not exist.

EXAMPLE 5 Infinite limits

Find $\lim\limits_{x \to 2^-} \dfrac{3x - 5}{x - 2}$ and $\lim\limits_{x \to 2^+} \dfrac{3x - 5}{x - 2}$.

Solution

Notice that $\dfrac{1}{x - 2}$ increases without bound as x approaches 2 from the right and $\dfrac{1}{x - 2}$ decreases without bound as x approaches 2 from the left. That is,

$$\lim_{x \to 2^+} \frac{1}{x - 2} = +\infty \qquad \text{and} \qquad \lim_{x \to 2^-} \frac{1}{x - 2} = -\infty$$

We also have $\lim\limits_{x \to 2}(3x - 5) = 1$, and it follows that

$$\lim_{x \to 2^+} \frac{3x - 5}{x - 2} = +\infty \qquad \text{and} \qquad \lim_{x \to 2^-} \frac{3x - 5}{x - 2} = -\infty \qquad \blacksquare$$

GRAPHS WITH ASYMPTOTES

Figure 4.43 shows a graph that approaches the horizontal line $y = 2$ as $x \to +\infty$ and $y = -1$ as $x \to -\infty$, and the vertical line $x = 3$ as x approaches 3 from either side.

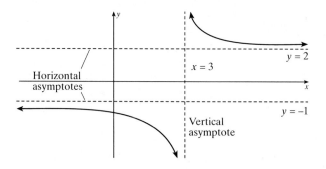

Figure 4.43 A typical graph with asymptotes

Vertical and Horizontal Asymptotes

> The line $x = c$ is a **vertical asymptote** of the graph of f if either of the one-sided limits
>
> $$\lim_{x \to c^-} f(x) \qquad \text{or} \qquad \lim_{x \to c^+} f(x)$$
>
> is infinite. The line $y = L$ is a **horizontal asymptote** of the graph of f if
>
> $$\lim_{x \to +\infty} f(x) = L \qquad \text{or} \qquad \lim_{x \to -\infty} f(x) = L$$

EXAMPLE 6   Graphing a rational function with asymptotes

Sketch the graph of $f(x) = \dfrac{3x - 5}{x - 2}$.

Solution

Vertical Asymptotes First, make sure the rational function is written in simplified (reduced) form. Because vertical asymptotes for $f(x) = \dfrac{3x - 5}{x - 2}$ occur at values of c for which $\lim_{x \to c^-} f(x)$ or $\lim_{x \to c^+} f(x)$ is infinite, we look for values that cause the denominator to be zero (and the numerator not to be zero); that is, we solve $d(c) = 0$, where $d(x)$ is the denominator of $f(x)$, and then evaluate $\lim_{x \to c^-} f(x)$ and $\lim_{x \to c^+} f(x)$ to ascertain the behavior of the function at $x = c$. For this example, $x = 2$ is a value that causes division by zero, so we find

$$\lim_{x \to 2^+} \frac{3x - 5}{x - 2} = +\infty \qquad \text{and} \qquad \lim_{x \to 2^-} \frac{3x - 5}{x - 2} = -\infty$$

(We found these limits in Example 5.) This means that $x = 2$ is a vertical asymptote and that the graph is moving downward as $x \to 2$ from the left and upward as $x \to 2$ from the right. This information is recorded on the preliminary graph shown in Figure 4.44a by a dashed vertical line with upward ($\uparrow$) and downward ($\downarrow$) arrows.

Horizontal Asymptotes To find the horizontal asymptotes we compute

$$\lim_{x \to +\infty} \frac{3x - 5}{x - 2} = \lim_{x \to +\infty} \frac{3x - 5}{x - 2} \cdot \frac{\frac{1}{x}}{\frac{1}{x}} = \lim_{x \to +\infty} \frac{3 - \frac{5}{x}}{1 - \frac{2}{x}} = \frac{3 - 0}{1 - 0} = 3$$

and

$$\lim_{x \to -\infty} \frac{3x - 5}{x - 2} = 3 \qquad \text{(The steps here are the same as for } x \to +\infty.)$$

This means that $y = 3$ is a horizontal asymptote. This information is recorded on the preliminary graph shown in Figure 4.44a by a dashed horizontal line with outbound arrows ($\leftarrow, \rightarrow$).

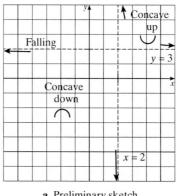
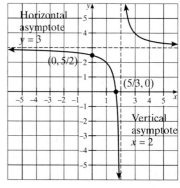

a. Preliminary sketch   **b.** Completed sketch

Figure 4.44 Graph of $f(x) = \dfrac{3x - 5}{x - 2}$

The preliminary sketch gives us some valuable information about the graph, but it does not present the entire picture. Next, we use calculus to find where the function is increasing and decreasing (first derivative) and where it is concave up and concave down (second derivative):

$$f'(x) = \frac{-1}{(x - 2)^2} \qquad \text{and} \qquad f''(x) = \frac{2}{(x - 2)^3}$$

Neither derivative is ever zero, and both are undefined at $x = 2$. Checking the signs of the first and second derivatives, we find that the graph is always falling and that it is concave up for $x > 2$ and concave down for $x < 2$. However, it does not have a point of inflection (the function is not defined at $x = 2$). This information is added to the preliminary sketch shown in Figure 4.44a. The completed graph is shown in Figure 4.44b, which also shows the x- and y-intercepts at $(\frac{5}{3}, 0)$ and $(0, \frac{5}{2})$. ∎

EXAMPLE 7 Sketching a curve with asymptotes

Discuss and sketch the graph of $f(x) = \dfrac{x^2 - x - 2}{x - 3}$.

Solution We find that

$$f'(x) = \frac{x^2 - 6x + 5}{(x - 3)^2} \qquad \text{and} \qquad f''(x) = \frac{8}{(x - 3)^3}$$

Solving $f'(x) = 0$, we see that the critical numbers are $x = 1$ and $x = 5$. Testing on each side of the critical numbers and $x = 3$, where $f(x)$ is not defined, we obtain the intervals of increase and decrease and concavity shown in Figure 4.45.

Note that there is a relative maximum at $x = 1$ and a relative minimum at $x = 5$. The concavity changes (from ↓ to ↑) at $x = 3$, but this does not correspond to an inflection point since $f(3)$ is not defined. We look for vertical asymptotes where $f(x)$ (in reduced form) is not defined; in this case, at $x = 3$. Testing with limits, we find that

$$\lim_{x \to 3^-} \frac{x^2 - x - 2}{x - 3} = -\infty \qquad \text{and} \qquad \lim_{x \to 3^+} \frac{x^2 - x - 2}{x - 3} = +\infty$$

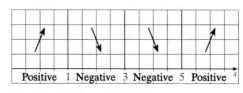

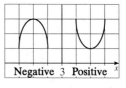

a. Intervals of increase and decrease   **b.** Intervals of concavity

Figure 4.45   Intervals of increase and decrease and concavity for $f(x) = \dfrac{x^2 - x - 2}{x - 3}$

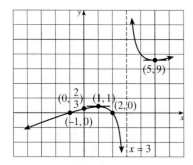

Figure 4.46 Graph of
$f(x) = \dfrac{x^2 - x - 2}{x - 3}$

To check for horizontal asymptotes, we compute

$$\lim_{x \to +\infty} \frac{x^2 - x - 2}{x - 3} = +\infty \qquad \text{and} \qquad \lim_{x \to -\infty} \frac{x^2 - x - 2}{x - 3} = -\infty$$

Since neither limit of $f(x)$ at infinity is finite, there are no horizontal asymptotes.

We plot some points: the relative maximum $(1, 1)$; the relative minimum $(5, 9)$; the x-intercepts $(2, 0)$, $(-1, 0)$; and the y-intercept $(0, \frac{2}{3})$. We also show the vertical asymptote $x = 3$, and, using the intervals of increase and decrease and concavity indicated in Figure 4.45, we obtain the graph shown in Figure 4.46. ■

VERTICAL TANGENTS AND CUSPS

Suppose the function f is continuous at the point P where $x = c$ and that $f'(x)$ becomes infinite as x approaches c. Then the graph of f has a *vertical tangent* at P if the graph turns smoothly through P and a *cusp* at P if the graph changes direction abruptly there. These graphical features can be defined in terms of limits, as follows:

Vertical Tangents and Cusps

> Suppose the function f is continuous at the point $P(c, f(c))$. Then the graph of f has
>
> a **vertical tangent** at P if $\lim\limits_{x \to c^-} f'(x)$ and $\lim\limits_{x \to c^+} f'(x)$ are either both $+\infty$ or both $-\infty$;
>
> a **cusp** at P if $\lim\limits_{x \to c^-} f'(x)$ and $\lim\limits_{x \to c^+} f'(x)$ are both infinite with opposite signs (one $+\infty$ and the other $-\infty$).

These possibilities are shown in Figure 4.47.

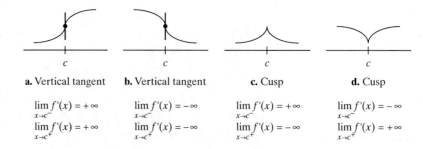

a. Vertical tangent

$\lim\limits_{x \to c^-} f'(x) = +\infty$

$\lim\limits_{x \to c^+} f'(x) = +\infty$

b. Vertical tangent

$\lim\limits_{x \to c^-} f'(x) = -\infty$

$\lim\limits_{x \to c^+} f'(x) = -\infty$

c. Cusp

$\lim\limits_{x \to c^-} f'(x) = +\infty$

$\lim\limits_{x \to c^+} f'(x) = -\infty$

d. Cusp

$\lim\limits_{x \to c^-} f'(x) = -\infty$

$\lim\limits_{x \to c^+} f'(x) = +\infty$

Figure 4.47   Vertical tangents and cusps

EXAMPLE 8   Identifying vertical tangents and cusps

In each of the following cases, determine whether the graph of the given function has a vertical tangent or a cusp:

a. $f(x) = x^{2/3}(2x + 5)$ **b.** $g(x) = x^{1/3}(x + 4)$

Solution

a. Writing $f(x) = 2x^{5/3} + 5x^{2/3}$, we find that

$$f'(x) = \tfrac{10}{3}x^{2/3} + \tfrac{10}{3}x^{-1/3} = \tfrac{10}{3}x^{-1/3}(x + 1)$$

so $f'(x)$ becomes infinite only at $x = 0$. Since

$$\lim_{x \to 0^-} f'(x) = \lim_{x \to 0^-} \tfrac{10}{3}x^{-1/3}(x + 1) = -\infty$$

and

$$\lim_{x \to 0^+} f'(x) = \lim_{x \to 0^+} \tfrac{10}{3}x^{-1/3}(x + 1) = +\infty$$

it follows that there is a cusp on the graph of f at $(0, 0)$. The graph is shown in Figure 4.48a.

b. The derivative

$$g'(x) = \tfrac{4}{3}x^{-2/3}(x + 1)$$

becomes infinite only when $x = 0$. We find that

$$\lim_{x \to 0^-} g'(x) = \lim_{x \to 0^-} \tfrac{4}{3}x^{-2/3}(x + 1) = +\infty$$

and

$$\lim_{x \to 0^+} g'(x) = \lim_{x \to 0^+} \tfrac{4}{3}x^{-2/3}(x + 1) = +\infty$$

Since the limit approaches $+\infty$ as x approaches zero from both the left and the right, we conclude that a vertical tangent occurs at the origin $(0, 0)$. The graph is shown in Figure 4.48b.

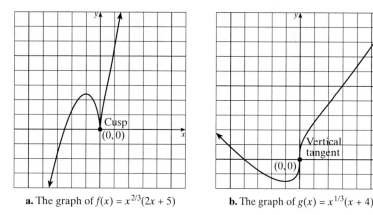

a. The graph of $f(x) = x^{2/3}(2x + 5)$ **b.** The graph of $g(x) = x^{1/3}(x + 4)$

Figure 4.48   A graph with a cusp and another with a vertical tangent

A GENERAL GRAPHING STRATEGY

It is worthwhile to combine the techniques of curve sketching from calculus with those techniques studied in precalculus courses. You may be familiar with **extent** (finding the domain and the range of the function) and **symmetry** (with respect to the x-axis, y-axis, or origin). These features are reviewed in Chapter 8 of the *Student Mathematics Handbook*. We now have all the tools we need to describe a general procedure for curve sketching, and this procedure is summarized in Table 4.1.

TABLE 4.1   Graphing Strategy for a Function Defined by $y = f(x)$

Step	Procedure
Simplify.	If possible, simplify algebraically the function you wish to graph. For example, if $f(x) = \dfrac{(x-2)(x+3)}{x-2}$, you must write this as $f(x) = x + 3$, $x \neq 2$ before beginning the procedure listed here.
Find derivatives and critical numbers.	Compute the first and second derivatives; set each equal to zero and solve (by factoring, if possible), and find the first- and second-order critical numbers.
Determine intervals of increase and decrease.	Use the first-order critical numbers of f : $f'(x) > 0$, curve rising (indicate these regions by ↑) $f'(x) < 0$, curve falling (indicate these regions by ↓)
Apply the second-derivative test.	Use the second-derivative test to find the relative maxima or minima: Substitute the first-order critical numbers, c_1, with the following test: $f''(x) > 0$, relative minimum $f''(x) < 0$, relative maximum $f''(x) = 0$, test fails; use first-derivative test
Determine concavity and points of inflection.	Find the points of inflection. These are located where the concavity changes from up to down or down to up, and are found by checking the intervals on either side of the second-order critical numbers.

Apply the first-derivative test.
 	
 ↗ ↘
 Maximum
 	
 ↘ ↗
 Minimum
	Use the first-derivative test if the second-derivative test fails or is too complicated.
	
	 1. Let c_1 be a first-order critical number of a continuous function f.
	 2. **a.** $(c_1, f(c_1))$ is a relative maximum if
	
	      $f'(x) > 0$ for all x in an open interval (a, c_1) to the left of c_1
	      $f'(x) < 0$ for all x in an open interval (c_1, b) to the right of c_1.
	
	 b. $(c_1, f(c_1))$ is a relative minimum if
	
	      $f'(x) < 0$ for all x in an open interval (a, c_1) to the left of c_1
	      $f'(x) > 0$ for all x in an open interval (c_1, b) to the right of c_1.
	
	 c. $(c_1, f(c_1))$ is not an extremum if $f'(x)$ has the same sign in open intervals (a, c_1) and (c_1, b) on both sides of c_1.

Find asymptotes, vertical tangents, and cusps.	1. *Vertical asymptotes*—Vertical asymptotes, if any exist, will occur at values $x = c$ for which f is not defined. Use the limits $\lim_{x \to c^-} f(x)$ and $\lim_{x \to c^+} f(x)$ to determine the behavior of the graph near $x = c$. Show this behavior with arrows (↑↓). 2. *Horizontal asymptotes*—Compute $\lim_{x \to +\infty} f(x)$ and $\lim_{x \to -\infty} f(x)$. If either is finite, plot the associated horizontal asymptote. 3. *Vertical tangents* and *cusps*—Find the vertical tangents and cusps; the graph has a vertical tangent at P if $\lim_{x \to c^-} f'(x)$ and $\lim_{x \to c^+} f'(x)$ are either both $+\infty$ or both $-\infty$. It has a cusp at P if $\lim_{x \to c^-} f'(x)$ and $\lim_{x \to c^+} f'(x)$ are both infinite with opposite signs.
Plot points.	1. If $f(c)$ is a relative maximum, relative minimum, or inflection point, plot $(c, f(c))$. Show the relative maximum points by using a "cap" (∩) and relative minimum points by using a "cup" (∪). 2. x-intercepts: Set $y = 0$ and if $x = a$ is a solution, plot $(a, 0)$. y-intercepts: Set $x = 0$ and if $y = b$ is a solution, plot $(0, b)$; a function will have, at most, one y-intercept.
Sketch the curve.	Draw a curve using the above information.

4.4 PROBLEM SET

A 1. **WHAT DOES THIS SAY?** Outline a method for curve sketching.

2. **WHAT DOES THIS SAY?** What are critical numbers? Discuss the importance of critical numbers in curve sketching.

3. **Exploration Problem** Discuss the importance of concavity and points of inflection in curve sketching.

4. **Exploration Problem** Discuss the importance of asymptotes in curve sketching.

Evaluate the limits in Problems 5–24.

5. $\lim\limits_{x\to+\infty} \dfrac{2,000}{x+1}$

6. $\lim\limits_{x\to+\infty} \dfrac{7,000}{\sqrt{x}+1}$

7. $\lim\limits_{x\to+\infty} \dfrac{3x+5}{x-2}$

8. $\lim\limits_{x\to+\infty} \dfrac{x+2}{3x-5}$

9. $\lim\limits_{t\to+\infty} \dfrac{9t^5+50t^2+800}{t^5-1,000}$

10. $\lim\limits_{x\to-\infty} \dfrac{(2x+5)(x-3)}{(7x-2)(4x+1)}$

11. $\lim\limits_{x\to+\infty} \dfrac{x}{\sqrt{x^2+1,000}}$

12. $\lim\limits_{x\to-\infty} \dfrac{3x}{\sqrt{4x^2+10}}$

13. $\lim\limits_{x\to+\infty} \dfrac{x^{5.916}+1}{x^{\sqrt{35}}}$

14. $\lim\limits_{x\to+\infty} \dfrac{x^{6.083}+1}{x^{\sqrt{37}}}$

15. $\lim\limits_{x\to1^-} \dfrac{x-1}{|x^2-1|}$

16. $\lim\limits_{x\to3^+} \dfrac{x^2-4x+3}{x^2-6x+9}$

17. $\lim\limits_{x\to0^+} \dfrac{x^2-x+1}{x-\sin x}$

18. $\lim\limits_{x\to(\pi/4)^+} \dfrac{\sec x}{\tan x-1}$

19. $\lim\limits_{x\to+\infty} \left(x\sin\dfrac{1}{x}\right)$

20. $\lim\limits_{x\to0^+} \dfrac{x^2}{1-\cos x}$

21. $\lim\limits_{x\to0^+} \dfrac{\ln\sqrt[3]{x}}{\sin x}$

22. $\lim\limits_{x\to+\infty} \dfrac{\ln\sqrt[3]{x}}{\sin x}$

23. $\lim\limits_{x\to-\infty} e^x \sin x$

24. $\lim\limits_{x\to+\infty} \dfrac{\tan^{-1}x}{e^{0.1x}}$

B *Find all vertical and horizontal asymptotes of the graph of each function given in Problems 25–44. Find where each graph is rising and where it is falling, determine concavity, and locate all critical points and points of inflection. Finally, sketch the graph. Be sure to show any special features, such as cusps or vertical tangents.*

25. $f(x) = \dfrac{3x+5}{7-x}$

26. $g(x) = \dfrac{15}{x+4}$

27. $f(x) = 4 + \dfrac{2x}{x-3}$

28. $g(x) = 1 - \dfrac{x}{4-x}$

29. $f(x) = \dfrac{x^3+1}{x^3-8}$

30. $f(x) = \dfrac{2x^2-5x+7}{x^2-9}$

31. $g(x) = \dfrac{8}{x-1} + \dfrac{27}{x+4}$

32. $f(x) = \dfrac{1}{x+1} + \dfrac{1}{x-1}$

33. $g(t) = (t^3+t)^2$

34. $g(t) = t^{-1/2} + \frac{1}{3}t^{3/2}$

35. $f(x) = (x^2-9)^2$

36. $g(x) = x(x^2-12)$

37. $f(x) = x^{1/3}(x-4)$

38. $f(u) = u^{2/3}(u-7)$

39. $f(x) = \tan^{-1}x^2$

40. $f(x) = \ln(4-x^2)$

41. $t(\theta) = \sin\theta - \cos\theta$ for $0 \le \theta \le 2\pi$

42. $f(x) = x - \sin 2x$ for $0 \le x \le \pi$

43. $f(x) = \sin^2 x - 2\sin x + 1$ for $0 \le x \le \pi$

44. $T(\theta) = \tan^{-1}\theta - \tan^{-1}\dfrac{\theta}{3}$

45. The *ideal speed* v for a banked curve on a highway is modeled by the equation

$$v^2 = gr\tan\theta$$

where g is the constant acceleration due to gravity, r is the radius of the curve, and θ is the angle of the bank. Assuming that r is constant, sketch the graph of v as a function of θ for $0 \le \theta \le \frac{\pi}{2}$.*

46. According to Einstein's special theory of relativity, the mass of a body is modeled by the expression

$$m = \dfrac{m_0}{\sqrt{1 - \dfrac{v^2}{c^2}}}$$

where m_0 is the mass of the body at rest in relation to the observer, m is the mass of the body when it moves with speed v in relation to the observer, and c is the speed of light. Sketch the graph of m as a function of v. What happens as $v \to c^-$?

47. Sketch a graph of a function f with all the following properties: The graph has $y = 1$ and $x = 3$ as asymptotes; f is increasing for $x < 3$ and $3 < x < 5$ and is decreasing elsewhere; the graph is concave up for $x < 3$ and for $x > 7$ and concave down for $3 < x < 7$; $f(0) = 4 = f(5)$ and $f(7) = 2$.

48. Sketch a graph of a function g with all of the following properties:

(i) g is increasing for $x < -1$ and $-1 < x < 1$ and decreasing for $1 < x < 3$ and $x > 3$;

(ii) The graph has only one critical point $(1, -1)$, no inflection points;

(iii) $\lim\limits_{x\to-\infty} g(x) = -1$; $\lim\limits_{x\to+\infty} g(x) = 2$;

$\lim\limits_{x\to-1^+} g(x) = \lim\limits_{x\to3^-} g(x) = -\infty$.

49. **Exploration Problem** Frank Kornerkutter has put off doing his math homework until the last minute, and he is now trying to evaluate

$$\lim\limits_{x\to0^+} \left(\dfrac{1}{x^2} - \dfrac{1}{x}\right)$$

At first he is stumped, but suddenly he has an idea: Because

$$\lim\limits_{x\to0^+} \dfrac{1}{x^2} = +\infty \quad \text{and} \quad \lim\limits_{x\to0^+} \dfrac{1}{x} = +\infty$$

it must surely be true that the limit in question has the value $+\infty - (+\infty) = 0$. Having thus "solved" his problem, he celebrates by taking a nap. Is he right, and, if not, what is wrong with his argument?

---

*In physics it is shown that if one travels around the curve at the ideal speed, no frictional force is required to prevent slipping. This greatly reduces wear on tires and contributes to safety.

50. In an experiment, a biologist introduces a toxin into a bacterial colony and then measures the effect on the population of the colony. Suppose that at time t (in minutes) the population is

$$P(t) = 5 + e^{-0.04t}(t + 1)$$

thousand. At what time will the population be the largest? What happens to the population in the long run (as $t \to +\infty$)? Find where the graph of P has an inflection point, and interpret this point in terms of the population. Sketch the graph of P.

51. Let $P(x) = a_n x^n + a_{n-1} x^{n-1} + \cdots + a_1 x + a_0$ be a polynomial with $a_n \neq 0$ and let $L = \lim_{x \to -\infty} P(x)$ and $M = \lim_{x \to +\infty} P(x)$. Fill in the missing entries in the following table:

Sign of a_n	n	L	M
+	even	**a.**	$+\infty$
+	odd	$-\infty$	**b.**
−	even	**c.**	**d.**
−	odd	**e.**	$-\infty$

52. **a.** Show that, in general, the graph of the function

$$f(x) = \frac{ax^2 + bx + c}{rx^2 + sx + t}$$

will have $y = \dfrac{a}{r}$ as a horizontal asymptote and that when $br \neq as$, the graph will cross this asymptote at the point where

$$x = \frac{at - cr}{br - as}$$

   b. Sketch the graph of each of the following functions:

$$g(x) = \frac{x^2 - 4x - 5}{2x^2 + x - 10} \qquad h(x) = \frac{3x^2 - x - 7}{-12x^2 + 4x + 8}$$

53. Find constants a and b that guarantee that the graph of the function defined by

$$f(x) = \frac{ax + 5}{3 - bx}$$

will have a vertical asymptote at $x = 5$ and a horizontal asymptote at $y = -3$.

54. **Journal Problem:** *Parabola.** ■ Draw a careful sketch of the curve $y = \dfrac{x^2}{x^2 - 1}$, indicating clearly any vertical or horizontal asymptotes, turning points, or points of inflection.

55. HISTORICAL QUEST   The possibility of division by zero is a fact that causes special concern to mathematicians. One of the first recorded observations of division by zero comes from the twelfth-century Hindu mathematician Bhaskaracharya (also known as Bhaskara), who made the following observation: "The fraction whose denominator is zero is termed an infinite quantity." Bhaskaracharya then went on to give a very beautiful conception of infinity that involved his view of God

and creation. Bhaskaracharya gave a solution for the so-called Pell equation

$$x^2 = 1 + py^2 \qquad x, y \text{ both nonnegative}$$

which is related to the problem of cutting a given sphere so the volumes of the two parts have a specified ratio.

Solve this equation for $p = 2/3$ and write this Pell equation as $y = f(x)$.[†] Find $\lim_{x \to +\infty} f(x)$.

❰ᶜ❱ Counterexample Problems   *In Problems 56—59, either show that the statement is generally true or find a counterexample.*

56. If f is concave up and g is concave down on an interval I, then fg is neither concave up nor concave down on I.

57. If f and g are concave up on the interval I, then so is $f + g$.

58. If $f(x) > 0$ and $g(x) > 0$ for all x on I and if f and g are concave up on I, then fg is also concave up on I.

59. If $f(x) < 0$ and $f''(x) > 0$ for all x on I, then the function $g = f^2$ is concave up on I.

60. **Exploration Problem**   State what you think should be the formal definition of each of the following limit statements:

   a. $\lim_{x \to c^+} f(x) = -\infty$ **b.** $\lim_{x \to c^-} f(x) = +\infty$

61. Consider the rational function

$$f(x) = \frac{a_n x^x + a_{n-1} x^{n-1} + \cdots + a_1 x + a_0}{b_m x^m + b_{m-1} x^{m-1} + \cdots + b_1 x + b_0}$$

   a. If $m > n$ and $b_m \neq 0$, show that the x-axis is the only horizontal asymptote of the graph of f.

   b. If $m = n$, show that the line $y = a_n/b_m$ is the only horizontal asymptote of the graph of f.

   c. If $m < n$, is it possible for the graph to have a horizontal asymptote? Explain.

62. Prove the following limit rule. If $\lim_{x \to c} f(x) = +\infty$ and $\lim_{x \to c} g(x) = A$ $(A > 0)$, then

$$\lim_{x \to c} [f(x)g(x)] = +\infty$$

   Hint: Notice that because $\lim_{x \to c} g(x) = A$, the function $g(x)$ is near A when x is near c. Therefore, because $\lim_{x \to +\infty} f(x) = +\infty$, the product $f(x)g(x)$ is large if x is near c. Formalize these observations for the proof.

63. Prove that if $\lim_{x \to +\infty} f(x)$ and $\lim_{x \to +\infty} g(x)$ both exist, so do $\lim_{x \to +\infty} [f(x) + g(x)]$ and

$$\lim_{x \to +\infty} [f(x) + g(x)] = \lim_{x \to +\infty} f(x) + \lim_{x \to +\infty} g(x)$$

   Hint: The key is to show that if $|f(x) - L| < \dfrac{\epsilon}{2}$ for $x > N_1$ and $|g(x) - M| < \dfrac{\epsilon}{2}$ for $x > N_2$, then whenever $x > N$ for some number N,

$$|[f(x) + g(x)] - (L + M)| < \epsilon$$

   You should also show that N relates to N_1 and N_2.

[†]From "Mathematics in India in the Middle Ages," by Chandra B. Sharma, *Mathematical Spectrum*, Volume 14(1), pp. 6–8, 1982.

4.5 l'Hôpital's Rule

IN THIS SECTION a rule to evaluate indeterminate forms, indeterminate forms 0/0 and ∞/∞, other indeterminate forms, special limits involving e^x and $\ln x$

A RULE TO EVALUATE INDETERMINATE FORMS

In curve sketching, optimization, and other applications, it is often necessary to evaluate a limit of the form $\lim\limits_{x \to c} \dfrac{f(x)}{g(x)}$, where $\lim\limits_{x \to c} f(x)$ and $\lim\limits_{x \to c} g(x)$ are either both 0 or both ∞. Such limits are called $0/0$ *indeterminate forms* and ∞/∞ *indeterminate forms*, respectively, because their value cannot be determined without further analysis. There is a rule to evaluate such indeterminate forms, known as *l'Hôpital's rule*, which relates the evaluation to a computation of $\lim\limits_{x \to c} \dfrac{f'(x)}{g'(x)}$, the limit of the ratio of the derivatives of f and g. Here is a precise statement of the rule.

WARNING First check the hypotheses (make sure it is of the form 0/0 or ∞/∞), and then take f'/g', not $(f/g)'$.

THEOREM 4.9 l'Hôpital's Rule

Let f and g be differentiable functions with $g'(x) \neq 0$ on an open interval containing c (except possibly at c itself). Suppose $\lim\limits_{x \to c} \dfrac{f(x)}{g(x)}$ produces an indeterminate form $\frac{0}{0}$ or $\frac{\infty}{\infty}$ and that

$$\lim_{x \to c} \frac{f'(x)}{g'(x)} = L$$

where L is either a finite number, $+\infty$, or $-\infty$. Then

$$\lim_{x \to c} \frac{f(x)}{g(x)} = L$$

The theorem also applies to one-sided limits and to limits at infinity (where $x \to +\infty$ and $x \to -\infty$).

Proof The proof of an important special case is given in Appendix B. However, we can obtain a sense of why it is true in the following argument. Suppose $f(x)$ and $g(x)$ are differentiable functions such that $f(a) = g(a) = 0$. Then, using the linearization formula for a differentiable function F

$$F(x) \approx F(a) + F'(a)(x - a) \qquad \text{See Section 3.8.}$$

we can write

$$\frac{f(x)}{g(x)} \approx \frac{f(a) + f'(a)(x - a)}{g(a) + g'(a)(x - a)} = \frac{0 + f'(a)(x - a)}{0 + g'(a)(x - a)} = \frac{f'(a)}{g'(a)}$$

so

$$\lim_{x \to a} \frac{f(x)}{g(x)} = \frac{f'(a)}{g'(a)} \qquad \Box$$

l'Hôpital's rule is named after Guillaume François Antoine de l'Hôpital (1661–1704), the author of the first textbook on differential calculus, published in 1696. However, the result that bears l'Hôpital's name was actually due to Johann Bernoulli (see the Historical Quest in Problem 58).

INDETERMINATE FORMS 0/0 and ∞/∞

We now consider a variety of problems involving indeterminate forms. We begin with a limit first computed in Chapter 2, but instead of using a geometric argument together with the squeeze rule of limits, we use l'Hôpital's rule.

EXAMPLE 1   Using l'Hôpital's rule to compute a familiar trigonometric limit

Evaluate $\lim\limits_{x \to 0} \dfrac{\sin x}{x}$.

Solution

Note that this is an indeterminate form because $\sin x$ and x both approach 0 as $x \to 0$. This means that l'Hôpital's rule applies:

$$\lim_{x \to 0} \frac{\sin x}{x} = \lim_{x \to 0} \frac{\cos x}{1} = 1$$

  ∎

EXAMPLE 2   l'Hôpital's rule with a 0/0 form

Evaluate $\lim\limits_{x \to 2} \dfrac{x^7 - 128}{x^3 - 8}$.

Solution

For this example, $f(x) = x^7 - 128$ and $g(x) = x^3 - 8$, and the form is 0/0.

$$\lim_{x \to 2} \frac{x^7 - 128}{x^3 - 8} = \lim_{x \to 2} \frac{7x^6}{3x^2} \qquad \text{l'Hôpital's rule}$$

$$= \lim_{x \to 2} \frac{7x^4}{3} \qquad \text{Simplify.}$$

$$= \frac{7(2)^4}{3} = \frac{112}{3} \qquad \text{Limit of a quotient}$$

  ∎

EXAMPLE 3   Limit is not an indeterminate form

Evaluate $\lim\limits_{x \to 0} \dfrac{1 - \cos x}{\sec x}$.

Solution

You must always remember to check that you have an indeterminate form before applying l'Hôpital's rule. The limit is

$$\lim_{x \to 0} \frac{1 - \cos x}{\sec x} = \frac{\lim\limits_{x \to 0}(1 - \cos x)}{\lim\limits_{x \to 0} \sec x} = \frac{0}{1} = 0$$

  ∎

WARNING   If you blindly apply l'Hpital's rule in Example 3, you obtain the WRONG answer:

$$\lim_{x \to 0} \frac{1 - \cos x}{\sec x} = \lim_{x \to 0} \frac{\sin x}{\sec x \tan x} \qquad \text{This is NOT correct.}$$

$$= \lim_{x \to 0} \frac{\cos x}{\sec x} = \frac{1}{1} = 1$$

This answer is blatantly WRONG, as you can see by looking at the Technology Note.

You can use a graphing calculator to help find many indeterminate-form limits. For instance, the limit in Example 3 can easily be checked by looking at the graph. If you have a graphing calculator, you can see that as $x \to 0$ from either the left or the right, the limit looks the same, namely, 0.

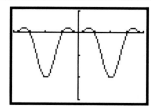

```
Y₁█(1-cos X)cos
X
Xmin=-6.283185…
Xmax=6.2831853…
Xscl=1.5707963…
Ymin=-3
Ymax=1
Yscl=1
```

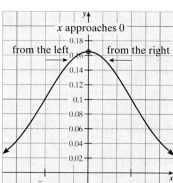
By looking at the graph, you can reinforce the result obtained using l'Hôpital's rule.

EXAMPLE 4 l'Hôpital's rule applied more than once

Evaluate $\lim\limits_{x\to 0} \dfrac{x - \sin x}{x^3}$.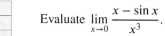

Solution

This is a 0/0 indeterminate form, and we find that

$$\lim_{x\to 0} \frac{x - \sin x}{x^3} = \lim_{x\to 0} \frac{1 - \cos x}{3x^2}$$

This is still the indeterminate form 0/0, so l'Hôpital's rule can be applied once again:

$$\lim_{x\to 0} \frac{1 - \cos x}{3x^2} = \lim_{x\to 0} \frac{-(-\sin x)}{6x} = \frac{1}{6}\lim_{x\to 0}\frac{\sin x}{x} = \frac{1}{6}(1) = \frac{1}{6} \quad \blacksquare$$

EXAMPLE 5 l'Hôpital's rule with an ∞/∞ form

Evaluate $\lim\limits_{x\to +\infty} \dfrac{2x^2 - 3x + 1}{3x^2 + 5x - 2}$.

Solution

Using the methods of Section 2.2, we could compute this limit by multiplying by $(1/x^2)/(1/x^2)$. Instead, we note that this is of the form ∞/∞ and apply l'Hôpital's rule:

$$\lim_{x\to +\infty} \frac{2x^2 - 3x + 1}{3x^2 + 5x - 2} = \lim_{x\to +\infty} \frac{4x - 3}{6x + 5} \quad \text{Apply l'Hôpital's rule again.}$$

$$= \lim_{x\to +\infty} \frac{4}{6} = \frac{2}{3} \quad \blacksquare$$

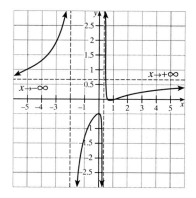

It may happen that even when l'Hôpital's rule applies to a limit, it is not the best way to proceed, as illustrated by the following example.

EXAMPLE 6 Using l'Hôpital's rule with other limit properties

Evaluate $\lim\limits_{x\to 0} \dfrac{(1 - \cos x)\sin 4x}{x^3 \cos x}$.

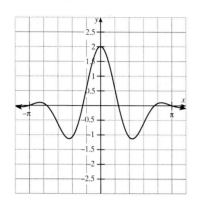

Solution

This limit has the form 0/0, but direct application of l'Hôpital's rule leads to a real mess (try it!). Instead, we compute the given limit by using the product rule for limits first, followed by two simple applications of l'Hôpital's rule. Specifically, using the product rule for limits (assuming the limits exist), we have

$$\lim_{x \to 0} \frac{(1 - \cos x)\sin 4x}{x^3 \cos x} = \left[\lim_{x \to 0} \frac{1 - \cos x}{x^2}\right] \left[\lim_{x \to 0} \frac{\sin 4x}{x}\right] \left[\lim_{x \to 0} \frac{1}{\cos x}\right]$$

$$= \left[\lim_{x \to 0} \frac{\sin x}{2x}\right] \left[\lim_{x \to 0} \frac{4\cos 4x}{1}\right] \left[\lim_{x \to 0} \frac{1}{\cos x}\right]$$

$$= \left(\frac{1}{2}\right)(4)(1) = 2 \qquad \blacksquare$$

EXAMPLE 7 Hypotheses of l'Hôpital's rule are not satisfied

Evaluate $\displaystyle\lim_{x \to +\infty} \frac{x + \sin x}{x - \cos x}$.

Solution

This limit has the indeterminate form ∞/∞. If you try to apply l'Hôpital's rule, you find

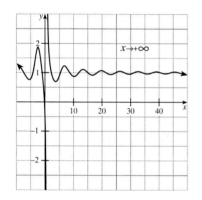

$$\lim_{x \to +\infty} \frac{x + \sin x}{x - \cos x} = \lim_{x \to +\infty} \frac{1 + \cos x}{1 + \sin x}$$

The limit on the right does not exist, because both $\sin x$ and $\cos x$ oscillate between -1 and 1 as $x \to +\infty$. Recall that l'Hôpital's rule applies only if $\displaystyle\lim_{x \to c} \frac{f'(x)}{g'(x)} = L$ or is $\pm\infty$. This does not mean that the limit of the original expression does not exist or that we cannot find it; it simply means that we cannot apply l'Hôpital's rule. To find this limit, factor out an x from the numerator and denominator and proceed as follows:

$$\lim_{x \to +\infty} \frac{x + \sin x}{x - \cos x} = \lim_{x \to +\infty} \frac{x(1 + \frac{\sin x}{x})}{x(1 - \frac{\cos x}{x})} = \lim_{x \to +\infty} \frac{1 + \frac{\sin x}{x}}{1 - \frac{\cos x}{x}} = \frac{1 + 0}{1 - 0} = 1 \qquad \blacksquare$$

OTHER INDETERMINATE FORMS

WARNING l'Hpital's rule itself applies only to the indeterminate form 0/0 and ∞/∞.

Other indeterminate forms, such as 1^∞, 0^0, ∞^0, $\infty - \infty$, and $0 \cdot \infty$, can often be manipulated algebraically into one of the standard forms 0/0 or ∞/∞ and then evaluated using l'Hôpital's rule. The following examples illustrate such procedures.

We begin by deriving a formula given without proof in Section 2.4.

EXAMPLE 8 Limit of the form 1^∞

Show that $\displaystyle\lim_{x \to +\infty} \left(1 + \frac{1}{x}\right)^x = e$.

Solution

Note that this limit is indeed of the indeterminate form 1^∞. Let

$$L = \lim_{x \to +\infty} \left(1 + \frac{1}{x}\right)^x$$

Take the logarithm of both sides:

$$\ln L = \ln \left[\lim_{x \to +\infty} \left(1 + \frac{1}{x} \right)^x \right]$$

$$= \lim_{x \to +\infty} \ln \left(1 + \frac{1}{x} \right)^x \qquad \ln x \text{ is continuous}$$

$$= \lim_{x \to +\infty} x \ln \left(1 + \frac{1}{x} \right) \qquad \text{Property of logarithms}$$

$$= \lim_{x \to +\infty} \frac{\ln \left(1 + \frac{1}{x} \right)}{\frac{1}{x}} \qquad \text{Form } \frac{0}{0}$$

$$= \lim_{x \to +\infty} \frac{\frac{1}{1 + 1/x} \left(-\frac{1}{x^2} \right)}{-\frac{1}{x^2}} \qquad \text{l'Hôpital's rule}$$

$$= \lim_{x \to +\infty} \frac{1}{1 + \frac{1}{x}} \qquad \text{Simplify}$$

$$= \frac{1}{1 + 0}$$

$$= 1$$

Thus, $\ln L = 1$ and $L = e^1 = e$. ∎

EXAMPLE 9   l'Hôpital's rule with the form $0 \cdot \infty$

Evaluate $\displaystyle \lim_{x \to \pi/2^-} \left(x - \frac{\pi}{2} \right) \tan x$.

Solution

This limit has the form $0 \cdot \infty$, because

$$\lim_{x \to \pi/2^-} \left(x - \frac{\pi}{2} \right) = 0 \qquad \text{and} \qquad \lim_{x \to \pi/2^-} \tan x = +\infty$$

Write $\tan x = \dfrac{1}{\cot x}$ to obtain

$$\lim_{x \to \pi/2^-} \left(x - \frac{\pi}{2} \right) \tan x = \lim_{x \to \pi/2^-} \frac{x - \frac{\pi}{2}}{\cot x} \qquad \text{Form } \frac{0}{0}$$

$$= \lim_{x \to \pi/2^-} \frac{1}{-\csc^2 x} \qquad \text{l'Hôpital's rule}$$

$$= \lim_{x \to \pi/2^-} (-\sin^2 x) = -1 \qquad ∎$$

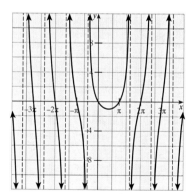

Look at the graph as $x \to \frac{\pi}{2}$ from both the left and the right.

EXAMPLE 10   Limit of the form 0^0

Find $\displaystyle \lim_{x \to 0^+} x^{\sin x}$.

Solution

This is a 0^0 indeterminate form. From the graph shown in Figure 4.49, it looks as though the desired limit is 1. We can verify this conjecture analytically.

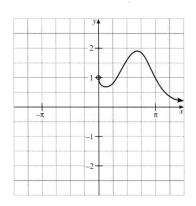

Figure 4.49 Graph of $x^{\sin x}$

As in Example 8, we begin by using properties of logarithms.

$$L = \lim_{x \to 0^+} x^{\sin x}$$

$$\ln L = \ln \lim_{x \to 0^+} x^{\sin x}$$

$$= \lim_{x \to 0^+} \ln x^{\sin x} \qquad \text{ln is continuous}$$

$$= \lim_{x \to 0^+} (\sin x) \ln x \qquad \text{This is } 0 \cdot \infty \text{ form.}$$

$$= \lim_{x \to 0^+} \frac{\ln x}{\csc x} \qquad \text{This is } \frac{\infty}{\infty} \text{ form.}$$

$$= \lim_{x \to 0^+} \frac{1/x}{-\csc x \cot x} \qquad \text{l'Hôpital's rule}$$

$$= \lim_{x \to 0^+} \frac{-\sin^2 x}{x \cos x}$$

$$= \lim_{x \to 0^+} \left(\frac{\sin x}{x} \right) \left(\frac{-\sin x}{\cos x} \right)$$

$$= (1)(0) = 0$$

Thus, $L = e^0 = 1$.   ■

EXAMPLE 11   Limit of the form ∞^0

Find $\lim\limits_{x \to +\infty} x^{1/x}$.

Solution

This is a limit of the indeterminate form ∞^0.

If $L = \lim\limits_{x \to +\infty} x^{1/x}$, then

$$\ln L = \ln \lim_{x \to +\infty} x^{1/x}$$

$$= \lim_{x \to +\infty} \ln x^{1/x} \qquad \text{The limit of a log is the log of the limit.}$$

$$= \lim_{x \to +\infty} \frac{1}{x} \ln x$$

$$= \lim_{x \to +\infty} \frac{\ln x}{x} \qquad \text{This is } \frac{\infty}{\infty} \text{ form.}$$

$$= \lim_{x \to +\infty} \frac{\frac{1}{x}}{1} \qquad \text{l'Hôpital's rule}$$

$$= 0$$

Thus, we have $\ln L = 0$; therefore, $L = e^0 = 1$.   ■

EXAMPLE 12   Horizontal asymptotes with l'Hôpital's rule

Find all horizontal asymptotes of the graph of $y = xe^{-2x}$.

Solution

To test for horizontal asymptotes, we compute

$$\lim_{x \to -\infty} xe^{-2x} \qquad \text{and} \qquad \lim_{x \to +\infty} xe^{-2x}$$

For the first limit, we find

$$\lim_{x \to -\infty} xe^{-2x} = -\infty$$

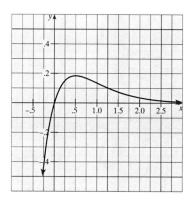

Figure 4.50 Graph of $y = xe^{-2x}$ showing the x-axis as a horizontal asymptote

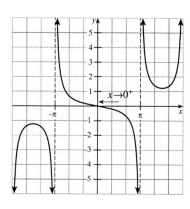

and for the second,

$$\lim_{x \to +\infty} xe^{-2x} = \lim_{x \to +\infty} \frac{x}{e^{2x}} \qquad \frac{\infty}{\infty} \text{ form}$$

$$= \lim_{x \to +\infty} \frac{1}{2e^{2x}} \qquad \text{l'Hôpital's rule}$$

$$= 0$$

Thus, $y = 0$ (the x-axis) is a horizontal asymptote. The graph of $y = xe^{-2x}$ is shown in Figure 4.50. ∎

EXAMPLE 13   l'Hôpital's rule with the form $\infty - \infty$

Evaluate $\displaystyle \lim_{x \to 0^+} \left(\frac{1}{x} - \frac{1}{\sin x} \right)$.

Solution

As it stands, this has the form $\infty - \infty$, because $\dfrac{1}{x} \to +\infty$ and $\dfrac{1}{\sin x} \to +\infty$ as $x \to 0$ from the right. However, using a little algebra, we find

$$\lim_{x \to 0^+} \left(\frac{1}{x} - \frac{1}{\sin x} \right) = \lim_{x \to 0^+} \frac{\sin x - x}{x \sin x}$$

This limit is now of the form $0/0$, so the hypotheses of l'Hôpital's rule are satisfied. Thus,

$$\lim_{x \to 0^+} \frac{\sin x - x}{x \sin x} = \lim_{x \to 0^+} \frac{\cos x - 1}{\sin x + x \cos x} \qquad \text{Again, the form } \frac{0}{0}$$

$$= \lim_{x \to 0^+} \frac{-\sin x}{\cos x + x(-\sin x) + \cos x} = \frac{0}{2} = 0 \qquad ∎$$

WARNING Not all limits that appear indeterminate actually are indeterminate. For example,

$$\lim_{x \to 0^+} (\sin x)^{1/x} = 0 \qquad 0^\infty \text{ form}$$

$$\lim_{x \to 0^+} (\csc x - \ln x) = +\infty \qquad +\infty - (-\infty) \text{ form}$$

$$\lim_{x \to 0^+} \frac{\tan x}{\ln x} = 0 \qquad \frac{0}{\infty} \text{ form}$$

Other such "false indeterminate forms" include $+\infty + (+\infty)$, $\infty/0$, and $\infty \cdot \infty$, which are all actually infinite.

SPECIAL LIMITS INVOLVING e^x AND $\ln x$

We close this section with a theorem that summarizes the behavior of certain important special functions involving e^x and $\ln x$ near 0 and at $\pm\infty$.

THEOREM 4.10   Limits involving natural logarithms and exponentials

If k and n are positive numbers, then

$$\lim_{x \to 0^+} \frac{\ln x}{x^n} = -\infty \qquad \lim_{x \to +\infty} \frac{\ln x}{x^n} = 0$$

$$\lim_{x \to +\infty} \frac{e^{kx}}{x^n} = +\infty \qquad \lim_{x \to +\infty} x^n e^{-kx} = 0$$

Proof   These can all be verified directly or by applying l'Hôpital's rule. For example,

$$\lim_{x\to+\infty}\frac{\ln x}{x^n} = \lim_{x\to+\infty}\frac{\frac{1}{x}}{nx^{n-1}} = \lim_{x\to+\infty}\frac{1}{nx^n} = 0$$

The other parts are left for you to verify.   ❑

> ➡ **What This Says**   The limit statements
>
> $$\lim_{x\to+\infty}\frac{e^{kx}}{x^n} = +\infty \qquad \text{and} \qquad \lim_{x\to+\infty}\frac{\ln x}{x^n} = 0$$
>
> are especially important. They tell us that, in the long run, any exponential e^{kx} dominates any power x^n, for k and n positive, which, in turn, dominates any logarithm.

4.5   PROBLEM SET

Ⓐ 1. An incorrect use of l'Hôpital's rule is illustrated in the following limit computations. In each case, explain what is wrong and find the correct value of the limit.

a. $\displaystyle\lim_{x\to\pi}\frac{1-\cos x}{x} = \lim_{x\to\pi}\frac{\sin x}{1} = 0$

b. $\displaystyle\lim_{x\to\pi/2}\frac{\sin x}{x} = \lim_{x\to\pi/2}\frac{\cos x}{1} = 0$

2. Exploration Problem   Sometimes l'Hôpital's rule leads to faulty computations. For example, observe what happens when the rule is applied to

$$\lim_{x\to+\infty}\frac{x}{\sqrt{x^2-1}}$$

Use any method you wish to evaluate this limit.

Find each of the limits in Problems 3–36.

3. $\displaystyle\lim_{x\to1}\frac{x^3-1}{x^2-1}$

4. $\displaystyle\lim_{x\to2}\frac{x^3-27}{x^2-9}$

5. $\displaystyle\lim_{x\to1}\frac{x^{10}-1}{x-1}$

6. $\displaystyle\lim_{x\to-1}\frac{x^{10}-1}{x+1}$

7. $\displaystyle\lim_{x\to0}\frac{1-\cos^2 x}{\sin^3 x}$

8. $\displaystyle\lim_{x\to0}\frac{1-\cos^2 x}{3\sin x}$

9. $\displaystyle\lim_{x\to\pi}\frac{\cos\frac{x}{2}}{\pi-x}$

10. $\displaystyle\lim_{x\to0}\frac{1-\cos x}{x^2}$

11. $\displaystyle\lim_{x\to0}\frac{\sin ax}{\cos bx}$, $ab\neq0$

12. $\displaystyle\lim_{x\to0}\frac{\tan 3x}{\sin 5x}$

13. $\displaystyle\lim_{x\to0}\frac{x-\sin x}{\tan x-x}$

14. $\displaystyle\lim_{x\to0}\frac{1-\cos^2 x}{x\tan x}$

15. $\displaystyle\lim_{x\to\pi/2}\frac{3\sec x}{2+\tan x}$

16. $\displaystyle\lim_{x\to0}\frac{x+\sin^3 x}{x^2+2x}$

17. $\displaystyle\lim_{x\to0}\frac{\sin 3x\sin 2x}{x\sin 4x}$

18. $\displaystyle\lim_{x\to\pi/2}\frac{\sin 2x\cos x}{x\sin 4x}$

19. $\displaystyle\lim_{x\to0}\frac{x^2+\sin x^2}{x^2+x^3}$

20. $\displaystyle\lim_{x\to0}x^2\sin\frac{1}{x}$

21. $\displaystyle\lim_{x\to+\infty}x^{3/2}\sin\frac{1}{x}$

22. $\displaystyle\lim_{x\to0}\left(\cot x-\frac{1}{x}\right)$

23. $\displaystyle\lim_{x\to1}\frac{(x-1)\sin(x-1)}{1-\cos(x-1)}$

24. $\displaystyle\lim_{\theta\to0}\frac{\theta-1+\cos^2\theta}{\theta^2+5\theta}$

25. $\displaystyle\lim_{x\to0}\frac{x+\sin(x^2+x)}{3x+\sin x}$

26. $\displaystyle\lim_{x\to\pi/2^-}\sec 3x\cos 9x$

27. $\displaystyle\lim_{x\to0}\left(\frac{1}{\sin 2x}-\frac{1}{2x}\right)$

28. $\displaystyle\lim_{x\to+\infty}x^{-5}\ln x$

29. $\displaystyle\lim_{x\to0^+}x^{-5}\ln x$

30. $\displaystyle\lim_{x\to0^+}(\sin x)\ln x$

31. $\displaystyle\lim_{x\to+\infty}\frac{\ln(\ln x)}{x}$

32. $\displaystyle\lim_{x\to-\infty}\left(1-\frac{3}{x}\right)^{2x}$

33. $\displaystyle\lim_{x\to+\infty}\left(1+\frac{1}{2x}\right)^{3x}$

34. $\displaystyle\lim_{x\to+\infty}(\ln x)^{1/x}$

35. $\displaystyle\lim_{x\to0^+}(e^x+x)^{1/x}$

36. $\displaystyle\lim_{x\to0^+}(\sin x)^{1/\ln\sqrt{x}}$

Ⓑ *Find each of the limits in Problems 37–51.*

37. $\displaystyle\lim_{x\to(\pi/2)^-}\left(\frac{1}{\pi-2x}+\tan x\right)$

38. $\displaystyle\lim_{x\to+\infty}\left(\sqrt{x^2-x}-x\right)$

39. $\displaystyle\lim_{x\to+\infty}[x-\ln(x^3-1)]$ *Hint*: $\ln e^x = x$

40. $\displaystyle\lim_{x\to+\infty}[x-\ln(e^x+e^{-x})]$ *Hint*: $\ln e^x = x$

41. $\displaystyle\lim_{x\to0^+}\left(\frac{1}{x^2}-\ln\sqrt{x}\right)$

42. $\displaystyle\lim_{x\to0}(e^x-1-x)^x$

43. $\displaystyle\lim_{x\to0^+}(\ln x)(\cot x)$

44. $\displaystyle\lim_{x\to0^+}(e^x-1)^{1/\ln x}$

45. $\displaystyle\lim_{x\to+\infty}\frac{x+\sin 3x}{x}$

46. $\displaystyle\lim_{x\to+\infty}\frac{x(\pi+\sin x)}{x^2+1}$

47. $\displaystyle\lim_{x\to0^+}\left(\frac{2\cos x}{\sin 2x}-\frac{1}{x}\right)$

48. $\displaystyle\lim_{x\to+\infty}\left(\frac{x^3}{x^2-x+1}-\frac{x^3}{x^2+x-1}\right)$

49. $\displaystyle\lim_{x\to0}\frac{(2-x)(e^x-x-2)}{x^3}$

50. $\lim\limits_{x\to 0} \dfrac{\tan^{-1}(3x) - 3\tan^{-1} x}{x^3}$

51. $\lim\limits_{x\to +\infty} x^5 \left[\sin\left(\dfrac{1}{x}\right) - \dfrac{1}{x} + \dfrac{1}{6x^3} \right]$

52. Find A so that $\lim\limits_{x\to +\infty} \left(\dfrac{x+A}{x-2A}\right)^x = 5$.

In Problems 53–56, use l'Hôpital's rule to determine all horizontal asymptotes to the graph of the given function. You are NOT required to sketch the graph.

53. $f(x) = x^3 e^{-0.01x}$

54. $f(x) = \dfrac{\ln x^5}{x^{0.02}}$

55. $f(x) = (\ln\sqrt{x})^{2/x}$

56. $f(x) = \left(\dfrac{x+3}{x+2}\right)^{2x}$

57. Exploration Problem Write a paper on using technology to evaluate limits.

58. HISTORICAL QUEST The French mathematician Guillaume de l'Hpital is best known today for the rule that bears his name, but the rule was discovered by l'Hpital's teacher, Johann Bernoulli. Not only did l'Hpital neglect to cite his sources in his book, but there is also evidence that he paid Bernoulli for his results and for keeping their arrangements for payment confidential. In a letter dated March 17, 1694, he asked Bernoulli "to communicate to me your discoveries ..."—with the request not to mention them to others—"... it would not please me if they were made public." L'Hpital's argument, which was originally given without using functional notation, can easily be reproduced*:

$$\frac{f(a+dx)}{g(a+dx)} = \frac{f(a) + f'(a)\,dx}{g(a) + g'(a)\,dx}$$
$$= \frac{f'(a)\,dx}{g'(a)\,dx}$$
$$= \frac{f'(a)}{g'(a)} \quad \blacksquare$$

Supply reasons for this argument, and give necessary conditions for the functions f and g.

59. HISTORICAL QUEST The remarkable Bernoulli family of Switzerland produced at least eight noted mathematicians over three generations. Two brothers, Jacob (1654–1705) and Johann (1667–1748), were bitter rivals. These brothers were extremely influential advocates of the newly born calculus. Johann was the most prolific of the clan and was responsible for the discovery of l'Hpital's rule (see Problem 58), Bernoulli numbers, Bernoulli polynomials, the lemniscate of Bernoulli, the Bernoulli equation, the Bernoulli theorem, and the Bernoulli

*D. J. Struik, A Source Book in Mathematics, 1200–1800. Cambridge, MA: Harvard University Press, 1969, pp. 313–316.

distribution. He did a great deal of work with differential equations. Johann was jealous and cantankerous; he tossed a son (Daniel) out of the house for winning an award he had expected to win himself. ■

Write a report on the Bernoulli family.

Find the limits in Problems 60–62 using the following methods.

 a. graphically   b. analytically   c. numerically

Compare, contrast, and reconcile the three methods.

60. $\lim\limits_{x\to 0^+} x^x$

61. $\lim\limits_{x\to 0^+} (x^x)^x$

62. $\lim\limits_{x\to +\infty} \left[x\sin^{-1}\left(\dfrac{1}{x}\right)\right]^{x^2}$

63. Find constants a and b so that

$$\lim\limits_{x\to 0} \left(\frac{\sin 2x}{x^3} + \frac{a}{x^2} + b\right) = 1$$

64. Find all values of A and B so that

$$\lim\limits_{x\to 0} \frac{\sin Ax + Bx}{x^3} = 36$$

65. For a certain value of C, the limit

$$\lim\limits_{x\to +\infty} (x^4 + 5x^3 + 3)^C - x$$

is finite and nonzero. Find C and then compute the limit.

66. For which values of constants D and E is it true that

$$\lim\limits_{x\to 0}(x^{-3}\sin 7x + Dx^{-2} + E) = -2?$$

67. A weight hanging by a spring is made to vibrate by applying a sinusoidal force, and the displacement at time t is given by

$$f(t) = \frac{C}{\beta^2 - \alpha^2}(\sin\alpha t - \sin\beta t)$$

where C, α, and β are constants such that $\alpha \neq \beta$. What happens to the displacement as $\beta \to \alpha$? You may assume that α is fixed.

68. For F and G positive constants, define

$$f(x) = (e^x + Fx)^{G/x}$$

 a. Compute $L_1 = \lim\limits_{x\to 0} f(x)$ and $L_2 = \lim\limits_{x\to +\infty} f(x)$.

 b. What is the largest value of F for which the equation $L_1 = GL_2$ has a solution? What are L_1 and L_2 in this case?

4.6   Optimization in the Physical Sciences and Engineering

IN THIS SECTION   optimization procedure, Fermat's principle of optics and Snell's law

We introduced the process of mathematical modeling in Chapter 3, and now that we have developed the necessary calculus skills, we will use mathematical modeling and calculus to solve optimization problems.

OPTIMIZATION PROCEDURE

NOTHING TAKES PLACE in the world whose meaning is not that of some maximum or minimum.

——Leonhard Euler

When light travels from one medium to another—say, from air into water—which path does it follow? In a mechanical system involving pulleys, which arrangement results in minimal potential energy? At what temperature does a given mass of water occupy the least volume (the answer is not 0°C)? These are typical *optimization problems* from the physical sciences and engineering and will be examined in the examples and exercises of this section. The process of finding the maximum or minimum of a function is called **optimization**. Then, in the next section, we will explore optimization involving applications to business, economics, and the social and life sciences. We begin by outlining a general optimization procedure based on ideas originally suggested by George Pólya (1887–1985), one of the great problem solvers of twentieth-century mathematics (see the Historical Quest in Problem 61 of Section 7.4).

Optimization Procedure

Step 1.   Draw a figure (if appropriate) and label all quantities relevant to the problem.

Step 2.   Focus on the quantity to be optimized. Name it. Find a formula for the quantity to be maximized or minimized.

Step 3.   Use conditions in the problem to eliminate variables in order to express the quantity to be maximized or minimized in terms of a single variable.

Step 4.   Find the practical domain for the variables in Step 3; that is, the interval of possible values determined from the physical restrictions in the problem.

Step 5.   If possible, use the methods of calculus to obtain the required optimum value.

EXAMPLE 1   Maximizing a constrained area

You need to fence a rectangular play zone for children. What is the maximum area for this play zone if it is to fit into a right-triangular plot with sides measuring 4 m and 12 m?

Solution

A picture of the play zone is shown in Figure 4.51. Let x and y denote the length and width of the inscribed rectangle. The appropriate formula for the area is

$$A = (\text{LENGTH})(\text{WIDTH}) = xy$$

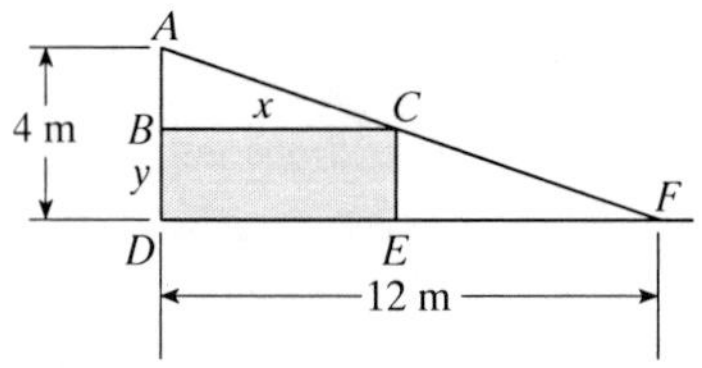

We wish to maximize A, where $A = xy$, but first we must express A as a function of a single variable. To do this, note that, because $\triangle ABC$ is similar to $\triangle ADF$, the corresponding sides of these triangles are proportional,

$$\frac{4 - y}{4} = \frac{x}{12}$$

$$y = 4 - \tfrac{1}{3}x$$

Figure 4.51 Children's play zone

 SMH   See Section 1.5 of the *Student Mathematics Handbook* for similar triangles.

We can now write A as a function of x alone:

$$A(x) = x(4 - \tfrac{1}{3}x) = 4x - \tfrac{1}{3}x^2$$

The domain for A is $0 \le x \le 12$. The critical numbers for A are values such that $A'(x) = 0$ (since $A'(x)$ exists for all x). Since

$$A'(x) = 4 - \tfrac{2}{3}x$$

the only critical number is $x = 6$. Evaluate $A(x)$ at the endpoints and the critical number:

$$A(6) = 4(6) - \tfrac{1}{3}(6)^2 = 12; \quad A(0) = 0; \quad A(12) = 0$$

The maximum area occurs when $x = 6$. This means that

$$y = 4 - \tfrac{1}{3}(6) = 2$$

Thus, the largest rectangular play zone that can be built in the triangular plot is a rectangle 6 m long and 2 m wide. ∎

EXAMPLE 2 Maximizing a volume

A carpenter wants to make an open-topped box out of a rectangular sheet of tin 24 in. wide and 45 in. long. The carpenter plans to cut congruent squares out of each corner of the sheet and then bend and solder the edges of the sheet upward to form the sides of the box, as shown in Figure 4.52.

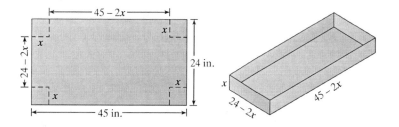

Figure 4.52 A box cut from a 24 in. by 45 in. piece of tin

For what dimensions does the box have the greatest possible volume?

Solution

If each square corner cut out has side x, the box will be x inches deep, $45 - 2x$ inches long, and $24 - 2x$ inches wide. The volume of the box shown in Figure 4.52 is

$$V(x) = x(45 - 2x)(24 - 2x) = 4x^3 - 138x^2 + 1{,}080x$$

and this is the quantity to be maximized. To find the domain, we note that the dimensions must all be nonnegative; therefore, $x \ge 0$, $45 - 2x \ge 0$ (or $x \le 22.5$), and $24 - 2x \ge 0$ (or $x \le 12$). This implies that the domain is $[0, 12]$.

To find the critical numbers (the derivative is defined everywhere in the domain), we find values for which the derivative is 0:

$$V'(x) = 12x^2 - 276x + 1{,}080 = 12(x - 18)(x - 5)$$

The critical numbers are $x = 5$ and $x = 18$, but $x = 18$ is not in the domain, so the only relevant critical number is $x = 5$. Evaluating $V(x)$ at the critical number $x = 5$ and the endpoints $x = 0$, $x = 12$, we find

$$V(5) = 5(45 - 10)(24 - 10) = 2{,}450; \quad V(0) = 0; \quad V(12) = 0$$

Thus, the box with the largest volume is found when $x = 5$. Such a box has dimensions 5 in. × 14 in. × 35 in. ∎

You will note in Example 2 we did not have to test whether the critical point was a maximum or a minimum, but knew that it was a maximum because the continuous function V is nonnegative on the interval $[0, 12]$ and is indeed zero at the endpoints. Since there is only one critical number $x = 5$, that must yield the maximum. Similar reasoning can be used in many examples, allowing us to forgo having to test for a maximum or minimum with the first- or second-derivative test. We summarize this procedure with the following definition.

EVT Convention

> If the hypotheses of the extreme value theorem apply to a particular problem, we can often avoid testing a candidate to see whether it is a maximum or a minimum. Suppose we have three candidates and two are obviously minima—the third *must be a maximum*. We will refer to this principle of not testing a candidate as the **EVT convention** because it is shorthand for using the extreme value theorem.

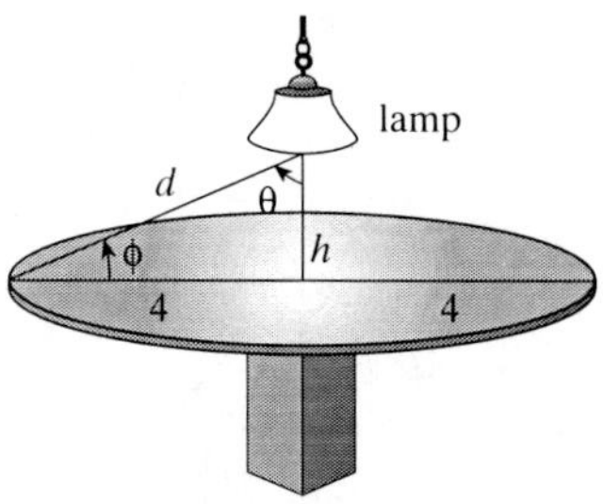

Figure 4.53 Illumination on a kitchen table

EXAMPLE 3   Maximizing illumination

A lamp with adjustable height hangs directly above the center of a circular kitchen table that is 8 ft in diameter. Model the illumination I at the edge of the table to be directly proportional to the cosine of the angle θ and inversely proportional to the square of the distance d, where θ and d are as shown in Figure 4.53. How close to the table should the lamp be lowered to maximize the illumination at the edge of the table?

Solution

We note that

$$I(\theta) = \frac{k \cos \theta}{d^2}$$

where k is a (positive) constant of proportionality. Moreover, from the right triangle shown in Figure 4.53,

$$\sin \theta = \frac{4}{d} \quad \text{or} \quad d = \frac{4}{\sin \theta}$$

Hence,

$$I(\theta) = k \cos \theta \left[\frac{1}{(4/\sin \theta)^2} \right]$$

$$= \frac{k}{16} \cos \theta \sin^2 \theta$$

Only values of θ between 0 and $\frac{\pi}{2}$ are meaningful in the context of this problem. Hence, the goal is to find the absolute maximum of the function $I(\theta)$ on $[0, \frac{\pi}{2}]$.

Using the product rule and the chain rule to differentiate $I(\theta)$, we obtain

$$I'(\theta) = \frac{k}{16}[\cos \theta(2 \sin \theta \cos \theta) + \sin^2 \theta(-\sin \theta)]$$

$$= \frac{k}{16}(2 \cos^2 \theta \sin \theta - \sin^3 \theta)$$

$$= \frac{k}{16} \sin \theta(2 \cos^2 \theta - \sin^2 \theta)$$

This is zero when $\theta = 0$ (since $\sin 0 = 0$) and when

$$2 \cos^2 \theta - \sin^2 \theta = 0$$

$$\frac{\sin^2 \theta}{\cos^2 \theta} = 2$$

$$\tan^2 \theta = 2$$

$$\theta = \tan^{-1} \sqrt{2}$$

Evaluating $I(\theta)$ at the endpoints, $\theta = 0$ and $\theta = \frac{\pi}{2}$, and at the interior critical number $\tan^{-1}\sqrt{2} \approx 0.9553$, we find that

$$I(0) = \frac{k}{16}(\cos 0)(\sin^2 0) = 0$$

$$I\left(\frac{\pi}{2}\right) = \frac{k}{16}\left(\cos\frac{\pi}{2}\right)\left(\sin^2\frac{\pi}{2}\right) = 0$$

$$I(\tan^{-1}\sqrt{2}) \approx I(0.9553) \approx \frac{k}{16}(\cos 0.9553)(\sin^2 0.9553) \approx 0.0241k$$

Finally, to find the height h that maximizes the illumination I, observe from Figure 4.53 that

$$\tan\theta = \frac{4}{h}$$

Since $\tan\theta = \sqrt{2}$ when I is maximized, it follows that

$$h = \frac{4}{\tan\theta} = \frac{4}{\sqrt{2}} \approx 2.83$$

To maximize the illumination, the lamp should be placed about 2.8 ft (2 ft 10 in.) above the table. ∎

EXAMPLE 4   Minimizing time of travel

A dune buggy is on the desert at a point A located 40 km from a point B, which lies on a long, straight road, as shown in Figure 4.54. The driver can travel at 45 km/h on the desert and 75 km/h on the road. The driver will win a prize if she arrives at the finish line at point D, 50 km from B, in 84 min or less. What route should she travel to minimize the time of travel? Does she win the prize?

Solution

Suppose the driver heads for a point C located x km down the road from B toward her destination, as shown in Figure 4.54. We want to minimize the time. We will need to remember the formula $d = rt$, or in terms of time, $t = \frac{d}{r}$.

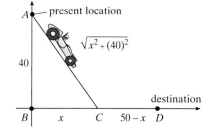

Figure 4.54 A path traveled by a dune buggy

TIME = TIME FROM A TO C + TIME FROM C TO D

$$= \frac{\text{DISTANCE FROM } A \text{ TO } C}{\text{RATE FROM } A \text{ TO } C} + \frac{\text{DISTANCE FROM } C \text{ TO } D}{\text{RATE FROM } C \text{ TO } D}$$

$$T(x) = \frac{\sqrt{x^2 + 1{,}600}}{45} + \frac{50 - x}{75}$$

The domain of T is $[0, 50]$. Next, find the derivative of time T with respect to x:

$$T'(x) = \frac{1}{45}\left[\frac{1}{2}(x^2 + 1{,}600)^{-1/2}(2x)\right] + \frac{1}{75}(-1)$$

$$= \frac{x}{45\sqrt{x^2 + 1{,}600}} - \frac{1}{75}$$

$$= \frac{5x - 3\sqrt{x^2 + 1{,}600}}{225\sqrt{x^2 + 1{,}600}}$$

The derivative exists for all x and is zero when

$$5x - 3\sqrt{x^2 + 1{,}600} = 0$$

Solving this equation, we find $x = 30$ (-30 is extraneous). Evaluating $T(x)$ here and at the endpoints, we find that

$$T(30) = \frac{\sqrt{30^2 + 1{,}600}}{45} + \frac{50 - 30}{75} \approx 1.3778 \text{ hr} \approx 83 \text{ min}$$

$$T(0) = \frac{\sqrt{0^2 + 1{,}600}}{45} + \frac{50 - 0}{75} \approx 1.5556 \text{ hr} \approx 93 \text{ min}$$

$$T(50) = \frac{\sqrt{50^2 + 1{,}600}}{45} + \frac{50 - 50}{75} \approx 1.4229 \text{ hr} \approx 85 \text{ min}$$

The driver can minimize the total driving time by heading for a point that is 30 miles from the point B and then traveling on the road to point D. She wins the prize because this minimal route requires only 83 minutes.   ■

EXAMPLE 5   Optimizing a constrained area

A wire of length L is to be cut into two pieces, one of which will be bent to form a circle and the other to form a square. Determine how the wire should be cut to

a. maximize the sum of the areas enclosed by the two pieces.
b. minimize the sum of the areas enclosed by the two pieces.

Solution

To understand the problem we draw a sketch, as shown in Figure 4.55, and label the radius of the circle r and the side of the square s.

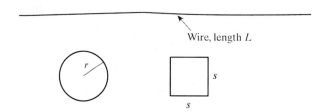

Figure 4.55   Forming a circle and a square from a wire with length L

We find that the combined area is

$$\text{AREA} = \text{AREA OF CIRCLE} + \text{AREA OF SQUARE} = \pi r^2 + s^2$$

We need to write the radius r and the side s in terms of the length of wire, L.

$$L = \text{CIRCUMFERENCE OF CIRCLE} + \text{PERIMETER OF SQUARE}$$
$$= 2\pi r + 4s$$

so $s = \frac{1}{4}(L - 2\pi r)$. (We could just as easily have solved for r.) By substitution,

$$A(r) = \pi r^2 + \left[\tfrac{1}{4}(L - 2\pi r)\right]^2 = \pi r^2 + \tfrac{1}{16}(L - 2\pi r)^2$$

To find the domain, we note that $r \geq 0$ and that $L - 2\pi r \geq 0$, so the domain is $0 \leq r \leq \dfrac{L}{2\pi}$. Note when $r = 0$ there is no circle, and when $r = \dfrac{L}{2\pi}$ there is no square. The derivative of $A(r)$ is

$$A'(r) = 2\pi r + \tfrac{1}{8}(L - 2\pi r)(-2\pi)$$
$$= 2\pi r - \tfrac{\pi}{4}(L - 2\pi r)$$
$$= \tfrac{\pi}{4}(8r - L + 2\pi r)$$

Solve $A'(r) = 0$ to find $r = \dfrac{L}{2(\pi + 4)}$.

Thus, the extreme values of the area function on $\left[0, \dfrac{L}{2\pi}\right]$ must occur either at the endpoints or at the critical number $\dfrac{L}{2\pi + 8}$. Evaluating $A(r)$ at each of these numbers, we find

$$A(0) = \pi(0)^2 + \frac{1}{16}[L - 2\pi(0)]^2 = \frac{L^2}{16}$$

$$A\left(\frac{L}{2\pi}\right) = \pi\left(\frac{L}{2\pi}\right)^2 + \frac{1}{16}\left[L - 2\pi\left(\frac{L}{2\pi}\right)\right]^2 = \frac{L^2}{4\pi}$$

$$A\left(\frac{L}{2\pi + 8}\right) = \pi\left(\frac{L}{2\pi + 8}\right)^2 + \frac{1}{16}\left[L - 2\pi\left(\frac{L}{2\pi + 8}\right)\right]^2 = \frac{L^2}{4(\pi + 4)}$$

Comparing these values, we see that the smallest area occurs at $r = \dfrac{L}{2\pi + 8}$ and the largest area occurs at $x = L/(2\pi)$. To summarize,

1. To maximize the sum of the areas, do not cut the wire at all. Bend the wire to form a circle of radius $r = \dfrac{L}{2\pi}$.

2. To minimize the sum of the areas, cut the wire at the point located $2\pi r = \dfrac{2\pi L}{2\pi + 8}$

$= \dfrac{\pi L}{\pi + 4}$ units from one end, and form the circular part with resulting radius $r = \dfrac{L}{2\pi + 8}$.

If you use a graphing calculator or a computer, you can verify this result (for $L = 1$) by looking at the graph of the area function, as shown in Figure 4.56. ∎

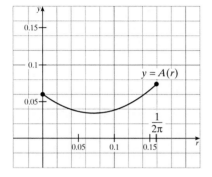

Figure 4.56 Graph of $A(r) = \pi r^2 + \frac{1}{16}(1 - 2\pi r)^2$

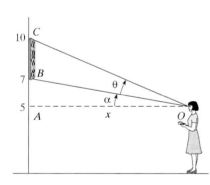

Figure 4.57 The angle θ is subtended by the observer's eye

EXAMPLE 6 Optimizing an angle of observation

A painting is hung on a wall in such a way that its upper and lower edges are 10 ft and 7 ft above the floor, respectively. An observer whose eyes are 5 ft above the floor stands x feet from the wall, as shown in Figure 4.57. How far away from the wall should the observer stand to maximize the angle subtended by the painting?

Solution

In Figure 4.57, θ is the angle whose vertex occurs at the observer's eyes at a point O located x feet from the wall. Note that α is the angle between the line $\overline{OA}$ drawn horizontally from the observer's eyes to the wall and the line $\overline{OB}$ from the eyes to the bottom edge of the painting. In $\triangle OAB$, the angle at O is α, with $\cot \alpha = \frac{x}{7}$. In $\triangle OAC$, the angle at O is $(\alpha + \theta)$, and $\cot(\alpha + \theta) = \frac{x}{5}$. By using the definition of inverse cotangent, we have

$$\theta = (\alpha + \theta) - \alpha = \cot^{-1}\left(\frac{x}{5}\right) - \cot^{-1}\left(\frac{x}{2}\right)$$

To maximize θ, we first compute the derivative:

$$\frac{d\theta}{dx} = \frac{-1}{\left[1 + \left(\frac{x}{5}\right)^2\right]}\left(\frac{1}{5}\right) - \frac{-1}{\left[1 + \left(\frac{x}{2}\right)^2\right]}\left(\frac{1}{2}\right) = \frac{-5}{25 + x^2} + \frac{2}{4 + x^2}$$

Solving the equation $\dfrac{d\theta}{dx} = 0$ yields

$$-5(4 + x^2) + 2(25 + x^2) = 0$$

$$-3x^2 + 30 = 0$$

$$x = \pm\sqrt{10}$$

Because distance must be nonnegative, we reject the negative value. We apply the first-derivative test to show that the positive critical number $\sqrt{10}$ corresponds to a relative maximum (verify). Thus, the angle θ is maximized when the observer stands $\sqrt{10}$ ft away from the wall. ∎

FERMAT'S PRINCIPLE OF OPTICS AND SNELL'S LAW

Light travels at different rates in different media; the more optically dense the medium, the slower the speed of transit. Consider the situation shown in Figure 4.58, in which a beam of light originates at a point A in one medium, then strikes the upper surface of a second, denser medium at a point P, and is refracted to a point B in the second medium.

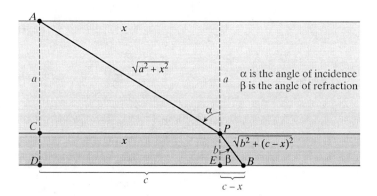

Figure 4.58   The path of a light beam through two media of different density

Suppose light travels with speed v_1 in the first medium and speed v_2 in the second. What can be said about the path followed by the beam of light?

Our method of investigating this question is based on the following optical property.

Fermat's Principle of Optics

Light travels between two points in such a way as to minimize the time of transit.

This problem is very similar to the dune buggy problem of Example 4: Light minimizes the time, and determining minimum time was the goal of that example. In Figure 4.58, let $a = \left| \overline{AC} \right|$, $b = \left| \overline{CD} \right|$, and $c = \left| \overline{DB} \right|$, and let x denote the distance from C to P. Because A and B are fixed points, the path APB is determined by the location of P, which, in turn, is determined by x. Because v_1 is a given constant, the time required for the light to travel from A to P is given by

$$T_1 = \frac{\left| \overline{AP} \right|}{v_1} = \frac{\sqrt{a^2 + x^2}}{v_1}$$

and the time required for the light to go from P to B is

$$T_2 = \frac{\left| \overline{PB} \right|}{v_2} = \frac{\sqrt{b^2 + (c - x)^2}}{v_2}$$

for another given constant v_2. Therefore, the total time of transit is

$$T = T_1 + T_2 = \frac{\sqrt{a^2 + x^2}}{v_1} + \frac{\sqrt{b^2 + (c - x)^2}}{v_2}$$

where it is clear that $0 \le x \le c$. According to Fermat's principle, the path followed by the beam of light is the one that corresponds to the smallest possible value of T; that is, we want to minimize T as a function of x.

Toward this end, we begin by finding $\dfrac{dT}{dx}$.

$$\frac{dT}{dx} = \frac{x}{v_1 \sqrt{a^2 + x^2}} - \frac{c - x}{v_2 \sqrt{b^2 + (c - x)^2}}$$

Note from Figure 4.58 that if α is the angle of incidence of the beam of light and β is the angle of refraction, then (from the definition of sine)

$$\sin \alpha = \frac{x}{\sqrt{a^2 + x^2}} \quad \text{and} \quad \sin \beta = \frac{c - x}{\sqrt{b^2 + (c - x)^2}}$$

Therefore (by substitution), we see the derivative of T can be expressed as

$$\frac{dT}{dx} = \frac{\sin \alpha}{v_1} - \frac{\sin \beta}{v_2}$$

and it follows that the only critical number occurs when

$$\frac{\sin \alpha}{\sin \beta} = \frac{v_1}{v_2}$$

By using the first-derivative test, it can be shown that this critical number corresponds to an absolute minimum. The corresponding value of x enables us to locate P and hence to determine the path followed by the beam of light. We have established the following law of optics.

Snell's Law of Refraction

If a beam of light strikes the boundary between two media with angle of incidence α and is refracted through an angle β, then

$$\frac{\sin \alpha}{\sin \beta} = \frac{v_1}{v_2}$$

where v_1 and v_2 are the rates at which light travels through the first and second medium, respectively. The constant ratio

$$n = \frac{\sin \alpha}{\sin \beta}$$

is called the **relative index of refraction** of the two media.

4.6 PROBLEM SET

A 1. **WHAT DOES THIS SAY?** Describe an optimization procedure.

2. **WHAT DOES THIS SAY?** What is Fermat's principle of optics?

B 3. A woman plans to fence off a rectangular garden whose area is 64 ft². What should be the dimensions of the garden if she wants to minimize the amount of fencing used?

4. The highway department is planning to build a rectangular picnic area for motorists along a major highway. It is to have an area of 5,000 yd² and is to be fenced off on the three sides not adjacent to the highway. What is the least amount of fencing that will be needed to complete the job?

5. **Exploration Problem** Pull out a sheet of $8\frac{1}{2}$-in. by 11-in. engineering or binder paper. Cut squares from the corners and fold the sides up to form a container. Show that the maximum volume of such a container is about 1 liter.

6. **Journal Problem:** *Parabola.** ■ Farmer Jones has to build a fence to enclose a 1,200 m² rectangular area $ABCD$. Fencing

costs \$3 per meter, but Farmer Smith has agreed to pay half the cost of fencing $\overline{CD}$, which borders the property. Given x is the length of side $\overline{CD}$, what is the minimum amount (to the nearest cent) Jones has to pay?

7. Find the rectangle of largest area that can be inscribed in a semicircle of radius R, assuming that one side of the rectangle lies on the diameter of the semicircle.

8. A cylindrical container with no top is to be constructed to hold a fixed volume V_0 of liquid. The cost of the material used for the bottom is 50¢/in.², and the cost of the material used for the curved lateral side is 30¢/in.² Use calculus to find the radius (in terms of V_0) of the least expensive container.

9. Find the dimensions of the right circular cylinder of largest volume that can be inscribed in a sphere of radius R.

10. Given a sphere of radius R, find the radius r and altitude $2h$ of the right circular cylinder with largest lateral surface area that can be inscribed in the sphere.

11. Each edge of a square has length L, as shown in Figure 4.59.

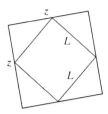

Figure 4.59   Square in a square

Determine the edge of the square of largest area that can be circumscribed about the given square.

12. Find the dimensions of the right circular cylinder of largest volume that can be inscribed in a right circular cone of radius R and altitude H. *Hint:* Begin with Figure 4.60.

Figure 4.60   Cylinder in a cone

13. A truck is 250 mi due east of a sports car and is traveling west at a constant speed of 60 mi/h. Meanwhile, the sports car is going north at 80 mi/h. When will the truck and the car be closest to each other? What is the minimum distance between them? *Hint:* Minimize the square of the distance.

14. Show that of all rectangles with a given perimeter, the square has the largest area.

15. Show that of all rectangles with a given area, the square has the smallest perimeter.

16. A closed box with square base is to be built to house an ant colony. The bottom of the box and all four sides are to be made of material costing $1/ft², and the top is to be constructed of glass costing $5/ft². What are the dimensions of the box of greatest volume that can be constructed for $72?

17. According to postal regulations, the girth plus the length of a parcel sent by fourth-class mail may not exceed 108 in. What is the largest possible volume of a rectangular parcel with two square sides that can be sent by fourth-class mail?

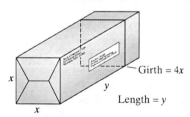

18. The bottom of an 8-ft-high mural painted on a vertical wall is 13 ft above the ground. The lens of a camera fixed to a tripod is 4 ft above the ground. How far from the wall should

the camera be placed to photograph the mural with the largest possible angle?

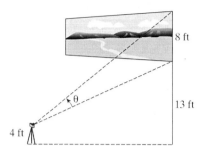

19. Missy Smith is at a point A on the north bank of a long, straight river 6 mi wide. Directly across from her on the south bank is a point B, and she wishes to reach a cabin C located s mi down the river from B, as shown in Figure 4.61.

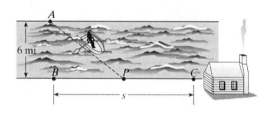

Figure 4.61   Getting Missy home

Given that Missy can row at 6 mi/h (including the effect of the current) and run at 10 mi/h, what is the minimum time (to the nearest minute) required for her to travel from A to C in each case?

   a. $s = 4$ **b.** $s = 6$

20. **Modeling Problem**   Two towns A and B are 12.0 mi apart and are located 5.0 and 3.0 mi, respectively, from a long, straight highway, as shown in Figure 4.62.

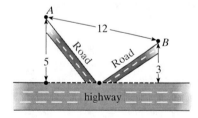

Figure 4.62   Building the shortest road

A construction company has a contract to build a road from A to the highway and then to B. Analyze a model to determine the length (to the nearest tenth of a mile) of the *shortest* road that meets these requirements.

21. A poster is to contain 108 cm² of printed matter, with margins of 6 cm each at top and bottom and 2 cm on the sides. What is the minimum cost of the poster if it is to be made of material costing 20 ¢/cm²?

22. An isosceles trapezoid has a base of 14 cm and slant sides of 6 cm, as shown in Figure 4.63. What is the largest area of such a trapezoid?

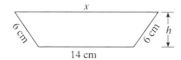

Figure 4.63 Area of a trapezoid

23. **Spy Problem** It is noon. The Spy has returned from space (Problem 63 of Section 3.4) and is driving a jeep through the sandy desert in the tiny principality of Alta Loma. He is 32 km from the nearest point on a straight, paved road. Down the road 16 km is a power plant in which a band of international terrorists has placed a time bomb set to explode at 12:50 P.M. The jeep can travel at 48 km/h on the sand and at 80 km/h on the paved road. If he arrives at the power plant in the shortest possible time, how long will our hero have to defuse the bomb?

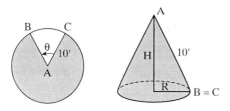

24. A storage bin is to be constructed by removing a sector with central angle θ from a circular piece of tin of radius 10 ft and folding the remainder of the tin to form a cone, as shown in Figure 4.64. What is the maximum volume of a storage bin formed in this fashion?

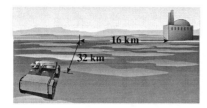

Figure 4.64 Fabricating a cone from a sheet of tin

25. **Exploration Problem** Use the fact that 12 oz $\approx$ 355 mL = 355 cm^3 to find the dimensions of the 12-oz Coke® can that can be constructed by using the least amount of metal. Compare these dimensions with a Coke from your refrigerator. What do you think accounts for the difference? An interesting article that discusses a similar question regarding tuna fish cans and the resulting responses is "What Manufacturers Say about a Max/Min Application," by Robert F. Cunningham, Trenton State College, *The Mathematics Teacher*, March 1994, pp. 172–175.

26. A stained glass window in the form of an equilateral triangle is built on top of a rectangular window, as shown in Figure 4.65.

Figure 4.65 Maximizing the amount of light

The rectangular part of the window is of clear glass and transmits twice as much light per square foot as the triangular part, which is made of stained glass. If the entire window has a perimeter of 20 ft, find the dimensions (to the nearest ft) of the window that will admit the most light.

27. Figure 4.66 shows a thin lens located p cm from an object AB and q cm from the image RS.

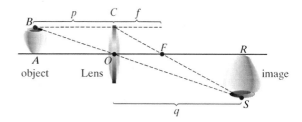

Figure 4.66 Image from a lens

The distance f from the center O of the lens to the point labeled F is called the focal length of the lens.

a. Using similar triangles, show that

$$\frac{1}{p} + \frac{1}{q} = \frac{1}{f}$$

b. Suppose a lens maker wishes to have $p + q = 24$. What is the largest value of f for which this condition can be satisfied?

28. One end of a cantilever beam of length L is built into a wall and the other end is supported by a single post. The deflection, or "sag," of the beam at a point located x units from the built-in end is modeled by the formula

$$D = k(2x^4 - 5Lx^3 + 3L^2x^2)$$

where k is a positive constant. Where does the maximum deflection occur on the beam?

29. When a mechanical system is at rest in an equilibrium position, its potential energy is minimized with respect to any small change in its position. Figure 4.67 shows a system involving a pulley, two small weights of mass m, and a larger weight of mass M.

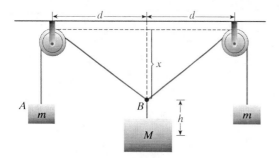

Figure 4.67 A pulley system

In physics, the total potential energy of the system is modeled by

$$E = -Mg(x + h) - 2mg(L - \sqrt{x^2 + d^2})$$

where x, h, and d are the distances shown in Figure 4.67, L is the length of the cord from A around one pulley to B, and g is the constant acceleration due to gravity. All the other symbols represent constants. Use this information to find the critical value(s) for E.

30. A resistor of R ohms is connected across a battery of E volts whose internal resistance is r ohms. According to the principles of electricity, the formula

$$I = \frac{E}{R + r}$$

gives the current (amperes) in the circuit, while

$$P = I^2 R$$

gives the power (watts) in the external resistor. Assuming that E and r are constant, what value of R will result in maximum power in the external resistor?

31. **Modeling Problem** One model of a computer disk storage system uses the function

$$T(x) = N \left(k + \frac{c}{x} \right) p^{-x}$$

for the average time needed to send a file correctly by modem (including all retransmission of messages in which errors are detected), where x is the number of information bits, p is the (fixed) probability that any particular file will be received correctly, and N, k, and c are positive constants.[*]

a. Find $T'(x)$.

b. For what value of x is $T(x)$ minimized?

c. Sketch the graph of T.

32. **Modeling Problem** In crystallography, a fundamental problem is the determination of the *packing fraction* of a crystal lattice, which is defined as the fraction of space occupied by the atoms in the lattice, assuming the atoms are hard spheres. When the

lattice contains exactly two different kinds of atoms, the packing fraction is modeled by the formula

$$F(x) = \frac{K(1 + c^2 x^3)}{(1 + x)^3}$$

where $x = r/R$ is the ratio of the radii of the two kinds of atoms in the lattice and c and K are positive constants.[†]

a. The function F has exactly one critical number. Find it and use the second-derivative test to determine whether it corresponds to a relative maximum or a relative minimum.

b. The numbers c and K and the domain of F depend on the cell structure in the lattice. For ordinary rock salt, it turns out that $c = 1$, $K = 2\pi/3$, and the domain is $[\sqrt{2} - 1, 1]$. Find the largest and smallest values of F on this domain.

c. Repeat part **b** for β-cristobalite, for which $c = \sqrt{2}$, $K = \sqrt{3}\pi/6$, and the domain is $[0, 1]$.

33. If air resistance is neglected, it can be shown that the stream of water emitted by a fire hose will have height

$$y = -16(1 + m^2)(x/v)^2 + mx$$

above a point located x ft from the nozzle, where m is the slope of the nozzle, and v is the velocity of the stream of water as it leaves the nozzle. (See Figure 4.68.) Assume v is constant.

a. For fixed m, determine the distance x that results in maximum height.

b. If m is allowed to vary but the firefighter must stand $x = x_0$ ft from the base of a burning building, what is the highest point on the building that the firefighter can reach with the water from her hose?

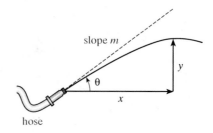

Figure 4.68 Stream of water from a fire hose

34. A telecommunications satellite is located

$$r(t) = \frac{4,831}{1 + 0.15 \cos 0.06t}$$

miles above the center of the earth t minutes after achieving orbit.

a. Sketch the graph of $r(t)$.

b. What are the lowest and highest points on the satellite's orbit? These are called the *perigee* and *apogee* positions, respectively.

[*]Paul J. Campbell, "Calculus Optimization in Information Technology," *UMAP module 1991: Tools for Teaching*. Lexington, MA: CUPM Inc., 1992; pp. 175–199.

[†]John C. Lewis and Peter P. Gillis, "Packing Factors in Diatomic Crystals," *American Journal of Physics*, Vol. 61, No. 5 (1993), pp. 434–438.

35. According to relativity theory, a particle's energy is related to its rest mass m_0, and its wavelength λ by the formula

$$E = \sqrt{\left(\frac{hc}{\lambda}\right)^2 + m_0^2 c^4}$$

where m_0 is the rest mass of the particle and h is a constant (Planck's constant). This equation is used mostly in atomic, nuclear, and particle physics where the masses are not very large. Sketch the graph of $E(\lambda)$. What happens to E as $\lambda \to +\infty$?

36. The theory of relativity models the Doppler shift s of an object traveling at a velocity v:

$$s = \sqrt{\frac{c+v}{c-v}} - 1$$

where c is the speed of light and $v < c$.

a. Express v as a function of s and sketch the graph of $v(s)$.

b. Certain stellar objects called quasars appear to be moving away at velocities approaching c. The fastest one has a redshift of $s = 3.78$. What is its velocity in relation to c?

c. How fast is the velocity changing with respect to s when $s = 3.78$?

37. The lower right-hand corner of a piece of paper is folded over to reach the leftmost edge, as shown in Figure 4.69.

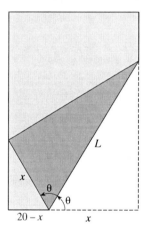

Figure 4.69 Paper folding problem

If the page is 20 cm wide and 30 cm long, what is the length L of the shortest possible crease? *Hint:* First express $\cos\theta$ and $\cos 2\theta$ in terms of x and then use the trigonometric identity

$$\cos 2\theta = 2\cos^2\theta - 1$$

to eliminate θ and express L in terms of x alone.

38. Find the length of the longest pipe that can be carried horizontally around a corner joining two corridors that are $2\sqrt{2}$ ft wide. *Hint:* Show that the length L can be written as

$$L(\theta) = \frac{2\sqrt{2}}{\sin\theta} + \frac{2\sqrt{2}}{\cos\theta}$$

and find the absolute minimum of $L(\theta)$ on an appropriate interval, as shown in Figure 4.70.

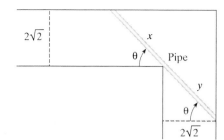

Figure 4.70 Corner problem

39. It is known that water expands and contracts according to its temperature. Physical experiments suggest that an amount of water that occupies 1 liter at $0°C$ will occupy

$$V(T) = 1 - 6.42 \times 10^{-5}T$$
$$+ 8.51 \times 10^{-6}T^2 - 6.79 \times 10^{-8}T^3$$

liters when the temperature is $T°C$. At what temperature is $V(T)$ minimized? How is this result related to the fact that ice forms only at the upper levels of a lake during winter?

40. Modeling Problem Light emanating from a source A is reflected by a mirror to a point B, as shown in Figure 4.71. Use Fermat's principle of optics to show that the angle of incidence α equals the angle of reflection β.

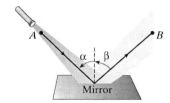

Figure 4.71 Angle of incidence is equal to the angle of reflection

41. Congruent triangles are cut out of a square piece of paper 20 cm on a side, leaving a starlike figure that can be folded to form a pyramid, as indicated in Figure 4.72.

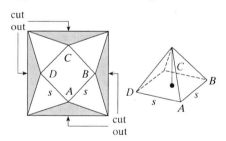

Figure 4.72 Constructing a pyramid

What is the largest volume of the pyramid that can be formed in this manner?

42. Modeling Problem A universal joint is a coupling used in cars and other mechanical systems to join rotating shafts together at an angle. In a model designed to explore the mechanics of the universal joint mechanism, the angular velocity $\beta(t)$ of the output (driven) shaft is modeled by the formula

$$\beta(t) = \frac{\alpha\cos\gamma}{1 - \sin^2\gamma\sin^2(\alpha t)}$$

where α (in rad/s) is the angular velocity of the input (driving) shaft, and γ is the angle between the two shafts, as shown in Figure 4.73.[*]

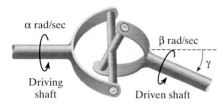

α rad/sec

β rad/sec

γ

Driving shaft

Driven shaft

Figure 4.73 Universal joint

a. Sketch the graph of $\beta(t)$ for the case where α and γ are both positive constants.

b. What are the largest and smallest values of $\beta(t)$?

43. **Modeling Problem** Rainbows are formed when sunlight traveling through the air is both reflected and refracted by raindrops.[†] Figure 4.74 shows a raindrop, which we assume to be a sphere for simplicity. An incoming beam of sunlight strikes the raindrop at point A with angle of incidence α, and some of the light is refracted through the angle β to point B. The process is then reversed, as indicated in the figure, and the light finally exits the drop at point C.

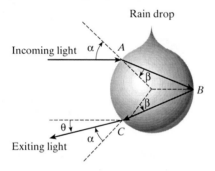

Rain drop

Incoming light   α   A

β

B

θ

α   C

Exiting light

Figure 4.74 Light passing through a raindrop

*Thomas O'Neil, "A Mathematical Model of a Universal Joint," *UMAP Modules 1982: Tools for Teaching*. Lexington, MA: Consortium for Mathematics and Its Applications, Inc., 1983, pp. 393–405.

†This problem is based on an article by Steve Janke, "Somewhere Within the Rainbow," *UMAP Modules 1992: Tools for Teaching*. Lexington, MA: Consortium for Mathematics and Its Applications, Inc., 1993.

a. At the interface points, A, B, and C, the light beam is deflected (from a straight line path) and loses intensity. For instance, at A, the incoming beam is deflected through a clockwise rotation of $(\alpha - \beta)$ radians. Show that the total deflection (at all three interfaces) is

$$D = \pi + 2\alpha - 4\beta$$

b. For raindrops falling through the air, Snell's law of refraction has the form $\sin \alpha = 1.33 \sin \beta$. Use this fact to express the derivative $D'(\alpha)$ in terms of α and β.

c. The intensity of rainbow light reaching the eye of an observer will be greatest when the total deflection $D(\alpha)$ is minimized. If the minimum deflection occurs when $\alpha = \alpha_0$, the corresponding angle of observation $\theta = \pi - D(\alpha_0)$ is called the *rainbow angle* because the rainbow is brightest when viewed in that direction (see Figure 4.75).

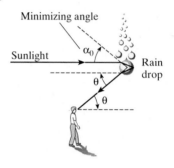

Minimizing angle

Sunlight α_0

Rain drop

θ

θ

Figure 4.75 A rainbow is brightest when viewed at the rainbow angle

Solve $D'(\alpha) = 0$ and show that the critical number you find minimizes $D(\alpha)$. Then find the rainbow angle θ. *Hint*: You may assume $0 \le \alpha - \beta \le \frac{\pi}{2}$.

4.7   Optimization in Business, Economics, and the Life Sciences

IN THIS SECTION   **economics**: maximizing profit and marginal analysis, **business management**: an inventory model and optimal holding time, **physiology**: concentration of a drug in the bloodstream and optimal angle for vascular branching

In the previous section, we saw how differentiation can be used to solve optimization problems in the physical sciences and engineering. The methods of calculus are also used in business and economics and are becoming increasingly prominent in the social and life sciences. We will examine a selection of such applications, and we begin with two modeling problems involving maximization of profit.

ECONOMICS

Maximizing Profit

EXAMPLE 1 Maximizing profits

A manufacturer can produce a pair of earrings at a cost of \$3. The earrings have been selling for \$5 per pair and at this price, consumers have been buying 4,000 pairs per month. The manufacturer is planning to raise the price of the earrings and estimates that for each \$1 increase in the price, 400 fewer pairs of earrings will be sold each month. At what price should the manufacturer sell the earrings to maximize profit?

Solution

Let x denote the number of \$1 price increases, and let $P(x)$ represent the corresponding profit.

$$\text{PROFIT} = \text{REVENUE} - \text{COST}$$
$$= (\text{NUMBER SOLD})(\text{PRICE PER PAIR}) - (\text{NUMBER SOLD})(\text{COST PER PAIR})$$
$$= (\text{NUMBER SOLD})(\text{PRICE PER PAIR} - \text{COST PER PAIR})$$

Recall that 4,000 pairs of earrings are sold each month when the price is \$5 per pair and 400 fewer pairs will be sold each month for each added dollar in the price. Thus,

$$\text{NUMBER OF PAIRS SOLD} = 4{,}000 - 400(\text{NUMBER OF \$1 INCREASES})$$
$$= 4{,}000 - 400x$$

Knowing that the price per pair is $5 + x$, we can now write the profit as a function of x:

$$P(x) = (\text{NUMBER SOLD})(\text{PRICE PER PAIR} - \text{COST PER PAIR})$$
$$= (4{,}000 - 400x)[(5 + x) - 3]$$
$$= 400(10 - x)(2 + x)$$

To find the domain, we note that $x \geq 0$. And $400(10 - x)$, the number of pairs sold, should be nonnegative, so $x \leq 10$. Thus, the domain is $[0, 10]$.

The critical numbers are found when the derivative is 0 (P is a polynomial function, so there are no values for which the derivative is not defined):

$$P'(x) = 400(10 - x)(1) + 400(-1)(2 + x)$$
$$= 400(8 - 2x) = 800(4 - x)$$

The critical number is $x = 4$ and the endpoints are $x = 0$ and $x = 10$. Checking for the maximum profit,

$$P(4) = 400(10 - 4)(2 + 4) = 14{,}400; \quad P(0) = 8{,}000; \quad P(10) = 0$$

The maximum possible profit is \$14,400, which will be generated if the earrings are sold for \$5.00 + \$4.00 = \$9.00 per pair. The graph of the profit function is shown in Figure 4.76. ∎

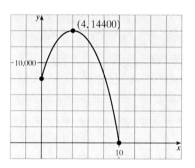

Figure 4.76 The profit function $P(x)$

Sometimes the function to be optimized has practical meaning only when its independent variable is a positive integer. Such functions are said to have a discrete domain and are called **discrete functions**. Technically, the methods of calculus cannot be applied to discrete functions because the theorems we have developed apply only to continuous functions. However, useful information about a discrete function $f(n)$ can often be obtained by analyzing the related continuous function $f(x)$ obtained by replacing the discrete variable n by a real variable x. Here is an example that illustrates the general procedure.

EXAMPLE 2   Maximizing a discrete revenue function

A travel company plans to sponsor a special tour to Africa. There will be accommodations for no more than 40 people, and the tour will be canceled if no more than 10 people book reservations. Based on past experience, the manager determines that if n people book the tour, the profit (in dollars) may be modeled by the function

$$P(n) = -n^3 + 27.6n^2 + 970.2n - 4{,}235$$

For what size tour group is profit maximized?

Solution

The domain of $P(n)$ is the set of integers n between 10 and 40. To optimize this function, we apply the methods developed in this chapter to the related continuous function

$$P(x) = -x^3 + 27.6x^2 + 970.2x - 4{,}235$$

where x is a real variable defined on the interval $10 \le x \le 40$. To determine the critical numbers of $P(x)$, we solve

$$P'(x) = -3x^2 + 55.2x + 970.2 = 0$$

and obtain $x = 29.4$ and $x = -11$. Only $x = 29.4$ is in the domain, and by testing the sign of $P'(x)$ on each side of this critical number, we find that the continuous function $P(x)$ is increasing for $0 < x < 29.4$ and decreasing for $29.4 < x < 40$. Therefore, the original discrete function $P(n)$ is maximized either at $n = 29$ or at $n = 30$. Since

$$P(29) = 22{,}723.4 \quad \text{and} \quad P(30) = 22{,}711$$

we conclude that the maximum profit is $22,723.40, and occurs when 29 people book the tour. The graphs of $P(n)$ and the related continuous function $P(x)$ are shown in Figure 4.77.   ■

Marginal Analysis   In Section 3.8, we described *marginal analysis* as that branch of economics that is concerned with the way quantities such as price, cost, revenue, and profit vary with small changes in the level of production. Specifically, recall that if x is the number of units produced and brought to market, then the total cost of producing the units is denoted by $C(x)$. The **demand** function $p(x)$ is defined to be the price that consumers will pay for each unit of the commodity when x units are brought to market. Then $R(x) = xp(x)$ is the **total revenue** derived from the sale of the x units and $P(x) = R(x) - C(x)$ is the **total profit**. The relationship among revenue, cost, and profit is shown in Figure 4.78.

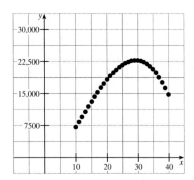

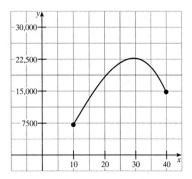

Figure 4.77 Discrete and continuous graphs of the profit function P

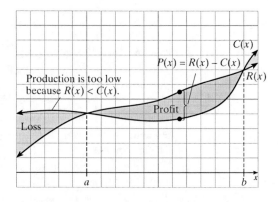

Figure 4.78 Cost, revenue, and profit functions

In Section 3.8, we worked with marginal quantities and their role as rates of change, namely, $C'(x)$, the *marginal cost*, and $R'(x)$, the *marginal revenue*.*

We will now consider these functions in optimization problems. For example, the manufacturer certainly would like to know what level of production results in maximum profit. To solve this problem, we want to maximize the profit function

$$P(x) = R(x) - C(x)$$

We differentiate with respect to x and find that

$$P'(x) = R'(x) - C'(x)$$

Thus, $P'(x) = 0$ when $R'(x) = C'(x)$, and by using economic arguments we can show that a maximum occurs at the corresponding critical point.

Maximum Profit

Profit is maximized when marginal revenue equals marginal cost.

EXAMPLE 3   Using marginal analysis to maximize profit

A manufacturer estimates that when x units of a particular commodity are produced each month, the total cost (in dollars) will be

$$C(x) = \tfrac{1}{8}x^2 + 4x + 200$$

and all units can be sold at a price of $p(x) = 49 - x$ dollars per unit. Determine the price that corresponds to the maximum profit.

Solution

The marginal cost is $C'(x) = \tfrac{1}{4}x + 4$. The revenue is

$$
\begin{aligned}
R(x) &= xp(x) \\
&= x(49 - x) \\
&= 49x - x^2
\end{aligned}
$$

The marginal revenue is $R'(x) = 49 - 2x$. The profit is maximized when $R'(x) = C'(x)$:

$$
\begin{aligned}
R'(x) &= C'(x) \\
49 - 2x &= \tfrac{1}{4}x + 4 \\
x &= 20
\end{aligned}
$$

Thus, the price that corresponds to the maximum profit is $p(20) = 49 - 20 = 29$ dollars/unit.   ∎

A second general principle of economics involves the following relationship between marginal cost and the *average cost* $A(x) = \dfrac{C(x)}{x}$.

Minimum Average Cost

Average cost is minimized at the level of production where the marginal cost equals the average cost.

---

*Recall (from Section 3.8) that marginal cost is the instantaneous rate of change of production cost C with respect to the number of units x_0 produced and the marginal revenue is the instantaneous rate of change of revenue with respect to the number of units x_0 produced.

To justify this second business principle, find the derivative of the average cost function:

$$A'(x) = \frac{xC'(x) - C(x)}{x^2} = \frac{C'(x) - \dfrac{C(x)}{x}}{x} = \frac{C'(x) - A(x)}{x}$$

Thus, $A'(x) = 0$ when $C'(x) = A(x)$. Once again, economic theory can be used to justify this result as a minimum.

EXAMPLE 4   Using marginal analysis to minimize average cost

A manufacturer estimates that when x units of a particular commodity are produced each month, the total cost (in dollars) will be

$$C(x) = \tfrac{1}{8}x^2 + 4x + 200$$

and they can all be sold at a price of $p(x) = 49 - x$ dollars per unit. Determine the level of production at which the average cost is minimized.

Solution

The average cost is $A(x) = \dfrac{C(x)}{x} = \dfrac{1}{8}x + 4 + 200x^{-1}$ and $A(x)$ is minimized when $C'(x) = A(x)$. Thus,

$$\tfrac{1}{4}x + 4 = \tfrac{1}{8}x + 4 + 200x^{-1}$$
$$x^2 = 1600 \qquad \text{Multiply both sides by } 8x \text{ and simplify.}$$

If we disregard the negative solution, it follows that the minimal average cost occurs when $x = 40$ units.

You might have noticed that we did not need the information $p(x) = 49 - x$ in arriving at the solution to this example. When doing real-world modeling, you must often make a choice about which parts of the available information are necessary to solve the problem. ∎

BUSINESS MANAGEMENT

Sometimes mathematical methods can be used to assist managers in making certain business decisions. As an illustration, we will show how calculus can be applied to a problem involving inventory control.

An Inventory Model   For each shipment of raw materials, a manufacturer must pay an ordering fee to cover handling and transportation. When the raw materials arrive, they must be stored until needed and storage costs result. If each shipment of raw materials is large, few shipments will be needed and ordering costs will be low, but storage costs will be high. If each shipment is small, ordering costs will be high because many shipments will be needed, but storage cost will be low. Managers want to determine the shipment size that will minimize the total cost. Here is an example of how such a problem may be solved using calculus.

EXAMPLE 5   Modeling Problem: Managing inventory to minimize cost

A retailer buys 6,000 calculator batteries a year from a distributor and is trying to decide how often to order the batteries. The ordering fee is $20 per shipment, the storage cost is $0.96 per battery per year, and each battery costs the retailer $0.25. Suppose that the batteries are sold at a constant rate throughout the year and that each shipment arrives uniformly throughout the year just as the preceding shipment has been used up. How many batteries should the retailer order each time to minimize the total cost?

Solution

We begin by writing the cost function:

TOTAL COST = STORAGE COST + ORDERING COST + COST OF BATTERIES

We need to find an expression for each of these unknowns. Assume that the same number of batteries must be ordered each time an order is placed; denote this number by x so that $C(x)$ is the corresponding total cost. The average number of batteries in storage during the year is half of a given order (that is, $x/2$), and we assume that the total yearly storage cost is the same as if the $x/2$ batteries were kept in storage for the entire year. This situation is shown in Figure 4.79.

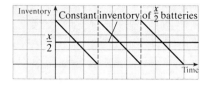

Figure 4.79 Inventory graph

$$\text{STORAGE COST} = \begin{pmatrix} \text{AVERAGE NUMBER} \\ \text{IN STORAGE PER YR} \end{pmatrix} \begin{pmatrix} \text{COST OF STORING 1} \\ \text{BATTERY FOR 1 YR} \end{pmatrix}$$

$$= \left(\frac{x}{2}\right)(0.96)$$

$$= 0.48x$$

To find the total ordering cost, we can multiply the ordering cost per shipment by the number of shipments. We also note that because 6,000 batteries are ordered during the year and because each shipment contains x batteries, the number of shipments is $6{,}000/x$.

$$\text{ORDERING COST} = \begin{pmatrix} \text{ORDERING COST} \\ \text{PER SHIPMENT} \end{pmatrix} \begin{pmatrix} \text{NUMBER OF} \\ \text{SHIPMENTS} \end{pmatrix}$$

$$= (20)\left(\frac{6{,}000}{x}\right) = \frac{120{,}000}{x}$$

Finally, we must also include the cost of purchasing the batteries:

$$\text{COST OF BATTERIES} = \begin{pmatrix} \text{TOTAL NUMBER} \\ \text{OF BATTERIES} \end{pmatrix} \begin{pmatrix} \text{COST PER} \\ \text{BATTERY} \end{pmatrix}$$

$$= 6{,}000(0.25) = 1{,}500$$

Thus, we model the total cost by the function

$$C(x) = 0.48x + \frac{120{,}000}{x} + 1{,}500$$

The goal is to minimize $C(x)$ on $(0, 6000]$. To obtain the critical numbers, we find the derivative

$$C'(x) = 0.48 - 120{,}000x^{-2}$$

and then solve $C'(x) = 0$:

$$0.48 - 120{,}000x^{-2} = 0$$

$$0.48x^2 = 120{,}000$$

$$x = \pm 500$$

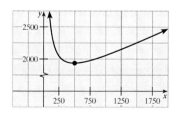

Figure 4.80 The total cost function $C(x) = 0.48x + 120{,}000x^{-1} + 1{,}500$

The root $x = -500$ does not lie in the interval $(0, 6000]$. It is easy to check that C is decreasing on $(0, 500)$ and increasing on $(500, 6000]$, as shown in Figure 4.80. Thus, the absolute minimum of C on the interval $(0, 6000]$ occurs when $x = 500$, and we conclude that to minimize cost, the manufacturer should order the batteries in lots of 500. ∎

Optimal Holding Time   Even with an asset that increases in value, there often comes a time when continuing to hold the asset is less advantageous than selling it and investing the proceeds of the sale. How should the investor decide when to sell? One way is to hold the asset until the time its present value at the current prevailing rate of interest is maximized. In other words, hold until today's dollar equivalent of the selling price is as large as possible, and then sell. Here is an example that illustrates this strategy.

EXAMPLE 6   Modeling Problem: Optimal holding time

Suppose you own an asset whose market price t years from now is modeled by $V(t) = 10,000e^{\sqrt{t}}$ dollars. If the prevailing rate of interest is 8% compounded continuously, when should the asset be sold?

Solution

The present value of the asset in t years is modeled by the function $P(t) = V(t)e^{-rt}$, where r is the annual interest rate and t is the time in years. Thus,

$$P(t) = 10,000e^{\sqrt{t}}e^{-0.08t}$$
$$= 10,000\exp(\sqrt{t} - 0.08t)$$

To maximize P, find $P'(t)$ and solve $P'(t) = 0$:

$$P'(t) = 10,000\exp(\sqrt{t} - 0.08t)\left(\frac{1}{2} \cdot \frac{1}{\sqrt{t}} - 0.08\right)$$

$P'(t) = 0$ when $\dfrac{1}{2\sqrt{t}} - 0.08 = 0$ or $t \approx 39.06$ years. Thus, the asset should be held for 39 years and then sold.   ■

PHYSIOLOGY

Calculus can be used to model a variety of situations in the biological and life sciences. We will consider two examples from physiology. In the first, we use a model for the concentration of a drug in the bloodstream of a patient to determine when the maximum concentration occurs.

Concentration of a Drug in the Bloodstream

EXAMPLE 7   Modeling Problem: Maximum concentration of a drug

Let $C(t)$ denote the concentration in the blood at time t of a drug injected into the body intramuscularly. In a classic paper by E. Heinz, it was observed that the concentration may be modeled by

$$C(t) = \frac{k}{b - a}(e^{-at} - e^{-bt}) \qquad t \geq 0$$

where a, b (with $b > a$), and k are positive constants that depend on the drug.* At what time does the largest concentration occur? What happens to the concentration as $t \to +\infty$?

Solution

To locate the extrema, we solve $C'(t) = 0$.

$$C'(t) = \frac{d}{dt}\left[\frac{k}{b - a}(e^{-at} - e^{-bt})\right]$$

$$= \frac{k}{b - a}[(-a)e^{-at} - (-b)e^{-bt}] = \frac{k}{b - a}(be^{-bt} - ae^{-at})$$

---

*E. Heinz, "Probleme bei der Diffusion kleiner Substanzmengen innerhalb des menschlichen Körpers," *Biochem.*, Vol. 319 (1949), pp. 482–492.

We see that $C'(t) = 0$ when

$$be^{-bt} = ae^{-at}$$

$$\frac{b}{a} = e^{bt}e^{-at} = e^{bt-at}$$

$$bt - at = \ln \frac{b}{a} \qquad \text{Definition of logarithm}$$

$$t = \frac{1}{b - a} \ln \frac{b}{a}$$

The second-derivative test can be used to show that the largest value of $C(t)$ occurs at this t (see Problem 49).

To see what happens to the concentration as $t \to +\infty$, we compute the limit

$$\lim_{t \to +\infty} C(t) = \lim_{t \to +\infty} \frac{k}{b - a}[e^{-at} - e^{-bt}]$$

$$= \frac{k}{b - a}\left[\lim_{t \to +\infty} \frac{1}{e^{at}} - \lim_{t \to +\infty} \frac{1}{e^{bt}}\right]$$

$$= \frac{k}{b - a}[0 - 0]$$

$$= 0$$

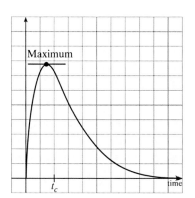

Figure 4.81 Graph of
$$C(t) = \frac{k}{b - a}(e^{-at} - e^{-bt})$$

This tells us that the longer the drug is in the blood, the closer the concentration is to 0. The graph of C is shown in Figure 4.81.

Intuitively, we would expect the Heinz concentration function to begin at 0, increase to a maximum, and then gradually drop off to 0 in a finite amount of time. Figure 4.81 indicates that $C(t)$ does not have these characteristics, because it does not quite get back to 0 in finite time. This suggests that the Heinz model may apply most reliably to the period of time right after the drug has been injected. ∎

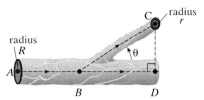

Figure 4.82 Vascular branching

Optimal Angle for Vascular Branching The blood vascular system operates in such a way that the circulation of blood—from the heart, through the organs of the body, and back to the heart—is accomplished with as little expenditure of energy as possible. Thus, it is reasonable to expect that when an artery branches, the angle between the "parent" artery and its "daughter" should minimize the total resistance to the flow of blood. Figure 4.82 shows a small artery of radius r branching from a larger artery of radius R. Blood flows in the direction of the arrows from point A to the branch at B and then to points C and D. For simplicity, we assume that C and D are located in such a way that $\overline{CD}$ is perpendicular to the main line through A, B, and D. We wish to find the value of the branching angle θ that minimizes the total resistance to the flow of blood as it moves from A to B and then to point C, which is located a fixed perpendicular distance h from the line through A and B.* (See Figure 4.82.)

Poiseuille's Resistance To Flow Law

The resistance to the flow of blood in an artery is directly proportional to the artery's length and inversely proportional to the fourth power of its radius.

---

*The key to solving this problem is a result due to work of the nineteenth-century French physiologist Jean Louis Poiseuille (1789–1869). Our discussion of vascular branching is adapted from *Introduction to Mathematics for Life Scientists*, 2nd edition, by Edward Batschelet (New York: Springer-Verlag, 1976, pp. 278–280). In this excellent little book, Batschelet develops a number of interesting applications of calculus, several of which appear in the problem set.

According to Poiseuille's law, the resistance to flow, f_1, from A to B is

$$f_1 = \frac{ks_1}{R^4}$$

where R is the radius of the larger artery, and the resistance to flow, f_2, from B to C is

$$f_2 = \frac{ks_2}{r^4}$$

where r is the radius of the smaller artery, k is a viscosity constant, $s_1 = \left| \overline{AB} \right|$, and $s_2 = \left| \overline{BC} \right|$. Thus, the total resistance to flow may be modeled by the sum

$$f = f_1 + f_2 = \frac{ks_1}{R^4} + \frac{ks_2}{r^4} = k\left(\frac{s_1}{R^4} + \frac{s_2}{r^4} \right)$$

The next task is to write f as a function of θ. To do this, reconsider Figure 4.82 by labeling s_1, s_2, h, and ℓ as shown in Figure 4.83.

We want to find equations for s_1 and s_2 in terms of h and θ; to this end we notice that

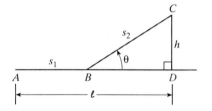

$$\sin \theta = \frac{h}{s_2} \qquad\qquad \tan \theta = \frac{h}{\ell - s_1}$$

$$s_2 = \frac{h}{\sin \theta} \qquad\qquad \ell - s_1 = \frac{h}{\tan \theta}$$

$$= h \csc \theta \qquad\qquad s_1 = \ell - \frac{h}{\tan \theta}$$

$$\qquad\qquad\qquad = \ell - h \cot \theta$$

Figure 4.83 Minimizing the resistance to blood flow

We can now write f as a function of θ:

$$f(\theta) = k\left(\frac{s_1}{R^4} + \frac{s_2}{r^4} \right) = k\left(\frac{\ell - h\cot\theta}{R^4} + \frac{h\csc\theta}{r^4} \right)$$

To minimize f, we need to find the critical numbers (remember that h and k are positive constants):

$$\frac{df}{d\theta} = k\left[\frac{-h(-\csc^2\theta)}{R^4} + \frac{h(-\csc\theta\cot\theta)}{r^4} \right]$$

$$= kh\csc\theta \left(\frac{\csc\theta}{R^4} - \frac{\cot\theta}{r^4} \right)$$

$$\left(\frac{\csc\theta}{R^4} - \frac{\cot\theta}{r^4} \right) = 0$$

$$\frac{\csc\theta}{R^4} = \frac{\cot\theta}{r^4}$$

$$\frac{1}{R^4 \sin\theta} = \frac{\cos\theta}{r^4 \sin\theta}$$

$$\frac{r^4}{R^4} = \cos\theta$$

By finding the second derivative and noting that both r and R are positive, we can show that any value θ_m that satisfies this equation yields a value $f(\theta_m)$ that is a minimum. Thus, the required optimal angle is $\theta_m = \cos^{-1}(r^4/R^4)$.

4.7 PROBLEM SET

A *In Problems 1–3, we give the cost C of producing x units of a particular commodity and the selling price p when x units are produced. In each case, determine the level of production that maximizes profit.*

1. $C(x) = \frac{1}{8}x^2 + 5x + 98$ and $p(x) = \frac{1}{2}(75 - x)$

2. $C(x) = \frac{2}{3}x^2 + 3x + 10$ and $p(x) = \frac{1}{5}(45 - x)$

3. $C(x) = \frac{1}{5}(x + 30)$ and $p(x) = \dfrac{70 - x}{x + 30}$

4. Suppose the total cost of producing x units of a certain commodity is

$$C(x) = 2x^4 - 10x^3 - 18x^2 + x + 5$$

Determine the largest and smallest values of the marginal cost for $0 \le x \le 5$.

5. Suppose the total cost of manufacturing x units of a certain commodity is

$$C(x) = 3x^2 + x + 48$$

dollars. Determine the minimum average cost.

6. A toy manufacturer produces an inexpensive doll (Flopsy) and an expensive doll (Mopsy) in units of x hundreds and y hundreds, respectively. Suppose it is possible to produce the dolls in such a way that

$$y = \frac{82 - 10x}{10 - x} \qquad 0 \le x \le 8$$

and that the company receives *twice* as much for selling a Mopsy doll as for selling a Flopsy doll. Find the level of production for both x and y for which the total revenue derived from selling these dolls is maximized. What vital assumption must be made about sales in this model?

7. A business manager estimates that when p dollars are charged for every unit of a product, the sales will be $x = 380 - 20p$ units. At this level of production, the average cost is modeled by

$$A(x) = 5 + \frac{x}{50}$$

   a. Find the total revenue and total cost functions, and express the profit as a function of x.

   b. What price should the manufacturer charge to maximize profit? What is the maximum profit?

8. Suppose a manufacturer estimates that, when the market price of a certain product is p, the number of units sold will be

$$x = -6 \ln \left(\frac{p}{40} \right)$$

It is also estimated that the cost of producing these x units will be

$$C(x) = 4xe^{-x/6} + 30$$

   a. Find the average cost, the marginal cost, and the marginal revenue for this production process.

   b. What level of production x corresponds to maximum profit?

9. A manufacturer can produce shoes at a cost of $50 a pair and estimates that if they are sold for x dollars a pair, consumers will buy approximately

$$s(x) = 1{,}000e^{-0.1x}$$

pairs of shoes per week. At what price should the manufacturer sell the shoes to maximize profit?

10. A certain industrial machine depreciates in such a way that its value (in dollars) after t years is

$$Q(t) = 20{,}000e^{-0.4t}$$

   a. At what rate is the value of the machine changing with respect to time after 5 years?

   b. At what percentage rate is the value of the machine changing with respect to time after t years?

11. It is projected that t years from now, the population of a certain country will be $P(t) = 50e^{0.02t}$ million.

   a. At what rate will the population be changing with respect to time 10 years from now?

   b. At what percentage rate will the population be changing with respect to time t years from now?

12. Some psychologists model a child's ability to memorize by a function of the form

$$g(t) = \begin{cases} t \ln t + 1 & \text{if } 0 < t \le 4 \\ 1 & \text{if } t = 0 \end{cases}$$

where t is time, measured in years. Determine when the largest and smallest values of g occur.

13. It is estimated that t years from now the population of a certain country will be

$$p(t) = \frac{160}{1 + 8e^{-0.01t}}$$

million. When will the population be growing most rapidly?

B 14. **Modeling Problem** The owner of the Pill Boxx drugstore expects to sell 600 bottles of hair spray each year. Each bottle costs $4, and the ordering fee is $30 per shipment. In addition, it costs 90¢ per year to store each bottle. Assuming that the hair spray sells at a uniform rate throughout the year and that each shipment arrives just as the last bottle from the previous shipment is sold, how frequently should shipments of hair spray be ordered to minimize the total cost?

15. **Modeling Problem** An electronics firm uses 18,000 cases of connectors each year. The cost of storing one case for a year is $4.50, and the ordering fee is $20 per shipment. Assume that the connectors are used at a constant rate throughout the year and that each shipment arrives just as the preceding shipment has been used up. How many cases should the firm order each time to keep total cost to a minimum?

16. Suppose the total cost (in dollars) of manufacturing x units of a certain commodity is

$$C(x) = 3x^2 + 5x + 75$$

   a. At what level of production is the average cost per unit the smallest?

   b. At what level of production is the average cost per unit equal to the marginal cost?

   c. Graph the average cost and the marginal cost functions on the same set of axes, for $x > 0$.

17. Suppose the total revenue (in dollars) from the sale of x units of a certain commodity is

$$R(x) = -2x^2 + 68x - 128$$

a. At what level of sales is the average revenue per unit equal to the marginal revenue?

b. Verify that the average revenue is increasing if the level of sales is less than the level in part **a** and decreasing if the level of sales is greater than the level in part **a**.

c. On the same set of axes, graph the relevant portions of the average and marginal revenue functions.

18. A manufacturer finds that the demand function for a certain product is

$$x(p) = \frac{73}{\sqrt{p}}$$

Should the price p be raised or lowered to increase consumer expenditure? Explain your answer.

19. Suppose you own a rare book whose value t years from now is modeled as $300e^{\sqrt{3t}}$. If the prevailing rate of interest remains constant at 8% compounded continuously, when will be the most advantageous time to sell?

20. Suppose you own a parcel of land whose value t years from now is modeled as

$$P(t) = 200 \ln \sqrt{2t}$$

thousand dollars. If the prevailing rate of interest is 10% compounded continuously, when will be the most advantageous time to sell?

21. A store has been selling skateboards at the price of $40 per board, and at this price skaters have been buying 45 boards a month. The owner of the store wishes to raise the price and estimates that for each $1 increase in price, 3 fewer boards will be sold each month. If each board costs the store $29, at which price should the store sell the boards to maximize profit?

22. **Modeling Problem** As more and more industrial areas are constructed, there is a growing need for standards ensuring control of the pollutants released into the air. Suppose that the pollution at a particular location is based on the distance from the source of the pollution according to the principle that for distances greater than or equal to 1 mi, the concentration of particulate matter (in parts per million, ppm) decreases as the reciprocal of the distance from the source. This means that if you live 3 mi from a plant emitting 60 ppm, the pollution at your home is $\frac{60}{3} = 20$ ppm. On the other hand, if you live 10 mi from the plant, the pollution at your home is $\frac{60}{10} = 6$ ppm. Suppose that two plants 10 mi apart are releasing 60 and 240 ppm, respectively. At what point between the plants is the pollution a minimum? Where is it a maximum?

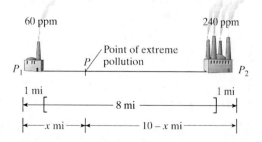

23. A tour agency is booking a tour and has 100 people signed up. The price of a ticket is $2,000 per person. The agency has booked a plane seating 150 people at a cost of $125,000. Additional costs to the agency are incidental fees of $500 per person. For each $10 that the price is lowered, a new person will sign up. How much should the price be lowered for all participants to maximize the profit to the tour agency?

24. A bookstore can obtain the best-seller *20,000 Leagues Under the Majors* from the publisher at a cost of $6 per book. The store has been offering the book at a price of $30 per copy and has been selling 200 copies per month at this price. The bookstore is planning to lower its price to stimulate sales and estimates that for each $2 reduction in the price, 20 more books will be sold per month. At what price should the bookstore sell the book to generate the greatest possible profit?

25. A Florida citrus grower estimates that if 60 orange trees are planted, the average yield per tree will be 400 oranges. The average yield will decrease by 4 oranges for each additional tree planted on the same acreage. How many trees should the grower plant to maximize the total yield?

26. Farmers can get $2 per bushel for their potatoes on July 1, and after that the price drops 2¢ per bushel per day. On July 1, a farmer has 80 bushels of potatoes in the field and estimates that the crop is increasing at the rate of 1 bushel per day. When should the farmer harvest the potatoes to maximize revenue?

27. A viticulturist estimates that if 50 grapevines are planted per acre, each grapevine will produce 150 lb of grapes. Each additional grapevine planted per acre (up to 20) reduces the average yield per vine by 2 lb. How many grapevines should be planted to maximize the yield per acre?

28. A commuter train carries 600 passengers each day from a suburb to a city. It now costs $5 per person to ride the train. A study shows that 50 additional people will ride the train for each 25¢ reduction in fare. What fare should be charged to maximize total revenue?

29. **Modeling Problem** To raise money, a service club has been collecting used bottles, which it plans to deliver to a local glass company for recycling. Since the project began 80 days ago, the club has collected 24,000 pounds of glass, for which the glass company offers 1¢ per pound. However, because bottles are accumulating faster than they can be recycled, the company plans to reduce the price it will pay by 1¢ per 100 pounds of used glass.

a. What is the most advantageous time for the club to conclude its project and deliver all the bottles?

b. What assumptions must be made in part **a** to solve the problem with the given information?

30. Suppose that the demand function for a certain commodity is expressed as

$$p(x) = \sqrt{\frac{120 - x}{0.1}} \quad \text{for} \quad 0 \le x \le 120$$

where x is the number of items sold.

a. Find the total revenue function explicitly and use its first derivative to determine the price at which revenue is maximized.

b. Graph the relevant portions of the demand and revenue functions.

31. Suppose the demand function for a certain commodity is linear, that is,

$$p(x) = \frac{b - x}{a} \quad \text{for} \quad 0 \le x \le b$$

where a and b are positive constants.

a. Find the total revenue function explicitly and use its first derivative to determine its intervals of increase and decrease.

b. Graph the relevant portions of the demand and revenue functions.

32. Modeling Problem Homing pigeons will rarely fly over large bodies of water unless forced to do so, presumably because it requires more energy to maintain altitude in flight over the cool water. Suppose a pigeon is released from a boat floating on a lake 3 mi from a point A on the shore and 10 mi away from the pigeon's loft, as shown in Figure 4.84.

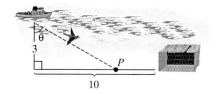

Figure 4.84 Flight path for a pigeon

Assuming the pigeon requires twice as much energy to fly over water as over land and it follows a path that minimizes total energy, find the angle θ of its heading as it leaves the boat. (This is the situation in the Perspective section of the chapter introduction.)

33. Modeling Problem In an experiment, a fish swims s meters upstream at a constant velocity v m/sec relative to the water, which itself has velocity v_1 relative to the ground. The results of the experiment suggest that if the fish takes t seconds to reach its goal (that is, to swim s meters), the energy it expends may be modeled by

$$E = cv^k t$$

where $c > 0$ and $k > 2$ are physical constants. Assuming v_1 is known, what velocity v minimizes the energy?

34. In a learning model, two responses (A and B) are possible for each of a series of observations. If there is a probability p of getting response A in any observation, the probability of getting a response A exactly n times in a series of M observations is

$$F(p) = p^n (1 - p)^{M-n}$$

The *maximum likelihood estimate* is the value of p that maximizes $F(p)$ on $[0, 1]$. For what value of p does this occur?

35. Modeling Problem The production of blood cells plays an important role in medical research involving leukemia and other so-called *dynamical diseases*. In 1977, a mathematical model

was developed by A. Lasota that involved the cell production function

$$P(x) = Ax^s e^{-sx/r}$$

where A, s, and r are positive constants and x is the number of granulocytes (a type of white blood cell) present.[*]

a. Find the granulocyte level x that maximizes the production function P. How do you know it is a maximum?

b. If $s > 1$, show that the graph of P has two inflection points. Sketch the graph of P and give a brief interpretation of the inflection points.

c. Sketch the graph for the case where $0 < s < 1$. What is different about this case?

36. Modeling Problem During a cough, the diameter of the trachea decreases. The velocity v of air in the trachea during a cough may be modeled by the formula

$$v = Ar^2(r_0 - r)$$

where A is a constant, r is the radius of the trachea during the cough, and r_0 is the radius of the trachea in a relaxed state. Find the radius of the trachea when the velocity is greatest, and find the maximum velocity of air. (Notice that $0 \le r \le r_0$.)

37. Modeling Problem The work of V. A. Tucker and K. Schmidt-Koenig[†] models the energy expended in flight by a certain kind of bird by the function

$$E = \frac{1}{v}[a(v - b)^2 + c]$$

where a, b, and c are positive constants, v is the velocity of the bird, and the domain of v is $[16, 60]$. Which value of v will minimize the energy expenditure in the case where $a = 0.04$, $b = 36$, and $c = 9$?

38. Modeling Problem A plastics firm has received an order from the city recreation department to manufacture 8,000 special styrofoam kickboards for its summer swimming program. The firm owns 10 machines, each of which can produce 50 kickboards per hour. The cost of setting up the machines to produce the kickboards is $800 per machine. Once the machines have been set up, the operation is fully automated and can be overseen by a single production supervisor earning $35 per hour.

a. How many machines should be used to minimize the cost of production?

b. How much will the supervisor earn during the production run if the optimal number of machines is used?

39. Modeling Problem After hatching, the larva of the codling moth goes looking for food. The period between hatching and finding food is called the *searching period*. According to a model developed by P. L. Shaffer and H. J. Gold[‡] the length (in days) of the searching period is given by

$$S(T) = (-0.03T^2 + 1.67T - 13.67)^{-1}$$

[*]See "A Blood Cell Population Model, Dynamical Diseases, and Chaos," by W. B. Gearhart and M. Martelli, *UMAP Modules 1990: Tools for Teaching.* Arlington, MA: Consortium for Mathematics and Its Applications (CUPM) Inc., 1991.

[†]V. A. Tucker and K. Schmidt-Koenig, "Flight of Birds in Relation to Energetics and Wind Directions," *The Auk*, Vol. 88 (1971), pp. 97–107.

[‡]P. L. Shaffer and H. J. Gold, "A Simulation Model of Population Dynamics of the Codling Moth *Cydia Pomonella*," *Ecological Modeling*, Vol. 30 (1985) pp. 247–274.

where T (°C) is the air temperature ($20 \leq T \leq 30$), and the percentage of larvae that survive the searching period is

$$N(T) = -0.85T^2 + 45.45T - 547$$

a. Sketch the graph of N and find the largest and smallest survival percentages for the allowable range of temperatures, $20 \leq T \leq 30$.

b. Find $S'(T)$ and solve $S'(T) = 0$. Sketch the graph of S for $20 \leq T \leq 30$.

c. The percentage of codling moth eggs that hatch at a given temperature T is given by

$$H(T) = -0.53T^2 + 25T - 209$$

for $20 \leq T \leq 30$. Sketch the graph of H and determine the temperatures at which the largest and smallest hatching percentages occur.

40. According to a certain logistic model, the world's population (in billions) t years after 1960 is modeled by the function

$$P(t) = \frac{40}{1 + 12e^{-0.08t}}$$

a. If this model is correct, at what rate will the world's population be increasing with respect to time in the year 2010? At what percentage rate will it be increasing at this time?

b. Sketch the graph of P. What feature on the graph corresponds to the time when the population is growing most rapidly? What happens to $P(t)$ as $t \to +\infty$ (that is, "in the long run")?

C 41. **Modeling Problem** Generalize Problem 38. Specifically, a manufacturing firm received an order for Q units of a certain commodity. Each of the firm's machines can produce n units per hour. The setup cost is S dollars per machine, and the operating cost is p dollars per hour.

a. Derive a formula for the number of machines that should be used to minimize the total cost of filling the order.

b. Show that when the total cost is minimal, the setup cost is equal to the cost of operating the machines.

42. **Modeling Problem** (Continuation of Problem 39) Suppose you have 10,000 codling moth eggs. Find a function F for the number of moths that hatch and survive to have their first meal when the temperature is T. For what temperature T on $[20, 30]$ is the number of dining moths the greatest? How large is the optimum dining party and how long did it take to find its meal?

43. An epidemic spreads through a community in such a way that t weeks after its outbreak, the number of residents who have been infected is modeled by a function of the form

$$f(t) = \frac{A}{1 + Ce^{-kt}}$$

where A is the total number of susceptible residents. Show that the epidemic is spreading most rapidly when half the susceptible residents have been infected.

44. In certain tissues, cells exist in the shape of circular cylinders. Suppose such a cylinder has radius r and height h. If the volume is fixed (say, at v_0), find the value of r that minimizes the total surface area ($S = 2\pi rh + 2\pi r^2$) of the cell.

45. **Modeling Problem** A store owner expects to sell Q units of a certain commodity each year. It costs S dollars to order each new shipment of x units; and it costs t dollars to store each unit for a year. Assuming that the commodity is used at a constant rate throughout the year and that each shipment arrives just as the preceding shipment has been used up, show that the total cost of maintaining inventory is minimized when the ordering cost equals the storage cost.

46. **Modeling Problem** Sometimes investment managers determine the optimal holding time of an asset worth $V(t)$ dollars by finding when the relative rate of change $V'(t)/V(t)$ equals the prevailing rate of interest r. Show that the optimal time determined by this criterion is the same as that found by maximizing the present value of $V(t)$.

47. An important quantity in economic analysis is *elasticity of demand*, defined by

$$E(x) = \frac{p}{x}\frac{dx}{dp}$$

where x is the number of units of a commodity demanded when the price is p dollars per unit.[*] Show that

$$\frac{dR}{dx} = \frac{R}{x}\left[1 + \frac{1}{E(x)}\right]$$

That is, marginal revenue is $[1 + 1/E(x)]$ times average revenue.

48. **Modeling Problem** There are alternatives to the inventory model analyzed in Example 5. Suppose a company must supply N units/month at a uniform rate. Assume the storage cost/unit is S_1 dollars/month and that the setup cost is S_2 dollars. Further assume that production is at a uniform rate of m units/month (with no units left over in inventory at the end of the month). Let x be the number of items produced in each run.

a. Explain why the total average cost per month may be modeled by

$$C(x) = \frac{S_1 x}{2}\left(1 - \frac{N}{m}\right) + \frac{S_2 N}{x}$$

b. Find an expression for the number of items that should be produced in each run in order to minimize the total average cost C.

Economists refer to the optimum found in this inventory model as the *economic production quantity* (EPQ), whereas the optimum found in the model analyzed in Example 5 is called the *economic order quantity* (EOQ).

49. In this section we showed that the Heinz concentration function,

$$C(t) = \frac{k}{b - a}(e^{-at} - e^{-bt})$$

for $b > a$ has exactly one critical number, namely,

$$t_c = \frac{1}{b - a}\ln\left(\frac{b}{a}\right)$$

Find $C''(t)$ and use the second-derivative test to show that a relative maximum for the concentration $C(t)$ occurs at time $t = t_c$.

---

[*] See the module with the intriguing title, "Price Elasticity of Demand: Gambling, Heroin, Marijuana, Prostitution, and Fish," by Yves Nievergelt, *UMAP Modules 1987: Tools for Teaching*. Arlington, MA: CUPM Inc., 1988, pp. 153–181.

50. Let $f(\theta)$ be the resistance to blood flow obtained on page 257, namely

$$f(\theta) = k\left(\frac{\ell - h\cot\theta}{R^4} + \frac{h\csc\theta}{r^4}\right)$$

We found that $\theta_m = \cos^{-1}(r^4/R^4)$ is a critical number of f. Find $f''(\theta)$ and use the second-derivative test to verify that a relative minimum occurs at $\theta = \theta_m$. Explain why this must be an *absolute* minimum.

51. Beehives are formed by packing together cells that may be modeled as regular hexagonal prisms open at one end, as shown in Figure 4.85. It can be shown that a cell with hexagonal side of length s and prism height h has surface area

$$S(\theta) = 6sh + 1.5s^2(-\cot\theta + \sqrt{3}\csc\theta)$$

for $0 < \theta < \frac{\pi}{2}$. What is the angle θ (to the nearest degree)

that minimizes the surface area of the cell (assuming that s and h are fixed)?

 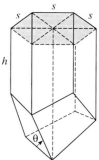

Figure 4.85 Beehive (left) and beehive cell (right)

CHAPTER 4 REVIEW

Proficiency Examination

CONCEPT PROBLEMS

1. What is the difference between absolute and relative extrema of a function?
2. State the extreme value theorem.
3. What are the critical numbers of a function? What is the difference between critical numbers and critical points?
4. Outline a procedure for finding the absolute extrema of a continuous function on a closed interval $[a, b]$.
5. State both Rolle's theorem and the mean value theorem, and discuss the relationship between them.
6. What is the zero-derivative theorem?
7. State the first-derivative and second-derivative tests, and discuss when and in which order you would use them.
8. What is a vertical asymptote? A horizontal asymptote?
9. How would you identify a cusp? A vertical tangent?
10. State l'Hôpital's rule.
11. Define $\lim_{x \to +\infty} f(x) = L$ and $\lim_{x \to c} f(x) = +\infty$.
12. Outline a graphing strategy for a function defined by $y = f(x)$.
13. What do we mean by optimization? Outline an optimization procedure.
14. What is Fermat's principle of optics?
15. What is Snell's law of refraction?
16. When is the profit maximized in terms of marginal revenue and marginal cost? When is the average cost minimized?
17. What is Poiseuille's law of resistance to flow?

PRACTICE PROBLEMS

Evaluate the limits in Problems 18–21.

18. $\lim_{x \to \pi/2} \dfrac{\sin 2x}{\cos x}$

19. $\lim_{x \to 1} \dfrac{1 - \sqrt{x}}{x - 1}$

20. $\lim_{x \to +\infty} \left(\dfrac{1}{x} - \dfrac{1}{\sqrt{x}}\right)$

21. $\lim_{x \to +\infty} \left(1 + \dfrac{2}{x}\right)^{3x}$

Sketch the graph of each function in Problems 22–27. Include all key features, such as relative extrema, inflection points, asymptotes, intercepts, cusps, and vertical tangents.

22. $f(x) = x^3 + 3x^2 - 9x + 2$

23. $f(x) = x^{1/3}(27 - x)$

24. $f(x) = \dfrac{x^2 - 1}{x^2 - 4}$

25. $f(x) = (x^2 - 3)e^{-x}$

26. $f(x) = x + \tan^{-1} x$

27. $f(x) = \sin^2 x - 2\cos x$ on $[0, 2\pi]$

28. Determine the largest and smallest values of

$$f(x) = x^4 - 2x^5 + 5$$

on the closed interval $[0, 1]$.

29. A box is to have a square base, an open top, and volume of $2\ \text{ft}^3$. Find the dimensions of the box (to the nearest inch) that uses the least amount of material.

30. The personnel manager of a department store estimates that if N temporary salespersons are hired for the holiday season, the total net revenue derived (in hundreds of dollars) from their efforts may be modeled by the function

$$R(N) = -3N^4 + 50N^3 - 261N^2 + 540N$$

for $0 \le N \le 9$. How many salespersons should be hired to maximize total net revenue?

Supplementary Problems

Sketch the graph of each function in Problems 1–20. Use as many as possible of the key features such as domain, relative extrema, inflection points, concavity, asymptotes, intercepts, cusps, and vertical tangents.

1. $f(x) = x^3 + 6x^2 + 9x - 1$
2. $f(x) = x^4 + 4x^3 + 4x^2 + 1$
3. $f(x) = 3x^4 - 4x^3 + 1$
4. $f(x) = 3x^4 - 4x^2 + 1$
5. $f(x) = 6x^5 - 15x^4 + 10x^3$
6. $f(x) = 3x^5 - 10x^3 + 15x + 1$

7. $f(x) = \dfrac{9 - x^2}{3 + x^2}$ 8. $f(x) = \dfrac{x}{1 - x}$

9. $f(x) = \sin 2x - \sin x$ on $[-\pi, \pi]$

10. $f(x) = \sin x \sin 2x$ on $[-\pi, \pi]$

11. $f(x) = \dfrac{x^2 - 4}{x^2}$ 12. $f(x) = \dfrac{x^2 + 2x - 3}{x^2 - 3x + 2}$

13. $f(x) = \dfrac{3x - 2}{(x + 1)^2(x - 2)}$ 14. $f(x) = \dfrac{x^3 + 3}{x(x + 1)(x + 2)}$

15. $f(x) = x^2 \ln \sqrt{x}$ 16. $f(x) = \sin^{-1} x + \cos^{-1} x$

17. $f(x) = x(e^{-2x} + e^{-x})$ 18. $f(x) = \ln\left(\dfrac{x - 1}{x + 1}\right)$

19. $f(x) = \dfrac{5}{1 + e^{-x}}$ 20. $f(x) = xe^{1/x}$

In Problems 21–24, the graph of the given function $f(x)$ for $x > 0$ is one of the six curves shown in Figure 4.86. In each case, match the function to a graph.

21. $f(x) = x2^{-x}$ 22. $f(x) = \dfrac{\ln \sqrt{x}}{x}$

23. $f(x) = \dfrac{e^x}{x}$ 24. $f(x) = e^{-x} \sin x$

a.   b.

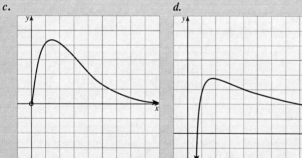

c.   d.

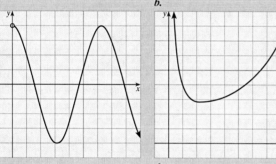

e.   f.

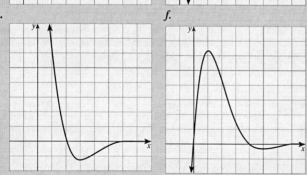

Figure 4.86 Problems 21–24

Determine the absolute maximum and absolute minimum value of each function on the interval given in Problems 25–28.

25. $f(x) = x^4 - 8x^2 + 12$ on $[-1, 2]$

26. $f(x) = \sqrt{x}(x - 5)^{1/3}$ on $[0, 6]$

27. $f(x) = 2x - \sin^{-1} x$ on $[0, 1]$

28. $f(x) = e^{-x} \ln x$ on $\left[\frac{1}{2}, 2\right]$

Evaluate the limits in Problems 29–50.

29. $\displaystyle\lim_{x \to +\infty} \dfrac{x \sin^2 x}{x^2 + 1}$ 30. $\displaystyle\lim_{x \to +\infty} \dfrac{2x^4 - 7}{6x^4 + 7}$

31. $\displaystyle\lim_{x \to +\infty} (\sqrt{x^2 - x} - x)$ 32. $\displaystyle\lim_{x \to +\infty} [\sqrt{x(x + b)} - x]$

33. $\displaystyle\lim_{x \to 0} \dfrac{x \sin x}{x + \sin^3 x}$ 34. $\displaystyle\lim_{x \to 0} \dfrac{x \sin x}{x^2 - \sin^3 x}$

35. $\displaystyle\lim_{x \to 0} \dfrac{x \sin^2 x}{x^2 - \sin^2 x}$ 36. $\displaystyle\lim_{x \to 0} \dfrac{x - \sin x}{\tan^3 x}$

37. $\displaystyle\lim_{x \to 0} \dfrac{\sin^2 x}{\sin x^2}$ 38. $\displaystyle\lim_{x \to 0} \left(\dfrac{1}{x^2} - \dfrac{1}{x^2 \sec x}\right)$

39. $\displaystyle\lim_{x \to \pi/2^-} \dfrac{\sec^2 x}{\sec^2 3x}$ 40. $\displaystyle\lim_{x \to \pi/2^-} (1 - \sin x)\tan x$

41. $\displaystyle\lim_{x \to \pi/2^-} (\sec x - \tan x)$

42. $\displaystyle\lim_{x \to +\infty} \left(\sqrt{x^2 + 4} - \sqrt{x^2 - 4}\right)$

43. $\displaystyle\lim_{x \to 0^+} (1 + x)^{4/x}$ 44. $\displaystyle\lim_{x \to 1^-} \left(\dfrac{1}{1 - x}\right)^x$

45. $\displaystyle\lim_{x \to 0^+} x^{\tan x}$ 46. $\displaystyle\lim_{x \to 0} \dfrac{5^x - 1}{x}$

47. $\displaystyle\lim_{x \to 0} \dfrac{\ln(x^2 + 1)}{x}$ 48. $\displaystyle\lim_{x \to +\infty} \left(\dfrac{1}{x}\right)^x$

49. $\displaystyle\lim_{x \to +\infty} \left(4 - \dfrac{1}{x}\right)^x$ 50. $\displaystyle\lim_{x \to +\infty} \dfrac{e^x \cos x - 1}{x}$

51. **Journal Problem** *Mathematics Teacher.*[*] ■ Which of the graphs in Figure 4.87 is the derivative and which is the function?

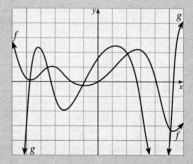

Figure 4.87 A function and its derivative

52. Determine a, b, and c such that the graph of $f(x) = ax^3 + bx^2 + c$ has an inflection point and slope 1 at $(-1, 2)$.

53. **Exploration Problem** Explain why the graph of a quadratic polynomial cannot have a point of inflection. How many inflection points does the graph of a cubic polynomial have?

54. Find the points on the hyperbola $x^2 - y^2 = 4$ that are closest to the point $(0, 1)$.

55. Find numbers A, B, C, and D that guarantee that the function

$$f(x) = Ax^3 + Bx^2 + Cx + D$$

will have a relative maximum at $(-1, 1)$ and a relative minimum at $(1, -1)$.

56. A Norman window consists of a rectangle with a semicircle surmounted on the top. What are the dimensions of the Norman window of largest area with a fixed perimeter of P_0 meters?

57. An apartment complex has 200 units. When the monthly rent for each unit is $600, all units are occupied. Experience indicates that for each $20-per-month increase in rent, 5 units will become vacant. Each rented apartment costs the owners of the complex $80 per month to maintain. What monthly rent should be charged to maximize the owner's profit? What is maximum profit? How many units are rented when profit is a maximum?

58. A farmer wishes to enclose a rectangular pasture with 320 ft of fence. Find the dimensions that give the maximum area in these situations:

a. The fence is on all four sides of the pasture.

b. The fence is on three sides of the pasture and the fourth side is bounded by a wall.

59. A peach grower has determined that if 30 trees are planted per acre, each tree will average 200 lb of peaches per season. However, for each tree grown in addition to the 30 trees, the average yield for each of the trees in the grove drops by 5 lb per tree. How many peach trees should be planted on each acre in order to maximize the yield of peaches per acre? What is the maximum yield?

60. Modeling Problem To obtain the maximum price, a shipment of fruit should reach the market as early as possible after the fruit has been picked. If a grower picks the fruit immediately for shipment, 100 cases can be shipped at a profit of $10 per case. By waiting, the grower estimates that the crop will yield an additional 25 cases per week, but because the competitor's yield will also increase, the grower's profit will decrease by $1 per case per week. Use calculus to determine when the grower should ship the fruit to maximize profit. What will be the maximum profit?

61. Modeling Problem Oil from an offshore rig located 3 mi from the shore is to be pumped to a location on the edge of the shore that is 8 mi east of the rig. The cost of constructing a pipe in the ocean from the rig to the shore is 1.5 times as expensive as the cost of construction on land. Set up and analyze a model to determine how the pipe should be laid to minimize cost.

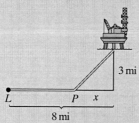

62. The owner of a novelty store can obtain joy buzzers from the manufacturer for 40¢ apiece. It is estimated that 60 buzzers will be sold when the price is $1.20 per buzzer and that 10 more buzzers will be sold for every 10¢ decrease in price. What price should be charged to maximize profit?

63. Journal Problem *AMATYC Review** ■ You are to build a rectangular enclosure with front side made of material costing $10 per foot and with the other three sides (back, left, right) of material costing $5 per foot. If the enclosure is to contain exactly 600 square feet and to be built at minimum total cost, how long should the side be and what is the total cost?

Answer: $600.

Here is the real question: By coincidence, the answer matches the constrained area (both 600, aside from units, of course). *Question:* Characterize when this happens more generally, and thus describe the relationship that exists in such problems in which the resultant minimum cost matches the given area (all in appropriate units).

64. Journal Problem *Quantum*[†] ■ Two students are pondering the following problem: A tin can takes the form of a right circular cylinder with radius R and height H. An ant is sitting on the border circle of one of its bases (point A in Figure 4.88). It wants to crawl to the most distant point B at the border circle of the other base (symmetric to A with respect to the center of the tin). Find the shortest path for the ant.

Figure 4.88 Shortest path from A to B?

a. What is the length of the shortest path?

b. *After* finding a solution, compare your solution with that of the first student as follows: "It's a simple problem!" the first student says confidently. "We just have to consider the planar development of the tin. Let's say, for the sake of definiteness, that the ant first crawls along the side surface and then across the upper base (of course, it's possible that the ant takes the symmetric route: first crawling across the lower base, then along the side surface; but the length of this route is the same)."

c. Compare your solution with that of the second student, as follows: "Wait a second," the other student replies. "One can very comfortably develop the tin can in a different way! Just throw away the lids and spread the side surface on the plane so that we get a rectangle. Then the shortest path will be the segment connecting points A and B, where the image of the ant's route on the tin can will be part of a corkscrew line."

d. Either your solution matched one of the students' solutions or it did not. Which of the two (or possibly three) solutions provides the minimum? Before you answer, find out the conditions whereby the lengths of both of the students' routes are the same. Critique the solutions given by the two students.

65. Westel Corporation manufactures telephones and has developed a new cellular phone. Production analysis shows that its price must not be less than $50; if x units are sold, then the price per unit is given by the formula $p(x) = 150 - x$. The total cost of producing x units is given by the formula $C(x) = 2,500 + 30x$. Find the maximum profit, and determine the price that should be charged to maximize the profit.

66. **Modeling Problem** A manufacturer receives an order for 5,000 items. There are 12 machines available, each of which can produce 25 items per hour. The cost of setting up a machine for a production run is $50. Once the machines are in operation, the procedure is fully automated and can be supervised by a single worker earning $20 per hour. Set up and analyze a model to determine the number of machines that should be used to minimize the total cost of filling the order. State any assumptions that must be made.

67. Show that the graph of a polynomial of degree n, with $n > 2$, has at most $n - 2$ inflection points.

68. Show that the graph of the function $f(x) = x^n$ with $n > 1$ has either one or no inflection points, depending on whether n is odd or even.

69. Each tangent line to the circle $x^2 + y^2 = 1$ at a point in the first quadrant will intersect the coordinate axes at points $(x_1, 0)$ and $(0, y_1)$. Determine the line for which $x_1 + y_1$ is a minimum.

70. An accelerated particle moving at speed close to the speed of light emits power P in the direction θ given by

$$P(\theta) = \frac{a \sin \theta}{(1 - b \cos \theta)^5} \qquad \text{for} \quad 0 < b < 1 \quad \text{and} \quad a > 0$$

Find the value of θ ($0 \le \theta \le \pi$) for which P has the greatest value.

71. Suppose that f is a continuous function defined on the closed interval $[a, b]$ and that $f'(x) = c$ on the open interval (a, b) for some constant c. Use the MVT to show that

$$f(x) = c(x - a) + f(a)$$

for all x in the interval $[a, b]$.

72. Find the point of inflection of the curve

$$y = (x + 1) \tan^{-1} x$$

73. Find the critical numbers for the function

$$f(x) = \tan^{-1}\left(\frac{x}{a}\right) - \tan^{-1}\left(\frac{x}{b}\right), \qquad a > b$$

Classify each as corresponding to a relative maximum, a relative minimum, or neither.

74. Suppose that $f''(x)$ exists for all x and that $f''(x) + c^2 f(x) = 0$ for some number c with $f'(0) = 1$. Show that for any $x = x_0$, there is a number w between 0 and x_0 for which $f'(x_0) + c^2 f(w)x_0 = 1$.

75. **Modeling Problem** According to the *Mortality and Morbidity Report* of the U.S. Centers for Disease Control, the following table gives the number of annual deaths from acquired immune deficiency syndrome (AIDS) in the United States for the years 1982–1991.[*]

[*]For an interesting discussion of how mathematical modeling can be applied to a problem of great public and personal interest, see "Modeling the AIDS Epidemic," by Allyn Jackson, *Notices of the American Mathematical Society*, Vol. 36, No. 8 (October 1989), pp. 981–983.

Year	Deaths	Year	Deaths
1982	400	1987	13,900
1983	1,400	1988	17,300
1984	3,200	1989	32,000
1985	6,200	1990	39,000
1986	10,660	1991	45,000

a. To model the number of annual AIDS deaths, a data analysis program produced the cubic polynomial

$$N(x) = -8.58197x^3 + 732.727x^2 - 3,189.9x + 4,375.09$$

Sketch the graph of N and determine the time when its highest point occurs for $0 \le x \le 20$, where $x = 0$ represents 1982.

b. The same report gives the number of cases of reported AIDS for the period 1984–1991:

Year	Deaths	Year	Deaths
1984	4,445	1988	31,001
1985	8,249	1989	33,722
1986	12,932	1990	41,595
1987	21,070	1991	43,672

The same data analysis program used in part a yields

$$C(x) = -171.247x^3 + 3,770.90x^2 - 19,965.1x + 34,893.9$$

as a modeling polynomial for the number of cases as a function of time x. When does this model predict the number of reported cases will be the largest? When does it predict the number of reported cases will drop to 0?

c. When the data in part b are modeled exponentially, the data analysis program produces the function

$$y = 1,676e^{0.3256x}$$

Sketch the cubic modeling formula $y = C(x)$ from part b and this exponential formula on the same set of coordinate axes along with the data points from the table in part b. Which formula do you think does a better job of fitting the data?

d. Explore other modeling formulas for the data given in part a.

e. Call the Centers for Disease Control or check the World Wide Web (www.cdc.gov) for the most recent updates for the data in parts a and b. Do the formulas in this problem correctly model the current information? Explain the discrepancies.

f. Based on the information you obtained in part **e**, find new models for the information in parts **a** and **b** using all the data you have available.

Using the graphing and differentiation programs of your computer or calculator, graph $f(x)$, $f'(x)$, $f''(x)$ for each function in Problems 76–79. Print out a copy, if possible. On each graph, indicate where

a. $f'(x) > 0$ **b.** $f'(x) < 0$ **c.** $f''(x) > 0$
d. $f''(x) < 0$ **e.** $f'(x) = 0$ **f.** $f'(x)$ *does not exist*
g. $f''(x) = 0$

Describe how these inequalities qualitatively determine the shape of the graph of the functions over the given interval.

76. $f(x) = \sin 2x$ on $[-\pi, \pi]$

77. $f(x) = x^3 - x^2 - x + 1$ on $\left[-\frac{3}{2}, 2\right]$

78. $f(x) = x^4 - 2x^2$ on $[-2, 2]$

79. $f(x) = x^3 - x + \dfrac{1}{x} + 1$ on $[-2, 2]$

80. Consider a string 60 in. long that is formed into a rectangle. Using a graphing calculator or a graphing program, graph the area $A(x)$ enclosed by the string as a function of the length x of a given side ($0 < x < 30$). From the graph, deduce that the maximum area is enclosed when the rectangle is a square. What is the minimum area enclosed? Compare this problem to the exact solution. What conclusions do you draw about the desirability of analytical solutions and the role of the computer?

81. Modeling Problem The beach of a lake follows contours that are approximated by the curve $4x^2 + y^2 = 1$, and a nearby road lies along the curve $y = 1/x$ for $x > 0$. Using your graphing calculator or computer software, determine the closest approach of the road to the lake in the north-south direction. Take the positive y-axis as pointing north.

82. Using your graphing and differentiation programs, locate and identify all the relative extrema for the function defined by

$$f(x) = \tfrac{1}{5}x^5 - \tfrac{5}{4}x^4 + 2x^2$$

This may require judicious choices of the window settings.

83. Modeling Problem Suppose you are a manager of a fleet of delivery trucks. Each truck is driven at a constant speed of x mi/h ($15 \leq x \leq 55$), and gas consumption (gal/mi) is modeled by the function

$$\frac{1}{250}\left(\frac{750}{x} + x\right)$$

Using a graphing and differentiation program (and/or root-solving program on your computer or calculator), answer the following questions:

a. If gas costs $1.70/gal, estimate the steady speed that will minimize the cost of fuel for a 500-mi trip.

b. Estimate the steady speed that minimizes the cost if the driver is paid $28 per hour and the price of gasoline remains constant at $1.70/gal.

84. HISTORICAL QUEST   Leonhard Euler is one of the giants in the history of mathematics. His name is attached to almost every branch of mathematics. He was the most prolific writer on the subject of mathematics, and his mathematical textbooks were masterfully written. His writing was not at all slowed down by his total blindness for the last 17 years of his life. He possessed a phenomenal memory, had almost total recall, and could mentally calculate long and complicated problems. The basis for the historical development of calculus, as well as modern-day analysis, is the notion of a function. Euler's book *Introductio in analysin infinitorum* (1784) first used the function concept as the basic idea. It was the identification of functions, rather than curves, as the principal object of study, that permitted the advancement of mathematics in general, and calculus in particular. In Chapter 2, we noted that the number e is named in honor of Euler. Euler did not use the definition we use today, namely,

LEONHARD EULER
1707–1783

$$e = \lim_{n \to +\infty}\left(1 + \frac{1}{n}\right)^n$$

Instead, Euler used series in his work (which we will study in Chapter 8). ■

In this Historical Quest problem we will lay the groundwork for a Historical Quest in Chapter 8. Euler introduced $\log_a x$ (which he wrote as ℓx) as that exponent y such that $a^y = x$. This was done in 1748, which makes it the first appearance of a logarithm interpreted explicitly as an exponent. He does not define $a^0 = 1$, but instead writes

$$a^\epsilon = 1 + k\epsilon$$

for an infinitely small number ϵ. In other words,

$$k = \lim_{\epsilon \to 0}\frac{a^\epsilon - 1}{\epsilon}$$

Explain why $k = \ln a$.

When Euler was 13, he registered at the University of Basel and was introduced to another famous mathematician, Johann Bernoulli, who was an instructor there at the time (see Historical Quest, Section 4.5, Problems 58–59). If Bernoulli thought that a student was promising, he would provide, sometimes gratis, private instruction. Here is Euler's own account of this first encounter with Bernoulli

I soon found an opportunity to gain introduction to the famous professor Johann Bernoulli, whose good pleasure it was to advance me further in the mathematical sciences. True, because of his business he flatly refused me private lessons, but he gave me much wiser advice, namely, to get some more difficult mathematical books and work through them with all industry, and wherever I should find some check or difficulties, he gave me free access to him every Saturday afternoon and was so kind as to elucidate all difficulties, which happened with such greatly desired advantage that whenever he had obviated one check for me, because of that ten others disappeared right away, which is certainly the way to make a happy advance in the mathematical sciences.*

**From *Elements of Algebra* by Leonhard Euler, 1840. London: Longman, Orme, and Co. Reprinted by Springer-Verlag.

85. **Putnam Examination Problem** Given the parabola $y^2 = 2mx$, what is the length of the shortest chord that is normal to the curve at one end? *Hint*: If $\overline{AB}$ is normal to the parabola, where A and B are the points $(2mt^2, 2mt)$ and $(2ms^2, 2ms)$, show that the slope of the tangent at A is $1/(2t)$.

86. **Putnam Examination Problem** Prove that the polynomial

$$(a-x)^6 - 3a(a-x)^5 + \tfrac{5}{2}a^2(a-x)^4 - \tfrac{1}{2}a^4(a-x)^2$$

has only negative values for $0 < x < a$. *Hint*: Show that if $x = g(1-y)$, the polynomial becomes $a^6 y^2 g(y)$, where

$$g(y) = y^4 - 3y^3 + \tfrac{5}{2}y^2 - \tfrac{1}{2}$$

and then prove that $g(y) < 0$ for $0 < y < 1$.

87. **Putnam Examination Problem** Find the maximum value of $f(x) = x^3 - 3x$ on the set of all real numbers x satisfying $x^4 + 36 \le 13x^2$.

88. **Putnam Examination Problem** Let T be an acute triangle. Inscribe a pair R and S of rectangles in T, as shown in Figure 4.89. Let $A(X)$ denote the area of polygon X. Find the maximum value, or show that no maximum exists, of the ratio

$$\frac{A(R) + A(S)}{A(T)}$$

where T ranges over all triangles, and R and S range over all rectangles as shown in Figure 4.89.

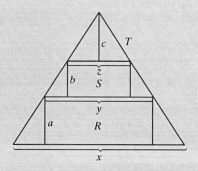

Figure 4.89 Problem 88

89. **Putnam Examination Problem** Which is greater

$$(\sqrt{n})^{\sqrt{n+1}} \qquad \text{or} \qquad (\sqrt{n+1})^{\sqrt{n}}$$

where $n > 8$? *Hint*: Use the function $f(x) = \dfrac{\ln x}{x}$, and show that $x^y > y^x$ when $e \le x < y$.

90. **Putnam Examination Problem** The graph of the equation $x^y = y^x$ for $x > 0$, $y > 0$ consists of a straight line and a curve. Find the coordinates of the point where the line and the curve intersect.

Group Research Project*

Wine Barrel Capacity*

This project is to be done in groups of three or four students. Each group will submit a single written report.

A wine barrel has a hole in the middle of its side called a **bung hole**. To determine the volume of wine in the barrel, a **bung rod** is inserted in the hole until it hits the lower seam. Determine how to calibrate such a rod so that it will measure the volume of the wine in the barrel. You should make the following assumptions:

1. The barrel is cylindrical.
2. The distance from the bung hole to the corner is λ.
3. The ratio of the height to the diameter of the barrel is t. This ratio should be chosen so that for a given λ value, the volume of the barrel is maximal.

Your paper is not limited to the following questions, but it should include these concerns: You should show that the volume of the cylindrical barrel is

$$V = 2\pi \lambda^3 t (4 + t^2)^{-3/2}$$

and you should find the approximate ideal value for t. Johannes Kepler was the first person to show mathematically why coopers were guided in their construction of wine barrels by one rule: *make the staves* (the boards that make up the sides of the barrel) *one and one-half times as long as the diameter.* (This is the approximate t-value.) You should provide dimensions for the barrel as well as for the bung rod.

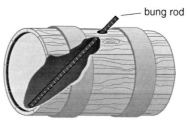

bung rod

JOHANNES KEPLER (1571–1630) is usually remembered for his work in astronomy, in particular for his three laws of planetary motion. Tycho Brahe (1546-1601) was working for Rodolf II, Holy Roman Emperor in Prague in 1599, and he asked Kepler to work with him. The historian Burton describes this as a fortunate alliance. "Tycho was a splendid observer but a poor mathematician, while Kepler was a splendid mathematician but a poor observer." Because Kepler was a Protestant during a time when most intellectuals were required to be Catholic, Kepler had trouble supporting himself, and consequently worked for many benefactors. While serving the Austrian emperor Matthew I, Kepler observed with admiration the ability of a young vintner to declare quickly and easily the capacities of a number of different wine casks. He describes how this can be done in his book *The New Stereometry of Wine Barrels, Mostly Austrian.*

*The idea for this group research project comes from research done at Iowa State University as part of a National Science Foundation grant. Our thanks to Elgin Johnston of Iowa State University.

5

Integration

PREVIEW

A traveler, driving a car down a straight, level road at 40 mi/h, applies the brakes, which decelerate the car at the rate of 21 ft/s². How far does the car travel before coming to a full stop? An ecologist measures the width of an oil spill at intervals of 5 ft along its length. What is the approximate area of the spill? On Christmas day, it starts snowing at a steady rate. A snowplow starts out at noon, going 2 mi during the first hour and 1 mi during the second hour. When did it start to snow?

We will examine questions such as these in the examples and problems of this chapter, as we study **integral calculus**, the companion to the **differential calculus** developed in Chapters 3 and 4.

PERSPECTIVE

The key concept in integral calculus is *integration*, a procedure that involves computing a special kind of limit of sums called the *definite integral*. We will find that such limits can often be computed by reversing the process of differentiation; that is, given a function f, we find a function F such that $F' = f$. This is called *indefinite integration*, and the equation $F' = f$ is an example of a *differential equation*.

Finding integrals and solving differential equations are extremely important processes in calculus. We begin our study of these topics by defining definite and indefinite integration and showing how they are connected by a remarkable result called the *fundamental theorem of calculus*. Then we examine several techniques of integration and show how area, average value, and other quantities can be set up and analyzed by integration. Our study of differential equations begins in this chapter and will continue in appropriate sections throughout this text. We also establish a mean value theorem for integrals and develop numerical procedures for estimating the value of a definite integral.

5.1   Antidifferentiation

IN THIS SECTION   reversing differentiation, antiderivative notation, antidifferentiation formulas, applications, area as an antiderivative

REVERSING DIFFERENTIATION

A physicist who knows the acceleration of a particle may want to determine its velocity or its position at a particular time. An ecologist who knows the rate at which a certain pollutant is being absorbed by a particular species of fish might want to know the actual amount of pollutant in the fish's system at a given time. In each of these cases, a derivative f' is given and the problem is that of finding the corresponding function f. Toward this end, we make the following definition.

Antiderivative

> A function F is called an **antiderivative** of a given function f on an interval I if
> $$F'(x) = f(x)$$
> for all x in I.

Suppose we know $f(x) = 3x^2$. We wish to find a function $F(x)$ such that $F'(x) = 3x^2$. It is not difficult to use the power rule in reverse to discover that $F(x) = x^3$ is such a function. However, that is not the only possibility:

Given: $F(x) = x^3$ $G(x) = x^3 - 5$ $H(x) = x^3 + \pi^2$

Find: $F'(x) = 3x^2$ $G'(x) = 3x^2$ $H'(x) = 3x^2$

In fact, if F is an antiderivative of f, then so is $F + C$ for any constant C, because

$$[F(x) + C]' = F'(x) + 0 = f(x)$$

In the following theorem, we use the constant difference theorem of Section 4.2 to show that *any* antiderivative of f can be expressed in this form.

THEOREM 5.1   Antiderivatives of the same function differ by a constant

If F is an antiderivative of the continuous function f, then any other antiderivative, G, of f must have the form

$$G(x) = F(x) + C$$

> ➡ **What This Says**   Two antiderivatives of the same function differ by a constant.

Proof   If F and G are both antiderivatives of f, then $F' = f$ and $G' = f$ and Theorem 4.6 (the constant difference theorem) tells us that

$$G(x) - F(x) = C$$

so $G(x) = F(x) + C$.   ❑

EXAMPLE 1   Finding antiderivatives

Find general antiderivatives for the given functions.

a. $f(x) = x^5$ **b.** $s(x) = \sin x$ **c.** $y'(x) = \dfrac{1}{x}$

Solution

a. If $F(x) = x^6$, then $F'(x) = 6x^5$, so we see that a particular antiderivative of f is $F(x) = \dfrac{x^6}{6}$ to obtain $F'(x) = \dfrac{6x^5}{6} = x^5$. By Theorem 5.1, the most general antiderivative is $G(x) = \dfrac{x^6}{6} + C$.

b. If $S(x) = -\cos x$, then $S'(x) = \sin x$, so $G(x) = -\cos x + C$.

c. If $y(x) = \ln|x|$, then $y'(x) = \dfrac{1}{x}$, so $G(x) = \ln|x| + C$. ■

Recall that the slope of a function $y = f(x)$ at any point (x, y) on its graph is given by the derivative $f'(x)$. We can exploit this fact to obtain a "picture" of the graph of f. Reconsider Example 1c where $y' = 1/x$. There is an antiderivative $F(x)$ of $1/x$ such that the slope of F at each point $(x, F(x))$ is $1/x$ for each nonzero value of x. Let us draw a graph of these slopes:

If $x = 1$, then the slope is $\frac{1}{1} = 1$. Draw short line segments at $x = 1$, each with slope 1, for different y-values as shown in Figure 5.1a.

If $x = -3$, then the slope is $-1/3$, so draw short line segments at $x = -3$, each with slope $-1/3$, also shown in Figure 5.1a.

If we continue to plot these slope points for different values of x, we obtain many little slope lines. The resulting graph shown in Figure 5.1c is known as a **slope field** for the equation $y' = 1/x$. Beginning in Section 5.6 slope fields are also called *direction fields*.

Finally, notice the relationship between the slope field for $y' = 1/x$ and its antiderivative $y = \ln|x| + C$ (found in Example 1c). If we choose particular values for C, say $C = 0$, $C = -\ln 2$, or $C = 2$, and draw these particular antiderivatives in Figure 5.1c, we notice that these particular solutions are anticipated by the slope field drawn in part b. That is, the slope field shows the entire family of antiderivatives of the original equation.

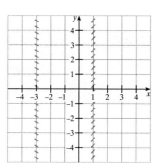
a. Slopes for x = 1 and x = −3

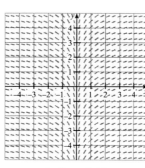
b. Slope field

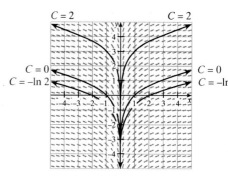
c. Sample antiderivatives

Figure 5.1 Slope field for the equation $y' = \dfrac{1}{x}$

Slope fields will be discussed in more detail in Section 5.6. In general, slope fields, and antiderivatives obtained by using slope fields, are usually generated using technology in computers and calculators.

Here is an example in which the antiderivatives cannot be obtained as elementary functions.

EXAMPLE 2   Finding an antiderivative using a slope field

Consider the slope field for $y' = e^{x^2}$, which is shown in Figure 5.2. Draw a possible graph of the antiderivative of e^{x^2} that passes through the point $(0, 0)$.

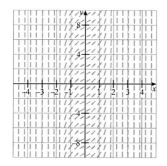
Figure 5.2 Slope field for $y' = e^{x^2}$

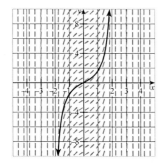

Figure 5.3 Antiderivative of $y' = e^{x^2}$ passing through $(0,0)$

Indefinite Integral

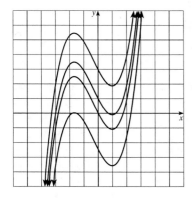

Figure 5.4 Several members of the family of curves $y = F(x) + C$

Solution

Each little segment represents the slope of e^{x^2} for a particular x value. For example, if $x = 0$, the slope is 1, if $x = 1$, the slope is e, and if $x = 2$, the slope is e^4 (quite steep). However, to draw the antiderivative, step back and take a large view of the graph, and "go with the flow." We sketch the apparent graph that passes through $(0,0)$, as shown in Figure 5.3.   ∎

ANTIDERIVATIVE NOTATION

It is worthwhile to define a notation to indicate the operation of antidifferentiation.

The notation
$$\int f(x)\,dx = F(x) + C$$
where C is an arbitrary constant means that F is an antiderivative of f. It is called the **indefinite integral of f** and satisfies the condition that $F'(x) = f(x)$ for all x in the domain of f.

➡ **What This Says**   This is nothing more than the definition of the antiderivative, along with a convenient notation. We also agree that in the context of antidifferentiation, C is an arbitrary constant.

The graph of $F(x) + C$ for different values of C is called **a family of functions** (see Figure 5.4).

WARNING➡   It is important to remember that $\int f(x)\,dx$ represents a family of functions, not just a single function.

Because each member of the family $y = F(x) + C$ has the same derivative at x, the slope of the graph at x is the same. This means that the graph of all functions of the form $y = F(x) + C$ is a collection of parallel curves, as shown in Figure 5.4.

The process of finding indefinite integrals is called **indefinite integration**. Notice that this process amounts to finding an antiderivative of f and adding an arbitrary constant C, which is called the **constant of integration**.

EXAMPLE 3   Antidifferentiation

Find each of the following indefinite integrals.

a. $\int 5x^3\,dx$ **b.** $\int \sec^2 x\,dx$ **c.** $\int e^x\,dx$

Solution

a. Since $\dfrac{d}{dx}(x^4) = 4x^3$, it follows that $\dfrac{d}{dx}\left(\dfrac{5x^4}{4}\right) = 5x^3$. Thus,

$$\int 5x^3\,dx = \frac{5x^4}{4} + C$$

b. Because $\dfrac{d}{dx}(\tan x) = \sec^2 x$, we have $\int \sec^2 x\,dx = \tan x + C$.

c. Since $\dfrac{d}{dx}(e^x) = e^x$, we have $\int e^x\,dx = e^x + C$.   ∎

ANTIDIFFERENTIATION FORMULAS

Example 3 leads us to state formulas for antidifferentiation. Theorem 5.2 summarizes several fundamental properties of indefinite integrals, each of which can be derived by reversing an appropriate differentiation formula. Assume that f and g are functions; u is a variable; a, b, c are given constants; and C is an arbitrary constant.

THEOREM 5.2 Basic integration rules

	Differentiation Formulas	*Integration Formulas*

PROCEDURAL RULES

Constant multiple: $\dfrac{d}{du}(cf) = c\dfrac{df}{du}$ $\displaystyle\int cf(u)\,du = c\int f(u)\,du$

Sum rule: $\dfrac{d}{du}(f + g) = \dfrac{df}{du} + \dfrac{dg}{du}$ $\displaystyle\int [f(u) + g(u)]\,du = \int f(u)\,du + \int g(u)\,du$

Difference rule: $\dfrac{d}{du}(f - g) = \dfrac{df}{du} - \dfrac{dg}{du}$ $\displaystyle\int [f(u) - g(u)]\,du = \int f(u)\,du - \int g(u)\,du$

Linearity rule: $\dfrac{d}{du}(af + bg) = a\dfrac{df}{du} + b\dfrac{dg}{du}$ $\displaystyle\int [af(u) + bg(u)]\,du = a\int f(u)\,du + b\int g(u)\,du$

BASIC FORMULAS

Constant rule: $\dfrac{d}{du}(c) = 0$ $\displaystyle\int 0\,du = 0 + C$

Exponential rule: $\dfrac{d}{du}(e^u) = e^u$ $\displaystyle\int e^u\,du = e^u + C$

Power rule: $\dfrac{d}{du}(u^n) = nu^{n-1}$ $\displaystyle\int u^n\,du = \begin{cases} \dfrac{u^{n+1}}{n+1} + C; & n \neq -1 \\[2mm] \ln|u| + C; & n = -1 \end{cases}$

Logarithmic rule:* $\dfrac{d}{du}(\ln|u|) = \dfrac{1}{u}$

Trigonometric rules: $\dfrac{d}{du}(\cos u) = -\sin u$ $\displaystyle\int \sin u\,du = -\cos u + C$

$\dfrac{d}{du}(\sin u) = \cos u$ $\displaystyle\int \cos u\,du = \sin u + C$

$\dfrac{d}{du}(\tan u) = \sec^2 u$ $\displaystyle\int \sec^2 u\,du = \tan u + C$

$\dfrac{d}{du}(\sec u) = \sec u \tan u$ $\displaystyle\int \sec u \tan u\,du = \sec u + C$

$\dfrac{d}{du}(\csc u) = -\csc u \cot u$ $\displaystyle\int \csc u \cot u\,du = -\csc u + C$

$\dfrac{d}{du}(\cot u) = -\csc^2 u$ $\displaystyle\int \csc^2 u\,du = -\cot u + C$

---

*Note the absolute value. This is the result of reversing Theorem 3.13, Section 3.6.

Inverse trigonometric rules:

$$\frac{d}{du}(\sin^{-1} u) = \frac{1}{\sqrt{1 - u^2}} \qquad \int \frac{du}{\sqrt{1 - u^2}} = \sin^{-1} u + C$$

The other three inverse trigonometric rules are not needed since, for example, $\sin^{-1} u + \cos^{-1} u = \frac{\pi}{2}$, so that

$$\frac{d}{du}(\tan^{-1} u) = \frac{1}{1 + u^2} \qquad \int \frac{du}{1 + u^2} = \tan^{-1} u + C$$

$$\frac{d}{du}(\sec^{-1} u) = \frac{1}{|u|\sqrt{u^2 - 1}} \qquad \int \frac{du}{|u|\sqrt{u^2 - 1}} = \sec^{-1} u + C$$

$$\int \frac{du}{\sqrt{1 - u^2}} = \frac{\pi}{2} - \cos^{-1} u + C_1$$

$$= -\cos^{-1} u + C$$

Proof   Each of these parts can be derived by reversing the accompanying derivative formula. For example, to obtain the power rule, note that if n is any number other than -1, then

$$\frac{d}{du}\left[\frac{1}{n + 1} u^{n+1}\right] = \frac{1}{n + 1}\left[(n + 1)u^n\right] = u^n$$

so that $\frac{1}{n + 1} u^{n+1}$ is an antiderivative of u^n and

$$\int u^n \, du = \frac{1}{n + 1} u^{n+1} + C \quad \text{for} \quad n \neq -1 \qquad \Box$$

Now we will use these rules to compute a number of indefinite integrals.

EXAMPLE 4   Indefinite integral of a polynomial function

Evaluate $\int (x^5 - 3x^2 - 7) \, dx$.

Solution

The first two steps are usually done mentally:

$$\int (x^5 - 3x^2 - 7) \, dx = \int x^5 \, dx - \int 3x^2 \, dx - \int 7 \, dx \quad \text{Sum and difference rules}$$

$$= \int x^5 \, dx - 3\int x^2 \, dx - 7\int dx \quad \text{Constant multiple}$$

$$= \frac{x^{5+1}}{5 + 1} - 3\frac{x^{2+1}}{2 + 1} - 7x + C \quad \text{Power rule}$$

$$= \frac{1}{6}x^6 - x^3 - 7x + C \qquad \blacksquare$$

EXAMPLE 5   Indefinite integral with a mixture of forms

Evaluate $\int (5\sqrt{x} + 4\sin x) \, dx$.

Solution

$$\int (5\sqrt{x} + 4\sin x) \, dx = 5\int x^{1/2} \, dx + 4\int \sin x \, dx \quad \text{Sum and constant rules}$$

$$= 5\frac{x^{3/2}}{\frac{3}{2}} + 4(-\cos x) + C \quad \text{Power and trig rules}$$

$$= \tfrac{10}{3} x^{3/2} - 4\cos x + C \qquad \blacksquare$$

Antiderivatives will be used extensively in integration in connection with a marvelous result called the fundamental theorem of calculus (Section 5.4).

APPLICATIONS

In Chapter 3, we used differentiation to compute the slope at each point on the graph of a function. Example 6 shows how this procedure can be reversed.

EXAMPLE 6   Finding the function with a given slope through a particular point

The graph of a certain function F has slope $4x^3 - 5$ at each point (x, y) and contains the point $(1, 2)$. Find the function F.

Solution

We will work this problem twice; first we find an analytic solution and the second time we approximate the solution using technology, which is often sufficient.

Analytic solution: Because the slope of the tangent at each point (x, y) is given by $F'(x)$, we have

$$F'(x) = 4x^3 - 5$$

and it follows that

$$\int F'(x)\, dx = \int (4x^3 - 5)\, dx$$
$$F(x) = 4\left(\frac{x^4}{4}\right) - 5x + C$$
$$= x^4 - 5x + C$$

The family of curves is $y = x^4 - 5x + C$. To find the one that passes through $(1, 2)$, substitute:

$$2 = 1^4 - 5(1) + C$$
$$6 = C$$

The curve is $y = x^4 - 5x + 6$.

Technology solution: Begin by drawing the slope field, as shown in Figure 5.5a. We are interested in drawing the particular solution passing through $(1, 2)$. Remember to "go with the flow," as shown in Figure 5.5b. If we compare the analytic solution and the graphical solution, we see that the graph of the equation in the analytic solution is the same as the one found by technology.

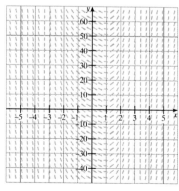

a. Slope field

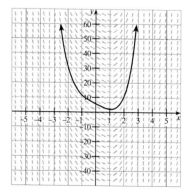

b. Particular solution

Figure 5.5   Slope field for $F'(x) = 4x^3 - 5$

In Section 3.4, we observed that an object moving along a straight line with position $s(t)$ has velocity $v(t) = \dfrac{ds}{dt}$ and acceleration $a(t) = \dfrac{dv}{dt}$. Thus, we have

$$v(t) = \int a(t)\, dt \qquad \text{and} \qquad s(t) = \int v(t)\, dt$$

These formulas are used in Examples 7 and 8.

EXAMPLE 7   Modeling Problem: The motion of a particle

A particle moves along a coordinate axis in such a way that its acceleration is modeled by $a(t) = 2t^{-2}$ for time $t > 0$. If the particle is at $s = 5$ when $t = 1$ and has velocity $v = -3$ at this time, where is it (to four decimal places) when $t = 4$?

Solution

Because $a(t) = v'(t)$, it follows that

$$v(t) = \int a(t)\, dt = \int 2t^{-2}\, dt = -2t^{-1} + C_1$$

and since $v(1) = -3$, we have

$$-3 = v(1) = \frac{-2}{1} + C_1 \qquad \text{so} \qquad C_1 = -3 + 2 = -1$$

We also know $v(t) = s'(t)$, so

$$s(t) = \int v(t)\, dt = \int (-2t^{-1} - 1)\, dt = -2\ln|t| - t + C_2$$

Since $s(1) = 5$, we have

$$5 = s(1) = -2\ln|1| - 1 + C_2 \qquad \text{or} \qquad C_2 = 6$$

Thus, $s(t) = -2\ln|t| - t + 6$ so that $s(4) \approx -0.7726$. The particle is at -0.7726 when $t = 4$. ∎

EXAMPLE 8   Stopping distance for an automobile

The brakes of a certain automobile produce a constant deceleration of 22 ft/s². If the car is traveling at 60 mi/h (88 ft/s) when the brakes are applied, how far will it travel before coming to a complete stop?

Solution

Let $a(t)$, $v(t)$, and $s(t)$ denote the acceleration, velocity, and position of the car t seconds after the brakes are applied. We will assume that s is measured from the point where the brakes are applied, so that $s(0) = 0$.

$$v(t) = \int a(t)\, dt$$

$$= \int (-22)\, dt \qquad \text{Negative because the car is decelerating}$$

$$= -22t + C_1 \qquad v(0) = -22(0) + C_1 = 88, \text{ so that } C_1 = 88$$
$$\qquad\qquad\qquad \text{Starting velocity is 88.}$$

$$= -22t + 88$$

Similarly,

$$s(t) = \int v(t)\, dt$$

$$= \int (-22t + 88)\, dt$$

$$= -11t^2 + 88t + C_2 \qquad s(0) = -11(0)^2 + 88(0) + C_2 = 0$$
$$\qquad\qquad\qquad\qquad \text{so that } C_2 = 0$$

$$= -11t^2 + 88t \qquad\qquad \text{Starting distance is 0.}$$

Finally, the car comes to rest when its velocity is 0, so we need to solve $v(t) = 0$ for t:

$$-22t + 88 = 0$$
$$t = 4$$

This means that the car decelerates for 4 sec before coming to rest, and in that time it travels

$$s(4) = -11(4)^2 + 88(4) = 176 \text{ ft} \qquad \blacksquare$$

Indefinite integration also has applications in business and economics. Recall from Section 4.7 that the *demand function* for a particular commodity is the function $p(x)$, which gives the price p that consumers will pay for each unit of the commodity when x units are brought to market. Then the total revenue is $R(x) = xp(x)$, and the marginal revenue is $R'(x)$. The next example shows how the demand function can be determined from the marginal revenue.

EXAMPLE 9   Finding the demand function given the marginal revenue

A manufacturer estimates that the marginal revenue of a certain commodity is $R'(x) = 240 + 0.1x$ when x units are produced. Find the demand function $p(x)$.

Solution

$$R(x) = \int R'(x)\, dx$$
$$= \int (240 + 0.1x)\, dx$$
$$= 240x + 0.1 \left(\tfrac{1}{2}x^2\right) + C$$
$$= 240x + 0.05x^2 + C$$

Because $R(x) = xp(x)$, where $p(x)$ is the demand function, we must have $R(0) = 0$ so that

$$240(0) + 0.05(0)^2 + C = 0 \quad \text{or} \quad C = 0$$

Thus, $R(x) = 240x + 0.05x^2$. It follows that the demand function is

$$p(x) = \frac{R(x)}{x} = \frac{240x + 0.05x^2}{x} = 240 + 0.05x \qquad \blacksquare$$

AREA AS AN ANTIDERIVATIVE

In the next section, we will consider area as the limit of a sum, and we conclude this section by showing how area can be computed by antidifferentiation. The connection between area as a limit and area as an antiderivative is then made by a result called the fundamental theorem of calculus (see Section 5.4).

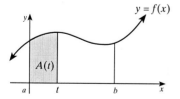

Figure 5.6 Area function $A(t)$

THEOREM 5.3   Area as an antiderivative

If f is a continuous function such that $f(x) \geq 0$ for all x on the closed interval $[a, b]$, then the area bounded by the curve $y = f(x)$, the x-axis, and the vertical lines $x = a$, $x = t$, viewed as a function of t, is an antiderivative of $f(t)$ on $[a, b]$.

Proof   Define an **area function**, $A(t)$, as the area of the region bounded by the curve $y = f(x)$, the x-axis, and the vertical lines $x = a$, $x = t$ for $a \leq t \leq b$, as shown in Figure 5.6. We need to show that $A(t)$ is an antiderivative of f on the interval $[a, b]$; that is, we need to show that $A'(t) = f(t)$.

Let $h > 0$ be small enough so that $t + h < b$ and consider the numerator of the difference quotient for $A(t)$, namely, the difference $A(t + h) - A(t)$. Geometrically this difference is the area under the curve $y = f(x)$ between $x = t$ and $x = t + h$, as shown in Figure 5.7a.

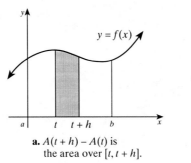
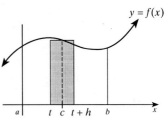

a. $A(t+h) - A(t)$ is the area over $[t, t+h]$.

b. $A(t+h) - A(t)$ is approximated by the area of a rectangle.

Figure 5.7 The area under the curve $y = f(x)$

If h is small enough, this area is approximately the same as the area of a rectangle with base h and height $f(c)$, where c is the midpoint of the interval $[t, t+h]$, as shown in Figure 5.7b. Thus, we have

$$\underbrace{A(t+h) - A(t)}_{\text{Area under the curve on } [t, t+h]} \approx \underbrace{hf(c)}_{\text{Area of rectangle}}$$

The difference quotient for $A(t)$ satisfies

$$\frac{A(t+h) - A(t)}{h} \approx f(c)$$

Finally, by taking the limit as $h \to 0^+$, we find the derivative of the area function $A(t)$ satisfies

$$\lim_{h \to 0^+} \frac{A(t+h) - A(t)}{h} = \lim_{h \to 0^+} f(c)$$
$$A'(t) = f(t)$$

The limit on the left is the definition of derivative, and on the right we see that since f is continuous and c is the midpoint of the interval $[t, t+h]$, c must approach t as $h \to 0^+$. A similar argument works as $h \to 0^-$. Thus, $A(t)$ is an antiderivative of $f(t)$. ❑

EXAMPLE 10　Area as an antiderivative

Find the area under the parabola $y = x^2$ over the interval $[0, 1]$. This area is shown in Figure 5.8.

Solution

Let $A(t)$ be the area function for this example—namely, the area under $y = x^2$ on $[0, t]$. Since f is continuous and $f(x) \geq 0$ on $[0, 1]$, Theorem 5.3 tells us that $A(t)$ is an antiderivative of $f(t) = t^2$ on $[0, 1]$. That is,

$$A(t) = \int t^2 \, dt = \tfrac{1}{3}t^3 + C$$

for all t in the interval $[0, 1]$. Clearly, $A(0) = 0$, so

$$A(0) = \tfrac{1}{3}(0)^3 + C \quad \text{or} \quad C = 0$$

and the area under the curve is

$$A(1) = \tfrac{1}{3}(1)^3 + 0 = \tfrac{1}{3}$$

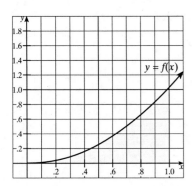

Figure 5.8 Area of $y = f(x)$ over $[0, 1]$

5.1 PROBLEM SET

A *Find the indefinite integral in Problems 1–30.*

1. $\int 2\,dx$

2. $\int -4\,dx$

3. $\int (2x+3)\,dx$

4. $\int (4-5x)\,dx$

5. $\int (4t^3 + 3t^2)\,dt$

6. $\int (-8t^3 + 15t^5)\,dt$

7. $\int \frac{dx}{2x}$

8. $\int 14e^x\,dx$

9. $\int (6u^2 - 3\cos u)\,du$

10. $\int (5t^3 - \sqrt{t})\,dt$

11. $\int \sec^2 \theta\,d\theta$

12. $\int \sec\theta\tan\theta\,d\theta$

13. $\int 2\sin\theta\,d\theta$

14. $\int \frac{\cos\theta}{3}\,d\theta$

15. $\int \frac{5}{\sqrt{1-y^2}}\,dy$

16. $\int \frac{dx}{10(1+x^2)}$

17. $\int (u^{3/2} - u^{1/2} + u^{-10})\,du$

18. $\int (x^3 - 3x + \sqrt[4]{x} - 5)\,dx$

19. $\int x(x+\sqrt{x})\,dx$

20. $\int y(y^2 - 3y)\,dy$

21. $\int \left(\frac{1}{t^2} - \frac{1}{t^3} + \frac{1}{t^4} \right)\,dt$

22. $\int \frac{1}{t}\left(\frac{2}{t^2} - \frac{3}{t^3} \right)\,dt$

23. $\int (2x^2 + 5)^2\,dx$

24. $\int (3 - 4x^3)^2\,dx$

25. $\int \left(\frac{x^2 + 3x - 1}{x^4} \right)\,dx$

26. $\int \frac{x^2 + \sqrt{x} + 1}{x^2}\,dx$

27. $\int \frac{x^2 + x - 2}{x^2}\,dx$

28. $\int \left(1 + \frac{1}{x}\right)\left(1 - \frac{4}{x^2}\right)\,dx$

29. $\int \frac{\sqrt{1-x^2} - 1}{\sqrt{1-x^2}}\,dx$

30. $\int \frac{x^2}{x^2 + 1}\,dx$

The slope $F'(x)$ at each point on a graph is given in Problems 31–38 along with one point (x_0, y_0) on the graph. Use this information to find F both graphically and analytically.

31. $F'(x) = x^2 + 3x$
with point $(0, 0)$

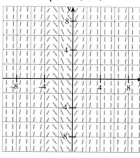

32. $F'(x) = (2x-1)^2$
with point $(1, 3)$

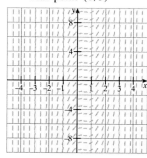

33. $F'(x) = (\sqrt{x} + 3)^2$
with point $(4, 36)$

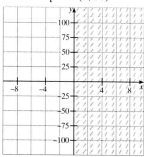

34. $F'(x) = 3 - 2\sin x$
with point $(0, 0)$

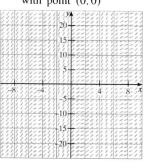

35. slope $\dfrac{x+1}{x^2}$
with point $(1, -2)$

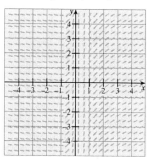

36. slope $\dfrac{2}{x\sqrt{x^2-1}}$
with point $(4, 1)$

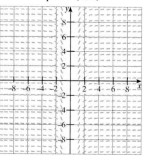

37. slope $x + e^x$
with point $(0, 2)$

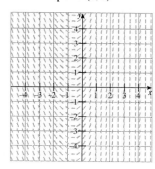

38. slope $\dfrac{x^2 - 1}{x^2 + 1}$
with point $(0, 0)$

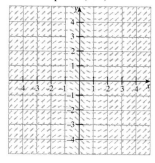

B **39. a.** If $F(x) = \int \left(\dfrac{1}{\sqrt{x}} - 4 \right)\,dx$, find F so that $F(1) = 0$.

b. Sketch the graphs of $y = F(x)$, $y = F(x) + 3$, and $y = F(x) - 1$.

c. Find a constant C_0 so that the largest value of $G(x) = F(x) + C_0$ is 0.

40. A ball is thrown directly upward from ground level with an initial velocity of 96 ft/s. Assuming that the ball's only acceleration is that due to gravity (that is, $a(t) = -32$ ft/s^2), determine the maximum height reached by the ball and the time it takes to return to ground level.

41. The marginal cost of a certain commodity is $C'(x) = 6x^2 - 2x + 5$, where x is the level of production. If it costs \$5 to produce 1 unit, what is the total cost of producing 5 units?

42. The marginal revenue of a certain commodity is
$R'(x) = -3x^2 + 4x + 32$, where x is the level of production (in thousands). Assume $R(0) = 0$.
   a. Find the demand function $p(x)$.
   b. Find the level of production that results in maximum revenue. What is the market price per unit at this level of production?

43. It is estimated that t months from now, the population of a certain town will be changing at the rate of $4 + 5t^{2/3}$ people per month. If the current population is 10,000, what will the population be 8 months from now?

44. A particle travels along the x-axis in such a way that its acceleration at time t is $a(t) = \sqrt{t} + t^2$. If it starts at the origin with an initial velocity of 2 (that is, $s(0) = 0$ and $v(0) = 2$), determine its position and velocity when $t = 4$.

45. An automobile starts from rest (that is, $v(0) = 0$) and travels with constant acceleration $a(t) = k$ in such a way that 6 sec after it begins to move, it has traveled 360 ft from its starting point. What is k?

46. The price of bacon is currently $1.80/lb in Styxville. A consumer service has conducted a study predicting that t months from now, the price will be changing at the rate of $0.084 + 0.012\sqrt{t}$ cents per month. How much will a pound of bacon cost 4 months from now?

47. An airplane has a constant acceleration while moving down the runway from rest. What is the acceleration of the plane at liftoff if the plane requires 900 ft of runway before lifting off at 88 ft/s (60 mi/h)?

48. After its brakes are applied, a certain sports car decelerates at a constant rate of 28 ft/s². Compute the stopping distance if the car is going 60 mi/h (88 ft/s) when the brakes are applied.

49. The brakes of a certain automobile produce a constant deceleration of k ft/s². The car is traveling at 60 mi/h (88 ft/s) when the driver is forced to hit the brakes, and it comes to rest at a point 121 ft from the point where the brakes were applied. What is k?

50. **Spy Problem**   The Spy, having defused the bomb in Problem 23, Section 4.6, is driving the sports car in Problem 48 at a speed of 60 mi/h on Highway 1 in the remote republic of San Dimas. Suddenly he sees a camel in the road 199 ft in front of the car.

After a reaction time of 00.7 seconds, he steps on the brakes. Will he stop before hitting the camel?

51. A particle moves along the x-axis in such a way that at time $t > 0$, its velocity (in ft/s) is

$$v(t) = t^{-1} + t$$

How far does it move between times $t = 1$ and $t = e^2$?

52. A manufacturer estimates that the marginal cost in a certain production process is

$$C'(x) = 0.1e^x + 21\sqrt{x}$$

when x units are produced. If the cost of producing 1 unit is $100, what does it cost (to the nearest cent) to produce 4 units?

In Problems 53–58, find the area under the curve defined by the given equation, above the x-axis, and over the given interval.

53. $y = x^2$ over $[1, 4]$ 54. $y = \sqrt{x}$ over $[1, 4]$

55. $y = e^x - x$ over $[0, 2]$ 56. $y = \dfrac{x+1}{x}$ over $[1, 2]$

57. $y = \cos x$ over $\left[0, \frac{\pi}{2}\right]$ 58. $y = (1 - x^2)^{-1/2}$ over $\left[0, \frac{1}{2}\right]$

59. Evaluate $\displaystyle\int \frac{dy}{2y\sqrt{y^2 - 1}}$ using the indicated methods.
   a. Use an inverse trigonometric differentiation rule.
   b. Use technology (TI-92, *Maple*, *Mathematica*, or *Derive*) to evaluate this integral.
   c. Reconcile your answers for parts **a** and **b**.

60. If a, b, and c are constants, use the linearity rule twice to show that

$$\int [af(x) + bg(x) + ch(x)]\,dx$$
$$= a\int f(x)\,dx + b\int g(x)\,dx + c\int h(x)\,dx$$

61. Use the area as an antiderivative theorem (Theorem 5.3) to find the area under the line $y = mx + b$ over the interval $[c, d]$, where $m > 0$ and $mc + b > 0$. Check your result by using geometry to find the area of a trapezoid.

5.2   Area as the Limit of a Sum

IN THIS SECTION   area as the limit of a sum, the general approximation scheme, summation notation, area using summation formulas

AREA AS THE LIMIT OF A SUM

Computing area has been a problem of both theoretical and practical interest since ancient times, but except for a few special cases, the problem is not easy. For example, you may know the formulas for computing the area of a rectangle, square, triangle, circle, and even a trapezoid. You have probably found the areas of regions that were more complicated but could be broken up into parts using these formulas. In Example 10 of the previous section we found the area between the parabola $y = x^2$ and the

x-axis on the interval $[0, 1]$ (see Figure 5.9a). We revisit this example to demonstrate a general procedure for computing area.

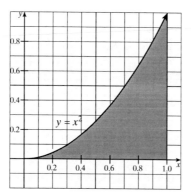 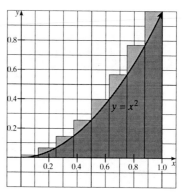

a. Problem: Compute the area under the curve $y = x^2$, above the x-axis, and between the lines $x = 0$ and $x = 1$.

b. The required area is approximately the same as the total area bounded by the shaded rectangles.

Figure 5.9   Example of the area problem

EXAMPLE 1   Estimating an area using rectangles and right endpoints

Estimate the area under the parabola $y = x^2$ on the interval $[0, 1]$.

Solution

In the previous section we found this area using the area function. In this example, we will *estimate* the area by adding the areas of approximating rectangles constructed on subintervals of $[0, 1]$, as shown in Figure 5.9b. To simplify computations, we will require all approximating rectangles to have the same width and will take the height of each rectangle to be the y-coordinate of the parabola above the *right endpoint* of the subinterval on which it is based.*

For the first estimate, we divide the interval $[0, 1]$ into 5 subintervals, as shown in Figure 5.10a. Because the approximating rectangles all have the same width, the right endpoints are $x_1 = 0.2$, $x_2 = 0.4$, $x_3 = 0.6$, $x_4 = 0.8$, and $x_5 = 1$. This subdivision is called a *partition* of the interval. The width of each subdivision is denoted by Δx and is found by dividing the length of the interval by the number of subintervals:

$$\Delta x = \frac{1 - 0}{5} = \frac{1}{5} = 0.2$$

Let S_n be the total area of n rectangles. For the case where $n = 5$,

$$\begin{aligned}
S_5 &= f(x_1)\Delta x + f(x_2)\Delta x + f(x_3)\Delta x + f(x_4)\Delta x + f(x_5)\Delta x \\
&= [f(x_1) + f(x_2) + f(x_3) + f(x_4) + f(x_5)]\Delta x \\
&= [f(0.2) + f(0.4) + f(0.6) + f(0.8) + f(1)](0.2) \\
&= [0.2^2 + 0.4^2 + 0.6^2 + 0.8^2 + 1^2](0.2) \\
&= 0.44
\end{aligned}$$

Even though $S_5 = 0.44$ serves as a reasonable approximation of the area, we see from Figure 5.10b that this approximation seems too large. Let us rework Example 1

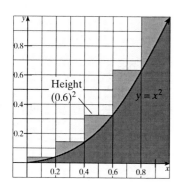

a. Partition into 5 subdivisions

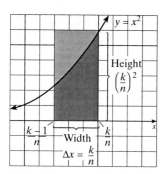

b. Detail showing one rectangle

Figure 5.10 Partitioning of Figure 5.8a into 5 subdivisions

---

*Actually, there is nothing special about right endpoints, and we could just as easily have used any other point in the base subinterval—say, the left endpoint or the midpoint.

using a general scheme rather than a specified number of rectangles. Partition the interval $[0, 1]$ into n equal parts, each with width

$$\Delta x = \frac{1 - 0}{n} = \frac{1}{n}$$

For $k = 1, 2, 3, \ldots, n$, the kth subinterval is $\left[\dfrac{k-1}{n}, \dfrac{k}{n}\right]$, and on this subinterval we then construct an approximating rectangle with width $\Delta x = \dfrac{1}{n}$ and height $\left(\dfrac{k}{n}\right)^2$, since $y = x^2$. The total area bounded by all n rectangles is

$$S_n = \left[\left(\frac{1}{n}\right)^2 + \left(\frac{2}{n}\right)^2 + \cdots + \left(\frac{n}{n}\right)^2\right]\left(\frac{1}{n}\right)$$

Consider different choices for n, as shown in Figure 5.11.

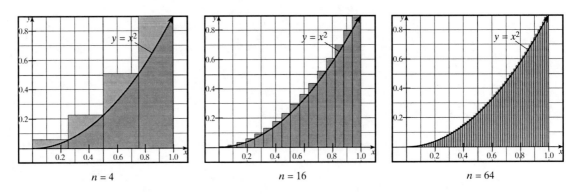

$n = 4$ $\qquad\qquad$ $n = 16$ $\qquad\qquad$ $n = 64$

Figure 5.11   The area estimate is improved by taking more rectangles.

n	S_n	
5	0.440	(Example 1 result)
4	0.469	(Figure 5.11a result)
16	0.365	(Figure 5.11b result)
64	0.341	(Figure 5.11c result)
100	0.338	
1,000	0.334	
5,000	0.333	

If we increase the number of subdivisions n, the width $\Delta x = \frac{1}{n}$ of each approximating rectangle will decrease, and we would expect the area estimates S_n to improve. Thus, it is reasonable to *define* the area A under the parabola to be the *limit* of S_n as $\Delta x \to 0$ or, equivalently, as $n \to +\infty$. We can attempt to predict its value by seeing what happens to the sum as n grows large without bound. It is both tedious and difficult to evaluate such sums by hand, but fortunately we can use a calculator or computer to obtain some (rounded) values for S_n, as shown in the following table. Notice that for $n = 5$, the value 0.44 corresponds to the calculation in Example 1 and that as n increases, S_n appears to approach $1/3$.

Figure 5.12 displays some computer-generated drawings showing the area under the curve $y = x^2$ on $[1, 5]$ as approximated by rectangles using left endpoints (as contrasted with right endpoints in Example 1). The sums in these outputs are called *Riemann sums*, which we will discuss in the next section.

THE GENERAL APPROXIMATION SCHEME

We now compute the area under any curve $y = f(x)$ on an interval $[a, b]$, where f is a nonnegative continuous function. We first partition the interval $[a, b]$ into n equal subintervals, each of width

$$\Delta x = \frac{b - a}{n}$$

For $k = 1, 2, 3, \ldots, n$ the kth subinterval is $[a + (k - 1)\Delta x, a + k\Delta x]$, and the kth approximating rectangle is constructed with width Δx and height $f(a + k\Delta x)$ equal to the height of the curve $y = f(x)$ above the right endpoint of the subinterval. Adding the areas of these n rectangles, we obtain

$$S_n = \overbrace{f(a + \Delta x)\Delta x}^{\text{Area of first rectangle}} + \overbrace{f(a + 2\Delta x)\Delta x}^{\text{Area of second rectangle}} + \cdots + \overbrace{f(a + n\Delta x)\Delta x}^{\text{Area of }n\text{th rectangle}}$$

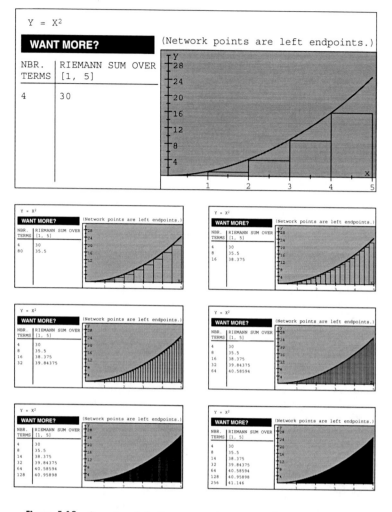

Figure 5.12 Sample of finding successive rectangular approximations

as an estimate of the area under the curve. In advanced calculus, it is shown that the continuity of f guarantees the existence of $\lim_{\Delta x \to 0} S_n$, and we use this limit to define the required area, as shown in the following box.

Area as the Limit of a Sum

Suppose f is continuous and $f(x) \geq 0$ throughout the interval $[a, b]$. Then the **area** of the region under the curve $y = f(x)$ over this interval is

$$A = \lim_{\Delta x \to 0} [f(a + \Delta x) + f(a + 2\Delta x) + \cdots + f(a + n\Delta x)]\Delta x$$

where $\Delta x = \dfrac{b - a}{n}$.

The definition of area as a limit of a sum is consistent with the area concept introduced in plane geometry, and with the area function defined in Section 5.1. For example, it would not be difficult to use this formula to show that a rectangle has area $A = \ell w$ or that a triangle has area $A = \frac{1}{2}bh$. You will also note that we maintained everyday usage in saying that the *formula* for the area of a rectangle is $A = \ell w$ or the *area* of the region under the curve $y = f(x)$ is a limit, but what we are really doing is *defining* area as a limit.

The problem we now face is how to implement this definition of area as the limit of a sum. The immediate answer (discussed in this section) is to use summation formulas and technology. The long-range goal is to develop integral calculus, which is discussed in the next section.

SUMMATION NOTATION

The expanded form of the sum for the definition of area makes it awkward to use. Therefore, we will digress to introduce a more compact notation for sums, and that notation will motivate integral notation. Using this **summation notation**, we express the sum $a_1 + a_2 + \cdots + a_n$ as follows:

$$a_1 + a_2 + \cdots + a_n = \sum_{k=1}^{n} a_k$$

The summation notation is sometimes called the **sigma notation** because the uppercase Greek letter sigma (Σ) is used to denote the summation process. The **index** k is called the **index of summation** (or *running index*). The terminology used in connection with the summation notation is shown:

Upper limit of summation

General term

$$\sum_{k=1}^{n} a_k$$

Index of summation

Lower limit of summation

Note that in the summation process, the choice of summation index is immaterial. For example, the following sums are all exactly the same:

$$\sum_{k=3}^{7} k^2 = \sum_{j=3}^{7} j^2 = \sum_{i=3}^{7} i^2 = \sum_{\lambda=3}^{7} \lambda^2$$

In general, an index (k, j, i, or λ) that represents a process in which it has no direct effect on the result is called a **dummy variable**.

Several useful properties of sums and sum formulas are listed in Theorem 5.4. We will use the summation notation throughout the rest of this text, especially in this chapter, Chapter 6, and Chapter 8.

THEOREM 5.4 Basic rules for sums

For any numbers c and d and positive integers m and n,

1. Constant term rule $\displaystyle\sum_{k=1}^{n} c = \underbrace{c + c + \cdots + c}_{n \text{ terms}} = nc$

2. Sum rule $\displaystyle\sum_{k=1}^{n} (a_k + b_k) = \sum_{k=1}^{n} a_k + \sum_{k=1}^{n} b_k$

3. Scalar multiple rule $\displaystyle\sum_{k=1}^{n} ca_k = c \sum_{k=1}^{n} a_k = \left(\sum_{k=1}^{n} a_k\right) c$

4. Linearity rule $\displaystyle\sum_{k=1}^{n} (ca_k + db_k) = c \sum_{k=1}^{n} a_k + d \sum_{k=1}^{n} b_k$

5. Subtotal rule If $1 < m < n$, then $\displaystyle\sum_{k=1}^{n} a_k = \sum_{k=1}^{m} a_k + \sum_{k=m+1}^{n} a_k$

6. Dominance rule If $a_k \leq b_k$ for $k = 1, 2, \ldots, n$, then $\displaystyle\sum_{k=1}^{n} a_k \leq \sum_{k=1}^{n} b_k$

Proof These properties can all be established by applying well-known algebraic rules (see Problem 50). ❑

AREA USING SUMMATION FORMULAS

Using summation notation, we can streamline the symbolism in the formula for the area under the curve $y = f(x)$, $f(x) \geq 0$ on the interval $[a, b]$. In particular, note that the approximating sum S_n is

$$S_n = [f(a + \Delta x) + f(a + 2\Delta x) + \cdots + f(a + n\Delta x)]\Delta x$$

$$= \sum_{k=1}^{n} f(a + k\Delta x)\Delta x$$

where $\Delta x = \dfrac{b - a}{n}$. Thus, the formula for the definition of area is shown:

n is the number of approximating rectangles

Area under $y = f(x)$ above the
x-axis between $x = a$ and $x = b$
$\downarrow$

Width of each rectangle

$$A = \lim_{n \to +\infty} S_n = \lim_{\Delta x \to 0} \sum_{k=1}^{n} \underbrace{f(a + k\Delta x)}_{\text{Height of the } k\text{th rectangle}} \overbrace{\Delta x}$$

From algebra we recall certain summation formulas (which can be proved using mathematical induction) that we will need in order to find areas using the limit definition.

Summation Formulas

$$\sum_{k=1}^{n} 1 = n$$

$$\sum_{k=1}^{n} k = 1 + 2 + 3 + \cdots + n = \frac{n(n + 1)}{2}$$

$$\sum_{k=1}^{n} k^2 = 1^2 + 2^2 + 3^2 + \cdots + n^2 = \frac{n(n + 1)(2n + 1)}{6}$$

$$\sum_{k=1}^{n} k^3 = 1^3 + 2^3 + 3^3 + \cdots + n^3 = \frac{n^2(n + 1)^2}{4}$$

EXAMPLE 2   Area using the definition and summation formulas

Use the summation definition of area to find the area under the parabola $y = x^2$ on the interval $[0, 1]$. You estimated this area in Example 1.

Solution

Partition the interval $[0, 1]$ into n subintervals with width $\Delta x = \dfrac{1 - 0}{n}$. The right endpoint of the kth subinterval is $a + k\Delta x = \dfrac{k}{n}$ and $f\left(\dfrac{k}{n}\right) = \dfrac{k^2}{n^2}$. Thus, from the definition of area we have

$$A = \lim_{\Delta x \to 0} \sum_{k=1}^{n} f(a + k\Delta x)\Delta x$$

$$= \lim_{n \to +\infty} \sum_{k=1}^{n} \left(\frac{k^2}{n^2}\right)\left(\frac{1}{n}\right)$$

$$= \lim_{n \to +\infty} \sum_{k=1}^{n} \frac{k^2}{n^3} \qquad \text{Note that } 1/n^3 \text{ is independent of the index of summation, } k.$$

$$= \lim_{n \to +\infty} \frac{1}{n^3} \sum_{k=1}^{n} k^2 \qquad \text{Scalar multiple rule}$$

$$= \lim_{n \to +\infty} \frac{1}{n^3} \left[\frac{n(n+1)(2n+1)}{6}\right] \qquad \text{Summation formula for squares}$$

$$= \lim_{n \to +\infty} \frac{1}{6} \left[2 + \frac{3}{n} + \frac{1}{n^2}\right] = \frac{1}{3}$$

This is the same as the answer found by antidifferentiation in Example 10 of Section 5.1 and is consistent with the table on page 284.   ∎

EXAMPLE 3   Tabular approach for finding area

Use a computer to estimate the area under the curve $y = \sin x$ on the interval $\left[0, \frac{\pi}{2}\right]$.

Solution

We see $a = 0$ and $b = \frac{\pi}{2}$, so $\Delta x = \dfrac{\frac{\pi}{2} - 0}{n} = \dfrac{\pi}{2n}$. The right endpoints are

$$a + \Delta x = 0 + \left(\frac{\pi}{2n}\right) = \frac{\pi}{2n}; a + 2\Delta x = \frac{2\pi}{2n} = \frac{\pi}{n}; a + 3\Delta x = \frac{3\pi}{2n}; \ldots$$

$$a + n\Delta x = \frac{n\pi}{2n} = \frac{\pi}{2} = b$$

Thus, $S_n = \displaystyle\sum_{k=1}^{n} f\left(0 + \frac{k\pi}{2n}\right)\left(\frac{\pi}{2n}\right) = \sum_{k=1}^{n} \left[\sin\left(\frac{k\pi}{2n}\right)\right]\left(\frac{\pi}{2n}\right)$. Now we know from the definition that the actual area is

$$S = \lim_{n \to +\infty} \sum_{k=1}^{n} \left[\sin\left(\frac{k\pi}{2n}\right)\right]\left(\frac{\pi}{2n}\right) = \frac{\pi}{2} \lim_{n \to +\infty} \sum_{k=1}^{n} \frac{1}{n} \sin\left(\frac{k\pi}{2n}\right)$$

n	S_n
10	1.07648
20	1.03876
50	1.01563
100	1.00783
500	1.00157

which we can estimate by computing S_n for successively large values of n, as summarized in the table in this margin. Note that the table suggests that

$$\lim_{\Delta x \to 0} S_n = \lim_{n \to +\infty} S_n = 1$$

Thus, we expect the actual area under the curve to be 1 square unit.   ∎

5.2   PROBLEM SET

Ⓐ *Evaluate the sums in Problems 1–8 by using the summation formulas.*

4. $\displaystyle\sum_{k=1}^{10}(k+1)$ **5.** $\displaystyle\sum_{k=1}^{5}k^3$ **6.** $\displaystyle\sum_{k=1}^{7}k^2$

1. $\displaystyle\sum_{k=1}^{6}1$ **2.** $\displaystyle\sum_{k=1}^{250}2$ **3.** $\displaystyle\sum_{k=1}^{15}k$ **7.** $\displaystyle\sum_{k=1}^{100}(2k-3)$ **8.** $\displaystyle\sum_{k=1}^{100}(k-1)^2$

Use the properties of summation notation in Problems 9–12 to evaluate the given limits.

9. $\displaystyle\lim_{n\to+\infty}\sum_{k=1}^{n}\frac{k}{n^2}$

10. $\displaystyle\lim_{n\to+\infty}\sum_{k=1}^{n}\frac{k^3}{n^4}$

11. $\displaystyle\lim_{n\to+\infty}\sum_{k=1}^{n}\left(1+\frac{k}{n}\right)\left(\frac{2}{n}\right)$

12. $\displaystyle\lim_{n\to+\infty}\sum_{k=1}^{n}\left(1+\frac{2k}{n}\right)^2\left(\frac{2}{n}\right)$

First sketch the region under the graph of $y=f(x)$ on the interval $[a,b]$ in Problems 13–21. Then approximate the area of each region by using right endpoints and the formula

$$S_n=\sum_{k=1}^{n}f(a+k\Delta x)\Delta x$$

for $\Delta x=\dfrac{b-a}{n}$ and the indicated values of n.

13. $f(x)=4x+1$ on $[0,1]$ for

    a. $n=4$ **b.** $n=8$

14. $f(x)=3-2x$ on $[0,1]$ for

    a. $n=3$ **b.** $n=6$

15. $f(x)=x^2$ on $[1,2]$ for

    a. $n=4$ **b.** $n=6$

16. $f(x)=\cos x$ on $\left[-\dfrac{\pi}{2},0\right]$ for $n=4$

17. $f(x)=x+\sin x$ on $\left[0,\dfrac{\pi}{4}\right]$ for $n=3$

18. $f(x)=\dfrac{1}{x^2}$ on $[1,2]$ for $n=4$

19. $f(x)=\dfrac{2}{x}$ on $[1,2]$ for $n=4$

20. $f(x)=\sqrt{x}$ on $[1,4]$ for $n=4$

21. $f(x)=\sqrt{1+x^2}$ on $[0,1]$ for $n=4$

B *Find the exact area under the given curve on the interval prescribed in Problems 22–27 by using area as the limit of a sum and the summation formulas.*

22. $y=4x^3+2x$ on $[0,2]$

23. $y=4x^3+2x$ on $[1,2]$

24. $y=6x^2+2x+4$ on $[0,3]$

25. $y=6x^2+2x+4$ on $[1,3]$

26. $y=3x^2+2x+1$ on $[0,1]$

27. $y=4x^3+3x^2$ on $[0,1]$

Counterexample Problems *Show that each statement about area in Problems 28–33 is generally true or provide a counterexample. It will probably help to sketch the indicated region for each problem.*

28. If $C>0$ is a constant, the region under the line $y=C$ on the interval $[a,b]$ has area $A=C(b-a)$.

29. If $C>0$ is a constant and $b>a\geq 0$, the region under the line $y=Cx$ on the interval $[a,b]$ has area $A=\frac{1}{2}C(b-a)$.

30. The region under the parabola $y=x^2$ on the interval $[a,b]$ has area less than $\frac{1}{2}(b^2+a^2)(b-a)$.

31. The region under the curve $y=\sqrt{1-x^2}$ on the interval $[-1,1]$ has area $A=\dfrac{\pi}{2}$.

32. Let f be a function that satisfies $f(x)\geq 0$ for x in the interval $[a,b]$. Then the area under the curve $y=f^2(x)$ on the interval $[a,b]$ must always be greater than the area under $y=f(x)$ on the same interval.

33. Recall that a function f is said to be **even** if $f(-x)=f(x)$ for all x. If f is even and $f(x)\geq 0$ throughout the interval $[-a,a]$, then the area under the curve $y=f(x)$ on this interval is *twice* the area under $y=f(x)$ on $[0,a]$.

34. Show that the region under the curve $y=x^3$ on the interval $[0,1]$ has area $\frac{1}{4}$ square units.

35. Use the definition of area to show that the area of a rectangle equals the product of its length ℓ and its width w.

36. Show that the triangle with vertices $(0,0)$, $(0,h)$, and $(b,0)$ has area $A=\frac{1}{2}bh$ using the area as the limit of a sum.

37. a. Compute the area under the parabola $y=2x^2$ on the interval $[1,2]$ as the limit of a sum.

    b. Let $f(x)=2x^2$ and note that $g(x)=\frac{2}{3}x^3$ defines a function that satisfies $g'(x)=f(x)$ on the interval $[1,2]$. Verify that the area computed in part **a** satisfies $A=g(2)-g(1)$.

    c. The function defined by

$$h(x)=\tfrac{2}{3}x^3+C$$

for any constant C also satisfies $h'(x)=f(x)$. Is it true that the area in part **a** satisfies $A=h(2)-h(1)$?

Use a tabular approach to compute the area under the curve $y=f(x)$ on each interval given in Problems 38–44 as the limit of a sum of terms.

38. $f(x)=4x$ on $[0,1]$

39. $f(x)=x^2$ on $[0,4]$

40. $f(x)=\cos x$ on $[-\frac{\pi}{2},0]$ (Compare with Problem 16.)

41. $f(x)=x+\sin x$ on $[0,\frac{\pi}{4}]$ (Compare with Problem 17.)

42. $f(x)=\ln(x^2+1)$ on $[0,3]$

43. $f(x)=e^{-3x^2}$ on $[0,1]$

44. $f(x)=\cos^{-1}(x+1)$ on $[-1,0]$

45. a. Use the tabular approach to compute the area under the curve $y=\sin x+\cos x$ on the interval $[0,\frac{\pi}{2}]$ as the limit of a sum.

    b. Let $f(x)=\sin x+\cos x$ and note that $g(x)=-\cos x+\sin x$ satisfies $g'(x)=f(x)$ on the interval $[0,\frac{\pi}{2}]$. Verify that the area computed in part **a** satisfies $A=g(\frac{\pi}{2})-g(0)$.

    c. The function $h(x)=-\cos x+\sin x+C$ for constant C also satisfies $h'(x)=f(x)$. Is it true that the area in part **a** satisfies $A=h(\frac{\pi}{2})-h(0)$?

C 46. Derive the formula

$$\sum_{k=1}^{n}k=1+2+3+\cdots+n=\frac{n(n+1)}{2}$$

by completing these steps:

a. Use the basic rules for sums to show that

$$\sum_{k=1}^{n}k=\frac{1}{2}\sum_{k=1}^{n}[k^2-(k-1)^2]+\frac{1}{2}\sum_{k=1}^{n}1$$

$$=\frac{1}{2}\sum_{k=1}^{n}[k^2-(k-1)^2]+\frac{1}{2}n$$

b. Show that

$$\sum_{k=1}^{n}[k^2-(k-1)^2]=n^2$$

Hint: Expand the sum by writing out a few terms. Note the internal cancellation.

c. Combine parts **a** and **b** to show that

$$\sum_{k=1}^{n} k = \frac{n(n+1)}{2}$$

47. a. First find constants a, b, c, and d such that

$$k^3 = a[k^4 - (k-1)^4] + bk^2 + ck + d$$

b. Modify the approach outlined in Problem 46 to establish the formula

$$\sum_{k=1}^{n} k^2 = \frac{n(n+1)(2n+1)}{6}$$

48. The purpose of this problem is to verify the results shown in Figure 5.11. Specifically, we will find the area A under the parabola $y = x^2$ on the interval $[0, 1]$ using approximating rectangles with heights taken at the *left* endpoints.

Verify that

$$\lim_{n \to +\infty} \sum_{k=1}^{n} \left(\frac{k-1}{n}\right)^2 \left(\frac{1}{n}\right) = \frac{1}{3}$$

Compare this with the procedure outlined in Example 1. Note that when the interval $[0, 1]$ is subdivided into n equal parts, the kth subinterval is

$$\left[\frac{k-1}{n}, \frac{k}{n}\right]$$

49. Develop a formula for area based on approximating rectangles with heights taken at the *midpoints* of subintervals.

50. Use the properties of real numbers to establish the summation formulas in Theorem 5.4. For example, to prove the linearity rule, use the associative, commutative, and distributive properties of real numbers to note that

$$\sum_{k=1}^{n}(ca_k + db_k)$$

$$= (ca_1 + db_1) + (ca_2 + db_2) + \cdots + (ca_n + db_n)$$

$$= (ca_1 + ca_2 + \cdots + ca_n) + (db_1 + db_2 + \cdots + db_n)$$

$$= c(a_1 + a_2 + \cdots + a_n) + d(b_1 + b_2 + \cdots + b_n)$$

$$= c\sum_{k=1}^{n} a_k + d\sum_{k=1}^{n} b_k$$

5.3   Riemann Sums and the Definite Integral

IN THIS SECTION   Riemann sums, the definite integral, area as an integral, properties of the definite integral, distance as an integral

We will soon discover that not just area, but other useful quantities such as distance, volume, mass, and work, can be first approximated by sums and then obtained exactly by taking a limit involving the approximating sums. The special kind of limit of a sum that appears in this context is called the *definite integral*, and the process of finding integrals is called *definite integration* or *Riemann integration* in honor of the German mathematician Georg Bernhard Riemann (1826–1866), who pioneered the modern approach to integration theory. We begin by introducing some special notation and terminology.

RIEMANN SUMS

Recall from Section 5.2 that to find the area under the graph of the function $y = f(x)$ on the closed interval $[a, b]$ using sums where f is continuous and $f(x) \geq 0$, we proceed as follows:

1. Partition the interval into n subintervals of equal width $\Delta x = \dfrac{b-a}{n}$.

2. Evaluate f at the right endpoint $a + k\Delta x$ of the kth subinterval for $k = 1, 2, \ldots, n$.

3. Form the approximating sum of the areas of the n rectangles, which we denote by

$$S_n = \sum_{k=1}^{n} f(a + k\Delta x)\Delta x.$$

4. Because we expect the estimates S_n to improve as Δx decreases, we *define* the area A under the curve, above the x-axis, and bounded by the lines $x = a$ and $x = b$, to be the limit of S_n as $\Delta x \to 0$. Thus, we write

$$A = \lim_{n \to +\infty} \sum_{k=1}^{n} f(a + k\Delta x)\Delta x$$

if this limit exists. This means that A can be estimated to any desired degree of accuracy by approximating the sum S_n with Δx sufficiently small (or, equivalently, n sufficiently large).

This approach to the area problem contains the essentials of integration, but there is no compelling reason for the partition points to be evenly spaced or to insist on evaluating f at right endpoints. These conventions are for convenience of computation, but to accommodate easily as many applications as possible, it is useful to consider a more general type of approximating sum and to specify what is meant by the limit of such sums. The approximating sums that occur in integration problems are called **Riemann sums,** and the following definition contains a step-by-step description of how such sums are formed.

Riemann Sum

Suppose a bounded function f is given along with a closed interval $[a, b]$ on which f is defined. Then

Step 1. Partition the interval $[a, b]$ into n subintervals by choosing points $\{x_0, x_1, \ldots, x_n\}$ arranged in such a way that

$$a = x_0 < x_1 < x_2 < \cdots < x_{n-1} < x_n = b$$

Call this partition P. For $k = 1, 2, \ldots, n$, the kth subinterval width is $\Delta x_k = x_k - x_{k-1}$. The largest of these widths is called the **norm** of the partition P and is denoted by $\|P\|$; that is,

$$\|P\| = \max_{k=1,2,\ldots,n} \{\Delta x_k\}$$

Step 2. Choose a number arbitrarily from each subinterval. For $k = 1, 2, \ldots, n$, the number x_k^* chosen from the kth subinterval $[x_{k-1}, x_k]$ is called the *kth subinterval representative* of the partition P.

Step 3. Form the sum

$$R_n = f(x_1^*)\Delta x_1 + f(x_2^*)\Delta x_2 + \cdots + f(x_n^*)\Delta x_n = \sum_{k=1}^{n} f(x_k^*)\Delta x_k$$

This is the **Riemann sum** associated with f, the given partition P, and the chosen subinterval representatives $x_1^*, x_2^*, \ldots, x_n^*$.

➡ **What This Says** We will express quantities from geometry, physics, economics, and other applications in terms of a Riemann sum

$$\sum_{k=1}^{n} f(x_k^*)\Delta x_k$$

Riemann sums are generally used to model a quantity for a particular application. Note that the Riemann sum *does not* require that the function f be nonnegative, nor does it require that all the intervals must be the same length. In addition, x_k^* is *any* point in the kth subinterval and does not need to be something "nice" like the left or right endpoint, or the midpoint.

EXAMPLE 1   Formation of the Riemann sum for a given function

Suppose the interval $[-2, 1]$ is partitioned into 6 subintervals with subdivision points $a = x_0 = -2$, $x_1 = -1.6$, $x_2 = -0.93$, $x_3 = -0.21$, $x_4 = 0.35$, $x_5 = 0.82$, and

$x_6 = 1 = b$. Find the norm of this partition P and the Riemann sum associated with the function $f(x) = 2x$, the given partition, and the subinterval representatives $x_1^* = -1.81$, $x_2^* = -1.12$, $x_3^* = -0.55$, $x_4^* = -0.17$, $x_5^* = 0.43$, and $x_6^* = 0.94$.

Solution

Before we can find the norm of the partition or the required Riemann sum, we must compute the subinterval width Δx_k and evaluate f at each subinterval representative x_k^*. These values and computations are shown in Figure 5.13.

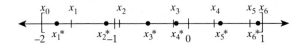

k	Given $x_k - x_{k-1} = \Delta x_k$	Given x_k^*	$f(x_k^*) = 2(x_k^*)$
1	$-1.6 - (-2) = 0.40$	-1.81	$f(-1.81) = -3.62$
2	$-0.93 - (-1.6) = 0.67$	-1.12	$f(-1.12) = -2.24$
3	$-0.21 - (-0.93) = 0.72$	-0.55	$f(-0.55) = -1.10$
4	$0.35 - (-0.21) = 0.56$	-0.17	$f(-0.17) = -0.34$
5	$0.82 - 0.35 = 0.47$	0.43	$f(0.43) = 0.86$
6	$1.00 - 0.82 = 0.18$	0.94	$f(0.94) = 1.88$

Figure 5.13 Riemann sum

WARNING Notice from Example 1 that the Riemann sum does not necessarily represent an area. The sum found is negative (and area must be nonnegative).

From the table, we see that the largest subinterval width is $\Delta x_3 = 0.72$, so the partition has norm $\|P\| = 0.72$. Finally, by using the definition, we compute the Riemann sum:

$$R_6 = (-3.62)(0.40) + (-2.24)(0.67) + (-1.10)(0.72) + (-0.34)(0.56)$$
$$+ (0.86)(0.47) + (1.88)(0.18)$$
$$\approx -3.1886 \approx -3.19$$

∎

THE DEFINITE INTEGRAL

By comparing the formula for the Riemann sum with that of area in the previous section, we recognize that the sum S_n used to approximate area is actually a special kind of Riemann sum that has

$$\Delta x_k = \Delta x = \frac{b - a}{n} \quad \text{and} \quad x_k^* = a + k \Delta x$$

for $k = 1, 2, \ldots, n$. Because the subintervals in the partition P associated with S_n are equally spaced, it is called a **regular partition**. When we express the area under the curve $y = f(x)$ as $A = \lim_{\Delta x \to 0} S_n$, we are actually saying that A can be estimated to any desired accuracy by finding a Riemann sum of the form S_n with norm

$$\|P\| = \frac{b - a}{n}$$

sufficiently small. We use this interpretation as a model for the following definition.

Definite Integral

If f is defined on the closed interval $[a, b]$, we say f is **integrable on** $[a, b]$ if

$$I = \lim_{\|P\| \to 0} \sum_{k=1}^{n} f(x_k^*) \Delta x_k$$

exists. This limit is called the **definite integral** of f from a to b. The definite integral is denoted by

$$I = \int_a^b f(x)\, dx$$

→ What This Says To say that f is *integrable* with definite integral I means the number I can be approximated to any prescribed degree of accuracy by *any* Riemann sum of f with norm sufficiently small. As long as the conditions of this definition are satisfied (that is, f is defined on $[a, b]$ and the Riemann sum exists), we can write

$$\int_a^b f(x)\, dx = \lim_{\|P\| \to 0} \sum_{k=1}^{n} f(x_k^*) \Delta x_k$$

Formally, I is the definite integral of f on $[a, b]$ if for each number $\epsilon > 0$, there exists a number $\delta > 0$ such that if

$$\sum_{k=1}^{n} f(x_k^*) \Delta x_k$$

is any Riemann sum of f whose norm satisfies $\|P\| < \delta$, then

$$\left| I - \sum_{k=1}^{n} f(x_k^*) \Delta x_k \right| < \epsilon$$

In advanced calculus, it is shown that when this limit exists, it is unique. Moreover, its value is independent of the particular way in which the partitions of $[a, b]$ and the subinterval representatives x_k^* are chosen.

WARNING Take a few minutes to make sure you understand the integral notation and terminology.

$$\int_a^b \overbrace{f(x)}^{\text{integrand}} dx$$

↓ upper limit of integration

↑ lower limit of integration

The "dx" indicates the variable of integration.

The function f that is being integrated is called the **integrand**; the interval $[a, b]$ is the **interval of integration**; and the endpoints a and b are called, respectively, the **lower and upper limits of integration**.

In the special case where $a = b$, the interval of integration $[a, b]$ is really just a point, and the integral of any function on this "interval" is defined to be 0; that is,

$$\int_a^a f(x)\, dx = 0 \qquad \text{Why does this makes sense?}$$

Also, at times, we will consider integrals in which the lower limit of integration is a larger number than the upper limit. To handle this case, we specify that the integral from b to a is the negative of the integral from a to b:

$$\int_b^a f(x)\, dx = -\int_a^b f(x)\, dx$$

To summarize,

Definite Integral at a Point

$$\int_a^a f(x)\,dx = 0$$

Interchanging the Limits of a Definite Integral

$$\int_b^a f(x)\,dx = -\int_a^b f(x)\,dx$$

At first, the definition of the definite integral may seem rather imposing. How are we to tell whether a given function f is integrable on an interval $[a, b]$? If f is integrable, how are we supposed to actually compute the definite integral? Answering these questions is not easy, but in advanced calculus, it is shown that f is integrable on a closed interval $[a, b]$ if it is continuous on the interval except at a finite number of points and if it is bounded on the interval (that is, there is a number $A > 0$ such that $|f(x)| < A$ for all x in the interval). We will state a special case of this result as a theorem.

THEOREM 5.5   Integrability of a continuous function

If f is continuous on an interval $[a, b]$, then f is integrable on $[a, b]$.

Proof   The proof requires the methods of advanced calculus and is omitted here.   ❑

Our next example illustrates how to use the definition to find a definite integral.

EXAMPLE 2   Evaluating a definite integral using the definition

Evaluate $\displaystyle\int_{-2}^{1} 4x\,dx$.

Solution

The integral exists because $f(x) = 4x$ is continuous on $[-2, 1]$. Because the integral can be computed by any partition whose norm approaches 0 (that is, the integral is independent of the sequence of partitions *and* the subinterval representatives), we will simplify matters by choosing a partition in which the points are evenly spaced. Specifically, we divide the interval $[-2, 1]$ into n subintervals, each of width

$$\Delta x = \frac{1 - (-2)}{n} = \frac{3}{n}$$

For each k, we choose the kth subinterval representative to be the right endpoint of the kth subinterval; that is,

$$x_k^* = -2 + k\,\Delta x = -2 + k\left(\frac{3}{n}\right)$$

Finally, we form the Riemann sum

$$\int_{-2}^{1} 4x\,dx = \lim_{\|P\| \to 0} \sum_{k=1}^{n} f(x_k^*)\Delta x$$

$$= \lim_{n \to +\infty} \sum_{k=1}^{n} 4\left(-2 + \frac{3k}{n}\right)\left(\frac{3}{n}\right) \qquad n \to +\infty \text{ as } \|P\| \to 0$$

$$= \lim_{n \to +\infty} \frac{12}{n^2} \sum_{k=1}^{n} (-2n + 3k)$$

$$= \lim_{n \to +\infty} \frac{12}{n^2} \left(\sum_{k=1}^{n} (-2n) + \sum_{k=1}^{n} 3k \right)$$

$$= \lim_{n \to +\infty} \frac{12}{n^2} \left((-2n)n + 3 \left[\frac{n(n+1)}{2} \right] \right) \quad \text{Summation formulas}$$

$$= \lim_{n \to +\infty} \frac{12}{n^2} \left(\frac{-4n^2 + 3n^2 + 3n}{2} \right)$$

$$= \lim_{n \to +\infty} \frac{-6n^2 + 18n}{n^2} = -6 \qquad \blacksquare$$

AREA AS AN INTEGRAL

Because we have used the development of area in Section 5.2 as the model for our definition of the definite integral, it is no surprise to discover that the area under a curve can be expressed as a definite integral. However, integrals can be positive, zero, or negative (as in Example 2), and we certainly would not expect the area under a curve to be a negative number! The actual relationship between integrals and area under a curve is contained in the following observation, which follows from the definition of area as the limit of a sum, along with Theorem 5.5.

WARNING We will find areas using a definite integral, but not every definite integral can be interpreted as an area.

> **Area as an Integral**
>
> Suppose f is continuous and $f(x) \geq 0$ on the closed interval $[a, b]$. Then the area under the curve $y = f(x)$ on $[a, b]$ is given by the definite integral of f on $[a, b]$. That is,
>
> $$\text{AREA} = \int_a^b f(x)\, dx$$

Usually we find area by evaluating a definite integral, but sometimes area can be used to help us evaluate the integral. At this stage of our study, it is not easy to evaluate Riemann sums, so if you happen to recognize that the integral represents the area of some common geometric figure, you can use the known formula instead of the definite integral, as shown in Example 3.

EXAMPLE 3 Evaluating an integral using an area formula

Evaluate $\displaystyle\int_{-3}^{3} \sqrt{9 - x^2}\, dx$.

Solution

Let $f(x) = \sqrt{9 - x^2}$. The curve $y = \sqrt{9 - x^2}$ is a semicircle centered at the origin of radius 3, as shown in Figure 5.14. The given integral can be interpreted as the area under the semicircle on the interval $[-3, 3]$. From geometry, we know the area of the circle is $A = \pi r^2 = \pi(3)^2 = 9\pi$. Thus, the area of the semicircle is $\frac{9\pi}{2}$, and we conclude that

$$\int_{-3}^{3} \sqrt{9 - x^2}\, dx = \frac{9\pi}{2} \qquad \blacksquare$$

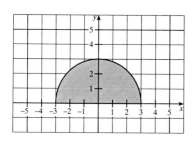

Figure 5.14 The curve $y = \sqrt{9 - x^2}$ is a semicircle of radius 3.

If f is continuous and $f(x) \le 0$ on the closed interval $[a, b]$, then the area between the curve $y = f(x)$ and the x-axis on $[a, b]$ is the opposite of the definite integral of f on $[a, b]$, since $-f(x) \ge 0$. That is,

$$\text{AREA} = -\int_a^b f(x)\, dx$$

More generally, as illustrated in Figure 5.15, if a continuous function f is sometimes positive and sometimes negative, then

$$\int_a^b f(x)\, dx = A_1 - A_2$$

where

A_1 is the sum of all areas of the region above the x-axis and below the graph of f (that is, where $f(x) \ge 0$).

A_2 is the sum of all areas of the region below the x-axis and above the graph of f (that is, where $f(x) \le 0$).

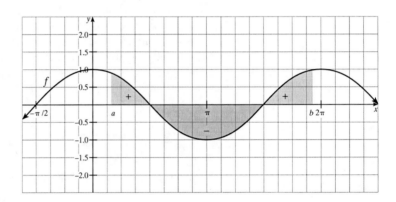

Figure 5.15 A_1 is the sum of the areas marked "+" and A_2 is the sum of the areas marked "–".

We just worked Example 2 (see Figure 5.16) using a Riemann sum, and it is easy to see from our knowledge of areas of triangles that the area of Triangle I (above the x-axis) is

$$A_1 = \tfrac{1}{2}bh = \tfrac{1}{2}(4)(1) = 2$$

and the area of Triangle II (below the x-axis) is

$$A_2 = \tfrac{1}{2}bh = \tfrac{1}{2}(8)(2) = 8$$

and we see that

$$A_1 - A_2 = 2 - 8 = -6$$

is the same as the value of the integral.

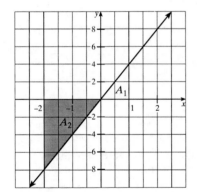

Figure 5.16 Area interpretation of Example 2

PROPERTIES OF THE DEFINITE INTEGRAL

In computations involving integrals, it is often helpful to use the three general properties listed in the following theorem.

THEOREM 5.6   General Properties of the Definite Integral

Linearity rule   If f and g are integrable on $[a, b]$, then so is $rf + sg$ for constants r, s, and

$$\int_a^b [rf(x) + sg(x)]\, dx = r\int_a^b f(x)\, dx + s\int_a^b g(x)\, dx$$

Dominance rule   If f and g are integrable on $[a, b]$ and $f(x) \le g(x)$ throughout this interval, then

$$\int_a^b f(x)\,dx \le \int_a^b g(x)\,dx$$

Subdivision rule   For any number c such that $a < c < b$,

$$\int_a^b f(x)\,dx = \int_a^c f(x)\,dx + \int_c^b f(x)\,dx$$

assuming all three integrals exist.

Proof   Each of these rules can be established by using a familiar property of sums or limits with the definition of the definite integral. For example, to derive the linearity rule, we note that any Riemann sum of the function $rf + sg$ can be expressed as

$$\sum_{k=1}^{n} [rf(x_k^*) + sg(x_k^*)]\Delta x_k = r\left[\sum_{k=1}^{n} f(x_k^*)\Delta x_k\right] + s\left[\sum_{k=1}^{n} g(x_k^*)\Delta x_k\right]$$

and the linearity rule then follows by taking the limit on each side of this equation as the norm of the partition tends to 0.   ❑

The dominance rule and the subdivision rule are interpreted geometrically for non-negative functions in Figure 5.17.

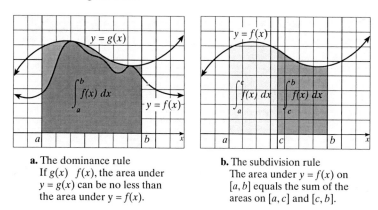

a. The dominance rule
If $g(x)\ f(x)$, the area under $y = g(x)$ can be no less than the area under $y = f(x)$.

b. The subdivision rule
The area under $y = f(x)$ on $[a, b]$ equals the sum of the areas on $[a, c]$ and $[c, b]$.

Figure 5.17   The dominance and subdivision rules

Notice that if $g(x) \ge f(x) \ge 0$, the curve $y = g(x)$ is always above (or touching) the curve $y = f(x)$, as shown in Figure 5.17a. The dominance rule expresses the fact that the area under the upper curve $y = g(x)$ cannot be less than the area under $y = f(x)$. The subdivision rule says that the area under $y = f(x)$ above $[a, b]$ is the sum of the area on $[a, c]$ and the area on $[c, b]$, as shown in Figure 5.17b. The following example illustrates one way of using the subdivision rule.

EXAMPLE 4   Subdivision rule

If $\displaystyle\int_{-2}^{1} f(x)\,dx = 3$ and $\displaystyle\int_{-2}^{7} f(x)\,dx = -5$, what is $\displaystyle\int_{1}^{7} f(x)\,dx$?

Solution

According to the subdivision rule, we have

$$\int_{-2}^{7} f(x)\,dx = \int_{-2}^{1} f(x)\,dx + \int_{1}^{7} f(x)\,dx$$

Therefore,

$$\int_{1}^{7} f(x)\,dx = \int_{-2}^{7} f(x)\,dx - \int_{-2}^{1} f(x)\,dx = (-5) - 3 = -8 \qquad \blacksquare$$

DISTANCE AS AN INTEGRAL

Many quantities other than area can be computed as the limit of a sum. For example, suppose an object moving along a line is known to have continuous velocity $v(t)$ for each time t between $t = a$ and $t = b$, and we wish to compute the total distance traveled by the object during this time period.

Let the interval $[a, b]$ be partitioned into n equal subintervals, each of length $\Delta t = \dfrac{b - a}{n}$ as shown in Figure 5.18.

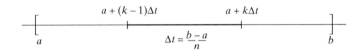

Figure 5.18   The distance traveled during the kth time subinterval

The kth subinterval is $[a + (k - 1)\Delta t, a + k\Delta t]$, and if Δt is small enough, the velocity $v(t)$ will not change much over the subinterval so it is reasonable to approximate $v(t)$ by the constant velocity of $v[a + (k - 1)\Delta t]$ throughout the entire subinterval.

The corresponding change in the object's position will be approximated by the product

$$v[a + (k - 1)\Delta t]\Delta t$$

and will be positive if $v[a + (k - 1)\Delta t]$ is positive and negative if $v[a + (k - 1)\Delta t]$ is negative. Both cases may be summarized by the formula

$$|v[a + (k - 1)\Delta t]|\, \Delta t$$

and the total distance traveled by the object as t varies from $t = a$ to $t = b$ is given by the sum

$$S_n = \sum_{k=1}^{n} |v[a + (k - 1)\Delta t]|\, \Delta t$$

which we recognize as a Riemann sum. We can make the approximation more precise by taking more refined partitions (that is, shorter and shorter time intervals Δt). Therefore, it is reasonable to *define* the exact distance S traveled as the *limit* of the sum S_n as $\Delta t \to 0$ or, equivalently, as $n \to +\infty$, so that

$$S = \lim_{n \to +\infty} \sum_{k=1}^{n} |v[a + (k - 1)\Delta t]|\, \Delta t = \int_{a}^{b} |v(t)|\, dt$$

The reason that we use $|v|$ is that if we travel 300 miles east and then 300 miles west, for example, the *net* distance traveled is $300 - 300 = 0$ miles, but we are usually interested in the total distance traveled, $300 + 300 = 600$ miles.

Distance

> The **total distance traveled** by an object with continuous velocity $v(t)$ along a straight line from time $t = a$ to $t = b$ is
>
> $$S = \int_{a}^{b} |v(t)|\, dt$$

Note: There is a difference between the *total distance* traveled by an object over a given time interval $[a, b]$, and the **net distance** or **displacement** of the object over the same interval, which is defined as the difference between the object's final and initial positions. It is easy to see that displacement is given by

$$D = \int_a^b v(t) \, dt$$

EXAMPLE 5 Distance traveled by an object whose velocity is known

An object moves along a straight line with velocity $v(t) = t^2$ for $t > 0$. How far does the object travel between times $t = 1$ and $t = 2$?

Solution

We have $a = 1$, $b = 2$, and $\Delta t = \dfrac{2 - 1}{n} = \dfrac{1}{n}$; therefore, the required distance is

$$S = \int_1^2 |v(t)| \, dt$$

$$= \lim_{n \to +\infty} \sum_{k=1}^n \left| v \left[1 + (k - 1) \left(\frac{1}{n} \right) \right] \right| \left(\frac{1}{n} \right)$$

$$= \lim_{n \to +\infty} \sum_{k=1}^n \left| v \left(\frac{n + k - 1}{n} \right) \right| \left(\frac{1}{n} \right)$$

$$= \lim_{n \to +\infty} \sum_{k=1}^n \frac{(n + k - 1)^2}{n^2} \left(\frac{1}{n} \right)$$

$$= \lim_{n \to +\infty} \frac{1}{n^3} \sum_{k=1}^n [(n^2 - 2n + 1) + k^2 + 2(n - 1)k]$$

$$= \lim_{n \to +\infty} \frac{1}{n^3} \left[(n^2 - 2n + 1) \sum_{k=1}^n 1 + \sum_{k=1}^n k^2 + 2(n - 1) \sum_{k=1}^n k \right]$$

$$= \lim_{n \to +\infty} \frac{1}{n^3} \left[(n^2 - 2n + 1)n + \frac{n(n + 1)(2n + 1)}{6} + 2(n - 1)\frac{n(n + 1)}{2} \right]$$

$$= \lim_{n \to +\infty} \frac{14n^3 - 9n^2 + n}{6n^3} = \frac{14}{6} = \frac{7}{3}$$

Thus, we expect the object to travel $\frac{7}{3}$ units during the time interval $[1, 2]$. ∎

By considering the distance as an integral, we see again that zero or negative values of a definite integral can also be interpreted geometrically. When $v(t) > 0$ on a time interval $[a, b]$, then the total distance S traveled by the object between times $t = a$ and $t = b$ is the same as the area under the graph of $v(t)$ on $[a, b]$.

When $v(t) > 0$, the object moves forward (to the right), but when $v(t) < 0$, it reverses direction and moves backward (to the left). In the general case, where $v(t)$ changes sign on the time interval $[a, b]$, the integral

$$\int_a^b v(t) \, dt$$

measures the net distance or displacement of the object, taking into account both forward ($v > 0$) and backward ($v < 0$) motion. For instance, an object that moves forward 2 units and back 3 on a given time interval has moved a total distance of 5 units, but its displacement is -1 because it ends up 1 unit to the left of its initial position.

For example, for the velocity function $v(t)$ graphed in Figure 5.19a, the net displacement is 0 because the area above the t-axis is the same as the area below, but in Figure 5.19b, there is more area below the t-axis, which means the net displacement is negative, and the object ends up "behind" (to the left of) its starting position.

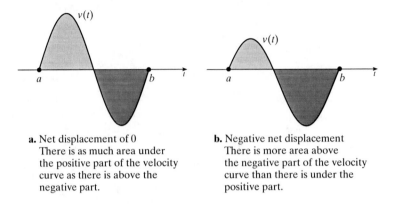

a. Net displacement of 0
There is as much area under the positive part of the velocity curve as there is above the negative part.

b. Negative net displacement
There is more area above the negative part of the velocity curve than there is under the positive part.

Figure 5.19   Definite integral in terms of displacement

PREVIEW

Students often become discouraged at this point, thinking they will have to compute all definite integrals using the limit of a Riemann sum definition, so we offer an encouraging word. Recall the definition of derivative in Chapter 3. It was difficult to find derivatives using the definition, but we soon proved some theorems to make it easier to find and evaluate derivatives. The same is true of integration. It is difficult to apply the definition of a definite integral, but you will soon discover that computing most definite integrals is no harder than finding an antiderivative.

As a preview of this result, consider an object moving along a straight line. We assume that its position is given by $s(t)$ and that its velocity $v(t) = s'(t)$ is positive ($v(t) > 0$) so that it is always moving forward. The total distance traveled by such an object between times $t = a$ and $t = b$ is clearly $S = s(b) - s(a)$, but earlier in this section, we showed that this distance is also given by the definite integral of $v(t)$ over the interval $[a, b]$. Thus we have

$$\text{TOTAL DISTANCE} = \int_a^b v(t)\, dt = s(b) - s(a)$$

where $s(t)$ is an antiderivative of $v(t)$.

This observation anticipates the *fundamental theorem of calculus*, which provides a vital link between differential and integral calculus. We will formally introduce the fundamental theorem in the next section. To illustrate, notice how our observation applies to Example 5, where $v(t) = t^2$ and the interval is $[1, 2]$. Since an antiderivative of $v(t)$ is $s(t) = \frac{1}{3}t^3$, we have

$$S = \int_1^2 t^2\, dt = s(2) - s(1) = \left[\frac{1}{3}(2)^3 - \frac{1}{3}(1)^3 \right] = \frac{7}{3}$$

which coincides with the result found numerically in Example 5.

5.3   PROBLEM SET

A *In Problems 1–10, estimate (using right endpoints) the given integral*
$\int_a^b f(x)\,dx$ *by using a Riemann sum*

$$S_n = \sum_{k=1}^n f(a + k\Delta x)\Delta x \text{ for } n = 4.$$

1. $\int_0^1 (2x + 1)\,dx$ **2.** $\int_0^1 (4x^2 + 2)\,dx$

3. $\int_1^3 x^2\,dx$ **4.** $\int_0^2 x^3\,dx$

5. $\int_0^1 (1 - 3x)\,dx$ **6.** $\int_1^3 (x^2 - x^3)\,dx$

7. $\int_{-\pi/2}^0 \cos x\,dx$ **8.** $\int_0^{\pi/4} (x + \sin x)\,dx$

9. $\int_0^1 e^x\,dx$ **10.** $\int_1^2 \frac{dx}{x}$

In Problems 11–16, $v(t)$ is the velocity of an object moving along a straight line. Use the formula

$$S_n = \sum_{k=1}^n |v(a + k\Delta t)|\,\Delta t$$

where $\Delta t = \dfrac{b - a}{n}$ to estimate (using right endpoints) the total distance traveled by the object during the time interval $[a, b]$. Let $n = 4$.

11. $v(t) = 3t + 1$ on $[1, 4]$ **12.** $v(t) = 1 + 2t$ on $[1, 2]$

13. $v(t) = \sin t$ on $[0, \pi]$ **14.** $v(t) = \cos t$ on $[0, \frac{\pi}{2}]$

15. $v(t) = e^{-t}$ on $[0, 1]$ **16.** $v(t) = \dfrac{1}{t + 1}$ on $[0, 1]$

Evaluate each of the integrals in Problems 17–22 by using the following information together with the linearity and subdivision properties:

$$\int_{-1}^2 x^2\,dx = 3; \quad \int_{-1}^0 x^2\,dx = \frac{1}{3}; \quad \int_{-1}^2 x\,dx = \frac{3}{2}; \quad \int_0^2 x\,dx = 2$$

17. $\int_0^{-1} x^2\,dx$ **18.** $\int_{-1}^2 (x^2 + x)\,dx$

19. $\int_{-1}^2 (2x^2 - 3x)\,dx$ **20.** $\int_0^2 x^2\,dx$

21. $\int_{-1}^0 x\,dx$ **22.** $\int_{-1}^0 (3x^2 - 5x)\,dx$

Use the dominance property of integrals to establish the given inequality in Problems 23–24.

23. $\int_0^1 x^3\,dx \le \dfrac{1}{2}$ *Hint*: Note that $x^3 \le x$ on $[0, 1]$.

24. $\int_0^\pi \sin x\,dx \le \pi$ *Hint*: $\sin x \le 1$ for all x.

B **25.** Given $\int_{-2}^4 [5f(x) + 2g(x)]\,dx = 7$ and $\int_{-2}^4 [3f(x) + g(x)]\,dx = 4$, find

$$\int_{-2}^4 f(x)\,dx \quad \text{and} \quad \int_{-2}^4 g(x)\,dx$$

26. Suppose $\int_0^2 f(x)\,dx = 3$, $\int_0^2 g(x)\,dx = -1$, and $\int_0^2 h(x)\,dx = 3$.

a. Evaluate $\int_0^2 [2f(x) + 5g(x) - 7h(x)]\,dx$.

b. Find a constant s such that

$$\int_0^2 [5f(x) + sg(x) - 6h(x)]\,dx = 0$$

27. Evaluate $\int_{-1}^2 f(x)\,dx$ given that

$$\int_{-1}^1 f(x)\,dx = 3; \quad \int_2^3 f(x)\,dx = -2; \quad \int_1^3 f(x)\,dx = 5$$

28. Let $f(x) = \begin{cases} 2 & \text{for } -1 \le x \le 1 \\ 3 - x & \text{for } 1 < x < 4 \\ 2x - 9 & \text{for } 4 \le x \le 5 \end{cases}$

Sketch the graph of f on the interval $[-1, 5]$ and show that f is continuous on this interval. Then use Theorem 5.6 to evaluate

$$\int_{-1}^5 f(x)\,dx$$

29. Let $f(x) = \begin{cases} 5 & \text{for } -3 \le x \le -1 \\ 4 - x & \text{for } -1 < x < 2 \\ 2x - 2 & \text{for } 2 \le x \le 5 \end{cases}$

Sketch the graph of f on the interval $[-3, 5]$ and show that f is continuous on this interval. Then use Theorem 5.6 to evaluate

$$\int_{-3}^5 f(x)\,dx$$

30. HISTORICAL QUEST
During the eighteenth century, integrals were considered simply as antiderivatives. That is, there were no underpinnings for the concept of an integral until Cauchy formulated the definition of the integral in 1823 (see Historical Quest 49, Problem Set 2.1). This formulation was later completed by Georg Friedrich Riemann. In this section, we see

GEORG FRIEDRICH RIEMANN
1826–1866

that history honored Riemann by naming the process after him. In his personal life he was frail, bashful, and timid, but in his professional life he was one of the giants in mathematical history. Riemann used what are called topological methods in his theory of functions and in his work with surfaces and spaces. Riemann is remembered for his work in geometry (Riemann surfaces) and analysis. In his book *Space Through the Ages*, Cornelius Lanczos wrote, "Although Riemann's collected papers fill only one single volume of 538 pages, this volume weighs tons if measured intellectually. Every one of his many discoveries was destined to change the course of mathematical science." ∎

For this Historical Quest, investigate the Königsberg bridge problem, and its solution.

This famous problem was formulated by Leonhard Euler (1707–1783). The branch of mathematics known today as *topology* began with Euler's work on the bridge problem and other related questions and was extended in the nineteenth century by Riemann and others.

⊙ 31. Generalize the subdivision property by showing that for $a \leq c \leq d \leq b$

$$\int_a^b f(x)\, dx = \int_a^c f(x)\, dx + \int_c^d f(x)\, dx + \int_d^b f(x)\, dx$$

whenever all these integrals exist.

32. If $Cx + D \geq 0$ for $a \leq x \leq b$, show that

$$\int_a^b (Cx + D)\, dx = (b - a)\left[\frac{C}{2}(b + a) + D\right]$$

Hint: Sketch the region under the line $y = Cx + D$, and express the integral as an area.

33. For $b > a > 0$, show that

$$\int_a^b x^2\, dx = \frac{1}{3}(b^3 - a^3)$$

In Problems 34–36, use the partition $P = \{-1, -0.2, 0.9, 1.3, 1.7, 2\}$ *on the interval* $[-1, 2]$.

34. Find the subinterval widths

$$\Delta x_k = x_k - x_{k-1}$$

for $k = 1, 2, \ldots, 5$. What is the norm of P?

35. Compute the Riemann sum on $[-1, 2]$ associated with $f(x) = 4 - 5x$; the partition P with $\Delta x_1 = 0.8$, $\Delta x_2 = 1.1$, $\Delta x_3 = 0.4$, $\Delta x_4 = 0.4$, and $\Delta x_5 = 0.3$; and the subinterval representatives $x_1^* = -0.5$, $x_2^* = 0.8$, $x_3^* = 1$, $x_4^* = 1.3$, $x_5^* = 1.8$. What is the norm of P?

36. Compute the Riemann sum on $[-1, 2]$ associated with $f(x) = x^3$; the partition P with $\Delta x_1 = 0.8$, $\Delta x_2 = 1.1$, $\Delta x_3 = 0.4$, $\Delta x_4 = 0.4$, and $\Delta x_5 = 0.3$; and subinterval representatives $x_1^* = -1$, $x_2^* = 0$, $x_3^* = 1$, $x_4^* = \frac{128}{81}$, and $x_5^* = \frac{125}{64}$. What is the norm of P?

37. If the numbers a_k and b_k satisfy $a_k \leq b_k$ for $k = 1, 2, \ldots, n$, then $\sum_{k=1}^n a_k \leq \sum_{k=1}^n b_k$. Use this dominance property of sums to establish the dominance property of integrals.

38. Counterexample Problem   Either prove that the following result is generally true or find a counterexample: If f and g are continuous on $[a, b]$, then

$$\int_a^b f(x)g(x)\, dx = \left[\int_a^b f(x)\, dx\right]\left[\int_a^b g(x)\, dx\right]$$

39. Counterexample Problem   Either prove that the following result is generally true or find a counterexample: There exists a nonzero continuous function f defined on $[a, b]$ with a nonzero area between the x-axis and the function f on the interval such that

$$\int_a^b f(x)\, dx = 0$$

40. Recall that a function f is **odd** if $f(-x) = -f(x)$ for all x. If f is odd, show that

$$\int_{-a}^a f(x)\, dx = 0$$

for all a. This problem is analogous to Problem 33 of the previous section.

41. Prove the *bounding rule* for definite integrals: If f is integrable on the closed interval $[a, b]$ and $m \leq f(x) \leq M$ for constants m, M, and all x in the closed interval, then

$$m(b - a) \leq \int_a^b f(x)\, dx \leq M(b - a)$$

42. Use the definition of the definite integral to prove that

$$\int_a^b C\, dx = C(b - a)$$

5.4   The Fundamental Theorems of Calculus

IN THIS SECTION   the first fundamental theorem of calculus, the second fundamental theorem of calculus

THE FIRST FUNDAMENTAL THEOREM OF CALCULUS

In the previous section we observed that if $v(t)$ is the velocity of an object at time t as it moves along a straight line, then

$$\int_a^b v(t)\, dt = s(b) - s(a)$$

where $s(t)$ is the displacement of the object and satisfies $s'(t) = v(t)$. This result is an application of the following general theorem which was discovered by the English mathematician Isaac Barrow (1630–1677), Newton's mentor at Cambridge.

THEOREM 5.7 The first fundamental theorem of calculus

If f is continuous on the interval $[a, b]$ and F is any function that satisfies $F'(x) = f(x)$ throughout this interval, then

$$\int_a^b f(x)\,dx = F(b) - F(a)$$

Proof Let $P = \{x_0, x_1, x_2, \ldots, x_n\}$ be a regular partition of the interval, with subinterval widths $\Delta x = \dfrac{b-a}{n}$. Note that F satisfies the hypotheses of the mean value theorem (Theorem 4.4, Section 4.2) on each of the closed subintervals $[x_{k-1}, x_k]$. Thus, the MVT tells us that there is a point x_k^* in each open subinterval (x_{k-1}, x_k) for which

$$\frac{F(x_k) - F(x_{k-1})}{x_k - x_{k-1}} = F'(x_k^*)$$

$$F(x_k) - F(x_{k-1}) = F'(x_k^*)(x_k - x_{k-1})$$

Because $F'(x_k^*) = f(x_k^*)$ and $x_k - x_{k-1} = \Delta x = \dfrac{b-a}{n}$, we can write $F(x_k) - F(x_{k-1}) = f(x_k^*)\Delta x$, so that

$$F(x_1) - F(x_0) = f(x_1^*)\Delta x$$
$$F(x_2) - F(x_1) = f(x_2^*)\Delta x$$
$$\vdots$$
$$F(x_n) - F(x_{n-1}) = f(x_n^*)\Delta x$$

Thus, by adding both sides of all the equations, we obtain

$$\sum_{k=1}^n f(x_k^*)\Delta x = f(x_1^*)\Delta x + f(x_2^*)\Delta x + \cdots + f(x_n^*)\Delta x$$
$$= [F(x_1) - F(x_0)] + [F(x_2) - F(x_1)] + \cdots + [F(x_n) - F(x_{n-1})]$$
$$= F(x_n) - F(x_0)$$

Because $x_0 = a$ and $x_n = b$, we have

$$\sum_{k=1}^n f(x_k^*)\Delta x = F(b) - F(a)$$

Finally, we take the limit of the left side as $\|P\| \to 0$ (i.e., $n \to +\infty$), and because $F(b) - F(a)$ is a constant, we have

$$\int_a^b f(x)\,dx = F(b) - F(a)$$
❑

➜ What This Says The definite integral $\int_a^b f(x)\,dx$ can be computed by finding an antiderivative on the interval $[a, b]$ and evaluating it at the limits of integration a and b. It is a consequence of the first fundamental theorem of calculus that our two definitions of area between the graph of $y = f(x)$ for $y \geq 0$ and the x-axis from the first two sections of this chapter agree. Also notice that this theorem does not say *how* to find the antiderivative, nor does it say that an antiderivative F *exists*. The existence of an antiderivative is asserted by the second fundamental theorem of calculus, which is examined later in this section (page 306).

To give you some insight into why this theorem is important enough to be named *the fundamental theorem of calculus*, we repeat Example 2 from Section 5.3 on the left and then work the same example using the fundamental theorem, on the right.

EXAMPLE 1   Evaluating a definite integral

Evaluate $\int_{-2}^{1} 4x \, dx$ using the definition of the definite integral and also using the fundamental theorem.

Solution

Solution from Section 5.3 using Riemann sums:

$$\int_{-2}^{1} 4x \, dx = \lim_{\|P\| \to 0} \sum_{k=1}^{n} f(x_k^*) \Delta x$$

$$= \lim_{n \to +\infty} \sum_{k=1}^{n} 4 \left(-2 + \frac{3k}{n} \right) \left(\frac{3}{n} \right)$$

$$= \lim_{n \to +\infty} \frac{12}{n^2} \sum_{k=1}^{n} (-2n + 3k)$$

$$= \lim_{n \to +\infty} \frac{12}{n^2} \left(\sum_{k=1}^{n} (-2n) + \sum_{k=1}^{n} 3k \right)$$

$$= \lim_{n \to +\infty} \frac{12}{n^2} \left((-2n)n + 3 \left[\frac{n(n+1)}{2} \right] \right)$$

$$= \lim_{n \to +\infty} \frac{12}{n^2} \left(\frac{-4n^2 + 3n^2 + 3n}{2} \right)$$

$$= \lim_{n \to +\infty} \frac{-6n^2 + 18n}{n^2}$$

$$= -6$$

Solution using the fundamental theorem of calculus:

If $F(x) = 2x^2$, then $F'(x) = 4x$, so F is an antiderivative of f. Thus,

$$\int_{-2}^{1} 4x \, dx = F(1) - F(-2)$$

$$= 2(1)^2 - 2(-2)^2 = -6$$

Note that if we choose a *different* antiderivative, say $G(x) = 2x^2 + 3$, then $G(1) - G(-2) = -6$, as well.

∎

The variable used in a definite integral is a **dummy variable** in the sense that it can be replaced by any other variable with no effect on the value of the integral. For instance, we have just found that

$$\int_{-2}^{1} 4x \, dx = -6$$

and without further computation, it follows that

$$\int_{-2}^{1} 4t \, dt = -6 \qquad \int_{-2}^{1} 4u \, du = -6 \qquad \int_{-2}^{1} 4N \, dN = -6$$

Henceforth, when evaluating an integral by the fundamental theorem, we will denote the difference

$$F(b) - F(a) \quad \text{by} \quad F(x)\big|_a^b$$

Sometimes we also write $[F(x)]_a^b$, where $F'(x) = f(x)$ on $[a, b]$. This notation is illustrated in Example 2.

EXAMPLE 2   Finding the area under a curve using the fundamental theorem of calculus

Find the area under the curve $y = \cos x$ on $\left[-\frac{\pi}{2}, \frac{\pi}{2} \right]$.

Solution

Note that $f(x) = \cos x$ is continuous and $f(x) \geq 0$ on $\left[-\frac{\pi}{2}, \frac{\pi}{2}\right]$, as shown in Figure 5.20. Because the derivative of $\sin x$ is $\cos x$, it follows (from the definition of the antiderivative) that $\sin x$ is an antiderivative of $\cos x$. Thus, the required area is given by the integral

$$A = \int_{-\pi/2}^{\pi/2} \cos x \, dx = \sin x \big|_{-\pi/2}^{\pi/2} = \sin \tfrac{\pi}{2} - \sin \left(-\tfrac{\pi}{2}\right) = 1 - (-1) = 2$$

The region has area $A = 2$ square units.

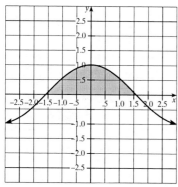

If you look at the graph of $f(x) = \cos x$ on $\left[-\frac{1}{2}, \frac{1}{2}\right]$, you can see that an area of 2 seems reasonable.

Figure 5.20 Graph to estimate area

WARNING It is important to remember that, for fixed numerical values of a and b, the definite integral $\int_a^b f(x)\, dx$ is a number, whereas the indefinite integral $\int f(x)\, dx$ is a family of functions. The relationship between the indefinite and definite integral is given by

$$\int_a^b f(x)\, dx = \left[\int f(x)\, dx \right] \Big|_a^b$$ ■

EXAMPLE 3   Evaluating an integral using the fundamental theorem

Evaluate

a. $\displaystyle\int_{-3}^{5} (-10)\, dx$ **b.** $\displaystyle\int_{4}^{9} \left[\frac{1}{\sqrt{x}} + x \right] dx$ **c.** $\displaystyle\int_{-2}^{2} |x|\, dx$

Solution

a. $\displaystyle\int_{-3}^{5} (-10)\, dx = -10x\big|_{-3}^{5} = -10(5 + 3) = -80$

b. $\displaystyle\int_{4}^{9} \left[\frac{1}{\sqrt{x}} + x \right] dx = \int_{4}^{9} \left[x^{-1/2} + x \right] dx = \left[\left(\frac{x^{1/2}}{\frac{1}{2}} \right) + \frac{x^2}{2} \right] \Bigg|_{4}^{9}$

$$= \left(6 + \tfrac{81}{2} \right) - \left(4 + \tfrac{16}{2} \right) = 34\tfrac{1}{2}$$

c. $\displaystyle\int_{-2}^{2} |x|\, dx = \int_{-2}^{0} |x|\, dx + \int_{0}^{2} |x|\, dx$ Subdivision rule

$$= \int_{-2}^{0} (-x)\, dx + \int_{0}^{2} x\, dx \qquad \text{Recall,} \quad \begin{aligned} |x| &= x \quad \text{if } x \geq 0 \\ |x| &= -x \quad \text{if } x < 0 \end{aligned}$$

$$= -\frac{x^2}{2} \bigg|_{-2}^{0} + \frac{x^2}{2} \bigg|_{0}^{2} = -\left(0 - \frac{4}{2} \right) + \left(\frac{4}{2} + 0 \right) = 4$$

Note that we must use the subdivision rule because we do not know an antiderivative of the function $|x|$, where x is defined on an interval containing zero. ■

THE SECOND FUNDAMENTAL THEOREM OF CALCULUS

In certain circumstances, it is useful to consider an integral of the form

$$\int_a^x f(t)\, dt$$

where the upper limit of integration is a variable instead of a constant. As x varies, so does the value of the integral, and

$$F(x) = \int_a^x f(t)\, dt$$

is a function of the variable x. (Note that the integrand does not contain x.) For instance,

$$F(x) = \int_2^x t^2 \, dt = \tfrac{1}{3}x^3 - \tfrac{1}{3}(2)^3 = \tfrac{1}{3}x^3 - \tfrac{8}{3}$$

The first fundamental theorem of calculus tells us that if f is continuous on $[a, b]$, then

$$\int_a^b f(x) \, dx = F(b) - F(a)$$

where F is an antiderivative of f on $[a, b]$. But in general, what guarantee do we have that such an antiderivative even exists? The answer is provided by the following theorem, which is often referred to as the second fundamental theorem of calculus.

THEOREM 5.8   The second fundamental theorem of calculus

Let $f(t)$ be continuous on the interval $[a, b]$ and define the function G by the integral equation

$$G(x) = \int_a^x f(t) \, dt$$

for $a \le x \le b$. Then G is an antiderivative of f on $[a, b]$; that is,

$$G'(x) = \frac{d}{dx}\left[\int_a^x f(t) \, dt\right] = f(x)$$

on $[a, b]$.

Proof   Apply the definition of the derivative to G:

$$G'(x) = \lim_{\Delta x \to 0} \frac{G(x + \Delta x) - G(x)}{\Delta x} \qquad \text{x is fixed, only } \Delta x \text{ changes}$$

$$= \lim_{\Delta x \to 0} \frac{1}{\Delta x}[G(x + \Delta x) - G(x)]$$

$$= \lim_{\Delta x \to 0} \frac{1}{\Delta x}\left[\int_a^{x+\Delta x} f(t) \, dt - \int_a^x f(t) \, dt\right]$$

$$= \lim_{\Delta x \to 0} \frac{1}{\Delta x}\left[\int_a^{x+\Delta x} f(t) \, dt + \int_x^a f(t) \, dt\right]$$

$$= \lim_{\Delta x \to 0} \frac{1}{\Delta x}\left[\int_x^{x+\Delta x} f(t) \, dt\right] \qquad \text{Subdivision rule}$$

Since f is continuous on $[a, b]$, it is continuous on $[x, x + \Delta x]$ for any x in $[a, b]$. Let $m(x)$ and $M(x)$ be the smallest and largest values, respectively, for $f(t)$ on $[x, x+\Delta x]$. (*Note*: In general, m and M depend on x and Δx but are constants as far as t-integration is concerned.) Since $m(x) \le f(t) \le M(x)$, we have (by the dominance rule)

$$\int_x^{x+\Delta x} m(x) \, dt \le \int_x^{x+\Delta x} f(t) \, dt \le \int_x^{x+\Delta x} M(x) \, dt$$

so

$$m(x)[(x + \Delta x) - x] \le \int_x^{x+\Delta x} f(t) \, dt \le M(x)[(x + \Delta x) - x]$$

or

$$m(x) \le \frac{1}{\Delta x}\int_x^{x+\Delta x} f(t) \, dt \le M(x)$$

Since

$$m(x) \le f(x) \le M(x)$$

on $[x, x + \Delta x]$, it follows that $m(x)$ and $M(x)$ are both "squeezed" toward $f(x)$ as $\Delta x \to 0$ and we have

$$G'(x) = \lim_{\Delta x \to 0} \frac{1}{\Delta x}\int_x^{x+\Delta x} f(t) \, dt = f(x) \qquad \Box$$

We also note that the function G is continuous, since it is differentiable. If F is *any* antiderivative of f on the interval $[a, b]$, then the antiderivative

$$G(x) = \int_a^x f(t)\, dt$$

found in Theorem 5.8 satisfies $G(x) = F(x) + C$ for some constant C and all x on the interval $[a, b]$. In particular, when $x = a$, we have

$$0 = \int_a^a f(t)\, dt = G(a) = F(a) + C$$

so that $C = -F(a)$. Finally, by letting $x = b$, we find that

$$\int_a^b f(t)\, dt = G(b) = F(b) + C = F(b) + [-F(a)] = F(b) - F(a)$$

as claimed by the first fundamental theorem.

EXAMPLE 4   Using the second fundamental theorem

Differentiate $F(x) = \int_7^x (2t - 3)\, dt$.

Solution

From the second fundamental theorem, we can obtain $F'(x)$ by simply replacing t with x in the integrand $f(t) = 2t - 3$. Thus,

$$F'(x) = \frac{d}{dx}\left[\int_7^x (2t - 3)\, dt\right] = 2x - 3 \qquad \blacksquare$$

The second fundamental theorem of calculus can also be applied to an integral function with a variable *lower* limit of integration. For example, to differentiate

$$G(z) = \int_z^5 \frac{\sin u}{u}\, du$$

reverse the order of integration and apply the second fundamental theorem of calculus as before:

$$G'(z) = \frac{d}{dz}\left[\int_z^5 \frac{\sin u}{u}\, du\right] = \frac{d}{dz}\left[-\int_5^z \frac{\sin u}{u}\, du\right] = -\frac{d}{dz}\left[\int_5^z \frac{\sin u}{u}\, du\right] = -\frac{\sin z}{z}$$

EXAMPLE 5   Second fundamental theorem with the chain rule

Find the derivative of $F(x) = \int_0^{x^2} t^2\, dt$.

Solution

$$F'(x) = \frac{d}{dx}\left[\int_0^{x^2} t^2\, dt\right] = \frac{d}{du}\left[\int_0^u t^2\, dt\right]\frac{du}{dx} \qquad \text{Chain rule; } u = x^2$$

$$= u^2\frac{du}{dx} \qquad \text{Second fundamental theorem of calculus}$$

$$= \left(x^2\right)^2 (2x)$$

$$= 2x^5 \qquad \blacksquare$$

5.4 PROBLEM SET

Ⓐ *In Problems 1–30, evaluate the definite integral.*

1. $\displaystyle\int_{-10}^{10} 7\,dx$

2. $\displaystyle\int_{-5}^{7} (-3)\,dx$

3. $\displaystyle\int_{-3}^{5} (2x + a)\,dx$

4. $\displaystyle\int_{-2}^{2} (b - x)\,dx$

5. $\displaystyle\int_{-1}^{2} ax^3\,dx$

6. $\displaystyle\int_{-1}^{1} (x^3 + bx^2)\,dx$

7. $\displaystyle\int_{1}^{2} \frac{c}{x^3}\,dx$

8. $\displaystyle\int_{-2}^{-1} \frac{p}{x^2}\,dx$

9. $\displaystyle\int_{0}^{9} \sqrt{x}\,dx$

10. $\displaystyle\int_{0}^{27} \sqrt[3]{x}\,dx$

11. $\displaystyle\int_{0}^{1} (5u^7 + \pi^2)\,du$

12. $\displaystyle\int_{0}^{1} (7x^8 + \sqrt{\pi})\,dx$

13. $\displaystyle\int_{1}^{2} x^{2a}\,dx,\ a \neq -\tfrac{1}{2}$

14. $\displaystyle\int_{1}^{2} (2x)^{\pi}\,dx$

15. $\displaystyle\int_{\ln 2}^{\ln 5} 5e^x\,dx$

16. $\displaystyle\int_{e^{-2}}^{e} \frac{dx}{x}$

17. $\displaystyle\int_{0}^{4} \sqrt{x}(x + 1)\,dx$

18. $\displaystyle\int_{0}^{1} \sqrt{t}(t - \sqrt{t})\,dt$

19. $\displaystyle\int_{1}^{2} \frac{x^3 + 1}{x^2}\,dx$

20. $\displaystyle\int_{1}^{4} \frac{x^2 + x - 1}{\sqrt{x}}\,dx$

21. $\displaystyle\int_{1}^{\sqrt{3}} \frac{6a}{1 + x^2}\,dx$

22. $\displaystyle\int_{0}^{0.5} \frac{b\,dx}{\sqrt{1 - x^2}}$

23. $\displaystyle\int_{-2}^{3} (\sin^2 x + \cos^2 x)\,dx$

24. $\displaystyle\int_{0}^{\pi/4} (\sec^2 x - \tan^2 x)\,dx$

25. $\displaystyle\int_{0}^{1} (1 - e^t)\,dt$

26. $\displaystyle\int_{1}^{2} \frac{x^3 + 1}{x}\,dx$

27. $\displaystyle\int_{0}^{1} \frac{x^2 - 4}{x - 2}\,dx$

28. $\displaystyle\int_{0}^{1} \frac{x^2 - 1}{x^2 + 1}\,dx$

29. $\displaystyle\int_{-1}^{2} (x + |x|)\,dx$

30. $\displaystyle\int_{0}^{2} (x - |x - 1|)\,dx$

In Problems 31–38, find the area of the region under the given curve over the prescribed interval.

31. $y = x^2 + 1$ on $[-1, 1]$

32. $y = \sqrt{t}$ on $[0, 1]$

33. $y = \sec^2 x$ on $\left[0, \frac{\pi}{4}\right]$

34. $y = \sin x + \cos x$ on $\left[0, \frac{\pi}{2}\right]$

35. $y = e^t - t$ on $[0, 1]$

36. $y = (x^2 + x + 1)\sqrt{x}$ on $[1, 4]$

37. $y = \dfrac{x^2 - 2x + 3}{x}$ on $[1, 2]$

38. $y = \dfrac{2}{1 + t^2}$ on $[0, 1]$

In Problems 39–44, find the derivative of the given function.

39. $F(x) = \displaystyle\int_{0}^{x} \frac{t^2 - 1}{\sqrt{t + 1}}\,dt$

40. $F(x) = \displaystyle\int_{-2}^{x} (t + 1)\sqrt[3]{t}\,dt$

41. $F(t) = \displaystyle\int_{1}^{t} \frac{\sin x}{x}\,dx$

42. $F(t) = \displaystyle\int_{t}^{2} \frac{e^x}{x}\,dx$

43. $F(x) = \displaystyle\int_{x}^{1} \frac{dt}{\sqrt{1 + 3t^2}}$

44. $F(x) = \displaystyle\int_{\pi/3}^{x} \sec^2 t \tan t\,dt$

Ⓑ *The formulas in Problems 45–50 are taken from a table of integrals. In each case, use differentiation to verify that the formula is correct.*

45. $\displaystyle\int \cos^2 au\,du = \frac{u}{2} + \frac{\sin 2au}{4a} + C$

46. $\displaystyle\int u \cos^2 au\,du = \frac{u^2}{4} + \frac{u \sin 2au}{4a} + \frac{\cos 2au}{8a^2} + C$

47. $\displaystyle\int \frac{u\,du}{(a^2 - u^2)^{3/2}} = \frac{1}{\sqrt{a^2 - u^2}} + C$

48. $\displaystyle\int \frac{du}{u^2 - a^2} = \frac{1}{2a} \ln \left| \frac{u - a}{u + a} \right| + C$

49. $\displaystyle\int \frac{u\,du}{\sqrt{a^2 - u^2}} = -\sqrt{a^2 - u^2} + C$

50. $\displaystyle\int (\ln |u|)^2\,du = u(\ln |u|)^2 - 2u \ln |u| + 2u + C$

51. Exploration Problem   What is the relationship between finding an area and evaluating an integral?

52. Journal Problem   *FOCUS** ■ The area of the shaded region in Figure 5.21a is 8 times the area of the shaded region in Figure 5.21b. What is c in terms of a?

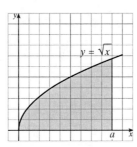
a.

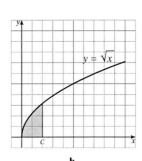
b.

Figure 5.21   Comparing areas

53. Exploration Problem   If you use the first fundamental theorem for the following integral, you find

$$\int_{-1}^{1} \frac{dx}{x^2} = \left[-\frac{1}{x} \right] \Bigg|_{-1}^{1} = -1 - 1 = -2$$

But the function $y = \dfrac{1}{x^2}$ is never negative. What's wrong with this "evaluation"?

54. Evaluate

$$\int_{0}^{2} f(x)\,dx \quad \text{where} \quad f(x) = \begin{cases} x^3 & \text{if } 0 \leq x < 1 \\ x^4 & \text{if } 1 \leq x \leq 2 \end{cases}$$

55. Evaluate

$$\int_{0}^{\pi} f(x)\,dx \quad \text{where} \quad f(x) = \begin{cases} \cos x & \text{if } 0 \leq x < \pi/2 \\ x & \text{if } \pi/2 \leq x \leq \pi \end{cases}$$

*February 1995, p. 15.

56. a. If $F(x) = \int \left(\dfrac{1}{\sqrt{x}} - 4\right) dx$, find F so that $F(1) = 0$.

b. Sketch the graphs of $y = F(x)$, $y = F(x) + 3$, and $y = F(x) - 1$.

c. Find a constant K such that the largest value of $G(x) = F(x) + K$ is 0.

57. Let $g(x) = \int_0^x f(t)\, dt$, where f is the function defined by the following graph. Note that f crosses the x-axis at 3 points on $[0, 2]$; label these (from left to right), $x = a$, $x = b$, and $x = c$.

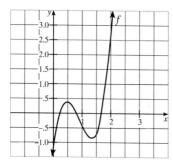

a. What can you say about $g(a)$?

b. Estimate $g(1)$.

c. Where does g have a maximum value on $[0, 2]$?

d. Sketch a rough graph of g.

58. Let $g(x) = \int_0^x f(t)\, dt$, where f is the function defined by the following graph.

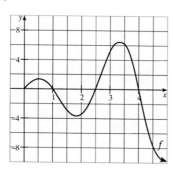

a. Where does g have a relative minimum on $[0, 5]$?

b. Where does g have a relative maximum value on $[0, 5]$?

c. If $g(1) = 1$, $g(2.5) = -2.5$, and $g(4) = 4$, sketch a rough graph of g.

59. Counterexample Problem The purpose of this problem is to provide a counterexample showing that the integral of a product (or quotient) is not necessarily equal to the product (quotient) of the respective integrals.

a. Show that $\int x\sqrt{x}\, dx \neq (\int x\, dx)(\int \sqrt{x}\, dx)$.

b. Show that $\int \dfrac{\sqrt{x}}{x}\, dx \neq \dfrac{\int \sqrt{x}\, dx}{\int x\, dx}$.

60. Suppose f is a function with the property that $f'(x) = f(x)$ for all x.

a. Show that $\int_a^b f(x)\, dx = f(b) - f(a)$.

b. Show that $\int_a^b [f(x)]^2\, dx = \dfrac{1}{2}\{[f(b)]^2 - [f(a)]^2\}$.

61. Find $\dfrac{d}{dx}\int_0^{x^4} (2t - 3)\, dt$ using the second fundamental theorem of calculus. Check your work by evaluating the integral directly and then taking the derivative of your answer.

62. Find $\dfrac{d}{dx}\int_0^{x^2} \sin t\, dt$ using the second fundamental theorem of calculus. Check your work by evaluating the integral directly and then taking the derivative of your answer.

63. Find an equation for the tangent line to the curve $y = F(x)$ at the point P where $x = 1$ and

$$F(x) = \int_1^{\sqrt{x}} \dfrac{2t + 1}{t + 2}\, dt$$

64. Find an equation for the tangent line to the curve $y = F(x)$ at the point P where $x = 1$ and

$$F(x) = \int_1^{x^3} \dfrac{t^2 + 1}{t - 2}\, dt$$

65. Suppose $F(x)$ is the integral function $F(x) = \int_{u(x)}^{v(x)} f(t)\, dt$. What is $F'(x)$? This result is called *Leibniz' rule*.

66. Suppose $F(x) = \int_{-x}^x e^t\, dt$. Find $F'(x)$.

5.5 Integration by Substitution

IN THIS SECTION substitution with indefinite integration, substitution with definite integration

SUBSTITUTION WITH INDEFINITE INTEGRATION

Recall that according to the chain rule, the derivative of $(x^2 + 3x + 5)^9$ is

$$\dfrac{d}{dx}(x^2 + 3x + 5)^9 = 9(x^2 + 3x + 5)^8(2x + 3)$$

Thus,

$$\int 9(x^2 + 3x + 5)^8(2x + 3)\, dx = (x^2 + 3x + 5)^9 + C$$

Note that the product is of the form $g(u)\dfrac{du}{dx}$ where, in this case, $g(u) = 9u^8$ and $u = x^2 + 3x + 5$. The following theorem generalizes this procedure by showing how products of the form $g(u)\dfrac{du}{dx}$ can be integrated by reversing the chain rule.

THEOREM 5.9   Integration by substitution

Let f, g, and u be differentiable functions of x such that

$$f(x) = g(u)\frac{du}{dx}$$

Then

$$\int f(x)\, dx = \int g(u)\frac{du}{dx}\, dx = \int g(u)\, du = G(u) + C$$

where G is an antiderivative of g.

Proof   If G is an antiderivative of g, then $G'(u) = g(u)$ and, by the chain rule,

$$f(x) = \frac{d}{dx}[G(u)] = G'(u)\frac{du}{dx} = g(u)\frac{du}{dx}$$

Integrating both sides of this equation, we obtain

$$\int f(x)\, dx = \int \left[g(u)\frac{du}{dx} \right] dx = \int \left[\frac{d}{dx}G(u) \right] dx = G(u) + C$$

as required. $\square$

EXAMPLE 1   Indefinite integral by substitution

Find $\displaystyle\int 9(x^2 + 3x + 5)^8 (2x + 3)\, dx$.

Solution

Look at the integral and make the observations as shown in the boxes:

If $u = x^2 + 3x + 5$,
Let $u = x^2 + 3x + 5$. $\leftarrow$ then $du = (2x + 3)\, dx$.

$$\int \underbrace{9(x^2 + 3x + 5)^8}_{\text{This is } g(u).} \underbrace{(2x + 3)\, dx}_{\text{This is } du.} = \int 9u^8\, du$$

Now complete the integration of $g(u)$ and, when you are finished, back-substitute to express u in terms of x:

$$\int 9u^8\, du = 9\left(\frac{u^9}{9} \right) + C = (x^2 + 3x + 5)^9 + C \qquad \blacksquare$$

EXAMPLE 2   Finding an integral by substitution

Find $\displaystyle\int (2x + 7)^5\, dx$.

Solution

$$\int (2x + 7)^5\, dx = \int u^5 \left(\tfrac{1}{2}\, du \right) \qquad \text{Note: If } du = 2\, dx, \text{ then } dx = \tfrac{1}{2}\, du.$$

Let $u = 2x + 7$, so $du = 2\, dx$.

$$= \tfrac{1}{2}\left[\tfrac{1}{6}u^6 \right] + C \qquad \text{Power rule for integrals}$$

$$= \tfrac{1}{12}(2x + 7)^6 + C \qquad \text{Replace } u = 2x + 7. \qquad \blacksquare$$

When choosing a substitution to evaluate $\int f(x)\,dx$, where $f(x)$ is a composite function $f(x) = g(u(x))$, it is usually a good idea to pick the "inner" function $u = u(x)$. In Example 2, we chose $u = 2x + 7$, **NOT** the entire power $(2x + 7)^5$.

When making a substitution $u = u(x)$, remember that $du = u'(x)\,dx$, so you cannot simply replace dx by du in the transformed integral. For example, when you use the substitution $u = \sin x$, you have $du = \cos x\,dx$ and then replace the entire expression $\cos x\,dx$ by du in the transformed integral, as shown in the following example.

EXAMPLE 3   Substitution with a trigonometric function

Find $\int (4 - 2\cos\theta)^3 \sin\theta\,d\theta$.

Solution

Let $u = 4 - 2\cos\theta$, so $\dfrac{du}{d\theta} = -2(-\sin\theta) = 2\sin\theta$ and $d\theta = \dfrac{du}{2\sin\theta}$; substitute:

$$\int (4 - 2\cos\theta)^3 \sin\theta\,d\theta = \int u^3 \sin\theta\,\frac{du}{2\sin\theta} = \frac{1}{2}\int u^3\,du$$

$$= \frac{1}{2}\left(\frac{u^4}{4}\right) + C = \frac{1}{8}(4 - 2\cos\theta)^4 + C \qquad\blacksquare$$

Note: We will use a shorthand notation for substitution by placing a "box" under the integrand as follows:

$$\int (4 - 2\cos\theta)^3 \sin\theta\,d\theta = \int u^3 \sin\theta\,\frac{d\theta}{2\sin\theta}$$
$$\boxed{u = 4 - 2\cos\theta;\ du = -2(-\sin\theta)\,d\theta}$$

This notation is used in the following example.

EXAMPLE 4   Substitution in an exponential integral

Evaluate $\int xe^{4-x^2}\,dx$.

Solution
$$\int xe^{4-x^2}\,dx = \int e^u\left(-\tfrac{1}{2}\,du\right)$$
$$\boxed{u = 4 - x^2;\ du = -2x\,dx}$$
$$= -\tfrac{1}{2}e^u + C$$
$$= -\tfrac{1}{2}e^{4-x^2} + C \qquad\blacksquare$$

WARNING   When using the method of substitution, all terms involving x in the original integral $\int f(x)\,dx$ must be converted into terms involving u in the transformed integral $\int g(u)\,du$. That is, after you have made your substitution and simplified, there should be no "leftover" x-values in the integrand.

EXAMPLE 5   Substitution with leftover x-values

Find $\int x(4x - 5)^3\,dx$.

Solution

$$\int x(4x-5)^3\,dx = \int xu^3\left(\frac{du}{4}\right) = \frac{1}{4}\int xu^3\,du$$

$$\boxed{u = 4x-5;\ du = 4\,dx}$$
$$\uparrow$$
$$\text{There is a leftover } x\text{-value.}$$

We are not ready to integrate until the leftover *x*-term has been eliminated. Because $u = 4x - 5$, we can solve for *x*:

$$x = \frac{u+5}{4}$$

so

$$\frac{1}{4}\int xu^3\,du = \frac{1}{4}\int\left(\frac{u+5}{4}\right)u^3\,du = \frac{1}{16}\int(u^4 + 5u^3)\,du$$

$$= \frac{1}{16}\left(\frac{u^5}{5} + 5\frac{u^4}{4}\right) + C = \frac{1}{80}(4x-5)^5 + \frac{5}{64}(4x-5)^4 + C \qquad \blacksquare$$

Note: Always introduce the constant of integration immediately after the last integration.

The next example derives formulas that will be used many times throughout the text, often enough, in fact, that you should remember them or mark them for future reference.

EXAMPLE 6   Integral formulas for the tangent and cotangent functions

Show that $\displaystyle\int \tan x\,dx = -\ln|\cos x| + C$ and $\displaystyle\int \cot x\,dx = \ln|\sin x| + C$.

Solution

$$\int \tan x\,dx = \int \frac{\sin x}{\cos x}\,dx \qquad \text{Trigonometric identity } \tan x = \frac{\sin x}{\cos x}$$

$$= \int\left(\frac{1}{\cos x}\right)(\sin x\,dx) \qquad \text{Let } u = \cos x,\ du = -\sin x\,dx.$$

$$= -\int \frac{du}{u}$$

$$= -\ln|u| + C$$

$$= -\ln|\cos x| + C$$

This can also be written as $\ln\left|(\cos x)^{-1}\right| + C = \ln|\sec x| + C$. Similarly,
$$\int \cot x\,dx = \int \frac{\cos x}{\sin x}\,dx = \ln|\sin x| + C. \qquad \blacksquare$$

Here is a problem in which the rate of change of a quantity is known and we use the method of substitution to find an expression for the quantity itself.

EXAMPLE 7   Find the volume when the rate of flow is known

Water is flowing into a tank at the rate of $\sqrt{3t+1}$ ft^3/min. If the tank is empty when $t = 0$, how much water does it contain 5 min later?

Solution

Because the rate at which the volume V is changing is dV/dt,

$$\frac{dV}{dt} = \sqrt{3t+1}$$

$$V = \int \sqrt{3t+1}\, dt = \int \sqrt{u}\,\frac{du}{3}$$

$$\boxed{u = 3t+1;\ du = 3\,dt}$$

$$V = \frac{1}{3}\int u^{1/2}\, du$$

$$= \frac{1}{3}\cdot\frac{2}{3}u^{3/2} + C$$

$$V = \tfrac{2}{9}(3t+1)^{3/2} + C$$

$V(0) = \tfrac{2}{9}(3\cdot 0 + 1)^{3/2} + C = 0$ so that $C = -\tfrac{2}{9}$ The initial volume is 0.

$V(t) = \tfrac{2}{9}(3t+1)^{3/2} - \tfrac{2}{9}$ and $V(5) = \tfrac{2}{9}(16)^{3/2} - \tfrac{2}{9} = 14$

The tank contains 14 ft^3 of water after 5 minutes. ∎

SUBSTITUTION WITH DEFINITE INTEGRATION

Example 7 could be considered as a definite integral:

$$\int_0^5 \sqrt{3t+1}\, dt = \frac{2}{9}(3t+1)^{3/2}\Big|_0^5 = \tfrac{2}{9}(16)^{3/2} - \tfrac{2}{9}(1)^{3/2} = 14$$

Notice that the definite integral eliminates the need for finding C. Furthermore, the following theorem eliminates the need for returning to the original variable (even though sometimes it is more convenient to do so).

THEOREM 5.10 Substitution with the definite integral

If $f(u)$ is a continuous function of u and $u(x)$ is a differentiable function of x, then

$$\int_a^b f[u(x)]u'(x)\, dx = \int_{u(a)}^{u(b)} f(u)\, du$$

Proof Let $F(u) = \int f(u)\, du$ be an antiderivative of $f(u)$. Then the first fundamental theorem of calculus tells us that

$$\int_a^b f[u(x)]u'(x)\, dx = F[u(x)]\big|_{x=a}^{x=b} = F[u(b)] - F[u(a)]$$

But since $F(u)$ is an antiderivative of $f(u)$, it also follows that

$$\int_{u(a)}^{u(b)} f(u)\, du = F(u)\big|_{u=u(a)}^{u=u(b)} = F[u(b)] - F[u(a)]$$

Thus,

$$\int_a^b f[u(x)]u'(x)\, dx = \int_{u(a)}^{u(b)} f(u)\, du$$ ❑

We now have two valid methods for evaluating a definite integral of the form $\int_a^b f[u(x)]u'(x)\,dx$:

1. Use substitution to evaluate the indefinite integral and then evaluate it between the limits of integration $x = a$ and $x = b$.
2. Change the limits of integration to conform with the change of variable $u = u(x)$ and evaluate the transformed definite integral between the limits of integration $u = u(a)$ and $u = u(b)$.

These two methods are illustrated in Example 8.

EXAMPLE 8   Substitution with the definite integral

Evaluate $\int_1^2 (4x - 5)^3\,dx$.

Solution

Method I: We first use a substitution with an indefinite integral.

$$\int (4x - 5)^3\,dx = \int u^3 \left(\frac{1}{4}\,du\right) = \frac{1}{4}\left(\frac{u^4}{4}\right) + C = \frac{1}{16}(4x - 5)^4 + C$$

$$\boxed{\text{Let } u = 4x - 5; \; du = 4\,dx}$$

Now evaluate the definite integral of $f(x)$ between $x = 1$ and $x = 2$ by using the fundamental theorem of calculus:

$$\int_1^2 (4x - 5)^3\,dx = \tfrac{1}{16}(4x - 5)^4 \Big|_{x=1}^{x=2}$$

$$= \tfrac{1}{16}[4(2) - 5]^4 - \tfrac{1}{16}[4(1) - 5]^4$$

$$= \tfrac{1}{16}(81) - \tfrac{1}{16}(1)$$

$$= 5$$

Method II: This is similar to method I, except that as part of the integration process, we change the limits of integration when we are doing the substitution.

$$\boxed{\text{Let } u = 4x - 5; \; du = 4\,dx.}$$

If $x = 2$, then $u = 4(2) - 5 = 3$.

$$\int_1^2 (4x - 5)^3\,dx = \int_{-1}^3 u^3\,\frac{du}{4}$$

If $x = 1$, then $u = 4(1) - 5 = -1$.

WARNING You cannot change variables and keep the orginal limits of integration because the limits of integration are expressed in terms of the variable of integration.

$$= \frac{1}{4} \cdot \frac{u^4}{4} \Big|_{-1}^{3}$$

$$= \tfrac{1}{16}(81 - 1) = 5 \qquad \blacksquare$$

5.5 PROBLEM SET

A *Problems 1–8 present pairs of integration problems, one of which will require substitution and one of which will not. As you are working these problems, think about when substitution may be appropriate.*

1. **a.** $\int_0^4 (2t + 4)\, dt$ **b.** $\int_0^4 (2t + 4)^{-1/2}\, dt$

2. **a.** $\int_0^{\pi/2} \sin\theta\, d\theta$ **b.** $\int_0^{\pi/2} \sin 2\theta\, d\theta$

3. **a.** $\int_0^{\pi} \cos t\, dt$ **b.** $\int_0^{\sqrt{\pi}} t\cos t^2\, dt$

4. **a.** $\int_0^4 \sqrt{x}\, dx$ **b.** $\int_{-4}^0 \sqrt{-x}\, dx$

5. **a.** $\int_0^{16} \sqrt[4]{x}\, dx$ **b.** $\int_{-16}^0 \sqrt[4]{-x}\, dx$

6. **a.** $\int x(3x^2 - 5)\, dx$ **b.** $\int x(3x^2 - 5)^{50}\, dx$

7. **a.** $\int x^2\sqrt{2x^3}\, dx$ **b.** $\int x^2\sqrt{2x^3 - 5}\, dx$

8. **a.** $\int \dfrac{dx}{\sqrt{1 - x^2}}$ **b.** $\int \dfrac{x\, dx}{\sqrt{1 - x^2}}$

Use substitution to evaluate the indefinite integrals in Problems 9–34.

9. $\int (2x + 3)^4\, dx$

10. $\int \sqrt{3t - 5}\, dt$

11. $\int [\tan(x^2 + 5x + 3)(2x + 5)]\, dx$

12. $\int (11 - 2x)^{-4/5}\, dx$

13. $\int (x^2 - \cos 3x)\, dx$

14. $\int \csc^2 5t\, dt$

15. $\int \sin(4 - x)\, dx$

16. $\int \cot[\ln(x^2 + 1)]\dfrac{2x\, dx}{x^2 + 1}$

17. $\int \sqrt{t}(t^{3/2} + 5)^3\, dt$

18. $\int \dfrac{(6x - 9)\, dx}{(x^2 - 3x + 5)^3}$

19. $\int x\sin(3 + x^2)\, dx$

20. $\int \sin^3 t\cos t\, dt$

21. $\int \dfrac{x\, dx}{2x^2 + 3}$

22. $\int \dfrac{x^2\, dx}{x^3 + 1}$

23. $\int x\sqrt{2x^2 + 1}\, dx$

24. $\int \dfrac{4x\, dx}{2x + 1}$

25. $\int \sqrt{x}e^{x\sqrt{x}}\, dx$

26. $\int \dfrac{e^{\sqrt[3]{x}}\, dx}{x^{2/3}}$

27. $\int x(x^2 + 4)^{1/2}\, dx$

28. $\int x^3(x^2 + 4)^{1/2}\, dx$

29. $\int \dfrac{\ln x}{x}\, dx$

30. $\int \dfrac{\ln(x + 1)}{x + 1}\, dx$

31. $\int \dfrac{dx}{\sqrt{x}(\sqrt{x} + 7)}$

32. $\int \dfrac{dx}{x^{2/3}(\sqrt[3]{x} + 1)}$

33. $\int \dfrac{e^t\, dt}{e^t + 1}$

34. $\int \dfrac{e^{\sqrt{t}}\, dt}{\sqrt{t}(e^{\sqrt{t}} + 1)}$

Evaluate the definite integrals given in Problems 35–44. Approximate the answers to Problems 43 and 44 to two significant digits.

35. $\int_0^1 \dfrac{5x^2\, dx}{2x^3 + 1}$

36. $\int_1^4 \dfrac{e^{-\sqrt{x}}\, dx}{\sqrt{x}}$

37. $\int_{-\ln 2}^{\ln 2} \dfrac{1}{2}(e^x - e^{-x})\, dx$

38. $\int_0^2 (e^x - e^{-x})^2\, dx$

39. $\int_1^2 \dfrac{e^{1/x}}{x^2}\, dx$

40. $\int_0^2 x\sqrt{2x + 1}\, dx$

41. $\int_0^{\pi/6} \tan 2x\, dx$

42. $\int_0^1 x^2(x^3 + 9)^{1/2}\, dx$

43. $\int_0^5 \dfrac{0.58}{1 + e^{-0.2x}}\, dx$

44. $\int_0^{12} \dfrac{5,000}{1 + 10e^{-t/5}}\, dt$

45. HISTORICAL QUEST   Johann Peter Gustav Lejeune Dirichlet was a professor of mathematics at the University of Berlin and is known for his role in formulating a rigorous foundation for calculus. He was not known as a good teacher. His nephew wrote that the mathematics instruction he received from Dirichlet was the most dreadful experience of his life. Howard Eves tells of the time Dirichlet was to deliver a lecture on definite integrals, but because of illness he posted the following note:

LEJEUNE DIRICHLET
1805–1859

> *Because of illness I cannot lecture today*
> *Dirichlet*

The students then doctored the note to read as follows:

> *Michaelmas*
> $\int$ *Because of illness I cannot lecture today* d *(1 Frdor)*
> *Easter*
> *Dirichlet*

Michaelmas and Easter were school holidays, and 1 Frdor (Friedrichsd'or) was the customary honorarium for a semester's worth of lectures. ■

a. What is the answer when you integrate the student-doctored note?

b. The so-called *Dirichlet function* is often used for counterexamples in calculus. Look up the definition of this function. What special property does it have?

B *Find the area of the region under the curves given in Problems 46–49.*

46. $y = t\sqrt{t^2 + 9}$ on $[0, 4]$

47. $y = \dfrac{1}{t^2}\sqrt{5 - \dfrac{1}{t}}$ on $\left[\dfrac{1}{5}, 1\right]$

48. $y = x(x-1)^{1/3}$ on $[2,9]$ **49.** $y = \dfrac{x}{\sqrt{x^2+1}}$ on $[1,3]$

50. a. In Section 5.3 (Problem 40), you were asked to prove that if f is continuous and **odd** [that is, $f(-x) = -f(x)$] on the interval $[-a, a]$, then

$$\int_{-a}^{a} f(x)\,dx = 0$$

b. In Section 5.2 (Problem 33), you were asked to find a counterexample or informally show that if f is continuous and **even** [$f(-x) = f(x)$] on the interval $[-a, a]$, then

$$\int_{-a}^{a} f(x)\,dx = 2\int_{0}^{a} f(x)\,dx = 2\int_{-a}^{0} f(x)\,dx$$

For this problem, use the properties of integrals to prove each of these statements.

Use the results of Problem 50 to evaluate the integrals given in Problems 51–54.

51. $\displaystyle\int_{-\pi}^{\pi} \sin x\,dx$ **52.** $\displaystyle\int_{-\pi/2}^{\pi/2} \cos x\,dx$

53. $\displaystyle\int_{-3}^{3} x\sqrt{x^4+1}\,dx$ **54.** $\displaystyle\int_{-1}^{1} \dfrac{\sin x\,dx}{x^2+1}$

55. In each of the following cases, determine whether the given relationship is true or false.

a. $\displaystyle\int_{-175}^{175} (7x^{1001} + 14x^{99})\,dx = 0$

b. $\displaystyle\int_{0}^{\pi} \sin^2 x\,dx = \int_{0}^{\pi} \cos^2 x\,dx$

c. $\displaystyle\int_{-\pi/2}^{\pi/2} \cos x\,dx = \int_{-\pi}^{0} \sin x\,dx$

56. The slope at each point (x, y) on the graph of $y = F(x)$ is given by $x(x^2-1)^{1/3}$, and the graph passes through the point $(3, 1)$. Use this information to find F. Sketch the graph of F.

57. The slope at each point (x, y) on the graph of $y = F(x)$ is given by $\dfrac{2x}{1-3x^2}$. What is $F(x)$ if the graph passes through $(0, 5)$?

58. A particle moves along the t-axis in such a way that at time t, its velocity is $v(t) = t^2(t^3-8)^{1/3}$.

a. At what time does the particle turn around?

b. If the particle starts at a position which we denote as 1, where does it turn around?

59. A rectangular storage tank has a square base 10 ft on a side. Water is flowing into the tank at the rate modeled by the function

$$R(t) = t(3t^2 + 1)^{-1/2} \quad \text{ft}^3/\text{s}$$

at time t seconds. If the tank is empty at time $t = 0$, how much water does it contain 4 sec later? What is the depth of the water (to the nearest quarter inch) at that time?

60. Journal Problem *College Mathematics Journal.** ■ Evaluate

$$\int [(x^2-1)(x+1)]^{-2/3}\,dx$$

61. Modeling Problem A group of environmentalists model the rate at which the ozone level is changing in a suburb of Los Angeles by the function

$$L'(t) = \dfrac{0.24 - 0.03t}{\sqrt{36 + 16t - t^2}}$$

parts per million per hour (ppm/h) t hours after 7:00 A.M.

a. Express the ozone level $L(t)$ as a function of t if L is 4 ppm at 7:00 A.M.

b. Use the graphing utility of your calculator to find the time between 7:00 A.M. and 7:00 P.M. when the highest level of ozone occurs. What is the highest level?

c. Use your graphing utility or another utility of your calculator to determine a second time during the day when the ozone level is the same as it is at 11:00 A.M.

62. A *logistic* function is one of the form $Q(t) = \dfrac{B}{1 + Ae^{-rt}}$. Evaluate $\displaystyle\int Q(t)\,dt$.

*Vol. 20, No. 4, Sept. 1989, p. 343. Problem by Murray Klamkin.

5.6   Introduction to Differential Equations

IN THIS SECTION   introduction and terminology, direction fields, separable differential equations, modeling exponential growth and decay, orthogonal trajectories, modeling fluid flow through an orifice, modeling the motion of a projectile: escape velocity

The study of differential equations is as old as calculus itself. Today, it would be virtually impossible to make a serious study of physics, astronomy, chemistry, or engineering without encountering physical models based on differential equations. In addition, differential equations are beginning to appear more frequently in the biological and social sciences, especially in economics. We begin by introducing some basic terminology and examining a few modeling procedures.

INTRODUCTION AND TERMINOLOGY

Any equation that contains a derivative or differential is called a **differential equation**. For example, the equations

$$\frac{dy}{dx} = 3x^3 + 5, \quad \frac{dP}{dt} = kP^2, \quad \left(\frac{dy}{dx}\right)^2 + 3\frac{dy}{dx} + 2y = xy, \quad \frac{d^2x}{dt^2} + 2\frac{dx}{dt} + 5t = \sin t$$

are all differential equations.

Many practical situations, especially those involving rates, can be described mathematically by differential equations. For example, the assumption that population P grows at a rate proportional to its size can be expressed by the differential equation

$$\frac{dP}{dt} = kP$$

where t is time and k is the constant of proportionality.

A **solution** of a given differential equation is a function that satisfies the equation. A **general solution** is a characterization of all possible solutions of the equation. We say that the differential equation is **solved** when we find a general solution.

For example, $y = x^2$ is a solution of the differential equation

$$\frac{dy}{dx} = 2x$$

because

$$\frac{dy}{dx} = \frac{d}{dx}(y) = \frac{d}{dx}(x^2) = 2x$$

Moreover, because any solution of this equation must be an indefinite integral of $2x$, it follows that

$$y = \int 2x \, dx = x^2 + C$$

is the general solution of the differential equation.

EXAMPLE 1   Verifying that a given function is a solution to a differential equation

If $4x - 3y^2 = 10$, verify that $\dfrac{dy}{dx} = \dfrac{2}{3y}$.

Solution

$$4x - 3y^2 = 10$$

$$\frac{d}{dx}(4x - 3y^2) = \frac{d}{dx}(10) \qquad \text{Take the derivative of both sides.}$$

$$4 - 6y\frac{dy}{dx} = 0 \qquad \text{Don't forget the chain rule, since } y \text{ is a function of } x.$$

$$\frac{dy}{dx} = \frac{4}{6y} = \frac{2}{3y} \qquad \text{Solve for } \frac{dy}{dx}. \qquad ■$$

EXAMPLE 2   Finding future revenue

An oil well that yields 300 barrels of crude oil a day will run dry in 3 years. It is estimated that t days from now the price of the crude oil will be $p(t) = 30 + 0.3\sqrt{t}$ dollars per barrel. If the oil is sold as soon as it is extracted from the ground, what will be the total future revenue from the well?

Solution

Let $R(t)$ denote the total revenue up to time t. Then the rate of change of revenue is $\frac{dR}{dt}$, the number of dollars received per barrel is $p(t) = 30 + 0.3\sqrt{t}$, and the number of barrels sold per day is 300. Thus, we have

$$\begin{bmatrix} \text{RATE OF CHANGE} \\ \text{OF TOTAL REVENUE} \end{bmatrix} = \begin{bmatrix} \text{NUMBER OF DOLLARS} \\ \text{PER BARREL} \end{bmatrix} \begin{bmatrix} \text{NUMBER OF BARRELS} \\ \text{SOLD PER DAY} \end{bmatrix}$$

$$\frac{dR}{dt} = (30 + 0.3\sqrt{t})(300)$$

$$= 9,000 + 90\sqrt{t}$$

This is actually a statement of the chain rule: $\frac{dR}{dt} = \frac{dR}{dB} \cdot \frac{dB}{dt}$, where B denotes the number of barrels extracted and R denotes the revenue. It is often helpful to use the chain rule in this way when setting up differential equations.

We solve this differential equation by integration:

$$R = \int \frac{dR}{dt}\,dt = \int (9,000 + 90\sqrt{t})\,dt$$

$$R(t) = 9,000t + 60t^{3/2} + C$$

Since $R(0) = 0$, it follows that $C = 0$. We also are given that the well will run dry in 3 years or 1,095 days, so that the total revenue obtained during the life of the well is

$$R(1,095) = 9,000(1,095) + 60(1,095)^{3/2}$$

$$\approx 12,029,064.52$$

The total future revenue is approximately \$12 million.   ■

DIRECTION FIELDS

We can use slope fields to help with a visualization of a differential equation. In Section 5.1 we looked at small segments with slope defined by the derivative of some function. The collection of all such line segments is called the *slope field* or **direction field** of the differential equation. Today, with the assistance of computers, we can sometimes draw the direction field in order to obtain a particular solution (or a family of solutions) as shown in the following example.

EXAMPLE 3   Finding a solution, given the direction field

The direction field for the differential equation

$$\frac{dy}{dx} = y - x^2$$

is shown in Figure 5.22.

a. Sketch a solution to the initial value problem passing through $(2, 1)$.
b. Sketch a solution to the initial value problem passing through $(0, 1)$.

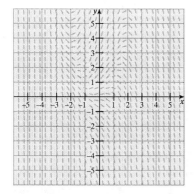

Figure 5.22 Direction field for $y' = y - x^2$

Solution

a. The initial value $y(2) = 1$ means the solution passes through $(2, 1)$ and is shown in Figure 5.23a.
b. Since $y(0) = 1$, the solution passes through $(0, 1)$, as shown in Figure 5.23b.

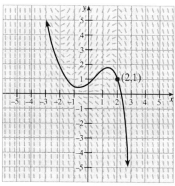
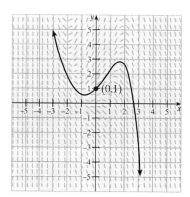

a. Solution passes through $(2, 1)$ **b.** Solution passes through $(0, 1)$

Figure 5.23 Particular solutions from a given direction field   ■

SEPARABLE DIFFERENTIAL EQUATIONS

Solving a differential equation is often a complicated process. However, many important equations can be expressed in the form

$$\frac{dy}{dx} = \frac{g(x)}{f(y)}$$

To solve such an equation, first separate the variables into the differential form

$$f(y)\,dy = g(x)\,dx$$

and then integrate both sides separately to obtain

$$\int f(y)\,dy = \int g(x)\,dx$$

A differential equation expressible in the form $dy/dx = g(x)/f(y)$ is said to be **separable**. This procedure is illustrated in Example 4.

EXAMPLE 4 Solving a separable differential equation

Solve $\dfrac{dy}{dx} = \dfrac{x}{y}$.

Solution

$$\frac{dy}{dx} = \frac{x}{y}$$
$$y\,dy = x\,dx$$
$$\int y\,dy = \int x\,dx$$
$$\tfrac{1}{2}y^2 + C_1 = \tfrac{1}{2}x^2 + C_2$$
$$x^2 - y^2 = C \qquad \text{where } C = 2(C_1 - C_2).$$

■

Notice the treatment of constants in Example 4. Because all constants can be combined into a single constant, it is customary not to write $2(C_1 - C_2)$ but rather to simply replace all the arbitrary constants in the problem by a single arbitrary constant, C, immediately after the last integral is found.

The remainder of this section is devoted to selected applications involving separable differential equations.

MODELING EXPONENTIAL GROWTH AND DECAY

A process is said to undergo **exponential change** if the relative rate of change of the process is modeled by a constant; in other words,

$$\frac{Q'(t)}{Q(t)} = k \quad \text{or} \quad \frac{dQ}{dt} = kQ(t)$$

If the constant k is positive, the exponential change is called **growth**, and if k is negative, it is called **decay**. Exponential growth occurs in certain populations, and exponential decay occurs in the disintegration of radioactive substances.

To solve the growth/decay equation, separate the variables and integrate both sides.

$$\frac{dQ}{dt} = kQ$$

$$\int \frac{dQ}{Q} = \int k\,dt$$

$$\ln|Q| = kt + C_1$$

$$e^{kt+C_1} = Q \qquad \text{Definition of natural logarithm}$$

$$e^{kt}e^{C_1} = Q$$

Thus, $Q = Ce^{kt}$, where $C = e^{C_1}$. Finally, if we let Q_0 be the initial amount (that is, when $t = 0$), we see that

$$Q_0 = Ce^0 \qquad \text{or} \qquad C = Q_0, \quad \text{so} \quad Q(t) = Q_0 e^{kt}$$

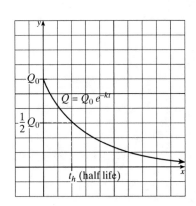

Figure 5.24 The decay curve for a radioactive substance

Growth/Decay Equation

The **growth/decay equation** of a substance is

$$Q(t) = Q_0 e^{kt}$$

where $Q(t)$ is the amount of the substance present at time t, Q_0 is the initial amount of the substance, and k is a constant that depends on the substance. If $k > 0$, it is a *growth* equation; if $k < 0$, it is a *decay* equation.

The graph of $Q = Q_0 e^{kt}$ for $k < 0$ is shown in Figure 5.24. In Figure 5.24 we have also indicated the time t_h required for half of a given substance to disintegrate. The time t_h is called the **half-life** of the substance, and it provides a measure of the substance's rate of disintegration.

EXAMPLE 5   Amount of a radioactive substance present

A particular radioactive substance has a half-life of 600 yr. Find k for this substance and determine how much of a 50-g sample will remain after 125 yr.

Solution

From the decay equation,

$$Q(t) = Q_0 e^{kt}$$

$$\frac{Q(t)}{Q_0} = e^{kt}$$

$$\frac{1}{2} = e^{k(600)} \qquad \text{Half-life is 600 years.}$$

$$k(600) = \ln \tfrac{1}{2} \qquad \text{Definition of logarithm}$$

$$k = \frac{\ln \tfrac{1}{2}}{600} \approx -0.0011552453$$

Next, to see how much of a 50-g sample will remain after 125 yr, substitute $Q_0 = 50$, $k = -0.0011552453$, and $t = 125$ into the decay equation:

$$Q(125) \approx 50e^{-0.0011552453(125)} \approx 43.27682805$$

There will be about 43 g present.   ■

One of the more interesting applications of radioactive decay is a technique known as **carbon dating**, which is used by geologists, anthropologists, and archaeologists to estimate the age of various specimens.* The technique is based on the fact that all animal and vegetable systems (whether living or dead) contain both stable carbon ^{12}C and a radioactive isotope ^{14}C. Scientists assume that the ratio of ^{14}C to ^{12}C in the air has remained approximately constant throughout history. Living systems absorb carbon dioxide from the air, so the ratio of ^{14}C to ^{12}C in a living system is the same as that in the air itself. When a living system dies, the absorption of carbon dioxide ceases. The ^{12}C already in the system remains while the ^{14}C decays, and the ratio of ^{14}C to ^{12}C decreases exponentially. The half-life of ^{14}C is approximately 5,730 years. The ratio of ^{14}C to ^{12}C in a specimen t years after it was alive is approximately

$$R = R_0 e^{kt}$$

where $k = \dfrac{\ln(1/2)}{5,730}$ and R_0 is the ratio of ^{14}C to ^{12}C in the atmosphere. By comparing $R(t)$ with R_0, scientists can estimate the age of the object. Here is an example.

EXAMPLE 6   Modeling Problem: Carbon dating

An archaeologist has found a specimen in which the ratio of ^{14}C to ^{12}C is 20% the ratio found in the atmosphere. Approximately how old is the specimen?

Solution

The age of the specimen is the value of t for which $R(t) = 0.20R_0$:

$$0.20R_0 = R_0 e^{kt}$$
$$0.20 = e^{kt}$$
$$kt = \ln 0.20$$
$$t = \frac{1}{k} \ln 0.2 \qquad k = \frac{\ln(1/2)}{5,730}$$
$$\approx 13,304.64798$$

The specimen is approximately 13,000 yr old.   ■

ORTHOGONAL TRAJECTORIES

A curve that intersects each member of a given family of curves at right angles is called an **orthogonal trajectory** of that family and is shown in Figure 5.25. Orthogonal families arise in many applications. For example, in thermodynamics, the heat flow across a planar surface is orthogonal to the curves of constant temperature, called *isotherms*. In the theory of fluid flow, the flow lines are orthogonal trajectories of *velocity potential curves*. The basic procedure for finding orthogonal trajectories involves differential equations and is demonstrated in Example 7.

---

*Carbon dating is used primarily for estimating the age of relatively "recent" specimens. For example, it was used (along with other methods) to determine that the Dead Sea Scrolls were written and deposited in the Caves of Qumran approximately 2,000 years ago. For dating older specimens, it is better to use techniques based on radioactive substances with longer half-lives. In particular, potassium 40 is often used as a "clock" for events that occurred between 5 and 15 million years ago. Paleoanthropologists find this substance especially valuable because it often occurs in volcanic deposits and can be used to date specimens trapped in such deposits. See Mathematical Essay 5 on page 352.

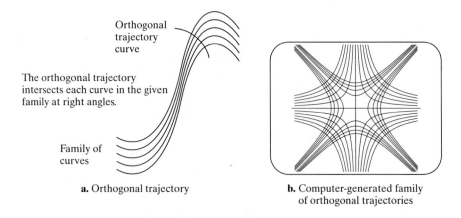

a. Orthogonal trajectory   **b.** Computer-generated family
of orthogonal trajectories

Figure 5.25   Orthogonal trajectories

EXAMPLE 7   Finding orthogonal trajectories

Find the orthogonal trajectories of the family of curves of the form $xy = C$.

Solution

We are seeking a family of curves. Each curve in that family intersects each curve in
the family $xy = C$ at right angles, as shown in Figure 5.26. Assume that a typical
point on a given curve in the family $xy = C$ has coordinates (x, y) and that a typical
point on the orthogonal trajectory curve has coordinates (X, Y).[*]

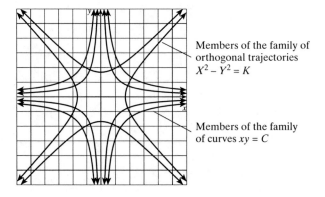

Members of the family of
orthogonal trajectories
$X^2 - Y^2 = K$

Members of the family
of curves $xy = C$

Figure 5.26   The family of curves $xy = C$ and their orthogonal trajectories

Let P be a point where a particular curve of the form $xy = C$ intersects the
orthogonal trajectory curve. At P, we have $x = X$ and $y = Y$, and the slope dY/dX
of the orthogonal trajectory is the same as the negative reciprocal of the slope dy/dx
of the curve $xy = C$. Using implicit differentiation, we find

$$xy = C$$

$$x\frac{dy}{dx} + y = 0 \qquad \text{Product rule}$$

$$\frac{dy}{dx} = \frac{-y}{x}$$

---

[*]We use uppercase letters for one kind of curve and lowercase for the other to make it easier to tell
which curve is being mentioned at each stage of the following discussion.

Thus, at the point of intersection P, the slope $\dfrac{dY}{dX}$ of the orthogonal trajectory is

$$\frac{dY}{dX} = -\frac{1}{\dfrac{dy}{dx}} = -\frac{1}{\dfrac{-y}{x}} = \frac{x}{y} = \frac{X}{Y}$$

According to this equation, the coordinates (X, Y) of the orthogonal trajectory curve satisfy the separable differential equation

$$\frac{dY}{dX} = \frac{X}{Y}$$

discussed in Example 4. Using the result of that example, we see that the orthogonal trajectories of the family $xy = C$ are the curves in the family

$$X^2 - Y^2 = K$$

where K is a constant. The given family of curves $xy = C$ and the family of orthogonal trajectory curves $X^2 - Y^2 = K$ are shown in Figure 5.26.   ∎

MODELING FLUID FLOW THROUGH AN ORIFICE

Consider a tank that is filled with a fluid being slowly drained through a small, sharp-edged hole in its base, as shown in Figure 5.27. By using a principle of physics known as Torricelli's law,[†] we can show that the rate of discharge dV/dt at time t is proportional to the square root of the depth h at that time. Specifically, if all dimensions are given in terms of feet, the drain hole has area A_0, and the height above the hole is h at time t (seconds), then

$$\frac{dV}{dt} = -4.8 A_0 \sqrt{h}$$

is the rate of flow of water in cubic feet per second. This formula is used in Example 8.

Fluid has height h above a hole of area A_0.

Figure 5.27 The flow of a fluid through an orifice

EXAMPLE 8   Fluid flow through an orifice

A cylindrical tank (with a circular base) is filled with a liquid that is draining through a small circular hole in its base. If the tank is 9 ft high with radius 4 ft and the drain hole has radius 1 in., how long does it take for the tank to empty?

Solution

Because the drain hole is a circle of radius $\frac{1}{12}$ ft (= 1 in.), its area is $\pi r^2 = \pi \left(\frac{1}{12}\right)^2$, and the rate of flow is

$$\frac{dV}{dt} = -4.8 \left(\frac{\pi}{144}\right) \sqrt{h}$$

Because the tank is cylindrical, the amount of fluid in the tank at any particular time will form a cylinder of radius 4 ft and height h. Also, because we are using $g = 32$ ft/s^2, it is implied that the time, t, is measured in seconds. The volume of such a liquid cylinder is

$$V = \pi r^2 h = \pi (4)^2 h = 16\pi h$$

[†]Torricelli's law says that the stream of liquid through the orifice has velocity $\sqrt{2gh}$, where $g = 32$ ft/s^2 is the acceleration due to gravity and h is the height of the liquid above the orifice. The factor 4.8 that appears in the rate of flow equation is required to compensate for the effect of friction.

and by differentiating both sides of this equation with respect to t, we obtain

$$\frac{dV}{dt} = 16\pi \frac{dh}{dt}$$

$$-4.8 \left(\frac{\pi}{144} \right) \sqrt{h} = 16\pi \frac{dh}{dt} \qquad \text{Torricelli's law}$$

$$\frac{dh}{dt} = \frac{-4.8\sqrt{h}}{144(16)} \approx -0.0021\sqrt{h}$$

$$\frac{1}{\sqrt{h}} dh = -0.0021\, dt \qquad \text{Separate the variables.}$$

$$\int h^{-1/2} dh = \int (-0.0021)\, dt \qquad \text{Integrate both sides.}$$

$$2h^{1/2} + C_1 = -0.0021t + C_2$$

$$2\sqrt{h} = -0.0021t + C$$

To evaluate C, recall that the tank is full at time $t = 0$. Thus, $h = 9$ when $t = 0$, so

$$2\sqrt{9} = -0.0021(0) + C, \quad \text{or} \quad C = 6$$

and the general formula is

$$2\sqrt{h} = -0.0021t + 6$$

where time t is in seconds (because g is 32 ft/s^2).

Now we can find the depth of the fluid at any given time or the time at which a prescribed depth occurs. In particular, the tank is empty at the time t_e when $h = 0$. By substituting $h = 0$ into this formula we find

$$2\sqrt{0} = -0.0021t_e + 6 \quad \text{so that} \quad t_e \approx 2,880 \text{ sec}$$

Thus, roughly 48 min are required to drain the tank.   ■

MODELING THE MOTION OF A PROJECTILE: ESCAPE VELOCITY

Consider a projectile that is launched with initial velocity v_0 from a planet's surface along a direct line through the center of the planet, as shown in Figure 5.28. We will find a general formula for the velocity of the projectile and the minimal value of v_0 required to guarantee that the projectile will escape the planet's gravitational attraction.

We assume that the only force acting on the projectile is that due to gravity, although in practice, factors such as air resistance must also be considered. With this assumption, Newton's law of gravitation can be used to show that when the projectile is at a distance s from the center of the planet, its acceleration is given by the formula

$$a = \frac{-gR^2}{s^2}$$

where R is the radius of the planet and g is the acceleration due to gravity at the planet's surface (see Problem 69).*

Our first goal is to express the velocity v of the projectile in terms of the height s. Because the projectile travels along a straight line, we know that

$$a = \frac{dv}{dt} \quad \text{and} \quad v = \frac{ds}{dt}$$

and by applying the chain rule, we see that

$$a = \frac{dv}{dt} = \frac{dv}{ds} \cdot \frac{ds}{dt} = \frac{dv}{ds} v$$

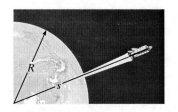

Figure 5.28 A projectile launched from the surface of a planet

---

*According to Newton's law of gravitation, the force of gravity acting on a projectile of mass m has magnitude $F = mk/s^2$, where k is constant. If this is the only force acting on the projectile, then $F = ma$, and we have $ma = F = mk/s^2$. By canceling the m's on each side of the equation, we obtain $a = k/s^2$.

Therefore, by substitution for a we have

$$\frac{dv}{ds}v = \frac{-gR^2}{s^2}$$

$$v\,dv = -gR^2 s^{-2}\,ds$$

$$\int v\,dv = \int -gR^2 s^{-2}\,ds$$

$$\tfrac{1}{2}v^2 + C_1 = gR^2 s^{-1} + C_2$$

$$v^2 = 2gR^2 s^{-1} + C$$

To evaluate the constant C, recall that the projectile was fired from the planet's surface with initial velocity v_0. Thus, $v = v_0$ when $s = R$, and by substitution

$$v_0^2 = 2gR^2 R^{-1} + C, \quad \text{which implies} \quad C = v_0^2 - 2gR$$

so

$$v^2 = 2gR^2 s^{-1} + v_0^2 - 2gR$$

Because the projectile is launched in a direction away from the center of the planet, we would expect it to keep moving in that direction until it stops. In other words, *the projectile will keep moving away from the planet until it reaches a point where $v = 0$.* Because $2gR^2 s^{-1} > 0$ for all $s > 0$, v^2 will always be positive if $v_0^2 - 2gR \geq 0$. On the other hand, if $v_0^2 - 2gR < 0$, then sooner or later v will become 0 and the projectile will eventually fall back to the surface of the planet.

Therefore, we conclude that the projectile will escape from the planet's gravitational attraction if $v_0^2 \geq 2gR$; that is, $v_0 \geq \sqrt{2gR}$. For this reason, the minimum speed for which this can occur, namely,

$$v_0 = \sqrt{2gR}$$

is called the **escape velocity** of the planet. In particular, for the earth, $R = 3,956$ mi and $g = 32$ ft/s^2 = 0.00606 mi/s^2, and the escape velocity is

$$v_0 = \sqrt{2gR} \approx \sqrt{2(0.00606)(3,956)} \approx 6.924357$$

The escape velocity for the earth is 6.92 mi/s.

5.6 PROBLEM SET

A *Verify in Problems 1–8 that if y satisfies the prescribed relationship with x, then it will be a solution of the given differential equation.*

1. If $x^2 + y^2 = 7$, then $\dfrac{dy}{dx} = -\dfrac{x}{y}$.

2. If $5x^2 - 2y^2 = 3$, then $\dfrac{dy}{dx} = \dfrac{5x}{2y}$.

3. If $xy = C$, then $\dfrac{dy}{dx} = \dfrac{-y}{x}$.

4. If $x^2 - 3xy + y^2 = 5$, then $(2x - 3y)\,dx + (2y - 3x)\,dy = 0$.

5. If $y = \sin(Ax + B)$, then $\dfrac{d^2y}{dx^2} + A^2 y = 0$.

6. If $y = \dfrac{x^4}{20} - \dfrac{A}{x} + B$, then $x\dfrac{d^2y}{dx^2} + 2\dfrac{dy}{dx} = x^3$.

7. If $y = 2e^{-x} + 3e^{2x}$, then $y'' - y' - 2y = 0$.

8. If $y = Ae^x + Be^x \ln x$, then $xy'' + (1 - 2x)y' - (1 - x)y = 0$.

Find the particular solution of the first-order linear differential equations in Problems 9–14. A graphical solution within its direction field is shown.

9. $\dfrac{dy}{dx} = -\dfrac{x}{y}$
passing through $(2, 2)$

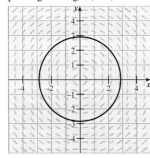

10. $\dfrac{dy}{dx} - y = 10$
passing through $(-2, -9)$

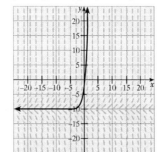

11. $\dfrac{dy}{dx} - y^2 = 1$
passing through $(\pi, 1)$

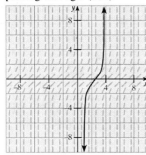

12. $\dfrac{dy}{dx} = e^{x+y}$
passing through $(0, 0)$

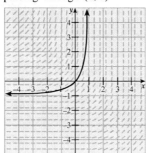

13. $\dfrac{dy}{dx} = \sqrt{\dfrac{x}{y}}$
passing through $(4, 1)$

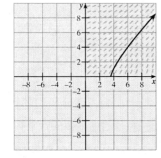

14. $\dfrac{dy}{dx} = y^2\sqrt{x}$
passing through $\left(9, -\dfrac{1}{18}\right)$

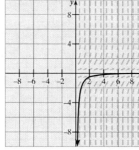

In each of Problems 15–20, sketch the particular solution passing through the given point for the differential equation whose direction field is given.

15. $(0, 1)$

16. $(0, 1)$

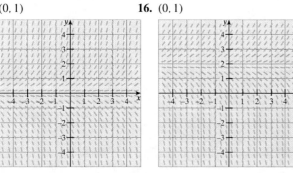

17. $(0, 0)$

18. $(3, 3)$

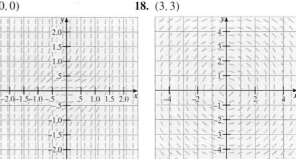

19. $(1, 0)$

20. $(0, 0)$

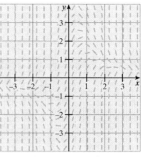

Find the general solution of the separable differential equations given in Problems 21–30. Note that for some problems, the general solution will be a relationship between x and y, rather than $y = f(x)$.

21. $\dfrac{dy}{dx} = 3xy$

22. $\dfrac{dy}{dx} = \sqrt{\dfrac{y}{x}}$

23. $\dfrac{dy}{dx} = \dfrac{x}{y}\sqrt{1 - x^2}$

24. $\dfrac{dy}{dx} = (y - 4)^2$

25. $xy\,dx + \sqrt{xy}\,dy = 0$

26. $\dfrac{dy}{dx} = \dfrac{y}{\sqrt{1 - 2x^2}}$

27. $\dfrac{dy}{dx} = \dfrac{\sin x}{\cos y}$

28. $x^2\,dy + \sec y\,dx = 0$

29. $xy\dfrac{dy}{dx} = \dfrac{\ln x}{\sqrt{1 - y^2}}$

30. $\dfrac{dy}{dx} = e^{y-x}$

In Problems 31–34, find the general solution of the given differential equation by using either the product or the quotient rule.

31. $x\,dy + y\,dx = 0$

32. $\dfrac{x\,dy - y\,dx}{x^2} = 0$

33. $y\,dx = x\,dy,\ x > 0,\ y > 0$

34. $x^2 y\,dy + xy^2\,dx = 0$

B *Find the orthogonal trajectories of the family of curves given in Problems 35–42. In each case, sketch several members of the given family of curves and several members of the family of orthogonal trajectories on the same coordinate axes.*

35. the lines $2x - 3y = C$

36. the lines $y = x + C$

37. the cubic curves $y = x^3 + C$

38. the curves $y = x^4 + C$

39. the curves $xy^2 = C$

40. the parabolas $y^2 = 4kx$

41. the circles $x^2 + y^2 = r^2$

42. the exponential curves $y = Ce^{-x}$

Modeling Problems Write a differential equation to model the situation given in each of Problems 43–48. Be sure to define your unknown function first. Do not solve.

43. The number of bacteria in a culture grows at a rate that is proportional to the number present.

44. A sample of radium decays at a rate that is proportional to the amount of radium present in the sample.

45. The rate at which the temperature of an object changes is proportional to the difference between its own temperature and the temperature of the surrounding medium.

46. When a person is asked to recall a set of facts, the rate at which the facts are recalled is proportional to the number of relevant facts in the person's memory that have not yet been recalled. *Hint:* Let Q denote the number of facts recalled and N the total number of relevant facts in the person's memory.

47. The rate at which an epidemic spreads through a community of P susceptible people is proportional to the product of the number of people who have caught the disease and the number who have not.

48. The rate at which people are implicated in a government scandal is proportional to the product of the number of people already implicated and the number of people involved who have not yet been implicated.

49. What do you think the orthogonal trajectories of the family of curves $x^2 - y^2 = C$ will be? Verify your conjecture. *Hint:* Take another look at Example 7.

50. The following is a list of six families of curves. Sketch several members of each family and then determine which pairs are orthogonal trajectories of one another.
    a. the circles $x^2 + y^2 = A$ b. the ellipses $2x^2 + y^2 = B^2$
    c. the ellipses $x^2 + 2y^2 = C$ d. the lines $y = Cx$
    e. the parabolas $y^2 = Cx$ f. the parabolas $y = Cx^2$

51. The Dead Sea Scrolls were written on parchment in about 100 B.C. What percentage of ^{14}C originally contained in the parchment remained when the scrolls were discovered in 1947?

52. Tests of an artifact discovered at the Debert site in Nova Scotia show that 28% of the original ^{14}C is still present. What is the probable age of the artifact?

53. HISTORICAL QUEST The Shroud of Turin is a rectangular linen cloth kept in the Chapel of the Holy Shroud in the cathedral of St. John the Baptist in Turin, Italy. It shows the image of a man whose wounds correspond with the biblical accounts of the crucifixion.

In 1389, Pierre d'Arcis, the Bishop of Troyes, wrote a memo to the Pope, accusing a colleague of passing off "a certain cloth, cunningly painted" as the burial shroud of Jesus Christ. Despite this early testimony of forgery, this so-called Shroud of Turin has survived as a famous relic. In 1988, a small sample of the Shroud of Turin was taken and scientists from Oxford University, the University of Arizona, and the Swiss Federal Institute of Technology were permitted to test

it. It was found that the cloth contained 92.3% of the original ^{14}C.

According to this information, how old is the Shroud?

54. A cylindrical tank of radius 3 ft is filled with water to a depth of 5 ft. Determine how long (to the nearest minute) it takes to drain the tank through a sharp-edged circular hole in the bottom with radius 2 in.

55. Rework Problem 54 for a tank with a sharp-edged drain hole that is square with side of length 1.5 in.

56. **Experiment** A rectangular tank has a square base 2 ft on a side that is filled with water to a depth of 4 ft. It is being drained from the bottom of the tank through a sharp-edged square hole that is 2 in. on a side.
    a. Show that at time t, the depth h satisfies the differential equation
    $$\frac{dh}{dt} = -\frac{1}{30}\sqrt{h}$$
    b. How long will it take to empty the tank?
    c. Construct this tank and then drain it out of the 4 in.^{2} hole. Is the time that it takes consistent with your answer to part **b**?

57. A toy rocket is launched from the surface of the earth with initial velocity $v_0 = 150$ ft/s. (The radius of the earth is roughly 3,956 mi, and $g = 32$ ft/s^2.)
    a. Determine the velocity (to the nearest ft/s) of the rocket when it is first 200 feet above the ground. (Remember, this is not the same as 200 ft from the center of the earth.)
    b. What is s when $v = 0$? Determine the maximum height above the ground that is attained by the rocket.

58. Determine the escape velocity of each of the following heavenly bodies:
    a. moon ($R = 1,080$ mi; $g = 5.5$ ft/s^2)
    b. Mars ($R = 2,050$ mi; $g = 12$ ft/s^2)
    c. Venus ($R = 3,800$ mi; $g = 28$ ft/s^2)

59. Population statistics indicate that t years after 1990, a certain city was growing at a rate of approximately $1,500t^{-1/2}$ people per year. In 1994, the population of the city was 39,000.
    a. What was the population in 1990?
    b. If this pattern continued, how many people were living in the city in the year 1999?

60. The radius of planet X is one-fourth that of planet Y, and the acceleration due to gravity at the surface of X is eight-ninths that at the surface of Y. If the escape velocity of planet X is 6 ft/s, what is the escape velocity of planet Y?

61. A survey indicates that the population of a certain town is growing in such a way that the rate of growth at time t is proportional to the square root of the population P at the time. If the population was 4,000 ten years ago and is observed to be 9,000 now, how long will it take before 16,000 people live in the town?

62. A scientist has discovered a radioactive substance that disintegrates in such a way that at time t, the rate of disintegration is proportional to the *square* of the amount present.
    a. If a 100-g sample of the substance dwindles to only 80 g in 1 day, how much will be left after 6 days?
    b. When will only 10 g be left?

63. The shape of a tank is such that when it is filled to a depth of h feet, it contains $V = 9\pi h^3$ ft^3 of water. The tank is being drained through a sharp-edged circular hole of radius 1 in. If the tank is originally filled to a depth of 4 ft, how long does it take for the tank to empty?

64. A rectangular tank has a square base 4 ft on a side and is 10 ft high. Originally, it was filled with water to a depth of 6 feet, but now is being drained from the bottom of the tank through a sharp-edged square hole 1 in. on a side.
    a. Find an equation involving the rate dh/dt.
    b. How long will it take to drain the tank?

65. The radioactive substance neptunium-139 decays to 73.36% of its original amount after 24 hours. How long would it take for 43% of the original neptunium to be present? What is the half-life of neptunium-139?

66. A certain artifact is tested by carbon dating and found to contain 73% of its original carbon-14. As a cross-check, it is also dated using radium and is found to contain 32% of the original amount. Assuming the dating procedures are accurate, what is the half-life of radium?

67. The radioactive isotope gallium-67 (symbol ^{67}Ga) used in the diagnosis of malignant tumors has a half-life of 46.5 hours. If we start with 100 mg of ^{67}Ga, what percent is lost between the 30th and 35th hours? Is this the same as the percent lost over any other 5-hour period?

C 68. **Modeling Problem** A projectile is launched from the surface of a planet whose radius is R and where the acceleration due to gravity at the surface is g.
    a. If the initial velocity v_0 of the projectile satisfies $v_0 < \sqrt{2gR}$, show that the maximum height above the surface of the planet reached by the projectile is
    $$h = \frac{v_0^2 R}{2gR - v_0^2}$$
    b. On a certain planet, it is known that $g = 25$ ft/s^2. A projectile is fired with an initial velocity of $v_0 = 2$ mi/s and attains a maximum height of 450 mi. What is the radius of the planet?

69. A projectile is launched from the surface of a planet whose radius is R and where the constant acceleration due to gravity

is g. According to Newton's law of gravitation, the force of gravity acting on a projectile of mass m has magnitude
$$F = \frac{mk}{s^2}$$
where k is a constant. If this is the only force acting on the projectile, then $F = ma$, where a is the acceleration of the projectile. Show that
$$a = \frac{-gR^2}{s^2}$$

70. **Modeling Problem** In physics, it is shown that the amount of heat Q (calories) that flows through an object by conduction will satisfy the differential equation
$$\frac{dQ}{dt} = -kA\frac{dT}{ds}$$
where t (seconds) is the time of flow, k is a physical constant (the *thermal conductivity* of the object), A is the surface area of the object measured at right angles to the direction of flow, and T is the temperature at a point s centimeters within the object, measured in the direction of the flow, as shown in Figure 5.29.

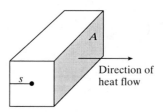

Figure 5.29 Heat conduction through an object

Under certain conditions (equilibrium), the rate of heat flow dQ/dt will be constant. Assuming these conditions exist, find the number of calories that will flow each second across the face of a square pane of glass 2 cm thick and 50 cm on a side if the temperature on one side of the pane is 5°C and on the other side is 60°C. The thermal conductivity of glass is approximately $k = 0.0025$.

5.7   The Mean Value Theorem for Integrals; Average Value

IN THIS SECTION   mean value theorem for integrals, modeling average value of a function

MEAN VALUE THEOREM FOR INTEGRALS

In Section 4.2 we established a very useful theoretical tool called the mean value theorem, which said that under reasonable conditions, there is at least one number c in the interval (a, b) such that
$$\frac{f(b) - f(a)}{b - a} = f'(c)$$

The mean value theorem for integrals is similar, and in the special case where $f(x) \geq 0$ it has a geometric interpretation that makes the theorem easy to understand.

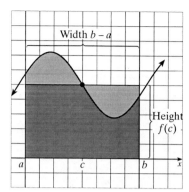

Width $b - a$

Height $f(c)$

a c b x

The shaded rectangle has the same area as the region under the curve $y = f(x)$ on $[a, b]$.

Figure 5.30 Geometric interpretation of the mean value theorem for integrals

In particular, the theorem says that it is possible to find at least one number c on the interval (a, b) such that the area of the rectangle with height $f(c)$ and width $(b - a)$ has exactly the same area as the region under the curve $y = f(x)$ on $[a, b]$. This is illustrated in Figure 5.30.

THEOREM 5.11 Mean value theorem for integrals

If f is continuous on the interval $[a, b]$, then there is at least one number c between a and b such that

$$\int_a^b f(x)\, dx = f(c)(b - a)$$

Proof Suppose M and m are the absolute maximum and the absolute minimum of f, respectively, on $[a, b]$. This means that

$$m \leq \qquad f(x) \qquad \leq M \quad \text{when } a \leq x \leq b$$

$$\int_a^b m\, dx \leq \quad \int_a^b f(x)\, dx \quad \leq \int_a^b M\, dx \qquad \text{Dominance rule}$$

$$m(b - a) \leq \quad \int_a^b f(x)\, dx \quad \leq M(b - a)$$

$$m \leq \frac{1}{b - a} \int_a^b f(x)\, dx \leq M$$

Because f is continuous on the closed interval $[a, b]$ and because the number

$$I = \frac{1}{b - a} \int_a^b f(x)\, dx$$

lies between m and M, the intermediate value theorem (Theorem 2.6 of Section 2.3) says that there exists a number c between a and b for which $f(c) = I$; that is,

$$\frac{1}{b - a} \int_a^b f(x)\, dx = f(c)$$

$$\int_a^b f(x)\, dx = f(c)(b - a) \qquad \qquad \square$$

The mean value theorem for integrals does not specify how to determine c. It simply guarantees the existence of at least one number c in the interval. However, Example 1 shows how to find a value of c guaranteed by this theorem for a particular function and interval.

EXAMPLE 1 Finding c using the mean value theorem for integrals

Find a value of c guaranteed by the mean value theorem for integrals for $f(x) = \sin x$ on $[0, \pi]$.

Solution

$$\int_0^\pi \sin x\, dx = -\cos x \big|_0^\pi = -\cos \pi + \cos 0 = -(-1) + 1 = 2$$

The region bounded by f and the x-axis on $[0, \pi]$ is shaded in Figure 5.31.

The mean value theorem for integrals asserts the existence of a number c on $[0, \pi]$ such that $f(c)(b - a) = 2$. We can solve this equation to find this value:

$$f(c)(b - a) = 2$$

$$(\sin c)(\pi - 0) = 2$$

$$\sin c = \frac{2}{\pi}$$

$$c \approx 0.690107 \quad \text{or} \quad 2.451486$$

Because each choice of c is between 0 and π, we have found two values of c guaranteed by the mean value theorem for integrals. ∎

y

1.5

$\int_0^\pi \sin x\, dx = 2$

$f(c)$ 1.0

$f(x) = \sin x$ on $[0, \pi]$

0.5

c π x

Find c such that area of the rectangle equals the area under the curve.

Figure 5.31 Graph of $f(x) = \sin x$ illustrating the mean value theorem on $[0, \pi]$

MODELING AVERAGE VALUE OF A FUNCTION

There are many practical situations in which one is interested in the *average value* of a continuous function on an interval, such as the average level of air pollution over a 24-hour period, the average speed of a truck during a 3-hour trip, or the average productivity of a worker during a production run.

You probably know that the average value of n numbers $x_1, x_2, \ldots, x_n$ is

$$\frac{x_1 + x_2 + \cdots + x_n}{n}$$

but what if there are infinitely many numbers? Specifically, what is the average value of $f(x)$ on the interval $a \leq x \leq b$? To see how the definition of finite average value can be used, imagine that the interval $[a, b]$ is divided into n equal subintervals, each of width

$$\Delta x = \frac{b - a}{n}$$

For $k = 1, 2, \ldots, n$, let x_k^* be a number chosen arbitrarily from the kth subinterval. Then the average value AV of f on $[a, b]$ is estimated by the sum

$$S_n = \frac{f(x_1^*) + f(x_2^*) + \cdots + f(x_n^*)}{n} = \frac{1}{n} \sum_{k=1}^{n} f(x_k^*)$$

Because $\Delta x = \dfrac{b - a}{n}$, we know that $\dfrac{1}{n} = \dfrac{1}{b - a} \Delta x$ and

$$S_n = \frac{1}{n} \sum_{k=1}^{n} f(x_k^*) = \left[\frac{1}{b - a} \Delta x \right] \sum_{k=1}^{n} f(x_k^*) = \frac{1}{b - a} \sum_{k=1}^{n} f(x_k^*) \Delta x$$

The sum on the right is a Riemann sum with norm $\|P\| = \dfrac{b - a}{n}$. It is reasonable to expect the estimating average S_n to approach the "true" average value AV of $f(x)$ on $[a, b]$ as $n \to +\infty$. Thus, we model average value by

$$AV = \lim_{n \to +\infty} \frac{1}{b - a} \sum_{k=1}^{n} f(x_k^*) \Delta x = \frac{1}{b - a} \int_a^b f(x)\, dx$$

We use this integral as the definition of average value.

Average Value

> If f is continuous on the interval $[a, b]$, the **average value** (AV) of f on this interval is given by the integral
>
> $$AV = \frac{1}{b - a} \int_a^b f(x)\, dx$$

EXAMPLE 2   Modeling average speed of traffic

Suppose a study suggests that between the hours of 1:00 P.M. and 4:00 P.M. on a normal weekday the speed of the traffic at a certain expressway exit is modeled by the formula

$$S(t) = 2t^3 - 21t^2 + 60t + 20$$

kilometers per hour, where t is the number of hours past noon. Compute the average speed of the traffic between the hours of 1:00 P.M. and 4:00 P.M.

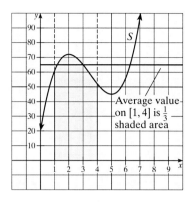

Figure 5.32 Graph of S and the average value

Solution

Our goal is to find the average value of $S(t)$ on the interval $[1, 4]$. The average speed is

$$\frac{1}{4-1}\int_1^4 (2t^3 - 21t^2 + 60t + 20)\, dt = \frac{1}{3}\left[\frac{1}{2}t^4 - 7t^3 + 30t^2 + 20t\right]_1^4$$

$$= \frac{1}{3}(240 - 43.5) = 65.5$$

The function, as well as the average value, is shown in Figure 5.32. ■

According to the mean value theorem for integrals, we have

$$\frac{1}{b-a}\int_a^b f(x)\, dx = f(c)$$

which says that the *average value of a continuous function f on $[a, b]$ equals the value of f for at least one number c between a and b.* This is quite reasonable since the intermediate value theorem for continuous functions assures us that a continuous function f assumes every value between its maximum M and minimum m, and we would expect the average value to be between these two extremes. Example 3 illustrates one way of using these ideas.

EXAMPLE 3   Modeling average temperature

Suppose that during a typical winter day in Minneapolis, the temperature (in degrees Celsius) x hours after midnight is modeled by the formula

$$T(x) = 2 - \tfrac{1}{7}(x - 13)^2$$

A graph of this formula is shown in Figure 5.33. Find the average temperature over the time period from 2:00 A.M. to 2:00 P.M., and find a time when the average temperature actually occurs.

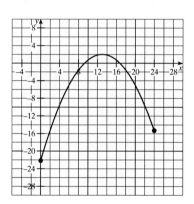

Figure 5.33 Graph of temperatures in Minneapolis over a 24-hour period

Solution

We wish to find the average temperature T on the interval $[2, 14]$ (because 2 P.M. is 14 hours after midnight). The average value is

$$T = \frac{1}{14-2}\int_2^{14}\left[2 - \frac{1}{7}(x - 13)^2\right] dx = \frac{1}{12}\left[2x - \frac{1}{7}\cdot\frac{1}{3}(x - 13)^3\right]\Bigg|_2^{14}$$

$$= \frac{1}{12}\left[\frac{587}{21} - \frac{1,415}{21}\right] \approx -3.2857143$$

Thus, the average temperature on the given time period is approximately 3.3°C below zero. To determine when this temperature actually occurs, solve the equation

$$\text{AVERAGE TEMPERATURE} = \text{TEMPERATURE AT TIME } x$$

$$-3.2857143 = 2 - \tfrac{1}{7}(x - 13)^2$$

$$37 = (x - 13)^2$$

$$x = 13 \pm \sqrt{37} \approx 19.082763 \quad \text{or} \quad 6.9172375$$

The first value is to be rejected because it is not in the interval $[2, 14]$, so we find that the average temperature occurs 6.917 hr after midnight, or at approximately 6:55 A.M. ■

EXAMPLE 4   Modeling average population

The logistic formula

$$P(t) = \frac{202.31}{1 + e^{3.938 - 0.314t}}$$

was developed by the United States Bureau of the Census to represent the population of the United States (in millions) during the period 1790–1990. Time t in the formula is the number of decades after 1790. Thus, $t = 0$ for 1790, $t = 20$ for 1990. Use this formula to compute the average population of the United States between 1790 and 1990. When did the average population actually occur?

Solution

The average population is given by the integral

$$A = \frac{1}{20 - 0} \int_0^{20} \frac{202.31 \, dt}{1 + e^{3.938 - 0.314t}} \qquad \text{Multiply by } \frac{e^{0.314t}}{e^{0.314t}}.$$

$$= \frac{1}{20} \int_0^{20} \frac{202.31 e^{0.314t}}{e^{0.314t} + e^{3.938}} \, dt \qquad \text{Let } u = e^{0.314t} + e^{3.938};$$
$$du = 0.314 e^{0.314t} \, dt.$$

$$= \frac{1}{20} \left(\frac{202.31}{0.314} \right) \int_{t=0}^{t=20} \frac{du}{u}$$

$$= \frac{1}{20} \left(\frac{202.31}{0.314} \right) \ln \left| e^{0.314t} + e^{3.938} \right| \Big|_0^{20} \approx 77.7827445296$$

To find when the average population of 77.7827 million actually occurred, solve $P(t) = 77.7827$:

$$\frac{202.31}{1 + e^{3.938 - 0.314t}} = 77.7827$$

$$e^{3.938 - 0.314t} = \frac{202.31}{77.7827} - 1$$

$$3.938 - 0.314t = \ln \left(\frac{202.31}{77.7827} - 1 \right)$$

$$t \approx 11.043$$

The average population occurred approximately 11 decades after 1790, around the year 1900.   ∎

5.7   PROBLEM SET

A *In Problems 1–10, find c such that*

$$\int_a^b f(x) \, dx = f(c)(b - a)$$

as guaranteed by the mean value theorem for integrals. If you cannot find such a value, explain why the theorem does not apply.

1. $f(x) = 4x^3$ on $[1, 2]$

2. $f(x) = x^2 + 4x + 1$ on $[0, 2]$

3. $f(x) = 15x^{-2}$ on $[1, 5]$

4. $f(x) = 12x^{-3}$ on $[-3, 3]$

5. $f(x) = 2 \csc^2 x$ on $\left[-\frac{\pi}{3}, \frac{\pi}{3} \right]$

6. $f(x) = \cos x$ on $\left[-\frac{\pi}{2}, \frac{\pi}{2} \right]$

7. $f(x) = e^{2x}$ on $\left[-\frac{1}{2}, \frac{1}{2} \right]$

8. $f(x) = \dfrac{x}{1 + x}$ on $[0, 1]$

9. $f(x) = \dfrac{x + 1}{1 + x^2}$ on $[-1, 1]$

10. $f(x) = \tan x$ on $[0, 2]$

Determine the area of the indicated region in Problems 11–16 and then draw a rectangle with base $(b - a)$ and height $f(c)$ for some c on $[a, b]$ so that the area of the rectangle is equal to the area of the given region.

11. $y = \frac{1}{2}x$ on $[0, 10]$

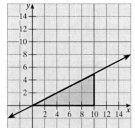

12. $y = x^2$ on $[0, 3]$

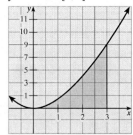

13. $y = x^2 + 2x + 3$ on $[0, 2]$ **14.** $y = \dfrac{1}{x^2}$ on $[0.5, 2]$

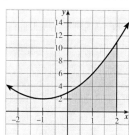 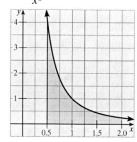

15. $y = \cos x$ on $[-1, 1.5]$ **16.** $y = x + \sin x$ on $[0, 10]$

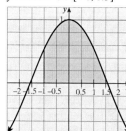 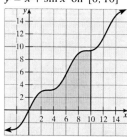

Find the average value of the function given in Problems 17–30 on the prescribed interval.

17. $f(x) = x^2 - x + 1$ on $[-1, 2]$

18. $f(x) = x^3 - 3x^2$ on $[-2, 1]$

19. $f(x) = e^x - e^{-x}$ on $[-1, 1]$

20. $f(x) = \dfrac{x}{2x + 3}$ on $[0, 1]$

21. $f(x) = \sin x$ on $\left[0, \frac{\pi}{4}\right]$

22. $f(x) = 2 \sin x - \cos x$ on $\left[0, \frac{\pi}{2}\right]$

23. $f(x) = \sqrt{4 - x}$ on $[0, 4]$

24. $f(x) = \sqrt[3]{1 - x}$ on $[-7, 0]$

25. $f(x) = (2x - 3)^3$ on $[0, 1]$

26. $f(x) = x\sqrt{2x^2 + 7}$ on $[0, 1]$

27. $f(x) = x(x^2 + 1)^3$ on $[-2, 1]$

28. $f(x) = \dfrac{x}{\sqrt{x^2 + 1}}$ on $[0, 3]$

29. $f(x) = \sqrt{9 - x^2}$ on $[-3, 3]$ *Hint:* The integral can be evaluated as the area of part of a circle.

30. $f(x) = \sqrt{2x - x^2}$ on $[0, 2]$ *Hint:* The integral can be evaluated as the area of part of a circle.

Ⓑ 31. If an object is propelled upward from ground level with an initial velocity v_0, then its height at time t is given by

$$s = -\tfrac{1}{2}gt^2 + v_0 t$$

where g is the constant acceleration due to gravity. Show that between times t_0 and t_1, the average height of the object is

$$s = -\tfrac{1}{6}g[t_1^2 + t_1 t_0 + t_0^2] + \tfrac{1}{2}v_0(t_1 + t_0)$$

32. What is the average velocity for the object described in Problem 31 during the same time period?

33. Records indicate that t hours past midnight, the temperature at the local airport was

$$f(t) = -0.1t^2 + t + 50$$

degrees Fahrenheit. What was the average temperature at the airport between 9:00 A.M. and noon?

34. Suppose a study indicates that t years from now, the level of carbon dioxide in the air of a certain city will be

$$L(t) = te^{-0.01t^2}$$

parts per million (ppm) for $0 \le t \le 20$.

a. What is the average level of carbon dioxide in the first 3 years?

b. At what time (or times) does the average level of carbon dioxide actually occur? Answer to the nearest month.

35. The number of bacteria (in thousands) present in a certain culture after t minutes is modeled by

$$Q(t) = \dfrac{2{,}000}{1 + 0.3e^{-0.276t}}$$

a. What was the average population during the *second* ten minutes ($10 \le t \le 20$)?

b. At what time during the period $10 \le t \le 20$ is the average population actually attained?

Ⓒ 36. Let $f(t)$ be a function that is continuous and satisfies $f(t) \ge 0$ on the interval $\left[0, \frac{\pi}{2}\right]$. Suppose it is known that for any number x between 0 and $\frac{\pi}{2}$, the region under the graph of f on $[0, x]$ has area $A(x) = \tan x$.

a. Explain why $\displaystyle\int_0^x f(t)\, dt = \tan x$ for $0 \le x \le \frac{\pi}{2}$.

b. Differentiate both sides of the equation in part **a** and deduce the identity of f.

37. Exploration Problem Suppose that $f(t)$ is continuous for all t and that for any number x it is known that the average value of f on $[-1, x]$ is

$$A(x) = \sin x$$

Use this information to deduce the identity of f.

38. Modeling Problem In Example 7 of Section 4.7, we gave the Heinz function

$$f(t) = \dfrac{k}{b - a}(e^{-at} - e^{-bt}) \qquad t \ge 0$$

where $f(t)$ is the concentration of a drug in a person's bloodstream t hours after an intramuscular injection. The coefficients a and b ($b > a$) are characteristics of the drug and the patient's metabolism and are called the absorption and diffusion rates, respectively.

a. Show that for each fixed t, $f(t)$ can be thought of as the average value of a function of the form

$$g(\lambda) = (At^2 + Bt + C)e^{-\lambda t}$$

over the interval $a \le \lambda \le b$. Find A, B, and C.

b. Exploration Problem So what? In particular, can you see any value in the interpretation of the Heinz concentration function as an average value? Explain.

5.8   Numerical Integration: The Trapezoidal Rule and Simpson's Rule

IN THIS SECTION   approximation by rectangles, trapezoidal rule, Simpson's rule, error estimation

The fundamental theorem of calculus can be used to evaluate an integral whenever an appropriate antiderivative is known. However, certain functions, such as $f(x) = e^{x^2}$, have no simple antiderivatives. To find a definite integral of such a function, it is often necessary to use numerical approximation.

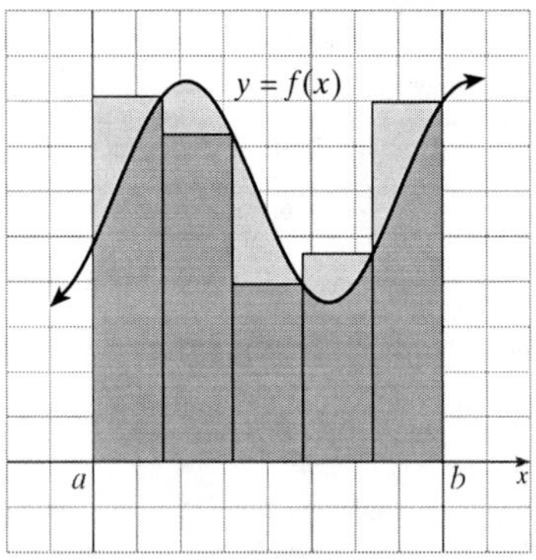

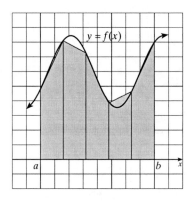

Figure 5.34 Approximation by rectangles

APPROXIMATION BY RECTANGLES

If $f(x) \geq 0$ on the interval $[a, b]$, the definite integral $\int_a^b f(x)\, dx$ is equal to the area under the graph of f on $[a, b]$. As we saw in Section 5.2, one way to approximate this area is to use n rectangles, as shown in Figure 5.34. In particular, divide the interval $[a, b]$ into n subintervals, each of width $\Delta x = \dfrac{b - a}{n}$, and let x_k^* denote the right endpoint of the kth subinterval. The base of the kth rectangle is the kth subinterval, and its height is $f(x_k^*)$. Hence, the area of the kth rectangle is $f(x_k^*)\Delta x$. The sum of the areas of all n rectangles is an approximation for the area under the curve and hence an approximation for the corresponding definite integral. Thus,

$$\int_a^b f(x)\, dx \approx f(x_1^*)\Delta x + f(x_2^*)\Delta x + \cdots + f(x_n^*)\Delta x$$

This approximation improves as the number of rectangles increases, and we can estimate the integral to any desired degree of accuracy by taking n large enough. However, because fairly large values of n are usually required to achieve reasonable accuracy, approximation by rectangles is rarely used in practice.

TRAPEZOIDAL RULE

The accuracy of the approximation generally improves significantly if trapezoids are used instead of rectangles. Figure 5.35 shows the area from Figure 5.34 approximated by n trapezoids instead of rectangles. Even from these rough illustrations you can see how much better the approximation is in this case.

Suppose the interval $[a, b]$ is partitioned into n equal parts by the subdivision points $x_0, x_1, \ldots, x_n$, where $x_0 = a$ and $x_n = b$. The kth trapezoid is shown in greater detail in Figure 5.36. Recall the formula for the area of a trapezoid:

$$A = \tfrac{1}{2}(b_1 + b_2)h$$

If we let T_n denote the sum of the areas of n trapezoids, we see that

$$T_n = \tfrac{1}{2}[f(x_0) + f(x_1)]\Delta x + \tfrac{1}{2}[f(x_1) + f(x_2)]\Delta x + \cdots + \tfrac{1}{2}[f(x_{n-1}) + f(x_n)]\Delta x$$
$$= \tfrac{1}{2}[f(x_0) + 2f(x_1) + 2f(x_2) + \cdots + 2f(x_{n-1}) + f(x_n)]\Delta x$$

The sum T_n estimates the total area under the curve $y = f(x)$ on the interval $[a, b]$ and hence also estimates the integral

$$\int_a^b f(x)\, dx$$

This approximation formula is known as the *trapezoidal rule* and applies as a means of approximating the integral, even if the function f is not positive.

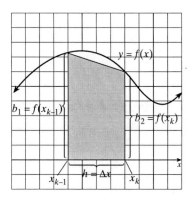

Figure 5.35 Approximation by trapezoids

Figure 5.36 The kth trapezoid has area $\tfrac{1}{2}[f(x_{k-1}) + f(x_k)]\Delta x$.

> **Trapezoidal Rule**
>
> Let f be continuous on $[a, b]$. The **trapezoidal rule** is
>
> $$\int_a^b f(x)\, dx \approx \tfrac{1}{2}[f(x_0) + 2f(x_1) + 2f(x_2) + \cdots + 2f(x_{n-1}) + f(x_n)]\Delta x$$
>
> where $\Delta x = \dfrac{b-a}{n}$ and, for the kth subinterval, $x_k = a + k\Delta x$. Moreover, the larger the value for n, the better the approximation.

Our first example uses the trapezoidal rule to estimate the value of an integral that we can compute exactly by using the fundamental theorem.

EXAMPLE 1   Trapezoidal rule approximation

Use the trapezoidal rule with $n = 4$ to estimate $\displaystyle\int_{-1}^{2} x^2\, dx$.

Solution

The interval is $[a, b] = [-1, 2]$, so $a = -1$ and $b = 2$. Then
$\Delta x = \dfrac{2 - (-1)}{4} = \dfrac{3}{4} = 0.75$. Thus,

$$x_0 = a = -1 \qquad\qquad f(x_0) = f(-1) = (-1)^2 = 1$$
$$x_1 = a + 1 \cdot \Delta x = -1 + \tfrac{3}{4} = -\tfrac{1}{4} \qquad 2f(x_1) = 2\left(-\tfrac{1}{4}\right)^2 = \tfrac{1}{8} = 0.125$$
$$x_2 = a + 2 \cdot \Delta x = -1 + \tfrac{6}{4} = \tfrac{1}{2} \qquad 2f(x_2) = 2\left(\tfrac{1}{2}\right)^2 = \tfrac{1}{2} = 0.5$$
$$x_3 = a + 3 \cdot \Delta x = -1 + \tfrac{9}{4} = \tfrac{5}{4} \qquad 2f(x_3) = 2\left(\tfrac{5}{4}\right)^2 = \tfrac{25}{8} = 3.125$$
$$x_4 = a + 4 \cdot \Delta x = b = 2 \qquad\qquad f(x_4) = 2^2 = 4$$
$$T_4 = \tfrac{1}{2}[1 + 0.125 + 0.5 + 3.125 + 4](0.75) = 3.28125$$

∎

The exact value of the integral in Example 1 is

$$\int_{-1}^{2} x^2\, dx = \left.\frac{x^3}{3}\right|_{-1}^{2} = \frac{8}{3} - \frac{-1}{3} = 3$$

Therefore, the trapezoidal estimate T_4 involves an error, which we denote by E_4. We find that

$$E_4 = \int_{-1}^{2} x^2\, dx - T_4 = 3 - 3.28125 = -0.28125$$

The negative sign indicates that the trapezoidal formula *overestimated* the true value of the integral in Example 1.

Software for numerical evaluation of integrals is common (see the *Technology Manual*). The output for Example 1 is shown in the margin.

Trapezoidal Rule to calculate estimate		
Type of estimate	# of sub-intervals	Estimate over [-1, 2]
Trapezoid	4	3.28125
Trapezoid	10	3.045
Trapezoid	100	3.00045
Trapezoid	1000	3.000005

SIMPSON'S RULE

Roughly speaking, the accuracy of a procedure for estimating the area under a curve depends on how well the upper boundary of each approximating area fits the shape of the given curve. Trapezoidal strips often result in a better approximation than rectangular strips, and it is reasonable to expect even greater accuracy to occur if the approximating regions have curved upper boundaries, as shown in Figure 5.37.

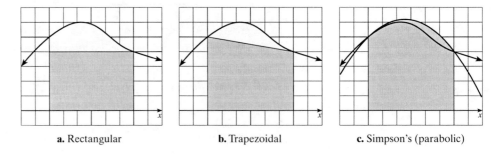

a. Rectangular   **b.** Trapezoidal   **c.** Simpson's (parabolic)

Figure 5.37 A comparison of approximation methods

The name given to the procedure in which the approximating strip has a parabolic arc for its upper boundary is called **Simpson's rule.**[*]

As with the trapezoidal rule, we will derive Simpson's rule as a means for approximating the area under the curve $y = f(x)$ on the interval $[a, b]$, where f is continuous and satisfies $f(x) \geq 0$. First, we partition the given interval into a number of equal subintervals, but this time, we require the number of subdivisions to be an *even* number (because this requirement will simplify the formula associated with the final result).

If $x_0, x_1, \ldots, x_n$ are the subdivision points in our partition (with $x_0 = a$ and $x_n = b$), we pass a parabolic arc through the points, three at a time (the points with x-coordinates x_0, x_1, x_2, then those with x_2, x_3, x_4, and so on). It can be shown (see Problem 42) that the region under the parabolic curve $y = f(x)$ on the interval $[x_{2k-2}, x_{2k}]$ has area

$$\tfrac{1}{3}[f(x_{2k-2}) + 4f(x_{2k-1}) + f(x_{2k})]\Delta x$$

where $\Delta x = \dfrac{b - a}{n}$. This procedure is illustrated in Figure 5.38.

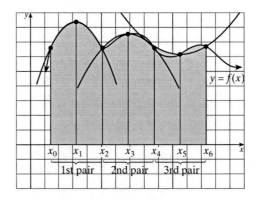

Figure 5.38 Approximation using parabolas

By adding the area of the approximating parabolic strips and combining terms, we obtain the sum S_n of n parabolic regions:

$$S_n = \tfrac{1}{3}[f(x_0) + 4f(x_1) + f(x_2)]\Delta x + \tfrac{1}{3}[f(x_2) + 4f(x_3) + f(x_4)]\Delta x$$
$$+ \cdots + \tfrac{1}{3}[f(x_{n-2}) + 4f(x_{n-1}) + f(x_n)]\Delta x$$
$$= \tfrac{1}{3}[f(x_0) + 4f(x_1) + 2f(x_2) + 4f(x_3) + \cdots + 4f(x_{n-1}) + f(x_n)]\Delta x$$

These observations are summarized in the following box:

---

[*]This rule is named for Thomas Simpson (1710–1761), an English mathematician who, curiously, neither discovered nor made any special use of the formula that bears his name.

> **Simpson's Rule**
>
> Let f be continuous on $[a, b]$. **Simpson's rule** is
>
> $$\int_a^b f(x)\, dx \approx \frac{1}{3}[f(x_0) + 4f(x_1) + 2f(x_2) + 4f(x_3) + 2f(x_4) + \cdots$$
> $$+ 4f(x_{n-1}) + f(x_n)]\Delta x$$
>
> where $\Delta x = \dfrac{b-a}{n}$, $x_k = a + k\Delta x$, k an integer and n an even integer. Moreover, the larger the value for n, the better the approximation.

EXAMPLE 2 Approximation by Simpson's rule

Use Simpson's rule with $n = 10$ to approximate $\displaystyle\int_1^2 \frac{dx}{x}$.

Solution

We have $\Delta x = \dfrac{2-1}{10} = 0.1$, and $x_0 = a = 1$, $x_1 = 1.1$, $x_2 = 1.2$, ..., $x_9 = 1.9$, $x_{10} = b = 2$.

$$\int_1^2 \frac{1}{x}\, dx \approx S_{10}$$

$$= \frac{1}{3}\left(\frac{1}{1} + \frac{4}{1.1} + \frac{2}{1.2} + \frac{4}{1.3} + \frac{2}{1.4} + \frac{4}{1.5} + \frac{2}{1.6} + \frac{4}{1.7} + \frac{2}{1.8} + \frac{4}{1.9} + \frac{1}{2}\right)(0.1)$$

$$\approx 0.6931502$$

This estimate compares well with the value found directly by applying the fundamental theorem of calculus:

$$\int_1^2 \frac{dx}{x} = \ln 2 - \ln 1 \approx 0.6931472$$

An example of the output of a computer program for this type of problem is shown in the margin. ∎

Comparison of Simpson's and trapezoidal rules		
Type of estimate	# of sub-intervals	Estimate over [1, 2]
Trapezoid	10	.693771403175
Simpson	10	.693150230689
Trapezoid	100	.693153430482
Simpson	100	.693147180872
Trapezoid	1000	.693147243060
Simpson	1000	.693147100560

Comparison of Simpson's and trapezoidal rules

ERROR ESTIMATION

The difference between the value of an integral and its estimated value is called its error. Since this error is a function of n we denote it by E_n.

THEOREM 5.12 Error in the trapezoidal rule and Simpson's rule

If f has a continuous second derivative on $[a, b]$, then the error E_n in approximating $\int_a^b f(x)\, dx$ by the trapezoidal rule satisfies the following:

Trapezoidal error:
$$|E_n| \le \frac{(b-a)^3}{12n^2} M, \text{ where } M \text{ is the maximum value of } |f''(x)| \text{ on } [a, b].$$

Moreover, if f has a continuous fourth derivative on $[a, b]$, then the error E_n (n even) in approximating $\int_a^b f(x)\, dx$ by Simpson's rule satisfies the following:

Simpson's error:
$$|E_n| \le \frac{(b-a)^5}{180n^4} K, \text{ where } K \text{ is the maximum value of } \left|f^{(4)}(x)\right| \text{ on } [a, b].$$

Proof The proofs of these error estimates are beyond the scope of this book and can be found in many advanced calculus textbooks and in most numerical analysis books. ❑

EXAMPLE 3   Estimate of error when using Simpson's rule

Estimate the accuracy of the approximation of $\int_1^2 \frac{dx}{x}$ by Simpson's rule with $n = 10$ in Example 2.

Solution

If $f(x) = \frac{1}{x}$, we find that $f^{(4)}(x) = 24x^{-5}$. The maximum value of this function will occur at a critical number (there is none on $[1, 2]$) or at an endpoint. Thus, the largest value of $\left| f^{(4)}(x) \right|$ on $[1, 2]$ is $\left| f^{(4)}(1) \right| = 24$. Now, apply the error formula with $K = 24$, $a = 1$, $b = 2$, and $n = 10$ to obtain

$$|E_{10}| \le \frac{k(b-a)^5}{180n^4} = \frac{24(2-1)^5}{180(10)^4} \approx 0.0000133$$

That is, the error in the approximation in Example 2 is guaranteed to be no greater than 0.0000133. ∎

With the aid of the error estimates, we can decide in advance how many subintervals to use to achieve a desired degree of accuracy.

EXAMPLE 4   Choosing the number of subintervals to guarantee given accuracy

How many subintervals are required to guarantee that the error will be correct to four decimal places in the approximation of

$$\int_1^2 \frac{dx}{x}$$

on $[1, 2]$ using the trapezoidal rule?

Solution

To be correct to four decimal places means that $|E_n| < 0.00005$. Because $f(x) = x^{-1}$, we have $f''(x) = 2x^{-3}$. On $[1, 2]$ the largest value of $|f''(x)|$ is $|f''(1)| = 2$, so $M = 2$, $a = 1$, $b = 2$, and

$$|E_n| \le \frac{2(2-1)^3}{12n^2} = \frac{1}{6n^2}$$

The goal is to find the smallest positive integer n for which

$$\frac{1}{6n^2} < 0.00005$$

$$10,000 < 3n^2 \qquad \text{Multiply by the positive number } 60,000n^2.$$

$$10,000 - 3n^2 < 0$$

$$(100 - \sqrt{3}n)(100 + \sqrt{3}n) < 0$$

$$n < -\frac{100}{\sqrt{3}} \quad \text{or} \quad n > \frac{100}{\sqrt{3}} \approx 57.735$$

The smallest positive integer that satisfies this condition is $n = 58$; therefore, 58 subintervals are required to ensure the desired accuracy. ∎

If f is the linear function $f(x) = Ax + B$, then $f''(x) = 0$ and we can take $M = 0$ as the error estimate. In this case, the error in applying the trapezoidal rule satisfies $|E_n| \le 0$. That is, the trapezoidal rule is exact for a linear function, which is what we would expect, because the region under a line on an interval is a trapezoid.

In discussing the accuracy of the trapezoidal rule as a means of estimating the value of the definite integral

$$I = \int_a^b f(x)\, dx$$

we have focused attention on the "error term," but this only measures the error that comes from estimating I by the trapezoidal or Simpson approximation sum. There are other kinds of errors that must be considered in this or any other method of approximation. In particular, each time we cut off digits from a decimal, we incur what is known as a round-off error. For example, a round-off error occurs when we use 0.66666667 in place of $\frac{2}{3}$ or 3.1415927 for the number π. Round-off errors occur even in large computers and can accumulate to cause real problems. Specialized methods for dealing with these and other errors are studied in numerical analysis.

The examples of numerical integration examined in this section are intended as illustrations and thus involve relatively simple computations, whereas in practice, such computations often involve hundreds of terms and can be quite tedious. Fortunately, these computations are extremely well suited to automatic computing, and the reader who is interested in pursuing computer methods in numerical integration will find an introduction to this topic in the *Technology Manual*.

5.8 PROBLEM SET

A *Approximate the integrals in Problems 1–2 using the trapezoidal rule and Simpson's rule with the specified number of subintervals and then compare your answers with the exact value of the definite integral.*

1. $\int_1^2 x^2 \, dx$ with $n = 4$ **2.** $\int_0^4 \sqrt{x} \, dx$ with $n = 6$

Approximate the integrals given in Problems 3–8 with the specified number of subintervals using

   a. the trapezoidal rule   *b. Simpson's rule*

3. $\int_0^1 \dfrac{dx}{1 + x^2}$ with $n = 4$

4. $\int_{-1}^0 \sqrt{1 + x^2} \, dx$ with $n = 4$

5. $\int_2^4 \sqrt{1 + \sin x} \, dx$ with $n = 4$

6. $\int_0^2 x \cos x \, dx$ with $n = 6$

7. $\int_0^2 x e^{-x} \, dx$ with $n = 6$

8. $\int_1^2 \ln x \, dx$ with $n = 6$

B **9. WHAT DOES THIS SAY?** Describe the trapezoidal rule.

10. WHAT DOES THIS SAY? Describe Simpson's rule.

Estimate the value of the integrals in Problems 11–18 to within the prescribed accuracy.

11. $\int_0^1 \dfrac{dx}{x^2 + 1}$ with error less than 0.05. Use the trapezoidal rule.

12. $\int_{-1}^2 \sqrt{1 + x^2} \, dx$ with error less than 0.05. Use Simpson's rule.

13. $\int_0^1 \cos 2x \, dx$ accurate to three decimal places. Use Simpson's rule.

14. $\int_1^2 x^{-1} \, dx$ accurate to three decimal places. Use Simpson's rule.

15. $\int_0^2 x\sqrt{4 - x} \, dx$ with error less than 0.01. Use the trapezoidal rule.

16. $\int_0^\pi \theta \cos^2 \theta \, d\theta$ with error less than 0.01. Use Simpson's rule.

17. $\int_0^1 \tan^{-1} x \, dx$ with error less than 0.01. Use Simpson's rule.

18. $\int_0^\pi e^{-x} \sin x \, dx$ to three decimal places. Use Simpson's rule.

In Problems 19–23, determine how many subintervals are required to guarantee accuracy to within 0.00005 using

   a. the trapezoidal rule   *b. Simpson's rule*

19. $\int_1^3 x^{-1} \, dx$ **20.** $\int_{-1}^4 (x^3 + 2x^2 + 1) \, dx$

21. $\int_1^4 \dfrac{dx}{\sqrt{x}}$ **22.** $\int_0^2 \cos x \, dx$

23. $\int_1^2 \ln \sqrt{x} \, dx$ **24.** $\int_0^1 e^{-2x} \, dx$

25. A quarter-circle of radius 1 has the equation $y = \sqrt{1 - x^2}$ for $0 \le x \le 1$, which implies that

$$\int_0^1 \sqrt{1 - x^2} \, dx = \frac{\pi}{4}$$

   a. Estimate π correct to one decimal place by applying the trapezoidal rule to this integral.

   b. Estimate π correct to one decimal place by applying Simpson's rule to this integral.

26. Find the smallest value of n for which the trapezoidal rule estimates the value of the integral

$$\int_1^2 x^{-1} \, dx$$

with six-decimal-place accuracy.

27. The width of an irregularly shaped dam is measured at 5-m intervals, with the results indicated in Figure 5.39. Use the trapezoidal rule to estimate the area of the face of the dam.

Figure 5.39 Area of the face of a dam

28. Jack and Jill are traveling in a car with a broken odometer. In order to determine the distance they traveled between noon and 1:00 P.M., Jack (the passenger) takes a speedometer reading every 5 minutes.

Minutes (after noon)	0	5	10	15	20
Speedometer reading	54	57	50	51	55

Minutes	25	30	35	40	45	50	55	60
Speedometer	60	49	53	47	39	42	48	53

Use the trapezoidal rule to estimate the total distance traveled by the couple from noon to 1:00 P.M.

29. An industrial plant spills pollutant into a lake. The pollutant spread out to form the pattern shown in Figure 5.40. All distances are in feet.

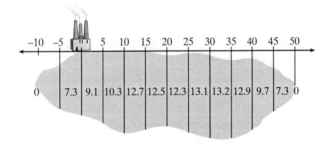

Figure 5.40 Pollutant spill

Use Simpson's rule to estimate the area of the spill.

30. Apply the trapezoidal rule to estimate $\int_0^3 f(x)\,dx$, where the values for f are found on the following spreadsheet (table):

	A	B
1	x	$f(x)$
2	0	3.7
3	0.3	3.9
4	0.6	4.1
5	0.9	4.1
6	1.2	4.2
7	1.5	4.4
8	1.8	4.6
9	2.1	4.9
10	2.4	5.2
11	2.7	5.5
12	3	6

31. Apply Simpson's rule to estimate $\int_0^5 f(x)\,dx$, where the values for f are found on the following spreadsheet (table):

	A	B
1	x	$f(x)$
2	0	10
3	0.5	9.75
4	1	10
5	1.5	10.75
6	2	12
7	2.5	13.75
8	3	16
9	3.5	18.75
10	4	22
11	4.5	25.75
12	5	30

32. In this problem, we explore the "order of convergence" of three numerical integration methods. A method is said to have "order of convergence n^k" if $E_n \cdot n^k = C$, where n is the number of intervals in the approximation and k is a constant power. In other words, the error $E_n \to 0$ as $C/n^k \to 0$. In each of the following cases, use the fact that

$$I = \int_0^\pi \sin x\,dx = -\cos x\big|_0^\pi = 2$$

a. Use the trapezoidal rule to estimate I for $n = 10, 20, 40$, and 80. Compute the error E_n in each case and compute $E_n \cdot n^k$ for $k = 1, 2, 3, 4$. Based on your results, you should be able to conclude that the order of convergence of the trapezoidal approximation is n^2.

b. Repeat part **a** using Simpson's rule. Based on your results, what is the order of convergence for Simpson's rule?

c. Repeat part **a** using a rectangular approximation with right endpoints. What is the order of convergence for this method?

33. Let $I = \int_0^\pi (9x - x^3)\,dx$.

a. Estimate I using rectangles, the trapezoidal rule, and Simpson's rule, for $n = 10, 20, 40, 80$. Something interesting happens with Simpson's rule. Explain.

b. **Simpson struggles!** In contrast to part **a**, here is an example where Simpson's rule does not live up to expectations. For $n = 10, 20, 40$, and 80, use Simpson's rule and the rectangular rule (select midpoints) for this integral and make a table of errors. Then try to explain Simpson's poor performance. *Hint*: Look at the formula for the error.

$$\int_0^2 \sqrt{4 - x^2}\,dx = \pi$$

34. HISTORICAL QUEST The mathematician Seki Kōwa was born in Fujioka, Japan, the son of a samurai, but was adopted by a patriarch of the Seki family. Seki invented and used an early form of determinants for solving systems of equations, and he also invented a method for approximating areas that is very similar to the rectangular

TAKAKAZU SEKI KŌWA
1642–1708

method introduced in this section. This method, known as the yenri (circle principle), found the area of a circle by dividing the circle into small rectangles, as shown in Figure 5.41.

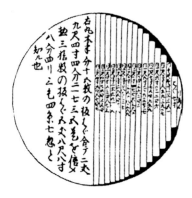

Figure 5.41 Early Asian calculus

The sample shown in Figure 5.41 was drawn by a student of Seki Kōwa. ∎

For this quest, draw a circle with radius 10 cm. Draw vertical chords through each centimeter on a diameter (you should have 18 rectangles). Measure the heights of the rectangles and approximate the area of the circle by adding the areas of the rectangles. Compare this with the formula for the area of this circle.

35. HISTORICAL QUEST In 1670, a predecessor of Seki Kōwa (see Problem 34), Kazuyuki Sawaguchi wrote seven volumes that concluded with fifteen problems that he believed were unsolvable. In 1674, Seki Kōwa published solutions to all fifteen of Kazuyuki's unsolvable problems. One of the "unsolvable" problems was the following: Three circles are inscribed in a circle, each tangent to the other two and to the original circle. All three cover all but 120 square units of the circumscribing circle. The diameters of the two smaller inscribed circles are equal, and each is five units less than the diameter of the larger inscribed circle. Find the diameters of the three inscribed circles.

The solution to this "impossible" problem is beyond the scope of this course (it involves solving a 6th degree equation with a horrendous amount of computation), but we can replace it with a simpler problem: Consider two circles inscribed in a circle, each tangent to the other and to the original circle. The diameter of the smaller circle is five units less than the diameter of the larger inscribed circle. The sum of the areas of the larger circle and twice the smaller circle cover all but 120 square units of the circumscribing circles. Find the diameters of the two inscribed circles.

36. HISTORICAL QUEST Isaac Newton (see Historical Quest essay at the end of Chapter 1 on page 48) invented a preliminary version of Simpson's rule. In 1779, Newton wrote an article to an addendum to *Methodus Differentials* (1711) in which he gave the following example: If there are four ordinates at equal intervals, let A be the sum of the first and fourth, B the sum of the second and third, and R the interval

ROGER COTES
1682–1716

between the first and fourth; then ... the area between the first and fourth ordinates is approximated by $\frac{1}{8}(A + 3B)R$. This is known today as the "Newton-Cotes three-eighths rule," which can be expressed in the form

$$\int_{x_0}^{x_3} f(x)\, dx \approx \tfrac{3}{8}(y_0 + 3y_1 + 3y_2 + y_3)\Delta x$$

Roger Cotes and James Stirling (1692–1770) both knew this formula, as well as what we called in this section Simpson's rule. In 1743, this rule was rediscovered by Thomas Simpson (1710–1761). ∎

Estimate the integral

$$\int_0^3 \tan^{-1} x\, dx$$

using the Newton-Cotes three-eighths rule, and then compare with approximation using left endpoints (rectangles) and trapezoids with $n = 4$. Which of the three rules gives the most accurate estimate?

37. Show that if $p(x)$ is any polynomial of degree less than or equal to 3, then

$$\int_a^b p(x)\, dx = \frac{b-a}{6}\left[p(a) + 4p\left(\frac{a+b}{2}\right) + p(b)\right]$$

This result is often called the *prismoidal rule*.

38. Use the prismoidal rule (Problem 37) to evaluate

$$\int_{-1}^2 (x^3 - 3x + 4)\, dx$$

39. Use the prismoidal rule (Problem 37) to evaluate

$$\int_{-1}^3 (x^3 + 2x^2 - 7)\, dx$$

40. Let $p(x)$ be a polynomial of degree at most 3.
    a. Find a number c between 0 and 1 such that

$$\int_{-1}^1 p(x)\, dx = p(c) + p(-c)$$

    b. Find a number c between $-\frac{1}{2}$ and $\frac{1}{2}$ such that

$$\int_{-1/2}^{1/2} p(x)\, dx = \tfrac{1}{3}[p(-c) + p(0) + p(c)]$$

41. Let $p(x) = Ax^3 + Bx^2 + Cx + D$ be a cubic polynomial. Show that Simpson's rule gives the exact value for

$$\int_a^b p(x)\, dx$$

42. The object of this exercise is to prove Simpson's rule for the special case involving three points.
    a. Let $P_1(-h, f(-h))$, $P_2(0, f(0))$, $P_3(h, f(h))$. Find the equation of the form $y = Ax^2 + Bx + C$ for the parabola through the points P_1, P_2, and P_3.

b. If $y = p(x)$ is the quadratic function found in part **a**, show that

$$\int_{-h}^{h} p(x)\, dx = \frac{h}{3}[p(-h) + 4p(0) + p(h)]$$

c. Let $Q_1(x_1, f(x_1))$, $Q_2(x_2, f(x_2))$, $Q_3(x_3, f(x_3))$ be points with $x_2 = x_1 + h$, and $x_3 = x_1 + 2h$. Explain why

$$\int_{x_1}^{x_3} p(x)\, dx = \frac{h}{3}[p(x_1) + 4p(x_2) + p(x_3)]$$

5.9   An Alternative Approach: The Logarithm as an Integral

IN THIS SECTION   natural logarithm as an integral, geometric interpretation, the natural exponential function

NATURAL LOGARITHM AS AN INTEGRAL

You may have noticed in Section 2.4 that we did not prove the properties of exponential functions for all real number exponents. To treat exponentials and logarithms *rigorously*, we use the alternative approach provided in this section. Specifically, we use a definite integral to introduce the *natural logarithmic function* and then use this function to *define* the *natural exponential function*.

"When I use a word," Humpty Dumpty said, "it means just what I choose it to mean—nothing more or less."
——Lewis Carroll (1832–1898)

Natural Logarithm

> The **natural logarithm** is the function defined by
>
> $$\ln x = \int_{1}^{x} \frac{dt}{t} \qquad x > 0$$

At first glance, it appears there is nothing "natural" about this definition, but if this integral function has the properties of a logarithm, why should we not call it a logarithm? We begin with a theorem that shows that $\ln x$ does indeed have the properties we would expect of a logarithm.

THEOREM 5.13   Properties of a logarithm as defined by $\ln x = \int_{1}^{x} \frac{dt}{t}$

Let $x > 0$ and $y > 0$ be positive numbers. Then

a. $\ln 1 = 0$

b. $\ln xy = \ln x + \ln y$

c. $\ln \dfrac{x}{y} = \ln x - \ln y$

d. $\ln x^p = p \ln x$ for all rational numbers p

Proof

a. Let $x = 1$. Then $\displaystyle\int_{1}^{1} \frac{dt}{t} = 0.$

b. For fixed positive numbers x and y, we use the additive property of integrals as follows:

$$\ln(xy) = \int_{1}^{xy} \frac{dt}{t} = \int_{1}^{x} \frac{dt}{t} + \int_{x}^{xy} \frac{dt}{t}$$

> Let $u = \dfrac{t}{x}$, so $t = ux$;
> $dt = x\, du.$
> If $t = x$, then $u = 1$;
> if $t = xy$, then $u = y$.

$$= \ln x + \int_{1}^{y} \frac{x\, du}{ux}$$

$$= \ln x + \int_{1}^{y} \frac{du}{u}$$

$$= \ln x + \ln y$$

c. and **d.** The proofs are outlined in the problem set.   ❑

GEOMETRIC INTERPRETATION

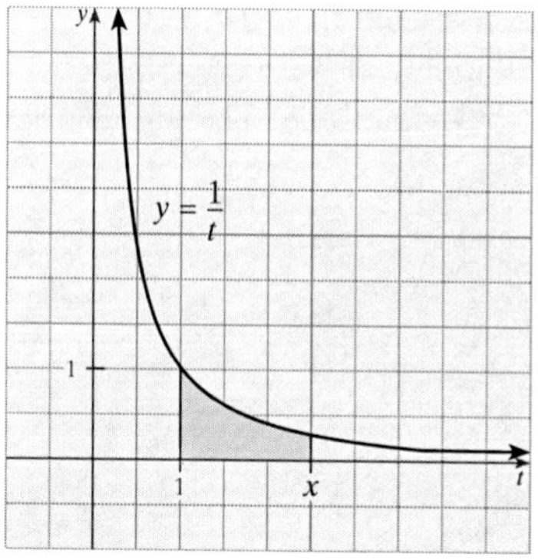

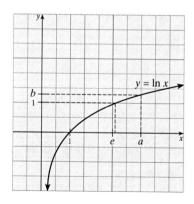

Figure 5.42 If $x > 1$, $\ln x = \int_1^x \frac{dt}{t}$ is the area under $y = \frac{1}{t}$ on $[1, x]$.

An advantage of defining the logarithm by the integral formula is that calculus can be used to study the properties of $\ln x$ from the beginning. For example, note that if $x > 1$, the integral

$$\ln x = \int_1^x \frac{dt}{t}$$

may be interpreted geometrically as the area under the graph of $y = \frac{1}{t}$ from $t = 1$ to $t = x$, as shown in Figure 5.42. If $x > 1$, then $\ln x > 0$. On the other hand, if $0 < x < 1$, then

$$\ln x = \int_1^x \frac{dt}{t} = -\int_x^1 \frac{dt}{t} < 0$$

so that

$$\ln x > 0 \quad \text{if } x > 1$$
$$\ln 1 = 0$$
$$\ln x < 0 \quad \text{if } 0 < x < 1$$

The definition $\ln x = \int_1^x \frac{dt}{t}$ makes it easy to differentiate $\ln x$. Recall from Section 5.4 that according to the second fundamental theorem of calculus, if f is continuous on $[a, b]$, then

$$F(x) = \int_a^x f(t)\, dt$$

is a differentiable function of x with derivative $\frac{dF}{dx} = f(x)$ on any interval $[a, x]$. Therefore, because $\frac{1}{t}$ is continuous for all $t > 0$, it follows that $\ln x = \int_1^x \frac{dt}{t}$ is differentiable for all $x > 0$ with derivative $\frac{d}{dx}(\ln x) = \frac{1}{x}$. By applying the chain rule, we also find that

$$\frac{d}{dx}(\ln u) = \frac{1}{u}\frac{du}{dx}$$

for any differentiable function u of x with $u > 0$.

To analyze the graph of $f(x) = \ln x$, we use the curve-sketching methods of Chapter 4:

a. $\ln x$ is continuous for all $x > 0$ (because it is differentiable), so its graph is "unbroken."

b. The graph of $\ln x$ is always *rising*, because the derivative

$$\frac{d}{dx}(\ln x) = \frac{1}{x}$$

is positive for $x > 0$. (Recall that the natural logarithm is defined only for $x > 0$.)

c. The graph of $\ln x$ is *concave down*, because the second derivative

$$\frac{d^2}{dx^2}(\ln x) = \frac{d}{dx}\left(\frac{1}{x}\right) = \frac{-1}{x^2}$$

is negative for all $x > 0$.

d. Note that $\ln 2 > 0$ (because $\int_1^2 \frac{dt}{t} > 0$) and because $\ln 2^p = p \ln 2$, it follows that $\lim_{p \to +\infty} \ln 2^p = +\infty$. But the graph of $f(x) = \ln x$ is always rising, and thus $\lim_{x \to +\infty} \ln x = +\infty$. Similarly, it can be shown that $\lim_{x \to 0^+} \ln x = -\infty$.

e. If b is any positive number, there is exactly one number a such that $\ln a = b$ (because the graph of $\ln x$ is always rising for $x > 0$). In particular, we define $x = e$ as the unique number that satisfies $\ln x = 1$.

Figure 5.43 The graph of the natural logarithm function, $\ln x$

These features are shown in Figure 5.43.

THE NATURAL EXPONENTIAL FUNCTION

Originally, we introduced the natural exponential function e^x and then defined the natural logarithm $\ln x$ as the inverse of e^x. In this alternative approach, we note that because the natural logarithm is an increasing function, it must be one-to-one. Therefore, it has an inverse function, which we denote by $E(x)$.

Because $\ln x$ and $E(x)$ are inverses, we have

$$E(x) = y \quad \text{if and only if} \quad \ln y = x$$

From the definition of inverse formulas we have

$$E(\ln x) = x \quad \text{and} \quad \ln[E(x)] = x$$

We call these formulas the **inversion formulas**. Therefore,

$$
\begin{aligned}
E(0) &= E(\ln 1) && \text{Because } \ln 1 = 0 \\
&= 1 && \text{Because } E(\ln x) = x
\end{aligned}
$$

and

$$
\begin{aligned}
E(1) &= E(\ln e) && \text{Because } \ln e = 1 \\
&= e && \text{Because } E(\ln e) = e
\end{aligned}
$$

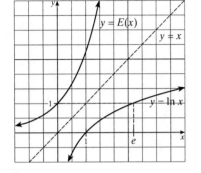

Figure 5.44 The graph of $E(x)$ is the reflection of the graph of $\ln x$ in the line $y = x$.

To obtain the graph of $E(x)$, we reflect the graph of $y = \ln x$ in the line $y = x$. The graph is shown in Figure 5.44. Notice that $\ln x = 1$ has the unique solution $x = e$.

The following algebraic properties of the natural exponential function can be obtained by using the properties of the natural logarithm given in Theorem 5.13 along with the inversion formulas.

THEOREM 5.14 Properties of the exponential as defined by $E(x)$

For any numbers x and y,

a. $E(0) = 1$ **b.** $E(x + y) = E(x)E(y)$

c. $E(x - y) = \dfrac{E(x)}{E(y)}$ **d.** $[E(x)]^p = E(px)$

Proof

a. Proved above (inversion formula).

b. We use the fact that $\ln AB = \ln A + \ln B$ to show that

$$
\begin{aligned}
\ln[E(x)E(y)] &= \ln E(x) + \ln E(y) && \text{Property of logarithms} \\
&= x + y && \text{Inversion formula} \\
&= \ln E(x + y) && \text{Inversion formula}
\end{aligned}
$$

Because $\ln x$ is a one-to-one function, we conclude that

$$E(x)E(y) = E(x + y)$$

c. and **d.** The proofs are similar and are left as exercises. ❏

Next, we use implicit differentiation along with the differentiation formula

$$\frac{d}{dx}(\ln x) = \frac{1}{x}$$

to obtain a differentiation formula for $E(x)$.

THEOREM 5.15 Derivative of $E(x)$

The function defined by $E(x)$ is differentiable and

$$\frac{dE}{dx} = E(x)$$

Proof It can be shown that the inverse of any differentiable function is also differentiable so long as the derivative is never zero (see Appendix B). Since $\ln x$ is differentiable, it follows that its inverse $E(x)$ is also differentiable, and using implicit differentiation, we find that

$$\ln y = \ln[E(x)] \qquad y = E(x)$$

$$\ln y = x \qquad\qquad \text{Inversion formula}$$

$$\frac{1}{y}\frac{dy}{dx} = 1 \qquad\qquad \text{Differentiate implicitly.}$$

$$\frac{dy}{dx} = y$$

$$\frac{dE}{dx} = E(x) \qquad\qquad \text{Because } \frac{dy}{dx} = \frac{dE}{dx} \text{ and } E(x) = y \qquad\qquad ❑$$

Finally, we observe that if r is a rational number, then

$$\ln(e^r) = r \ln e = r$$

so that

$$E(r) = e^r$$

This means that $E(x) = e^x$ when x is a rational number, and we **define** $E(x)$ to be e^x for irrational x as well. In particular, we now have an alternative definition for e: $E(1) = e^1 = e$.

5.9 PROBLEM SET

1. Use the integral definition

$$\ln x = \int_1^x \frac{dt}{t}$$

to show that $\ln x \to -\infty$ as $x \to 0^+$. *Hint*: What happens to $\ln(2^{-N})$ as N grows large without bound?

2. Use Simpson's rule with $n = 8$ subintervals to estimate

$$\ln 3 = \int_1^3 \frac{dt}{t}$$

Compare your estimate with the value of $\ln 3$ obtained from your calculator.

3. Use the error estimate for Simpson's rule to determine the accuracy of the estimate in Problem 2. How many subintervals should be used in Simpson's rule to estimate $\ln 3$ with an error not greater than 0.00005?

4. Prove the quotient rule for logarithms,

$$\ln\left(\frac{x}{y}\right) = \ln x - \ln y$$

for all $x > 0$, $y > 0$. *Hint*: Use the product rule for logarithms.

5. Show that $\ln(x^p) = p \ln x$ for $x > 0$ and all rational exponents p by completing the following steps.

a. Let $F(x) = \ln(x^p)$ and $G(x) = p \ln x$. Show that $F'(x) = G'(x)$ for $x > 0$. Conclude that $F(x) = G(x) + C$.

b. Let $x = 1$ and conclude that $F(x) = G(x)$. That is, $\ln(x^p) = p \ln x$.

6. Use Rolle's theorem to show that

$$\ln M = \ln N$$

if and only if $M = N$. *Hint*: Show that if $M \neq N$, Rolle's theorem implies that

$$\frac{d}{dx}(\ln x) = 0$$

for some number c between M and N. Why is this impossible?

7. The product rule for logarithms states

$$\log_b(MN) = \log_b M + \log_b N$$

For this reason, we want the natural logarithm function $\ln x$ to satisfy the functional equation

$$f(xy) = f(x) + f(y)$$

Suppose $f(x)$ is a function that satisfies this equation throughout its domain D.

a. Show that if $f(1)$ is defined, then $f(1) = 0$.

b. Show that if $f(-1)$ is defined, then $f(-1) = 0$.

c. Show that $f(-x) = f(x)$ for all x in D.

d. If $f'(x)$ is defined for each $x \neq 0$, show that

$$f'(x) = \frac{f'(1)}{x}$$

Then show that

$$f(x) = f'(1) \int_1^x \frac{dt}{t} \quad \text{for} \quad x > 0$$

e. Conclude that any solution of

$$f(xy) = f(x) + f(y)$$

that is not identically 0 and has a derivative for all $x \neq 0$ must be a multiple of

$$L(x) = \int_1^{|x|} \frac{dt}{t} \quad \text{for } x \neq 0$$

8. Show that for each number A, there is only one number x for which $\ln x = A$. *Hint:* If not, then $\ln x = \ln y = A$ for $x \neq y$. Why is this impossible?

9. **a.** Use an area argument to show that $\ln 2 < 1$.

   b. Show that $\ln 3 > 1$, and then explain why $2 < e < 3$.

10. Prove $E(x - y) = \dfrac{E(x)}{E(y)}$.

11. Prove $E(x)^p = E(px)$.

CHAPTER 5 REVIEW

Proficiency Examination

CONCEPT PROBLEMS

1. What is an antiderivative?
2. State the integration rule for powers.
3. State the exponential rule for integration.
4. State the integration rules we have learned for the trigonometric functions.
5. State the integration rules for the inverse trigonometric functions.
6. What is an area function? What do we mean by area as an antiderivative? What conditions are necessary for an integral to represent an area?
7. What is the formula for area as the limit of a sum?
8. What is a Riemann sum?
9. Define a definite integral.
10. Complete these statements summarizing the general properties of the definite integral.

    a. Definite integral at a point: $\displaystyle\int_a^a f(x)\,dx = $ _____

    b. Switching limits of a definite integral: $\displaystyle\int_b^a f(x)\,dx = $ _____

11. How can distance traveled by an object be expressed as an integral?
12. State the first fundamental theorem of calculus.
13. State the second fundamental theorem of calculus.
14. Describe in your own words the process of integration by substitution.
15. What is a differential equation?
16. What is a separable differential equation? How do you solve such an equation?
17. What is the growth/decay equation? Describe carbon dating.
18. What is an orthogonal trajectory?
19. State the mean value theorem for integrals.
20. What is the formula for the average value of a continuous function?
21. State the following approximation rules:

    a. rectangular approximation

    b. trapezoidal rule

    c. Simpson's rule

PRACTICE PROBLEMS

22. Given that $\displaystyle\int_0^1 [f(x)]^4\,dx = \frac{1}{5}$ and $\displaystyle\int_0^1 [f(x)]^2\,dx = \frac{1}{3}$, find

$$\int_0^1 [f(x)]^2 \{2[f(x)]^2 - 3\}\,dx$$

23. Find $F'(x)$ if $F(x) = \displaystyle\int_3^x t^5 \sqrt{\cos(2t + 1)}\,dt$.

Evaluate the integrals in Problems 24–29.

24. $\displaystyle\int \frac{dx}{1 + 4x^2}$

25. $\displaystyle\int x e^{-x^2}\,dx$

26. $\displaystyle\int_1^4 (\sqrt{x} + x^{-3/2})\,dx$

27. $\displaystyle\int_0^1 (2x - 6)(x^2 - 6x + 2)^2\,dx$

28. $\displaystyle\int_0^{\pi/2} \frac{\sin x\,dx}{(1 + \cos x)^2}$

29. $\displaystyle\int_{-2}^1 (2x + 1)\sqrt{2x^2 + 2x + 5}\,dx$

30. Find the area under the curve $f(x) = 3x^2 + 2$ over $[-1, 3]$.

31. Approximate the area under the curve $g(x) = e^{x^2}$ over $[1, 2]$.[*]

32. Find the average value of $y = \cos 2x$ on the interval $\left[0, \frac{\pi}{2}\right]$.

33. **Modeling Problem** In 1995, a team of archaeologists led by Michel Brunet of the University of Poitiers announced the identification in Chad of *Australopithecus* specimens believed to be about 3.5 Myr (million years) old.[†] Using the exponential decay equation, explain why the archaeologists were reluctant to use carbon-14 to date their find.

---

[*]There is an interesting discussion of this integral in the May 1999 issue of *The American Mathematical Monthly* in an article entitled, "What Is a Closed-Form Number?" The function $\int e^{x^2}$ is an example of a function that is **not** an elementary function (that we mentioned in Section 1.3).

[†]"Early Hominid Fossils from Africa," by Meave Leakey and Alan Walker, *Scientific American*, June 1997, p. 79.

34. A slope field for the differential equation

$$y' = x + y$$

is given in Figure 5.45.

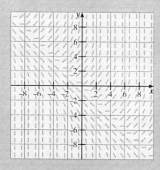

Figure 5.45 Direction field

Draw the particular solutions passing through the points requested in parts **a–d**.

a. $(0, -4)$ **b.** $(0, 2)$ **c.** $(4, 0)$ **d.** $(-4, 0)$

e. All of the curves you have drawn in parts **a–d** seem to have a common asymptote. From the slope field, write the equation for this asymptote.

35. a. Find the necessary n to estimate the value of $\int_0^{\pi/2} \cos x \, dx$ to within 0.0005 of its correct value using the trapezoidal rule.

b. What is n if Simpson's rule is used?

Supplementary Problems

Find the definite integrals of the functions in Problems 1–3.

1. Given that $\int_{-1}^0 f(x)\,dx = 3$, $\int_0^1 f(x)\,dx = -1$, and $\int_{-1}^1 g(x)\,dx = 7$, find $\int_{-1}^1 [3g(x) + 2f(x)]\,dx$.

2. Use the definition of the definite integral to find $\int_0^1 (3x^2 + 2x - 1)\,dx$.

3. Use the definition of the definite integral to find $\int_0^1 (4x^3 + 6x^2 + 3)\,dx$.

Find the definite and indefinite integrals in Problems 4–31. If you do not have a technique for finding a closed (exact) answer, approximate the integral using numerical integration.

4. $\int_0^1 (5x^4 - 8x^3 + 1)\,dx$ **5.** $\int_{-1}^2 30(5x - 2)^2\,dx$

6. $\int_0^1 (x\sqrt{x} + 2)^2\,dx$ **7.** $\int_1^2 \dfrac{x^2\,dx}{\sqrt{x^3 + 1}}$

8. $\int_2^2 (x + \sin x)^3\,dx$ **9.** $\int_{-1}^0 \dfrac{dx}{\sqrt{1 - 2x}}$

10. $\int_1^2 \dfrac{dx}{\sqrt{3x - 1}}$ **11.** $\int_{-1}^0 \dfrac{dx}{\sqrt[3]{1 - 2x}}$

12. $\int \dfrac{1}{x^3}\,dx$ **13.** $\int \dfrac{5x^2 - 2x + 1}{\sqrt{x}}\,dx$

14. $\int \dfrac{x + 1}{2x}\,dx$ **15.** $\int \dfrac{3 - x}{\sqrt{1 - x^2}}\,dx$

16. $\int (e^{-x} + 1)e^x\,dx$ **17.** $\int \dfrac{\sin x - \cos x}{\sin x + \cos x}\,dx$

18. $\int \sqrt{x}(x^2 + \sqrt{x} + 1)\,dx$ **19.** $\int (x - 1)^2\,dx$

20. $\int \dfrac{x^2 + 1}{x^2}\,dx$ **21.** $\int (\sin^2 x + \cos^2 x)\,dx$

22. $\int x(x + 4)\sqrt{x^3 + 6x^2 + 2}\,dx$

23. $\int x(2x^2 + 1)\sqrt{x^4 + x^2}\,dx$

24. $\int \dfrac{dx}{\sqrt{x}(\sqrt{x} + 1)^2}$ **25.** $\int x\sqrt{1 - 5x^2}\,dx$

26. $\int \sqrt{\sin x - \cos x}(\sin x + \cos x)\,dx$

27. $\int x^3 \cos(\tan^{-1} x)\,dx$

28. $\int (\cos^{11} x \sin^9 x - \cos^9 x \sin^{11} x)\,dx$

29. $\int \dfrac{\ln x}{x}\sqrt{1 + \ln(2x)}\,dx$

30. $\int_{-10}^{10} [3 + 7x^{73} - 100x^{101}]\,dx$

31. $\int_{-\pi/4}^{\pi/4} [\sin(4x) + 2\cos(4x)]\,dx$

In Problems 32–35, draw the indicated particular solution for the differential equations whose direction fields are given.

32. $y(4) = 0$ **33.** $y(10) = 1$

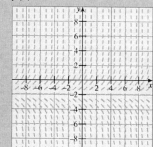 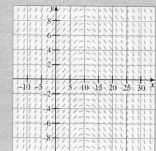

34. $y(0) = 2$ **35.** $y(0) = 0$

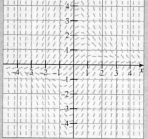 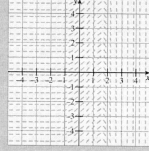

36. Find $F'(x)$, where $F(x) = \int_5^x t^2 \cos^4 t \, dt$

37. Find the area under $f(x) = x^{-1}$ on $[1, 4]$.

38. Find the area under $f(x) = 2 + x - x^2$ on $[-1, 1]$.

39. Find the area under $f(x) = e^{4x}$ on $[0, 2]$.

40. Find the area bounded by the curve $y = x\sqrt{x^2 + 5}$, the x-axis, and the vertical lines $x = -1$ and $x = 2$.

41. Find $f(t)$ if $f''(t) = \sin 4t - \cos 2t$ and $f\left(\frac{\pi}{2}\right) = f'\left(\frac{\pi}{2}\right) = 1$.

42. Find $f(x)$ if $f'''(x) = 2x^3 + x^2$, given that $f''(1) = 2$, $f'(1) = 1$, and $f(1) = 0$.

Solve the differential equations in Problems 43–50.

43. $\dfrac{dy}{dx} = (1 - y)^2$

44. $\dfrac{dy}{dx} = \dfrac{\cos 4x}{y}$

45. $\dfrac{dy}{dx} = \left(\dfrac{\cos y}{\sin x}\right)^2$

46. $\dfrac{dy}{dx} = \dfrac{x}{y}$

47. $\dfrac{dy}{dx} = y(x^2 + 1)$

48. $\dfrac{dy}{dx} = \dfrac{x}{y}\sqrt{\dfrac{y^2 + 2}{x^2 + 1}}$

49. $\dfrac{dy}{dx} = \dfrac{\cos^2 y}{\cot x}$

50. $\dfrac{dy}{dx} = \sqrt{\dfrac{x}{y}}$

51. Find the average value of $f(x) = \dfrac{\sin x}{\cos^2 x}$ on the interval $\left[0, \frac{\pi}{4}\right]$.

52. Find the average value of $f(x) = \sin x$
   a. on $[0, \pi]$ **b.** on $[0, 2\pi]$

53. Use the trapezoidal rule with $n = 6$ to approximate $\displaystyle\int_0^\pi \sin x\, dx$. Compare your result with the exact value of this integral.

54. Estimate $\displaystyle\int_0^1 \sqrt{1 + x^3}\, dx$ using the trapezoidal rule with $n = 6$.

55. Estimate $\displaystyle\int_0^1 \dfrac{dx}{\sqrt{1 + x^3}}$ using the trapezoidal rule with $n = 8$.

56. Estimate $\displaystyle\int_0^1 \sqrt{1 + x^3}\, dx$ using Simpson's rule with $n = 6$.

57. Use the trapezoidal rule to approximate $\displaystyle\int_0^1 \dfrac{x^2\, dx}{1 + x^2}$ with an error no greater than 0.005.

58. Use the trapezoidal rule to estimate to within 0.00005 the value of the integral
$$\int_1^2 \sqrt{x + \frac{1}{x}}\, dx$$

59. HISTORICAL QUEST Karl Gauss is considered to be one of the four greatest mathematicians of all time, along with Archimedes (Historical Quest, Problem 53, Section 3.8), Newton (Historical Quest, Problem 1, Mathematical Essays of Chapter 1, p. 48), and Euler (Historical Quest, Chapter 4 supplementary Problem 84). Gauss graduated from college at the age of 15 and proved what was to become the fundamental theorem of algebra for his doctoral thesis at the age of 22. He published only a small portion of the ideas that seemed to storm his mind, because he believed that each published result had to be complete, concise, polished, and convincing. His motto was "Few, but ripe." Carl B. Boyer, in *A History of Mathematics*, describes Gauss as the last mathematician to know everything in his subject, and we could relate Gauss to nearly every topic of this book. Such a generalization is bound to be inexact, but it does emphasize the breadth of interest Gauss displayed.

KARL GAUSS
1777–1855

A **prime number**, p, is a counting number that has exactly two divisors. **The prime number theorem**, conjectured by Gauss in 1793, says that the number of primes $\pi(x)$ less than a real number x is a function that behaves like $x/\ln x$ as $x \to \infty$; that is,

$$\lim_{x \to +\infty} \frac{\pi(x)}{x/\ln x} = 1$$

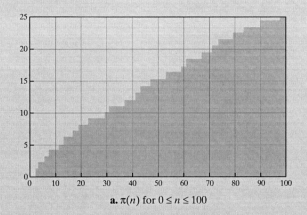

a. $\pi(n)$ for $0 \le n \le 100$

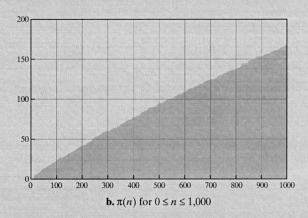

b. $\pi(n)$ for $0 \le n \le 1{,}000$

Figure 5.46 Graphs of $\pi(n)$

Gauss estimated the prime distribution function $\pi(x)$ by the integral
$$G(x) = \int_2^x \frac{dt}{\ln t}$$
known as the *integral logarithm* function. History records many who constructed tables for $\pi(n)$, and Figure 5.46 shows values for $\pi(n)$ for various choices of n. ∎

Your Quest is to examine this estimate by using the trapezoidal rule to approximate $G(x)$ for $x = 100$, $1{,}000$, and $10{,}000$. The actual value of $\pi(x)$ for selected values of x are as follows:

n	$\pi(n)$
10^3	168
10^4	1,229
10^5	9,592
10^6	78,498
10^{10}	455,052,511

60. HISTORICAL QUEST There are many ways to estimate the prime distribution function $\pi(x)$ defined in Problem 59 other than by the integral function $G(x)$ used by Gauss. Adrien-Marie Legendre is best known for his work with elliptic integrals and mathematical physics. In 1794, he proved that π was an irrational number and formulated a conjecture that is equivalent to the prime number theorem. He made his estimate using the function

ADRIEN-MARIE
LEGENDRE
1752–1833

$$\pi(x) \approx L(x) = \frac{x}{\ln x - 1.08366} \quad \blacksquare$$

For this Quest, use $L(x)$ to estimate $\pi(x)$ for $x = 100$, 1,000, and 10,000, and then compare with the results found using $G(x)$ in Problem 59.

61. Approximate the average value of the function defined by

$$f(x) = \frac{\cos x}{1 - \dfrac{x^2}{2}}$$

on $[0, 1]$. *Hint*: Use the trapezoidal rule with $n = 6$.

62. The brakes of a certain automobile produce a constant deceleration of k m/s^2. The car is traveling at 25 m/s when the driver is forced to hit the brakes. If it comes to rest at a point 50 m from the point where the brakes are applied, what is k?

63. A particle moves along the t-axis in such a way that $a(t) = -4s(t)$, where $s(t)$ and $a(t)$ are its position and acceleration, respectively, at time t. The particle starts from rest at $s = 5$.

  a. Show that $v^2 + 4s^2 = 100$, where $v(t)$ is the velocity of the particle. *Hint*: First use the chain rule to show that $a(t) = v(dv/ds)$.

  b. What is the velocity when the particle first reaches $s = 3$? *Note*: At the time in question, the sign of v is determined by the direction the particle is moving.

64. An object experiences linear acceleration given by

$$a(t) = 2t + 1 \quad \text{ft/s}^2$$

Find the velocity and position of the object, given that it starts its motion (at $t = 0$) at $s = 4$ with initial velocity 2 ft/s.

65. When it is x years old, a certain industrial machine generates revenue at the rate of $R'(x) = 1,575 - 5x^2$ thousand dollars per year. Find a function that measures the amount of revenue, and find the revenue for the first five years.

66. A manufacturer estimates marginal revenue to be $100x^{-1/3}$ dollars per unit when the level of production is x units. The corresponding marginal cost is found to be $0.4x$ dollars per unit. Suppose the manufacturer's profit is \$520 when the level of production is 16 units. What is the manufacturer's profit when the level of production is 25 units?

67. A tree has been transplanted and after t years is growing at a rate of

$$1 + \frac{1}{(t + 1)^2}$$

feet per year. After 2 years it has reached a height of 5 ft. How tall was the tree when it was transplanted?

68. A manufacturer estimates that the marginal revenue of a certain commodity is

$$R'(x) = \sqrt{x}(x^{3/2} + 1)^{-1/2}$$

dollars per unit when x units are produced. Assuming no revenue is obtained when $x = 0$, how much revenue is obtained from producing $x = 4$ units?

69. Find a function whose tangent has slope $x\sqrt{x^2 + 5}$ for each value of x and whose graph passes through the point $(2, 10)$.

70. A particle moves along the x-axis in such a way that after t seconds its acceleration is $a(t) = 12(2t + 1)^{-3/2}$. If it starts at rest at $x = 3$, where will it be 4 seconds later?

71. An environmental study of a certain community suggests that t years from now, the level of carbon monoxide in the air will be changing at the rate of $0.1t + 0.2$ parts per million per year. If the current level of carbon monoxide in the air is 3.4 parts per million, what will the level be 3 years from now?

72. A woman, driving on a straight, level road at the constant speed v_0, is forced to apply her brakes to avoid hitting a cow. The car comes to a stop 3 seconds later, s_0 ft from the point where the brakes were applied. Continuing on her way, she increases her speed by 20 ft/s to make up time but is again forced to hit the brakes, and this time it takes her 5 seconds and s_1 feet to come to a full stop. Assuming that her brakes supplied a constant deceleration k ft/s^2 each time they were used, find k and determine v_0, s_0, and s_1.

73. A study indicates that x months from now the population of a certain town will be increasing at the rate of $10 + 2\sqrt{x}$ people per month. By how much will the population of the town increase over the next 9 months?

74. It is estimated that t days from now a farmer's crop will be increasing at the rate of $0.3t^2 + 0.6t + 1$ bushels per day. By how much will the value of the crop increase during the next 6 days if the market price remains fixed at \$2 per bushel?

75. Records indicate that t months after the beginning of the year, the price of turkey in local supermarkets was

$$P(t) = 0.06t^2 - 0.2t + 1.2$$

dollars per pound. What was the average price of turkey during the first 6 months of the year?

76. Modeling Problem V. A. Tucker and K. Schmidt-Koenig have investigated the relationship between the velocity v (km/h) of a bird in flight and the energy $E(v)$ expended by the bird.* Their study showed that for a certain kind of parakeet, the rate of change of the energy expended with respect to velocity is modeled (for $v > 0$) by

$$\frac{dE}{dv} = \frac{0.074v^2 - 112.65}{v^2}$$

  a. What is the most economical velocity for the parakeet? That is, find the velocity v_0 that minimizes the energy.

  b. Suppose it is known that $E = E_0$ when $v = v_0$. Express E in terms of v_0 and E_0.

  c. Express the average energy expended as the parakeet's velocity ranges from $v = \frac{1}{2}v_0$ to $v = v_0$ in terms of E_0.

*Adapted from "Flight Speeds of Birds in Relation to Energies and Wind Directions," by V. A. Tucker and K. Schmidt-Koenig. *The Auk*, Vol. 88 (1971), pp. 97–107.

77. **Modeling Problem** A toxin is introduced into a bacterial culture, and t hours later, the population $P(t)$ of the culture is found to be changing at the rate

$$\frac{dP}{dt} = -(\ln 2)2^{5-t}$$

If there were 1 million bacteria in the culture when the toxin was introduced, when will the culture die out?

78. **Modeling Problem** *The Snowplow Problem of R. P. Agnew*[*] ■
(This problem was mentioned in the preview for this chapter.) One day it starts snowing at a steady rate sometime before noon. At noon, a snowplow starts to clear a straight, level section of road. If the plow clears 1 mile of road during the first hour but requires 2 hr to clear the second mile, at what time did it start snowing? Answer this question by completing the following steps:

a. Let t be the time (in hours) from noon. Let h be the depth of the snow at time t, and let s be the distance moved by the plow. If the plow has width w and clears snow at the constant rate p, explain why $wh\dfrac{ds}{dt} = p$.

b. Suppose it started snowing t_0 hours before noon. Let r denote the (constant) rate of snowfall. Explain why

$$h(t) = r(t + t_0)$$

By combining this equation with the differential equation in part **a**, note that

$$wr(t + t_0)\frac{ds}{dt} = p$$

Solve this differential equation (with appropriate conditions) to obtain t_0 and answer the question posed in the problem.

79. **a.** If f is continuous on $[a, b]$, show that

$$\left| \int_a^b f(x)\, dx \right| \le \int_a^b |f(x)|\, dx$$

b. Show that $\left| \displaystyle\int_1^4 \frac{\sin x}{x}\, dx \right| \le \frac{3}{2}.$

80. A company plans to hire additional advertising personnel. Suppose it is estimated that if x new people are hired, they will bring in additional revenue of $R(x) = \sqrt{2x}$ thousand dollars and that the cost of adding these x people will be $C(x) = \frac{1}{3}x$ thousand dollars. How many new people should be hired? How much total net revenue (that is, revenue minus cost) is gained by hiring these people?

81. The half-life of the radioactive isotope cobalt-60 is 5.25 years.

a. What percentage of a given sample of cobalt-60 remains after 5 years?

b. How long will it take for 90% of a given sample to disintegrate?

82. The rate at which salt dissolves in water is directly proportional to the amount that remains undissolved. If 8 lb of salt is placed in a container of water and 2 lb dissolves in 30 min, how long will it take for 1 lb to dissolve?

*There is an interesting discussion of this problem, along with a BASIC computer simulation, in the November 1995 (Vol. 26, No. 5) issue of *The College Mathematics Journal* in the article "The Meeting of the Plows: A Simulation" by Jerome Lewis (pp. 395–400).

83. Scientists are observing a species of insect in a certain swamp region. The insect population is estimated to be 10 million and is expected to grow at the rate of 2% per year. Assuming that the growth is exponential and stays that way for a period of years, what will the insect population be in 10 yr? How long will it take to double?

84. Solve the system of differential equations

$$\begin{cases} 2\dfrac{dx}{dt} + 5\dfrac{dy}{dt} = t \\[2mm] \dfrac{dx}{dt} + 3\dfrac{dy}{dt} = 7\cos t \end{cases}$$

Hint: Solve for $\dfrac{dx}{dt}$ and $\dfrac{dy}{dt}$ algebraically, and then integrate.

85. **Spy Problem** While lunching on cassoulet de chameau at his favorite restaurant in San Dimas (recall Problem 50, Section 5.1), the Spy finds a message from his esteemed superior, Lord Newton Fleming, spelled out in his alphabet soup, "The average of the temperature $F(t) = at^3 + bt^2 + ct + d$ over the time period from 9 A.M. to 3 P.M. is the average temperature between two fixed times t_1 and t_2. Mother waits at the well."

The Spy knows that "Mother" is the codename of Lord Newton himself, and "the well" is a sleazy bar at the edge of town. He decides that time t is measured from noon because the soup was served at that time. The cryptic nature of the message suggests that t_1 and t_2 are independent of a, b, c, and d and that one of them is the rendezvous time. When should he arrive for the meeting? (Remember, it's not wise to go to the well too often.)

86. **Putnam Examination Problem** Where on the parabola $4ay = x^2$ ($a > 0$) should a chord be drawn so that it will be normal to the parabola and cut off a parabolic sector of minimum area? That is, find P so that the shaded area in Figure 5.47 is as small as possible.

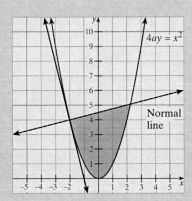

Figure 5.47 Minimum area problem

87. **Putnam Examination Problem** If $a_0, a_1, \ldots, a_n$ are real numbers that satisfy

$$\frac{a_0}{1} + \frac{a_1}{2} + \cdots + \frac{a_n}{n+1} = 0$$

show that the equation $a_0 + a_1 x + a_2 x^2 + \cdots + a_n x^n = 0$ has at least one real root. *Hint*: Use the mean value theorem for integrals.

Kinematics of Jogging

Ralph Boas (1912–1992), who was a professor of mathematics at Northwestern University, wrote this guest essay. Professor Boas was well known for his many papers and professional activities. In addition to his work in real and complex analysis, he wrote many expository articles, such as this guest essay, about teaching or using mathematics.

NATURE HERSELF EXHIBITS to us measurable and observable quantities in definite mathematical dependence; the conception of a function is suggested by all the processes of nature where we observe natural phenomena varying according to distance or to time. Nearly all the "known" functions have presented themselves in the attempt to solve geometrical, mechanical, or physical problems.

——J. T. Mertz
*A History of European Thought
in the Nineteenth Century*
(Edinburgh and London, 1903), p. 696.

Some people think that calculus is dull, but it did not seem so three centuries ago, when it was invented. Then, it produced unexpected results; and, now and then, it still does. This essay is about such a result.

You have learned about the intermediate value theorem (see Section 2.3), which tells you, for instance, that if you jog at 8 min per mile, there must be some instant when your speed is exactly $\frac{1}{8}$ mi per minute—assuming, as is only natural in a course in calculus, that your elapsed time is a continuous function of the distance covered. This principle is very intuitive and was recognized before calculus was invented: Galileo was aware of it in 1638, and thought that it had been known to Plato. On the other hand, there is a question with a much less intuitive answer that was noticed only recently (and, as happens more often than mathematicians like to admit, by a physicist). Suppose that you average 8 min/mi; must you cover some one continuous mile (such as a "measured mile" on a highway) in exactly 8 min? The answer is not intuitive at all: It depends on whether or not your total distance was an integral number of miles. More precisely, if you cover an integral number of miles, then you cover exactly one mile in some 8 min. However, if you cover a nonintegral number of miles, there is not necessarily any one continuous mile that you cover in 8 min.

To prove this, let x be the distance (in miles) covered at any point during your trip, and suppose that when you stop you have covered an integral number of n miles. Let $f(x)$ be the time (in minutes) that it took to cover the first x miles; we will suppose that f is a continuous function. If you averaged 8 min/mi, then $f(x) - 8x = 0$ when $x = 0$ and when $x = n$. Now suppose that you never did cover any consecutive mile in 8 min; in mathematical terms,

$$f(x + 1) - f(x) \neq 8$$

Because

$$f(x + 1) - f(x) - 8$$

is continuous and never 0, it must either always be positive, or else always negative; let us suppose the former. Write the corresponding facts for $x = 0, 1, \ldots, n$:

$$f(1) - f(0) > 8$$
$$f(2) - f(1) > 8$$
$$\vdots$$
$$f(n) - f(n - 1) > 8$$

If we add these inequalities, we obtain

$$f(n) - f(0) > 8n$$

But we started with the assumption that $f(n) = 8n$ and $f(0) = 0$, so assuming that $f(x + 1) - f(x)$ is never 8 leads to a contradiction.

351

It is somewhat harder to show that only integral values of n will work. Suppose you jog so that your time to cover x miles is

$$J(x) = k \sin^2 \frac{\pi x}{n} + 8x$$

where n is not an integer and k is a small number. This is a legitimate assumption, because J is an increasing function (as a time has to be), if k is small enough. To be sure of this, we calculate $J'(x)$—and here we actually have to use some calculus (or have a calculator that will do it for us). We find

$$J'(x) = \frac{k\pi}{n} \sin \frac{2\pi x}{n} + 8$$

If k is small enough ($k < \frac{8n}{\pi}$), then $J'(x) > 0$. This shows not only that J increases but also that

$$J(x + 1) - J(x)$$

cannot be eight. Because $J(x + 1) - J(x)$ is never negative, if you jog so that your time is $J(x)$, you will never cover a whole mile in less than 8 min.

Mathematical Essays

Use the Internet, a library, or references other than this textbook to research the information necessary to answer questions in Problems 1–11

1. HISTORICAL QUEST The derivative is one of the great ideas of calculus. Write an essay of at least 500 words about some application of the derivative that is not discussed in this text.

2. HISTORICAL QUEST The concept of the integral is one of the great ideas of calculus. Write an essay of at least 500 words about the relationship of integration and differentiation as it relates to the history of calculus.

3. HISTORICAL QUEST Write a report on Georg Riemann. (See Historical Quest in Section 5.3.) Include the 1984 development in the solution of the Riemann hypothesis.

4. HISTORICAL QUEST As we saw in a Historical Quest in Section 5.8, the mathematician Seki Kōwa was doing a form of integration at about the same time that Newton and Leibniz were inventing the calculus. Write a paper on the history of calculus from the Eastern viewpoint.

5. "Lucy," the famous prehuman whose skeleton was discovered in East Africa, has been found to be approximately 3.8 million years old. About what percentage of ^{14}C would you expect to find if you tried to "date" Lucy by the usual carbon dating procedure? The answer you get to this question illustrates why it is reasonable to use carbon dating only on more recent artifacts, usually less than 50,000 years old (roughly the time since the last major ice age). Read an article on alternative dating procedures such as potassium-argon and rubidium-strontium dating. Write a paper comparing and contrasting such methods.

6. In the guest essay it was assumed that the time to cover x miles is

$$J(x) = k \sin^2 \frac{\pi x}{n} + 8x$$

Suppose that $n = 5$. What choices for k seem reasonable?

7. Suppose that the time to cover x miles is given by

$$J(x) = \sin^2 \frac{\pi x}{5} + 8x$$

Graph this function on $[0, 8]$.

8. Use calculus to find how small k (from the guest essay) needs to be in the expression

$$J(x) = k \sin^2 \frac{\pi x}{n} + 8x$$

so that $J'(x) > 0$.

9. a. Find a number x, $x \neq 0$, that, when divided by 2, gives a display of 0 on your calculator. Write a paper describing your work as well as the processes on your calculator.

   b. Calculate $\sqrt{2}$ using a calculator. Next, repeatedly subtract the integer part of the displayed number and multiply the result by 10. Describe the outcome, and then devise a method for finding $\sqrt{2}$ using calculus. Write a paper comparing these answers.

10. **Book Report** Eli Maor, a native of Israel, has a long-standing interest in the relations between mathematics and the arts. Read the fascinating book *To Infinity and Beyond, A Cultural History of the Infinite* (Boston: Birkhäuser, 1987), and prepare a book report.

11. **Book Report** In Section 3.1, we told the story of Fermat's last theorem. The book *Fermat's Enigma* by Simon Singh (New York: Walker & Company, 1997) tells the story of how Andrew Wiles solved the greatest mathematical puzzle of our age: He locked himself in a room and emerged seven years later. Read this book and prepare a book report.

12. Make up a word problem involving an application of the integral. Send your problem and solution to

   Strauss, Bradley, and Smith
   Prentice Hall Publishing Company
   1 Lake Street
   Upper Saddle River, NJ 07458

The best one submitted will appear in the next edition (along with credit to the problem poser).

CHAPTERS 1–5   Cumulative Review

1. **WHAT DOES THIS SAY?** Define limit. Explain what this definition is saying using your own words.

2. **WHAT DOES THIS SAY?** Define derivative. Explain what this definition is saying using your own words.

3. **WHAT DOES THIS SAY?** Define a definite integral. Explain what this definition is saying using your own words.

4. **WHAT DOES THIS SAY?** Define a differential equation, and in your own words describe the procedure for solving a separable differential equation.

Evaluate the limits in Problems 5–13.

5. $\lim\limits_{x \to 2} \dfrac{3x^2 - 5x - 2}{3x^2 - 7x + 2}$

6. $\lim\limits_{x \to +\infty} \dfrac{3x^2 + 7x + 2}{5x^2 - 3x + 3}$

7. $\lim\limits_{x \to +\infty} (\sqrt{x^2 + x} - x)$

8. $\lim\limits_{x \to \pi/2} \dfrac{\cos^2 x}{\cos x^2}$

9. $\lim\limits_{x \to 0} \dfrac{x \sin x}{x + \sin^2 x}$

10. $\lim\limits_{x \to 0} \dfrac{\sin 3x}{x}$

11. $\lim\limits_{x \to +\infty} (1 + x)^{2/x}$

12. $\lim\limits_{x \to 0} \dfrac{\tan^{-1} x - x}{x^3}$

13. $\lim\limits_{x \to 0^+} x^{\sin x}$

Find the derivatives in Problems 14–22.

14. $y = 6x^3 - 4x + 2$

15. $y = (x^2 + 1)^3 (3x - 4)^2$

16. $y = \dfrac{x^2 - 4}{3x + 1}$

17. $y = \dfrac{x}{x + \cos x}$

18. $x^2 + 3xy + y^2 = 0$

19. $y = \sec^2 3x$

20. $y = e^{5x - 4}$

21. $y = \ln(5x^2 + 3x - 2)$

22. $y = \tan^{-1}(x^2 - 3)$

Find the integrals in Problems 23–28.

23. $\displaystyle\int_4^9 d\theta$

24. $\displaystyle\int_{-1}^1 50(2x - 5)^3 \, dx$

25. $\displaystyle\int_0^1 \dfrac{x \, dx}{\sqrt{9 + x^2}}$

26. $\displaystyle\int \csc 3\theta \cot 3\theta \, d\theta$

27. $\displaystyle\int \dfrac{e^x \, dx}{e^x + 2}$

28. $\displaystyle\int \dfrac{x^3 + 2x - 5}{x} \, dx$

29. Approximate $\displaystyle\int_0^4 \dfrac{dx}{\sqrt{1 + x^3}}$ using Simpson's rule with $n = 6$.

30. Sketch the graph of $y = x^3 - 5x^2 + 2x + 8$.

31. Sketch the graph of $y = \dfrac{4 + x^2}{4 - x^2}$.

32. Find the largest value of $f(x) = \frac{1}{3}x^3 - 2x^2 + 3x - 10$ on $[0, 6]$.

Solve the differential equations in Problems 33–34.

33. $\dfrac{dy}{dx} = x^2 y^2 \sqrt{4 - x^3}$

34. $(1 + x^2) \, dy = (x + 1) y \, dx$

Find the particular solution of the differential equations in Problems 35–36.

35. $\dfrac{dy}{dx} = 2(5 - y);\ y = 3$ when $x = 0$

36. $\dfrac{dy}{dx} = e^y \sin x;\ y = 5$ when $x = 0$

37. The graph of a function f consists of a semicircle of radius 3 and two line segments as shown in Figure 5.48. Let F be the function defined by

$$F(x) = \int_0^x f(t) \, dt$$

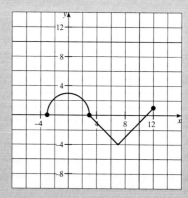

Figure 5.48   Graph of f

a. Find $F(7)$.

b. Find all values on the interval $(-3, 12)$ at which F has a relative maximum.

c. Write an equation for the line tangent to the graph of F at $x = 7$.

d. Find the x-coordinate of each point of inflection of the graph of F on the interval $(-3, 12)$.

38. An electric charge Q_0 is distributed uniformly over a ring of radius R. The electric field intensity at any point x along the axis of the ring is given by

$$E(x) = \dfrac{Q_0 x}{(x^2 + R^2)^{3/2}}$$

At what point on the axis is $E(x)$ maximized?

39. A rocket is launched vertically from a point on the ground 5,000 ft from a TV camera. If the rocket is rising vertically at the rate of 850 ft/s at the instant the rocket is 4,000 ft above the ground, how fast must the TV camera change the angle of elevation to keep the rocket in the picture?

40. A particle moves along the x-axis so that its velocity at any time $t \geq 0$ is given by $v(t) = 6t^2 - 2t - 4$. It is known that the particle is at position $x = 6$ for $t = 2$.

a. Find the position of the particle at any time $t \geq 0$.

b. For what value(s) of t, $0 \leq t \leq 3$, is the particle's instantaneous velocity the same as its average velocity over the interval $[0, 3]$.

c. Find the total distance traveled by the particle from time $t = 0$ to $t = 3$.

41. Let f be the function defined by $f(x) = 2 \cos x$. Let $P(0, 2)$ and $Q\left(\frac{\pi}{2}, 0\right)$ be the points where f crosses the y-axis and x-axis, respectively.

a. Write an equation for the secant line passing through points P and Q.

b. Write an equation for the tangent line of f at point Q.

c. Find the x-coordinate of the point on the graph of f, between point P and Q, at which the line tangent to the graph of f is parallel to $\overline{PQ}$. Cite a theorem or result that assures the existence of such a tangent.

42. Let f be the function defined by $f(x) = \sqrt{x-2}$.

   a. Sketch f and shade the region R enclosed by the graph of f, the x-axis, and the vertical line $x = 5$.

   b. Find the area of R.

43. Let f be the function defined by $f(x) = x^3 - 6x^2 + k$ for k an arbitrary constant.

   a. Find the relative maximum and minimum of f in terms of k.

   b. For which values of k does f have three distinct roots?

   c. Find the values of k for which the average value of f over $[-1, 2]$ is 2.

44. An object is thrown directly downward with velocity 5 ft/s from an airplane, and t seconds later is falling with acceleration

$$a(t) = 32 - 0.08v$$

where $v(t)$ is the object's velocity at time t.

   a. Find an expression for v in terms of t.

   b. If the terminal velocity is defined as $\lim_{t \to +\infty} v(t)$, find the terminal velocity of the object (to the nearest ft/s).

   c. The object can land safely if the impact velocity is no greater than 60 ft/s. What is the maximum altitude the airplane can fly to guarantee a safe landing for the object?

45. Solve the differential equation $\dfrac{dy}{dx} = y^2 \sin 3x$.

Appendices

Introduction to the Theory of Limits

In Section 2.1 we defined the limit of a function as follows:
The notation

$$\lim_{x \to c} f(x) = L$$

is read "the limit of $f(x)$ as x approaches c is L" and means that the function values $f(x)$ can be made arbitrarily close to L by choosing x sufficiently close to c but not equal to c.

This informal definition was valuable because it gave you an intuitive feeling for the limit of a function and allowed you to develop a working knowledge of this fundamental concept. For theoretical work, however, this definition will not suffice, because it gives no precise, quantifiable meaning to the terms "arbitrarily close to L" and "sufficiently close to c." The following definition, derived from the work of Cauchy and Weierstrass, gives precision to the limit definition and was also first stated in Section 2.1.

Limit of a Function (Formal definition)

The limit statement

$$\lim_{x \to c} f(x) = L$$

means that for each number $\epsilon > 0$, there corresponds a number $\delta > 0$ with the property that

$$|f(x) - L| < \epsilon \qquad \text{whenever} \qquad 0 < |x - c| < \delta$$

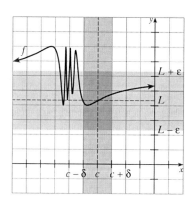

Figure A.1 The epsilon-delta definition of limit

Behind the formal language is a fairly straightforward idea. In particular, to establish a specific limit, say $\lim_{x \to c} f(x) = L$, a number $\epsilon > 0$ is chosen first to establish a desired degree of proximity to L, and then a number $\delta > 0$ is found that determines how close x must be to c to ensure that $f(x)$ is within ϵ units of L.

The situation is illustrated in Figure A.1, which shows a function that satisfies the conditions of the definition. Notice that whenever x is within δ units of c (but not equal to c), the point $(x, f(x))$ on the graph of f must lie in the rectangle (shaded region) formed by the intersection of the horizontal band of width 2ϵ centered at L and the vertical band of width 2δ centered at c. The smaller the ϵ-interval around the proposed limit L, generally the smaller the δ-interval will need to be in order for $f(x)$ to lie in the ϵ-interval. If such a δ can be found no matter how small ϵ is, then L must be the limit.

THE BELIEVER/DOUBTER FORMAT

The limit process can be thought of as a "contest" between a "believer" who claims that $\lim_{x \to c} f(x) = L$ and a "doubter" who disputes this claim. The contest begins with the doubter choosing a positive number ϵ and the believer countering with a positive number δ.

When will the believer win the argument and when will the doubter win? As you can see from Figure A.1, if the believer has the "correct limit" L, then no matter how the doubter chooses ϵ, the believer can find a δ so that the graph of $y = f(x)$ for $c - \delta < x < c + \delta$ will lie inside the heavily shaded rectangle in Figure A.1 (with the possible exception of $x = c$); that is, inside the rectangular region

$$R: \quad \text{width: } [c - \delta, c + \delta]; \quad \text{height: } [L - \epsilon, L + \epsilon]$$

On the other hand, if the believer tries to defend an incorrect value w (for "wrong") as the limit, then it will be possible for the doubter to choose an ϵ so that at least part of the curve $y = f(x)$ will lie outside the heavily shaded rectangle R, no matter what value of δ is chosen by the believer (see Figure A.2).

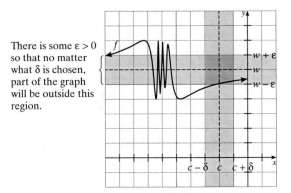

There is some $\epsilon > 0$ so that no matter what δ is chosen, part of the graph will be outside this region.

Figure A.2 False limit scenario

To avoid an endless chain of ϵ-δ challenges, the believer usually tries to settle the issue by producing a formula relating the choice of δ to the doubter's ϵ that will satisfy the requirement no matter what ϵ is chosen. The believer/doubter format is used in Example 1 to verify a given limit statement (believer "wins") and in Example 2 to show that a certain limit does not exist (doubter "wins").

EXAMPLE 1   Verifying a limit claim (believer wins)

Show that $\lim_{x \to 2}(2x + 1) = 5$.

Solution

Let $f(x) = 2x + 1$. To verify the given limit statement, we begin by having the doubter choose a positive number ϵ. To help the believer, choose $\delta > 0$, and note the computation in the following box.

$$|(2x + 1) - 5| = |2x - 4| = 2|x - 2|$$
Thus, if $0 < |x - c| < \delta$ or $0 < |x - 2| < \delta$, then
$$|(2x + 1) - 5| < 2\delta$$

The believer *wants* $|f(x) - L| < \epsilon$, so we see that the believer should choose $2\delta = \epsilon$, or $\delta = \frac{\epsilon}{2}$

With the information shown in this box, we can now make the following argument, which uses the formal definition of limit:

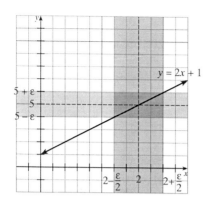

Figure A.3 Verifying $\lim_{x \to 2}(2x + 1) = 5$: Given $\epsilon > 0$, choose $\delta = \dfrac{\epsilon}{2}$.

Let $\epsilon > 0$ be given. The believer chooses $\delta = \frac{\epsilon}{2} > 0$ so that

$$|f(x) - L| = |(2x + 1) - 5| < 2\delta = 2\left(\frac{\epsilon}{2}\right) = \epsilon$$

whenever $0 < |x - 2| < \delta$, and the limit statement is verified. The graphical relationship between ϵ and δ is shown in Figure A.3. Notice that no matter what ϵ is chosen by the doubter, by choosing a number that is one-half of that ϵ, the believer will force the function to stay within the shaded portion of the graph, as shown in Figure A.3. ∎

EXAMPLE 2   Disproving a limit claim (doubter wins)

Determine whether $\lim_{x \to 2} \dfrac{2x^2 - 3x - 2}{x - 2} = 6$.

Solution

Let $f(x) = \dfrac{2x^2 - 3x - 2}{x - 2} = \dfrac{(2x + 1)(x - 2)}{x - 2} = 2x + 1$, $x \neq 2$. Once again, the doubter will choose a positive number ϵ and the believer must respond with a δ. As before, the believer does some preliminary work with $f(x) - L$:

$$\left| \frac{2x^2 - 3x - 2}{x - 2} - 6 \right| = \left| \frac{2x^2 - 3x - 2 - 6x + 12}{x - 2} \right|$$

$$= \left| \frac{2x^2 - 9x + 10}{x - 2} \right|$$

$$= \left| \frac{(2x - 5)(x - 2)}{x - 2} \right|$$

$$= |2x - 5|$$

The believer wants to write this expression in terms of $x - c = x - 2$. This example does not seem to "fall into place" as did Example 1. Let's analyze the situation shown in Figure A.4.

The doubter observes that if $\epsilon > 0$ is small enough, at least part of the line $y = 2x + 1$ for $0 < |x - 2| < \delta$ lies outside the shaded rectangle

$$R: \quad \text{width:} \quad [2 - \delta, 2 + \delta]; \quad \text{height:} \quad [6 - \epsilon, 6 + \epsilon]$$

regardless of the value of $\delta > 0$. For instance, suppose $\epsilon < 1$. Then, if δ is any positive number, we have

$$\left| f\left(2 - \frac{\delta}{2}\right) - 6 \right| = \left| \left[2\left(2 - \frac{\delta}{2}\right) + 1 \right] - 6 \right| = |-\delta - 1| > 1$$

so $|f(x) - 6| < \epsilon$ is not satisfied for all $0 < |x - 2| < \delta$ (in particular, not for $x = 2 - \frac{\delta}{2}$). Thus, $\lim_{x \to 2} \dfrac{2x^2 - 3x - 2}{x - 2} = 6$ is false. ∎

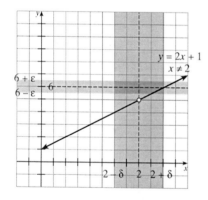

Figure A.4 Example of an incorrect limit statement

The believer/doubter format is a useful device for dramatizing the way certain choices are made in epsilon-delta arguments, but it is customary to be less "chatty" in formal mathematical proofs.

EXAMPLE 3   An epsilon-delta proof of a limit of a rational function

Show that $\lim_{x \to 2} \dfrac{x^2 - 2x + 2}{x - 4} = -1$.

Solution

Let $f(x) = \dfrac{x^2 - 2x + 2}{x - 4}$. We have

$$|f(x) - L| = \left| \frac{x^2 - 2x + 2}{x - 4} - (-1) \right|$$

$$= \left| \frac{x^2 - x - 2}{x - 4} \right|$$

$$= \underbrace{|x - 2| \left| \frac{x + 1}{x - 4} \right|}$$

This must be less than the given ϵ whenever x is near 2, but not equal to 2.

Certainly $|x - 2|$ is small if x is near 2, and the factor $\left| \dfrac{x + 1}{x - 4} \right|$ is not large (it is close to $\frac{3}{2}$). Note that if $|x - 2|$ is small it is reasonable to assume

$$|x - 2| < 1 \quad \text{so that} \quad 1 < x < 3$$

Let $g(x) = \dfrac{x + 1}{x - 4} = 1 + \dfrac{5}{x - 4}$; $g'(x) = -\dfrac{5}{(x - 4)^2} < 0$ on $(1, 3)$. Thus $g(x)$ is decreasing on $(1, 3)$ and

$$g(3) = \frac{4}{-1} < \frac{x + 1}{x - 4} < \frac{2}{-3} = g(1)$$

Hence, if $|x - 2| < 1$, then

$$-4 < \frac{x + 1}{x - 4} < 4 \qquad \text{Because } -\frac{2}{3} < 4$$

and

$$\left| \frac{x + 1}{x - 4} \right| < 4$$

Now let $\epsilon > 0$ be given. If simultaneously

$$|x - 2| < \frac{\epsilon}{4} \quad \text{and} \quad \left| \frac{x + 1}{x - 4} \right| < 4$$

then

$$|f(x) - L| = |x - 2| \left| \frac{x + 1}{x - 4} \right| < \frac{\epsilon}{4}(4) = \epsilon$$

Thus, we have only to take δ to be the smaller of the two numbers 1 and $\frac{\epsilon}{4}$ in order to guarantee that

$$|f(x) - L| < \epsilon$$

That is, given $\epsilon > 0$, choose δ to be the smaller of the numbers 1 and $\frac{\epsilon}{4}$. We write this as $\delta = \min\left(1, \frac{\epsilon}{4}\right)$. We can confirm this result by looking at the graph of $y = f(x)$ in Figure A.5). ■

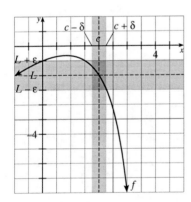

Figure A.5 $\displaystyle \lim_{x \to 2} \frac{x^2 - 2x + 2}{x - 4} = -1$

EXAMPLE 4   An epsilon-delta proof that a limit does not exist

Show that $\displaystyle \lim_{x \to 0} \frac{1}{x}$ does not exist.

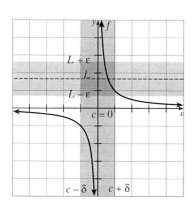

Figure A.6 $\lim\limits_{x\to 0}\dfrac{1}{x}$

Solution

Let $f(x) = \dfrac{1}{x}$ and L be any number. Suppose that $\lim\limits_{x\to 0} f(x) = L$. Look at the graph of f, as shown in Figure A.6. It would seem that no matter what value of ϵ is chosen, it would be impossible to find a corresponding δ. Consider the absolute value expression required by the definition of limit: If

$$|f(x) - L| < \epsilon, \qquad \text{or, for this example,} \qquad \left|\frac{1}{x} - L\right| < \epsilon$$

then

$$-\epsilon < \frac{1}{x} - L < \epsilon \qquad \text{Property of absolute value (Table 1.1, p. 3)}$$

and

$$L - \epsilon < \frac{1}{x} < L + \epsilon$$

If $\epsilon = 1$ (not a particularly small ϵ), then

$$\left|\frac{1}{x}\right| < |L| + 1$$

$$|x| > \frac{1}{|L| + 1}$$

and thus x is not close to zero which proves (since L was chosen arbitrarily) that $\lim\limits_{x\to 0}\dfrac{1}{x}$ does not exist. In other words, since $|x|$ can be chosen so that $0 < |x| < \dfrac{1}{|L| + 1}$, then $\dfrac{1}{|x|}$ will be very large, and it will be impossible to squeeze $\dfrac{1}{x}$ between $L - \epsilon$ and $L + \epsilon$ for any L. ∎

SELECTED THEOREMS WITH FORMAL PROOFS

Next, we will prove two theoretical results using the formal definition of the limit. These two theorems are useful tools in the development of calculus. The first states that the points on a graph that are on or above the x-axis cannot possibly "tend toward" a point *below* the axis, as shown in Figure A.7.

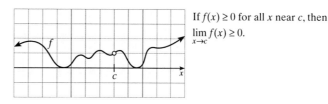

If $f(x) \geq 0$ for all x near c, then $\lim\limits_{x\to c} f(x) \geq 0$.

Figure A.7 Limit limitation theorem

THEOREM A.1 **Limit limitation theorem**

Suppose $\lim\limits_{x\to c} f(x)$ exists and $f(x) \geq 0$ throughout an open interval containing the number c, except possibly at c itself. Then

$$\lim_{x\to c} f(x) \geq 0$$

Proof   Let $L = \lim\limits_{x \to c} f(x)$. To show that $L \geq 0$, assume the contrary; that is, assume $L < 0$. According to the definition of limit (with $\epsilon = -L$), there is a number $\delta > 0$ such that

$$|f(x) - L| < -L \qquad \text{whenever} \qquad 0 < |x - c| < \delta$$

Thus,

$$f(x) - L < -L$$
$$f(x) < 0$$

whenever $0 < |x - c| < \delta$, which contradicts the hypothesis that $f(x) \geq 0$ throughout an open interval containing c (with the possible exception of $x = c$). The contradiction forces us to reject the assumption that $L < 0$, so $L \geq 0$, as required.   ❑

WARNING ➡ It may seem reasonable to conjecture that if $f(x) > 0$ throughout an open interval containing c, then $\lim\limits_{x \to c} f(x) > 0$. This is not necessarily true, and the most that can be said in this situation is that $\lim\limits_{x \to c} f(x) \geq 0$, if the limit exists. For example, if

$$f(x) = \begin{cases} x^2 & \text{for } x \neq 0 \\ 1 & \text{for } x = 0 \end{cases}$$

then $f(x) > 0$ for all x, but $\lim\limits_{x \to 0} f(x) = 0$.

Useful information about the limit of a given function f can often be obtained by examining other functions that bound f from above and below. For example, in Section 2.1 we discovered

$$\lim_{x \to 0} \frac{\sin x}{x} = 1$$

by using a table. We justified the limit statement in Section 2.2 by using a geometric argument to show that

$$\cos x \leq \frac{\sin x}{x} \leq 1$$

for all x near 0 and then noting that since $\cos x$ and 1 both tend toward 1 as x approaches 0, the function

$$\frac{\sin x}{x}$$

which is "squeezed" between them, must converge to 1 as well. Theorem A.2 provides the theoretical basis for this method of proof.

THEOREM A.2   The squeeze rule

If $g(x) \leq f(x) \leq h(x)$ for all x in an open interval containing c (except possibly at c itself) and if

$$\lim_{x \to c} g(x) = \lim_{x \to c} h(x) = L$$

then $\lim\limits_{x \to c} f(x) = L$. (This is stated, without proof, in Section 2.2.)

Proof   Let $\epsilon > 0$ be given. Since $\lim\limits_{x \to c} g(x) = L$ and $\lim\limits_{x \to c} h(x) = L$, there are positive numbers δ_1 and δ_2 such that

$$|g(x) - L| < \epsilon \quad \text{and} \quad |h(x) - L| < \epsilon$$

whenever

$$0 < |x - c| < \delta_1 \quad \text{and} \quad 0 < |x - c| < \delta_2$$

respectively. Let δ be the smaller of the numbers δ_1 and δ_2. Then, if x is a number that satisfies $0 < |x - c| < \delta$, we have

$$-\epsilon < g(x) - L \leq f(x) - L \leq h(x) - L < \epsilon$$

and it follows that $|f(x) - L| < \epsilon$. Thus, $\lim\limits_{x \to c} f(x) = L$, as claimed.   ❑

The geometric interpretation of the squeeze rule is shown in Figure A.8. Notice that since $g(x) \leq f(x) \leq h(x)$, the graph of f is "squeezed" between those of g and h in the neighborhood of c. Thus, if the bounding graphs converge to a common point P as x approaches c, then the graph of f must also converge to P as well.

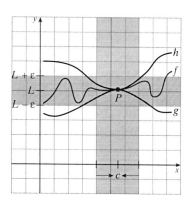

Figure A.8   The squeeze rule

A.1 PROBLEM SET

B *In Problems 1–6, use the believer/doubter format to prove or disprove the given limit statement.*

1. $\lim\limits_{x \to 1}(2x - 5) = -3$

2. $\lim\limits_{x \to -2}(3x + 7) = 1$

3. $\lim\limits_{x \to 1}(3x + 1) = 5$

4. $\lim\limits_{x \to 2}(x^2 - 2) = 5$

5. $\lim\limits_{x \to 2}(x^2 + 2) = 6$

6. $\lim\limits_{x \to 1}(x^2 - 3x + 2) = 0$

In Problems 7–12, use the formal definition of the limit to prove or disprove the given limit statement.

7. $\lim\limits_{x \to 2}(x + 3) = 5$

8. $\lim\limits_{t \to 0}(3t - 1) = 0$

9. $\lim\limits_{x \to -2}(3x + 7) = 1$

10. $\lim\limits_{x \to 1}(2x - 5) = -3$

11. $\lim\limits_{x \to 2}(x^2 + 2) = 6$

12. $\lim\limits_{x \to 2}\dfrac{1}{x} = \dfrac{1}{2}$

13. Prove that $f(x) = \begin{cases} \sin \dfrac{1}{x} & \text{if } x \neq 0 \\ 0 & \text{if } x = 0 \end{cases}$

is not continuous at $x = 0$. *Hint*: To show that $\lim\limits_{x \to 0} f(x) \neq 0$, choose $\epsilon = 0.5$ and note that for any $\delta > 0$, there exists an x of the form $x = \dfrac{2}{\pi(2n + 1)}$ with n a natural number for which $0 < |x| < \delta$.

C *In Problems 14–19, construct a formal ϵ-δ proof to show that the given limit statement is valid for any number c.*

14. If $\lim\limits_{x \to c} f(x)$ exists and k is a constant, then
$\lim\limits_{x \to c} k f(x) = k \lim\limits_{x \to c} f(x)$.

15. If $\lim\limits_{x \to c} f(x)$ and $\lim\limits_{x \to c} g(x)$ both exist, then
$\lim\limits_{x \to c}[f(x) - g(x)] = \lim\limits_{x \to c} f(x) - \lim\limits_{x \to c} g(x)$.

16. If $\lim\limits_{x \to c} f(x)$ and $\lim\limits_{x \to c} g(x)$ both exist and a and b are constants, then $\lim\limits_{x \to c}[a f(x) + b g(x)] = a \lim\limits_{x \to c} f(x) + b \lim\limits_{x \to c} g(x)$.

17. If $\lim\limits_{x \to c} f(x) = 0$ and $\lim\limits_{x \to c} g(x) = 0$, then $\lim\limits_{x \to c} f(x)g(x) = 0$.

18. If $f(x) \geq g(x) \geq 0$ for all x and $\lim\limits_{x \to c} f(x) = 0$, then $\lim\limits_{x \to c} g(x) = 0$.

19. If $f(x) \geq g(x)$ for all x in an open interval containing the number c and $\lim\limits_{x \to c} f(x)$ and $\lim\limits_{x \to c} g(x)$ both exist, then $\lim\limits_{x \to c} f(x) \geq \lim\limits_{x \to c} g(x)$. *Hint*: Apply the limit limitation theorem (Theorem A.1) to the function $h(x) = f(x) - g(x)$.

Problems 20–23 lead to a proof of the product rule for limits.

20. If $\lim\limits_{x \to c} f(x) = L$, show that $\lim\limits_{x \to c} |f(x)| = |L|$. *Hint*: Note that $\big||f(x)| - |L|\big| \leq |f(x) - L|$.

21. If $\lim\limits_{x \to c} f(x) = L$, $L \neq 0$, show that there exists a $\delta > 0$ such that

$$\tfrac{1}{2}|L| < |f(x)| < \tfrac{3}{2}|L|$$

for all x for which $0 < |x - c| < \delta$. *Hint*: Use $\epsilon = \tfrac{1}{2}|L|$ in Problem 20.

22. If $\lim\limits_{x \to c} f(x) = L$ and $L \neq 0$, show that $\lim\limits_{x \to c}[f(x)]^2 = L^2$ by completing these steps:

a. Use Problem 21 to show that there exists a $\delta_1 > 0$ so that

$$|f(x) + L| < \tfrac{5}{2}|L|$$

whenever $0 < |x - c| < \delta_1$.

b. Given $\epsilon > 0$, show that there exists a $\delta_2 > 0$ such that

$$\left|[f(x)]^2 - L^2\right| < \tfrac{5}{2}|L|\,\epsilon$$

whenever $0 < |x - c| < \delta_2$.

c. Complete the proof that

$$\lim_{x \to c}[f(x)]^2 = L^2$$

23. Prove the product rule for limits: If $\lim_{x \to c} f(x) = L$ and $\lim_{x \to c} g(x) = M$, then $\lim_{x \to c} f(x)g(x) = LM$. *Hint*: Use the result of Problem 22 along with the identity

$$fg = \tfrac{1}{4}[(f + g)^2 - (f - g)^2]$$

24. Show that if f is continuous at c and $f(c) > 0$, then $f(x) > 0$ throughout an open interval containing c. *Hint*: Note that $\lim_{x \to c} f(x) = f(c)$ and use $\epsilon = \tfrac{1}{2}f(c)$ in the definition of limit.

25. Show that if f is continuous at L and $\lim_{x \to c} g(x) = L$, then, $\lim_{x \to c} f[g(x)] = f(L)$ by completing the following steps:

a. Explain why there exists a $\delta_1 > 0$ such that $|f(w) - f(L)| < \epsilon$ whenever $|w - L| < \delta_1$.

b. Complete the proof by setting $w = g(x)$ and using part **a.**

26. For linear functions, the relation between ϵ and δ is clear; but for complicated functions, it is not. However, the correct graph can illustrate this relationship. For the following function, illustrate not only that f is continuous at $x = 3$, but determine graphically how you would pick δ to accommodate a given ϵ. (For example, $\delta = K^{-1}\epsilon$.)

$$f(x) = \frac{x^4 - 2x^3 + 3x^2 - 5x + 2}{x - 2}$$

APPENDIX B   Selected Proofs

CHAIN RULE (Chapter 3)

Suppose f is a differentiable function of u and u is a differentiable function of x. Then, $f[u(x)]$ is a differentiable function of x and

$$\frac{df}{dx} = \frac{df}{du}\frac{du}{dx}$$

Proof Define an auxiliary function g by

$$g(t) = \frac{f[u(x) + t] - f[u(x)]}{t} - \frac{df}{du} \quad \text{if } t \neq 0 \quad \text{and} \quad g(t) = 0 \quad \text{if } t = 0$$

You can verify that g is continuous at $t = 0$. Notice that for $t = \Delta u$ and $t \neq 0$,

$$g(\Delta u) = \frac{f[u(x) + \Delta u] - f[u(x)]}{\Delta u} - \frac{df}{du}$$

$$g(\Delta u) + \frac{df}{du} = \frac{f[u(x) + \Delta u] - f[u(x)]}{\Delta u}$$

$$\left[g(\Delta u) + \frac{df}{du}\right]\Delta u = f[u(x) + \Delta u] - f[u(x)]$$

We now use the definition of derivative for f.

$$\frac{df}{dx} = \lim_{\Delta x \to 0} \frac{f[u(x + \Delta x)] - f[u(x)]}{\Delta x}$$

$$= \lim_{\Delta x \to 0} \frac{f[u(x) + \Delta u] - f[u(x)]}{\Delta x} \qquad \text{Where } \Delta u = u(x + \Delta x) - u(x)$$

$$= \lim_{\Delta x \to 0} \frac{\left[g(\Delta u) + \dfrac{df}{du}\right]\Delta u}{\Delta x} \qquad \text{Substitution}$$

$$= \lim_{\Delta x \to 0} \left[g(\Delta u) + \frac{df}{du}\right]\frac{\Delta u}{\Delta x}$$

$$= \lim_{\Delta x \to 0} \left[g(\Delta u) + \frac{df}{du}\right] \lim_{\Delta x \to 0} \frac{\Delta u}{\Delta x}$$

$$= \left[\lim_{\Delta x \to 0} g(\Delta u) + \lim_{\Delta x \to 0} \frac{df}{du}\right] \lim_{\Delta x \to 0} \frac{\Delta u}{\Delta x}$$

$$= \left[0 + \frac{df}{du}\right] \frac{du}{dx}$$

Since g is continuous at $t = 0$

$$= \frac{df}{du} \frac{du}{dx}$$

CAUCHY'S GENERALIZED MEAN VALUE THEOREM (Chapter 4)

Let f and g be functions that are continuous on the closed interval $[a, b]$ and differentiable on the open interval (a, b). If $g(b) \neq g(a)$ and $g'(x) \neq 0$ on (a, b), then

$$\frac{f(b) - f(a)}{g(b) - g(a)} = \frac{f'(c)}{g'(c)}$$

for at least one number c between a and b.

Proof We begin by defining a special function, just as in the proof of the MVT as presented in Section 4.2. Specifically, let

$$F(x) = f(x) - f(a) - \frac{f(b) - f(a)}{g(b) - g(a)}[g(x) - g(a)]$$

for all x in the closed interval $[a, b]$. In the proof of the MVT in Section 4.2 we show that F satisfies the hypotheses of Rolle's theorem, which means that $F'(c) = 0$ for at least one number c in (a, b). For this number c, we have

$$0 = F'(c) = f'(c) - \frac{f(b) - f(a)}{g(b) - g(a)} g'(c)$$

and the result follows from this equation.

L'HÔPITAL'S RULE*(Chapter 4)

For any number a, let f and g be functions that are differentiable on an open interval (a, b), where $g'(x) \neq 0$. If $\lim_{x \to a^+} f(x) = 0$, $\lim_{x \to a^+} g(x) = 0$, and $\lim_{x \to a^+} \frac{f'(x)}{g'(x)}$ exists, then

$$\lim_{x \to a^+} \frac{f(x)}{g(x)} = \lim_{x \to a^+} \frac{f'(x)}{g'(x)}$$

Proof First, define auxiliary functions F and G by

$$F(x) = f(x) \quad \text{for } a < x \leq b \text{ and } F(a) = 0$$
$$G(x) = g(x) \quad \text{for } a < x \leq b \text{ and } G(a) = 0$$

These definitions guarantee that $F(x) = f(x)$ and $G(x) = g(x)$ for $a < x \leq b$ and that $F(a) = G(a) = 0$. Thus, if w is any number between a and b, the functions F and G are continuous on the closed interval $[a, w]$ and differentiable on the open interval (a, w). According to the Cauchy generalized mean value theorem, there exists a number t between a and w for which

$$\frac{F(w) - F(a)}{G(w) - G(a)} = \frac{F'(t)}{G'(t)}$$

$$\frac{F(w)}{G(w)} = \frac{F'(t)}{G'(t)} \qquad \text{Because } F(a) = G(a) = 0$$

$$\frac{f(w)}{g(w)} = \frac{f'(t)}{g'(t)} \qquad \text{Because } F(x) = f(x) \text{ and } G(x) = g(x)$$

*This is a special case of l'Hôpital's rule. The other cases can be found in most advanced calculus textbooks.

$$\lim_{w \to a^+} \frac{f(w)}{g(w)} = \lim_{w \to a^+} \frac{f'(t)}{g'(t)}$$

$$\lim_{w \to a^+} \frac{f(w)}{g(w)} = \lim_{t \to a^+} \frac{f'(t)}{g'(t)} \qquad \text{Because } t \text{ is "trapped" between } a \text{ and } w$$

$$\lim_{x \to a^+} \frac{f(x)}{g(x)} = \lim_{x \to a^+} \frac{f'(x)}{g'(x)} \qquad \qquad ❑$$

APPENDIX C   Significant Digits

Throughout this book, various Technology Notes appear, and in the answers to the problems you will frequently find approximate (decimal) answers. Sometimes your answer may not exactly agree with the answer found in the back of the book. This does not necessarily mean that your answer is incorrect, particularly if your answer is very close to the given answer.

To use your calculator intelligently and efficiently, you should become familiar with its functions and practice doing problems with the same calculator, whenever possible. Read the Technology Notes provided throughout this text, and consult the owner's manual for your particular calculator when you have questions. In addition, there are *Technology Manuals* accompanying this text which are available for TI and HP graphic calculators, as well as for Mathematica and for Maple.

SIGNIFICANT DIGITS

Applications involving measurements can never be exact. It is particularly important that you pay attention to the accuracy of your measurements when you use a computer or calculator, because using available technology can give you a false sense of security about the accuracy in a particular problem. For example, if you measure a triangle and find the sides are approximately 1.2 and 3.4 and then find the ratio of $1.2/3.4 \approx 0.35294117$, it appears that the result is more accurate than the original measurements! Some discussion about accuracy and significant digits is necessary.

The digits known to be correct in a number obtained by a measurement are called **significant digits**. The digits $1, 2, 3, 4, 5, 6, 7, 8,$ and 9 are always significant, whereas the digit 0 may or may not be significant.

1. Zeros that come between two other digits are significant, as in 203 or 10.04.
2. If the zero's only function is to place the decimal point, it is not significant, as in

$$\underbrace{0.00000}_{\text{Placeholders}} 23 \qquad \text{or} \qquad 23,\underbrace{000}_{\text{Placeholders}}$$

If a zero does more than fix the decimal point, it is significant, as in

$$0.0023\underbrace{0}_{\uparrow} \qquad \text{or} \qquad 23,000.0\underbrace{1}_{}$$
$$\text{This digit is significant.} \qquad \qquad \text{These are significant.}$$

This second rule can, of course, result in certain ambiguities, such as 23,000 (measured to the exact unit). To avoid such confusion, we use scientific notation in this case:

$$2.3 \times 10^4 \quad \text{has two significant digits}$$
$$2.3000 \times 10^4 \quad \text{has five significant digits}$$

Numbers that come about by counting are considered to be exact and are correct to any number of significant digits.

When you compute an answer using a calculator, the answer may have 10 or more digits. In the Technology Notes we generally show the 10 or 12 digits that result from the numerical calculation but frequently the number in the answer section will have only 5 or 6 digits in the answer. It seems clear that if the first 3 or 4 nonzero digits of the answer coincide, you probably have the correct method of doing the problem.

However, you might ask why there are discrepancies and how many digits you should use when you write down your final answer. Roughly speaking, the significant digits in a number are the digits that have meaning. To clarify the concept, we must for the moment assume that we know the exact answer. We then assume that we have been able to compute an approximation to this exact answer.

Usually we do this by some sort of iterative process, in which the answers are getting closer and closer to the exact answer. In such a process, we hope that the number of significant digits in our approximate answer is increasing at each trial. If our approximate answer is, say, 6 digits long (some of those digits might even be zero), and the difference between our answer and the exact answer is 4 units or less in the last place, then the first 5 digits are significant.

For example, if the exact answer is 3.14159 and our approximate answer is 3.14162, then our answer has 6 significant digits but is correct to 5 significant digits. Note that saying that our answer is correct to 5 significant digits does not guarantee that all of those 5 digits exactly match the first 5 digits of the exact answer. In fact, if an exact answer is 6.001 and our computed answer is 5.997, then our answer is correct to 3 significant digits and not one of them matches the digits in the exact answer. Also note that it may be necessary for an approximation to have more digits than are actually significant for it to have a certain number of significant digits. For example, if the exact answer is 6.003 and our approximation is 5.998, then it has 3 significant digits, but only if we consider the total 4-digit number and do not strip off the last nonsignificant digit.

Again, suppose you know that all digits are significant in the number 3.456; then you know that the exact number is less than 3.4565 and at least 3.4555. Some people may say that the number 3.456 is correct to 3 decimal places. This is the same as saying that it has 4 significant digits.Why bother with significant digits? If you multiply (or divide) two numbers with the same number of significant digits, then the product will generally be at least twice as long, but will have roughly the same number of significant digits as the original factors. You can then dispense with the unneeded digits. In fact, to keep them would be misleading about the accuracy of the result.

Frequently we can make an educated guess of the number of significant digits in an answer. For example, if we compute an iterative approximation such as

$$2.3123, \quad 2.3125, \quad 2.3126, \quad 2.31261, \quad 2.31262, \ldots$$

we would generally conclude that the answer is 2.3126 to 5 significant digits. Of course, we may very well be wrong, and if we continued iterating, the answer might end up as 2.4.

ROUNDING AND RULES OF COMPUTATION USED IN THIS BOOK

In hand and calculator computations, rounding a number is done to reduce the number of digits displayed and make the number easier to comprehend. Furthermore, if you suspect that the digit in the last place is not significant, then you might be tempted to round and remove this last digit. This can lead to error. For example, if the computed value is 0.64 and the true value is known to be between 0.61 and 0.67, then the computed value has only 1 significant digit. However, if we round it to 0.6 and the true value is really 0.66, then 0.6 is not correct to even 1 significant digit. In the interest of making the text easier to read, we have used the following rounding procedure:

Rounding Procedure

To round off numbers,

1. Increase the last retained digit by 1 if the remainder is greater than or equal to 5; or
2. Retain the last digit unchanged if the remainder is less than 5.

Elaborate rules for computation of approximate data can be developed when needed (in chemistry, for example), but in this text we will use three simple rules:

Rules For Significant Digits

Addition-subtraction: Add or subtract in the usual fashion, and then round off the result so that the last digit retained is in the column farthest to the right in which both given numbers have significant digits.

Multiplication-division: Multiply or divide in the usual fashion, and then round off the results to the smaller number of significant digits found in either of the given numbers.

Counting numbers: Numbers used to count or whole numbers used as exponents are considered to be correct to any number of significant digits.

Rounding Rule   We use the following rounding procedure in problems requiring rounding by involving several steps: Round only once, at the end. *That is, do not work with rounded results, because round-off errors can accumulate. If the problem does not ask for an approximate answer, but requires a calculator result, we will show the calculator result and leave it to the reader to write the appropriate number of digits.*

CALCULATOR EXPERIMENTS

You should be aware that you are much better than your calculator at performing certain computations. For example, almost all calculators will fail to give the correct answer to

$$(10.0 \text{ EE} + 50.0) + 911.0 - (10.0 \text{ EE} + 50.0)$$

Calculators will return the value of 0, but you know at a glance that the answer is 911.0. We must reckon with this poor behavior on the part of calculators, which is called *loss of accuracy* due to *catastrophic cancellation*. In this case, it is easy to catch the error immediately, but what if the computation is so complicated (or hidden by other computations) that we do not see the error?

First, we want to point out that the order in which you perform computations can be very important. For example, most calculators will correctly conclude that

$$(10.0 \text{ EE} + 50.0) - (10.0 \text{ EE} + 50.0) + 911.0 = 911$$

There are other cases besides catastrophic cancellation where the order in which a computation is performed will substantially affect the result. For example, you may not be able to calculate

$$(10.0 \text{ EE} + 50.0) * (911.0 \text{ EE} + 73.0)/(20.0 \text{ EE} + 60.0)$$

but rearranging the factors as

$$((10.0 \text{ EE} + 50.0)/(20.0 \text{ EE} + 60.0)) * (911.0 \text{ EE} + 73.0)$$

should provide the correct answer of 4.555 EE 65. So, for what do we need to watch? If you subtract two numbers that are close to each other in magnitude, you may obtain an inaccurate result. When you have a sequence of multiplications and divisions in a string, try to arrange the factors so that the result of each intermediate calculation stays as close as possible to 1.0.

Second, since a calculator performs all computations with a finite number of digits, it is unable to do exact computations involving nonterminating decimals. This enables us to see how many digits the calculator actually uses when it computes a result. For example, the computation

$$(7.0/17.0) * (17.0)$$

should give the result 7.0, but on most calculators it does not. The size of the answer gives an indication of how many digits "Accuracy" the calculator uses internally. That is, the calculator may display decimal numbers that have 10 digits, but use 12 digits internally. If the answer to the above computation is something similar to $1.0\ EE-12$, then the calculator is using 12 digits internally.

TRIGONOMETRIC EVALUATIONS

In many problems you will be asked to compute the values of trigonometric functions such as the sine, cosine, or tangent. In calculus, trigonometric arguments are usually assumed to be measured in radians. You must make sure the calculator is in radian mode. If it is in radian mode, then the sine of a small number will almost be equal to that number. For example,

$$\sin(0.00001) = 1\ E-5 \quad \text{(which is 0.00001)}$$

If not, then you are not using radian mode. Make sure you know how to put your calculator in radian mode.

GRAPHING BLUNDERS

When you are using the graphing features, you must always be careful to choose reasonable scales for the domain (horizontal scale) and range (vertical scale). If the scale is too large, you may not see important wiggles. If the scale is too small, you may not see important behavior elsewhere in the plane. Of course, knowing the techniques of graphing discussed in Chapter 4 will prevent you from making such blunders. Some calculators may have trouble with curves that jump suddenly at a point. An example of such a curve would be

$$y = \frac{e^x}{x}$$

which jumps at the origin. Try plotting this curve with your calculator using different horizontal and vertical scales, making sure that you understand how your calculator handles such graphs.

TECHNOLOGY NOTE

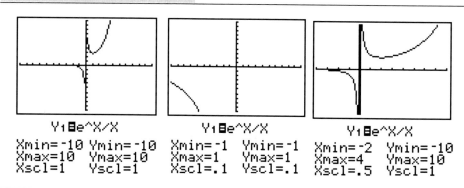

Y₁∎e^X/X
Xmin=-10 Ymin=-10
Xmax=10   Ymax=10
Xscl=1   Yscl=1

Y₁∎e^X/X
Xmin=-1   Ymin=-1
Xmax=1   Ymax=1
Xscl=.1   Yscl=.1

Y₁∎e^X/X
Xmin=-2   Ymin=-10
Xmax=4   Ymax=10
Xscl=.5   Yscl=1

APPENDIX D   Short Table of Integrals

Each formula is numbered for easy reference. The numbers in this short table are not sequential because this short table is truncated from the table of integrals found in the *Student Mathematics Handbook*.

BASIC FORMULAS

1. Constant rule

$$\int 0\, du = 0 + C$$

2. Power rule

$$\int u^n\, du = \frac{u^{n+1}}{n+1}; \quad n \neq -1$$

$$\int u^n\, du = \ln |u|; \quad n = -1$$

3. Natural Exponential rule

$$\int e^u\, du = e^u$$

4. Logarithmic rule

$$\int \ln |u|\, du = u \ln |u| - u$$

Trigonometric rules

5. $\displaystyle\int \sin u\, du = -\cos u$

6. $\displaystyle\int \cos u\, du = \sin u$

7. $\displaystyle\int \tan u\, du = -\ln |\cos u|$

8. $\displaystyle\int \cot u\, du = \ln |\sin u|$

9. $\displaystyle\int \sec u\, du = \ln |\sec u + \tan u|$

10. $\displaystyle\int \csc u\, du = -\ln |\csc u + \cot u|$

11. $\displaystyle\int \sec^2 u\, du = \tan u$

12. $\displaystyle\int \csc^2 u\, du = -\cot u$

13. $\displaystyle\int \sec u \tan u\, du = \sec u$

14. $\displaystyle\int \csc u \cot u\, du = -\csc u$

Exponential rule

15. $\displaystyle\int a^u\, du = \frac{a^u}{\ln a} \qquad a > 0,\ a \neq 1$

Hyperbolic rules

16. $\displaystyle\int \cosh u\, du = \sinh u$

17. $\displaystyle\int \sinh u\, du = \cosh u$

18. $\displaystyle\int \tanh u\, du = \ln \cosh u$

19. $\displaystyle\int \coth u\, du = \ln |\sinh u|$

20. $\displaystyle\int \operatorname{sech} u\, du = \tan^{-1}(\sinh u)$
$$= 2 \tan^{-1}(e^u)$$

21. $\displaystyle\int \operatorname{csch} u\, du = \ln \left| \tanh \frac{u}{2} \right|$

Inverse rules

22. $\displaystyle\int \frac{du}{\sqrt{a^2 - u^2}} = \sin^{-1} \frac{u}{a}$

23. $\displaystyle\int \frac{du}{\sqrt{u^2 - a^2}} = \cosh^{-1} \frac{u}{a}$

24. $\displaystyle\int \frac{du}{a^2 + u^2} = \frac{1}{a} \tan^{-1} \frac{u}{a}$

25. $\displaystyle\int \frac{du}{a^2 - u^2} = \begin{cases} \dfrac{1}{a}\tanh^{-1}\dfrac{u}{a} & \text{if } \left|\dfrac{u}{a}\right| < 1 \\[3mm] \dfrac{1}{a}\coth^{-1}\dfrac{u}{a} & \text{if } \left|\dfrac{u}{a}\right| > 1 \end{cases}$

26. $\displaystyle\int \frac{du}{u\sqrt{u^2 - a^2}} = \frac{1}{a}\sec^{-1}\left|\frac{u}{a}\right|$

27. $\displaystyle\int \frac{du}{u\sqrt{a^2 - u^2}} = -\frac{1}{a}\operatorname{sech}^{-1}\left|\frac{u}{a}\right| = -\frac{1}{a}\ln\left|\frac{a + \sqrt{a^2 - u^2}}{u}\right|$

28. $\displaystyle\int \frac{du}{\sqrt{a^2 + u^2}} = \ln\left(u + \sqrt{a^2 + u^2}\right) = \sinh^{-1}\frac{u}{a}$

29. $\displaystyle\int \frac{du}{u\sqrt{a^2 + u^2}} = -\frac{1}{a}\ln\left|\frac{\sqrt{a^2 + u^2} + a}{u}\right| = -\frac{1}{a}\operatorname{csch}^{-1}\left|\frac{u}{a}\right|$

INTEGRALS INVOLVING $au + b$

30. $\displaystyle\int (au + b)^n\, du = \frac{(au + b)^{n+1}}{(n + 1)a}$

31. $\displaystyle\int u(au + b)^n\, du = \frac{(au + b)^{n+2}}{(n + 2)a^2} - \frac{b(au + b)^{n+1}}{(n + 1)a^2}$

32. $\displaystyle\int u^2(au + b)^n\, du = \frac{(au + b)^{n+3}}{(n + 3)a^3} - \frac{2b(au + b)^{n+2}}{(n + 2)a^3} + \frac{b^2(au + b)^{n+1}}{(n + 1)a^3}$

33. $\displaystyle\int u^m(au + b)^n\, du = \begin{cases} \dfrac{u^{m+1}(au + b)^n}{m + n + 1} + \dfrac{nb}{m + n + 1}\displaystyle\int u^m(au + b)^{n-1}\, du \\[4mm] \dfrac{u^m(au + b)^{n+1}}{(m + n + 1)a} - \dfrac{mb}{(m + n + 1)a}\displaystyle\int u^{m-1}(au + b)^n\, du \\[4mm] \dfrac{-u^{m+1}(au + b)^{n+1}}{(n + 1)b} + \dfrac{m + n + 2}{(n + 1)b}\displaystyle\int u^m(au + b)^{n+1}\, du \end{cases}$

34. $\displaystyle\int \frac{du}{au + b} = \frac{1}{a}\ln|au + b|$

35. $\displaystyle\int \frac{u\, du}{au + b} = \frac{u}{a} - \frac{b}{a^2}\ln|au + b|$

36. $\displaystyle\int \frac{u^2\, du}{au + b} = \frac{(au + b)^2}{2a^3} - \frac{2b(au + b)}{a^3} + \frac{b^2}{a^3}\ln|au + b|$

37. $\displaystyle\int \frac{u^3\, du}{au + b} = \frac{(au + b)^3}{3a^4} - \frac{3b(au + b)^2}{2a^4} + \frac{3b^2(au + b)}{a^4} - \frac{b^3}{a^4}\ln|au + b|$

INTEGRALS INVOLVING $u^2 + a^2$

55. $\displaystyle\int \frac{du}{u^2 + a^2} = \frac{1}{a}\tan^{-1}\frac{u}{a}$

56. $\displaystyle\int \frac{u\, du}{u^2 + a^2} = \frac{1}{2}\ln(u^2 + a^2)$

57. $\displaystyle\int \frac{u^2\,du}{u^2+a^2} = u - a\tan^{-1}\frac{u}{a}$

58. $\displaystyle\int \frac{u^3\,du}{u^2+a^2} = \frac{u^2}{2} - \frac{a^2}{2}\ln(u^2+a^2)$

59. $\displaystyle\int \frac{du}{u(u^2+a^2)} = \frac{1}{2a^2}\ln\left(\frac{u^2}{u^2+a^2}\right)$

60. $\displaystyle\int \frac{du}{u^2(u^2+a^2)} = -\frac{1}{a^2u} - \frac{1}{a^3}\tan^{-1}\frac{u}{a}$

61. $\displaystyle\int \frac{du}{u^3(u^2+a^2)} = -\frac{1}{2a^2u^2} - \frac{1}{2a^4}\ln\left(\frac{u^2}{u^2+a^2}\right)$

INTEGRALS INVOLVING $u^2 - a^2$, $u^2 > a^2$

74. $\displaystyle\int \frac{du}{u^2-a^2} = \frac{1}{2a}\ln\left|\frac{u-a}{u+a}\right| \text{ or } -\frac{1}{a}\coth^{-1}\frac{u}{a}$

75. $\displaystyle\int \frac{u\,du}{u^2-a^2} = \frac{1}{2}\ln\left|u^2-a^2\right|$

76. $\displaystyle\int \frac{u^2\,du}{u^2-a^2} = u + \frac{a}{2}\ln\left|\frac{u-a}{u+a}\right|$

77. $\displaystyle\int \frac{u^3\,du}{u^2-a^2} = \frac{u^2}{2} + \frac{a^2}{2}\ln\left|u^2-a^2\right|$

78. $\displaystyle\int \frac{du}{u(u^2-a^2)} = \frac{1}{2a^2}\ln\left|\frac{u^2-a^2}{u^2}\right|$

79. $\displaystyle\int \frac{du}{u^2(u^2-a^2)} = \frac{1}{a^2u} + \frac{1}{2a^3}\ln\left|\frac{u-a}{u+a}\right|$

80. $\displaystyle\int \frac{du}{u^3(u^2-a^2)} = \frac{1}{2a^2u^2} - \frac{1}{2a^4}\ln\left|\frac{u^2}{u^2-a^2}\right|$

INTEGRALS INVOLVING $a^2 - u^2$, $u^2 < a^2$

93. $\displaystyle\int \frac{du}{a^2-u^2} = \frac{1}{2a}\ln\left|\frac{a+u}{a-u}\right| \text{ or } \frac{1}{a}\tanh^{-1}\frac{u}{a}$

94. $\displaystyle\int \frac{u\,du}{a^2-u^2} = -\frac{1}{2}\ln\left|a^2-u^2\right|$

95. $\displaystyle\int \frac{u^2\,du}{a^2-u^2} = -u + \frac{a}{2}\ln\left|\frac{a+u}{a-u}\right|$

96. $\displaystyle\int \frac{u^3\,du}{a^2-u^2} = -\frac{u^2}{2} - \frac{a^2}{2}\ln\left|a^2-u^2\right|$

97. $\displaystyle\int \frac{du}{u(a^2-u^2)} = \frac{1}{2a^2}\ln\left|\frac{u^2}{a^2-u^2}\right|$

98. $\displaystyle\int \frac{du}{u^2(a^2-u^2)} = -\frac{1}{a^2u} + \frac{1}{2a^3}\ln\left|\frac{a+u}{a-u}\right|$

99. $\int \dfrac{du}{u^3(a^2-u^2)} = -\dfrac{1}{2a^2u^2} + \dfrac{1}{2a^4} \ln \left| \dfrac{u^2}{a^2-u^2} \right|$

100. $\int \dfrac{du}{(a^2-u^2)^2} = \dfrac{u}{2a^2(a^2-u^2)} + \dfrac{1}{4a^3} \ln \left| \dfrac{a+u}{a-u} \right|$

101. $\int \dfrac{u\,du}{(a^2-u^2)^2} = \dfrac{1}{2(a^2-u^2)}$

102. $\int \dfrac{u^2\,du}{(a^2-u^2)^2} = \dfrac{u}{2(a^2-u^2)} - \dfrac{1}{4a} \ln \left| \dfrac{a+u}{a-u} \right|$

103. $\int \dfrac{u^3\,du}{(a^2-u^2)^2} = \dfrac{a^2}{2(a^2-u^2)} + \dfrac{1}{2} \ln \left| a^2-u^2 \right|$

104. $\int \dfrac{du}{u(a^2-u^2)^2} = \dfrac{1}{2a^2(a^2-u^2)} + \dfrac{1}{2a^4} \ln \left| \dfrac{u^2}{a^2-u^2} \right|$

105. $\int \dfrac{du}{u^2(a^2-u^2)^2} = \dfrac{-1}{a^4u} + \dfrac{u}{2a^4(a^2-u^2)} + \dfrac{3}{4a^5} \ln \left| \dfrac{a+u}{a-u} \right|$

106. $\int \dfrac{du}{u^3(a^2-u^2)^2} = \dfrac{-1}{2a^4u^2} + \dfrac{1}{2a^4(a^2-u^2)} + \dfrac{1}{a^6} \ln \left| \dfrac{u^2}{a^2-u^2} \right|$

INTEGRALS INVOLVING $\sqrt{au+b}$

135. $\int \dfrac{du}{\sqrt{au+b}} = \dfrac{2\sqrt{au+b}}{a}$

136. $\int \dfrac{u\,du}{\sqrt{au+b}} = \dfrac{2(au-2b)}{3a^2}\sqrt{au+b}$

137. $\int \dfrac{u^2\,du}{\sqrt{au+b}} = \dfrac{2(3a^2u^2-4abu+8b^2)}{15a^3}\sqrt{au+b}$

138. $\int \dfrac{du}{u\sqrt{au+b}} = \begin{cases} \dfrac{1}{\sqrt{b}} \ln \left| \dfrac{\sqrt{au+b}-\sqrt{b}}{\sqrt{au+b}+\sqrt{b}} \right| \\ \dfrac{2}{\sqrt{-b}} \tan^{-1} \sqrt{\dfrac{au+b}{-b}} \end{cases}$

139. $\int \dfrac{du}{u^2\sqrt{au+b}} = -\dfrac{\sqrt{au+b}}{bu} - \dfrac{a}{2b} \int \dfrac{du}{u\sqrt{au+b}}$

140. $\int \sqrt{au+b}\,du = \dfrac{2\sqrt{(au+b)^3}}{3a}$

141. $\int u\sqrt{au+b}\,du = \dfrac{2(3au-2b)}{15a^2}\sqrt{(au+b)^3}$

142. $\int u^2\sqrt{au+b}\,du = \dfrac{2(15a^2u^2-12abu+8b^2)}{105a^3}\sqrt{(au+b)^3}$

INTEGRALS INVOLVING $\sqrt{u^2 + a^2}$

168. $\displaystyle \int \sqrt{u^2 + a^2}\, du = \frac{u\sqrt{u^2 + a^2}}{2} + \frac{a^2}{2}\ln\left(u + \sqrt{u^2 + a^2}\right)$

169. $\displaystyle \int u\sqrt{u^2 + a^2}\, du = \frac{(u^2 + a^2)^{3/2}}{3}$

170. $\displaystyle \int u^2\sqrt{u^2 + a^2}\, du = \frac{u(u^2 + a^2)^{3/2}}{4} - \frac{a^2 u\sqrt{u^2 + a^2}}{8} - \frac{a^4}{8}\ln\left(u + \sqrt{u^2 + a^2}\right)$

171. $\displaystyle \int u^3\sqrt{u^2 + a^2}\, du = \frac{(u^2 + a^2)^{5/2}}{5} - \frac{a^2(u^2 + a^2)^{3/2}}{3}$

172. $\displaystyle \int \frac{du}{\sqrt{u^2 + a^2}} = \ln\left(u + \sqrt{u^2 + a^2}\right) \text{ or } \sinh^{-1}\frac{u}{a}$

173. $\displaystyle \int \frac{u\, du}{\sqrt{u^2 + a^2}} = \sqrt{u^2 + a^2}$

174. $\displaystyle \int \frac{u^2\, du}{\sqrt{u^2 + a^2}} = \frac{u\sqrt{u^2 + a^2}}{2} - \frac{a^2}{2}\ln\left(u + \sqrt{u^2 + a^2}\right)$

175. $\displaystyle \int \frac{u^3\, du}{\sqrt{u^2 + a^2}} = \frac{(u^2 + a^2)^{3/2}}{3} - a^2\sqrt{u^2 + a^2}$

176. $\displaystyle \int \frac{du}{u\sqrt{u^2 + a^2}} = -\frac{1}{a}\ln\left|\frac{a + \sqrt{u^2 + a^2}}{u}\right|$

177. $\displaystyle \int \frac{du}{u^2\sqrt{u^2 + a^2}} = -\frac{\sqrt{u^2 + a^2}}{a^2 u}$

178. $\displaystyle \int \frac{du}{u^3\sqrt{u^2 + a^2}} = -\frac{\sqrt{u^2 + a^2}}{2a^2 u^2} + \frac{1}{2a^3}\ln\left|\frac{a + \sqrt{u^2 + a^2}}{u}\right|$

179. $\displaystyle \int \frac{\sqrt{u^2 + a^2}}{u}\, du = \sqrt{u^2 + a^2} - a\ln\left|\frac{a + \sqrt{u^2 + a^2}}{u}\right|$

180. $\displaystyle \int \frac{\sqrt{u^2 + a^2}}{u^2}\, du = -\frac{\sqrt{u^2 + a^2}}{u} + \ln\left(u + \sqrt{u^2 + a^2}\right)$

INTEGRALS INVOLVING $\sqrt{u^2 - a^2}$

196. $\displaystyle \int \frac{du}{\sqrt{u^2 - a^2}} = \ln\left|u + \sqrt{u^2 - a^2}\right|$

197. $\displaystyle \int \frac{u\, du}{\sqrt{u^2 - a^2}} = \sqrt{u^2 - a^2}$

198. $\displaystyle \int \frac{u^2\, du}{\sqrt{u^2 - a^2}} = \frac{u\sqrt{u^2 - a^2}}{2} + \frac{a^2}{2}\ln\left|u + \sqrt{u^2 - a^2}\right|$

199. $\displaystyle \int \frac{u^3\, du}{\sqrt{u^2 - a^2}} = \frac{(u^2 - a^2)^{3/2}}{3} + a^2\sqrt{u^2 - a^2}$

200. $\displaystyle \int \frac{du}{u\sqrt{u^2 - a^2}} = \frac{1}{a}\sec^{-1}\left|\frac{u}{a}\right|$

201. $\displaystyle\int \frac{du}{u^2\sqrt{u^2-a^2}} = \frac{\sqrt{u^2-a^2}}{a^2 u}$

202. $\displaystyle\int \frac{du}{u^3\sqrt{u^2-a^2}} = \frac{\sqrt{u^2-a^2}}{2a^2 u^2} + \frac{1}{2a^3}\sec^{-1}\left|\frac{u}{a}\right|$

203. $\displaystyle\int \sqrt{u^2-a^2}\,du = \frac{u\sqrt{u^2-a^2}}{2} - \frac{a^2}{2}\ln\left|u+\sqrt{u^2-a^2}\right|$

204. $\displaystyle\int u\sqrt{u^2-a^2}\,du = \frac{(u^2-a^2)^{3/2}}{3}$

205. $\displaystyle\int u^2\sqrt{u^2-a^2}\,du = \frac{u(u^2-a^2)^{3/2}}{4} + \frac{a^2 u\sqrt{u^2-a^2}}{8} - \frac{a^4}{8}\ln\left|u+\sqrt{u^2-a^2}\right|$

206. $\displaystyle\int u^3\sqrt{u^2-a^2}\,du = \frac{(u^2-a^2)^{5}/2}{5} + \frac{a^2(u^2-a^2)^{3/2}}{3}$

INTEGRALS INVOLVING $\sqrt{a^2-u^2}$

224. $\displaystyle\int \frac{du}{\sqrt{a^2-u^2}} = \sin^{-1}\frac{u}{a}$

225. $\displaystyle\int \frac{u\,du}{\sqrt{a^2-u^2}} = -\sqrt{a^2-u^2}$

226. $\displaystyle\int \frac{u^2\,du}{\sqrt{a^2-u^2}} = -\frac{u\sqrt{a^2-u^2}}{2} + \frac{a^2}{2}\sin^{-1}\frac{u}{a}$

227. $\displaystyle\int \frac{u^3\,du}{\sqrt{a^2-u^2}} = \frac{(a^2-u^2)^{3/2}}{3} - a^2\sqrt{a^2-u^2}$

228. $\displaystyle\int \frac{du}{u\sqrt{a^2-u^2}} = -\frac{1}{a}\ln\left|\frac{a+\sqrt{a^2-u^2}}{u}\right| \text{ or } -\frac{1}{a}\operatorname{sech}^{-1}\left|\frac{u}{a}\right|$

229. $\displaystyle\int \frac{du}{u^2\sqrt{a^2-u^2}} = -\frac{\sqrt{a^2-u^2}}{a^2 u}$

230. $\displaystyle\int \frac{du}{u^3\sqrt{a^2-u^2}} = -\frac{\sqrt{a^2-u^2}}{2a^2 u^2} - \frac{1}{2a^3}\ln\left|\frac{a+\sqrt{a^2-u^2}}{u}\right|$

231. $\displaystyle\int \sqrt{a^2-u^2}\,du = \frac{u\sqrt{a^2-u^2}}{2} + \frac{a^2}{2}\sin^{-1}\frac{u}{a}$

232. $\displaystyle\int u\sqrt{a^2-u^2}\,du = -\frac{(a^2-u^2)^{3/2}}{3}$

233. $\displaystyle\int u^2\sqrt{a^2-u^2}\,du = -\frac{u(a^2-u^2)^{3/2}}{4} + \frac{a^2 u\sqrt{a^2-u^2}}{8} + \frac{a^4}{8}\sin^{-1}\frac{u}{a}$

234. $\displaystyle\int u^3\sqrt{a^2-u^2}\,du = \frac{(a^2-u^2)^{5/2}}{5} - \frac{a^2(a^2-u^2)^{3/2}}{3}$

235. $\displaystyle\int \frac{\sqrt{a^2-u^2}}{u}\,du = \sqrt{a^2-u^2} - a\ln\left|\frac{a+\sqrt{a^2-u^2}}{u}\right|$

INTEGRALS INVOLVING $\cos au$

311. $\displaystyle\int \cos au\, du = \frac{\sin au}{a}$

312. $\displaystyle\int u \cos au\, du = \frac{\cos au}{a^2} + \frac{u \sin au}{a}$

313. $\displaystyle\int u^2 \cos au\, du = \frac{2u}{a^2}\cos au + \left(\frac{u^2}{a} - \frac{2}{a^3}\right)\sin au$

314. $\displaystyle\int u^3 \cos au\, du = \left(\frac{3u^2}{a^2} - \frac{6}{a^4}\right)\cos au + \left(\frac{u^3}{a} - \frac{6u}{a^3}\right)\sin au$

315. $\displaystyle\int u^n \cos au\, du = \frac{u^n \sin au}{a} - \frac{n}{a}\int u^{n-1}\sin au\, du$

316. $\displaystyle\int u^n \cos au\, du = \frac{u^n \sin au}{a} + \frac{nu^{n-1}}{a^2}\cos au - \frac{n(n-1)}{a^2}\int u^{n-2}\cos au\, du$

317. $\displaystyle\int \cos^2 au\, du = \frac{u}{2} + \frac{\sin 2au}{4a}$

INTEGRALS INVOLVING $\sin au$

342. $\displaystyle\int \sin au\, du = -\frac{\cos au}{a}$

343. $\displaystyle\int u \sin au\, du = \frac{\sin au}{a^2} - \frac{u \cos au}{a}$

344. $\displaystyle\int u^2 \sin au\, du = \frac{2u}{a^2}\sin au + \left(\frac{2}{a^3} - \frac{u^2}{a}\right)\cos au$

345. $\displaystyle\int u^3 \sin au\, du = \left(\frac{3u^2}{a^2} - \frac{6}{a^4}\right)\sin au + \left(\frac{6u}{a^3} - \frac{u^3}{a}\right)\cos au$

346. $\displaystyle\int u^n \sin au\, du = -\frac{u^n \cos au}{a} + \frac{n}{a}\int u^{n-1}\cos au\, du$

347. $\displaystyle\int u^n \sin au\, du = -\frac{u^n \cos au}{a} + \frac{nu^{n-1}\sin au}{a^2} - \frac{n(n-1)}{a^2}\int u^{n-2}\sin au\, du$

348. $\displaystyle\int \sin^2 au\, du = \frac{u}{2} - \frac{\sin 2au}{4a}$

349. $\displaystyle\int u \sin^2 au\, du = \frac{u^2}{4} - \frac{u \sin 2au}{4a} - \frac{\cos 2au}{8a^2}$

350. $\displaystyle\int \sin^3 au\, du = -\frac{\cos au}{a} + \frac{\cos^3 au}{3a}$

351. $\displaystyle\int \sin^4 au\, du = \frac{3u}{8} - \frac{\sin 2au}{4a} + \frac{\sin 4au}{32a}$

INTEGRALS INVOLVING sin *au* and cos *au*

373. $\displaystyle\int \sin au \cos au \, du = \frac{\sin^2 au}{2a}$

374. $\displaystyle\int \sin pu \cos qu \, du = -\frac{\cos(p-q)u}{2(p-q)} - \frac{\cos(p+q)u}{2(p+q)}$

375. $\displaystyle\int \sin^n au \cos au \, du = \frac{\sin^{n+1} au}{(n+1)a}$

376. $\displaystyle\int \cos^n au \sin au \, du = -\frac{\cos^{n+1} au}{(n+1)a}$

377. $\displaystyle\int \sin^2 au \cos^2 au \, du = \frac{u}{8} - \frac{\sin 4au}{32a}$

378. $\displaystyle\int \frac{du}{\sin au \cos au} = \frac{1}{a} \ln |\tan au|$

379. $\displaystyle\int \frac{du}{\sin^2 au \cos au} = \frac{1}{a} \ln \left| \tan \left(\frac{\pi}{4} + \frac{au}{2} \right) \right| - \frac{1}{a \sin au}$

380. $\displaystyle\int \frac{du}{\sin au \cos^2 au} = \frac{1}{a} \ln \left| \tan \frac{au}{2} \right| + \frac{1}{a \cos au}$

INTEGRALS INVOLVING tan *au*

403. $\displaystyle\int \tan au \, du = -\frac{1}{a} \ln |\cos au| \text{ or } \frac{1}{a} \ln |\sec au|$

404. $\displaystyle\int \tan^2 au \, du = \frac{\tan au}{a} - u$

405. $\displaystyle\int \tan^3 au \, du = \frac{\tan^2 au}{2a} + \frac{1}{a} \ln |\cos au|$

406. $\displaystyle\int \tan^n au \, du = \frac{\tan^{n-1} au}{(n-1)a} - \int \tan^{n-2} au \, du$

407. $\displaystyle\int \tan^n au \sec^2 au \, du = \frac{\tan^{n+1} au}{(n+1)a}$

INTEGRALS INVOLVING cot *au*

414. $\displaystyle\int \cot au \, du = \frac{1}{a} \ln |\sin au|$

415. $\displaystyle\int \cot^2 au \, du = -\frac{\cot au}{a} - u$

416. $\displaystyle\int \cot^3 au \, du = -\frac{\cot^2 au}{2a} - \frac{1}{a} \ln |\sin au|$

417. $\displaystyle\int \cot^n au \, du = -\frac{\cot^{n-1} au}{(n-1)a} - \int \cot^{n-2} au \, du$

INTEGRALS INVOLVING sec *au*

425. $\int \sec au\, du = \dfrac{1}{a} \ln |\sec au + \tan au| = \dfrac{1}{a} \ln \left| \tan \left(\dfrac{au}{2} + \dfrac{\pi}{4} \right) \right|$

426. $\int \sec^2 au\, du = \dfrac{\tan au}{a}$

427. $\int \sec^3 au\, du = \dfrac{\sec au \tan au}{2a} + \dfrac{1}{2a} \ln |\sec au + \tan au|$

428. $\int \sec^n au\, du = \dfrac{\sec^{n-2} au \tan au}{a(n-1)} + \dfrac{n-2}{n-1} \int \sec^{n-2} au\, du$

INTEGRALS INVOLVING csc *au*

435. $\int \csc au\, du = \dfrac{1}{a} \ln |\csc au - \cot au| = \dfrac{1}{a} \ln \left| \tan \dfrac{au}{2} \right|$

436. $\int \csc^2 au\, du = -\dfrac{\cot au}{a}$

437. $\int \csc^3 au\, du = -\dfrac{\csc au \cot au}{2a} + \dfrac{1}{2a} \ln \left| \tan \dfrac{au}{2} \right|$

438. $\int \csc^n au\, du = -\dfrac{\csc^{n-2} au \cot au}{a(n-1)} + \dfrac{n-2}{n-1} \int \csc^{n-2} au\, du$

INTEGRALS INVOLVING INVERSE TRIGONOMETRIC FUNCTIONS

445. $\int \cos^{-1} \dfrac{u}{a}\, du = u \cos^{-1} \dfrac{u}{a} - \sqrt{a^2 - u^2}$

446. $\int u \cos^{-1} \dfrac{u}{a}\, du = \left(\dfrac{u^2}{2} - \dfrac{a^2}{4} \right) \cos^{-1} \dfrac{u}{a} - \dfrac{u\sqrt{a^2 - u^2}}{4}$

447. $\int u^2 \cos^{-1} \dfrac{u}{a}\, du = \dfrac{u^3}{3} \cos^{-1} \dfrac{u}{a} - \dfrac{(u^2 + 2a^2)\sqrt{a^2 - u^2}}{9}$

448. $\int \dfrac{\cos^{-1}(u/a)}{u}\, du = \dfrac{\pi}{2} \ln |u| - \int \dfrac{\sin^{-1}(u/a)}{u}\, du$

449. $\int \dfrac{\cos^{-1}(u/a)}{u^2}\, du = -\dfrac{\cos^{-1}(u/a)}{u} + \dfrac{1}{a} \ln \left| \dfrac{a + \sqrt{a^2 - u^2}}{u} \right|$

450. $\int \left(\cos^{-1} \dfrac{u}{a} \right)^2 du = u \left(\cos^{-1} \dfrac{u}{a} \right)^2 - 2u - 2\sqrt{a^2 - u^2} \cos^{-1} \dfrac{u}{a}$

451. $\int \sin^{-1} \dfrac{u}{a}\, du = u \sin^{-1} \dfrac{u}{a} + \sqrt{a^2 - u^2}$

452. $\int u \sin^{-1} \dfrac{u}{a}\, du = \left(\dfrac{u^2}{2} - \dfrac{a^2}{4} \right) \sin^{-1} \dfrac{u}{a} + \dfrac{u\sqrt{a^2 - u^2}}{4}$

453. $\int u^2 \sin^{-1} \dfrac{u}{a}\, du = \dfrac{u^3}{3} \sin^{-1} \dfrac{u}{a} + \dfrac{(u^2 + 2a^2)\sqrt{a^2 - u^2}}{9}$

454. $\int \dfrac{\sin^{-1}(u/a)}{u}\, du = \dfrac{u}{a} + \dfrac{(u/a)^3}{2 \cdot 3 \cdot 3} + \dfrac{1 \cdot 3(u/a)^5}{2 \cdot 4 \cdot 5 \cdot 5} + \dfrac{1 \cdot 3 \cdot 5(u/a)^7}{2 \cdot 4 \cdot 6 \cdot 7 \cdot 7} + \cdots$

455. $\displaystyle\int \frac{\sin^{-1}(u/a)}{u^2}\,du = -\frac{\sin^{-1}(u/a)}{u} - \frac{1}{a}\ln\left|\frac{a+\sqrt{a^2-u^2}}{u}\right|$

456. $\displaystyle\int \left(\sin^{-1}\frac{u}{a}\right)^2 du = u\left(\sin^{-1}\frac{u}{a}\right)^2 - 2u + 2\sqrt{a^2-u^2}\,\sin^{-1}\frac{u}{a}$

457. $\displaystyle\int \tan^{-1}\frac{u}{a}\,du = u\tan^{-1}\frac{u}{a} - \frac{a}{2}\ln\left(u^2+a^2\right)$

458. $\displaystyle\int u\tan^{-1}\frac{u}{a}\,du = \frac{1}{2}(u^2+a^2)\tan^{-1}\frac{u}{a} - \frac{au}{2}$

459. $\displaystyle\int u^2\tan^{-1}\frac{u}{a}\,du = \frac{u^3}{3}\tan^{-1}\frac{u}{a} - \frac{au^2}{6} + \frac{a^3}{6}\ln(u^2+a^2)$

INTEGRALS INVOLVING e^{au}

483. $\displaystyle\int e^{au}\,du = \frac{e^{au}}{a}$

484. $\displaystyle\int ue^{au}\,du = \frac{e^{au}}{a}\left(u-\frac{1}{a}\right)$

485. $\displaystyle\int u^2 e^{au}\,du = \frac{e^{au}}{a}\left(u^2 - \frac{2u}{a} + \frac{2}{a^2}\right)$

486. $\displaystyle\int u^n e^{au}\,du = \frac{u^n e^{au}}{a} - \frac{n}{a}\int u^{n-1} e^{au}\,du$

$$= \frac{e^{au}}{a}\left(u^n - \frac{nu^{n-1}}{a} + \frac{n(n-1)u^{n-2}}{a^2} - \cdots + \frac{(-1)^n n!}{a^n}\right)$$

if n = positive integer

487. $\displaystyle\int \frac{e^{au}}{u}\,du = \ln|u| + \frac{au}{1\cdot 1!} + \frac{(au)^2}{2\cdot 2!} + \frac{(au)^3}{3\cdot 3!} + \cdots$

488. $\displaystyle\int \frac{e^{au}}{u^n}\,du = \frac{-e^{au}}{(n-1)u^{n-1}} + \frac{a}{n-1}\int \frac{e^{au}}{u^{n-1}}\,du$

489. $\displaystyle\int \frac{du}{p+qe^{au}} = \frac{u}{p} - \frac{1}{ap}\ln|p+qe^{au}|$

490. $\displaystyle\int \frac{du}{(p+qe^{au})^2} = \frac{u}{p^2} + \frac{1}{ap(p+qe^{au})} - \frac{1}{ap^2}\ln|p+qe^{au}|$

491. $\displaystyle\int \frac{du}{pe^{au}+qe^{-au}} = \begin{cases} \dfrac{1}{a\sqrt{pq}}\tan^{-1}\left(\sqrt{\dfrac{p}{q}}\,e^{au}\right) \\[2em] \dfrac{1}{2a\sqrt{-pq}}\ln\left|\dfrac{e^{au}-\sqrt{-q/p}}{e^{au}+\sqrt{-q/p}}\right| \end{cases}$

492. $\displaystyle\int e^{au}\sin bu\,du = \frac{e^{au}(a\sin bu - b\cos bu)}{a^2+b^2}$

493. $\displaystyle\int e^{au}\cos bu\,du = \frac{e^{au}(a\cos bu + b\sin bu)}{a^2+b^2}$

494. $\displaystyle\int ue^{au}\sin bu\,du = \frac{ue^{au}(a\sin bu - b\cos bu)}{a^2+b^2}$

$$-\frac{e^{au}[(a^2-b^2)\sin bu - 2ab\cos bu]}{(a^2+b^2)^2}$$

495. $\int ue^{au} \cos bu \, du = \dfrac{ue^{au}(a \cos bu + b \sin bu)}{a^2 + b^2}$

$$- \dfrac{e^{au}[(a^2 - b^2) \cos bu + 2ab \sin bu]}{(a^2 + b^2)^2}$$

INTEGRALS INVOLVING $\ln |u|$

499. $\int \ln |u| \, du = u \ln |u| - u$

500. $\int (\ln |u|)^2 \, du = u(\ln |u|)^2 - 2u \ln |u| + 2u$

501. $\int (\ln |u|)^n \, du = u(\ln |u|)^n - n \int (\ln |u|)^{n-1} \, du$

502. $\int u \ln |u| \, du = \dfrac{u^2}{2} \left(\ln |u| - \dfrac{1}{2} \right)$

503. $\int u^m \ln |u| \, du = \dfrac{u^{m+1}}{m + 1} \left(\ln |u| - \dfrac{1}{m + 1} \right)$

APPENDIX E   Trigonometric Formulas

 See Chapter 4 of the *Student Mathematics Handbook* for a review of trigonometry.

Definition of the Trigonometric Functions

Let θ be any angle in standard position and let $P(x, y)$ be any point on the terminal side of the angle a distance of r from the origin ($r \neq 0$). Then

$$\cos \theta = \frac{x}{r} \qquad \sin \theta = \frac{y}{r}$$

$$\tan \theta = \frac{y}{x} \qquad \sec \theta = \frac{r}{x}$$

$$\csc \theta = \frac{r}{y} \qquad \cot \theta = \frac{x}{y}$$

Definition of the Inverse Trigonometric Functions

Inverse Trigonometric Function	Domain	Range
$y = \arccos x$ or $y = \cos^{-1} x$	$-1 \leq x \leq 1$	$0 \leq y \leq \pi$
$y = \arcsin x$ or $y = \sin^{-1} x$	$-1 \leq x \leq 1$	$-\frac{\pi}{2} \leq y \leq \frac{\pi}{2}$
$y = \arctan x$ or $y = \tan^{-1} x$	All reals	$-\frac{\pi}{2} < y < \frac{\pi}{2}$
$y = \text{arccot} \, x$ or $y = \cot^{-1} x$	All reals	$0 < y < \pi$
$y = \text{arcsec} \, x$ or $y = \sec^{-1} x$	$|x| \geq 1$	$0 \leq y \leq \pi, \ y \neq \frac{\pi}{2}$
$y = \text{arccsc} \, x$ or $y = \csc^{-1} x$	$|x| \geq 1$	$-\frac{\pi}{2} \leq y \leq \frac{\pi}{2}, \ y \neq 0$

The principal values of the inverse trigonometric relations are those values defined by these inverse trigonometric functions. These are the values obtained when using a calculator.

Trigonometric Identities   Fundamental identities

Reciprocal identities

1. $\sec \theta = \dfrac{1}{\cos \theta}$ **2.** $\csc \theta = \dfrac{1}{\sin \theta}$ **3.** $\cot \theta = \dfrac{1}{\tan \theta}$

Ratio identities

4. $\tan \theta = \dfrac{\sin \theta}{\cos \theta}$ **5.** $\cot \theta = \dfrac{\cos \theta}{\sin \theta}$

Pythagorean identities

6. $\cos^2 \theta + \sin^2 \theta = 1$ **7.** $1 + \tan^2 \theta = \sec^2 \theta$ **8.** $\cot^2 \theta + 1 = \csc^2 \theta$

Cofunction identities

9. $\cos\left(\dfrac{\pi}{2} - \theta\right) = \sin \theta$ **10.** $\sin\left(\dfrac{\pi}{2} - \theta\right) = \cos \theta$ **11.** $\tan\left(\dfrac{\pi}{2} - \theta\right) = \cot \theta$

Opposite-angle identities

12. $\cos(-\theta) = \cos \theta$ **13.** $\sin(-\theta) = -\sin \theta$ **14.** $\tan(-\theta) = -\tan \theta$

Addition laws

15. $\cos(\alpha + \beta) = \cos \alpha \cos \beta - \sin \alpha \sin \beta$

16. $\cos(\alpha - \beta) = \cos \alpha \cos \beta + \sin \alpha \sin \beta$

17. $\sin(\alpha + \beta) = \sin \alpha \cos \beta + \cos \alpha \sin \beta$

18. $\sin(\alpha - \beta) = \sin \alpha \cos \beta - \cos \alpha \sin \beta$

19. $\tan(\alpha + \beta) = \dfrac{\tan \alpha + \tan \beta}{1 - \tan \alpha \tan \beta}$ **20.** $\tan(\alpha - \beta) = \dfrac{\tan \alpha - \tan \beta}{1 + \tan \alpha \tan \beta}$

Double-angle identities

21. $\begin{aligned}\cos 2\theta &= \cos^2 \theta - \sin^2 \theta \\ &= 2\cos^2 \theta - 1 \\ &= 1 - 2\sin^2 \theta\end{aligned}$ **22.** $\sin 2\theta = 2 \sin \theta \cos \theta$

23. $\tan 2\theta = \dfrac{2 \tan \theta}{1 - \tan^2 \theta}$

Half-angle identities

24. $\cos \dfrac{1}{2}\theta = \pm\sqrt{\dfrac{1 + \cos \theta}{2}}$ **25.** $\sin \dfrac{1}{2}\theta = \pm\sqrt{\dfrac{1 - \cos \theta}{2}}$

26. $\begin{aligned}\tan \dfrac{1}{2}\theta &= \dfrac{1 - \cos \theta}{\sin \theta} \\[2mm] &= \dfrac{\sin \theta}{1 + \cos \theta}\end{aligned}$

Product-to-sum identities

27. $2 \cos \alpha \cos \beta = \cos(\alpha - \beta) + \cos(\alpha + \beta)$

28. $2 \sin \alpha \sin \beta = \cos(\alpha - \beta) - \cos(\alpha + \beta)$

29. $2 \sin \alpha \cos \beta = \sin(\alpha + \beta) + \sin(\alpha - \beta)$

30. $2 \cos \alpha \sin \beta = \sin(\alpha + \beta) - \sin(\alpha - \beta)$

Sum-to-product identities

31. $\cos \alpha + \cos \beta = 2 \cos\left(\dfrac{\alpha + \beta}{2}\right) \cos\left(\dfrac{\alpha - \beta}{2}\right)$

32. $\cos \alpha - \cos \beta = -2 \sin\left(\dfrac{\alpha + \beta}{2}\right) \sin\left(\dfrac{\alpha - \beta}{2}\right)$

33. $\sin \alpha + \sin \beta = 2 \sin\left(\dfrac{\alpha + \beta}{2}\right) \cos\left(\dfrac{\alpha - \beta}{2}\right)$

34. $\sin \alpha - \sin \beta = 2 \sin \left(\dfrac{\alpha - \beta}{2} \right) \cos \left(\dfrac{\alpha + \beta}{2} \right)$

Hyperbolic identities

35. $\operatorname{sech} x = \dfrac{1}{\cosh x}$ 　　　　　　　　　**36.** $\operatorname{csch} x = \dfrac{1}{\sinh x}$

37. $\coth x = \dfrac{1}{\tanh x}$ 　　　　　　　　　**38.** $\tanh x = \dfrac{\sinh x}{\cosh x}$

39. $\coth x = \dfrac{\cosh x}{\sinh x}$ 　　　　　　　　　**40.** $\cosh^2 x - \sinh^2 x = 1$

41. $1 - \tanh^2 x = \operatorname{sech}^2 x$ 　　　　　　　**42.** $\coth^2 x - 1 = \operatorname{csch}^2 x$

43. $\sinh(-x) = -\sinh x$ 　　　　　　　　**44.** $\cosh(-x) = \cosh x$

45. $\tanh(-x) = -\tanh x$

46. $\sinh(x \pm y) = \sinh x \cosh y \pm \cosh x \sinh y$

47. $\cosh(x \pm y) = \cosh x \cosh y \pm \sinh x \sinh y$

48. $\tanh(x \pm y) = \dfrac{\tanh x \pm \tanh y}{1 \pm \tanh x \tanh y}$

49. $\cosh 2x = \cosh^2 x + \sinh^2 x$ 　　　　　　**50.** $\sinh 2x = 2 \sinh x \cosh x$
$$= 2 \cosh^2 x - 1$$
$$= 1 + 2 \sinh^2 x$$

51. $\tanh 2x = \dfrac{2 \tanh x}{1 + \tanh^2 x}$ 　　　　　　**52.** $\cosh \dfrac{1}{2} x = \pm \sqrt{\dfrac{\cosh x + 1}{2}}$

53. $\sinh \dfrac{1}{2} x = \pm \sqrt{\dfrac{\cosh x - 1}{2}}$

54. $\tanh \dfrac{1}{2} x = \dfrac{\cosh x - 1}{\sinh x} = \dfrac{\sinh x}{\cosh x + 1}$

55. $\sinh^{-1} x = \ln(x + \sqrt{x^2 + 1})$

56. $\operatorname{csch}^{-1} x = \ln \left(\dfrac{1 + \sqrt{1 + x^2}}{x} \right)$ 　　if $x > 0$

57. $\cosh^{-1} x = \ln(x + \sqrt{x^2 - 1})$

58. $\operatorname{sech}^{-1} x = \ln \left(\dfrac{1 + \sqrt{1 - x^2}}{x} \right)$ 　　if $0 < x \leq 1$

59. $\tanh^{-1} x = \dfrac{1}{2} \ln \left(\dfrac{1 + x}{1 - x} \right)$ 　　if $-1 < x < 1$

60. $\coth^{-1} x = \dfrac{1}{2} \ln \left(\dfrac{x + 1}{x - 1} \right)$ 　　if $x^2 > 1$

APPENDIX F   Answers to Selected Problems

Many problems in this book are labeled WHAT DOES THIS SAY? *These problems solicit answers in your own words or a statement for you to rephrase as given statement in your own words. For this reason, it seems inappropriate to include the answers to these questions.* COUNTEREXAMPLE PROBLEMS *generally ask for counterexamples for which answers may vary so these answers are also not given.*

We also believe that an answer section should function as a check on work done, so for that reason, when an answer has both an exact answer and an approximate solution (from technology), we usually show only the approximate solution in this appendix. The exact solution (which may be the more appropriate answer) can be **checked** *by using the given approximation.*

The Student Survival and Solutions Manual *offers some review, survival hints, and added explanations for selected problems.*

Chapter 1: Functions and Graphs

1.1 Preliminaries (Pages 10–13)

1. a. $(-3, 4)$ **b.** $3 \le x \le 5$ **c.** $-2 \le x < 1$ **d.** $(2, 7]$

3. a.

b.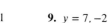

c.

d.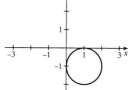

5. a.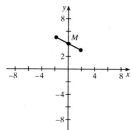

$M = (0, 4);\ d = 2\sqrt{5}$

b.

$M = (1, 2);\ d = 2\sqrt{10}$

7. $x = 0, 1$ **9.** $y = 7, -2$ **11.** $x = \dfrac{b \pm \sqrt{b^2 + 12c}}{6}$

13. $x = 6, -10$ **15.** $w = -2, 5$ **17.** $\emptyset$

19. $x = \dfrac{7\pi}{6}, \dfrac{11\pi}{6}$ **21.** $x = \dfrac{3\pi}{4}, \dfrac{5\pi}{4}, \dfrac{\pi}{3}, \dfrac{5\pi}{3}$ **23.** $x = \dfrac{2\pi}{3}$

25. $\left(-\infty, -\dfrac{5}{3}\right)$ **27.** $\left(-\dfrac{5}{3}, 0\right)$ **29.** $(-8, -3]$

31. $[-1, 3]$ **33.** $[7.999, 8.001]$

35. $(x + 1)^2 + (y - 2)^2 = 9$ **37.** $x^2 + (y - 1.5)^2 = 0.0625$

39. Center $(1, -1);\ r = 1$ **41.** Center $(-1, 5);\ r = 1$

43. $\dfrac{\sqrt{2} - \sqrt{6}}{4} \approx -0.2588$ **45.** $2 - \sqrt{3} \approx 0.2679$

51. a. period 2π **b.** period 2π

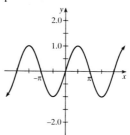
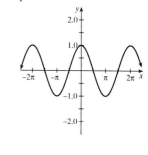

c. period π

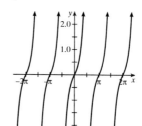

53. period $\pi/2$ **55.** period 4π

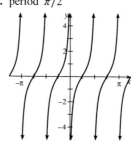
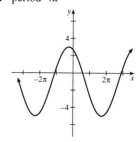

57.

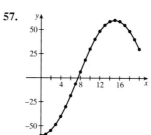

$A = 0,\ B = 60,\ C = \dfrac{\pi}{15},$ and $D = 7.5$

59. sun curve: $y = \cos \dfrac{\pi}{6} x$; moon curve: $y = 4\cos \dfrac{\pi}{6} x$; combined curve: $y = 5\cos \dfrac{\pi}{6} x$

61. a. The apparent depth is 3.4 m.

  b. The angle of incidence is 59°.

1.2 Lines in the Plane (Pages 17–19)

3. $2x + y - 5 = 0$ **5.** $2y - 1 = 0$

7. $x + 2 = 0$ **9.** $8x - 7y - 56 = 0$

11. $3x + y - 5 = 0$ **13.** $3x + 4y - 1 = 0$

15. $4x + y + 3 = 0$

17. $m = -5/7$;

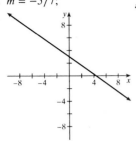

$(0, 3)$, $\left(\frac{21}{5}, 0\right)$

19. $m = 6.001$;

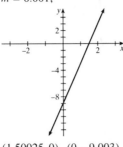

$(1.50025, 0)$, $(0, -9.003)$

21. $y = -\frac{3}{5}x - 3$; $m = -3/5$

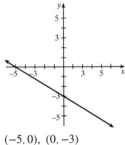

$(-5, 0)$, $(0, -3)$

23. $y = \frac{3}{5}x - 0.3$; $m = 3/5$

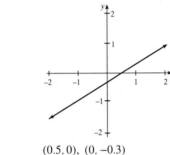

$(0.5, 0)$, $(0, -0.3)$

25. $m = 3/2$

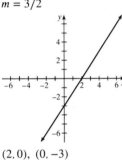

$(2, 0)$, $(0, -3)$

27. $y = \frac{1}{5}x$; $m = 1/5$

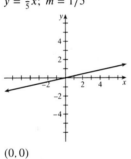

$(0, 0)$

29. no slope

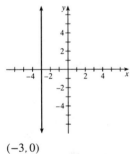

$(-3, 0)$

31. $y = 0$ and $y = 6$

33. $D(6, 6)$ or $E(2, 16)$; two parallelograms can be found

35. no values

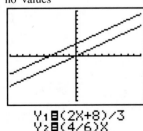

37. $(4, -1)$

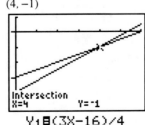

39. $\left(\frac{3}{4}, \frac{7}{2}\right)$

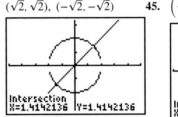

41. $\left(-\frac{64}{3}, \frac{100}{3}\right)$

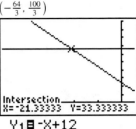

43. $(\sqrt{2}, \sqrt{2})$, $(-\sqrt{2}, -\sqrt{2})$

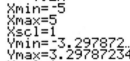

45. $\left(-\frac{15}{8}, \frac{7\sqrt{15}}{8}\right)$, $\left(-\frac{15}{8}, -\frac{7\sqrt{15}}{8}\right)$

47. a. $-38.2°F$ **b.** $-17.8°C$ **c.** $-40°$

49. The Spy escapes since freedom is reached at the border after only 83.8 km.

51. $V(t) = -19,000t + 200,000$

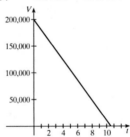

The value in 4 years is $124,000.

55. For the 8th month, 216 gallons

57. a. $48 **b.** not linear

59. $x = \dfrac{a \pm \sqrt{a^2 - 4}}{2}$, $y = \dfrac{2}{a \pm \sqrt{a^2 - 4}}$

1.3 Functions and Graphs (Pages 31–33)

Let D represent the domain in Problems 1–11.

1. $D = (-\infty, \infty)$; $f(-2) = -1$; $f(1) = 5$; $f(0) = 3$

3. $D = (-\infty, \infty)$; $f(1) = 6$; $f(0) = -2$; $f(-2) = 0$

5. $D = (-\infty, -3) \cup (-3, \infty)$; $f(2) = 0$; $f(0) = -2$; $f(-3)$ is undefined

7. $D = (-\infty, -2] \cup [0, \infty)$; $f(-1)$ is undefined; $f\left(\frac{1}{2}\right) = \frac{\sqrt{5}}{2}$; $f(1) = \sqrt{3}$

9. $D = (-\infty, \infty)$; $f(-1) = \sin 3 \approx 0.1411$; $f\left(\frac{1}{2}\right) = 0$; $f(1) = \sin(-1) \approx -0.8415$

11. $D = (-\infty, \infty)$; $f(3) = 4$; $f(1) = 2$; $f(0) = 4$

13. 9   **15.** $10x + 5h$ **17.** -1 **19.** $\dfrac{-1}{x(x+h)}$

21. not equal   **23.** equal   **25.** not equal

27. even   **29.** neither   **31.** neither   **33.** even

35. $(f \circ g)(x) = 4x^2 + 1$; $(g \circ f)(x) = 2x^2 + 2$

37. $(f \circ g)(t) = |t|$; $(g \circ f)(t) = t$

39. $(f \circ g)(x) = \sin(2x + 3)$; $(g \circ f)(x) = 2\sin x + 3$

41. $u(x) = 2x^2 - 1$; $g(u) = u^4$

43. $u(x) = 2x + 3$; $g(u) = |u|$

45. $u(x) = \tan x$; $g(u) = u^2$

47. $u(x) = \sqrt{x}$; $g(u) = \sin u$

49. $u(x) = \dfrac{x+1}{2-x}$; $g(u) = \sin u$

51. $P(5, f(5))$; $Q(x_0, f(x_0))$

53. $-\frac{1}{3}, 2$ **55.** $15, -\frac{25}{2}, \frac{65}{3}, -\frac{1}{4}$

57. 0   **59.** ± 1

61. a. The cost is \$4,500.   **b.** The cost of the 20th unit is \$371.

63. a. $I = \dfrac{30}{t^2(6-t)^2}$ **b.** $I(1) = \frac{6}{5}$ candles; $I(4) = \frac{15}{32}$ candles

65. a. $625t^2 + 25t + 900$ **b.** \$6,600   **c.** 4 hours

67. a.

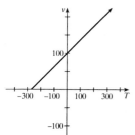

b. $T = 273$

69. a. The maximum height of the cannonball is 280 ft.

b. It hits the ground approximately 1,243 ft from the firing point.

c. The basic shape of a parabola (standard quadratic function).

71. a. 19,400 people   **b.** 67 people

c. The population will tend to 20,000 people in the long run.

73. Pythagorean theorem: $\triangle ABC$ with sides a, b, and c is a right triangle if and only if $c^2 = a^2 + b^2$. Proofs vary.

1.4 Inverse Functions; Inverse Trigonometric Functions (Pages 41–42)

3. These are inverse functions.

5. These are not inverse functions.

7. These are not inverse functions.

9. $\{(5,4), (3,6), (1,7), (4,2)\}$

11. $y = \frac{1}{2}x - \frac{3}{2}$ **13.** $y = \sqrt{x+5}$

15. $y = (x-5)^2$ **17.** $y = \dfrac{3x+6}{2-3x}$

19. a. $\frac{\pi}{3}$ **b.** $-\frac{\pi}{3}$ **21. a.** $-\frac{\pi}{4}$ **b.** $\frac{5\pi}{6}$

23. a. $-\frac{\pi}{3}$ **b.** π **25.** $\frac{\sqrt{3}}{2}$ **27.** 3   **29.** $-\frac{2\sqrt{6}}{5} \approx -0.9798$

33. no inverse

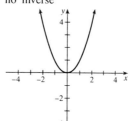

35. no inverse

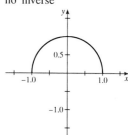

37. inverse exists

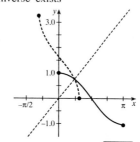

39. $\dfrac{2x}{x^2+1}$ **41.** $\dfrac{\sqrt{1-x^2}}{x}$ **43.** 1

47. a. 0.588   **b.** 2.5536   **c.** 2.1997   **d.** -0.5746

49. $h = \dfrac{x \tan \beta \tan \alpha}{\tan \alpha - \tan \beta}$

Chapter 1 Review
Proficiency Examination (Page 42–43)

18. a. $6x + 8y - 37 = 0$ **b.** $3x + 10y - 41 = 0$

c. $3x - 28y - 12 = 0$ **d.** $2x + 5y - 24 = 0$

e. $4x - 3y + 8 = 0$

19. $y = -\frac{3}{2}x + 6$

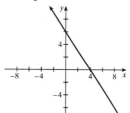

20. $y - 3 = |x + 1|$

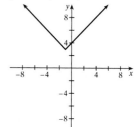

21. $y - 3 = -2(x-1)^2$

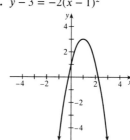

22. $y = (x-2)^2 - 14$

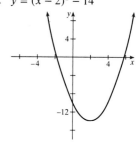

23. $y = 2\cos(x - 1)$

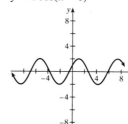

24. $y + 1 = \tan 2\left(x + \frac{3}{2}\right)$

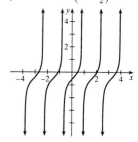

25. $y = \sin^{-1}(2x)$ **26.** $y = \tan^{-1} x^2$

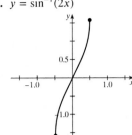   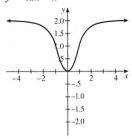

27. $-\frac{3}{2}, 1$

28. The two functions are not the same.

29. $f \circ g = \sin \sqrt{1 - x^2}$; $g \circ f = |\cos x|$

30. $V = \frac{2}{3}x(12 - x^2)$

Supplementary Problems (Pages 43–45)

1. $P = 30$; $A = 30$ **3.** $P \approx 27.1$; $A = 40$

5. $(x - 5)^2 + (y - 4)^2 = 16$ **7.** $5x - 3y + 3 = 0$

9. $A = -\frac{1}{4}$ and $B = \frac{3}{4}$

11. The medians meet at the point $\left(2, \frac{5}{3}\right)$.

13. 1,024 ft

15. a. 1.107149   **b.** 0.463647609   **c.** 1.899250945

17. $\frac{\pi^2}{4}$ **19.** $\frac{1}{2}(x^7 - 1)$ **21.** $\dfrac{7x + 5}{x - 1}$ **23.** $\dfrac{b - dx}{cx - a}$

27. a. 15 inches   **b.** 21 inches   **c.** 29 inches   **d.** 19 inches

29. a. The domain consists of all $x \neq 300$.

  b. x represents a percentage, so $0 \leq x \leq 100$ in order for $f(x) \geq 0$

  c. 120   **d.** 300

  e. The percentage of households should be 60%.

31. a. $V = \frac{256}{3}\pi$; $S = 64\pi$ **b.** $V = 30$; $S = 62$

  c. $V = 16\pi$; $S = 24\pi$ **d.** $V = 15\pi$; $A = 3\pi\sqrt{34}$

35. $c = -\frac{4}{5}$; $(-2, 0), (2, 0)$

37. $\theta = \frac{\pi}{4} - \tan^{-1}\frac{5}{12} \approx 0.3906$

39. a. $6 < p < 8$ **b.** $N(7) = 1$ is the maximum profit

41. The glass should be taken in on the 11th or 12th day.

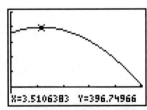

X=3.510b3B3   Y=39b.74966
Y1B-3X²+21X+360
Xmin=0   Ymin=-100
Xmax=15   Ymax=500
Xscl=3   Yscl=100

43. $C(x) = 4x^2 + 1{,}000x^{-1}$

45. This is Putnam Examination Problem 4 in the morning session for 1959.

Chapter 2: Limits and Continuity

2.1 The Limit of a Function (Pages 59–61)

1. a. 0   **b.** 2   **c.** 6

3. a. 2   **b.** 7   **c.** 7.5

5. a. 6   **b.** 6   **c.** 6

7. 15   **9.** 10   **11.** 8

13. 2   **15.** -1 **19.** 1.00

21. 5.00   **23.** -0.17 **25.** does not exist

27. a. 0.00   **b.** 0.64

29. 8.00   **31.** -2.00 **33.** 0.17

35. 0.25   **37.** does not exist   **39.** 2.00

41. 1.00   **43.** does not exist

45. a. $-32t + 40$ **b.** 40 ft/s

  c. 3; impact velocity is -56 ft/s

  d. $t = 1.25$ seconds

47. 228

2.2 Algebraic Computation of Limits (Pages 68–69)

1. -9 **3.** -8 **5.** $-\frac{1}{2}$ **7.** 2   **9.** $\frac{\sqrt{3}}{9}$

11. 4   **13.** -1 **15.** $\frac{1}{9}$ **17.** $\frac{1}{2}$ **19.** $\frac{1}{2}$

21. 0   **23.** 2   **25.** $\frac{5}{2}$ **27.** 0   **29.** 1

31. 0   **35.** a **37.** -1 **39.** 0

41. the limit does not exist   **43.** the limit does not exist

49. the limit does not exist   **51.** the limit does not exist

53. the limit does not exist   **55.** 4   **57.** 8

2.3 Continuity (Pages 78–80)

1. Temperature is continuous, so TEMPERATURE $= f(\text{TIME})$ would be a continuous function. The domain could be midnight to midnight say, $0 \leq t < 24$.

3. The charges (range of the function) consist of rational numbers only (dollars and cents to the nearest cent), so the function CHARGE $= f(\text{MILEAGE})$ would be a step function (that is, not continuous). The domain would consist of the mileage from the beginning of the trip to its end.

5. No suspicious points and no points of discontinuity with a polynomial.

7. The denominator factors to $x(x - 1)$, so suspicious points would be $x = 0, 1$. There will be a hole discontinuity at $x = 0$ and a pole discontinuity at $x = 1$.

9. $x = 0$ is suspicious point and is a point of discontinuity.

11. $x = 1$ is a suspicious point; there are no points of discontinuity.

13. The sine and cosine are continuous on the reals, but the tangent is discontinuous at $x = \pi/2 + n\pi$, n an integer. Each of these values will have a pole type discontinuity.

15. 3   **17.** π **19.** no value

21. a. continuous   **b.** discontinuous on $[0, 1]$

23. discontinuous at $t = 0$ **25.** discontinuous at $x = 0$

39. $a = 1$; $b = -18/5$ **41.** $a = 1$; $b = \frac{1}{2}$

43. $a = 5$; $b = 5$ **45.** 0

47. a. 1.25872   **b.** 0.785398

2.4 Exponential and Logarithm Functions (Pages 89–91)

1.

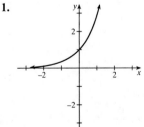

3.

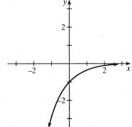

5. 31   7. 200.33681   9. 9,783.225896

11. 38,523.62544   13. 0   15. 2

17. −2   19. 3.5   21. $\frac{3}{10}$

23. 4   25. 0.23104906   27. −1.391662509

29. 729   31. 2, −1   33. 3

35. 2, −$\frac{5}{3}$ 37. −$\frac{3}{2}$ 39. 1

41. a. 0 b. e^{-1} 43. a. e b. 2

45. 2e 47. 27   49. 0.4

51. logarithmic   53. exponential

55. 3 m below surface   57. 0.7/r years to double

59. 6.9%

61. a. 793.7   b. 2 hr 40 min

63. a. $E^{1.5M+11.4}$ b. 1,000 times more energy

65. a.

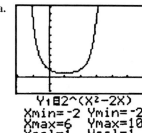

b. It crosses the y-axis at $(0,1)$. As $x \to +\infty$, $y \to +\infty$. As $x \to -\infty$, $y \to +\infty$.

c. The smallest value of $y = E$ is $E = 0.5$.

67. a. \$10,285.33   b. \$10,285.29

69. a. $\frac{4}{7}$ b. 59°   c. 70°

Chapter 2 Review
Proficiency Examination (Page 92)

19. $\frac{3}{2}$ 20. $\frac{1}{4}$ 21. −$\frac{1}{4}$

22. 0   23. $\frac{9}{5}$ 24. −1

25. a. exponential   b. exponential
c. logarithmic   d. logarithmic

26. We have suspicious points where the denominators are 0 at $t = 0, -1$. There are pole discontinuities at each of these points.

27. Suspicious points $x = -2$ and $x = 1$ are also points of discontinuity (since the denominator is 0).

28. a. 11 years, 3 quarters   b. 11 years, 6 months
c. 11 years, 166 days

29. $A = -1$; $B = 1$

30. Let $f(x) = x + \sin x - \frac{1}{\sqrt{x+3}}$. This function is continuous on $[0,\infty)$, and $f(0) = -\frac{1}{3}$, $f(\pi) = \pi - \frac{1}{\sqrt{\pi+3}} \approx 2.93$. So by the root location theorem there must be some value c in $(0,\pi)$ where $f(c) = 0$.

Supplementary Problems (Pages 92–95)

1. a. 1.504077397 b. 16.44464677 c. π d. $\sqrt{2}$

3. −2   5. 16, −1   7. 1.46085

9. 5   11. 1   13. 0

15. −$\frac{1}{2}$ 17. e^4 19. 5

21. $\frac{3}{2}$ 23. 0.8415   25. 1

27. 3   29. 0   31. $\frac{1}{\sqrt{2x}}$

33. $\frac{-4}{x^2}$ 35. e^x 37. continuous on $[-5,5]$

39. discontinuity is removable   41. not continuous anywhere

43. a. continuous on $[0,5]$ b. not continuous at $x = -2$
c. not continuous at $x = -2$ d. continuous on $[-5,5]$

45. a.

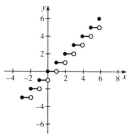

b. $\lim_{x\to 3} [\![x]\!]$ does not exist

c. The limit exists for all nonintegral values.

47. does not exist   49. $a = 2$ and $b = 1$

51. a. 0.2973   b. 0.8232   c. 0.07955

53. The rock concert is one million times as intense as normal conversation.

67. a. The windchill for 20 mi/h is 3.75° and for 50 mi/h is −7°.
b. $v \approx 25.2$
c. at $v = 4$, $T \approx 91.4$; at $v = 45$, $T \approx 868$

71. This is a Problem A1 of the morning session of the 1956 Putnam Examination.

Chapter 3: Differentiation

3.1 An Introduction to the Derivative: Tangents (Pages 107–110)

1. Some describe it as a five-step process:
(1) Find $f(x)$
(2) Find $f(x + \Delta x)$
(3) Find $f(x + \Delta x) - f(x)$
(4) Find $\dfrac{f(x + \Delta x) - f(x)}{\Delta x}$
(5) Find $\lim_{\Delta x \to 0} \dfrac{f(x + \Delta x) - f(x)}{\Delta x}$

3. Answers vary; continuity does not imply differentiability, but differentiability implies continuity.

5.

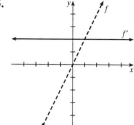

7.

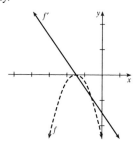

9.

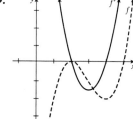

11. a. 0   **b.** 0   **13. a.** 2   **b.** 2

15. a. $-\Delta x$ **b.** 0   **17.** 0; differentiable for all x

19. 3; differentiable for all x **21.** $6x$; differentiable for all x

23. $2x - 1$; differentiable for all x

25. $2s - 2$; differentiable for all real s

27. $\dfrac{\sqrt{5x}}{2x}$; differentiable for $x > 0$

29. $3x - y - 7 = 0$ **31.** $3s - 4y + 1 = 0$

33. $x + 25y - 7 = 0$ **35.** $x + 3y - 9 = 0$

37. $216x - 6y - 647 = 0$ **39.** 2

41. 0   **43. a.** -3.9 **b.** -4

45. The derivative is 0 when $x = \frac{1}{2}$; the graph has a horizontal tangent at $\left(\frac{1}{2}, -\frac{1}{4}\right)$.

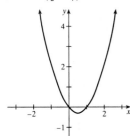

47. a. $-4x$ **b.** $y - 4 = 0$ **c.** $\left(\frac{2}{3}, \frac{28}{9}\right)$ **49.** yes

51. a.

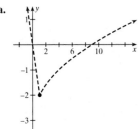

    b. f is not differentiable at $x = 1$, because the difference quotient has different limits from the left and right.

53. 4   **55.** $\frac{1}{2}$ **57.** $\frac{1}{4}$

59. The y-intercept is $\left(0, -Ac^2\right)$.   **61. a.** $2x$ **b.** $2x$

63. For $x < 0$, the tangent lines have negative slope and for $x > 0$ the tangent lines have positive slope. There is a corner at $x = 0$, and there is no tangent at $x = 0$, and consequently no derivative at that point.

65. Yes, the equation of the tangent line is $y = 1$.

67. The point $(6, 0)$ on the x-axis is the point through which the normal to the parabola at $(4, 4)$ passes. The required tangent is then the line through $(4, 4)$ perpendicular to this normal.

69. The equation of the normal line is $f'(c)y - f(c)f'(c) + x - c = 0$. If $f'(c) = 0$, then the normal line is vertical with equation $x = c$.

3.2 Techniques of Differentiation (Pages 117–118)

1. (11) 0   (12) 1   (13) 2   (14) 4   (15) 0   (16) -4

3. (23) $2x - 1$ (24) $-2t$ (25) $2s - 2$ (26) $-\frac{1}{2}x^{-2}$ (27) $\dfrac{\sqrt{5x}}{2x}$

5. a. $12x^3$ **b.** -1 **7. a.** $3x^2$ **b.** 1

9. $2t + 2t^{-3} - 20t^{-5}$ **11.** $-14x^{-3} + \frac{2}{3}x^{-1/3}$

13. $1 - x^{-2} + 14x^{-3}$ **15.** $-32x^3 - 12x^2 + 2$

17. $\dfrac{22}{(x+9)^2}$ **19.** $4x^3 + 12x^2 + 8x$

21. $f'(x) = 5x^4 - 15x^2 + 1$; $f''(x) = 20x^3 - 30x$; $f'''(x) = 60x^2 - 30$; $f^{(4)}(x) = 120x$

23. $f'(x) = 4x^{-3}$; $f''(x) = -12x^{-4}$; $f'''(x) = 48x^{-5}$; $f^{(4)}(x) = -240x^{-6}$

25. $\dfrac{d^2 y}{dx^2} = 18x - 14$ **27.** $7x + y + 9 = 0$

29. $6x + y - 6 = 0$ **31.** $x - 6y + 5 = 0$

33. $(1, 0)$ and $\left(\frac{4}{3}, -\frac{1}{27}\right)$ **35.** $\left(\frac{29}{6}, -\frac{361}{12}\right)$

37. $(1, -2)$ **39.** no horizontal tangents

41. d. $-4x^{-3} + 9x^{-4}$ **43.** $2x - y - 2 = 0$

45. a. $4x + y - 1 = 0$ **b.** $x = 0$

47. $(0, 0)$ and $(4, 64)$

49. The equation is not satisfied.

51. This function satisfies the given equation.

53. $\pi \approx \frac{62,832}{20,000} \approx 3.1416$ **63.** $y = x + 3$

3.3 Derivatives of Trigonometric, Exponential, and Logarithmic Functions (Page 125)

1. $\cos x - \sin x$ **3.** $2t - \sin t$ **5.** $\sin 2t$

7. $-\sqrt{x}\,\sin x + \frac{1}{2}x^{-1/2}\cos x - x\csc^2 x + \cot x$

9. $-x^2 \sin x + 2x \cos x$ **11.** $\dfrac{x \cos x - \sin x}{x^2}$

13. $e^t \csc t(1 - \cot t)$ **15.** $x + 2x \ln x$

17. $e^{2x}(3 \sin x - \cos x)$ **19.** $e^{-x}(\cos x - \sin x)$

21. $\dfrac{\sec^2 x - 2x \sec^2 x + 2 \tan x}{(1 - 2x)^2}$

23. $\dfrac{t \cos t + 2 \cos t - 2 - \sin t}{(t + 2)^2}$

25. $\dfrac{1}{\cos x - 1}$ **27.** $\dfrac{2 \cos x - \sin x - 1}{(2 - \cos x)^2}$

29. $\dfrac{-2}{(\sin x - \cos x)^2}$ **31.** $-\sin x$

33. $-\sin \theta$ **35.** $2 \sec^2 \theta \tan \theta$

37. $\sec^3 \theta + \sec \theta \tan^2 \theta$ **39.** $-\sin x - \cos x$

41. $-2e^x \sin x$ **43.** $-\frac{1}{4}t^{-3/2} \ln t$

45. $4x - 2y - \pi + 2 = 0$

47. $\sqrt{3}x - 2y + \left(1 - \frac{\sqrt{3}\pi}{6}\right) = 0$

49. $2x - y = 0$ **51.** $x - y + 1 = 0$

53. a. yes   **b.** yes   **c.** no   **d.** no

55. $A = 0$, $B = -\frac{3}{2}$; $y = -\frac{3}{2}x \sin x$

3.4 Rates of Change: Modeling Rectilinear Motion (Pages 134–137)

1. A mathematical model is a mathematical framework whose results approximate the real-world situation. It involves abstractions, predictions, and then interpretations and comparisons with real world events. An excellent exampler of real world modeling from *Scientific American* (March 1991) is mentioned on page 129.

3. 1   **5.** -3 **7.** $\frac{13}{4}$

9. -1 **11.** $\frac{1}{2}$ **13.** -1 **15.** -6

17. a. $2t - 2$ **b.** 2   **c.** 2

    d. Because $a(t) > 0$, the object is always accelerating.

19. a. $3t^2 - 18t + 15$ **b.** $6t - 18$ **c.** 46

    d. decelerating on $[0, 3)$; accelerating on $(3, 6]$

Appendix F **A–33**

21. **a.** $-2t^{-2} - 2t^{-3}$ **b.** $4t^{-3} + 6t^{-4}$
    c. $\frac{20}{9}$ **d.** accelerating on $[1,3]$

23. **a.** $-3\sin t$ **b.** $-3\cos t$ **c.** 12
    d. decelerating on $\left[0, \frac{\pi}{2}\right)$ and on $\left(\frac{3\pi}{2}, 2\pi\right]$; accelerating on $\left(\frac{\pi}{2}, \frac{3\pi}{2}\right)$

25. quadratic model   27. exponential model

29. quadratic model   31. cubic model

33. logarithmic model

35. **a.** -6 **b.** The decline will be the same each year.

37. 136   39. **a.** 9.91 m/min   **b.** 9.961 m

41. **a.** 64 ft/s   **b.** 336 ft   **c.** $-32t + 64$ ft/s   **d.** -160 ft/s

43. 30 ft   45. 144 ft   47. $v_0 = 24$ ft/s; 126 ft

49. **a.** $200t + 50\ln t + 450$ newspapers per year.
    b. 1,530 newspapers per year   **c.** 1,635 newspapers

51. **a.** 0.2 ppm/yr   **b.** 0.15 ppm   **c.** 0.25 ppm

53. 91 thousand/hr

55. **a.** 20 persons per mo   **b.** 0.39% per mo

57. 7.5% per year   59. $\frac{dP}{dT} = -\frac{4\pi\mu^2 N}{9k}T^{-2}$

61. **a.** $v(t) = -7\sin t$; $a(t) = -7\cos t$ **b.** 2π **c.** 7

63. The Spy is on Mars.

3.5 The Chain Rule (Pages 143–145)

3. $6(3x - 2)$ 5. $\frac{-8x}{(x^2 - 9)^3}$

7. $[\tan u + u\sec^2 u]\left[3 - \frac{6}{x^2}\right]$

9. **a.** $3u^2$ **b.** $2x$ **c.** $6x(x^2 + 1)^2$

11. **a.** $7u^6$ **b.** $-8 - 24x$ **c.** $-56(3x + 1)(12x^2 + 8x - 5)^6$

13. $25(5x - 2)^4$ 15. $8(3x - 1)(3x^2 - 2x + 1)^3$

17. $4\cos(4\theta + 2)$ 19. $(-2x + 3)e^{-x^2+3x}$

21. $e^{\sec x}\sec x\tan x$ 23. $(2t + 1)\exp(t^2 + t + 5)$

25. $5x\cos 5x + \sin 5x$ 27. $6(1 - 2x)^{-4}$

29. $(1 - 2x)e^{1-2x}$ 31. $2x\cos 2x^2$

33. $3x^2(2 - 3x)(2 - 5x)$

35. $\frac{1}{2}\left(\frac{x^2 + 3}{x^2 - 5}\right)^{-1/2}\left[\frac{-16x}{(x^2 - 5)^2}\right]$

37. $\frac{1}{3}(x + \sqrt{2x})^{-2/3}\left(1 + \frac{1}{\sqrt{2x}}\right)$

39. $\frac{\cos x - \sin x}{\sin x + \cos x}$ 41. $\frac{2}{9}$ 43. 1, 7   45. 0, $\frac{2}{3}$

47. **a.** 1   **b.** $\frac{3}{2}$ **c.** 1.5

49. **a.** $\frac{9}{40}$ **b.** $-\frac{3}{8}$ **c.** $\frac{3}{8}$

51. $-\frac{2}{3}$ 53. 0.31 ppm/yr

55. decreasing by 6 lb/wk

57. **a.** increasing by 0.035 lux/s.   **b.** 7.15 m

61. $T'(2) \approx 5.23$; it is getting hotter

63. $I'(\theta) = \frac{2a\pi I_0}{\lambda\beta^3}\sin\beta(\beta\cos\beta - \sin\beta)\cos\frac{\theta}{\lambda}$

67. **a.** $\frac{3}{(3x - 1)^2 + 1}$ **b.** $\frac{-1}{x^2 + 1}$

71. $\frac{d}{dx}[f'(f(x))] = f''(f(x))f'(x)$ and
    $\frac{d}{dx}[f(f'(x))] = f'(f'(x))f''(x)$

3.6 Implicit Differentiation (Pages 155–157)

1. $-\frac{x}{y}$ 3. $-\frac{y}{x}$

5. $\frac{-(2x + 3y)}{3x + 2y}$ 7. $-\frac{y^2}{x^2}$

9. $\frac{1 - \cos(x + y)}{\cos(x + y) + 1}$ 11. $\frac{2x - y\sin xy}{x\sin xy}$

13. $(2e^{2x} - x^{-1})y$

15. **a.** $-\frac{2x}{3y^2}$ **b.** $\frac{-2x}{3(12 - x^2)^{2/3}} = -\frac{2x}{3y^2}$

17. **a.** y^2 **b.** $\frac{1}{(x - 5)^2} = y^2$

19. $\frac{1}{\sqrt{-x^2 - x}}$ 21. $\frac{x}{(x^2 + 2)\sqrt{x^2 + 1}}$

23. $\frac{6(\sin^{-1} 2x)^2}{\sqrt{1 - 4x^2}}$ 25. $\frac{-1}{\sqrt{e^{-2x} - 1}}$

27. $\frac{-1}{x^2 + 1}$ 29. ± 1

31. $\frac{1 - \sin^{-1} y - \dfrac{y}{1 + x^2}}{\dfrac{x}{\sqrt{1 - y^2}} + \tan^{-1} x}$

33. $2x - 3y + 13 = 0$ 35. $(\pi + 1)x - y + \pi = 0$

37. $y = 0$ 39. $y' = 0$

41. $y' = \frac{5}{4}$ 43. $x - 1 = 0$

45. $y'' = -\frac{49}{100y^3}$

51. $\frac{dy}{dx} = y\left[\frac{10}{2x - 1} - \frac{1}{2(x - 9)} - \frac{2}{x + 3}\right]$

53. $\frac{dy}{dx} = y\left[6x - \frac{6x^2}{x^3 + 1} + \frac{8}{4x - 7}\right]$

55. $\frac{dy}{dx} = \frac{y\ln x}{x}$ 57. $(3, -4), (-3, 4)$

61. **c.** The derivative does not exist.

63. $(2, 0), \left(-\frac{1}{4}, \frac{\sqrt{3}}{4}\right), \left(-\frac{1}{4}, -\frac{\sqrt{3}}{4}\right)$

65. 0.44 rad/s   69. $\frac{d^2 y}{dx^2} = -\frac{ac}{b^2 y^3}$

73. The student was correct.

3.7 Related Rates and Applications (Pages 162–165)

1. -3 3. 1,000   5. 15

7. $\frac{4}{5}$ 9. $\frac{30}{13}$ 11. -3

13. $-10\sqrt{3}$ units/s   15. 0.637 ft/s

17. increasing at $34,000/yr

19. -30 lb/in.^{2}/s   23. -3π cm^3/s   25. 7.2 ft/s

27. decreasing at 7.5 ft/min

29. 200 ft/s toward the light.   31. 2.78 rad/s

33. Assume a sphere of radius r. The volume is changing at the rate of 60.3 cm^3/min.

35. 74.35 ft^3/min.

37. a. $\dfrac{dH}{dt} = \dfrac{3,125t - 6,250}{\sqrt{3,125t^2 - 12,500t + 62,500}}$

   b. $t = 2$ **c.** 224 mi

39. 1 rad/min   **41.** 3.927 mi/h

43. At $t = 2$ P.M., 8.875 knots; at $t = 5$ P.M., 10.417 knots

45. 0.001925 ft/min or 0.02310 in./min

47. a. $\theta = \cot^{-1}\dfrac{x}{150}$

   b. $d\theta/dt$ approaches 0.27 rad/s

   c. As v increases so will $d\theta/dt$ and it becomes more difficult to see the seals.

3.8 Linear Approximation and Differentials (Pages 173–176)

1. $6x^2\,dx$ **3.** $x^{-1/2}\,dx$

5. $(\cos x - x\sin x)\,dx$ **7.** $\dfrac{3x\sec^2 3x - \tan 3x}{2x^2}\,dx$

9. $\cot x\,dx$ **11.** $\dfrac{e^x}{x}(1 + x\ln x)\,dx$

13. $\dfrac{(x-3)(x^2\sec x\tan x + 2x\sec x) - x^2\sec x}{(x-3)^2}\,dx$

15. $\dfrac{x+13}{2(x+4)^{3/2}}\,dx$

19. 0.995; by calculator, 0.9949874371

21. 217.69; by calculator, 217.7155882 so we can see an error of approximately 0.0255882

23. 0.06 or 6%   **25.** 0.03 or 3%

27. 0.05 parts per million   **29.** reduced by 12,000 units

31. 28.37 in.^{3}

33. decrease of 2 beats every 3 minutes

35. ±2%

37. S increases by 2% and the volume increases by 3%

39. 0.0525 ft

41. −6.93 (or about 7) particles/unit area

43. a. 472.7   **b.** 468.70

45. 1.2 units   **47.** −1.4142   **49.** 0.5671

51. b. $x \approx 1.367$ **53.** 0.5183

57. $\Delta x = -3$, $f(97) = 9.85$; by calculator 9.848857802; if $\Delta x = 16$, $f(97) \approx 9.89$

61. $x_n = x_{n+1} = x_{n+2} = \cdots$

Chapter 3 Review
Proficiency Examination (Page 177)

21. $\dfrac{dy}{dx} = 3x^2 + \dfrac{3}{2}x^{1/2} - 2\sin 2x$

22. $\dfrac{dy}{dx} = \dfrac{\sqrt{3x}}{2x} - \dfrac{6}{x^3}$

23. $\dfrac{dy}{dx} = -x[\cos(3-x^2)][\sin(3-x^2)]^{-1/2}$

24. $\dfrac{dy}{dx} = \dfrac{-y}{x+3y^2}$ **25.** $y' = \dfrac{1}{2}xe^{-\sqrt{x}}(4 - \sqrt{x})$

26. $y' = \dfrac{\ln 1.5}{x(\ln 3x)^2}$ **27.** $y' = \dfrac{3}{\sqrt{1-(3x+2)^2}}$

28. $y' = \dfrac{2}{1+4x^2}$ **29.** $\dfrac{dy}{dx} = 0$

30. $y' = y\left[\dfrac{2x}{(x^2-1)\ln(x^2-1)} - \dfrac{1}{3x} - \dfrac{9}{3x-1}\right]$

31. $y'' = 2(2x-3)(40x^2 - 48x + 9)$

32. $\dfrac{dy}{dx} = 1 - 6x$ **33.** $14x - y - 6 = 0$

34. tangent line $y - \frac{1}{2} = \frac{\pi}{4}(x-1)$; normal line $y - \frac{1}{2} = -\frac{4}{\pi}(x-1)$

35. 2π ft^2/s

Supplementary Problems (Pages 177–180)

1. $y' = 4x^3 + 6x - 7$

3. $y' = \dfrac{-4x}{(x^2-1)^{1/2}(x^2-5)^{3/2}}$

5. $y' = \dfrac{4x - y}{x - 2}$

7. $y' = 10(x^3 + x)^9(3x^2 + 1)$

9. $y' = \dfrac{(x^3+1)^4(46x^3+1)}{3x^{2/3}}$

11. $y' = 8x^3(x^4-1)^9(2x^4+3)^6(17x^4 + 8)$

13. $y' = \dfrac{-\sin\sqrt{x}}{4\sqrt{x}\,\sqrt{\cos\sqrt{x}}}$

15. $y' = 5(x^{1/2} + x^{1/3})^4\left(\frac{1}{2}x^{-1/2} + \frac{1}{3}x^{-2/3}\right)$

17. $y' = (4x+5)\exp(2x^2 + 5x - 3)$

19. $y' = 3^{2-x}(1 - x\ln 3)$ **21.** $y' = \dfrac{y(1 + xye^{xy})}{x(1 - xye^{xy})}$

23. $y' = e^{\sin x}(\cos x)$ **25.** $y' = \dfrac{e^{-x}}{x\ln 5}(1 - x\ln 3x)$

27. $y' = \dfrac{2x^2 + 2xy^2 - 1}{2y - 2x - 2y^2}$ **29.** $y' = [\cos(\sin x)]\cos x$

31. $y' = \dfrac{2\sqrt{xy} - \sqrt{y}}{\sqrt{x}}$ **33.** $y' = \dfrac{1 - y\cos xy}{x\cos xy - 1}$

35. $\dfrac{dy}{dx} = \dfrac{\sin^{-1}x - x(1-x^2)^{-1/2}}{(\sin^{-1}x)^2} + \dfrac{1}{x^2}\left(\dfrac{x}{1+x^2} - \tan^{-1}x\right)$

37. $\dfrac{d^2y}{dx^2} = 20x^3 - 60x^2 + 42x - 6$

39. $y'' = -\dfrac{2(3y^3 + 4x^2)}{9y^5}$

41. $y'' = -2[1 + y^2 - 4x^2y - 4x^2y^3]$

43. $33x - y - 32 = 0$ **45.** $2\pi x + 4y - \pi^2 = 0$

47. $x + y - 2 = 0$ **49.** $4x - 2y - 1 = 0$

51. $y - 1 = 0$ **53.** $4x - y - 3 = 0$

55. tangent line, $12x - y - 11 = 0$; normal line, $x + 12y - 13 = 0$

57. $\dfrac{dy}{dt} = (3x^2 - 7)(t\cos t + \sin t)$

   or $(3t^2\sin^2 t - 7)(t\cos t + \sin t)$

59. $f'(x) = 4x^3 + 4x^{-5}$; $f''(x) = 12x^2 - 20x^{-6}$; $f'''(x) = 24x + 120x^{-7}$; $f^{(4)}(x) = 24 - 840x^{-8}$

61. $y' = \dfrac{-4x^3}{(x^4-2)^{4/3}(x^4+1)^{2/3}}$

63. $y' = \dfrac{x+2y}{y-2x}$; $y'' = \dfrac{5y^2 - 20xy - 5x^2}{(y-2x)^3}$

65. a. $f'(0) = 0$ **b.** $f'(x) = 2x\sin\frac{1}{x} - \cos\frac{1}{x}$

   c. f' is not continuous at $x = 0$

67. 0.8634074099; calculator 0.8633955506

69. 0.012 rad/min

71. $\dfrac{d}{dx}f(x^2 + x) = (2x+1)(x^4 + 2x^3 + 2x^2 + x)$

73. $4x\cos 2x^2 - 6x\sin 3x^2$

75. 75 mi/h

77. a. $\frac{4}{5}x + 3$ **b.** \$4.00 **c.** \$11.00 **d.** \$11.40

81. 0.09 radians/s $\approx 5°$/s

83. a. −0.2   **b.** −0.4   **c.** 0.3

85. $\frac{d\theta}{dt} = 0.05$ **87.** $\frac{dx}{dt} = 20\pi$ mi/min

93. For the velocity, $\frac{dx}{dt} = \frac{12\pi x \sin\theta}{2\cos\theta - x}$; for acceleration,

$$\frac{d^2x}{dt^2} = \frac{144\pi^2 x}{(2\cos\theta - x)^3}\left[2\sin^2\theta\cos\theta + (2\cos\theta - x)(1 - \tfrac{1}{2}x\cos\theta)\right]$$

95. This is Putnam Problem 1, morning session in 1946.

97. This is Putnam Problem 6, morning session in 1946.

Chapter 4: Additional Applications of the Derivative

4.1 Extreme Values of a Continuous Function (Pages 193–195)

1. critical number $x = 5$ is not in the interval; maximum value is 26 and the minimum value is −34

3. critical numbers, $x = 0$, $x = 2$; maximum value is 0 and minimum value is −4

5. critical number $x = 0$; maximum value is 1 and minimum value is $-\frac{1}{8}$

7. critical numbers $x = 0$, $\frac{4}{5}$; maximum value is 0 and minimum value is −2

9. critical number, $t = 1$; maximum value is e^{-1} and minimum value is 0

11. critical number $x = 0$; maximum value is 1 and minimum value is 0

13. critical numbers 0, $\frac{\pi}{3}$; maximum value is 1.25 and minimum value is approximately 0.41067

15. a. Find the value of the function at the endpoints of an interval.

    b. Find the critical points, that is, points at which the derivative of the function is zero or undefined.

    c. Find the value of the function at each critical point.

    d. State the absolute extrema.

17. The calculator does not seem to take the derivative at $x = 0$ and $x < 0$ into account. The derivative is not defined at $x = 0$, but it certainly is defined for $x < 0$. If you enter $(x^2)^\wedge(1/3)(5 - 2x)$ you will obtain the correct graph.

19. not defined at $t = -50$; the maximum value is 16 and the minimum value is 0.

21. the maximum value is 76 and the minimum value is −32

23. the maximum value is $\frac{5}{6}$ and the minimum value is $\frac{1}{6}$

25. the maximum value is 2π and the minimum value is $-\pi$

27. the maximum value is 0.2898 and the minimum value is −0.2898

29. the maximum value is 11 and the minimum value is −4

31. the smallest value is 3

33. the largest value is $\frac{9}{4}$

35. the largest value of g on [2, 3] is approximately −1.1

37. the maximum value is approximately 1.819 and the minimum value is 0

39. the maximum value is 6,496 and the minimum value is 0

41. the maximum value is 1.59 and the minimum value is −2.52

43. the maximum value is 1 and the minimum value is $-e^{-\pi}$

45. a. $f(x) = \begin{cases} x^2 & \text{for } -0.5 \le x \le 1 \\ -x + 3 & \text{for } 1 < x \le 1.5 \end{cases}$

    The minimum is 0, but there is no maximum.

    b. $f(x) = \begin{cases} -x^2 & \text{for } -1 < x \le 1 \\ x - 3 & \text{for } 1 < x \le 1.5 \end{cases}$

    The maximum is 0, but there is no minimum.

    c. $f(x) = \begin{cases} \sin x & \text{for } -\pi \le x \le \frac{\pi}{2} \\ 0.5 & \text{for } \frac{\pi}{2} < x \le 3 \end{cases}$

    The maximum is 1 and the minimum is −1.

    d. $f(x) = \begin{cases} (1 + x)/2 & -1 \le x < 1 \\ 0 & 1 \le x \le 2 \\ (x - 4)/2 & 2 < x \le 4 \end{cases}$

    There is no maximum and there is no minimum.

47. a. No such function can be found because of the extreme value theorem (Theorem 4.1).

    b. No such function can be found because of the extreme value theorem.

    c. $f(x) = \sin x$ for $[0, 2\pi]$.

    d. No such function can be found because of the extreme value theorem.

49. $f(x) = x^{-1}$ on (0, 1) has no extremum.

51. The maximum velocity is 60 when $t = 0$.

53. The largest product occurs when $x = 3$ and $y = 6$.

55. The largest product occurs when $x = 21$ and $y = 63$.

57. The largest area occurs when the length of a side is one-fourth of the length of the perimeter.

59. a. The greatest difference occurs at $x = \frac{1}{2}$.

    b. The greatest difference occurs at $x = 1/\sqrt{3}$.

    c. The greatest difference occurs at $x = \left(\dfrac{1}{n}\right)^{1/(n-1)}$.

4.2 The Mean Value Theorem (Pages 199–201)

3. $c = 1$ **5.** $c \approx 1.5275$ **7.** $c \approx 1.0772$

9. $c = 9/4$ **11.** $c \approx 0.73$ **13.** $c \approx 0.6901$

15. $c \approx 0.54$ **17.** $c \approx 1.082$ **19.** $c \approx 0.5227$

21. does not apply   **23.** applies   **25.** does not apply

27. does not apply   **29.** applies

31. $f(x) = 8x^3 - 6x + 10$ **33.** does not apply

35. applies   **37.** $c = 2.5$ and $c = 6.25$

41. does not apply   **43.** does not apply

47. does not apply   **55.** does not apply

4.3 Using Derivatives to Sketch the Graph of a Function (Pages 214–217)

7. The black curve is the function and the one in color is the derivative.

9.
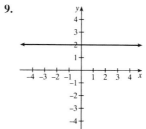

11.
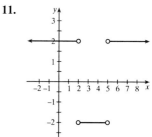

13. **a.** $x = 0$, $x = -2$

b. increasing on $(-\infty, -2) \cup (0, +\infty)$; decreasing on $(-2, 0)$

c. critical points: $(0, 1)$, relative minimum; $(-2, 5)$, relative maximum

d. $x = -1$; concave down on $(-\infty, -1)$; concave up on $(-1, \infty)$

e.

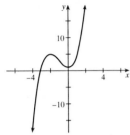

15. **a.** critical numbers: $x = \frac{5}{3}$, $x = -25$

b. increasing on $(-\infty, -25) \cup (\frac{5}{3}, +\infty)$; decreasing on $(-25, \frac{5}{3})$

c. critical points: $(\frac{5}{3}, -9,481)$, relative minimum; $(-25, 0)$, relative maximum

d. $x = -\frac{35}{3}$; concave down on $(-\infty, -\frac{35}{3})$; concave up on $(-\frac{35}{3}, \infty)$

e.

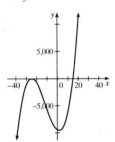

17. **a.** critical numbers: $x = -1$, $x = 3$

b. increasing on $(-1, 3)$; decreasing on $(-\infty, -1) \cup (3, +\infty)$

c. critical points: $(-1, -\frac{1}{2})$, relative minimum; $(3, \frac{1}{6})$, relative maximum

d. $x \approx -2.1$, $x \approx 0.3$, $x \approx 4.8$; concave down on $(-\infty, -2.1)$ and $(0.3, 4.8)$; concave up on $(-2.1, 0.3)$

e.

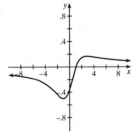

19. **a.** critical numbers: $t = -1$, $t = 3$

b. increasing on $(-\infty, -1) \cup (3, +\infty)$; decreasing on $(-1, 3)$

c. critical points: $(3, -32)$, relative minimum; $(-1, 0)$, relative maximum

d. $t = 1$; concave down on $(-\infty, 1)$; concave up on $(1, \infty)$

e.

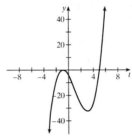

21. critical points: $(-3, -11)$, relative maximum; $(3, 13)$, relative minimum; increasing on $(-\infty, -3) \cup (3, +\infty)$; decreasing on $(-3, 0) \cup (0, 3)$; concave up on $(0, +\infty)$; concave down on $(-\infty, 0)$

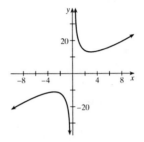

23. critical points: $(0, 26)$, relative maximum; $(-6.38, -852.22)$, relative minimum; $(1.88, -6.47)$, relative minimum; inflection points $(-4, -486)$, $(1, 9)$; increasing on $(-6.38, 0) \cup (1.88, +\infty)$; decreasing on $(-\infty, -6.38) \cup (0, 1.88)$; concave up on $(-\infty, -4) \cup (1, +\infty)$; concave down on $(-4, 1)$

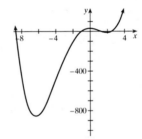

25. critical point: $(0, 0)$, relative minimum; increasing on $(0, +\infty)$; decreasing on $(-\infty, 0)$; concave up on $(-\infty, +\infty)$

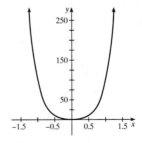

27. critical points: $(-1, -\frac{1}{2})$, relative minimum; $(1, \frac{1}{2})$, relative maximum; $(0, 0)$ is a point of inflection; points of inflection: $(\sqrt{3}, \frac{\sqrt{3}}{4})$, $(-\sqrt{3}, -\frac{\sqrt{3}}{4})$; increasing on $(-1, 1)$; decreasing on $(-\infty, -1) \cup (1, +\infty)$; concave up on $(-\sqrt{3}, 0) \cup (\sqrt{3}, +\infty)$; concave down on $(-\infty, -\sqrt{3}) \cup (0, \sqrt{3})$

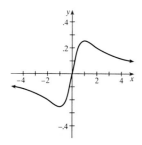

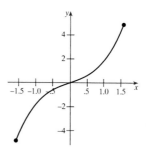

29. critical points: $(0,0)$, relative minimum; $(0.67, 0.06)$, relative maximum; $(0.195, 0.021)$, point of inflection; $(1.138, 0.043)$, point of inflection; decreasing on $(-\infty, 0), (0.67, +\infty)$; increasing on $(0, 0.67)$; concave up on $(-\infty, 0.195) \cup (1.138, +\infty)$; concave down on $(0.195, 1.138)$

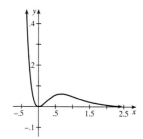

31. critical points $(1, 0)$, relative minimum; $(e, 1)$, point of inflection; decreasing on $(0, 1)$; increasing on $(1, +\infty)$; concave up for $(0, e)$; concave down for $(e, +\infty)$

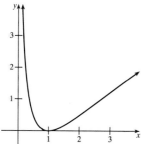

33. critical points: $\left(\frac{\pi}{12}, 1.13\right)$, relative maximum; $\left(\frac{5\pi}{12}, 0.44\right)$, relative minimum; inflection points: $\left(\frac{\pi}{4}, 0.79\right)$, $\left(\frac{3\pi}{4}, 2.36\right)$; increasing on $\left(0, \frac{\pi}{12}\right) \cup \left(\frac{5\pi}{12}, \pi\right)$; decreasing on $\left(\frac{\pi}{12}, \frac{5\pi}{12}\right)$; concave up on $\left(\frac{\pi}{4}, \frac{3\pi}{4}\right)$; concave down on $\left(0, \frac{\pi}{4}\right) \cup \left(\frac{3\pi}{4}, \pi\right)$

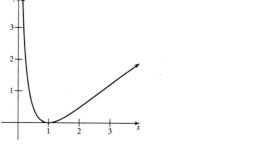

35. There are no critical points; the function is increasing for all x. Inflection point $(0, 0)$ concave down $(-1.57, 0)$; concave up $(0, 1.57)$

37. At $x = \frac{1}{2}$, relative maximum; at $x = 1$, relative minimum

39. At $x = 4$, relative minimum

41. $f(x) = \dfrac{x^2 - x + 5}{x + 4}$; $f'(x) = \dfrac{x^2 + 8x - 9}{(x + 4)^2}$; $f''(x) = \dfrac{50}{(x + 4)^3}$; $f''(1) = \frac{2}{5} > 0$; relative minimum $f''(-9) = -\frac{2}{5} < 0$; relative maximum

43. $f(x) = \sin x + \frac{1}{2} \cos 2x$; $f'(x) = \cos x - \sin 2x$; $f''(x) = -2 \cos 2x - \sin x$; $f''\left(\frac{\pi}{2}\right) = 1 > 0$; relative minimum; $f''\left(\frac{\pi}{6}\right) = -\frac{3}{2} < 0$; relative maximum

Answers for Problems 45–49 may vary.

45. 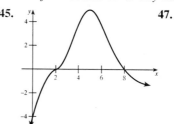   **47.**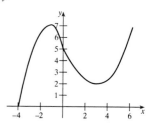

49.   **51.**

53. **a.** $-(2)^3 + 6(2)^2 + 13(2) = 42$; $-\frac{1}{3}(2)^3 + \frac{1}{2}(2)^2 + 25(2) = 49\frac{1}{3}$

  b. $N(x) = -x^3 + 6x^2 + 13x - \frac{1}{3}(4-x)^3 + \frac{1}{2}(4-x)^2 + 25(4-x)$

  c. $N'(x) = -2x^2 + 5x = 0$ when $x = 2.5$, so the optimum time for the break is 10:30 A.M. The optimum time is half the value for the diminishing return; $N''(2.5) < 0$.

55. Maximum deflection at $x = \dfrac{2\ell}{3}$

61. $f(x) = -3x^3 + 9x^2 - 1$

4.4 Curve Sketching with Asymptotes: Limits Involving Infinity (Pages 227–228)

5. 0   **7.** 3   **9.** 9

11. 1   **13.** 0   **15.** $-\frac{1}{2}$

17. $+\infty$ **19.** 1   **21.** $-\infty$

23. 0

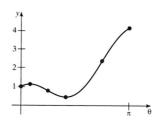

25. asymptotes: $x = 7, y = -3$; graph rising on
$(-\infty, 7) \cup (7, +\infty)$; concave up on $(-\infty, 7)$; concave down on
$(7, +\infty)$; no critical points; no points of inflection;

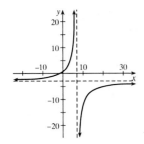

27. asymptotes: $x = 3, y = 6$; graph falling on
$(-\infty, 3) \cup (3, +\infty)$; concave up on $(3, +\infty)$; concave down on
$(-\infty, 3)$; no critical points; no points of inflection;

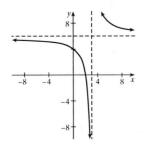

29. asymptotes: $x = 2, y = 1$; graph falling on
$(-\infty, 2) \cup (2, +\infty)$; concave up on $(-\sqrt[3]{4}, 0)$ or $(2, +\infty)$; concave down on $(-\infty, -\sqrt[3]{4})$ or $(0, 2)$; critical point is $(0, -\frac{1}{8})$;
points of inflection $(0, -\frac{1}{8})$, $(-\sqrt[3]{4}, \frac{1}{4})$;

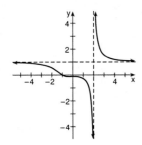

31. asymptotes: $x = -4, x = 1, y = 0$; graph falling on $(-\infty, -4) \cup (-4, 1) \cup (1, +\infty)$; concave up on $(-4, -1)$ or $(1, +\infty)$; concave down on $(-\infty, -4)$ or $(-1, 1)$; no critical points; point of inflection is $(-1, 5)$;

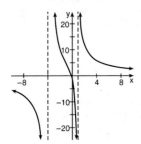

33. no asymptotes; graph rising on $(0, +\infty)$; graph falling on $(-\infty, 0)$; concave up on $(-\infty, +\infty)$; critical point is $(0, 0)$, which is a relative minimum; no points of inflection;

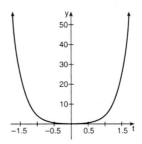

35. no asymptotes; graph rising on $(-3, 0) \cup (3, +\infty)$;
graph falling on $(-\infty, -3) \cup (0, 3)$; concave up on
$(-\infty, -\sqrt{3}) \cup (\sqrt{3}, +\infty)$; concave down on $(-\sqrt{3}, \sqrt{3})$;
critical points are $(-3, 0)$, relative minimum; $(0, 81)$,
relative maximum; $(3, 0)$, relative minimum; points
of inflection are $(-\sqrt{3}, 36), (\sqrt{3}, 36)$;

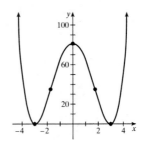

37. no asymptotes; graph rising on $(1, +\infty)$; graph falling on
$(-\infty, 1)$; concave up on $(-\infty, -2) \cup (0, +\infty)$; concave down
on $(-2, 0)$; critical points are $(1, -3)$, relative minimum; $(0, 0)$,
vertical tangent; $(0, 0)$ and $(-2, 6\sqrt[3]{2})$ are points of inflection;

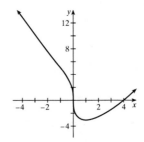

39. horizontal asymptote at $y = \frac{\pi}{2}$; relative minimum at $x = 0$;

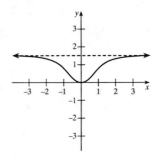

41. no asymptotes; graph rising on $(0, \frac{3\pi}{4}) \cup (\frac{7\pi}{4}, 2\pi)$; graph falling
on $(\frac{3\pi}{4}, \frac{7\pi}{4})$; concave up on $(0, \frac{\pi}{4})$ or $(\frac{5\pi}{4}, 2\pi)$; concave down
on $(\frac{\pi}{4}, \frac{5\pi}{4})$; critical points are $(\frac{3\pi}{4}, \sqrt{2})$, relative maximum;
$(\frac{7\pi}{4}, -\sqrt{2})$, relative minimum; points of inflection: $(\frac{\pi}{4}, 0)$,
$(\frac{5\pi}{4}, 0)$;

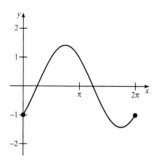

43. critical number at $x = \frac{\pi}{2}$; no asymptotes; graph rising on $(\frac{\pi}{2}, \pi)$; graph falling on $(0, \frac{\pi}{2})$; concave up on $(0, \pi)$; critical points are $(\frac{\pi}{2}, 0)$, relative minimum; $(0, 1)$, and $(\pi, 1)$ relative maxima; no points of inflection;

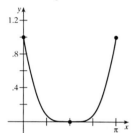

45. 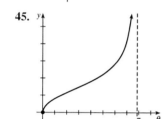 **47.**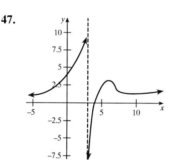

49. Frank is not correct.

51. a. $+\infty$ **b.** $+\infty$ **c.** $-\infty$

　　d. $-\infty$ **e.** $+\infty$

53. $a = \frac{9}{5}$, $b = \frac{3}{5}$ **55.** ∞ **57.** True   **59.** False

4.5 l'Hôpital's Rule (Pages 236–237)

1. a. The limit is not an indeterminate form. The correct limit is $\frac{2}{\pi}$.

　　b. The limit is not an indeterminate form. The correct limit is $\frac{2}{\pi}$.

3. $\frac{3}{2}$ **5.** 10   **7.** not defined

9. $\frac{1}{2}$ **11.** 0   **13.** $\frac{1}{2}$

15. 3   **17.** $\frac{3}{2}$ **19.** 2

21. $+\infty$ **23.** 2   **25.** $\frac{1}{2}$

27. 0   **29.** $-\infty$ **31.** 0

33. $e^{3/2}$ **35.** e^2 **37.** $+\infty$

39. $+\infty$ **41.** $+\infty$ **43.** $-\infty$

45. 1   **47.** 0   **49.** limit does not exist   **51.** $\frac{1}{120}$

53. horizontal asymptote, $y = 0$

55. horizontal asymptote, $y = 1$

61. b. 1   **63.** $a = -2$; $b = \frac{7}{3}$ **65.** If $C = \frac{1}{4}$, the limit is $\frac{5}{4}$.

67. $\lim\limits_{\beta \to \alpha} \left[\dfrac{C}{\beta^2 - \alpha^2} (\sin \alpha t - \sin \beta t) \right] = \dfrac{-Ct}{2\alpha} \cos \alpha t$

4.6 Optimization in the Physical Sciences and Engineering (Pages 245–250)

3. The dimensions of the garden should be 8 ft by 8 ft.

7. The largest rectangle has sides of length $R/\sqrt{2}$ and $\sqrt{2}\,R$.

9. The dimensions are $h = \dfrac{R}{3}\sqrt{3}$ and $r = \dfrac{R}{3}\sqrt{6}$.

11. A circumscribed square of side $s = \dfrac{L}{\sqrt{2}} + \dfrac{L}{\sqrt{2}} = \sqrt{2}L$ yields a maximum area.

13. The minimum distance is 200 mi.

15. The minimal perimeter is obtained when the rectangle is a square.

17. $11,664$ in.^{3} = 6.75 ft^3

19. a. When $s = 4$, Missy should row all the way.

　　b. When $s = 6$, she should land at a point 4.5 km from point B and run the rest of the way (1.5 km).

21. \$60.00

23. He has about 5 minutes 17 seconds to defuse the bomb.

25. $r \approx 3.84$ and $h \approx 7.67$ cm

27. b. When $p = 12$, the largest value of f is 6.

29. $x = \dfrac{Md}{\sqrt{4m^2 - M^2}}$

31. a. $T'(x) = -T\left[\dfrac{c}{(kx + c)x} + \ln p \right]$

　　b. $x = \dfrac{-c \ln p + \sqrt{c^2 (\ln p)^2 - 4kc \ln p}}{2k \ln p}$

　　c.

33. a. The maximum height occurs when $x = \dfrac{mv^2}{32(m^2 + 1)}$

　　b. The maximum height occurs when $y' = 0$ or when $m = v^2/(32x_0)$.

35.

As $\lambda \to +\infty$, $E(\lambda) \to m_0 c^2$.

37. 26 cm is a minimum.

39. The minimum value occurs when $T \approx 4°$.

41. 270 cm^3

43. b. $D'(\alpha) = 2 - 4\left[\dfrac{\cos \alpha}{1.33 \cos \beta} \right]$

　　c. The rainbow angle is 0.742 (or about 42.5°).

4.7 Optimization in Business, Economics, and the Life Sciences (Pages 259–263)

1. $x = 26$ **3.** $x = 20$

5. The minimum average cost is 25.

7. a. $C(x) = 5x + \dfrac{x^2}{50}$; $R(x) = x\left(\dfrac{380 - x}{20}\right)$;

$P(x) = -0.07x^2 + 14x$

b. The maximum profit occurs when the price is \$14/item. The maximum profit is \$700.

9. Profit is maximized when $x = 60$.

11. a. 1.22 million people/yr   **b.** The percentage rate is 2%.

13. 208 years from now   **15.** 45 times per year

17. a. $x = 8$ **c.**

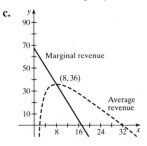

19. Since the optimum solution is over 100 years, you should will the book to your heirs so they can sell it in 117.19 years.

21. Sell the boards at a price of \$42, sell 39 per month, and have the maximum profit of \$507.

23. Lower the fare \$250.

25. Plant 80 total trees, have an average yield per tree of 320 oranges, and a maximum total crop of 25,600 oranges.

27. 62 vines

29. a. The most profitable time to conclude the project is 10 days from now.

b. Assume R is continuous over $[0, 10]$.

31. a. $R(x) = xp(x) = \dfrac{bx - x^2}{a}$ on $[0, b]$; R is increasing on $\left(0, \dfrac{b}{2}\right)$ and decreasing on $\left(\dfrac{b}{2}, b\right)$

b.

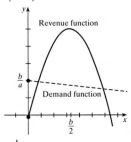

33. $v = \dfrac{kv_1}{k - 1}$

35. a. $x = r$ is a maximum

b. 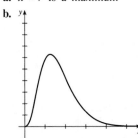   **c.**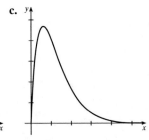

37. $v = 39$

39. a.

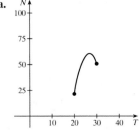

The largest survival percentage is 60.56%, and the smallest survival percentage is 22%.

b. $S'(T) = -(-0.06T + 1.67)(-0.03T^2 + 1.67T - 13.67)^{-2}$; $T \approx 27.83$

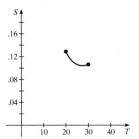

c.

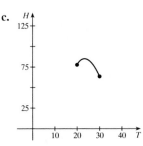

The largest hatching occurs when $T \approx 23.58$ and the smallest when $T = 30$.

41. a. $C = Sx + \dfrac{pQ}{nx}$; $x = \sqrt{\dfrac{pQ}{nS}}$

51. $\theta \approx 0.9553$; this is about 55°.

Chapter 4 Review

Proficiency Examination (Page 263)

18. 2   **19.** $-\frac{1}{2}$ **20.** 0   **21.** e^6

22. Relative maximum at $(-3, 29)$; relative minimum at $(1, -3)$; inflection point at $(-1, 13)$;

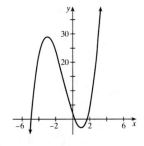

23. inflection points at approximately $\left(-\frac{27}{2}, -96.43\right)$ and $(0,0)$; relative maximum at $\left(\frac{27}{4}, 38.27\right)$;

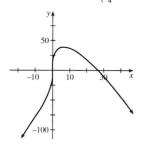

24. relative maximum at $\left(0, \frac{1}{4}\right)$

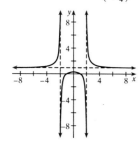

25. relative minimum at $(-1, -2e)$; relative maximum at $(3, 6e^{-3})$;

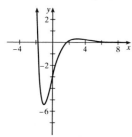

26. $(0,0)$ is a point of infection; the graph is concave up for $x < 0$ and down for $x > 0$.

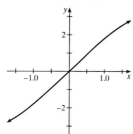

27. relative maximum where $x = \pi$; inflection points at $x = \frac{\pi}{3}$ and $x = \frac{5\pi}{3}$

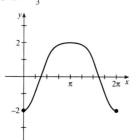

28. absolute maximum at $(0.4, 5.005)$; absolute minimum at $(1, 4)$

29. The dimensions of the box are 19 in. × 19 in. × 10 in.

30. hire 7 people

Supplementary Problems (Pages 263–268)

1.
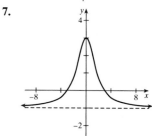

3.
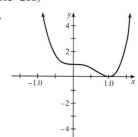

5.
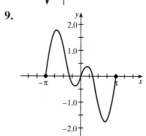

7.
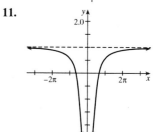

9.
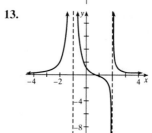

11.
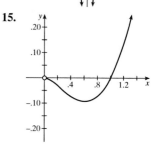

13.
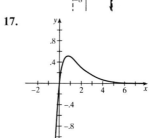

15.
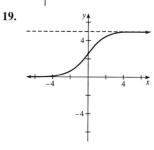

17.

19.

21. c   **23.** b

25. maximum $f(0) = 12$; minimum $f(2) = -4$

27. minimum $f(0) = 0$; maximum $f(\sqrt{3}/2) \approx 0.68$

29. 0   **31.** $-\frac{1}{2}$ **33.** 0

35. This limit does not exist.

37. 1   **39.** 9   **41.** 0

43. e^4 **45.** 1   **47.** 0

49. $+\infty$ **51.** f is the function and g is the derivative

55. $A = \frac{1}{2}$, $B = 0$, $C = -\frac{3}{2}$, $D = 0$

57. The maximum profit of $108,900 is reached when 165 units are rented at $740 each.

59. maximum yield of 6,125 for 35 trees per acre

61. 28,072 ft of pipe laid on the shore gives the minimum cost.

63. $c = 4ab$

65. The price is 90 and the maximum profit is 1,100.

73. $x = \sqrt{ab}$ leads to a relative minimum; $x = -\sqrt{ab}$ leads to a relative maximum.

75. a. The highest value is 165,000 when $N = 20$; this is in the year 2002.

  b. The model predicts that the highest point occurs when $x \approx 11.21$ or in the year 1991. This model predicts it will reach 0 when $x \approx 15.25$, or in the year 1995.

  c. This model seems to do a better job of fitting the data.

  d. Linear model: $y = 5,122x - 16,387$;
  exponential model: $y = 347e^{0.4888x}$;
  logarithmic model: $y = -21,712 \ln(12 - x) + 49,700$

77. a. $f'(x) > 0$ on $\left(-\frac{3}{2}, -\frac{1}{3}\right) \cup (1, 2)$ **b.** $f'(x) < 0$ on $\left(-\frac{1}{3}, 1\right)$

  c. $f''(x) > 0$ on $\left(\frac{1}{3}, +\infty\right)$ **d.** $f''(x) < 0$ on $\left(-\infty, \frac{1}{3}\right)$

  e. $f'(x) = 0$ at $x = -\frac{1}{3}, 1$ **f.** $f'(x)$ exists everywhere

  g. $f''(x) = 0$ at $x = -\frac{1}{3}$

79. a. $f'(x) > 0$ on $(-2, -0.876) \cup (0.876, 2)$

  b. $f'(x) < 0$ on $(-0.876, 0) \cup (0, 0.876)$

  c. $f''(x) > 0$ on $(0, 2)$ **d.** $f''(x) < 0$ on $(-2, 0)$

  e. $f'(x) = 0$ at $x \approx \pm 0.876$

  f. $f'(x)$ does not exist at $x = 0$ **g.** $f''(x) \neq 0$

81. Distance is minimized in the neighborhood of $x = 0.460355$.

83. a. Cost is minimized in the neighborhood of 27 mi/hr.

  b. The total cost is minimized at $x = 55$ mi/hr.

85. This is Putnam Problem 11 of the afternoon session of 1938.

87. This is Putnam Problem 1 of the morning session of 1987.

89. This is Putnam Problem 15 of the afternoon session of 1940.

Chapter 5: Integration

5.1 Antidifferention (Pages 281–282)

1. $2x + C$

3. $x^2 + 3x + C$

5. $t^4 + t^3 + C$

7. $\frac{1}{2} \ln|x| + C$

9. $2u^3 - 3\sin u + C$

11. $\tan \theta + C$

13. $-2\cos \theta + C$

15. $5 \sin^{-1} y + C$

17. $\frac{2}{5}u^{5/2} - \frac{2}{3}u^{3/2} - \frac{1}{9}u^{-9} + C$

19. $\frac{1}{3}x^3 + \frac{2}{5}x^{5/2} + C$

21. $-t^{-1} + \frac{1}{2}t^{-2} - \frac{1}{3}t^{-3} + C$

23. $\frac{4}{5}x^5 + \frac{20}{3}x^3 + 25x + C$

25. $-x^{-1} - \frac{3}{2}x^{-2} + \frac{1}{3}x^{-3} + C$

27. $x + \ln|x| + 2x^{-1} + C$

29. $x - \sin^{-1} x + C$

31. $F(x) = \frac{1}{3}x^3 + \frac{3}{2}x^2$

33. $F(x) = \frac{1}{2}x^2 + 4x^{3/2} + 9x - 40$

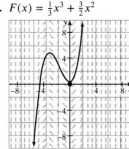

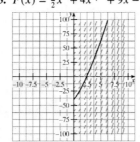

35. $F(x) = \ln|x| - x^{-1} - 1$ **37.** $F(x) = \frac{1}{2}x^2 + e^x + 1$

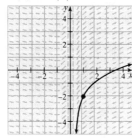

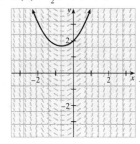

39. a. $F(x) = 2\sqrt{x} - 4x + 2$

  b.   **c.** $C_0 = -\frac{9}{4}$

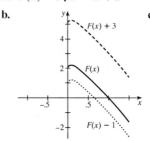

41. $249

43. The population in 8 months will be 10,128.

45. $k = 20$ ft/s^2

47. The acceleration of the plane at liftoff is 4.3 ft/s^2

49. $k = -32$ ft/s^2 **51.** 28.8   **53.** 21

55. $e^2 - 3$ **57.** 1

59. a. $\frac{1}{2}\sec^{-1} y + C$ **b.** $\frac{1}{2}\tan^{-1}\sqrt{y^2 - 1}$

  c. Technology does not use "+C," and to reconcile the inverse trigonometric functions, use a reference triangle where $\theta = \sec^{-1} y$, so $y = \sec \theta$. Then $\tan \theta = \sqrt{y^2 - 1}$ so that $\tan^{-1}(y^2 - 1) = \sec^{-1} y$.

61. $A = \frac{1}{2}(d - c)[m(d + c) + 2b]$

5.2 Area as the Limit of a Sum (Pages 288–290)

1. 6   **3.** 120   **5.** 225   **7.** 9,800

9. $\frac{1}{2}$ **11.** 3   **13. a.** 3.5   **b.** 3.25

15. a. 2.71875   **b.** 2.58796

17. 0.795   **19.** 1.269   **21.** 1.2033   **23.** 18

25. 68   **27.** 2   **29.** false   **31.** true

33. true   **37. a.** $\frac{14}{3}$ **c.** The statement is true.

39. 21.3646   **41.** 0.6018907   **43.** 0.5038795

45. a. 2   **c.** The statement is true.

49. $A = \lim\limits_{n \to +\infty} \left[\sum\limits_{k=1}^{n} f\left(a + \frac{(2k + 1)(b - a)}{2n}\right)\left(\frac{b - a}{n}\right) \right]$

5.3 Riemann Sums and the Definite Integral (Pages 301–302)

1. 2.25   **3.** 10.75   **5.** −0.875

7. 1.18   **9.** 1.94   **11.** 28.875

13. 1.896   **15.** 0.556   **17.** $-\frac{1}{3}$

19. $\frac{3}{2}$ **21.** $-\frac{1}{2}$ **23.** $\frac{1}{2}$

25. $\int_{-2}^{4} f(x)\,dx = 1$; $\int_{-2}^{4} g(x)\,dx = 1$ **27.** 10

29.
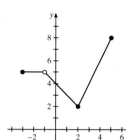
$$\int_{-3}^{5} f(x)\,dx = \frac{71}{2}$$

35. 2.3; $\|P\| = 1.1$

5.4 The Fundamental Theorems of Calculus (Pages 308–309)

1. 140

3. $16 + 8a$

5. $\frac{15}{4}a$

7. $\frac{3}{8}c$

9. 18

11. $\frac{5}{8} + \pi^2$

13. $\dfrac{2^{2a+1} - 1}{2a + 1}$

15. 15

17. $\frac{272}{15}$

19. 2

21. $\dfrac{a\pi}{2}$

23. 5

25. $2 - e$

27. $\frac{5}{2}$

29. 4

31. $\frac{8}{3}$

33. 1

35. $e - \frac{3}{2}$

37. $3\ln 2 - \frac{1}{2}$

39. $(x - 1)\sqrt{x + 1}$

41. $\dfrac{\sin t}{t}$

43. $\dfrac{-1}{\sqrt{1 + 3x^2}}$

55. $\frac{1}{8}(8 + 3\pi^2) \approx 4.7011$

57. a. relative minimum   **b.** $g(1) = 0$ **c.** $x = 0.75$
d.
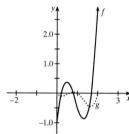

61. $8x^7 - 12x^3$

63. $y = \frac{1}{2}(x - 1)$

65. $F'(x) = f(v)\dfrac{dv}{dx} - f(u)\dfrac{du}{dx}$

5.5 Integration by Substitution (Pages 315–316)

1. a. 32   **b.** $2\sqrt{3} - 2$ **3. a.** 0   **b.** 0

5. a. $\frac{128}{5}$ **b.** $\frac{128}{5}$

7. a. $\frac{2}{9}\sqrt{2}\,x^{9/2} + C$ **b.** $\frac{1}{9}(2x^3 - 5)^{3/2} + C$

9. $\frac{1}{10}(2x + 3)^5 + C$

11. $-\ln\left|\cos(x^2 + 5x + 3)\right| + C$ or $\ln\left|\sec(x^2 + 5x + 3)\right| + C$

13. $\frac{1}{3}x^3 - \frac{1}{3}\sin 3x + C$

15. $\cos(4 - x) + C$

17. $\frac{1}{6}(t^{3/2} + 5)^4 + C$

19. $-\frac{1}{2}\cos(3 + x^2) + C$

21. $\frac{1}{4}\ln(2x^2 + 3) + C$

23. $\frac{1}{6}(2x^2 + 1)^{3/2} + C$

25. $\frac{2}{3}e^{x^{3/2}} + C$

27. $\frac{1}{3}(x^2 + 4)^{3/2} + C$

29. $\frac{1}{2}(\ln x)^2 + C$

31. $2\ln(\sqrt{x} + 7) + C$

33. $\ln(e^t + 1) + C$

35. $\frac{5}{6}\ln 3$

37. 0

39. $e - e^{1/2}$

41. $\frac{1}{2}\ln 2$

43. 1.80

45. a. We take 1 Frdor as the variable so the note from the students reads "Because of illness I cannot lecture between Easter and Michaelmas."

b. The Dirichlet function is defined as a function f so that $f(x)$ equals a determined constant c (usually 1) when the variable x takes a rational value, and equals another constant d (usually 0) when this variable is irrational. This famous function is one which is discontinuous everywhere.

47. $\frac{16}{3}$ **49.** $\sqrt{10} - \sqrt{2}$ **51.** 0   **53.** 0

55. a. true   **b.** true   **c.** false   **57.** $F(x) = -\frac{1}{3}\ln\left|1 - 3x^2\right| + 5$

59. The amount of water at 4 seconds is 2 ft^3. The depth at that time is about $\frac{1}{4}$ in.

61. a. $L(t) = 0.03\sqrt{36 + 16t - t^2} + 3.82$

b. The highest level is 4.12 ppm.
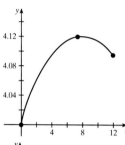

c. It is the same as 11:00 A.M. ($t = 4$) at 7:00 P.M. (when $t = 12$).
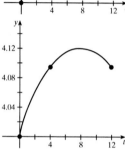

5.6 Introduction to Differential Equations (Pages 325–328)

9. $x^2 + y^2 = 8$ **11.** $y = \tan\left(x - \frac{3\pi}{4}\right)$ **13.** $x^{3/2} - y^{3/2} = 7$

15.
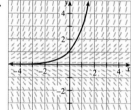
17.

19.

21. $y = Be^{(3/2)x^2}$

23. $2(1 - x^2)^{3/2} + 3y^2 = C$

25. $x^{3/2} + 3y^{1/2} = C$

27. $\cos x + \sin y = C$

29. $-\frac{1}{3}(1 - y^2)^{3/2} = \frac{1}{2}(\ln x)^2 + C$ **31.** $xy = C$ **33.** $y = Cx$

35.
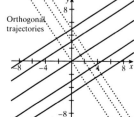
Orthogonal trajectories

37.
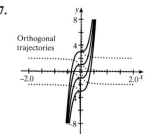
Orthogonal trajectories

39. 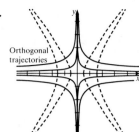   **41.**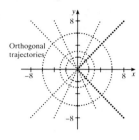

Orthogonal trajectories

Orthogonal trajectories

43. $\dfrac{dQ}{dt} = kQ$ **45.** $\dfrac{dT}{dt} = c(T - T_m)$ **47.** $\dfrac{dQ}{dt} = kQ(B - Q)$

49. Conjecture: The orthogonal trajectories are circles.

51. There was still 78% of the ^{14}C still present.

53. 1326 A.D.   **55.** 28 min

57. a. 98.5 ft/s **b.** $s = 3,956.067$; $h \approx 352$ ft

59. a. 33,000 **b.** 42,000

61. 10 years from now   **63.** 2 hr and 53 min

65. It will take about 65 hr for 43% to be left. Neptunium-139 has a half-life of 53.70 hours.

67. 7.182%; the percentage lost is always the same.

5.7 The Mean Value Theorem for Integrals; Average Value (Pages 332–333)

1. 1.55 is in the interval $[1, 2]$.

3. $\sqrt{5} \approx 2.24$ is in the interval.

5. The mean value theorem does not apply.

7. 0.0807 is in the interval.

9. -0.187 is in the interval.

11. $A = 25$ **13.** $A = 38/3$

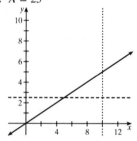

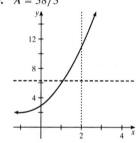

15. $A \approx 1.839$ **17.** $\frac{3}{2}$ **19.** 0

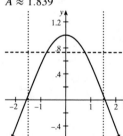

21. 0.3729   **23.** $\frac{4}{3}$

25. -10 **27.** -25.375

29. 2.36

33. Avg temperature $= 49.4$ °F

35. a. 1,987.24

  b. The average population is reached at just under 14 minutes.

37. $f(x) = (x + 1)\cos x + \sin x$

5.8 Numerical Integration: The Trapezoidal Rule and Simpson's Rule (Pages 339–342)

1. Trapezoidal rule; 2.34375; Simpson's rule, 2.33333; exact value, $\frac{7}{3}$

3. a. 0.7825   **b.** 0.785

5. a. 2.037871   **b.** 2.048596

7. a. 0.584   **b.** 0.594

11. $A \approx 0.775$; the exact answer is between $0.775 - 0.05$ and $0.775 + 0.05$

13. $A \approx 0.455$; the exact answer is between $0.455 - 0.0005$ and $0.455 + 0.0005$

15. $A \approx 3.25$; the exact answer is between $3.25 - 0.01$ and $3.25 + 0.01$

17. $A \approx 0.44$; the exact answer is between $0.44 - 0.01$ and $0.44 + 0.01$

19. a. $n = 164$ **b.** $n = 18$ **21. a.** $n = 184$ **b.** $n = 22$

23. a. $n = 82$ **b.** $n = 8$ **25. a.** 3.1 **b.** 3.1

27. 430   **29.** 613 ft^2 **31.** 79.17

33. a. Simpson error is 0. **b.** $f^{(4)}(x)$ is unbounded near $x = 2$

35. The inscribed circles have diameter $13\frac{1}{3}$ and $8\frac{1}{3}$.

39. $\frac{32}{3}$ **41.** Error is zero.

5.9 An Alternative Approach: The Logarithm as an Integral (Pages 345–346)

3. $E \approx 0.00104$; the number of subintervals should be 18

Chapter 5 Review
Proficiency Examination (Pages 346–347)

22. $-\frac{3}{5}$ **23.** $x^5 \sqrt{\cos(2x + 1)}$

24. $\frac{1}{2}\tan^{-1}(2x) + C$ **25.** $-\frac{1}{2}e^{-x^2} + C$ **26.** $\frac{17}{3}$

27. $-\frac{35}{3}$ **28.** $\frac{1}{2}$ **29.** 0   **30.** 36

31. $\displaystyle\int_1^2 e^{x^2} \, dx$ does not have a closed form, so we must use approximate integration or technology to find
$$\int_1^2 e^{x^2} \, dx \approx 14.99.$$

32. 0

33. The percent is approximately 1.33×10^{-184}, which exceeds the accuracy of most calculators and measuring devices.

34. 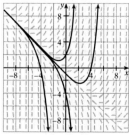   **e.** $y = -x - 1$

35. a. $n \geq 26$ **b.** $n \geq 4$

Supplementary Problems (Pages 347–350)

1. 25   **3.** 6   **5.** 1,710

7. $\dfrac{6 - 2\sqrt{2}}{3}$ **9.** $\sqrt{3} - 1$ **11.** $-\frac{3}{4}(1 - \sqrt[3]{9})$

13. $2x^{5/2} - \frac{4}{3}x^{3/2} + 2x^{1/2} + C$ **15.** $3\sin^{-1}x + \sqrt{1 - x^2} + C$

17. $-\ln|\sin x + \cos x| + C$ **19.** $\frac{1}{3}(x - 1)^3 + C$ **21.** $x + C$

23. $\dfrac{x^3(x^2 + 1)^{3/2}}{3} + C$ **25.** $-\frac{1}{15}(1 - 5x^2)^{3/2} + C$

27. $\frac{1}{3}(1 + x^2)^{3/2} - (1 + x^2)^{1/2} + C$

29. $\frac{2}{5}(1 + \ln 2x)^{5/2} - \frac{2}{3}(1 + \ln 2)(1 + \ln 2x)^{3/2} + C$ **31.** 0

33. 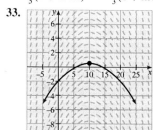   **35.**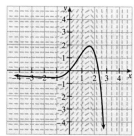

37. $\ln 4$ **39.** $\frac{1}{4}(e^8 - 1)$

41. $f(t) = -\frac{1}{16}\sin 4t + \frac{1}{4}\cos 2t + \frac{5}{4}t + \frac{5}{4} - \frac{5}{8}\pi$

43. $y = 1 - \dfrac{1}{x - C}$ **45.** $\tan y + \cot x = C$

47. $y = Ce^{(1/3)x^3 + x}$ **49.** $y = \tan^{-1}(C - \ln|\cos x|)$

51. 0.5274   **53.** 1.9541   **55.** 0.9091   **57.** $n = 6$

59. Number of primes less than x

x	$\pi(x)$	Gauss
10^3	168	178
10^4	1,229	1,246
10^5	9,592	9,628
10^6	78,498	78,628
10^{10}	455,052,511	455,055,614

61. 1.01297   **63. b.** ± 8 m/s

65. The revenue for the five years is \$7,666.67.

67. The tree was 2.33 ft tall when it was transplanted.

69. $y = \frac{1}{3}(x^2 + 5)^{3/2} + 1$ **71.** 4.45 ppm   **73.** 126 people

75. The average price was \$1.32 per pound.

77. about 2 min, 45 seconds

81. a. 51.7%

  b. The time for 90% to disintegrate is about $17\frac{1}{2}$ years.

83. 35 years   **85.** 1:44 P.M.

87. This is Putnam Problem 1 from the morning session in 1958.

Cumulative Review for Chapters 1–5 (Pages 353–354)

5. $\frac{7}{5}$ **7.** $\frac{1}{2}$ **9.** 0   **11.** 1   **13.** 1

15. $6(x^2 + 1)^2(3x - 4)(2x - 1)^2$ **17.** $\dfrac{\cos x + x\sin x}{(x + \cos x)^2}$

19. $6\sec^2 3x \tan 3x$ **21.** $\dfrac{10x + 3}{5x^2 + 3x - 2}$

23. 5   **25.** $\sqrt{10} - 3$ **27.** $\ln(e^x + 2) + C$ **29.** 1.812

31.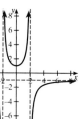

33. $y = \dfrac{9}{2(4 - x^3)^{3/2}} + C$

35. $y = 5 \pm 2e^{-2x}$

37. a. $\frac{9}{4}\pi - 8$ **b.** 3

  c. $4x + y - 20 - \frac{9}{4}\pi = 0$

  d. $x = 0$ and $x = 7$

39. 0.1 rad/s

41. a. $y = -\frac{4}{\pi}x + 2$ **b.** $y = -2x + \pi$

  c. $x \approx 0.690$; mean value theorem

43. a. relative maximum at $(0, k)$; relative minimum at $(4, k - 32)$

  b. $0 < k < 32$ **c.** $k = \frac{27}{4}$

45. $y = \dfrac{3}{\cos 3x + C}$

Appendix A (Pages A-7–A-8)

1. $\delta = \frac{\epsilon}{2}$ **3.** false   **5.** $\delta = \min(1, \frac{\epsilon}{5})$

7. $\delta = \epsilon$ **9.** $\delta = \frac{\epsilon}{3}$ **11.** $\delta = \min(1, \frac{\epsilon}{5})$

APPENDIX G   Credits

This page constitutes an extension of the copyright page.

CHAPTER 1

12   Problems 59 and 60 from *Introductory Oceanography*, 5th ed., by H. V. Thurman, p. 253. Reprinted with permission of Merrill, an imprint of Macmillan Publishing Company. Copyright ©1988 Merrill Publishing Company, Columbus, Ohio.

12   Problem 61 adapted from R. A. Serway, *Physics*, 3rd ed., Philadelphia: Saunders, 1992, p. 1007.

12   Journal problem (#62) by Murray Klamkin reprinted from *The Mathematics Student Journal*, Vol. 28, 1980, issue 3, p. 2.

18–19   Babylonian system of equations in Problem 58 and 59 taken from *A History of Mathematics*, 2nd ed., by Carl B. Boyer, revised by Uta C. Merzbach, John Wiley and Sons, Inc., New York, 1968.

19   Journal problem (#64) reprinted from *Ontario Secondary School Mathematics Bulletin*, Vol. 18, 1982, issue 2. p. 7.

33   Journal problem (#72) reprinted from *The Mathematics Student Journal*, Vol. 28, 1980, issue 3, p. 2.

45   Putnam examination problem (#45) 1959, reprinted by permission from The Mathematical Association of America.

45   Putnam examination problem (#46) 1960, reprinted by permission from The Mathematical Association of America.

46–47   Guest essay, "Calculus Was Inevitable," by John L. Troutman.

48   Historical Quest (#9) information from *Ethnomathematics* by Marcia Ascher, (Pacific Grove: Brooks/Cole, 1991) pp. 128–129 and 188–189.

CHAPTER 2

78   Graph (#36) from Michael D. La Grega, Philip L. Buckingham, and Jeffery C. Evans, *Hazardous Waste Management*, New York: McGraw-Hill, 1994, pp. 565–566.

79   Modeling problem (#37) from E. Batschelet, *Introduction to Mathematics for Life Scientists*, 2nd ed., New York: Springer-Verlag, 1976, p. 280.

95   Modeling problem (#67) from William Bosch and L. G. Cobb, "Windchill," *UMAP Module No. 658*, (1984), pp. 244–247.

95   Putnam examination problem (#71) 1956, reprinted by permission from The Mathematical Association of America.

95   Putnam examination problem (#72) 1986, reprinted by permission from The Mathematical Association of America.

CHAPTER 3

129   Global modeling illustration from *Scientific American*, March 1991.

157   Journal problem (#73) by Bruce W. King from *The Pi Mu Epsilon Journal*, Volume 7 (1981), p. 346.

174   Modeling problem (#30) by John A. Helms, "Environmental Control of Net Photosynthesis in Naturally Grown Pinus Ponderosa Nets," *Ecology* (Winter 1972) p. 92.

174   Modeling problems (#35, #36) from *Introduction to Mathematics for Life Scientists*, 2nd ed. New York: Springer-Verlag (1976), pp. 102–103.

178   Problem 65 from 1982 BC AP Examination.

180   Putnam examination problem (#95) 1946, reprinted by permission from The Mathematical Association of America.

180   Putnam examination problem (#96) 1939, reprinted by permission from The Mathematical Association of America.

180   Putnam examination problem (#97) 1946, reprinted by permission from The Mathematical Association of America.

181   Chaos example is by Jack Wadhams of Golden West College.

181   Photo courtesy of Gregory Sams/Photo Researchers, Inc.

CHAPTER 4

183   Energy expended by a pigeon by Edward Batschelet, *Introduction to Mathematics for Life Scientists*, 2nd ed., New York: Springer-Verlag, 1979, pp. 276–277.

209   MAL cartoon, © 1974, by permission from the estate of Malcolm Hancock.

216   Problem 54 from "The Mechanics of Bird Migration," by C. J. Pennycuick, *Ibis III*, pp. 525–556.

216   Journal problem (#57) from *Mathematics Magazine*, Volume 55 (1982), p. 300.

228   Journal problem (#54) from *Parabola*, Vol. 20, Issue 1, 1984.

228   Historical Quest (#55) from "Mathematics in India in the Middle Ages," by Chandra B. Sharma, *Mathematical Spectrum*, Volume 14(1), pp. 6–8, 1982.

237   Historical Quest (#58) from *A Source Book in Mathematics, 1200–1800* by D. J. Struik, Cambridge, MA: University Press, 1969, pp. 313–316.

245   Journal problem (#6) from *Parabola*, Vol. 19, Issue 1, 1983, p. 22.

248   Modeling problem (#31) by Paul J. Campbell, "Calculus Optimization in Information Technology," *UMAP Module 1991: Tool for Teaching*, Lexington, MA, CUPM Inc., 1992, pp. 175–199.

248   Modeling problem (#32) by John C. Lewis and Peter P. Gillis, "Packing Factors in Diatomic Crystals," *American Journal of Physics*, Vol. 61, No. 5 (1993), pp. 434–438.

249–250   Modeling problem (#42) by Thomas O'Neil, "A Mathematical Model of a Universal Joint," *UMAP Modules 1982: Tools for Teaching*. Lexington, MA: Consortium for Mathematics and Its Applications, Inc., 1983, pp. 393–405.

250   Modeling problem (#43) is based on an article by Steve Janke, "Somewhere Within the Rainbow," *UMAP Modules 1992: Tools for Teaching*. Lexington, MA: Consortium for Mathematics and Its Applications, Inc., 1993.

256   Concentration of drugs in the bloodstream application adapted from E. Heinz, "Probleme bei der Diffusion kleiner Substanzmengen innerhalb des menschlichen Körpers," *Biochem.*, Vol. 319 (1949), pp. 482–492.

257   Modeling vascular branching is adapted from *Introduction to Mathematics for Life Scientists*, 2nd ed., by Edward Batschelet, New York: Springer-Verlag, 1976, pp. 278–280.

261   Modeling problem (#35) from "A Blood Cell Population Model, Dynamical Diseases, and Chaos," by W. B. Gearhart and M. Martelli, *UMAP Modules 1990: Tools for Teaching*, Arlington, MA: Consortium for Mathematics and Its Applications (CUPM) Inc., 1991.

261   Modeling problem (#37) adapted from "Flight of Birds in Relation to Energetics and Wind Directions," by V. A. Tucker and K. Schmidt-Koening, *The Auk*, Vol. 88, 1971, pp. 97–107.

261   Modeling problem (#39) adapted from P. L. Shaffer and H. J. Gold, "A Simulation Model of Population Dynamics of the Codling Moth Cydia Pomonella," *Ecological Modeling*, Vol. 30, 1985, pp. 247–274.

262   Problem #47 adapted from "Price Elasticity of Demand: Gambling, Heroin, Marijuana, Prostitution, and Fish," by Yves Nievergelt, *UMAP Modules 1987: Tools for Teaching*. Arlingon, MA, CUPM Inc., 1988, pp. 153–181.

263   Photo of a beehive, courtesy of Scott Camazine/Photo Researchers, Inc.

264   Journal problem (#51) from the *Mathematics Teacher*, December 1990, p. 718.

265   Journal problem (#63) from the *AMATYC Review*, Spring 1995, pp. 67–68.

265   Journal problem (#64) from *Quantum*, 1997, Vol. 7, No. 4, pp. 50–53.

266   Modeling problem (#75) adapted from "Modeling the AIDS Epidemic," by Allyn Jackson, *Notices of the American Mathematical Society*, Vol. 36., No. 8 (October 1989), pp. 981–983.

267   Historical Quest (#84) quotation about Euler from *Elements of Algebra, 5th Ed*, by Leonhard Euler, London: Longman, Orme, and Co., 1840.

268   Putnam examination problem (#85) 1938, reprinted by permission from The Mathematical Association of America.

268   Putnam examination problem (#86) 1941, reprinted by permission from The Mathematical Association of America.

268   Putnam examination problem (#87) 1987, reprinted by permission from The Mathematical Association of America.

268   Putnam examination problem (#88) 1985, reprinted by permission from The Mathematical Association of America.

268   Putnam examination problem (#89) 1940, reprinted by permission from The Mathematical Association of America.

268   Putnam examination problem (#90) 1961, reprinted by permission from The Mathematical Association of America.

269   Photograph of a wine cellar showing wooden cask, courtesy of Peter Menzel/Stock Boston.

269   Group research project is from Elgin Johnston of Iowa State University. This group research project comes from research done at Iowa State University as part of a National Science Foundation grant.

CHAPTER 5

285   Software output from *Converge* by John R. Mowbray, JEMware, 567 South King Street, Suite 178, Honolulu, HI 96813.

308   Journal problem (#52) from *FOCUS*, February 1995, p. 15.

315   Historical Quest (#45) quotation from "A Short Account of the History of Mathematics," as quoted in *Mathematical Circles Adieu* by Howard Eves, Boston: Prindle, Weber & Schmidt, Inc., 1977.

316   Journal problem (#60) by Murray Klamkin from the *College Mathematics Journal*, Sept. 1989, p. 343. Problem by Murray Klamkin.

327   Shroud of Turin, courtesy of Gianni Tortoli/Science Source/Photo Researches, Inc.

341   Historical Quest (#34) Early Asian Calculus from *Mathematics*, by David Bergamini, p. 108. Reprinted by permission of Time, Incorporated, 1963.

349   Modeling problem (#76) adapted from "Flight Speeds of Birds in Relation to Energies and Wind Directions," by V. A. Tucker and K. Schmidt-Koenig, *The Auk*, Vol. 88 (1971), pp. 97–107.

350   Putnam examination problem (#86) 1951, reprinted by permission from The Mathematical Association of America.

350   Putnam examination problem (#87) 1958, reprinted by permission from The Mathematical Association of America.

351–352 Guest essay, "Kinematics of Jogging," by Ralph Boas.

Index

LICENSE AGREEMENT

YOU SHOULD CAREFULLY READ THE FOLLOWING TERMS AND CONDITIONS BEFORE BREAKING THE SEAL ON THE PACKAGE. AMONG OTHER THINGS, THIS AGREEMENT LICENSES THE ENCLOSED SOFTWARE TO YOU AND CONTAINS WARRANTY AND LIABILITY DISCLAIMERS. BY BREAKING THE SEAL ON THE PACKAGE, YOU ARE ACCEPTING AND AGREEING TO THE TERMS AND CONDITIONS OF THIS AGREEMENT. IF YOU DO NOT AGREE TO THE TERMS OF THIS AGREEMENT, DO NOT BREAK THE SEAL. YOU SHOULD PROMPTLY RETURN THE PACKAGE UNOPENED.

LICENSE.

Subject to the provisions contained herein, Prentice-Hall, Inc. ("PH") hereby grants to you a non-exclusive, non- transferable license to use the object code version of the computer software product ("Software") contained in the package on a single computer of the type identified on the package.

SOFTWARE AND DOCUMENTATION.

PH shall furnish the Software to you on media in machine-readable object code form and may also provide the standard documentation ("Documentation") containing instructions for operation and use of the Software.

LICENSE TERM AND CHARGES.

The term of this license commences upon delivery of the Software to you and is perpetual unless earlier terminated upon default or as otherwise set forth herein.

TITLE.

Title, and ownership right, and intellectual property rights in and to the Software and Documentation shall remain in PH and/or in suppliers to PH of programs contained in the Software. The Software is provided for your own internal use under this license. This license does not include the right to sublicense and is personal to you and therefore may not be assigned (by operation of law or otherwise) or transferred without the prior written consent of PH. You acknowledge that the Software in source code form remains a confidential trade secret of PH and/or its suppliers and therefore you agree not to attempt to decipher or decompile, modify, disassemble, reverse engineer or prepare derivative works of the Software or develop source code for the Software or knowingly allow others to do so. Further, you may not copy the Documentation or other written materials accompanying the Software.

UPDATES.

This license does not grant you any right, license, or interest in and to any improvements, modifications, enhancements, or updates to the Software and Documentation. Updates, if available, may be obtained by you at PH's then current standard pricing, terms, and conditions.

LIMITED WARRANTY AND DISCLAIMER.

PH warrants that the media containing the Software, if provided by PH, is free from defects in material and workmanship under normal use for a period of sixty (60) days from the date you purchased a license to it. THIS IS A LIMITED WARRANTY AND IT IS THE ONLY WARRANTY MADE BY PH. THE SOFTWARE IS PROVIDED 'AS IS' AND PH SPECIFICALLY DISCLAIMS ALL WARRANTIES OF ANY KIND, EITHER EXPRESS OR IMPLIED, INCLUDING, BUT NOT LIMITED TO, THE IMPLIED WARRANTY OF MERCHANTABILITY AND FITNESS FOR A PARTICULAR PURPOSE. FURTHER, COMPANY DOES NOT WARRANT, GUARANTY OR MAKE ANY REPRESENTATIONS REGARDING THE USE, OR THE RESULTS OF THE USE, OF THE SOFTWARE IN TERMS OF CORRECTNESS, ACCURACY, RELIABILITY, CURRENTNESS, OR OTHERWISE AND DOES NOT WARRANT THAT THE OPERATION OF ANY SOFTWARE WILL BE UNINTERRUPTED OR ERROR FREE. COMPANY EXPRESSLY DISCLAIMS ANY WARRANTIES NOT STATED HEREIN. NO ORAL OR WRITTEN INFORMATION OR ADVICE GIVEN BY PH, OR ANY PH DEALER, AGENT, EMPLOYEE OR OTHERS SHALL CREATE, MODIFY OR EXTEND A WARRANTY OR IN ANY WAY INCREASE THE SCOPE OF THE FOREGOING WARRANTY, AND NEITHER SUBLICENSEE OR PURCHASER MAY RELY ON ANY SUCH INFORMATION OR ADVICE. If the media is subjected to accident, abuse, or improper use; or if you violate the terms of this Agreement, then this warranty shall immediately be terminated. This warranty shall not apply if the Software is used on or in conjunction with hardware or programs other than the unmodified version of hardware and programs with which the Software was designed to be used as described in the Documentation.

LIMITATION OF LIABILITY.

Your sole and exclusive remedies for any damage or loss in any way connected with the Software are set forth below. UNDER NO CIRCUMSTANCES AND UNDER NO LEGAL THEORY, TORT, CONTRACT, OR OTHERWISE, SHALL PH BE LIABLE TO YOU OR ANY OTHER PERSON FOR ANY INDIRECT, SPECIAL, INCIDENTAL, OR CONSEQUENTIAL DAMAGES OF ANY CHARACTER INCLUDING, WITHOUT LIMITATION, DAMAGES FOR LOSS OF GOODWILL, LOSS OF PROFIT, WORK STOPPAGE, COMPUTER FAILURE OR MALFUNCTION, OR ANY AND ALL OTHER COMMERCIAL DAMAGES OR LOSSES, OR FOR ANY OTHER DAMAGES EVEN IF PH SHALL HAVE BEEN INFORMED OF THE POSSIBILITY OF SUCH DAMAGES, OR FOR ANY CLAIM BY ANY OTHER PARTY. PH'S THIRD PARTY PROGRAM SUPPLIERS MAKE NO WARRANTY, AND HAVE NO LIABILITY WHATSOEVER, TO YOU. PH's sole and exclusive obligation and liability and your exclusive remedy shall be: upon PH's election, (i) the replacement of your defective media; or (ii) the repair or correction of your defective media if PH is able, so will conform to the above warranty; or (iii) if PH is unable to replace or repair, you may terminate this license by returning the Software. Only if you inform PH of your problem during the applicable warranty period will PH be obligated to honor this warranty. You may contact PH to inform PH of the problem as follows: SOME STATES OR JURISDICTIONS DO NOT ALLOW THE EXCLUSION OF IMPLIED WARRANTIES OR LIMITATION OR EXCLUSION OF CONSEQUENTIAL DAMAGES, SO THE ABOVE LIMITATIONS OR EXCLUSIONS MAY NOT APPLY TO YOU. THIS WARRANTY GIVES YOU SPECIFIC LEGAL RIGHTS AND YOU MAY ALSO HAVE OTHER RIGHTS WHICH VARY BY STATE OR JURISDICTION.

MISCELLANEOUS.

If any provision of this Agreement is held to be ineffective, unenforceable, or illegal under certain circumstances for any reason, such decision shall not affect the validity or enforceability (i) of such provision under other circumstances or (ii) of the remaining provisions hereof under all circumstances and such provision shall be reformed to and only to the extent necessary to make it effective, enforceable, and legal under such circumstances. All headings are solely for convenience and shall not be considered in interpreting this Agreement. This Agreement shall be governed by and construed under New York law as such law applies to agreements between New York residents entered into and to be performed entirely within New York, except as required by U.S. Government rules and regulations to be governed by Federal law. YOU ACKNOWLEDGE THAT YOU HAVE READ THIS AGREEMENT, UNDERSTAND IT, AND AGREE TO BE BOUND BY ITS TERMS AND CONDITIONS. YOU FURTHER AGREE THAT IT IS THE COMPLETE AND EXCLUSIVE STATEMENT OF THE AGREEMENT BETWEEN US THAT SUPERSEDES ANY PROPOSAL OR PRIOR AGREEMENT, ORAL OR WRITTEN, AND ANY OTHER COMMUNICATIONS BETWEEN US RELATING TO THE SUBJECT MATTER OF THIS AGREEMENT.

U.S. GOVERNMENT RESTRICTED RIGHTS.

Use, duplication or disclosure by the Government is subject to restrictions set forth in subparagraphs (a) through (d) of the Commercial Computer-Restricted Rights clause at FAR 52.227-19 when applicable, or in subparagraph (c) (1) (ii) of the Rights in Technical Data and Computer Software clause at DFARS 252.227-7013, and in similar clauses in the NASA FAR Supplement.

INTEGRATION FORMULAS

PROCEDURAL RULES

Constant multiple rule
$$\int c f(u)\, du = c \int f(u)\, du$$

Sum rule
$$\int [f(u) + g(u)]\, du = \int f(u)\, du + \int g(u)\, du$$

Difference rule
$$\int [f(u) - g(u)]\, du = \int f(u)\, du - \int g(u)\, du$$

Linearity rule
$$\int [a f(u) + b g(u)]\, du = a \int f(u)\, du + b \int g(u)\, du$$

BASIC FORMULAS

Constant rule
$$\int 0\, du = C$$

Power rules
$$\int u^n\, du = \frac{u^{n+1}}{n+1} + C; \qquad n \neq -1$$
$$\int u^{-1}\, du = \ln |u| + C$$

Exponential rules
$$\int e^u\, du = e^u + C$$
$$\int a^u\, du = \frac{a^u}{\ln a} + C \quad a > 0,\ a \neq 1$$

Logarithmic rule
$$\int \ln u\, du = u \ln u - u + C,\ u > 0$$

Trigonometric rules

$$\int \sin u\, du = -\cos u + C \qquad \int \cos u\, du = \sin u + C$$

$$\int \tan u\, du = -\ln |\cos u| + C \qquad \int \cot u\, du = \ln |\sin u| + C$$
$$= \ln |\sec u| + C$$

$$\int \sec u\, du = \ln |\sec u + \tan u| + C \qquad \int \csc u\, du = -\ln |\csc u + \cot u| + C$$

$$\int \sec^2 u\, du = \tan u + C \qquad \int \csc^2 u\, du = -\cot u + C$$

$$\int \sec u \tan u\, du = \sec u + C \qquad \int \csc u \cot u\, du = -\csc u + C$$

Cosine squared formula
$$\int \cos^2 u\, du = \tfrac{1}{2}u + \tfrac{1}{4} \sin 2u + C$$

Sine squared formula
$$\int \sin^2 u\, du = \tfrac{1}{2}u - \tfrac{1}{4} \sin 2u + C$$

Hyperbolic rules

$$\int \sinh u\, du = \cosh u + C \qquad \int \cosh u\, du = \sinh u + C$$

$$\int \tanh u\, du = \ln(\cosh u) + C \qquad \int \coth u\, du = \ln |\sinh u| + C$$

Inverse rules

$$\int \frac{du}{\sqrt{a^2 - u^2}} = \sin^{-1} \frac{u}{a} + C \qquad \int \frac{du}{\sqrt{u^2 - a^2}} = \cosh^{-1} \frac{u}{a} + C$$

$$\int \frac{du}{a^2 + u^2} = \frac{1}{a} \tan^{-1} \frac{u}{a} + C \qquad \int \frac{du}{a^2 - u^2} = \begin{cases} \frac{1}{a} \tanh^{-1} \frac{u}{a} + C & \text{if } \left| \frac{u}{a} \right| < 1 \\ \frac{1}{a} \coth^{-1} \frac{u}{a} + C & \text{if } \left| \frac{u}{a} \right| > 1 \end{cases}$$

$$\int \frac{du}{u\sqrt{u^2 - a^2}} = \frac{1}{a} \sec^{-1} \frac{|u|}{a} + C$$

$$\int \frac{du}{u\sqrt{a^2 - u^2}} = -\frac{1}{a} \operatorname{sech}^{-1} \left| \frac{u}{a} \right| + C = -\frac{1}{a} \ln \left| \frac{a + \sqrt{a^2 - u^2}}{u} \right| + C$$

$$\int \frac{du}{\sqrt{a^2 + u^2}} = \sinh^{-1} \frac{u}{a} + C = \ln \left(\sqrt{a^2 + u^2} + u \right) + C$$

$$\int \frac{du}{u\sqrt{a^2 + u^2}} = -\frac{1}{a} \operatorname{csch}^{-1} \left| \frac{u}{a} \right| + C = -\frac{1}{a} \ln \left| \frac{\sqrt{a^2 + u^2} + a}{u} \right| + C$$

DIFFERENTIATION FORMULAS

PROCEDURAL RULES

Constant multiple rule
$$(cf)' = cf'$$

Sum rule
$$(f + g)' = f' + g'$$

Difference rule
$$(f - g)' = f' - g'$$

Linearity rule
$$(af + bg)' = af' + bg'$$

Product rule
$$(fg)' = fg' + f'g$$

Quotient rule
$$\left(\frac{f}{g}\right)' = \frac{gf' - fg'}{g^2}$$

Chain rule
$$\frac{dy}{dx} = \frac{dy}{du}\frac{du}{dx}$$

BASIC FORMULAS

Extended power rule
$$\frac{d}{dx}u^n = nu^{n-1}\frac{du}{dx}$$

Trigonometric rules
$$\frac{d}{dx}\sin u = \cos u \frac{du}{dx} \qquad \frac{d}{dx}\cos u = -\sin u \frac{du}{dx}$$

$$\frac{d}{dx}\tan u = \sec^2 u \frac{du}{dx} \qquad \frac{d}{dx}\cot u = -\csc^2 u \frac{du}{dx}$$

$$\frac{d}{dx}\sec u = \sec u \tan u \frac{du}{dx} \qquad \frac{d}{dx}\csc u = -\csc u \cot u \frac{du}{dx}$$

Inverse trigonometric rules
$$\frac{d}{dx}\sin^{-1} u = \frac{1}{\sqrt{1 - u^2}}\frac{du}{dx} \qquad \frac{d}{dx}\cos^{-1} u = \frac{-1}{\sqrt{1 - u^2}}\frac{du}{dx}$$

$$\frac{d}{dx}\tan^{-1} u = \frac{1}{1 + u^2}\frac{du}{dx} \qquad \frac{d}{dx}\cot^{-1} u = \frac{-1}{1 + u^2}\frac{du}{dx}$$

$$\frac{d}{dx}\sec^{-1} u = \frac{1}{|u|\sqrt{u^2 - 1}}\frac{du}{dx} \qquad \frac{d}{dx}\csc^{-1} u = \frac{-1}{|u|\sqrt{u^2 - 1}}\frac{du}{dx}$$

Logarithmic rules
$$\frac{d}{dx}\ln u = \frac{1}{u}\frac{du}{dx} \qquad \frac{d}{dx}\log_b u = \frac{\log_b e}{u}\frac{du}{dx} = \frac{1}{u \ln b}\frac{du}{dx}$$

Exponential rules
$$\frac{d}{dx}e^u = e^u \frac{du}{dx} \qquad \frac{d}{dx}b^u = b^u \ln b \frac{du}{dx}$$

Hyperbolic rules
$$\frac{d}{dx}\sinh u = \cosh u \frac{du}{dx} \qquad \frac{d}{dx}\cosh u = \sinh u \frac{du}{dx}$$

$$\frac{d}{dx}\tanh u = \operatorname{sech}^2 u \frac{du}{dx} \qquad \frac{d}{dx}\coth u = -\operatorname{csch}^2 u \frac{du}{dx}$$

$$\frac{d}{dx}\operatorname{sech} u = -\operatorname{sech} u \tanh u \frac{du}{dx} \qquad \frac{d}{dx}\operatorname{csch} u = -\operatorname{csch} u \coth u \frac{du}{dx}$$

Inverse hyperbolic rules
$$\frac{d}{dx}\sinh^{-1} u = \frac{1}{\sqrt{u^2 + 1}}\frac{du}{dx} \qquad \frac{d}{dx}\cosh^{-1} u = \frac{1}{\sqrt{u^2 - 1}}\frac{du}{dx}$$

$$\frac{d}{dx}\tanh^{-1} u = \frac{1}{1 - u^2}\frac{du}{dx} \qquad \frac{d}{dx}\coth^{-1} u = \frac{1}{1 - u^2}\frac{du}{dx}$$

$$\frac{d}{dx}\operatorname{sech}^{-1} u = \frac{-1}{u\sqrt{1 - u^2}}\frac{du}{dx} \qquad \frac{d}{dx}\operatorname{csch}^{-1} u = \frac{-1}{|u|\sqrt{1 + u^2}}\frac{du}{dx}$$